VAX/VMS Internals and Data Structures

10/4/84

VAX/VMS Internals and Data Structures

LAWRENCE J. KENAH

SIMON F. BATE

Digital Press

Order number EY-00014-DP.

Library of Congress Cataloging in Publication Data

Kenah, Lawrence J., 1946–
  VAX/VMS internals and data structures.

  Includes index.
  1. VAX/VMS (Computer operating system) 2. VAX-11 (Computer)—
Programming. 3. Data structures (Computer science) I. Bate,
Simon. II. Title. III. Title: V.A.X./V.M.S. internals and data structures.
QA76.6.K454 1984   001.64'2   83-26187
ISBN 0-932376-52-5

Preface

This book explains how the VAX/VMS executive works. It describes the data structures maintained and manipulated by the VMS operating system, discusses the mechanisms that transfer control between user processes and the VMS operating system (and among the components of the operating system itself), and describes some of the features of the VAX hardware as they are used by the VMS operating system. It also describes the VMS executive, including all the major components of the executive, as well as system initialization and the operation of all system services. It does not include a general discussion of the I/O subsystem, because that subject is already described in the *VAX/VMS Guide to Writing a Device Driver* (Digital Equipment Corporation, 1982). However, the details of some VAX/VMS device drivers, as well as the operations of I/O-related system services are included in this book.

This book is intended for system programmers and other users of the VAX/VMS operating system who wish to understand the internal workings of the executive. The detailed description of data structures should help system managers make better informed decisions when they configure systems for space-or time-critical applications. It will also help application designers to appreciate the effects (in speed or in memory consumption) of different design and implementation decisions. This book assumes that the reader is familiar with the VAX architecture and the VMS operating system, particularly with its use of system services and its techniques of memory management.

In explaining the operation of a subsystem of the executive, this book emphasizes the data structures manipulated by that component, rather than detailed flow diagrams of major routines.

This book differs from the reference manuals that make up the VAX/VMS documentation set in that it describes internal operations and data structures. While it is unlikely that any component described in this book will be drastically changed with any major release of the VAX/VMS operating system, there is no guarantee that a particular data structure or subroutine described here will remain the same from release to release. With each new version of the operating system, privileged application programs that rely on details contained in this book must be tested before they are used for production work with a standard load of users.

This book is divided into nine parts, each of which describes a different aspect of the operating system.

- Part 1 presents an overview of the VAX/VMS operating system and reviews those concepts that are crucial to understanding the workings of that system.

- Part 2 describes the mechanisms used to pass control between user programs and the operating system and within the VMS system itself.
- Part 3 describes scheduling and timer support, concluding with a discussion of the internals of the VAX/VMS lock manager.
- Part 4 discusses memory management.
- Part 5 describes the I/O subsystem.
- Part 6 describes the creation and deletion of a process and the activation and termination of an image in the context of a process.
- Part 7 deals with system initialization and also includes a discussion on the VAX-11/782.
- Part 8 discusses miscellaneous topics that are not conveniently classified in any conventional catalog of operating systems:

  —The implementation of logical names
  —The functions of miscellaneous system services
  —The use of listing and map files
  —The conventions used in naming symbols

- Part 9 provides information on VMS data structures.

Most of the operations of the VMS executive can be easily understood once the contents of the various data structures are known. Although selected structures are described throughout the book, Appendix B describes (or provides pointers to) all the structures used by the operating system. The structures related to device drivers and the file system are not described. The data structures related to device drivers are described in the *VAX/VMS Guide to Writing a Device Driver*. Data structures specific to the file system have yet to be documented.

Several documents in the VAX/VMS document set supply important background information for the topics discussed in this book. The following provide an especially valuable foundation: *VAX/VMS System Services Reference Manual*, the VAX-11 software installation guides, and the chapter in the *VAX-11 Run-Time Library Reference Manual* that describes condition handling.

The concepts underlying the operating system are discussed in the *VAX/VMS Summary Description and Glossary*, and the *VAX Software Handbook*. The following documents are also helpful references: the *VAX/VMS Guide to Writing a Device Driver*, the *VAX-11 Architecture Reference Manual*, and the *VAX Hardware Handbook*.

An excellent description of the VAX architecture, as well as a discussion of some of the design decisions made for its first implementation, the VAX-11/780, can be found in *Computer Programming and Architecture: The VAX-11* by Henry M. Levy and Richard H. Eckhouse, Jr. (Digital Press, 1980). This book also contains a bibliography of some of the literature dealing with operating system design.

The reader should be aware of several conventions used throughout this book. In all diagrams of memory, the lowest virtual address appears at the top of the page and addresses increase toward the bottom of the page. This convention means that the direction of stack growth is toward the top of the page. In diagrams that display more detail, such as bytes within longwords, addresses also increase from right to left. That is, the lowest addressed byte (or bit) in a longword is on the righthand side of a figure and the most significant byte (or bit) is on the lefthand side.

The words "system" or "VMS system" are used to describe the entire software package that is a part of a VAX-11 system, including privileged processes, utilities, and other support software as well as the executive itself.

The word "executive" refers to those parts of the VMS operating system that reside in system virtual address space. The executive includes the contents of the file SYS.EXE, device drivers, and other code and data structures loaded at initialization time, including RMS and the system message file.

When either "process control block" or "PCB" is used without a modifier, it refers to the software structure used by the scheduler. The data structure that contains copies of the general registers (that the hardware locates through the PR$_PCBB register) is always called the "hardware PCB."

When referring to access modes, the term "inner access modes" means those access modes with more privilege. The term "outer access modes" means those access modes with less privilege. Thus, the innermost access mode is kernel and the outermost access mode is user.

The term "SYSBOOT parameter" is used to describe any of the adjustable parameters that are used by the secondary bootstrap program SYSBOOT to configure the system. The adjustable parameters include both the dynamic parameters that can be changed on the running system and the static parameters that require a reboot in order for their values to change. These parameters are referred to by their parameter names rather than by the global locations where their values are stored. Appendix A relates the SYSBOOT parameter names to their corresponding global locations.

The terms "byte index," "word index," "longword index," and so on, refer to a method of access that uses the VAX-11 context indexing addressing capability. That is, the index value will be multiplied by one, two, four, or eight (depending on whether a byte, word, longword, or quadword is being referenced) as part of operand evaluation in order to calculate the effective address of the operand.

In general, the component called INIT refers to a module of that name in the executive and not the volume initialization utility. When that utility program is being referenced, it will be clearly specified.

Three conventions are observed for lists.

- In lists such as this one, where there is no order or hierarchy, list elements are indicated by leading bullets (•). Sublists without hierarchy are indicated by dashes (—).
- Lists that indicate an ordered set of operations are numbered. Sublists that indicate an ordered set of operations are lettered.
- Numbered lists with the numbers enclosed in circles indicate a correspondence between individual list elements and numbered items in a figure.

ACKNOWLEDGMENTS

Our first thanks must go to Joe Carchidi, for suggesting that this book be written, and to Dick Hustvedt, for his help and enlightening conversations.

We would like to thank John Lucas for putting together the initial versions of Chapters 7, 10, 11, and 30 and Vik Muiznieks for writing the initial versions of Chapters 5, 18, and 19.

Appreciation goes to all those who reviewed the drafts for both editions of the book (VAX/VMS Version 2.2 and 3.3). We would particularly like to thank Kathy Morse for reviewing the first edition in its entirety and Wayne Cardoza for reviewing the entire second edition. Our special thanks go to Ruth Goldenberg for reviewing both editions in their entirety, and for her many corrections, comments, and suggestions.

We owe a lot of thanks to our editing staff, especially to Jonathan Ostrowsky for his labors in preparing the first edition, and Betty Steinfeld for her help and suggestions. Many thanks go to Jonathan Parsons for reviewing and editing the second edition, and for all his help, patience, and suggestions.

We would like to thank the Graphic Services department at Spitbrook, particularily Pat Walker for her help in paging and production of the first edition, and Paul King for his help in transforming innumerable slides and rough sketches into figures. Thanks go to Kathy Greenleaf and Jackie Markow for converting the files to our generic markup language.

Thanks go to Larry Bohn, Sue Gault, Bill Heffner, Kathleen Jensen, and Judy Jurgens for their support and interest in this project.

Finally, we would like to thank all those who originally designed and implemented the VAX/VMS operating system, and all those who have contributed to later releases.

Lawrence J. Kenah
Simon F. Bate
August 1983

Contents

PART I/Introduction

1   System Overview 3

1.1   Process, Job, and Image 3
1.1.1   Process 3
1.1.2   Image 5
1.1.3   Job 6
1.2   Functionality Provided By VAX/VMS 6
1.2.1   Operating System Kernel 6
1.2.3   User Interface 9
1.2.4   Interface among Kernel Subsystems 11
1.3   Hardware Implementation of the Operating System Kernel 13
1.3.1   VAX Architecture Features Exploited by VMS 13
1.3.2   VAX-11 Instruction Set 14
1.3.3   Implementation of VMS Kernel Routines 15
1.3.4   Memory Management and Access Modes 19
1.3.5   Exceptions, Interrupts, and REI 20
1.3.6   Process Structure 21
1.4   Other System Concepts 22
1.4.1   Resource Control 22
1.4.2   Other System Primitives 23
1.5   Layout of Virtual Address Space 24
1.5.1   System Virtual Address Space 24
1.5.2   The Control Region (P1 Space) 26
1.5.3   The Program Region (P0 Space) 26

2   Synchronization Techniques 30

2.1   Elevated IPL 30
2.1.1   Use of IPL$_SYNCH 31
2.1.2   Other IPL Levels Used for Synchronization 32
2.1.3   IPL$_QUEUEAST 33
2.1.4   IPL 2 34
2.2   Serialized Access 35
2.2.1   Fork Processing 35
2.2.2   I/O Postprocessing 36
2.3   Mutual Exclusion Semaphores (Mutexes) 36
2.3.1   Locking a Mutex for Read Access 37
2.3.2   Locking a Mutex for Write Access 38
2.3.3   Mutex Wait State 39
2.3.4   Unlocking a Mutex 39
2.3.5   Resource Wait State 40
2.4   VAX/VMS Lock Management System Services 40

3   Dynamic Memory Allocation 42

3.1   Allocation Strategy and Implementation 42
3.1.1   Allocation of Dynamic Memory 43
3.1.2   Example of Allocation of Dynamic Memory 44
3.1.3   Deallocation of Dynamic Memory 45
3.1.4   Example of Deallocation of Dynamic Memory 45
3.1.5   Synchronization 47
3.1.6   Granularity of Allocation 49
3.2   Preallocated Request Packets 50
3.2.1   Allocation from One of the Lookaside Lists 50
3.2.2   Deallocation to the Lookaside List 51
3.3   Use of Dynamic Memory 53
3.3.1   Process Allocation Region 53

Contents

3.3.2   Paged Dynamic Memory   53
3.3.3   Nonpaged Dynamic
         Memory   56

PART II/Control Mechanisms

4   Condition Handling   61

4.1   Overview of the Condition
         Handling Facility   61
4.1.1   Goals of the VAX-11 Condition
         Handling Facility   61
4.1.2   Features of the VAX-11
         Condition Handling
         Facility   62
4.2   Generation of Exceptions   63
4.2.1   Exceptions That Originate in
         the Hardware   63
4.2.2   Exceptions Detected by
         Software   74
4.3   Uniform Exception
         Dispatching   75
4.3.1   Establishing a Condition
         Handler   77
4.3.2   The Search for a Condition
         Handler   78
4.3.3   Multiply Active Signals   81
4.4   Condition Handler Action   83
4.4.1   Continue or Resignal   84
4.4.2   Unwinding the Call Stack   84
4.4.3   Example of Unwinding the Call
         Stack   85
4.4.4   Potential Infinite Loop   88
4.4.5   Unwinding Multiply Active
         Signals   88
4.4.6   Correct Use of Default Depth
         in SYS$UNWIND   89
4.4.7   Unwinding AST's   92
4.5   Default (VMS-Supplied)
         Condition Handlers   95
4.5.1   Traceback Handler Established
         by Image Startup   95
4.5.2   Catch-All Condition
         Handler   95
4.5.3   Handlers Used by Other Access
         Modes   96

5   Hardware Interrupts   98

5.1   Hardware Interrupt
         Dispatching   98
5.1.1   Interrupt Dispatching   99
5.1.2   System Control Block   100
5.2   VAX/VMS Interrupt Service
         Routines   104
5.2.1   Restrictions Imposed on
         Interrupt Service
         Routines   104
5.2.2   Servicing UNIBUS
         Interrupts   105
5.2.3   MASSBUS Interrupt Service
         Routines   109
5.2.4   DR32 Interrupt Service
         Routine   112
5.2.5   MA780 Interrupt
         Dispatching   112
5.2.6   MA780 Interrupts on the
         VAX-11/782   114
5.3   Connect-to-Interrupt
         Mechanism   115

6   Software Interrupts   117

6.1   The Software Interrupt   117
6.1.1   Hardware Mechanism of
         Software Interrupts   117
6.1.2   Software Interrupt Service
         Routines   119
6.2   Software Interrupt Levels in
         VAX/VMS   119
6.2.1   Mount Verification
         Cancellation   120
6.2.2   Fork Processing   121
6.2.3   Software Timer   123
6.2.4   I/O Postprocessing   123
6.2.5   Rescheduling Interrupt   124
6.2.6   AST Delivery Interrupt   125

7   AST Delivery   126

7.1   Hardware Assistance to AST
         Delivery   126
7.1.1   REI Instruction   126
7.1.2   ASTLVL Processor Register
         (PR$_ASTLVL)   127

7.2	Queuing an AST to a Process 127		8.1.6	Error Log Mailbox 150
7.2.1	AST Control Block 127		8.2	System Crashes (BUGCHECKS) 150
7.2.2	Access Mode and AST Queuing 130		8.2.1	Bugcheck Mechanism 150
7.2.3	Special Kernel Mode ASTs 130		8.2.2	Operation of Bugcheck Routine 151
7.2.4	Piggyback Special Kernel Mode ASTs 130		8.2.3	System Dump File 154
7.2.5	Computation of a New Value for ASTLVL 132		8.3	Machine Check Mechanism 156
7.3	Delivering an AST to a Process 133		8.3.1	VAX-11/730 Machine Check 157
7.3.1	AST Delivery Interrupt 133		8.3.2	VAX-11/750 Machine Check 157
7.3.2	Argument List 135		8.3.3	VAX-11/780 Machine Check 159
7.3.3	AST Exit Path 136		8.3.4	Machine Check Recovery Blocks 160
7.4	Special Kernel Mode ASTs 137			
7.4.1	I/O Postprocessing in Process Context 137		**9**	**System Service Dispatching 162**
7.4.2	Process Suspension 138		9.1	System Service Vectors 162
7.4.3	Process Deletion 138		9.2	Change Mode Instructions 165
7.4.4	$GETJPI System Service 139		9.2.1	The CHMK and CHME Instructions 165
7.4.5	Power Recovery ASTs 140		9.2.2	The CHMS and CHMU Instructions 165
7.4.6	Other System Use of ASTs 140		9.3	Change Mode Dispatching in VMS 166
7.5	Attention and Out-of-Band ASTs 140		9.3.1	Operation of the Change Mode Dispatcher 167
7.5.1	Set Attention Mechanism 140		9.3.2	Change-Mode-to-Kernel Dispatcher 171
7.5.2	Delivery of Attention ASTs 141		9.3.3	Change-Mode-to-Executive Dispatcher 171
7.5.3	Flushing an Attention AST List 142		9.3.4	RMS Dispatching 171
7.5.4	Examples in VAX/VMS 142		9.3.5	Return Path for System Services 172
7.5.5	Out-of-Band ASTs 143		9.3.6	Return Path for RMS Services 173
			9.4	User-Written System Service Dispatching 174
8	**Error Handling 147**		9.4.1	Per-Process User-Written Dispatcher 174
8.1	Error Logging 147		9.4.2	Privileged Shareable Images 175
8.1.1	Overview of the Error Logging Subsystem 147			
8.1.2	Device Driver Errors 147			
8.1.3	Other Error Log Messages 148			
8.1.4	Operation of the Error Logger Routines 148			
8.1.5	Cursory Overview of the ERRFMT Process 149			

Contents

9.4.3   System-Wide User-Written
          Dispatcher   178
9.5   Related System Services   178
9.5.1   Set System Service Failure
          Exceptions System
          Service   179
9.5.2   Change Mode System
          Services   179
9.5.3   System Service Filtering   179

**PART III/Scheduling and Timer
Support**

10   Scheduling   183

10.1   Process States   183
10.1.1   Process Control Block   183
10.1.2   Software Priority   184
10.1.3   State Queues   191
10.2   System Events   197
10.2.1   Process State Changes   198
10.2.2   Wait States and AST
          Delivery   198
10.2.3   Event Reporting   200
10.2.4   System Events and Associated
          Priority Boosts   201
10.3   Rescheduling Interrupt   202
10.3.1   Hardware Context   203
10.3.2   Removal of Current Process
          from Execution   204
10.3.3   Selection of Next Process for
          Execution   205
10.3.4   Summary Longword and
          Computable State
          Queues   206
10.3.5   Hardware Assistance in
          Context Switching   207

11   Timer Support   212

11.1   Timekeeping in VAX/VMS   212
11.1.1   Hardware Clocks   212
11.1.2   Software Time   215
11.1.3   Set Time System Service   215
11.2   Hardware Clock Interrupt
          Service Routine   217
11.2.1   System Time Updating   217

11.2.2   Timer Queue Testing   217
11.3   Software Timer Interrupt
          Service Routine   218
11.3.1   Quantum Expiration   218
11.3.2   Timer Queue and Timer Queue
          Elements   218
11.3.3   Timer Request Servicing   220
11.3.4   Scheduled Wakeup   220
11.3.5   Periodic System
          Procedures   221
11.4   Timer System Services   222
11.4.1 $SETIMR Requests   222
11.4.2   Scheduled Wakeup
          Operations   223

**12   Process Control and
            Communication   225**

12.1   Event Flag Services   225
12.1.1   Local Event Flags   225
12.1.2   Common Event Flags   226
12.1.3   Event Flag Wait States   228
12.1.4   Setting and Clearing Event
          Flags   229
12.2   Affecting the Computability of
          Another Process   231
12.2.1   Common Event Flags   231
12.2.2   Process Control Services   231
12.2.3   Miscellaneous Process
          Attribute Changes   234
12.3   Interprocess
          Communication   235
12.3.1   Event Flags   238
12.3.2   VAX/VMS Lock Management
          system services   238
12.3.3   Mailboxes   238
12.3.4   Logical Names   239
12.3.5   Global Sections   239
12.3.6   Interprocessor Communication
          with the MA780   239

**13   VAX/VMS Lock
            Manager   244**

13.1   Lock Manager Data
          Structures   244
13.1.1   Lock Blocks   245
13.1.2   Resource Blocks   246

13.1.3	Accessing the Lock and Resource Blocks 247		14.3.4	Global Page Table and System Page Table 289
13.1.4	Relationships in the Lock Database 250		14.3.5	Process PTEs for Global Pages 292
13.2	Queuing and Dequeuing Locks 250		14.4	Swapping Data Structures 292
13.2.1	The $ENQ System Service 250		14.4.1	Balance Slots 292
			14.4.2	Balance Slot Arrays 293
13.2.2	Lock Conversions 254		14.4.3	Comment on Equal Size Balance Slots 294
13.2.3	The $DEQ System Service 255		14.5	Data Structures That Describe the Page and Swap Files 295
13.3	Handling Deadlocks 255			
13.3.1	Initiating a Deadlock Search 256		14.5.1	Structure of Page and Swap Files 295
13.3.2	Deadlock Detection 256		14.5.2	The SHELL process 297
13.3.3	Victim Selection 262		14.5.3	Structure of Swap Files 297
			14.5.4	Alternate Page and Swap Files 299
			14.6	Swapper and Modified Page Writer Page Table Arrays 299

PART IV/Memory Management

14	**Memory Management Data Structures 267**		14.6.1	Direct I/O and Scatter/Gather 299
			14.6.2	Swapper I/O 300
14.1	Process Data Structures (Process Header) 267		14.6.3	Modified Page Writer PTE Array 300
14.1.1	Process Page Tables 269		14.6.4	Nonreentrancy of Swapper and Modified Page Writer 301
14.1.2	Working Set List 273			
14.1.3	Process Section Table 276		14.7	Data Structures Used with Shared Memory 302
14.1.4	Process Header Page Arrays 279		14.7.1	Shared Memory Control Structures 302
14.2	PFN Database 279		14.7.2	Global Sections in Shared Memory 304
14.2.1	PTE Array 279			
14.2.2	BAK Array 280		14.7.3	Mailboxes in Shared Memory 307
14.2.3	STATE Array 282			
14.2.4	TYPE Array 283		14.7.4	Common Event Flag Clusters in Shared Memory 307
14.2.5	Forward and Backward Links 284			
14.2.6	REFCNT Array 284			
14.2.7	SHRCNT Array 285		**15**	**Paging Dynamics 308**
14.2.8	WSLX Array 286		15.1	Overview of Pager Operation 308
14.2.9	SWPVBN Array 286			
14.3	Data Structures for Global Pages 286		15.1.1	Hardware Action 308
14.3.1	Global Section Descriptor 286		15.1.2	Initial Pager Action 309
14.3.2	The System Header and Global Section Table Entries 287		15.2	Page Faults for Process Private Pages 310
14.3.3	Global Page Table Entries 288		15.2.1	Page Located in an Image File 311

Contents

15.2.2   Demand Zero Pages   317

15.2.3   Global Copy-on-Reference and
          Page-File Pages   317

15.2.4   Page Located in the Page
          File   319

15.3   Page Faults for Global
          Pages   319

15.3.1   Page Fault for Global
          Read-Only Page   319

15.3.2   Global Read/Write Pages   322

15.3.3   Global Copy-on-Reference
          Pages   323

15.3.4   Global Page-File Backing Store
          Pages   324

15.4   Working Set Replacement   326

15.4.1   Scan of Working Set List   326

15.4.2   Reusing Working Set List
          Entries   326

15.4.3   Using an Available Entry in the
          Working Set List   327

15.4.4   Skipping Working Set List
          Entries   328

15.5   Input and Output That Support
          Paging   328

15.5.1   Page Reads and
          Clustering   329

15.5.2   Modified Page Writing   333

15.5.3   Update Section System
          Service   338

15.6   Paging and Scheduling   339

15.6.1   Page Fault Wait State   339

15.6.2   Free Page Wait State   339

15.6.3   Collided Page Wait State   340

16   Memory Management
          System Services   341

16.1   Dispatch Method for Memory
          Management System
          Services   341

16.2   Virtual Address Creation and
          Deletion   342

16.2.1   Address Space Creation   342

16.2.2   Address Space Deletion   344

16.2.3   Controlled Allocation of
          Virtual Memory   346

16.3   Private and Global
          Sections   346

16.3.1   Create and Map Section System
          Service   346

16.3.2   Map Global Section System
          Service   349

16.3.3   Delete Global Section System
          Service   349

16.3.4   Update Section System
          Service   350

16.4   Related System Services   351

16.4.1   Working Set Size
          Adjustment   351

16.4.2   Locking and Unlocking
          Pages   357

16.4.3   Process Swap Mode   359

16.4.4   Altering Page Protection   359

17   Swapping

17.1   Swapping Overview   360

17.1.1   Swapper Responsibilities   360

17.1.2   Swapper Implementation   361

17.1.3   Comparison of Paging and
          Swapping   362

17.2   Swap Scheduling   362

17.2.1   Selection of Inswap
          Candidate   362

17.2.2   Selection of Shrink or Outswap
          Candidates   366

17.2.3   System Events That Trigger
          Swapper Activity   369

17.3   Swapper's Use of Memory
          Management Data
          Structures   370

17.3.1   Process Header   370

17.3.2   Swapper I/O Data
          Structures   372

17.4   Outswap Operation   373

17.4.1   Selection of Outswap
          Candidate   374

17.4.2   Outswap of the Process
          Body   374

17.4.3   Outswap of Process
          Header   379

17.5   Inswap Operation   381

17.5.1   Selection of an Inswap
          Candidate   382

17.5.2   Inswap of the Process
          Header   382

17.5.3   Rebuilding the Process
          Body   383

PART V/Input/Output

18   I/O System Services   393

18.1   Assigning and Deassigning
          Channels   393
18.1.1   Channel Assignment   393
18.1.2   Channel Deassignment   395
18.2   Device Allocation and
          Deallocation   396
18.2.1   Device Allocation   396
18.2.2   Device Deallocation   397
18.3 $QIO System Service   398
18.3.1   Device-Independent
          Preprocessing   398
18.3.2   FDT Routines   399
18.3.3   I/O Postprocessing   400
18.4   I/O Cancellation   402
18.5   Mailbox Creation and
          Deletion   402
18.5.1   Mailbox Creation   403
18.5.2   Mailbox Creation in Shared
          Memory   405
18.5.3   Mailbox Deletion   407
18.6   Broadcast System Service   408
18.7   Informational Services   411
18.7.1   Device-Independent
          Information   411
18.7.2   Device-Dependent
          Information   412

**19   VAX/VMS Device
          Drivers   414**

19.1   Disk Drivers   414
19.1.1   ECC Error Recovery   414
19.1.2   Offset Recovery   416
19.1.3   Dynamic Bad Block
          Handling   416
19.1.4   Multiple-Block Noncontiguous
          Virtual I/O   417
19.2   Magnetic Tape Drivers   419
19.3   Class and Port Drivers   420
19.3.1   Implementation of SCA on
          VAX/VMS   420

19.3.2   I/O Processing   422
19.4   Terminal Driver   422
19.4.1   Full Duplex Operation   426
19.4.2   Channels and Terminal
          Controllers   428
19.4.3   Type-Ahead Buffer   428
19.5   Pseudo Device Drivers   428
19.5.1   Null Device Driver   429
19.5.2   Network Device Driver   429
19.5.3   Remote Terminals   430
19.5.4   Mailbox Driver   430
19.6   Console Interface   435
19.6.1   VAX-11/730 Console
          Interface   435
19.6.2   VAX-11/750 Console
          Interface   436
19.6.3   VAX-11/780 Console
          Interface   436
19.6.4   Data Transfer Between the
          VAX-11 CPU and Console
          Devices   437
19.6.5   Console Interrupt
          Dispatching   437

PART VI/Process Creation and Deletion

20   Process Creation   443

20.1   Create Process System
          Service   443
20.1.1   Control Flow of Create
          Process   444
20.1.2   Establishing Quotas for the
          New Process   450
20.1.3   The PCB Vector   452
20.1.4   Fabrication of Process IDs   452
20.2   The Shell Process   454
20.2.1   Moving SHELL Into Process
          Context   454
20.2.2   Configuration of the Process
          Header   455
20.3   Process Creation in the
          Context of the New
          Process   458
20.3.1   Operation of PROCSTRT   458
20.3.2   Catch-All Condition
          Handler   462

Contents

21   **Image Activation and Termination**   **463**

21.1   Image Initiation   463
21.1.1   Image Activation   464
21.1.2   The Address Relocation Fixup System Service   476
21.1.3   Image Startup   480
21.2   Image Exit   482
21.2.1   Control Flow of the Exit System Service   483
21.2.2   Example of Termination Handler List Processing   484
21.3   Image and Process Rundown   485
21.3.1   Control Flow of Rundown   485
21.4   Process Privileges   488
21.4.1   Process Privilege Masks   488
21.4.2   Set Privilege System Service   490

22   **Process Deletion**   **492**

22.1   Process Deletion in Context of Caller   492
22.1.1   Delete Process System Service   492
22.2   Process Deletion in Context of Process Being Deleted   493
22.2.1   Special Kernel AST for Process Deletion   493
22.2.2   Deletion of a Process That Owns Subprocesses   496
22.2.3   Example of Process Deletion with Subprocesses   497

23   **Interactive and Batch Jobs**   **499**

23.1   The Job Controller and Unsolicited Input   499
23.1.1   Unsolicited Terminal Input   499
23.1.2   The SUBMIT Command   502
23.1.3   Unsolicited Card Reader Input   502
23.2   The LOGINOUT Image   503
23.2.1   Interactive Jobs   503
23.2.2   LOGINOUT Operation for Batch Jobs   505

23.2.3   The Logout Operation   506
23.3   Command Language Interpreters and Image Execution   508
23.3.1   CLI Initialization   509
23.3.2   Command Processing Loop   509
23.3.3   Image Initiation by DCL   511
23.3.4   Image Termination   513
23.3.5   Abnormal Image Termination   514
23.4   The LOGOUT Operation   516

PART VII/System Initialization

24   **Bootstrap Procedures**   **521**

24.1   Processor-Specific Initialization   521
24.1.1   VAX-11/730 Initial Bootstrap Operation   521
24.1.2   VAX-11/750 Initial Bootstrap Operation   524
24.1.3   VAX-11/780 Initial Bootstrap Operation   528
24.2   Primary Bootstrap Program   530
24.2.1   Motivation for Two Bootstrap Programs   534
24.2.2   Operation of VMB   535
24.2.3   Bootstrap Driver and I/O Subroutines   542
24.2.4   File Operations   542
24.3   Secondary Bootstrap Program (SYSBOOT)   542
24.3.1   Detailed Operation of SYSBOOT   543

25   **Operating System Initialization**   **548**

25.1   Initial Execution of the Executive (INIT)   548
25.1.1   Turning on Memory Management   548
25.1.2   Initialization of the Executive   550
25.1.3   I/O Adapter Initialization   557

25.1.4   CPU-Dependent
          Routines   558
25.2   Initialization in Process
          Context   559
25.2.1   SYSINIT Process   561
25.2.2   The STARTUP Process   564
25.3   The System Generation Utility
          (SYSGEN)   565
25.3.1   Contents of Parameter
          Block   566
25.3.2   Use of Parameter Files by
          SYSBOOT   566
25.3.3   Use of Parameter Files by
          SYSGEN   570

26   **Size of System Virtual
          Address Space   572**

26.1   Size of Process Header   572
26.1.1   Process Page Tables   573
26.1.2   Working Set List and Process
          Section Table   573
26.1.3   Process Header Page
          Arrays   575
26.2   System Virtual Address
          Space   576
26.2.1   System Virtual Address Space
          and SYSBOOT
          Parameters   576
26.2.2   System Page Table and the PFN
          Database   585
26.2.3   Approximation Used by
          SYSBOOT   586
26.2.4   Renormalization of
          SPTREQ   587
26.3   Physical Memory
          Requirements of the
          Executive   587
26.3.1   Physical Memory Used by the
          Executive   587
26.3.2   System Processes   589
26.4   Sizes of Pieces of P1 Space   590

27   **Powerfail Recovery   596**

27.1   Powerfail Sequence   596
27.2   Power Recovery   597
27.2.1   Initial Step in Power
          Recovery   598

27.2.2   Operation of the Restart
          Routine   601
27.2.3   Device Notification   603
27.2.4   Process Notification   604
27.3   Multiple Power Failures   605
27.3.1   Nested Power Fail
          Interrupts   605
27.3.2   Prevention of Nested
          Restarts   606
27.3.3   Device Driver Action   606
27.4   Power Failure on the
          UNIBUS   607
27.4.1   UNIBUS Power Failure on the
          VAX-11/730 and
          VAX-11/750   607
27.4.2   UNIBUS Power Failure on the
          VAX-11/780   607

28   **The VAX-11/782
          Multiprocessing
          System   609**

28.1   How the VMS System Supports
          Multiprocessing   610
28.1.1   Hooks in the Executive   611
28.1.2   Hardware Support for
          Multiprocessing   612
28.2   System Initialization on the
          VAX-11/782   613
28.2.1   System Initialization on the
          Primary Processor   613
28.2.2   System Initialization on the
          Attached Processor   613
28.2.3   Turning Multiprocessing
          On   614
28.2.4   Turning Multiprocessing
          Off   615
28.3   Scheduling and Interrupts on
          the VAX-11/782   616
28.3.1   Scheduling Processes on the
          VAX-11/782   617
28.3.2   Preventing Scheduling on the
          Attached Processor   618
28.3.3   Executing Jobs on the Attached
          Processor   618
28.3.4   Detecting Access Mode
          Transitions   620
28.3.5   Interrupt
          Communication   621

Contents

PART VIII/Miscellaneous Topics

29   Logical Names   625

29.1   Logical Name Tables   625
29.1.1 Logical Name Data
        Structures   625
29.1.2 Logical Name Block   627
29.1.3 Searching for a Logical
        Name   628
29.1.4 Hashing the Logical
        Names   628
29.1.5 Changes to Speed Logical
        Name Translation   629
29.2   Logical Name System
        Services   629
29.2.1 Privilege and Protection
        Checks   630
29.2.2 Logical Name Table
        Mutexes   630
29.2.3 Logical Name Creation   630
29.2.4 Logical Name Deletion   631
29.2.5 Logical Name Translation   631

30   Miscellaneous System
        Services

30.1   Communication with System
        Processes   632
30.1.1 Accounting Manager (Job
        Controller)   632
30.1.2 Symbiont Manager (Job
        Controller)   633
30.1.3 Operator
        Communications   634
30.1.4 Error Logger   634
30.2   System Message File
        Services   635
30.2.1 Get Message System
        Service   635
30.2.2 Put Message System
        Service   637
30.2.3 Procedure EXE$EXCMSG   638
30.3   Process Information
        ($GETJPI)   639
30.3.1 Operation of the $GETJPI
        System Service   639
30.3.2 $GETJPI Special Kernel Mode
        ASTs   641

30.3.3 Wildcard Support in
        $GETJPI   641
30.4   System Information
        ($GETSYI)   642
30.5   Formatting Support   642
30.5.1 Time Conversion
        Services   643
30.5.2 Formatted ASCII Output   643

31   Use of Listing and Map
        Files   645

31.1   Hints in Reading the Executive
        Listings   645
31.1.1 Structure of a MACRO Listing
        File   645
31.1.2 The VAX-11 Instruction Set and
        Addressing Modes   649
31.1.3 Use of the REI Instruction   653
31.1.4 Register Conventions   654
31.1.5 Elimination of Seldom-Used
        Code   655
31.1.6 Dynamically Locking Code or
        Data into Memory   656
31.2   Use of Map Files   658
31.2.1 The Executive Map
        SYS.MAP   658
31.2.2 RMS.MAP, DCL.MAP, and
        MP.MAP   659
31.2.3 Device Driver Map Files   660
31.2.4 CPU-Dependent
        Routines   660
31.2.5 Other Map Files   661
31.3   The System Dump Analyzer
        (SDA)   661
31.3.1 Global Locations   661
31.3.2 Layout of System Virtual
        Address Space   662
31.3.3 Layout of P1 Space   662
31.4   Interpreting MDL Files   662
31.4.1 Sample Structure
        Definitions   662
31.4.2 Commonly Used MDL
        Commands   663
31.4.3 Bit Field Definitions—The V
        Directive   670

32   Naming Conventions   671

32.1   Public Symbol Patterns   671
32.2   Object Data Types   676
32.3   Facility Prefix Table   677

APPENDIXES

A   Executive Data Areas   683

A.1   Statically Allocated Executive
        Data   683
A.2   Dynamically Allocated
        Executive Data   725

**B   Data Structure
          Definitions   733**

B.1   Executive Data
        Structures   736
B.2   Constants   764
B.3   Data Structures Used by the
        I/O System   771
B.4   Data Structures Used by Files-
        11   773
B.5   Miscellaneous Data Structures
        and Constants   774

PART I/Introduction

1 System Overview

For the fashion of Minas Tirith was such that it was built on
seven levels, each delved into a hill, and about each was set a
wall, and in each wall was a gate.

—J.R.R. Tolkien, *The Return of the King*

This chapter introduces the basic concepts that are used to describe the
VAX/VMS operating system. Special attention is paid to the features of the
VAX architecture that are either exploited by the operating system or exist
solely to support an operating system. In addition, some of the design goals
that guided the implementation of the VMS operating system are discussed.

1.1 PROCESS, JOB, AND IMAGE

The fundamental unit in the VAX/VMS operating system, the entity that is
selected for execution by the scheduler, is the process. If a process creates
subprocesses, the collection of the creator process, all the subprocesses created by it, and all subprocesses created by its descendants, is called a job. The
programs that a process executes in order to accomplish meaningful work are
called images.

1.1.1 Process

A process is fully described by hardware and software context and a virtual
address space description. This information is stored in several data structures located in different places in the process address space. The data structures that contain the various pieces of process context are pictured in Figure
1-1.

1.1.1.1 Hardware Context.

The hardware context consists of copies of the general
purpose registers, the four per-process stack pointers, the program counter
(PC), the processor status longword (PSL), and the process-specific processor
registers, including the memory management registers and the AST level
register. The hardware context resides in a data structure called the hardware
process control block that is used primarily when a process is removed from
or selected for execution.

Another part of process context that is related to hardware is the existence
of four per-process stacks, one for each of the four access modes. When any
code executes in the context of a process, the code uses the stack associated
with the code's current access mode.

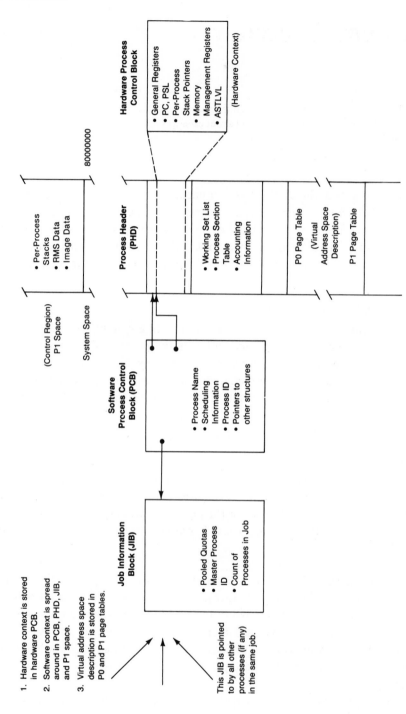

Figure 1-1
Data Structures That Describe Process Context

4

1.1.1.2   **Software Context.** Software context consists of all the data required by various parts of the operating system to make scheduling and other decisions about a process. This data includes the process software priority, its current scheduling state, process privileges, quotas and limits, and miscellaneous information such as process name and process identification.

The information about a process that must be in memory at all times is stored in a data structure called the software process control block (PCB). This data includes the software priority of the process, its unique process identification (PID), and the particular scheduling state that the process is in at a given point in time. Some process quotas and limits are stored in the software PCB. The quotas and limits shared among all processes in the same job are stored in a shared data structure called the job information block.

The information about a process that does not have to be permanently resident (swappable process context) is contained in a data structure called the process header. This information is only needed when the process is resident and consists mainly of information used by memory management when page faults occur. The data in the process header is also used by the swapper when the process is removed from memory (outswapped) or brought back into memory (inswapped). The hardware PCB, which contains the hardware context of a process, is a part of the process header. Some information in the process header is available to suitably privileged code whenever the process is resident (is in the balance set), and some information is only accessible from that process's context.

Other process-specific information is stored in the P1 portion of the process virtual address space (the control region). This data includes exception dispatching information, RMS data tables, and information about the image that is currently executing. Information that is stored in P1 space is only accessible when the process is executing (is the current process) because P1 space is process specific.

1.1.1.3   **Virtual Address Space Description.** The virtual address space of a process is described by the process P0 and P1 page tables, stored in the high address end of the process header. The process virtual address space is altered when an image is initially activated, during image execution through selected system services, and when an image terminates. The process page tables reside in system virtual address space and are in turn described by entries in the system page table. Unlike the other portions of the process header, the process page tables are themselves pageable, and they are faulted into the process working set only when they are needed.

1.1.2   **Image**

The programs that execute in the context of a process are called images. Images usually reside in files that are produced by the VAX/VMS linker.

When the user initiates image execution (as part of process creation or through a DCL or MCR command in an interactive or batch job), a component of the executive called the image activator sets up the process page tables to point to the appropriate sections of the image file. The VMS operating system uses the same paging mechanism that implements its virtual memory support to read image pages into memory as they are needed.

1.1.3 Job

The collection of subprocesses that have a common root process is called a job. The concept of a job exists solely for the purpose of sharing resources. Some quotas and limits, so-called pooled quotas, are shared among all processes in the same job. The current values of these quotas are contained in a data structure called a job information block (Figure 1-1) that is shared by all processes in the same job.

1.2 FUNCTIONALITY PROVIDED BY THE VAX/VMS SYSTEM

The VAX/VMS operating system provides services at many levels so that user applications may execute easily and effectively. The layered structure of the VAX/VMS operating system is pictured in Figure 1-2. In general, components in a given layer can make use of the facilities in all inner layers.

1.2.1 Operating System Kernel

The main topic of this book is the operating system kernel: the I/O subsystem, memory management, the scheduler, and the VAX/VMS system services that support and complement these components. The discussion of these three components and other miscellaneous parts of the operating system kernel focuses on the data structures that are manipulated by a given component. By discussing what each major data structure represents, and how that structure is altered by different sequences of events in the system, we will describe the detailed operations of each major piece of the executive.

1.2.1.1 I/O Subsystem.

The I/O subsystem consists of device drivers and their associated data structures, device-independent routines within the executive, and several system services, the most important of which is the $QIO request, the eventual I/O request that is issued by all outer layers of the system. The I/O subsystem is described in great detail from the point of view of adding a device driver to a VMS operating system in the *VAX/VMS Guide to Writing a Device Driver*. Chapters 18 and 19 of this book describe features of the I/O subsystem that are not described in that manual.

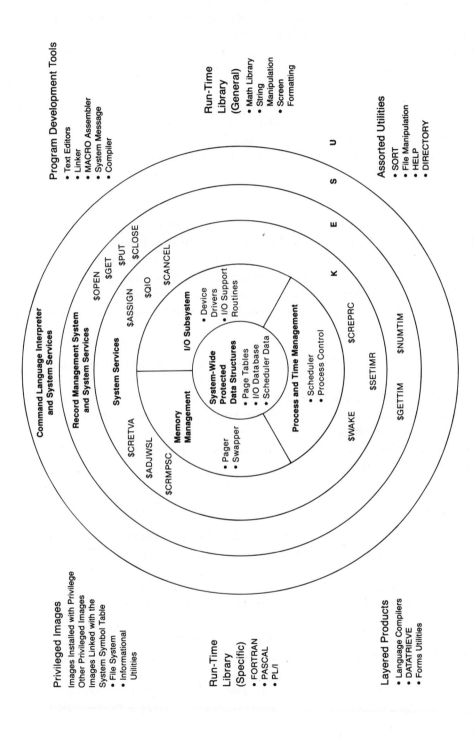

Figure 1-2
Layered Design of the VAX/VMS Operating System

1.2.1.2   **Memory Management.** The main components of the memory management subsystem are the page fault handler, which implements the virtual memory support of the VAX/VMS operating system, and the swapper, which allows the system to more fully utilize the amount of physical memory that is available. The data structures used and manipulated by the pager and swapper include the PFN database and the page tables of each process. The PFN database describes each page of physical memory that is available for paging and swapping. Virtual address space descriptions of each currently resident process are contained in their respective page tables.

System services are available to allow a user (or the system on behalf of the user) to create or delete specific portions of virtual address space or map a file into a specified virtual address range.

1.2.1.3   **Scheduling and Process Control.** The third major component of the kernel is the scheduler, which selects processes for execution and removes processes from execution that can no longer execute. The scheduler also handles clock servicing and includes timer-related system services. System services are available to allow a process (or programmer) to create or delete other processes. Other services provide one process the ability to control the execution of another.

1.2.1.4   **Miscellaneous Services.** One area of the operating system kernel that is not pictured in Figure 1-2 involves the many miscellaneous services that are available in the operating system kernel. Some of these services, for such tasks as logical name creation or string formatting, are available to the user in the form of system services. Others of these miscellaneous services, such as pool manipulation routines and synchronization techniques, are only used by the kernel and privileged utilities.

1.2.2   **Data Management**

The VAX/VMS operating system provides data management facilities at two levels. The record structure that exists within a file is interpreted by the VAX-11 Record Management Services (RMS), which exists in a layer just outside the kernel. RMS exists as a series of procedures located in system space, so it is in some ways just like the rest of the operating system kernel. Most of the procedures in RMS execute in executive access mode, providing a thin wall of protection between RMS and the kernel itself.

The placement of files on mass storage volumes is controlled by one of the disk or tape ACPs (Ancillary Control Process). ACPs are implemented as separate processes because many of their operations must be serialized to avoid synchronous access conflicts. These processes interact with the kernel both through the system service interface and by using some of the utility routines that are not accessible to the general user.

1.2.3 User Interface

The interface that is presented to the user (as distinct from the application programmer who is using system services and Run-Time Library procedures) is one of the command language interpreters (CLI). Some of the services performed by a CLI call RMS or the system services directly. Others result in the execution of an external image. These images are generally no different from user-written applications because their only interface to the executive is through the system services and RMS calls.

1.2.3.1 Images Installed with Privilege.
Some of the informational utilities and disk and tape volume manipulation utilities require that selected portions of protected data structures be read or written in a controlled fashion. Images that require privilege to perform their function can be installed (made known to the operating system) by the system manager so that they can perform their function in an ordinarily nonprivileged process environment. Images that fit this description are MAIL, MONITOR, VMOUNT (the volume mount utility), SET, and SHOW. Table 1-1 lists all those images that are installed with privilege in a typical VMS system.

1.2.3.2 Other Privileged Images.
Other images that perform privileged functions are not installed with privilege because their functions are less controlled and could destroy the system if executed by naive or malicious users. These images can only be executed by privileged users. Examples of these images include SYSGEN (for loading device drivers), INSTALL (which makes images privileged or shareable), or the images invoked by a CLI to manipulate print or batch queues. Images that require privilege to execute but are not installed with privilege in a typical VAX/VMS system are also listed in Table 1-1.

1.2.3.3 Images That Link with SYS$SYSTEM:SYS.STB.
Table 1-1 also lists those components that are linked with the system symbol table (SYS$SYSTEM: SYS.STB). These images access known locations in the system image (SYS.EXE) through global symbols and must be relinked each time the system itself is relinked. User applications or special components such as device drivers that include SYS.STB when they are linked must be relinked whenever a new version of the symbol table is released, usually at each major release of the VAX/VMS operating system.

Table 1-1: System Processes and Privileged Images

Image Name	Linked with SYS.STB	Description
F11AACP.EXE	Yes	Files-11 Structure Level 1 ACP
F11BACP.EXE	Yes	Files-11 Structure Level 2 ACP
MTAAACP.EXE	Yes	Magnetic Tape ACP
REMACP.EXE	Yes	Remote Terminal ACP
NETACP	Yes	Network ACP
ERRFMT.EXE	Yes	Error Log Buffer Format Process
INPSMB.EXE	Yes	Card Reader Input Symbiont
JOBCTL.EXE	Yes	Job Controller/Symbiont Manager
OPCOM.EXE	Yes	Operator Communication Facility
PRTSMB.EXE	Yes	Print Symbiont

Images Installed with Privilege (in a typical VMS system)

Image Name	Linked with SYS.STB	Description
DISMOUNT.EXE	Yes	Volume Dismount Utility
INIT.EXE	Yes	Volume Initialization Utility
LOGINOUT.EXE	Yes	Login/Logout Image
MAIL.EXE	No	Mail Utility
MONITOR.EXE	Yes	System Statistics Utility
PHONE.EXE	No	Phone Utility
REQUEST.EXE	Yes	Operator Request Facility
SET.EXE	Yes	SET Command Processor
SETP0.EXE	Yes	SET Command Processor
SHOW.EXE	Yes	SHOW Command Processor
SUBMIT.EXE	No	Batch and Print Job Submission Facility
VMOUNT.EXE	Yes	Volume Mount Utility

Images That Require Privilege That Are Typically Not Installed

Image Name	Linked with SYS.STB	Description
AUTHORIZE.EXE	Yes	Authorize Utility
INSTALL.EXE	Yes	Known Image Installation Utility
NCP.EXE	Yes	Network Control Program
OPCCRASH.EXE	Yes	System Shutdown Facility
QUEMAN.EXE	No	Queue Manipulation Command Processor
REPLY.EXE	No	Message Broadcasting Facility
RMSSHARE.EXE	Yes	File Sharing Utility
RUNDET.EXE	No	RUN Process Command Processor
SDA.EXE	Yes	System Dump Analyzer
SYSGEN.EXE	Yes	System Generation and Configuration Utility

Table 1-1: System Processes and Privileged Images *(continued)*

Images Whose Operations Are Protected by System UIC or Volume Ownership

Image Name	Linked with SYS.STB	Description
BAD.EXE	No	Bad Block Locator
BACKUP.EXE	No	Backup Utility
DSC1.EXE	No	Disk Save and Compress Utility for Structure Level 1
DSC2.EXE	No	Disk Save and Compress Utility for Structure Level 2
DISKQUOTA.EXE	Yes	Disk Quota Utility
VERIFY.EXE	No	File Structure Verification Utility

Miscellaneous Images Linked with SYS$SYSTEM:SYS.STB

Image Name	Linked with SYS.STB	Description
DCL.EXE	Yes	DCL Command Interpreter
MCR.EXE	Yes	MCR Command Interpreter
MP.EXE	Yes	Multiprocessing Loadable Code
RMS.EXE	Yes	Record Management Services Image

1.2.4   Interface among Kernel Subsystems

The coupling among the three major subsystems pictured in Figure 1-2 is somewhat misleading because there is actually little interaction between the three components. In addition, each of the three components has its own section of executive data structures that it is responsible for. When one of the other pieces of the system wishes to access such data structures, it does so through some controlled interface. Figure 1-3 shows the small amount of interaction that occurs between the three major subsystems in the operating system kernel.

1.2.4.1   I/O Subsystem Requests.
The I/O subsystem makes a request to memory management to lock down specified pages for a direct I/O request. The pager or swapper is notified directly when the I/O request that just completed was initiated by either one of them.

I/O requests can result in the requesting process being placed in a wait state, until the request completes. This change of state requires that the scheduler be notified. In addition, I/O completion can also cause a process to change its scheduling state. Again, the scheduler would be called.

1.2.4.2   Memory Management Requests.
Both the pager and swapper require input and output operations in order to fulfill their functions. Neither calls $QIO

11

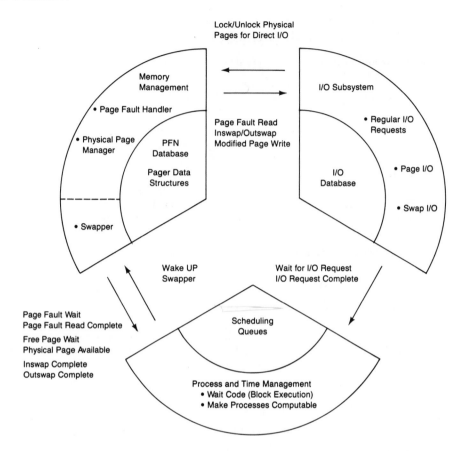

Figure 1-3
Interaction between Components of VMS Kernel

directly because many of the protection checks that $QIO makes are unnecessary and would slow down page I/O and swap I/O. Instead, the pager and swapper use special entry points into the I/O subsystem, and these points allow prebuilt I/O requests to be queued directly to a driver.

If a process incurs a page fault that results in a read from disk, or if a process requires physical memory and none is available, the process is put into one of the memory management wait states by the scheduler. When the page read completes or physical memory becomes available, the process is made computable again.

1.2.4.3 **Scheduler Requests.** The scheduler interacts very little with the rest of the system. It serves a more passive role when cooperation with memory management or the I/O subsystem is required. One exception to this passive role is that the scheduler awakens the swapper when a process that is not currently memory resident becomes computable.

**1.3   HARDWARE IMPLEMENTATION OF THE OPERATING
SYSTEM KERNEL**

The method of implementing the many services provided by the VAX/VMS
operating system illustrates the close connection between the hardware design and the operating system. Many of the general features of the VAX architecture are used to advantage by the VAX/VMS operating system. Other features of the architecture exist entirely to support an operating system.

1.3.1   VAX Architecture Features Exploited by VMS

Several features of the VAX architecture that are available to all users are
used for specific purposes by the operating system.

• The general purpose calling mechanism is the primary path into the operating system from all outer layers of the system. Because all system services are procedures, they are available to all native mode languages.
• The memory management protection scheme is used to protect code
  and data used by more privileged access modes from modification by less
  privileged modes. Read-only portions of the executive are protected in the
  same manner.
• There is implicit protection built into special instructions that may only
  be executed from kernel mode. Because only the executive (and suitably
  privileged process-based code) executes in kernel mode, such instructions
  as MTPR, LDPCTX, and HALT are protected from execution by nonprivileged users.
• The operating system uses interrupt priority level (IPL) for several purposes. At its most elementary level, IPL is elevated so that certain interrupts are blocked. For example, clock interrupts must be blocked while the
  system time (stored in a quadword) is checked because this checking takes
  more than one instruction. Clock interrupts are blocked to prevent the
  system time from being updated while it is being checked.
• IPL is also used as a synchronization tool. For example, any routine that
  accesses a system-wide data structure must raise IPL to 7 (called
  IPL$_SYNCH). The assignment of various hardware and software inter-
  rupts to specific IPL values establishes an order of importance to the hardware and software interrupt services that the VMS operating system performs.
• Several other features of the VAX architecture are used by specific components of the operating system and are described in later chapters. They
  include the following:

  —The change mode instructions (CHME and CHMK), which are used to
    decrease access mode (to greater privilege) (see Figure 1-4). Note that
    most exceptions and all interrupts result in changing mode to kernel (a

13

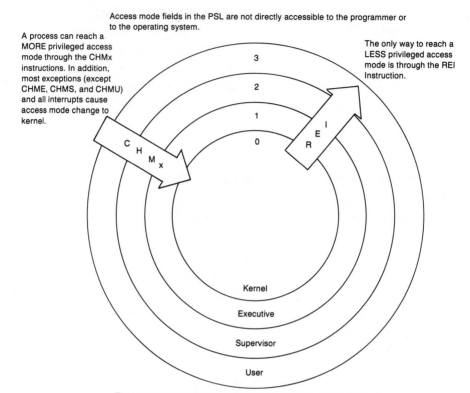

Access mode fields in the PSL are not directly accessible to the programmer or to the operating system.

A process can reach a MORE privileged access mode through the CHMx instructions. In addition, most exceptions (except CHME, CHMS, and CHMU) and all interrupts cause access mode change to kernel.

The only way to reach a LESS privileged access mode is through the REI Instruction.

The boundaries between the access modes are nearly identical to the layer boundaries pictured in Figure 1-2.
  • Nearly all of the system services execute in kernel mode.
  • RMS and some system services execute in executive mode.
  • Command Language Interpreters normally execute in supervisor mode.
  • Utilities, application programs, Run-Time Library procedures, and so on normally execute in user mode. Privileged utilities sometimes execute in kernel or executive mode.

Figure 1-4
Methods for Altering Access Mode

brief introduction to exceptions and interrupts is presented in Section 1.3.5).
—The inclusion of many protection checks and pending interrupt checks in the single instruction that is the common interrupt exit path, REI.
—Software interrupts.
—Hardware context and the single instructions (SVPCTX and LDPCTX) that save and restore it.
—The use of ASTs to obtain and pass information.

1.3.2   VAX-11 Instruction Set

While the VAX-11 instruction set, data types, and addressing modes were designed to be somewhat compatible with the PDP-11, several features that were missing in the PDP-11 were added to the VAX architecture. True context indexing allows array elements to be addressed by element number, with the hardware accounting for the size (byte, word, longword, or quadword) of each element. Short literal addressing was added in recognition of the fact that the majority of literals that appear in a program are small numbers. Variable length bit fields and character data types were added to serve the needs of several classes of users, including operating system designers.

The instruction set includes many instructions that are useful to any designer and occur often in the VMS executive. The queue instructions allow the construction of doubly linked lists as a common dynamic data structure. Character string instructions are useful when dealing with any data structure that can be treated as an array of bytes. Bit field instructions allow efficient operations on flags and masks.

One of the most important features of the VAX architecture is the calling standard. Any procedure that adheres to this standard can be called from any native language, an advantage for any large application that wishes to make use of the features of a wide range of languages. The VMS operating system adheres to this standard in its interfaces to the outside world through the system service interface, RMS entry points, and the Run-Time Library procedures. All system services and RMS routines are written as procedures that can be accessed by issuing a CALLx to absolute location SYS$service in the process P1 virtual address space. Run-Time Library procedures are included in a user's image instead of being located in system space.

1.3.3   Implementation of VMS Kernel Routines

In Section 1.2.1, the VMS kernel was divided into three functional pieces plus the system service interface to the rest of the world. Alternatively, the operating system kernel can be partitioned according to the method used to gain access to each part. Three classes of routines within the kernel are procedure-based code, exception service routines, and interrupt service routines. Other system-wide functions, the swapping and modified page writing performed by the swapper, are implemented as a separate process that resides in system space. Figure 1-5 shows the various entry paths into the operating system kernel.

1.3.3.1   **Process Context and System State.** The first section of this chapter discussed the pieces of the system that are used to describe a process. Process context includes a complete address space description, quotas, privileges, scheduling data, and so on. Any portion of the system that executes in the context of a process can count on all of these process attributes being available.

There is a portion of the kernel, however, that operates outside the context of a specific process. The largest class of routines that fall into this category is that of interrupt service routines, invoked in response to external events with

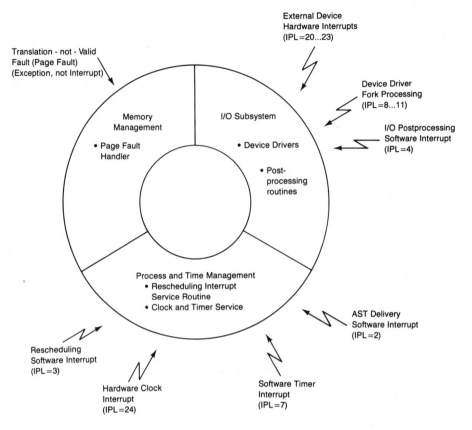

Figure 1-5
Paths into Components of VMS Kernel

no regard for the currently executing process. Portions of the initialization sequence also fall into this category. In any case, there are no process features such as a kernel stack or a page fault handler available when these routines are executing.

Because of the lack of a process, this system state or interrupt state can be characterized by the following limited context.

- All stack operations take place on the system-wide interrupt stack.
- The primary description of system or interrupt state is contained in the processor status longword (PSL). The PSL will indicate that the interrupt stack is being used, that the current access mode is kernel mode, and that the IPL is higher than IPL 2.
- The system control block, the data structure that controls the dispatching of interrupts and exceptions, can be thought of as the secondary structure that describes system state.

- Code that executes in this so-called system context can only refer to system virtual addresses. In particular, there is no P1 space available, so the system-wide interrupt stack must be located in system space.
- No page faults are allowed. The page fault handler generates a fatal bugcheck if a page fault occurs and the IPL is above IPL 2.
- No exceptions are allowed. Exceptions, like page faults, are associated with a process. The exception dispatcher generates a fatal bugcheck if an exception occurs above IPL 2 or while the processor is executing on the interrupt stack.
- ASTs, asynchronous events that allow a process to receive notification when external events have occurred, are not allowed. (The AST delivery interrupt is delivered when IPL drops below IPL 2, an indication that the processor is leaving the interrupt state.)
- No system services are allowed in the system state. (In fact, most system services can only be called from process context at IPL 0; only the memory management system services can be called at IPL 2. Process deletion requires that these system services be callable at IPL 2; doing so requires a great deal of care and is not recommended.)

1.3.3.2   **Process-Based Routines.** Procedure-based code (RMS services and the system services) and exception service routines usually execute in the context of the current process (on the kernel stack when in kernel mode).

The system services are implemented as procedures and are available to all native mode languages. In addition, the fact that they are procedures means that there is a call frame on the stack. Thus, errors detected by a utility subroutine used by a system service can return an error simply by putting the error status into R0 and issuing a RET instruction. All superfluous information is cleaned off the stack by the RET instruction. The system service dispatchers, actually the dispatchers for the CHMK and CHME exceptions, are exception service routines.

System services must be called from process context. They are not available from interrupt service routines or other code (such as portions of the initialization sequence) that executes outside the context of a process. One reason for requiring process context is that the various services assume that there is a process whose privileges can be checked and whose quotas can be charged as part of the normal operation of the service. Some system services reference locations in P1 space, a portion of address space only available while executing in process context. System services also make assumptions about IPL and synchronization that would be violated if they were called from other than process-based code executing at IPL 0.

The pager (the page fault exception handler) is an exception service routine that is invoked in response to a translation-not-valid fault. The pager thus satisfies page faults in the context of the process that incurred the fault. Because page faults are associated with a process, the system cannot tolerate page faults that occur in interrupt service routines or other routines that execute outside the context of a process. The actual restriction imposed by the pager is even more stringent. Page faults are not allowed above IPL 2. This restriction applies to process-based code executing at elevated IPL as well as to interrupt service code.

1.3.3.3   **Interrupt Service Routines.** By their asynchronous nature, interrupts execute without the support of process context (on the system-wide interrupt stack).

- I/O requests are initiated through the $QIO system service, which can be issued directly by the user or by some intermediary, such as RMS, on the user's behalf. Once an I/O request has been placed into a device queue, it remains there until the driver is triggered, usually by an interrupt generated in the external device.
    Two classes of software interrupt service routines exist solely to support the I/O subsystem. The fork level interrupts allow device drivers to lower IPL in a controlled fashion. Final processing of I/O requests is also done in a software interrupt service routine.
- The timer functions in the operating system include support in both the hardware clock interrupt service routine and a software interrupt service routine that actually services individual timer requests.
- Another software interrupt performs the rescheduling function, where one process is removed from execution and another selected and placed into execution.

1.3.3.4   **Special Processes—Swapper and Null.** The swapper and the null process are different from any other processes that exist in a VAX/VMS system. The differences lie not in their operations, which are completely normal, but in their limited context.

The limited context of either of these processes is due, in part, to the fact that these two processes exist as part of the system image SYS.EXE. They do not have to be created with the Create Process system service. Specifically, their PCBs and process headers are assembled (in module PDAT) and linked into the system image. Other characteristics of these two processes are listed here.

- Their process headers are static. There is no working set list and no process section table. Neither process supports page faults. All code executed by either process must be locked into memory in some way. In fact, the code of both of these processes is part of the nonpaged executive.
- Both processes execute entirely in kernel mode, thereby eliminating the need for stacks for the other three access modes.

- Neither process has a P1 space. The kernel stack for either process is located in system space.
- The null process does not have a P0 space either. The swapper uses an array allocated from nonpaged pool as its P0 page table for a special portion of process creation, the part that takes place in the context of the swapper process.

Despite their limited contexts, both of these processes behave in a normal fashion in every other way. The swapper and the null process are selected for execution by the scheduler just like any other process in the system. The swapper spends its idle time in the hibernate state until some component in the system recognizes a need for one of the swapper functions, at which time it is awakened. The null process is always computable, but set to the lowest priority in the system (priority 0). All CPU time not used by any other process in the system will be used by the null process.

1.3.3.5 **Special Subroutines.** There are several utility subroutines within the operating system related to scheduling and resource allocation that are called from both process-based code such as system services and from software interrupt service routines. These subroutines are constrained to execute with the limited context of interrupt or system state.

1.3.4 **Memory Management and Access Modes**

The address translation mechanism is described in the *VAX Hardware Handbook*. Two side effects of this operation are of special interest to the VMS operating system. When a page is not valid, a translation-not-valid exception is generated that transfers control to an exception service routine that can take whatever steps are required to make the page valid. This exception transfers control from a hardware mechanism, address translation, to a software exception service routine, the page fault handler, and allows the operating system to gain control on address translation failures in order to implement its dynamic mapping of pages while a program is executing.

Before the address translation mechanism checks the valid bit, a protection check is made to determine whether the requested access will be granted. The check uses both the current access mode in the PSL (PSL<25:24>), a protection code that is defined for each virtual page, and the type of access (read, modify, or write) to make its decision. This protection check allows the operating system to make read-only portions of the executive inaccessible to anyone (all access modes) for writing, preventing corruption of operating system code. In addition, privileged data structures can be protected from even read access by nonprivileged users, preserving the integrity of the operating system.

19

1.3.5   Exceptions, Interrupts, and REI

Before mentioning other features of the exception and interrupt mechanisms used by the VMS operating system, it would be helpful to compare and contrast these two mechanisms.

1.3.5.1   Comparison of Exceptions and Interrupts. The following list summarizes some of the characteristics of exceptions and interrupts.

- Interrupts occur asynchronously to the currently executing instruction stream. They are actually serviced between individual instructions or at well-defined points within the execution of a given instruction. Exceptions occur synchronously as a direct effect of the execution of the current instruction.
- Both mechanisms pass control to service routines whose addresses are stored in the system control block. These routines perform exception-specific or interrupt-specific processing.
- Exceptions are generally a part of the currently executing process. Their servicing is an extension of the instruction stream that is currently executing on behalf of that process. Interrupts are system-wide events that cannot rely on support of a process in their service routines.
- Because exceptions are usually caused by an executing process, the system-wide interrupt stack is usually used to store the PC and PSL of the process that was interrupted. Exceptions are usually serviced on the per-process kernel stack. Which stack to use is actually determined by control bits in the system control block entries for each exception or interrupt.
- Interrupts cause a PC/PSL pair to be pushed onto the stack. Exceptions often cause exception-specific parameters to be stored along with a PC/PSL pair.
- Interrupts cause the IPL to change. Exceptions usually do not have an IPL change associated with them. (Machine checks and kernel-stack-not-valid exceptions elevate IPL to 31.)
- A corollary of the previous step is that interrupts can be blocked by elevating IPL to a value at or above the IPL associated with the interrupt that is to be blocked. Exceptions, on the other hand, cannot be blocked. However, some exceptions can be disabled (by clearing associated bits in the PSW).
- When an interrupt or exception occurs, a new PSL is formed that summarizes the new IPL, the current access mode (almost always kernel), the stack being used (interrupt or other), and so on. One difference between exceptions and interrupts, a difference that reflects the fact that interrupts are not related to the interrupted instruction stream, is that the previous access mode field in the new PSL is set to kernel for interrupts, while the previous mode field for exceptions reflects the access mode in which the exception occurred.

1.3.5.2   **Other Uses of Exceptions and Interrupts.** In addition to the translation-not-valid fault used by memory management software, the operating system also uses the change-mode-to-kernel and change-mode-to-executive exceptions as entry paths to the executive. System services that must execute in a more privileged access mode use either the CHMK or CHME instruction to gain access mode rights (see Figure 1-4). The system handles most other exceptions by passing them through a common exception dispatcher described in Chapter 4.

Hardware interrupts temporarily suspend code that is executing so that an interrupt-specific routine can service the interrupt. Interrupts have an IPL associated with them. The internal processor priority level (IPL) is raised when the interrupt is recognized. High level interrupt service routines thus prevent the recognition of lower level interrupts. Lower level interrupt service routines can be interrupted by subsequent higher level interrupts. Kernel mode routines can also block interrupts at certain levels by specifically raising the IPL.

The VAX architecture also defines a series of software interrupt levels that can be used for a variety of purposes. The VMS operating system uses them for scheduling, I/O completion routines, and for synchronizing access to certain classes of data structures.

1.3.5.3   **The REI Instruction.** The REI instruction is the common exit path for interrupts and exceptions. Many protection and privilege checks are incorporated into this instruction. Because most fields in the processor status longword are not accessible to the programmer, the REI instruction provides the only means for changing access mode to a less privileged mode (see Figure 1-4). It is also the only way to reach compatibility mode.

Although the IPL field of the PSL is accessible through the PR$_IPL processor register, execution of an REI is a common way that IPL is lowered during normal execution. Because a change in IPL can alter the deliverability of pending interrupts, many hardware and software interrupts are delivered after an REI instruction is executed.

1.3.6   **Process Structure**

The VAX architecture also defines a data structure called a hardware process control block that contains copies of all a process's general registers when the process is not active. When a process is selected for execution, the contents of this block are copied into the actual registers inside the processor with a single instruction, LDPCTX. The corresponding instruction that saves the contents of the general registers when the process is removed from execution is SVPCTX.

1.4   OTHER SYSTEM CONCEPTS

This chapter began by discussing the most important concepts in the VMS operating system, process and image. There are several other fundamental ideas that should be mentioned before beginning a detailed description of VMS internals. Some of these ideas are briefly described here.

1.4.1   Resource Control

The VAX/VMS operating system protects itself and other processes in the system from careless or malicious users with hardware and software protection mechanisms, software privileges, and software quotas and limits.

1.4.1.1   Hardware Protection. The memory management protection mechanism that is related to access mode is used to prevent unauthorized users from modifying (or even reading) privileged data structures. Access mode protection is also used to protect system and user code, and other read-only data structures, from being modified by programming errors.

A more subtle but perhaps more important aspect of protection provided by the memory management architecture is that the process address space of one process (P0 space and P1 space) is not accessible to code running in the context of another process. When such accessibility is desired to share common routines or data, the operating system provides a controlled access through global sections. System virtual address space is available to all processes (although page-by-page protection may deny read or write access to specific system virtual pages for certain access modes).

1.4.1.2   Process Privileges. Many operations that are performed by system services could destroy operating system code or data or corrupt existing files if performed carelessly. Other services allow a process to adversely affect features in other processes in the system. The VMS operating system requires that processes wishing to execute these potentially damaging operations be suitably privileged. Process privileges are assigned when a process is created, either by the creator or through the user's record in the authorization file.

These privileges are described in the *VAX/VMS System Management and Operations Guide* and in the *VAX/VMS System Services Reference Manual*. The privileges themselves are specific bits in a quadword that is stored in the beginning of the process control block. (The locations and manipulations of the several process privilege masks that the operating system maintains are discussed in Chapter 21.) When a VMS service that requires privilege is called, the service checks to see whether the associated bit in the process privilege mask is set.

1.4.1.3   Quotas and Limits. The VMS operating system also controls allocation of its system-wide resources, such as nonpaged dynamic memory and page file space, through the use of quotas and limits. These process attributes are also assigned when the process is created. By restricting such items as the number of concurrent I/O requests or pending ASTs, the executive exercises control over the resource drain that a single process can exert on system resources such as nonpaged dynamic memory. In general, a process cannot perform certain operations (such as queue an AST) unless it has sufficient quota (nonzero PCB$W_ASTCNT in this case). The locations and values of the various quotas and limits used by the operating system are described in Chapter 20.

1.4.1.4   User Identification Code (UIC). The VMS operating system uses user identification code (UIC) for two different protection purposes. If a process wishes to perform some control operation (Suspend, Wake, Delete, and so on) on another process, it requires WORLD privilege in order to affect any process in the system. A process with GROUP privilege can affect only other processes with the same group number. A process with neither WORLD nor GROUP privilege can affect only other processes that are part of the same job. (A process with neither GROUP nor WORLD privilege cannot affect any other process in the system, even if it has the same UIC, unless the target process is in the same job as the process in question.)

The UIC is also the parameter that determines whether a user can read from or write to a given file. The owner of a file can determine how much access to his files he grants to himself, to other processes in the same group, and to other processes in the system.

The same UIC protection that exists for files is also used for other data structures in the system. Both logical names and global sections exist in two varieties, group names and sections or system names and sections. The group variety is only available to other processes in the same group. Common event flags, flags that can be shared among several processes, are restricted to processes in the same group.

1.4.2   Other System Primitives

Several other simple tools used by the VMS operating system are mentioned freely throughout this book and are described in Chapters 2, 3, and 29.

1.4.2.1   Synchronization. Any multiprogramming system must take measures to prevent simultaneous access to system data structures. The executive uses two simple synchronization techniques. By elevating IPL, a subset of interrupts can be blocked, allowing unrestricted access to system-wide data structures.

The most common synchronization IPL used by the operating system is IPL 7, called IPL$_SYNCH.

For some data structures, elevated IPL is either an unnecessary tool or a potential system degradation. For example, processes executing at or above IPL 3 cannot be rescheduled (removed from execution). Once a process gains control of a data structure protected by elevated IPL, it will not allow another process to execute until it gives up its ownership. In addition, page faults are not allowed above IPL 2 and so any data structure that exists in pageable address space cannot be synchronized with elevated IPL.

The VMS executive requires a second synchronization tool to allow synchronized access to pageable data structures. This tool must also allow a process to be removed from execution while it maintains ownership of the structure in question. The synchronization tool that fulfills these requirements is called a mutual exclusion semaphore (or mutex). Synchronization, including the use of mutexes, is discussed in Chapter 2.

1.4.2.2 **Dynamic Memory Allocation.** The system maintains three dynamic memory areas from which blocks of memory can be allocated and deallocated. Nonpaged pool contains those system-wide structures that might be manipulated by (hardware or software) interrupt service routines or process-based code executing above IPL 2. Paged pool contains system-wide structures that do not have to be kept memory resident. The process allocation region, a portion of the process P1 space, is used for pageable data structures that will not be shared among several processes. Dynamic memory allocation and deallocation are discussed in detail in Chapter 3.

1.4.2.3 **Logical Names.** The system uses logical names for many purposes, including a transparent way of implementing a device-independent I/O system. The use of logical names as a programming tool is discussed in the *VAX/VMS System Services Reference Manual.* The internal operations of the logical name system services, as well as the internal organization of the logical name tables, are described in Chapter 29.

1.5 **LAYOUT OF VIRTUAL ADDRESS SPACE**

This section shows the approximate contents of the three different parts of virtual address space.

1.5.1 **System Virtual Address Space**

The layout of system virtual address space is pictured in Figure 1-6. Details such as the no-access pages at either end of the interrupt stack are omitted to avoid cluttering the diagram. Table 26-2 gives a more complete description of

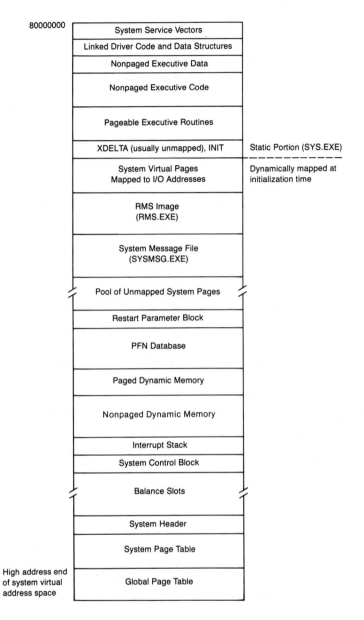

Figure 1-6
Layout of System Virtual Address Space

25

system space, including these guard pages, system pages allocated by disk drivers, and other details.

This figure was produced from two lists provided by the system dump analyzer (the system page table and the contents of all global data areas in system space) and from the system map SYS$SYSTEM:SYS.MAP. The relations between the variable size pieces of system space and their associated SYSBOOT parameters are given in Chapter 26.

1.5.2   The Control Region (P1 Space)

Figure 1-7 shows the layout of P1 space. This figure was produced mainly from information contained in module SHELL, which contains a prototype of a P1 page table that is used whenever a process is created. An SDA listing of process page tables was used to determine the order and size of the portions of P1 space not defined in SHELL.

Some of the pieces of P1 space are created dynamically when the process is created. These include a P1 map of process header pages, a command language interpreter if one is being used, and a symbol table for that CLI.

The two pieces of P1 space at the lowest virtual addresses (the user stack and the image I/O segment) are created dynamically each time an image executes and are deleted as part of image rundown. Chapter 26 contains a description of the sizes of the different pieces of P1 space. Table 26-4 gives a complete description of P1 space, including details such as memory management page protection and the name of the system component that maps a given portion.

1.5.3   The Program Region (P0 Space)

Figure 1-8 shows a typical layout of P0 space for both a native mode image (produced by the VAX-11 Linker) and a compatibility mode image (produced by the RSX-11M task builder). This figure is much more conceptual than the previous two illustrations because P0 space does not contain pieces of the executive as P1 space and system space do.

By default, the first page of P0 space (0 to 1FF) is not mapped (protection set to No Access). This no-access page allows easy detection of two common programming errors, using zero or a small number as the address of a data location or using such a small number as the destination of a control transfer. (A link-time request or a system service call can alter the protection of virtual page zero. Note also that page zero is accessible to compatibility mode images.)

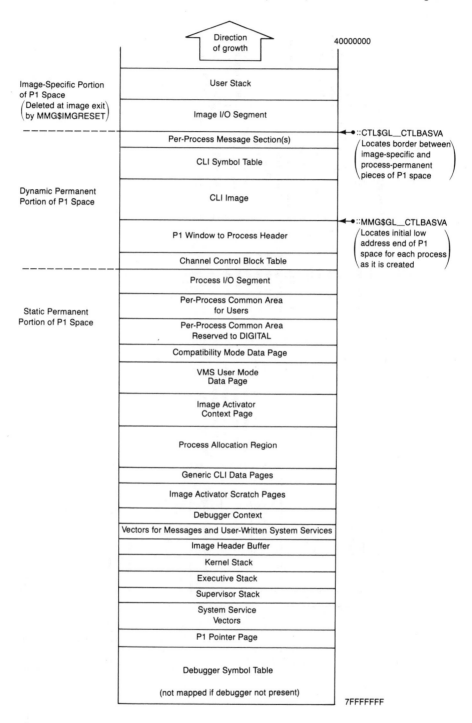

Figure 1-7
Layout of P1 Space

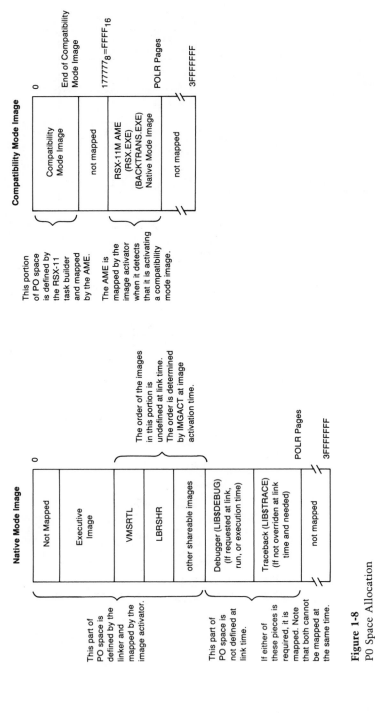

Figure 1-8
P0 Space Allocation

The main image is placed into P0 space, starting at address 200 (hex). Any shareable libraries that are position independent and shared (for example, VMSRTL) are placed at the end of the main image. The order in which these libraries are placed into the image is determined in image activation.

If the debugger or the traceback facility is required, these images are added at execution time (even if /DEBUG was selected at link time) by procedure SYS$IMGSTA. This mapping is described in detail in Chapter 21.

2 Synchronization Techniques

And now I see with eye serene
The very pulse of the machine.

—William Wordsworth, *She Was a Phantom of Delight*

One of the most important issues in the design of an operating system is synchronization. Especially in a system that is interrupt driven, certain sequences of instructions must be allowed to execute without interruption. The VMS operating system uses special IPL values to block certain interrupts during the execution of critical code paths.

Any operating system must also take precautions to insure that shared data structures are not being simultaneously modified by several routines or being read by one routine while another routine is modifying the structure. The VMS executive uses a combination of software techniques and features of the VAX hardware to synchronize access to shared data structures. The following techniques are described in this chapter:

- Elevated IPL
- Serialized access
- Mutual exclusion semaphores, called mutexes
- VAX/VMS lock management system services

2.1 ELEVATED IPL

The primary purpose of raising IPL is to block interrupts at the selected IPL value and all lower values of IPL. For example, by raising IPL to 23, all device interrupts are blocked; but the clock, which interrupts at IPL 24, can still cause interrupts. The operating system also uses selected IPL values for performing certain actions or for accessing certain structures.

The IPL, stored in PSL<20:16>, is altered by writing the desired IPL value to the privileged register PR$_IPL with the MTPR instruction. This change in IPL is usually accomplished in the operating system with one of two macros, SETIPL or DSBINT, whose macro definitions are as follows:

```
.MACRO   SETIPL  IPL = #31
MTPR     IPL,S^#PR$_IPL
.ENDM    SETIPL

.MACRO   DSBINT  IPL = #31 , DST = -(SP)
MFPR     S^#PR$_IPL,DST
MTPR     IPL,S^#PR$_IPL
.ENDM    DSBINT
```

The SETIPL macro changes IPL to the specified value. If no argument is present, IPL is elevated to 31. The DSBINT macro first saves the current IPL before elevating IPL to the specified value. If no alternate destination is specified, the old IPL is saved on the stack. The default IPL value is 31.

The DSBINT macro is usually used when a later sequence of code must restore the IPL to the saved value (with the ENBINT macro). This macro is especially useful when the caller's IPL level is unknown. The SETIPL macro is used when the IPL will later be explicitly lowered with another SETIPL or simply as a result of executing an REI instruction. That is, the value of the saved IPL is not important to the routine that is using the SETIPL macro.

The ENBINT macro is the counterpart of the DSBINT macro. It restores the IPL to the value found in the designated source argument.

```
.MACRO   ENBINT  SRC = (SP)+
MTPR     SRC,S^#PR$_IPL
.ENDM    ENBINT
```

Occasionally it is necessary to save an IPL value (to be restored later by the ENBINT macro) without changing the current IPL.

```
.MACRO   SAVIPL   DST = -(SP)
MFPR     S^#PR$_IPL,DST
.ENDM    SAVIPL
```

The successful use of IPL as a synchronization tool requires that IPL be raised (not lowered) to the appropriate synchronization level. Lowering IPL defeats any attempt at synchronization and runs the risk of a reserved operand fault when an REI instruction is later executed. (An REI instruction that attempts to elevate IPL causes a reserved operand fault.)

2.1.1 Use of IPL$_SYNCH

IPL 7 (IPL$_SYNCH) is used as the interrupt level for the software timer routines, those routines that service timer queue entries and handle quantum expiration. IPL 7 is also used as the level to which IPL must be raised for any routine to access a system-wide data structure. By raising IPL to 7, all other routines that might access the same system-wide data structure are blocked from execution until IPL is lowered.

While the processor is executing at IPL 7, certain system-wide events such as scheduling and I/O postprocessing are blocked. However, other, more important operations, such as hardware interrupt servicing and device driver fork processing, can continue. Thus, the amount of time that the operating system spends at IPL 7 does not affect more important activities such as servicing I/O requests. The fact that I/O processing, including fork processing, is more important than other system operations (such as satisfying a page fault) reflects one of the underlying philosophies of the executive, to keep external devices as busy as possible.

2.1.2 Other IPL Levels Used for Synchronization

Table 2-1 lists several IPL levels that are used for synchronization purposes by the system. Some of these levels are used to control access to shared data structures. Other levels are used to prevent certain events, such as a clock interrupt or process deletion, from occurring while a block of instructions is executed.

2.1.2.1 **IPL 31.** Routines in the operating system will raise IPL to 31 to block all interrupts for a short period of time (usually less than ten instructions once the system is initialized).

- Device drivers use IPL 31 just before they call IOC$WFIxxCH to prevent a powerfail interrupt from occurring.
- The entire bootstrap sequence operates at IPL 31 in order to put the system into a known state before allowing interrupts to occur.
- Because the error logger routines can be called from anywhere in the executive, including fault service routines that execute at IPL 31 (such as machine check handlers), allocation of an error log buffer can only execute at IPL 31. A corrolary of this requirement demands that the ERRFMT process execute at IPL 31 when it is altering data structures that describe the state of the error log buffer. (As Chapter 8 describes, the copy is done at two IPL levels. The error log buffer status flags and message counts are modified at IPL 31. Then IPL is lowered to zero; the contents of the error log buffer are copied to the ERRFMT process P0 space, and the messages are formatted and written to the error log file.)

2.1.2.2 **IPL 24.** When IPL is raised to 24, the level at which the hardware clock interrupts, clock interrupts are blocked. The software timer interrupt service rou-

---

Table 2-1: Common IPL Values Used by the Executive for Synchronization

Name	Value (decimal)	Meaning
IPL$_POWER	31	Disable all interrupts
IPL$_HWCLK	24	Block clock and device interrupts
UCB$B_DIPL (1)	20–23	Block interrupts from specific devices
UCB$B_FIPL (1)	8–11	Device driver fork levels
IPL$_SYNCH	7	Synchronize access to any system-wide data structures
IPL$_QUEUEAST	6	Device driver fork IPL that allows drivers to elevate IPL to 7
IPL$_ASTDEL	2	Block delivery of ASTs (prevent process deletion)

(1) These symbols are offsets into a device unit control block.

tine uses this IPL level when it is comparing two quadword system time values. An IPL value of 24 prevents the system time from being updated while it is being compared with some other time value. (This precaution is required because the VAX architecture does not contain a CMPQ—compare quadword—instruction.)

2.1.2.3 **Device IPL.** Device drivers will raise IPL to the level at which the associated device will interrupt in order to prevent other devices from generating interrupts while device registers are being read or written. This step usually precedes the further elevation of IPL to 31 just described.

2.1.2.4 **Fork IPL.** Fork IPL (a value specific to each device type) is used by the executive to synchronize access to each unit control block. These blocks are accessed by device drivers and by procedure-based code, such as the completion path of the $QIO system service and the Cancel I/O system service.

Device drivers also use their associated fork IPL as a synchronization level when accessing data structures that control shared resources, such as multiunit controllers or datapath registers or map registers. In order for this synchronization to work properly, all devices sharing a given resource must use the same fork IPL.

The use of fork IPL to synchronize access to unit control blocks works the same way that elevating IPL to 7 does. That is, one piece of code elevates IPL to the specified fork IPL (found at offset UCB$B_FIPL) and blocks all other potential accesses to the UCB. Fork processing, the technique whereby device drivers lower IPL below device interrupt level in a manner consistent with the interrupt nesting scheme, also uses the serialization technique described in Section 2.2.

2.1.3 **IPL$_QUEUEAST**

Perhaps the example that best illustrates the synchronization rules followed by the operating system is the use of IPL 6 (IPL$_QUEUEAST) by device drivers. There are instances where device drivers find it necessary to interact with the scheduler. For example, the terminal driver may notify a requesting process about unsolicited input or a CTRL/Y through an AST (see Chapter 7). The mailbox driver also can notify requesting processes about reads or writes to a mailbox.

The enqueuing of an AST must occur at IPL$_SYNCH to synchronize access to the scheduler's database. As already pointed out, IPL must be elevated (not lowered) to 7 to achieve this synchronization. The fork level at IPL 6 allows device drivers that execute at IPL 8 through IPL 11 to make these scheduling requests. Specifically, the driver calls a routine called COM$DELATTNAST that creates an IPL 6 fork request. That is, a fork block is placed into the IPL 6 fork queue and an IPL 6 software interrupt requested (software interrupts are described in Chapter 6). When that interrupt occurs, the fork block is used as an AST control block and passed to SCH$QAST, which will elevate IPL to 7, in keeping with the rule that IPL must be raised to IPL$_SYNCH to preserve proper interrupt nesting.

An obvious question in response to the above description is why the IPL 7 fork interrupt cannot be used to achieve the same result. The answer is that if the IPL 7 software interrupt were not being used for another purpose, that would be a perfectly acceptable solution. However, the software timer service routine is entered as a result of the IPL 7 software interrupt. So this synchronization technique uses the first free IPL below 7, the IPL 6 software interrupt called IPL$_QUEUEAST.

IPL 6 is used in a second instance by device drivers that interact with the scheduler. As described in the next chapter, nonpaged pool cannot be deallocated from code executing in response to an interrupt above IPL 7, because nonpaged pool is a system-wide resource whose availability must be reported to the scheduler. Routine COM$DRVDEALMEM creates an IPL 6 fork process that allows the deallocation to take place in response to an IPL 6 software interrupt, allowing the scheduler to properly synchronize its database accesses. The actual pool manipulation takes place at IPL 11 to synchronize with the allocation routine.

2.1.4   IPL 2

IPL 2 is the level at which the software interrupt associated with AST delivery occurs. When system service procedures raise IPL to 2, they are blocking the delivery of all ASTs, but particularly the special kernel AST that causes process deletion. In other words, if a process is executing at IPL 2 (or above), that process cannot be deleted.

This technique is used in several places to prevent process deletion between the time that some system resource (such as system dynamic memory) is allocated and the time that ownership of that resource is recorded (such as the insertion of a data structure into a list). For example, the $QIO system service executes at IPL 2 from the time that an I/O request packet is allocated from nonpaged dynamic memory until that packet is queued to a unit control block or placed into the I/O postprocessing queue.

The memory management subsystem uses IPL 2 in order to inhibit the special kernel mode AST that is queued on I/O completion. This inhibition is necessary at times when the memory management subsystem has some knowledge of the process's working set and yet the execution of the I/O completion AST could cause a modification to the working set, thereby invalidating that knowlege.

IPL 2 also has significance for an entirely different reason: it is the highest IPL level at which page faults are permitted. If a page fault occurs at IPL above

2, a fatal bugcheck (BUG$_PGFIPLHI) is issued. If there is any possibility that a page fault can occur, because either the code that is executing or the data that it references is pageable, then that code cannot execute above IPL 2. The converse of this constraint is that any code that executes above IPL 2, and all data referenced by such code, must be locked into memory in some way. Chapter 31 shows some of the techniques that the VMS executive uses to dynamically lock code or data into memory so that IPL can be elevated above IPL 2.

2.2 SERIALIZED ACCESS

The software interrupt capability described in Chapter 6 provides no method for counting the number of requested software interrupts. The VMS operating system uses a combination of software interrupts and doubly linked lists to cause several requests for the same data structure or procedure to be serialized. The most important example of this serialization in the operating system is the use of fork processes by device drivers. The I/O postprocessing software interrupt is a second example of serialized access.

2.2.1 Fork Processing

Fork processing is the technique that allows device drivers to lower IPL in a manner consistent with the interrupt nesting scheme defined by the VAX architecture. When a device driver receives control in response to a device interrupt, it performs whatever steps are necessary to service the interrupt at device IPL. For example, any device registers whose contents would be destroyed by another interrupt must be read before the driver dismisses the device interrupt.

Usually, there is some processing that can be deferred. For DMA devices, an interrupt signifies either completion of the operation or an error. The code that distinguishes these two cases and performs error processing is usually lengthy, and to execute at device IPL for extended periods of time would slow down the system. For non-DMA devices that do not interrupt at too rapid a rate, interrupt processing can be deferred in favor of other, more important device servicing.

In either case, the driver signals that it wishes to delay further processing until the IPL in the system drops below a predetermined value, the fork IPL associated with this driver. This signaling is accomplished by calling a routine in the executive that saves the address of the next instruction in the driver in a data structure called a fork block (see Figure 6-2). The fork block is then inserted at the end of the fork queue for that IPL value. A software interrupt at the appropriate IPL is requested.

2.2.2   I/O Postprocessing

Upon completion of an I/O request, there is a series of cleanup steps that must be performed. The event flag associated with the request must be set. A special kernel AST that will perform final cleanup in the context of the process that initially issued the $QIO call must be queued to the process. This cleanup must be completed for one I/O request before another is handled. In other words, I/O postprocessing must be serialized.

This serialization is accomplished by performing the postprocessing operation as a software interrupt service routine (at IPL 4). When a request is recognized as being complete, the I/O request packet is placed at the tail of the I/O postprocessing queue (at global listhead IOC$GL_PSBL), and a software interrupt at IPL 4 is requested.

When the device driver recognizes that an I/O request has completed (either successfully or unsuccessfully), it calls routine IOC$REQCOM, which makes the IPL 4 software interrupt request at fork IPL (IPL 8 to IPL 11), so the postprocessing interrupt is deferred until the IPL drops below 4.

Some I/O requests do not require driver action. When the Queue I/O Request ($QIO) system service or device-specific FDT routines detect that the request can be completed without driver intervention, or if they detect an error, they call one of the routines EXE$FINISHIO or EXE$FINISHIOC. These two routines execute at IPL 2 and so the requested software interrupt is taken immediately. ACPs also place I/O request packets directly into the postprocessing queue and request the IPL 4 software interrupt.

2.3   MUTUAL EXCLUSION SEMAPHORES (MUTEXES)

The synchronization techniques described so far all execute at elevated IPL, thus blocking certain operations, such as a rescheduling request, from taking place. There are some shared data structures that must be protected from multiple access where elevated IPL is an unacceptable technique for synchronization, because the processor would have to remain at an elevated IPL for an unspecified length of time. For example, two processes cannot allocate paged pool at the same time. In addition, when a system is low on paged pool or when the pool is highly fragmented, a search for an unused block that is the correct size can be very time consuming.

A second situation where elevated IPL is not acceptable as a synchronization tool occurs when the data structure that is being protected is paged. The memory management subsystem does not allow page faults to occur when IPL is above 2. Thus, any pageable data structure cannot be protected by elevating IPL to 7. For these two reasons, another mechanism is required for controlling access to shared data structures.

The VMS operating system uses mutexes, mutual exclusion semaphores, for this purpose. Mutexes are essentially flags that indicate whether a given data structure is being examined or modified by one of a group of cooperating

Table 2-2: List of Data Structures Protected by Mutexes

Data Structure	Global Address of Mutex (1)	Value in Version 3.0
System Logical Name Table	LOG$AL_MUTEX	80002750
Group Logical Name Table		80002754
I/O Database (2)	IOC$GL_MUTEX	800028C0
Common Event Block List	EXE$GL_CEBMTX	800028C4
Paged Dynamic Memory	EXE$GL_PGDYNMTX	800028C8
Global Section Descriptor List	EXE$GL_GSDMTX	800028CC
Shared Memory Global Section Descriptor Table	EXE$GL_SHMGSMTX	800028D0
Shared Memory Mailbox Descriptor Table	EXE$GL_SHMMBMTX	800028D4
Enqueue/Dequeue Tables (Not Currently Used)	EXE$GL_ENQMTX	800028D8
Known File Entry Table	EXE$GL_KFIMTX	800028DC
Line Printer Unit Control Block (3)	UCB$L_LP_MUTEX	(3)

(1) When a process is placed into an MWAIT state waiting for a mutex, the address of the mutex is placed into the PCB$L_EFWM field of the PCB. The symbolic contents of PCB$L_EFWM will probably remain the same from release to release. The numeric contents are almost certain to change with each major release of the operating system.

(2) This mutex is used by the Assign Channel and Allocate Device system services when searching through the linked list of device data blocks for a device with a given name. It is also used by the Mount Utility and the file system ACPs to lock the file system data structures.

(3) The mutex associated with each line printer unit does not have a fixed address like the other mutexes. Its value depends on where the UCB for that unit is allocated.

processes. The implementation allows either multiple readers or one writer of a data structure. Table 2-2 lists those data structures in the system that are protected by mutexes.

The mutex itself consists of a single longword that contains the number of owners of the mutex (MTX$W_OWNCNT) in the low-order word and status flags (MTX$W_STS) in the high-order word (see Figure 2-1). The owner count begins at -1 so that a mutex with a zero in the low-order word has one owner. The only flag currently implemented indicates whether a write operation is either in progress or pending for this mutex (MTX$V_WRT).

2.3.1   Locking a Mutex for Read Access

When a process wishes to gain read access to a data structure that is protected by a mutex, it passes the address of that mutex to a routine called

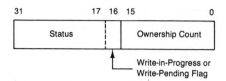

Figure 2-1
Format of Mutual Exclusion Semaphore (Mutex)

SCH$LOCKR. If there is no write operation either in progress or pending, the owner count of this mutex (MTX$W_OWNCNT) is incremented, the count of mutexes owned by this process (stored at offset PCB$W_MTXCNT in the software PCB) is also incremented, and control is passed back to the caller, unless this is the only mutex owned by this process (mutex count equals one).

If the mutex count for this process (PCB$W_MTXCNT) is one, indicating that the process owns no other mutexes, the current and base priorities are stored in the PCB at offsets PCB$B_PRISAV and PCB$B_PRIBSAV. In addition, if the process is not a real-time process (priority is less than 16), the software priority (both current priority and base priority) of the process is elevated to 16 to insure that the mutex will be owned for as little time as possible. Notice that the check on the number of owned mutexes prevents a process that gains ownership of two or more mutexes from receiving a permanent priority elevation into the real-time range.

Routine SCH$LOCKR always returns successfully in the sense that, if the mutex is currently unavailable, the process is placed into a mutex wait state (MWAIT) until the mutex is available for the process. When the process eventually gains ownership of the mutex, control will then be passed to the process. IPL is set to IPL$_ASTDEL (IPL 2) to prevent process deletion while the mutex is owned by this process. This preventative step must be taken because the Delete Process system service has no internal checks on whether the process being deleted owns any mutexes. If the deletion succeeded, the locked data structure would be lost to the system.

2.3.2   Locking a Mutex for Write Access

A process wishing to gain write access to a protected data structure passes the address of the appropriate mutex to a routine called SCH$LOCKW. This routine returns control to the caller with the mutex locked for write access if the mutex is currently unowned. In addition, both mutex counts (MTX$W_OWNCNT and PCB$W_MTXCNT) are incremented, the process software priority is possibly altered, and IPL is set to 2. An alternate entry point, SCH$LOCKNOWAIT, returns control to the caller with R0<0>

cleared (indicating failure) if the requested mutex is already owned. For the regular entry point (SCH$LOCKW), if this mutex is owned, the process is placed into the mutex wait state (MWAIT). However, the write pending bit is set so that future requests for read access will also be denied. In a sense, this scheme is placing requests for write access ahead of requests for read access. However, all that this check is really doing is preventing a continuous stream of read accesses keeping the mutex count (MTX$W_OWNCNT) nonzero. When the mutex count goes to −1 (no owners), it is declared available, and the highest priority process waiting for the mutex is the one that will get first access to the mutex, independent of whether it is requesting a read access or a write access.

2.3.3 Mutex Wait State

When a process is placed into a mutex wait state, its stack is set up so that the saved PC is the entry point of either the read-lock routine or the write-lock routine. (In the latter case, the PC points to a branch to SCH$LOCKW.) The PSL is adjusted so that the saved IPL is 2. The address of the mutex that is being requested is placed into the software PCB at offset PCB$L_EFWM. (Because the process is not waiting on an event flag, this field is available for other purposes.) Table 2-2 and part of Table 10-2 list the contents of the PCB$L_EFWM field for each MWAIT state.

2.3.4 Unlocking a Mutex

A process relinquishes ownership of a mutex by passing the address of the mutex to be released to a routine called SCH$UNLOCK. This routine decrements the number of mutexes owned by this process recorded in its PCB. If this process does not own any more mutexes (PCB$W_MTXCNT contains zero), the saved base and current priorities (in fields PCB$B_PRIBSAV and PCB$B_PRISAV) are established as the process's new base and current priorities. If there are computable (COM) processes with higher priorities than this process's new current priority, a rescheduling interrupt is requested.

SCH$UNLOCK also decrements the number of owners of this mutex (MTX$W_OWNCNT). If the owner count of this mutex does not go to −1, there are other outstanding owners of this mutex, so control is simply passed back to the caller.

If the count does become −1, this value indicates that this mutex is currently unowned. If the write-in-progress bit is clear, this indicates that there are no processes waiting on this mutex, and control is passed back to the caller. (A waiting writer would set this bit. A potential reader is only blocked if there is a current or pending writer.) If there are other processes waiting for this mutex, they are all made computable by scanning the MWAIT queue for all processes whose PCB$L_EFWM field matches the address of the unlocked mutex.

If the priority of any of the processes removed from the mutex wait state is greater than the priority of the current process, a rescheduling pass will occur that will select the highest priority process for execution. As noted above, there is no difference between processes waiting for read access and processes waiting for write access. The criterion that determines who will get first chance at ownership of the mutex is software priority.

2.3.5   Resource Wait State

The routines that place a process into a resource wait state and make resources available share some code with the mutex locking and unlocking routines and will be briefly described here. Details of resources that one process can access at a time can be found in Chapter 10.

When a process requires a resource that is unavailable, it is placed into a resource wait state, which shares the same scheduling state number and wait queue header with the mutex wait state. The resource number is stored in the PCB (at offset PCB$L_EFWM) instead of the mutex address (see Table 10-2). In addition, a bit corresponding to this resource is set in a resource wait mask (found at global location SCH$GL_RESMASK). The saved PC and PSL are determined by the caller of routine SCH$RWAIT. SCH$RWAIT saves the process's context, inserts the PCB into the MWAIT queue, and causes a new process to be selected for execution.

When a resource becomes available, the appropriate bit in the resource wait mask is cleared. If the bit was previously set, there are other processes waiting on this resource. The same routine that frees processes waiting on a mutex is entered at this point. Offset PCB$L_EFWM now contains a resource number instead of a mutex address, but this difference is a conceptual difference that is invisible to the code that is actually executing.

The MWAIT state queue is scanned for all processes whose PCB$L_EFWM field matches the number of the recently freed resource. All such processes are made computable. If the new priority of any of these processes is larger than the priority of the currently executing process, a rescheduling interrupt is requested. In any event, all processes waiting for the now available resource will compete for that resource based on software priority.

2.4   VAX/VMS LOCK MANAGEMENT SYSTEM SERVICES

So far, the methods of synchronization described in this chapter have required elevated IPL or execution in kernel access mode, or both. Though both are powerful and effective in synchronizing access to system data structures, there are other system applications in which elevated IPL or kernel mode access are not really necessary or desirable (for example, RMS).

The VAX/VMS lock management system services (or the lock manager) provide synchronization tools that can be invoked from all access modes. The use of the VAX/VMS lock management system services is described fully in the *VAX/VMS System Services Reference Manual*; the internals of the lock manager are described in Chapter 13 of this book.

3 Dynamic Memory Allocation

In this bright little package, now isn't it odd? You've a dime's
worth of something known only to God!

—Edgar A. Guest, *The Package of Seeds*

Some of the data structures described in this book are created when the system is initialized; many others are created when they are needed and destroyed when their useful life is finished. In order to store the data structures,
virtual memory needs to be allocated and deallocated in an orderly fashion. In
addition, different data structures have differing memory requirements; the
VAX/VMS operating system maintains three separate areas for dynamic allocation of storage.

- The process allocation region holds data structures that are required only
  by a single process.
- Paged dynamic memory contains data structures that are used by several
  processes but are not required to be permanently memory resident.
- The nonpaged pool contains data structures and code that are used by the
  portions of the VMS operating system that are not procedure based, such as
  interrupt service routines and device drivers. These portions of the operating system can use only system virtual address space and usually execute
  at elevated IPL, requiring nonpaged pool space rather than paged pool
  space.

    The nonpaged pool also contains data structures and code that are
  shared by several processes and must not be paged. This requirement is
  usually dictated by the constraint that page faults are not permitted
  above IPL 2.

3.1 ALLOCATION STRATEGY AND IMPLEMENTATION

Each of the three pool areas has the same structure, so common allocation
and deallocation routines can be used. The first two longwords of each unused block in one of the pool areas are used to describe the block. As illustrated in Figure 3-1, the first longword in a block contains the virtual address
of the next unused block in the list. The second longword contains the size in
bytes of the unused block. Each successive unused block is found at a higher
virtual address. Thus, each pool area forms a singly linked memory ordered
list.

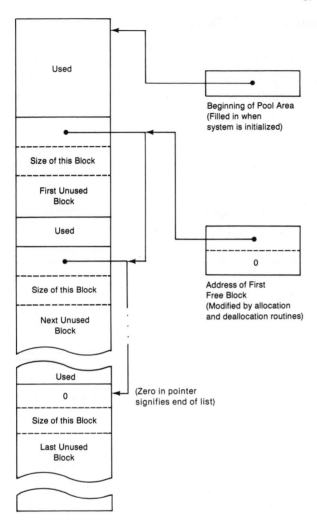

Figure 3-1
Layout of Unused Areas in Dynamic Memory Pools

3.1.1   Allocation of Dynamic Memory

When the allocation routine is called, it searches from the beginning of the list until it encounters the first unused block large enough to satisfy the call. If the fit is exact, the allocation routine simply adjusts the previous pointer to point to the next free block. If the fit is not exact, it subtracts the allocated size from the original size of the block, puts the new size into the remainder of the block, and adjusts the previous pointer to point to the remainder of the block. The two possible allocation situations (exact and inexact fit) are illustrated in Figure 3-1.

3.1.2 Example of Allocation of Dynamic Memory

The first part of Figure 3-2 (Initial Condition) shows a section of paged pool, including the pointers MMG$GL_PAGEDYN, which points to the beginning of paged pool, and EXE$GL_PAGED, which points to the first available block of paged pool. In this example, allocated blocks of memory are indicated only as the total number of bytes being used, ignoring either the number or size of the individual data structures within each block.

Following the allocation of a block of 60 bytes (an exact fit), the structure of the paged pool looks like the second part of Figure 3-2 (60 Bytes Allocated).

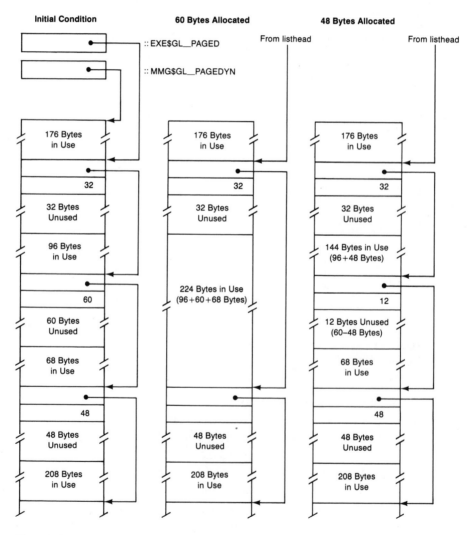

Figure 3-2
Examples of Allocation from Dynamic Memory

Note that the discreet portions of 96 bytes and 68 bytes in use and the 60 bytes that were allocated are now combined to show simply a 224-byte block of paged pool in use.

The third part of Figure 3-2 (48 Bytes Allocated) shows the case where a 48-byte block was allocated from the paged pool structure shown in the first part of the figure. The 48 bytes were taken from the first unused block large enough to contain it. (Note that allocation is done from the low address end of the unused block.) Because this allocation was not an exact fit, an unused block, 12 bytes long, remains.

3.1.3   Deallocation of Dynamic Memory

When a block is deallocated, it must be placed back into the list in its proper place, according to its address. This replacement is accomplished by following the unused area pointers until an address larger than the address of the block to be deallocated is encountered. If the deallocated block is adjacent to another unused block, the two blocks are merged into a single unused area. This merging, or agglomeration, can occur at the end of the preceding unused block or at the beginning of the following block (or both). Three sample deallocation situations, two of which illustrate merging, are shown in Figure 3-3 and are described in Section 3.1.4. Because merging occurs automatically as a part of deallocation, there is no need for any externally triggered cleanup routines.

The deallocation routine assumes that the word at offset 8 from the beginning of a block contains the size of the block being deallocated. All of the dynamically allocated blocks used by the executive adhere to this convention. The type code located in the byte at offset 10 is also used by the deallocation routine to distinguish between structures allocated from local memory (type code is positive) and structures allocated from shared memory (type code is negative). This size word and the type code stored in the adjacent byte at offset 10 allow SDA to correctly interpret the portions of nonpaged pool that are currently in use.

3.1.4   Example of Deallocation of Dynamic Memory

The first part of Figure 3-3 (Initial Condition) shows the structure of an area of paged pool containing logical name blocks for three logical names: ADAM, GREGORY, and ROSAMUND. These three logical name blocks are bracketed by two unused portions of paged pool, one 64 bytes long, the other 176 bytes long.

If the logical name ADAM were deleted, the structure of the pool would be altered to look like the structure shown in the second part of Figure 3-3 (ADAM Deleted). Because the logical name block was adjacent to the high

Dynamic Memory Allocation

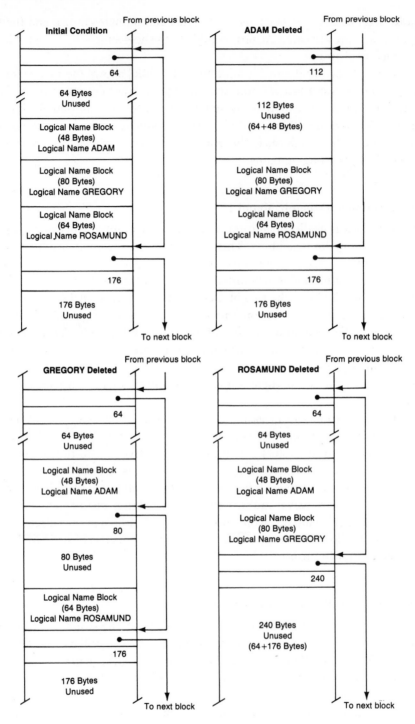

Figure 3-3
Examples of Deallocation of Dynamic Memory

address end of an unused block, the blocks are merged. The size of the deallocated block is added to the size of the unused block.

If the logical name GREGORY were deleted, the structure of the pool would be altered to look like the structure shown in the third part of Figure 3-3 (GREGORY Deleted). The pointer in the unused block of 64 bytes is altered to point to the deallocated block; a new pointer and size longword are created within the deallocated block.

The fourth part of Figure 3-3 (ROSAMUND Deleted) shows the case where the logical name ROSAMUND was deleted. In this case the deallocated block is adjacent to the low address end of an unused block, so the blocks are merged. The pointer to the next unused block that was previously in the adjacent block is moved to the beginning of the newly deallocated block. The following longword is loaded with the size of the merged block (240 bytes).

3.1.5 Synchronization

Some method is required to synchronize access to the pool areas to avoid several processes or executive routines searching one of these lists simultaneously.

There is no locking mechanism currently used for either the process allocation region or any of the lists (such as the process logical name table or the private mounted volume list) found there. However, the allocation routine executes in kernel mode at IPL 2, effectively blocking any other mainline or AST code from executing and perhaps attempting a simultaneous allocation from the process allocation region.

Paged pool is protected by a mutex. Before a block of memory is either allocated or deallocated from the paged pool, this mutex, found at global label EXE$GL_PGDYNMTX, is locked for write access.

Elevated IPL is used to control allocation of nonpaged pool. The IPL that is used is stored in the longword immediately preceding the pointer to the first unused block in the nonpaged pool (see Table 3-1). The allocation routine for nonpaged pool raises IPL to the value found here before proceeding. While the system is running, this longword usually contains an 11. The value of 11 was chosen because device drivers running at fork level frequently allocate dynamic storage, and IPL 11 represents the highest fork IPL currently used in the operating system. (An implication of this synchronization IPL value is that device drivers must not allocate nonpaged pool while executing at device IPL in response to a device interrupt.)

During initialization, the contents of this longword are set to 31 because the rest of the code in the system initialization routines (module INIT) executes at IPL 31 to block all interrupts. INIT is described in detail in Chapter 25. Changing the contents of this longword avoids lowering IPL as a side

Table 3-1: Global Listheads for Each Pool Area

Pool Area	Global Address of Pointer	Size	Use of These Fields	Static or Dynamic (1)
Nonpaged Pool	EXE$GL_NONPAGED	3 longwords		
		longword	Synchronization IPL for nonpaged pool allocation.	Dynamic (2)
		longword	Address of next (first) free block.	Dynamic
		longword	Dummy size (of zero) for listhead to speed up allocation routine.	Static
Nonpaged Pool Lookaside Lists	MMG$GL_NPAGEDYN	longword	Address of beginning of nonpaged pool area.	Static
	IOC$GL_LRPSPLIT	longword	Address of beginning of large request packet area.	Static
	EXE$GL_SPLITADR	longword	Address of beginning of I/O request packet area.	Static
	IOC$GL_SRPSPLIT	longword	Address of beginning of small request packet area.	Static
Paged Pool	EXE$GL_PAGED	2 longwords		
		longword	Address of next (first) free block.	Dynamic
		longword	Dummy size (of zero) for listhead to speed up allocation routine.	Static
Paged Pool	MMG$GL_PAGEDYN	longword	Address of beginning of paged pool area	Static
Process Allocation Region	CTL$GQ_ALLOCREG	2 longwords		
		longword	Address of next (first) free block.	Dynamic
		longword	Dummy size (of zero) for listhead to speed up allocation routine.	Static
Process Allocation Region			There is no global pointer that locates the beginning of the process allocation region.	

(1) Static pointers are loaded at initialization time. The contents of these locations do not change during the life of the system. Dynamic pointers generally change their contents each time a block is allocated from or deallocated to a pool area.

(2) The synchronization IPL is changed to 31 by INIT while it is executing but is reset to 11 and remains at that value for the life of the system.

effect of allocating space from nonpaged pool. The value of this longword is reset to 11 after INIT has finished its allocation but before INIT passes control to the scheduler.

IPL is also a consideration for deallocation of nonpaged pool, but for a different reason. Although nonpaged pool can be allocated from fork processes running at IPL levels up to IPL 11, it cannot be deallocated as a result of an interrupt above IPL 7. The reason for limiting the IPL is that nonpaged pool is a system-wide resource that processes might be waiting for. The deallocation routine notifies the scheduler that a resource is available. The scheduler in turn, checks whether any processes are waiting for the nonpaged pool resource. All of this scheduling must take place at IPL$_SYNCH, and the interrupt nesting scheme requires that IPL never be lowered below the IPL value at which the current interrupt occurred. This rule dictates that all pool be deallocated at IPL 7 or lower.

There may be instances where code executing above IPL 7 must deallocate nonpaged pool. Routine COM$DRVDEALMEM exists for this purpose. This routine takes the block that is to be deallocated, turns it into a fork block (see Figure 6-2), and requests an IPL 6 software interrupt. The code that executes as the fork process (the saved PC in the fork block) simply issues a JMP to EXE$DEANONPAGED to deallocate the block. However, because EXE$DEANONPAGED is entered at IPL 6 and not at fork IPL, the synchronized access to the scheduler's database is preserved. (This technique is similar to the one used by device drivers that need to interact with the scheduler by declaring ASTs. The attention AST mechanism is briefly described in Chapter 2 and discussed in greater detail in Chapter 7.)

3.1.6   Granularity of Allocation

The allocation routines for both paged and nonpaged pool round the requested size up to the next multiple of 16 bytes to impose a granularity on both the allocated and unused areas. Because both pool areas are initially page aligned, this rounding causes every structure allocated from one of the two system-wide pool areas to be at least quadword aligned.

There is no granularity imposed on the allocation size for the process allocation region. However, the two structures allocated from this pool by the system (logical name blocks for process logical names and mounted volume list entries for private volumes) are both an integral number of quadwords long so that any block allocated from the process allocation region is quadword aligned. Also, the smallest possible size of an unallocated block is eight bytes. Any user-written privileged program that allocates space from the process allocation region should insure that it requests an integral number of quadwords to keep this region quadword aligned.

3.2   **PREALLOCATED REQUEST PACKETS**

While most of the structures found in the nonpaged pool are allocated and
deallocated infrequently, pool is constantly being allocated and deallocated
for I/O request packets and other system data blocks. To avoid the overhead
of searching for blocks of free memory of sufficient size to accommodate
specific request packets, portions of nonpaged pool (called the lookaside lists)
are dedicated to the allocation and deallocation of I/O request packets (IRPs),
small request packets (SRPs), and large request packets (LRPs).

Specifically, at initialization time, a portion of the nonpaged system space
following the main portion of pool is partitioned into three pieces. One piece
is reserved for the IRP list, one is for the LRP list, and one is for the SRP list.
The pieces are then structured into a series of elements. The size of the IRP
list element is determined by the symbol IRP$C_LENGTH. The sizes of the
elements in the LRP and SRP lists are contained in the cells IOC$GL_LRPSIZE
and IOC$GL_SRPSIZE, which are defined in module SYSCOMMON. INIT
determines the values for LRPSIZE and SRPSIZE from SYSBOOT parameters.
In each of the lists, the elements are entered into a doubly linked list (with
the INSQUE instruction) so that the each list is a doubly linked list containing fixed size list elements.

3.2.1   **Allocation from One of the Lookaside Lists**

When a routine (such as the $QIO system service) needs an I/O request
packet, it simply issues a REMQUE from the beginning of this list (found
through global label IOC$GL_IRPFL). The SRP and LRP lookaside lists are
located by the global labels IOC$GL_SRPFL and IOC$GL_LRPFL respectively. Only if the list is empty (indicated by the V-bit set in the PSW) would
the more general allocation routine have to be called. Because allocation and
deallocation from the lookaside list are so much more efficient than the general routines that allow any size block to be allocated or deallocated, a special
check is built into the general nonpaged pool allocation routine to determine
whether the requested block can be allocated from one of the lookaside lists.
The logic of this routine is approximately the following.

1. The allocation size is rounded up to the next multiple of 16.
2. If the rounded size is greater than the size of an IRP (IRP$C_LENGTH), an
   attempt is made to allocate a packet from the LRP list. If the rounded size
   is still greater than the size of an LRP, the general allocation routine is
   called to search for the first free block large enough to accommodate the
   request. If the rounded size is less than the smallest request size for which
   an LRP can be allocated (IOC$GL_LRPMIN), the general allocation rou-
   tine is called.
3. The cell IOC$GL_IRPMIN indicates the smallest request size that can be

allocated an IRP. If the rounded size is less than IOC$GL_IRPMIN, an attempt is made to allocate a packet from the SRP list. If the rounded size is greater than the size of an SRP (IOC$GL_SRPSIZE), the general allocation routine is called.

4. Once the appropriate lookaside list is found, and if the list is not empty, the first packet is removed from the list and returned to the caller.
5. If a lookaside list is empty, an attempt is made to extend the list (see Section 3.3.3.2). If the list is extended, the allocation is attempted again. If the list cannot be extended, the general allocation routine is called.

Note that because allocation is done with a single instruction, there is no need for any other synchronization than that provided by the REMQUE instruction; however, IPL is raised to IPL$_SYNCH before determining if the allocation can be made from one of the lookaside lists or the main portion of pool (allocation from the main portion does require synchronization). The other concern of the general allocation routines, the block granularity, is also irrelevant here because all blocks on the lookaside list are the same size.

3.2.2   Deallocation to the Lookaside List

When the routine to deallocate a block of nonpaged pool is called, it first checks whether the block was allocated from the main portion of the pool or from one of the lookaside lists. The lookaside lists are divided by the following symbols, beginning with the smaller addresses:

IOC$GL_LRPSPLIT	Boundary between the main part of pool and the LRP list
EXE$GL_SPLITADR	Boundary between the LRP and the IRP list
IOC$GL_SRPSPLIT	Boundary between the IRP list and the SRP list

These addresses were determined by INIT when the lookaside lists were initialized. Figure 3-4 shows the relationship of the lookaside lists to the rest of nonpaged pool.

The deallocation routine determines the list to which the piece of pool is being returned by the following steps:

• The address of the block being deallocated is compared to the contents of global location IOC$GL_SRPSPLIT. If the address of the block is greater than IOC$GL_SRPSPLIT, the block came from the SRP list.
• If the address was less than IOC$GL_SRPSPLIT, the address is compared to EXE$GL_SPLITADR. If the address is greater, the block came from the IRP list.
• If the address was less than EXE$GL_SPLITADR, the address is compared to IOC$GL_LRPSPLIT. If the address is greater, the block came from the LRP list.

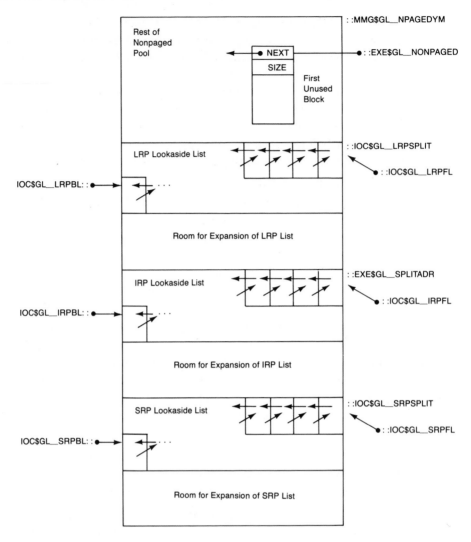

Figure 3-4
Preallocated Request Packets

- If the address was less than IOC$GL_LRPSPLIT, the block came from the main part of pool.

If the block was originally allocated from one of the lookaside lists, it is returned there by inserting it at the end of the list with an INSQUE instruction. The ends of the lookaside lists are indicated by the global labels IOCGL_SRPBL, IOCGL_IRPBL, and IOC$GL_LRPBL. Note that by allocating packets from one end of the list and putting them back at the other end, a transaction history as long as the list itself is maintained. If the block was originally allocated from the general pool area, the general deallocation routine is called. The differences between the lookaside list and the general nonpaged pool are summarized in Table 3-2.

Although the allocation from the lookaside list required no additional synchronization in addition to the REMQUE instruction, deallocation must be done at IPL 7 or below, because nonpaged pool is a resource whose availability must be reported to the scheduler, which will elevate IPL to 7. All deallocation to nonpaged pool is accomplished through the routines EXE$DEANONPAGED (which should not be called above IPL 7), and COM$DRVDEALMEM (which can be called from any IPL).

3.3   USE OF DYNAMIC MEMORY

Almost all of the data structures that are dynamically configured are placed in either the nonpaged or paged pool areas. Only the PFN database, the global and system page tables, the system header, and the interrupt stack have separate virtual address space allocated. Most per-process data structures, on the other hand, are assigned to dedicated areas of P1 space, as defined in the module SHELL and illustrated in Figure 1-7 and listed in Table 26-4. One per-process data structure, the process header, resides in the area of system space called the balance slot area.

3.3.1   Process Allocation Region

The process allocation region is currently 46 pages long. Its size is fixed by an assembly time parameter in module SHELL. Its protection is set to UREW (the page protection codes are described in Table 14-1). That is, it can be written from executive and kernel modes and read from any access mode. Only the process logical name table and the mounted volume list for private volumes are found in the process allocation region. There is enough room in the process allocation region for privileged application software to allocate reasonably sized process-specific data structures.

3.3.2   Paged Dynamic Memory

The following data structures are located in the paged pool area:

- The group and system logical name tables.
- Global section descriptors, which are required only when a section is mapped or unmapped.
- Data structures required by the Install Utility to describe known images. Any image that is installed has a known file entry created to describe it.

Table 3-2: Comparison of Different Pool Areas

Pool Area	Allocation Quantum	Type of List (1 and 2)	Synchronization Technique	Typical Structures Allocated Here
Nonpaged Pool	16 bytes	Variable size (1)	Elevated IPL	Buffered I/O buffer (GTRU 96 bytes) Driver Prolog Table (Driver Structure) Job Information Block Network Data Structures Process Control Block Process Quota Block Unit Control Block (Driver Structure)
Lookaside Lists SRP	@IOC$GL_SRPSIZE	Fixed size blocks (2)	None required	Buffered I/O buffer (LEQU @IOC$GL_IRPMIN bytes) Channel Request Block (Driver Structure) Device Data Block (Driver Structure) File Control Block Interrupt Dispatch Block (Driver Structure) Timer Queue Element Window Control Block
IRP	156 bytes			Buffered I/O buffer (GTR @IOC$GL_IRPMIN bytes) Common Event Block I/O Request Packet Volume Control Block
LRP	@IOC$GL_LRPSIZE			DECnet buffer

Table 3-2: Comparison of Different Pool Areas (continued)

Pool Area	Allocation Quantum	Type of List (1 and 2)	Synchronization Technique	Typical Structures Allocated Here
Paged Pool	16 bytes	Variable size (1)	Mutex	Global Section Descriptors Known File Entries Known File Headers Logical Name Blocks for group and system logical names Mounted Volume List Entry for volumes mounted /SYSTEM or /GROUP
Process Allocation Region	none	Variable size (1)	Access mode	Logical Name Blocks for process logical names Mounted Volume List Entry for private volumes (/SHARE OR /NOSHARE)

(1) The lookaside list has extremely efficient (single instruction) allocation and deallocation routines. Because the blocks are fixed size, internal fragmentation (unused space within individual blocks) can result.

(2) The general pool areas allow variable sized allocation requests (and contain variable sized empty areas). The allocation and deallocation routines must search at least a portion of the empty list. External fragmentation (unused blocks equal to the allocation quantum) near the beginning of the list can result from this type of allocation scheme.

Some frequently accessed known images also have their image headers permanently resident. These data structures are described in more detail in Chapter 21.

- The mounted volume list for volumes shared among several processes.

The size of paged dynamic memory is determined by the SYSBOOT parameter PAGEDYN. Its protection is set to URKW. The pages of paged dynamic memory used by RMS for the shared file database have their protection altered to EW (either read or write access from executive or kernel mode) by RMSSHARE, the image that executes as part of STARTUP.COM to initialize the shared file database.

3.3.3 Nonpaged Dynamic Memory

Nonpaged pool serves several purposes. At initialization time, data structures whose size and contents depend on SYSBOOT parameters will be allocated from nonpaged pool and initialized. These structures include the PCB vector and sequence vector, the swapper's I/O page table, the page file bitmap, modified page writer arrays, and the adapter control blocks for all external adapters located at bootstrap time. The detailed use of nonpaged pool by the initialization routines is described in Chapter 25.

A second general, somewhat static use of nonpaged pool is to contain device driver code and associated data structures for all devices that are either located through the autoconfigure phase of SYSGEN or explicitly loaded with the SYSGEN commands LOAD or CONNECT. The details of these structures are described in the *VAX/VMS Guide to Writing a Device Driver.*

3.3.3.1 The Sizes of Nonpaged Dynamic Memory Regions. The sizes of the variable nonpaged pool and the lookaside lists are determined by SYSBOOT parameters. Nonpaged dynamic memory differs from the paged dynamic area (and the process allocation area) in that it is potentially extensible during normal system operation (see Section 3.3.3.2). For each of the four regions of nonpaged pool there exist two SYSBOOT parameters, one to specify the initial size of the region, and another to specify the maximum size of the region.

The size in bytes of the variable length region of nonpaged pool is controlled by the SYSBOOT parameters NPAGEDYN and NPAGEVIR, both of which are rounded down to an integral number of pages. During system initialization, sufficient contiguous system page table entries (SPTEs) are allocated for the maximum size of the region (the larger of NPAGEDYN and NPAGEVIR). Physical pages of memory are allocated for the initial size of the region and are mapped using the first portion of allocated SPTEs. The protection of the valid pages is ERKW. The remaining SPTEs are left invalid. SPTEs and other memory management data structures are described in Chapter 14.

Table 3-3: SYSBOOT Parameters Controlling Lookaside List Sizes

List Type	Size of Packet	Initial Count	Maximum Count
IRP	160	IRPCOUNT	IRPCOUNTV
SRP	SRPSIZE	SRPCOUNT	SRPCOUNTV
LRP	LRPSIZE+64	LRPCOUNT	LRPCOUNTV

During system operation, failure to allocate from the variable nonpaged pool region will result in an attempted expansion of the region, with physical page(s) allocated to fill in the next invalid SPTE(s). The deallocation merge strategy described in Section 3.2.2 requires that the newly extended nonpaged dynamic area be virtually contiguous with the existing area and that the four regions be adjacent. It is because of these restrictions that the maximum number of SPTEs are allocated for each region, even if some of them are initially unused.

The lookaside lists are allocated during system initialization in the same manner as the variable length region. Table 3-3 lists the SYSBOOT parameters for each lookaside list. In each case, the initial count and maximum count are maximized. SRPSIZE is rounded up to a 16-byte boundary, and the maximum size in bytes of the SRP lookaside list is rounded up to a page boundary. The value 64 is added to LRPSIZE and the sum is rounded up to a 16-byte boundary, and the maximum size in bytes of the LRP lookaside list region is rounded up to a page boundary.

The parameter LRPSIZE is intended to be the DECnet buffer size, exclusive of a 64-byte internal buffer header. (Note that the output of SHOW MEMORY displays the inclusive packet size.)

Dynamic nonpaged pool expansion enables automatic system tuning. The penalty for setting an inadequate initial allocation size is the increased overhead encountered in allocating requests that cause expansion. An additional minor physical penalty is that unnecessary PFN database is built for those physical pages that are subsequently added to nonpaged pool as a result of expansion. The cost is about four percent of the size of the page (18 bytes) per added page. The penalty for a maximum allocation that is too large is one SPTE for each unused page, or less than one percent. If the maximum size of a lookaside list is too small, system performance may be adversely affected when the system is prevented from using the lookaside mechanism for pool requests. If the maximum size of the variable length region is too small, processes may be placed into the MWAIT state, waiting for nonpaged pool to become available.

3.3.3.2 **Expansion of Nonpaged Dynamic Pool.** When routine EXE$ALONONPAGED (in module MEMORYALC) fails to allocate nonpaged pool from any of the four regions, it attempts to expand nonpaged pool by invoking the routine EXE$EXTENDPOOL (found in module MEMORYALC).

EXE$EXTENDPOOL examines each lookaside list in turn. If a list is empty and is not at its maximum size, EXE$EXTENDPOOL attempts to allocate a page of physical memory. First a check is made to see if a physical page can be allocated without reducing the number of physical pages available to the system, that is, sufficient pages to accommodate the sum of the maximum working set size, the modified list low limit, and the free list low limit. If a page can be allocated, EXE$EXTENDPOOL places its page frame number (PFN) in the first invalid SPTE for that list, setting the valid bit. The new virtual page and any fragment from the previous virtual page are formatted into packets of the appropriate size and placed on the list. EXE$EXTENDPOOL records the size and address of any fragment left from the new page.

If EXE$EXTENDPOOL was called due to a failure to allocate space from the variable length region, EXE$EXTENDPOOL attempts to expand the region by a page and reports that the resource RSN$_NPAGEDYN is available for any waiting processes. (See Chapter 10 for more information on scheduling and event reporting.)

For proper synchronization of system databases, the resource availability report and the allocation of physical memory must not be done from a thread of execution running as the result of an interrupt above IPL 7. For this reason, EXE$EXTENDPOOL checks to see whether it has been entered in system context (that is, on the interrupt stack) as the result of attempted pool allocation from a device driver. If the interrupt stack bit in the PSL is set, EXE$EXTENDPOOL creates an IPL 6 fork process to expand the lists at some later time when IPL drops below 6 and returns an allocation failure status to its invoker.

PART II/Control Mechanisms

4   Condition Handling

"Would you tell me, please, which way I ought to go from here?"
  "That depends a good deal on where you want to get to," said the Cat.
—Lewis Carroll, *Alice's Adventures in Wonderland*

One of the design goals of the VAX architecture was a generalized uniform condition handling facility for both hardware-detected exceptions and software-generated conditions. In addition to making this facility available to users, the VAX/VMS operating system uses many of the features of the condition handling facility for its own purposes.

4.1   OVERVIEW OF THE CONDITION HANDLING FACILITY

The generalized condition handling facility that is included as part of the VAX architecture provides users and the system with a powerful tool in handling exceptional conditions that arise during normal program execution. In addition, software-detected conditions (not necessarily indicating an error) can be passed to the operating system to allow them to be handled in exactly the same manner as hardware-detected exceptions.

The options that are available to user programs to allow them to use the features of the VAX-11 condition handling facility are described in the *VAX/VMS System Services Reference Manual* and the *VAX-11 Run-Time Library Reference Manual*. This chapter discusses how the tools described in those two manuals actually implement their features.

4.1.1   Goals of the VAX-11 Condition Handling Facility

Some of the goals of the VAX-11 condition handling facility reflect goals of the VAX-11 procedure calling standard. Other goals reflect the desire to place an easy-to-use, general purpose mechanism into the operating system so that application programs and other layered products such as compilers can use this mechanism rather than inventing their own application-specific tools. Some of the explicit and implicit goals of the VAX-11 condition handling facility are the following.

1. The condition handling facility should be included in the base machine architecture so that it is available as a part of the base machine and not as part of some software component. The space reserved for condition handler addresses in the first longword of the call frame accomplishes this goal.

2. By including the handler specification as a part of the call frame, signal handling is an integral part of a procedure, rather than a global facility within a process. Including the handler specification as part of the call frame contributes to the general goal of modular procedures and allows condition handlers to be nested. The nested inner handlers can either service a detected exception or pass it along to some outer handler in the calling hierarchy.

3. Some languages such as BASIC and PL/I have signaling and error handling as part of the language specification. These languages can use the general mechanism rather than inventing their own procedures.

4. There should be little or no cost to procedures that do not establish handlers. Further, procedures that do establish handlers should incur little overhead for establishing them, with the expense in time being incurred when an error actually occurs.

5. As far as the user or application programmer is concerned, there should be no difference in the appearance of exceptions initially detected by the hardware and signals generated by software.

4.1.2   Features of the VAX-11 Condition Handling Facility

Some of the features of the VAX-11 condition handling facility show how these goals were attained. Others show the general desire to produce an easy-to-use but general condition handling mechanism. Features of the VAX-11 condition handling facility include the following.

1. A condition handler has three options available to it. The handler can fix the condition (continuing). The handler may not be capable of fixing the condition, so it passes the condition on to the next handler in the calling hierarchy (resignaling). The handler can alter the flow of control (unwinding the call stack).

2. Because condition handlers are themselves procedures, each has its own call frame with its own slot for a condition handler address. This condition handler address gives handlers the ability to establish their own handlers to field errors that they might cause.

3. The goals related to cost in space and time were realized by using only a single longword per procedure activation for handler address storage. There is no cost in time for procedures that do not establish handlers. Procedures that do establish handlers can do so with a single MOVAx instruction. No time is spent looking for condition handlers until a signal is actually generated.

4. The mechanism is designed to work even if a condition handler is written in a language that does not produce reentrant code. Thus, if a condition handler written in FORTRAN generated an error, that error would not be reported to the same handler.

    In fact, the special actions that are taken if multiple signals are active have a second benefit, namely that no condition handler has to worry about errors that it generates, because a handler would never be called in response to its own signals.

5. Uniform exception dispatching for hardware and software exceptions is accomplished by providing parallel mechanisms for the two forms of exceptions. Software-detected exceptions are generated by calling a procedure in the Run-Time Library. Hardware exceptions transfer control to an exception dispatcher in the executive. While the initial execution of these two mechanisms differs slightly to reflect their differing initial conditions, they eventually execute identical instruction sequences so that the information reported to condition handlers is independent of the initial detection mechanism.

6. By making condition handling a part of a procedure, high level languages can establish handlers that can examine a given signal and determine whether the signal was generated as a part of that language's support library. If so, the handler can attempt to fix the error in the manner defined by the language. If not, the handler passes the signal along to procedures further up the call stack.

4.2   GENERATION OF EXCEPTIONS

One way of classifying the conditions that occur in a running VAX/VMS system is to separate those conditions that originate in the VAX-11 hardware from those that are initiated by software. The primary differences between the two sets of initial conditions are the initial state of the stack that contains the exception parameters and the location of the routine that performs the dispatching.

4.2.1   Exceptions That Originate in the Hardware

When an exception is detected by the hardware, the exception PC and PSL (and possible exception-specific parameters) are pushed onto the appropriate stack. The appropriate stack is determined by the access mode in which the exception occurred and whether the CPU was previously executing on the interrupt stack.

- If the exception occurred in any mode other than kernel and the exception was not a CHMU, CHMS, or CHME exception, the kernel stack is used. (The interrupt stack is not a consideration in this case because it is impossible to be on the interrupt stack in other than kernel mode.)
- If the exception occurred in kernel mode and the kernel stack was in use, the kernel stack is also used as the exception stack.
- If the exception occurred in kernel mode and the interrupt stack was in use, the interrupt stack is used as the exception stack. The VMS system

does not expect exceptions to occur when it is operating on the interrupt stack. If an exception should occur on the interrupt stack, the exception dispatcher generates a VMS-requested system crash called a bugcheck (see Chapter 8) with a BUG$_INVEXCEPTN code.

The actual stack (interrupt or kernel) that is used to service an exception or interrupt is determined by the low-order two bits in the system control block (SCB) entry and whether the interrupt stack is already in use. These rules reflect the behavior of the VMS executive, where exceptions are associated with a process and serviced on that process's kernel stack (because the low-order two bits in the SCB entry are zero). The interrupt stack is only used if it was already in use when the exception occurred. Note that two serious aborts (machine check and kernel stack not valid), exceptions that also change IPL to 31, are serviced on the interrupt stack by the system.

After all of the exception information has been pushed onto the stack, control is then passed to an exception-specific service routine whose address is stored in the SCB (see Figure 4-1). The use of the first twenty

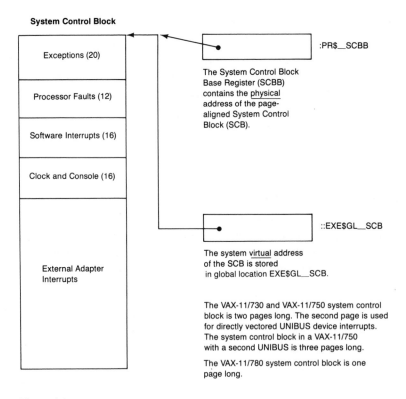

Figure 4-1
System Control Block

locations of this table are listed in Table 4-1. Most of the exceptions that are listed in this table are handled in a uniform way by the operating system. The actions that the VMS executive takes in response to these exceptions are the subject of most of this chapter. Some of the exceptions, however, result in special action on the part of the operating system. These exceptions are discussed in the paragraphs that follow and are indicated in Table 4-1 by an asterisk.

4.2.1.1 **Exceptions That the VMS Executive Treats in a Special Way.** Although the operating system provides uniform handling of most exceptions generated by users, several possible exceptions are used as entry points into privileged system procedures. Other exceptions can only be acted upon by the executive. It makes no sense for these procedures to pass information about the exceptions along to user's programs.

1. The machine check exception is a processor-specific condition that may or may not be recoverable. The machine check exception service routine is discussed in Chapter 8.
2. A kernel-stack-not-valid exception indicates that the kernel stack was not valid while the processor was pushing information onto the stack during the initiation of an exception or interrupt. The exception service routine for this exception generates a fatal bugcheck with a BUG$_KRNLSTAKNV code.
3. The powerfail entry point that appears as one of the first twenty entries in the SCB is not an exception. Because a power fluctuation occurs asynchronously with respect to the currently executing instruction stream, it is actually an interrupt. The fact that powerfail is an interrupt, with an associated IPL, implies that the powerfail interrupt can be blocked simply by raising IPL to 30 or 31. The steps that the VMS system takes in response to power failure as well as on power recovery are described in Chapter 27.
4. The translation-not-valid exception is a signal that a reference was made to a virtual address that is not currently mapped to physical memory. The page fault handler that is invoked in response to this exception is discussed in detail in Chapter 15.
5. The change-mode-to-kernel and change-mode-to-executive exceptions are the mechanisms used by the VMS system services and by RMS to reach a more privileged access mode. The dispatching scheme for system services and RMS calls is described in Chapter 9.

   The last two exceptions in the list (the two change mode exceptions) are paths into the operating system that allow nonprivileged users to reach a privileged access mode in a controlled fashion.

Table 4-1: Use of First 20 Locations in System Control Block

Byte Offset from SCB Base	Exception Name	Extra Parameters	Type (Abort, Fault, Trap)	Notes on VMS Dispatching	Comments
0	Unused				
4	*Machine Check	Note 1	Note 1	Note 1	(See Chapter 8.)
8	*Kernel Stack Not Valid	0	Abort	Note 2	IPL=31, Interrupt Stack
12	*Powerfail	0	Interrupt	Note 3	IPL=30 (See Chapter 27.)
16	Reserved/Privileged Instruction	0	Fault		
20	Customer Reserved Instruction	0	Fault		XFC Instruction
24	Reserved Operand	0	Abort/Fault		
28	Reserved Addressing Mode	0	Fault		
32	Access Violation	2	Fault		
36	*Translation Not Valid	2	Fault	Note 4	(See Chapter 14.)
40	Trace Pending	0	Fault	Note 5	
44	BPT Instruction	0	Fault	Note 5	
48	Compatibility Mode	1	Abort/Fault		
52	Arithmetic	1	Fault/Trap		VMS modifies code (See Table 4-3.)

Table 4-1: Use of First 20 Locations in System Control Block (continued)

Byte Offset from SCB Base	Exception Name	Extra Parameters	Type (Abort, Fault, Trap)	Notes on VMS Dispatching	Comments
56	Unused				
60	Unused				
64	*CHMK	1	Trap	Note 6	Uses Kernel Stack (See Chapter 9.)
68	*CHME	1	Trap	Note 6	Uses Executive Stack (See Chapter 9.)
72	CHMS	1	Trap		Uses Supervisor Stack
76	CHMU	1	Trap		Uses User Stack

*These exceptions result in special action on the part of the operating system.

(1) The machine check exception indicates a processor-detected internal error. Machine checks in executive and kernel mode cause bugchecks. Machine checks in supervisor and user mode are reported through the normal exception dispatch method.

(2) The exception service routine for the kernel-stack-not-valid abort issues a bugcheck.

(3) Powerfail causes an interrupt that passes control to the powerfail handler.

(4) The translation-not-valid fault is the entry path into the paging facility in VMS.

(5) If executive debugging (XDELTA) is selected at SYSBOOT time, the exception vectors for BPT and trace pending are altered to point into XDELTA fault handlers (see Chapter 25).

(6) The change-mode-to-kernel and change-mode-to-executive traps are the entry paths into system service and RMS procedures.

4.2.1.2 **Other Hardware Exceptions.** The rest of the exceptions detected by hardware are handled uniformly by their exception service routines. These exceptions are all reported to condition handlers established by the user or by the system, rather than resulting in special system action such as occurs following a change-mode-to-kernel exception or a translation-not-valid fault (page fault).

When a hardware-detected exception occurs, the PSL and PC at the time of the exception are pushed onto the stack. The usual stack that is used is the kernel stack but the CHMx exceptions use the stack of the destination mode. For example, a CHMS exception pushes the PC and PSL of the exception onto the supervisor stack. Note that a CHMx instruction issued from an inner access mode in an attempt to reach a less privileged (outer) access mode will not have the desired effect. The mode indicated by the instruction is minimized with the current access mode to determine the actual access mode that will be used. For example, a CHMS instruction issued from kernel mode will generate an exception through the correct SCB vector (the one for CHMS), but the final access mode will still be kernel. In other words, as illustrated in Figure 1-4, the CHMx instructions can only reach equal or more privileged access modes.

The PC that is pushed depends on the nature of the exception, that is, whether the exception is a fault, a trap, or an abort.

- Exceptions that are faults (see Table 4-1) cause the PC of the faulting instruction to be pushed onto the stack. When faults are dismissed with an REI instruction, the faulting instruction will execute again.
- Exceptions that are traps (see Table 4-1) push the PC of the next instruction onto the destination stack. Instructions that cause traps do not reexecute when the exception is dismissed with an REI instruction.
- A third class of exception, an abort, causes a PC in the middle of the instruction to be pushed onto the stack. Aborts are not restartable. Some aborts also raise IPL to 31, blocking all other activity on the system. IPL is usually not affected when exceptions occur. Independence from IPL is one of the features that distinguishes exceptions from interrupts. Exceptions that are aborts include kernel-stack-not-valid, some machine check codes, and some reserved operand exceptions.

For all exceptions that will eventually be reported to condition handlers, the hardware has pushed a PC/PSL pair onto the destination stack. In addition, from zero to two exception-specific parameters are pushed onto the destination stack (see Table 4-1). Finally, the hardware passes control to the exception service routine whose address VMS placed into the SCB when the system was initialized.

4.2.1.3 **Initial Action of Exception Service Routines.** These exception service routines all perform approximately the same action. The exception name (of the form SS$_exception-name) and the total number of exception parameters (from the exception name to the saved PSL inclusive) are pushed onto the stack so that the destination stack now contains a list, called the signal array, that resembles a VAX-11 argument list used by the CALLx instructions (see Figure 4-2). The exceptions that the operating system handles in this uniform way, including their names and total number of signal array elements, are listed in Table 4-2.

After the VMS system has built this array, control is passed to a general exception dispatcher that must locate any condition handlers that have been established in the access mode of the exception. The search method and the list of information passed to condition handlers is described in Section 4.3 below.

All hardware exceptions (except for CHME, CHMS, and CHMU) are initially reported on the kernel stack (assuming the processor is not already on the interrupt stack). In addition, the hardware exception reporting mechanism assumes that the kernel stack is valid. The decision to use the kernel stack was made to avoid the case of attempting to report an exception on, for example, the user stack, only to find that the user stack is corrupted in some way (invalid or otherwise inaccessible), resulting in another exception. If a kernel-stack-not-valid exception is generated while reporting an exception, the operating system causes a fatal bugcheck to occur.

However, the exception must eventually be reported back to the access mode in which the exception occurred. Before the dispatcher begins its search, it creates space on the stack of the mode in which the exception occurred. The exception parameter lists are then copied to that stack, where they will become the argument list that is passed to condition handlers.

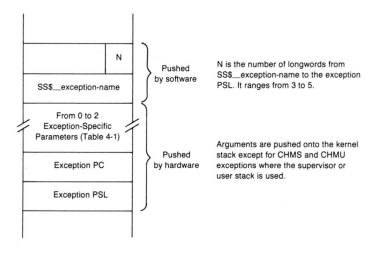

Figure 4-2
Signal Array Built by Hardware and Exception Routines

Table 4-2: Exceptions That Use the Dispatcher in Module EXCEPTION

Exception Name	Name in Signal Array	Notes on VMS Dispatching (Section 4.2.1.4)	Size of Signal Array	Extra Parameters in Signal Array (Note 1)
Access Violation	SS$_ACCVIO	Item 1	5	Signal (2) = Reason Mask Signal (3) = Inaccessible Virtual Address
Arithmetic Exception	(See Table 4-3.)	Item 2	3	Note 2
AST Delivery Stack Fault (Software exception)	SS$_ASTFLT	Item 3c	7	Signal (2) = SP Value at Fault Signal (3) = AST Parameter of failed AST (Note 3) Signal (4) = PC at AST delivery interrupt Signal (5) = PSL at AST delivery interrupt Signal (6) = PC to which AST would have been delivered Signal (7) = PSL at which AST would have been delivered
BPT Instruction	SS$_BREAK		3	
Change Mode to Supervisor	SS$_CMODSUPR	Item 4	4	Signal (2) = Change mode code
Change Mode to User	SS$_CMODUSER	Item 4	4	Signal (2) = Change mode code
Compatibility Mode	SS$_COMPAT	Item 4	4	Signal (2) = Compatibility exception code
Debug Signal (Software exception)	SS$_DEBUG	Item 3	3	
Machine Check	SS$_MCHECK		3	Note 4
Customer Reserved Instruction	SS$_OPCCUS		3	
Reserved/Privileged Instruction	SS$_OPCDEC	Item 5	3	

Table 4-2: Exceptions That Use the Dispatcher in Module EXCEPTION (continued)

Exception Name	Name in Signal Array	Notes on VMS Dispatching (Section 4.2.1.4)	Size of Signal Array	Extra Parameters in Signal Array (Note 1)
Page Fault Read Error (Software exception)	SS$_PAGRDERR	Item 3b	5	Signal (2) = Reason Mask Signal (3) = Inaccessible Virtual Address
Reserved Addressing Mode	SS$_RADRMOD		3	
Reserved Operand	SS$_ROPRAND		3	
System Service Failure (Software exception)	SS$_SSFAIL	Item 3a	4	Signal (2) = System service final status
Trace Pending	SS$_TBIT		3	

(1) Additional parameters in the signal array are represented in the following way.

Signal (0) = N   Number of additional longwords in signal array
Signal (1)   Exception name
Signal (2)   First additional parameter
Signal (3)   Second additional parameter

.
.

Signal [N − 1]   Exception PC
Signal [N]   Exception PSL

(2) The arithmetic exception has no extra parameters, despite the fact that the hardware pushes an exception code onto the kernel stack. VMS modifies this hardware code into an exception-specific exception name (see Table 4-3).
Signal (1) = 8 * code + SS$_ARTRES

(3) The AST delivery code exchanges the interrupt PC/PSL pair and the PC/PSL to which the AST would have been delivered.

(4) Machine check exceptions that are reported to a process do not have any extra parameters in the signal array. The machine check parameters have been examined, written to the error log, and discarded by the machine check handler (see Chapter 8).

71

4.2.1.4 **More Special Cases in Exception Dispatching.** Although the procedure described above is a reasonable approximation to the operation of the exception service routines in the operating system, there are detailed differences that occur in the dispatching of several exceptions that deserve special mention. These special cases are listed here.

1. User Stack Overflow is detected by the hardware as an access violation at the low address end of P1 space. The access violation fault handler tests whether the inaccessible virtual address is at the low end of P1 space. If it is, the stack is expanded and the exception dismissed. User and system condition handlers would only be notified about such an exception if the stack expansion were unsuccessful.

2. There are ten possible arithmetic exceptions that can occur. They are distinguished in the hardware by different exception parameters. However, the exception service routine does not simply push a generic exception name onto the stack, resulting in a four-parameter signal array. Rather, the exception parameter is used by the exception service routine to fashion a unique exception name for each of the possible arithmetic exceptions. The exception parameters and their associated signal names are listed in Table 4-3.

3. There are three exceptions listed in Table 4-2 that are detected by software rather than by hardware. However, these conditions are not generated by LIB$SIGNAL. Rather, they are detected by the executive, and control is passed to the same routines that are used for dispatching hardware-detected exceptions. The conditions are dispatched through the executive, because they are typically detected in kernel mode but must be reported back to some other access mode. The code to accomplish this access mode switch is contained in EXCEPTION. LIB$SIGNAL has no corresponding function. The three exceptions that fall into this category are system service failure exceptions, page fault read errors, and insufficient stack space while attempting to deliver an AST.

   - The SS$_SSFAIL exception is reported when a process has enabled system service failure exceptions and a system service returns unsuccessfully with a status of either STS$K_ERROR or STS$K_SEVERE.
   - The SS$_PAGRDERR exception is reported when a process incurs a page fault for a page on which a read error occurred in response to a previous page fault.
   - The SS$_ASTFLT exception is reported when an inaccessible stack is detected while attempting to deliver an AST to a process.

   A fourth software-detected exception is listed in Table 4-2 although it does not have a global entry point in module EXCEPTION. The signal SS$_DEBUG is generated by either the DCL or MCR command language interpreter in response to a DEBUG command while an image exists in an

Table 4-3: Signal Names for Arithmetic Exceptions

Exception Type	Code Pushed by Hardware	Resulting Exception Reported by VMS	Notes
Traps			
Integer Overflow	1	SS$_INTOVF	1
Integer Divide by Zero	2	SS$_INTDIV	
Floating Overflow	3	SS$_FLTOVF	3
Floating/Decimal			
Divide by Zero	4	SS$_FLTDIV	3
Floating Underflow	5	SS$_FLTUND	2, 3
Decimal Overflow	6	SS$_DECOVF	1
Subscript Range	7	SS$_SUBRNG	
Faults			
Floating Overflow	8	SS$_FLTOVF_F	3
Floating Divide by Zero	9	SS$_FLTDIV_F	3
Floating Underflow	10	SS$_FLTUND_F	3

(1) Integer overflow enable and decimal overflow enable bits in the PSW can be altered either directly or through the procedure entry mask.
(2) The floating underflow enable bit in the PSW can only be altered directly. There is no corresponding bit in the procedure entry mask.
(3) On the VAX-11/730 and VAX-11/750, these three floating point exceptions are faults. On the VAX-11/780 earlier than microcode revision (rev) level 7, they are traps. Rev level 7 ECO changes them to faults.

interrupted state. The DEBUG command processor pushes the PC and PSL of the interrupted image, the exception name (SS$_DEBUG), and the size of the signal array (3) onto the supervisor stack and jumps to EXE$REFLECT, a global entry address in module EXCEPTION.

The reason that a CLI uses this mechanism for the DEBUG signal rather than simply calling LIB$SIGNAL is that the DEBUG command is issued while in supervisor mode but the exception has to be reported back to user mode. Reporting information back to user mode involves moving the exception parameters from one stack to another (a function that does not exist in LIB$SIGNAL but does exist in EXCEPTION), because most hardware-detected exceptions are reported on the kernel stack.

4. The exception dispatching for the CHMS and CHMU exceptions and for compatibility mode exceptions can be short-circuited by use of the Declare Change Mode or Compatibility Mode Handler system service. When this system service is executed, one of three longword locations in the P1 pointer page (see Appendix A) is loaded with the address of the handler passed as a parameter to the system service.

When the dispatcher for the change-mode-to-supervisor or change-mode-to-user exception finds nonzero contents in the associated longword in P1 space, it transfers control to the routine whose address is stored in that location with the exception stack (supervisor or user) in exactly the same state it was in following the exception. That is, the change mode code is on the top of the stack, and the exception PC and exception PSL occupy the next two longwords.

The dispatcher for compatibility mode exceptions transfers control to the user-declared compatibility mode handler (if one was declared) with the user stack in the same state it was before the compatibility mode exception occurred. That is, no parameters are passed to the compatibility mode handler on the user stack. The compatibility mode code, the exception PC and PSL, and the contents of R0 through R6 are saved in the first ten longwords of the compatibility mode context page in P1 space at global location CTL$AL_CMCNTX (see Appendix A).

5. The reserved instruction fault is generated whenever an unrecognized opcode is detected by the instruction decoder. The same exception is generated when a privileged instruction is executed from other than kernel mode.

    VMS uses this fault as a path into the operating system crash code called the bugcheck mechanism. Opcode FF, followed by FE or FD, tells the reserved instruction exception service routine that the exception is actually a bugcheck. Control is passed to the bugcheck routine that is described in Chapter 8.

4.2.2   Exceptions Detected by Software

One of the goals of the design of the VAX architecture was to have a common condition handling facility for both hardware-detected and software-detected conditions. The dispatching for conditions that are initially detected by the hardware (and for four special software-detected exceptions) is performed by the routines in the executive module EXCEPTION. The Run-Time Library procedure called LIB$SIGNAL provides a similar capability to any user of a VAX/VMS system.

4.2.2.1   Passing Status from a Procedure.
There are usually two methods available for a procedure to indicate to its caller whether it completed successfully. One method is to indicate a return status in R0. The other is the signaling mechanism. The signaling mechanism involves a call to the VAX-11 Run-Time Library procedure LIB$SIGNAL to initiate a sequence of events exactly like those that occur in response to a hardware-detected exception. One of

the choices that must be made when designing a modular procedure is the method for reporting exceptional conditions back to the caller.

There are two reasons why signaling may be chosen over completion status. In some procedures, such as the mathematics procedures in the Run-Time Library, R0 is already used for another purpose, namely the return of a function value, and is therefore unavailable for error return status. In this case, the procedure must use the signaling mechanism to indicate exceptional conditions, such as an attempt to take the square root of a negative number.

The second common use of signaling occurs in an application that is using an indeterminate number of procedure calls to perform some action, such as a recursive procedure that parses a command line, where the use of a return status is often cumbersome and difficult to code. In this case, the VAX-11 signaling mechanism provides a graceful way not only to indicate that an error has occurred but also to return control (through SYS$UNWIND) to a known alternate return point in the calling hierarchy.

4.2.2.2 **Initial Operation of LIB$SIGNAL.** When the procedure that detects an error wishes to signal it, the procedure calls LIB$SIGNAL with the name of the exception and whatever additional parameters it wishes to pass to the condition handlers that have been established by the user and by the system. The state of the stack following a call to LIB$SIGNAL is pictured in Figure 4-3.

Before LIB$SIGNAL begins its search for condition handlers, it removes the call frame (and possibly the argument list) from the stack. Removing the call frame causes the stack to appear almost exactly the same to LIB$SIGNAL as it does to EXCEPTION following a hardware exception (see Figure 4-3). After building the exception argument list, LIB$SIGNAL uses the routines in EXCEPTION to search for condition handlers. The only difference between this procedure and the code contained in the executive is that no stack switch is required here. The search for condition handlers takes place on the stack of the caller of LIB$SIGNAL.

4.3 **UNIFORM EXCEPTION DISPATCHING**

Once information concerning the exception has been pushed onto the stack, the differences between hardware and software exceptions are no longer important. In the following discussion, the operation of exception dispatching will be discussed in general terms and explicit mention of EXCEPTION or LIB$SIGNAL will only be made where they depart from each other in their operation.

Before the search for a condition handler begins, the exception dispatcher must build a second data structure on the stack that will be used to report the

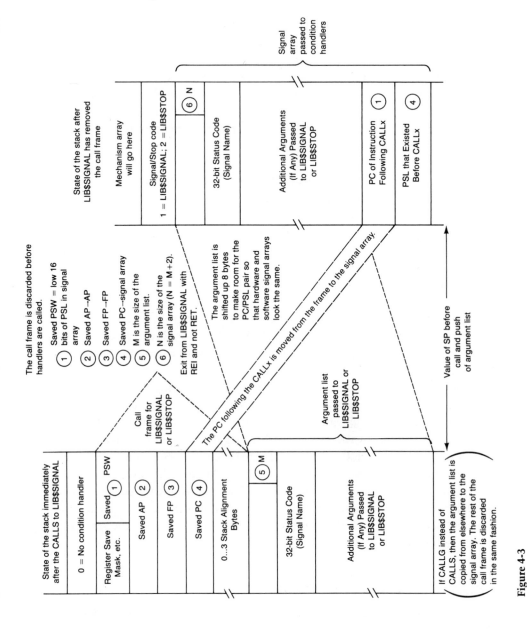

State of the stack immediately after the CALLS to LIB$SIGNAL

0 = No condition handler

Register Save Mask, etc.   Saved ① PSW

Saved AP ②

Saved FP ③

Saved PC ④

0...3 Stack Alignment Bytes

⑤ M

32-bit Status Code (Signal Name)

Additional Arguments (If Any) Passed to LIB$SIGNAL or LIB$STOP

If CALLG instead of CALLS, then the argument list is copied from elsewhere to the signal array. The rest of the call frame is discarded in the same fashion.

Argument list passed to LIB$SIGNAL or LIB$STOP

Value of SP before call and push of argument list

The PC following the CALLx is moved from the frame to the signal array.

The call frame is discarded before handlers are called.

① Saved PSW = low 16 bits of PSL in signal array

② Saved AP→AP

③ Saved FP→FP

④ Saved PC→signal array

⑤ M is the size of the argument list.

⑥ N is the size of the signal array (N = M + 2).

Exit from LIB$SIGNAL with REI and not RET.

The argument list is shifted up 8 bytes to make room for the PC/PSL pair so that hardware and software signal arrays look the same.

Call frame for LIB$SIGNAL or LIB$STOP

State of the stack after LIB$SIGNAL has removed the call frame

Mechanism array will go here

Signal/Stop code
1 = LIB$SIGNAL; 2 = LIB$STOP

⑥ N

32-bit Status Code (Signal Name)

Additional Arguments (If Any) Passed to LIB$SIGNAL or LIB$STOP

PC of Instruction Following CALLx ①

PSL that Existed Before CALLx ④

Signal array passed to condition handlers

Figure 4-3
Removal of Call Frame by LIB$SIGNAL

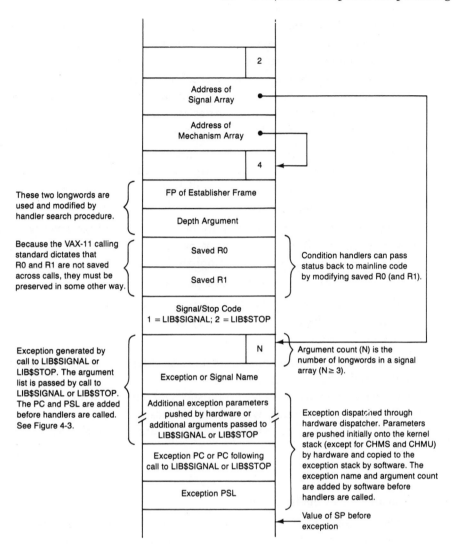

Figure 4-4
Signal and Mechanism Arrays

exception. The address of this structure, called the mechanism array, along with the address of the table containing the exception arguments will be the two arguments that are passed to any condition handlers that are called by the dispatcher (see Figure 4-4).

4.3.1   Establishing a Condition Handler

The VMS operating system provides two different methods for establishing condition handlers.

- One method uses the call stack associated with each access mode. Each call frame includes a longword to contain the address of a condition handler associated with that frame.
- The second method uses software exception vectors, set aside in the control region (P1 space) for each of the four access modes. Vectored handlers do not possess the modular properties associated with call frame handlers and are intended primarily for debuggers and performance monitors.

Call frame handlers are established by placing the address of the handler in the first longword of the currently active call frame. Thus, in assembly language, call frame handlers can be established with a single instruction:

```
MOVAB new-handler,(FP)
```

Because the frame pointer is generally not available to high level language programmers, the Run-Time Library procedure LIB$ESTABLISH can be called in the following way to accomplish the same result:

```
old-handler = LIB$ESTABLISH (new-handler)
```

Condition handlers are removed by clearing the first longword of the current call frame, as in the following assembly language instruction:

```
CLRL (FP)
```

The Run-Time Library procedure LIB$REVERT removes the condition handler established by LIB$ESTABLISH.

Exception vector handlers are established and removed with the Set Exception Vector system service, which simply loads the address of the specified handler into the specified exception vector, located in the pointer page in P1 space.

4.3.2   The Search for a Condition Handler

At this point in the dispatch sequence, the signal and mechanism arrays have been set up on the stack of the access mode that the exception will be reported to. The establisher frame argument in the mechanism array (see Figure 4-4) will be used by the search procedure to indicate how far along the search has gone. The depth argument in the mechanism array not only serves as useful information to condition handlers that wish to unwind but also allows the search procedure to distinguish call frame handlers (nonnegative depth) from exception vector handlers (negative depth).

4.3.2.1   Primary and Secondary Exception Vectors.

The search for a condition handler begins with the primary exception vector of the access mode in which the exception occurred. If the vector contains the address of a condition handler (any nonzero contents), the handler is called with a depth argument of -2 (third longword in mechanism array, Figure 4-4). If that handler resignals or if none exists, the same step is performed for the secondary exception vector, where the depth argument is now −1.

4.3.2.2   **Call Frame Condition Handlers.** If the search is to continue (no handler yet passed back a status of SS$_CONTINUE), the contents of the current call frame are examined next. If the first longword in the current call frame is nonzero, that handler is called next. If no handler is found there or if that handler resignals, the previous call frame is examined by using the saved frame pointer in the current call frame (see Figure 4-5). As each handler is called, the depth longword in the mechanism array is set to the number of frames that have already been examined for a handler.

The search continues until some handler passes back a status code of SS$_CONTINUE or until a saved frame pointer of zero is found (indicating the end of the call frame chain). When the exception dispatcher receives a return status of SS$_CONTINUE (any code with the low bit of R0 set will do), the stack is cleaned off, R0 and R1 are restored from the mechanism array, and the exception is dismissed by issuing an REI, using the saved PC and PSL that form the last two elements of the signal array.

Note that control is passed back with an REI instruction, even if the exception was caused by a call to LIB$SIGNAL, because it discarded the call frame that was set up when it was called. That is, LIB$SIGNAL modifies its stack to look just like the stack used by EXCEPTION (see Figure 4-3).

4.3.2.3   **Last Chance Condition Handler.** In the event that all handlers resignal, the search terminates when a saved frame pointer of zero is located. The exception dispatcher then calls the handler whose address is stored in the last chance exception vector with a depth argument of −3. (This handler is also called in the event that any errors occur while searching the stack for the existence of condition handlers.) The usual handler found in the last chance vector is the so-called catch-all condition handler established as part of image initiation. The action of this system-supplied handler is described at the end of this chapter.

If the last chance handler returns to the dispatcher (its status is ignored) or if the last chance vector is empty, the exception dispatcher indicates that no handler was found. This notification is performed by a procedure called EXE$EXCMSG (see Chapter 30) in the executive. Its two input parameters are an ASCIZ string containing message text and the argument list that was passed to any condition handlers. Following the call to EXE$EXCMSG (see Chapter 30), the image is terminated with a status indicating either that no handler was found or that a bad stack was detected while searching for a condition handler.

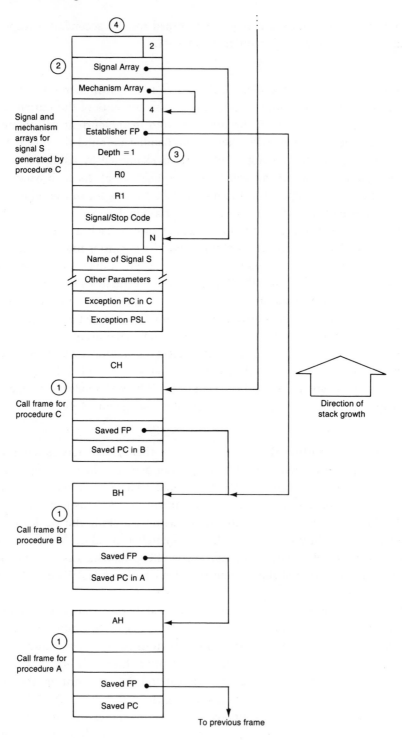

Figure 4-5
Order of Search for Condition Handler

4.3.3   Multiply Active Signals

If an exception occurs in a condition handler or in a procedure called by a condition handler, a situation called multiply active signals is reached. To avoid an infinite loop of exceptions, the procedure that searches for condition handlers modifies its search algorithm so that frames searched while servicing the first condition are skipped while servicing the second condition.

In order for this skipping to work correctly, call frames of condition handlers must be uniquely recognizable. The frames are made unique by always calling the condition handlers from a standard call site, located in the system service vector area.

4.3.3.1   Common Call Site for Condition Handlers. Before the dispatch to the handler occurs, the stack is set up to contain the signal and mechanism arrays and the handler argument list (see Figure 4-4). The handler address is loaded into R1 by the handler search procedure and control is passed to the common dispatch site with the following instruction:

```
JSB      @#SYS$CALL_HANDL
```

The code located at SYS$CALL_HANDL simply calls the procedure whose address is stored in R1 and returns to its caller with an RSB.

```
SYS$CALL_HANDL::
         CALLG     4(SP),(R1)
         RSB
```

The call instruction leaves the return address SYS$CALL_HANDL + 4, the address of the RSB instruction, in its call frame. Thus, the unique identifying characteristic of a condition handler is the address SYS$CALL_HANDL + 4 in the saved PC of its call frame. This signature is used not only by the search procedure but also by the Unwind system service, as described below.

4.3.3.2   Example of Multiply Active Signals. The modified search procedure can best be illustrated through an example. Figure 4-5 shows the stack after procedure C, called from B called from A, has generated signal S. We are assuming that the primary and secondary condition handlers (if they exist) resignaled. Condition handler CH also resignaled.

① Procedure A calls procedure B, which calls procedure C.
② Procedure C generates signal S.
③ The search procedure modifies the depth argument and establisher frame argument. If handler CH resignals, the depth argument is 1 when BH is called.
④ The call frame for handler BH is located (at lower virtual addresses) on top of the signal and mechanism arrays for signal S (see Figure 4-6). (The only intervening items are the saved registers and stack alignment bytes

81

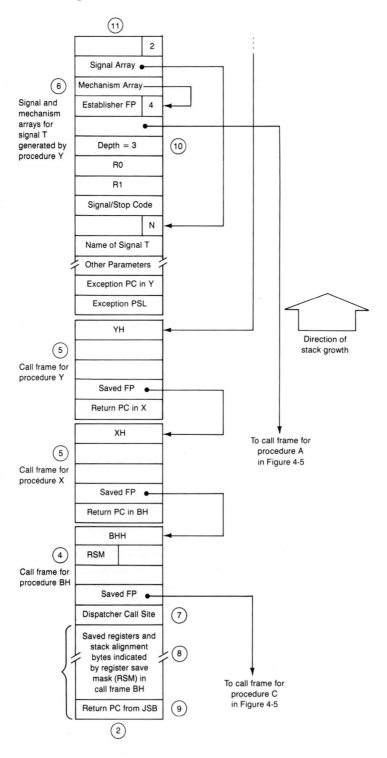

Figure 4-6
Modified Search with Multiply Active Signals

indicated by the register save mask in the upper byte of the second long-word of the call frame for handler BH.) The saved frame pointer in the call frame for BH points to the frame for procedure C.

⑤ Handler BH now calls procedure X, which calls procedure Y (see Figure 4-6).

⑥ Procedure Y generates signal T. The desired sequence of frames to be examined is: frame Y, frame X, frame BH, and then frame A. Frames B and C should be skipped because they were examined while servicing condition S.

⑦ The search procedure proceeds in its normal fashion. The primary and secondary vectors are examined first (no skipping here). Then frames Y, X, and BH are examined, resulting in handlers YH, XH, and BHH being called in turn. Let us assume that all these handlers resignal. After handler BHH returns to the dispatcher with a code of SS$_RESIGNAL, the search procedure notes that this is the frame of a condition handler, because its saved PC is SYS$CALL_HANDL + 4 (see Figure 4-6).

⑧ The skipping is accomplished by locating the frame that established this handler. The address of that frame is located in the mechanism array for signal S.

To locate the mechanism array for signal S, the value of SP before the call to BH must be calculated, using the register save mask and stack alignment bits in the call frame.

⑨ One extra longword, the return PC from the JSB to SYS$CALL_HANDL, must be skipped to locate the argument list (and thus the mechanism array) for signal S.

⑩ Because the frame pointed to by the mechanism array element has already been searched, the next frame examined by the search procedure is the frame pointed to by the saved frame pointer in the call frame of procedure B, which in this case is the frame for procedure A. The depths that are passed to handlers as a result of the modified search are 0 for YH, 1 for XH, 2 for BHH, and 3 for AH.

⑪ The frame for the search procedure, or for any of the handlers YH, XH, BHH, and AH when they are called, will be located on top of the signal and mechanism arrays for signal T (at lower virtual addresses). (One example is shown in Figure 4-8, which illustrates the operation of SYS$UNWIND.)

4.4   **CONDITION HANDLER ACTION**

Condition handlers have several options available to them.

• They can fix the exception and allow execution to continue at the interrupted point in the program.

- They can pass the exception along to another handler by resignaling.
- They can also allow execution to resume at any arbitrary place in the calling hierarchy by unwinding a number of frames from the call stack.

4.4.1 Continue or Resignal

A handler first determines the nature of the exception by examining the signal name in the signal array (see Figure 4-4). If the handler determines that it is not capable of resolving the current exception for whatever reason, it informs the exception dispatcher that the search for a handler must go on. This continuation is called resignaling and is performed by passing a return status code of SS$_RESIGNAL back to the dispatcher. (Recall that condition handlers are function procedures that return a status to their caller in R0.)

On the other hand, if the condition handler is able to resolve the exception (in some unspecified way), it indicates to the dispatcher that the program that was interrupted when the exception occurred can continue. To indicate that the program can continue, the return status code of SS$_CONTINUE is passed back to the caller.

When the dispatcher detects this return status code, it removes the argument list and mechanism array from the stack (see Figure 4-4), restoring R0 and R1 in the process. It then removes all of the signal array except the exception PC and PSL from the stack. Finally, these are removed with the REI instruction that dismisses the exception and passes control back to the program that was interrupted when the exception occurred.

If the exception that occurred was a hardware fault (such as an access violation), the instruction that caused the exception will be repeated because the PC of that instruction was pushed onto the stack when the exception occurred. If the exception was a hardware trap (such as integer overflow), the next instruction in the instruction stream will be the first to execute. In the event that a condition handler continues from an exception that was initiated through a call to LIB$SIGNAL, the first instruction to execute will be the instruction following the CALLx instruction.

4.4.2 Unwinding the Call Stack

Another powerful tool available to condition handlers allows them to alter the flow of control when an exception occurs. This tool is called unwinding and allows the condition handler to pass control back to a previous level in the calling hierarchy by throwing away a specified (or default) number of call frames.

The Unwind Call Stack system service is called with two optional arguments, the first of which indicates the number of frames to remove from the call stack and the second of which gives an alternate return PC to which control will be returned.

The Unwind system service does not actually remove frames from the stack. Rather, it changes the return PC in the specified number of frames to point to a special routine in the executive that will be entered as each procedure exits with a RET instruction. The effect of calling Unwind is pictured in Figure 4-7. If the alternate PC argument has also been passed to Unwind, the return PC in the next call frame is altered to the specified argument (see Figure 4-7).

As each procedure issues a RET instruction, control is passed to the executive routine that examines the current frame for the existence of a condition handler. If such a handler exists, it is called with the exception name SS$_UNWIND. When the condition handler returns to the unwind routine, a RET is issued by the unwind routine on behalf of the procedure to discard the current call frame. This sequence goes on until the specified number of call frames have been discarded. This technique of calling handlers as a part of the unwind sequence allows handlers that previously resignaled an exception to regain control and perform procedure-specific cleanup.

4.4.3   **Example of Unwinding the Call Stack**

An example of an unwind sequence is illustrated here with the help of Figure 4-7. The situation begins with a sequence exactly like the one pictured in Figure 4-5. Procedure A calls procedure B, which calls procedure C. Procedure C generates signal S. The primary and secondary handlers (if they exist) simply resignal. Handlers CH and BH, located next by the search procedure, also resignal.

Finally, handler AH is called. AH decides to unwind the call stack back to its establisher frame. (This unwinding is not the default case.) To accomplish the unwinding , AH must call SYS$UNWIND with a depth argument equal to the value contained in the mechanism array. In this example, the depth argument is 2. After the call to SYS$UNWIND, which executes in the access mode of its caller, but before the frame modification occurs, the stack has the form pictured on the left-hand side of Figure 4-7. The operation of frame modification by the $UNWIND system service now proceeds as follows.

① Unwind looks down the call stack until it locates a condition handler. Recall that a condition handler is identified by a saved PC of SYS$CALL_HANDL + 4. If handler AH had called another procedure in this example, nothing would have happened to that procedure's call frame. The first call frame modified by Unwind is the frame of the first handler that it encounters, which in the example in this figure is the frame for AH.

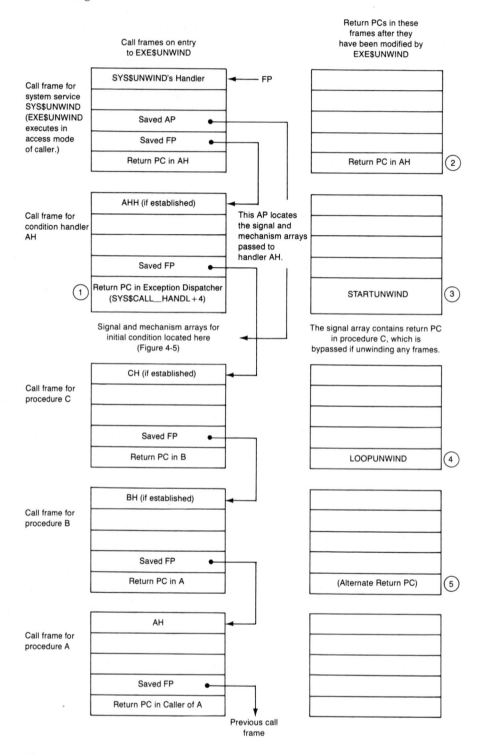

Figure 4-7
Call Frame Modification by SYS$UNWIND

② Unwind does not modify its own frame. When it issues a RET, control is passed back to handler AH.

③ The first frame that Unwind modifies is the frame of the first condition handler that it encounters by tracing back the call stack. It replaces the return address found there with the address of a routine (STARTUNWIND) internal to itself.

   When handler AH issues its RET, control will not go back to the exception dispatcher. Instead, the instructions beginning at STARTUNWIND execute. Note that not returning to the exception dispatcher means that control will never get back to procedure C, because its return PC is stored in the mechanism array and would be restored by the REI instruction issued by the exception dispatcher.

④ Unwind continues to modify the saved PC longwords in successive frames on the call stack until the number of frames specified (or implied) in the SYS$UNWIND argument list have been modified. All frames except the first have their saved PC replaced with address LOOPUNWIND, another label in the internal unwind routine (see Figure 4-7). It is this routine that checks whether the current frame has a handler established and, if so, calls that handler with the signal name SS$_UNWIND to allow the handler to perform procedure-specific cleanup.

   If a handler called in this way calls SYS$UNWIND (with the signal array containing SS$_UNWIND as the signal name), an error status of SS$_UNWINDING is returned, indicating that an unwind is already in progress.

⑤ If the alternate PC argument was also supplied to SYS$UNWIND, the call frame into which this argument would be inserted is the next frame beyond the last frame specified (or implied) in the first SYS$UNWIND argument. In this case; if an alternate PC argument were present, it would be placed into the call frame for procedure A.

   Now that all the frames have been modified, the actual unwinding occurs. The sequence of steps is approximately the following.

1. Unwind returns control to handler AH.
2. Handler AH does whatever else it needs to do to service the condition. When it has completed its work, it returns to the code beginning at label STARTUNWIND in module SYSUNWIND. (Because none of the unwind routines check return status, it does not matter what status is passed back by AH as it returns.)
3. The routine beginning at STARTUNWIND first restores R0 and R1 from the mechanism array. It then performs the following three steps.

   a. If a handler is established for this frame, the handler is called with the signal name SS$_UNWIND.

b. If either R0 or R1 is specified in the register save mask, the unwind routine replaces the value of that register in the register save area of the call frame with the current contents of the register. Note that this is rather an unusual case; the procedure calling standard specifies that R0 and R1 are to be used to return status codes and function values.

c. Control is returned to whatever address is specified in the saved PC longword of the current call frame by issuing a RET.

4. The RET issued in step 3c discards the call frame for procedure C, passing control to LOOPUNWIND where the three steps 3a through 3c are again executed.

5. The RET that discards the call frame for procedure B passes control back to the point in procedure A following the call to procedure B (if we assume no alternate PC argument) where execution will resume.

In effect, STARTUNWIND and LOOPUNWIND simulate returns from each nested procedure that is being unwound. These procedures never receive control again. However, the outermost procedure receives control as if all of the nested procedures had returned normally.

4.4.4 Potential Infinite Loop

There is one possible pitfall that can happen with this implementation. The previous section pointed out that the exception dispatcher takes care (when multiple signals are active) not to search frames for the second condition that were examined on the first pass. If a condition handler generates an exception, it is not called in response to its own signal (unless it establishes itself to handle its own signals!).

However, Unwind cannot perform such a check. It must call each condition handler that it encounters as it removes frames from the stack. Thus, a poorly written condition handler (one that generates an exception) could result in an infinite loop of exceptions if a handler higher up in the calling hierarchy unwinds the frame in which this poorly written handler is declared. This loop has no effect on the system but effectively destroys the process in which this handler exists.

4.4.5 Unwinding Multiply Active Signals

There is a slight change to the Unwind system service when multiple signals are active. While modifying saved PCs in call frames, Unwind counts the number of frames that have been modified until the requested number has been reached. The only change that occurs with multiply active signals is that the loop stops counting while the skipped frames are being modified.

The example of multiply active signals pictured in Figures 4-5 and 4-6 can be used to illustrate the unwinding. Recall that procedure A called procedure B, which called procedure C, which signaled S. Handler CH resignaled. Handler BH called procedure X, which called procedure Y, which signaled T. Handlers YH, XH, and BHH all resignaled. Finally, handler AH was called for signal T with a depth of 3.

If AH calls SYS$UNWIND, the top of the stack is as pictured in Figure 4-8, with the continuations of this figure in Figure 4-6. Assume that the depth argument passed to SYS$UNWIND is 3 (taken from the mechanism array and meaning unwind to the establisher of AH), and the alternate PC argument is not present.

The end result of the operation of Unwind in this case is as follows.

1. Unwind looks down the call stack until it locates a condition handler, which in this case is AH. The saved PC is modified to STARTUNWIND.
2. The saved PC longwords in frames Y and X are altered to contain address LOOPUNWIND. Note that SYS$UNWIND has now altered three frames.
3. Because the next frame on the stack, BH, indicates a condition handler (saved PC of SYS$CALL_HANDL + 4), its associated mechanism array is located (by climbing over saved registers, stack alignment bytes, and a saved PC from the JSB instruction). The saved PCs in all frames up to the frame pointed to by the mechanism array are modified (but not counted toward the number specified in the argument passed to SYS$UNWIND) to contain address LOOPUNWIND. This modification causes frames BH and C to get their saved PCs altered in the example.
4. The saved PC in the frame for procedure B is not altered so that when the unwind takes place, control will return to the call site of procedure B in procedure A.

4.4.6   Correct Use of Default Depth in SYS$UNWIND

A default depth argument to SYS$UNWIND (DEPADR = 0) specifies that the stack is to be unwound to the caller of the handler's establisher. In most cases, the caller of the handler's establisher is equivalent to the depth of the handler plus 1. However, because of an inherent ambiguity in counting the stack frames when multiply active signals are present, it is important that the default be used when unwinding to the caller of the establisher, rather than an explicit depth.

Consider the two following cases of nested exceptions. In Figure 4-9, routine A calls routine B. An exception causes handler BH to be invoked. An exception within BH causes handler AH to be invoked (because frame B is skipped, as described in Section 4.3.3). The depth of the mechanism vector in AH's argument list is 1. For AH to unwind to its establisher, it must specify an explicit depth of 1 to SYS$UNWIND. Then SYS$UNWIND removes one

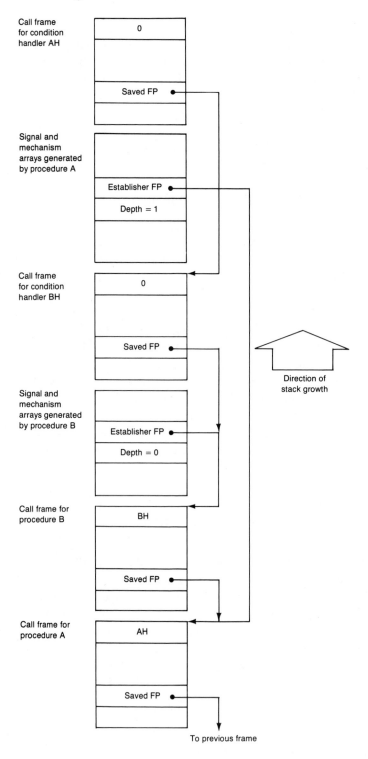

Figure 4-8
Modified Unwind with Multiply Active Signals

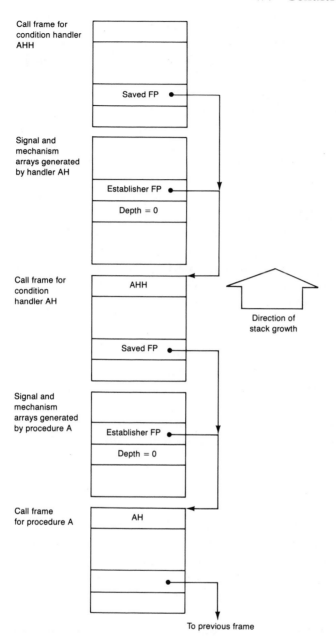

Call frame for
condition handler
AHH

Saved FP

Signal and
mechanism
arrays generated
by handler AH

Establisher FP

Depth = 0

Call frame for
condition
handler AH

AHH

Saved FP

Signal and
mechanism
arrays generated
by procedure A

Establisher FP

Depth = 0

Call frame
for procedure A

AH

Direction of
stack growth

To previous frame

Figure 4-9
Nested Exception, Type 1

frame, as specified by the count. The handler AH then notices that the next frame is a handler frame, and therefore continues to remove stack frames until it finds the establisher of the handler. This discovery completes the unwind to frame A.

Now consider Figure 4-10, in which routine A incurs an exception, resulting in the invoking of handler AH. Handler AH then causes an exception, causing its handler AHH to be invoked. The depth of AHH is zero. Now let us suppose that AHH wishes to unwind to the caller of its establisher. Now the establisher of AHH is AH. Since AH is a handler, its caller is the condition dispatcher, NOT routine A.

Compare Figure 4-10 with Figure 4-9 carefully and consider what happens if AHH calls SYS$UNWIND with an explicit depth of 1 (its depth plus 1). The depth of 1 causes AHH's frame to be removed. SYS$UNWIND then notices that the next frame is a handler frame and, therefore, unwinds it back to its establisher (frame A). Note that once AHH's frame is removed, the stack is indistinguishable from the stack in Figure 4-9 (down to frame B). Thus, SYS$UNWIND with an explicit depth of 1 results in control returning to routine A, which is incorrect.

Therefore, for AHH to unwind to the caller of its establisher (the condition dispatcher), it must specify a default depth. When this is done, $UNWIND's behavior upon encountering a handler frame after the count has been exhausted is modified so that the stack is not unwound further and control passes correctly back to the condition dispatcher.

Because of the inherent ambiguity of these two cases, it is important that handlers always use the default depth when unwinding to the caller of their establisher.

4.4.7 Unwinding ASTs

In VAX/VMS Version 3.0, the behavior of $UNWIND was changed so that it correctly handles unwinding out of ASTs. Doing so requires some special processing, because simply peeling off the stack frames ignores the presence of the AST and fails to dismiss the AST properly. The result is that execution continues in the user's main level code, with delivery of further ASTs blocked.

This situation is depicted in Figure 4-11. If handler XH unwinds to the caller of its establisher (procedure A), it will also unwind out of the AST. The problem is handled by having the $UNWIND service recognize the return PC of the AST call frame, which is set to the value EXE$ASTRET, the AST return point in the executive. When this PC is seen in a call frame, $UNWIND knows that located immediately beneath it is the AST parameter list. In this case, the unwind PC (STARTUNWIND or LOOPUNWIND) is stored not in the call frame, but rather in the PC of the AST parameter list.

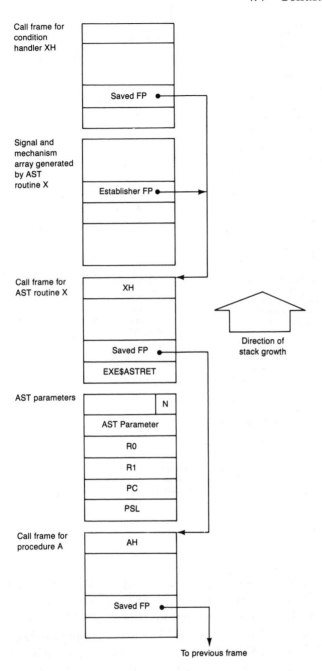

Call frame for
condition
handler XH

Saved FP

Signal and
mechanism
array generated
by AST
routine X

Establisher FP

Call frame for
AST routine X

XH

Saved FP

EXE$ASTRET

Direction of
stack growth

AST parameters

N

AST Parameter

R0

R1

PC

PSL

Call frame for
procedure A

AH

Saved FP

To previous frame

Figure 4-10
Nested Exception, Type 2

93

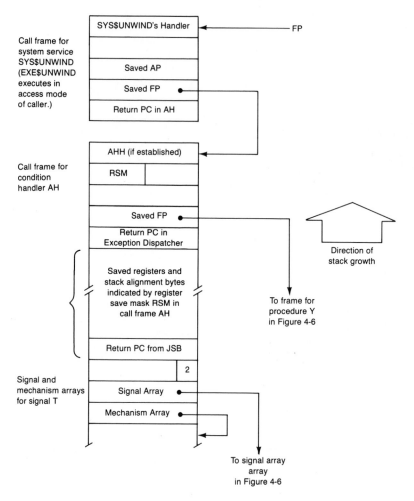

Figure 4-11
Exception during an AST

When the AST call returns during the actual unwinding of the stack, it returns to EXE$ASTRET, which dismisses the AST and returns to the interrupted code with an REI. The REI then returns back to STARTUNWIND or LOOPUNWIND because of the modified PC. In addition, immediately before returning to EXE$ASTRET, $UNWIND stores the current R0 and R1 in the AST parameter list so that they will propagate through the unwind process.

While it is technically possible to unwind out of an AST, doing so must be done with some caution. If the AST routine has any sort of side effects, it is essential to have a condition handler declared by the AST routine to clean up the side effects when the AST is unwound. (Note that issuing an I/O operation is a side effect of the highest order!) Note also that cleaning up any subroutines of the main line program from which an unwind was executed may be more difficult, because the asynchronous nature of ASTs means that unwinding could take place at any instant during the execution of a program.

4.5   DEFAULT (VMS-SUPPLIED) CONDITION HANDLERS

Although the use of condition handlers is totally general and completely in the hands of the user, some actions will always occur as the result of default condition handlers that are established by the executive as a part of process creation or image activation.

The discussions of process creation in Chapter 20 and image initiation in Chapter 21 point out exactly when and how each of the handlers described in this section is established. The action of each of these handlers, once they are invoked, is briefly described here.

4.5.1   Traceback Handler Established by Image Startup

When an image includes either the debugger or the traceback handler, another frame is put on the user stack before the image itself is called (see Chapter 21). The code that executes before calling the image places the address of a condition handler into this frame so that subsequent conditions that are not handled by an intervening condition handler will be picked up by this traceback handler.

This handler first checks whether the exception that occurred was SS$_DEBUG. If so, it maps the debugger into P0 space (if not already mapped) and passes control to it. This condition is signaled by a CLI in response to a DEBUG command. This feature allows an image that was not linked or run with debugger support to be interrupted and have that support added.

For all other exceptions, if the severity level is warning, error, or severe error, the handler maps the traceback facility into the top of P0 space and passes control to it. The traceback facility passes information about the exception to SYS$OUTPUT and terminates the image.

If the severity level is other than the three listed above, the traceback condition handler resignals the condition, which usually means that the condition is being passed on to the catch-all condition handler.

4.5.2   Catch-All Condition Handler

The address of this handler is placed in an initial call frame on the user stack and in the last chance exception vector for user mode either by PROCSTRT when the process is created or by a command language interpreter before an image is called. This handler is always called if no other handlers exist or if all other handlers resignal. Because the address of the handler is duplicated in the last chance vector, it will also be called in the event of some error while looking through the user stack.

The first step that this handler takes is to call SYS$PUTMSG (see Chapter 30). If the handler was called through the last chance exception vector (the depth argument in mechanism array is −3), or if the severity level of the exception name in the signal array indicates severe (exception name <2:0> GEQU 4), then SYS$EXCMSG (see Chapter 30) is called to print a summary message and the image is terminated. Otherwise, the image is continued.

4.5.3   Handlers Used by Other Access Modes

In addition to the handlers that the operating system supplies to handle exceptions that occur in user mode, it also sets up handlers that will determine system behavior if an exception occurs in one of the other three access modes.

4.5.3.1   Exceptions in Kernel or Executive Mode. In response to an exception in kernel mode, the exception dispatcher makes special checks to determine whether the processor was operating on the interrupt stack when the exception occurred, whether the process was the swapper process or null process, or whether IPL was above IPL$_ASTDEL (IPL 2). Any of these conditions could indicate that the exception is not associated with a normal process. In any case, if either of these conditions holds, an Invalid Exception fatal bugcheck (BUG$_INVEXCEPTN) is generated. Routines that forbid exceptions include interrupt service routines, device drivers (except for their FDT routines), and process-based code that happens to be executing above IPL$_ASTDEL (such as portions of certain system services).

If a kernel mode exception is associated with process-based code for which exceptions are allowed (IPL is less than or equal to 2 and the exception occurred on the kernel stack), then exception dispatching proceeds in its usual manner. The last chance exception vectors for both kernel and executive modes are initialized in module SHELL (see Chapter 20) to contain the addresses of routines that generate a bugcheck code of Unexpected System Service Exception. The difference between the bugchecks for the two access modes is that the bugcheck generated by the kernel mode primary exception handler is fatal while the corresponding bugcheck generated by the executive mode primary exception vector is not. Fatal bugchecks cause the system to crash. Nonfatal bugchecks generally result in error log entries and the deletion of the process that caused the bugcheck. The bugcheck operation is described in Chapter 8.

Routines that execute in executive mode include RMS, parts of the executive, and any user-written procedure that is entered through either a user-written system service dispatcher or through the Change Mode to Executive system service. Routines that execute in kernel mode (that can cause this bugcheck and not the Invalid Exception bugcheck because they execute at IPL 0 or IPL 2) include portions of all system services, many exception service routines, device driver FDT routines, including those that are written by users, and procedures that are called either by the user-written system service dispatcher or by the Change Mode to Kernel system service.

4.5.3.2 **Condition Handler Used by DCL or MCR.** The DCL and MCR command language interpreters establish nearly identical condition handlers at the beginning of their command loops to field exceptions that occur in supervisor mode.

Part of process creation involves image activation of the CLI (DCL or MCR). The first step that the CLI takes after image activation is to establish the supervisor mode condition handler that the CLI uses to handle its own internal errors. The condition handler performs two tasks when it is called:

- It cancels any exit handlers that have been established.
- It resignals the error.

The CLI is then allowed to run to completion, as a result of which the process is deleted.

5   Hardware Interrupts

While I nodded, nearly napping, suddenly there came a tapping,
As of some one gently rapping, rapping at my chamber door.
—Edgar Allan Poe, *The Raven*

The VMS operating system is an interrupt-driven operating system. It contains a collection of interrupt service routines that execute in response to hardware interrupts from external devices and internal devices such as the clock. The VMS operating system does not have a software-based central dispatching module that receives notification of all system events (that is, interrupts) and decides what to do next. Instead, the VMS operating system relies on a hardware-controlled interrupt dispatching scheme that always forces the highest priority interrupt on the system to be serviced first.

5.1   HARDWARE INTERRUPT DISPATCHING

The VAX architecture provides 16 hardware interrupt priority levels (IPL), from IPL 31 down to IPL 16. The top eight levels are for use by urgent conditions including serious errors (such as machine check), the system clock, and power failure. These conditions are discussed in Chapters 8, 11, and 27 respectively. The lower eight levels are used by peripheral devices.

When a peripheral device generates an interrupt, that interrupt is requested at a particular hardware IPL (fixed for a given device). As in the case of software interrupts, if the requested IPL value is higher than the level at which the processor is currently running (as determined by PSL <20:16>), then the interrupt service routine whose address is in the selected vector in the system control block (SCB) is entered immediately. Otherwise, servicing of the interrupt is deferred until IPL drops below the level associated with the interrupt.

When an interrupt is serviced, the current processor status must be preserved so that the interrupted thread of execution (either process-based code or an interrupt service routine executing at lower IPL) can continue normally after the interrupt is dismissed. Preserving the processor status is accomplished (by the hardware) by automatically saving the PC and PSL on the stack. These are later restored with an REI instruction that dismisses the interrupt. Other elements of the process context, such as general registers, must be saved and restored by the routine(s) handling the interrupt. In order to reduce interrupt overhead, no memory mapping information is changed when an interrupt occurs. Therefore, the instructions and data referenced by an interrupt service routine must be in system address space.

5.1.1   **Interrupt Dispatching**

The following list outlines the primary sequence of events that occur in interrupt dispatching.

1. An interrupt is requested.
2. The current instruction finishes or reaches a well-defined point where the instruction state is completely contained in the general registers, PC, and PSL (which happens in the execution of the string instructions). (Some instructions can also be interrupted at well-defined points so that, after the interrupt dismissal, they are restarted, rather than continued.)
3. The interrupt sequence is initiated by the hardware, pushing the current PC and PSL onto the stack. The VMS operating system uses the interrupt stack for all hardware interrupt servicing. Hardware interrupts are indicated by placing a 01 in bits <1:0> of each hardware interrupt vector in the system control block (see Figure 5-1).

   Most software interrupts are also serviced on the interrupt stack. On the other hand, the per-process interrupt associated with AST delivery and nearly all exceptions are serviced on the per-process kernel stack.
4. A new PC is loaded (from the appropriate SCB vector), and a new PSL is created (with PSL <20:16> containing the IPL associated with the interrupt, and the previous access mode, current access mode, CM, TP, FPD, DV, FU, IV, T, N, Z, and C bits cleared by the hardware). The current access mode bits are cleared to indicate that the service routine will run in kernel mode.
5. The interrupt service routine identified by the PC in the SCB executes and, eventually, exits with an REI instruction that dismisses the interrupt.
6. The PC and PSL are restored by the execution of the REI instruction, and the interrupted thread of execution (process or less important interrupt service routine) continues where it left off.

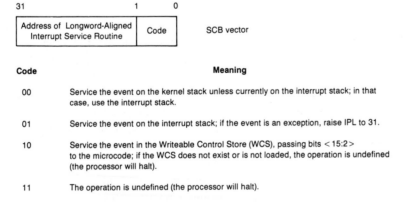

Figure 5-1
System Control Block Vector Format

Unlike software interrupt dispatching, there is not a one-to-one correspondence between hardware IPL and an interrupt service routine vector in the SCB (see Figure 5-2). The SCB contains the addresses of several interrupt service routines for a given device IPL. There are no registers corresponding to the Software Interrupt Request Register (PR$_SIRR) or Software Interrupt Summary Register (PR$_SISR); rather, the processor notes that a lower priority interrupt has been requested, but not granted. When IPL falls below the device interrupt level, and the device is still requesting the interrupt, the interrupt will be granted.

If, however, the device is no longer requesting an interrupt, the system will be unable to determine which interrupt service routine to call; such occurrences are called passive releases. If the adapter to which the device is connected is still requesting an interrupt, an adapter-specific error routine is called. If the adapter is no longer requesting an interrupt, the system is unable to determine which adapter requested the interrupt; in this case a nexus 0 interrupt service routine is called. In either case, the system increments the counter IO$GL_SCB_INT0.

5.1.2 System Control Block

The system control block (SCB) contains the vectors used to dispatch (software and hardware) interrupts and exceptions. The starting physical address of the SCB is found in the System Control Block Base Register (PR$_SCBB). The size of the SCB varies depending on processor type. The VAX-11/750 and the VAX-11/730 system control blocks are two pages long; a VAX-11/750 with a second UNIBUS has a three-page system control block; the VAX-11/780 system control block consists of a single page.

The first page of the system control block is the only page defined by the VAX architecture. It contains the addresses of software and hardware interrupt service routines as well as exception service routines. The layout of the first SCB page is pictured in Figure 4-1. Table 6-1 contains more details about the SCB vectors used for software interrupts. Figure 5-2 shows how the second half of the first page is divided among 16 possible external devices, each interrupting at four possible IPL values. The second SCB page on the VAX-11/730 and VAX-11/750 is used for directly vectored UNIBUS device interrupts. The third page on a VAX-11/750 with a second UNIBUS is used for directly vectored UNIBUS device interrupts to the second UNIBUS.

Each vector in the SCB is a longword that is examined by the processor when an exception or interrupt occurs, to determine how to service the event. Figure 5-1 illustrates the format of a vector in the SCB, and indicates which stack is used to service an exception or interrupt. In the VAX/VMS operating system, all hardware interrupts (and all software interrupts above IPL 3) are serviced on the system-wide interrupt stack. The rescheduling soft-

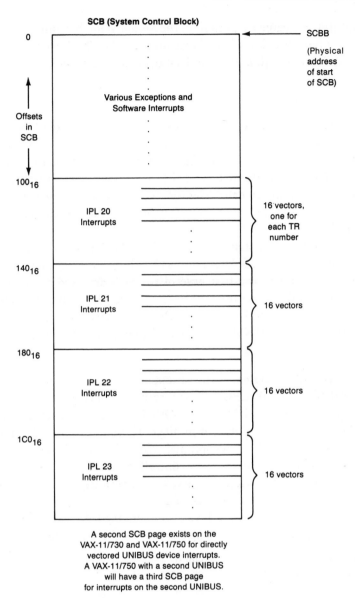

Figure 5-2
System Control Block Vectors for Hardware Interrupts

ware interrupt (IPL 3) begins execution on the kernel stack but immediately changes to the interrupt stack when it executes a SVPCTX instruction (see Chapter 10). AST delivery (IPL 2) is serviced using a process-specific kernel stack.

5.1.2.1 VAX-11/730 External Adapters. On the VAX-11/730 the CPU, the UNIBUS adapter, and the memory controller are connected by the Array Bus. In addition to the Array Bus, communications between the CPU and the integrated disk controller (IDC) are performed over the Accelerator Bus (the floating point accelerator also communicates over the Accelerator Bus). The IDC controls RL02 and R80 disks. The VAX-11/730 is not expandable and does not use expansion slots.

Because there are no expansion slots in the VAX-11/730, the first page of the SCB contains only one set of SCB vectors. The longwords located at SCB + 08 through SCB + 0B in the first page of the SCB are used as external adapters, one for each IPL value from 20 to 23. The second SCB page on the VAX-11/730 is used for directly vectored UNIBUS device interrupts. Each SCB vector corresponds to a UNIBUS vector in the range from 0 to 774 (octal).

5.1.2.2 VAX-11/750 External Adapters. The backplane interconnect on the VAX-11/750, called the CMI (CPU to memory interconnect), connects the CPU, memory controllers, and UNIBUS or MASSBUS adapters. Each connection to the CMI is identified by its slot number. There is a total of 32 slots, the first 16 of which are used for the optional writeable control store (WCS). The next 10 slots are reserved for memory controllers and UNIBUS or MASS-BUS adapters. These 10 slots are called fixed slots because the mapping of controller/adapter to slot number is fixed. That is, a particular slot can have only a particular adapter placed in it. Five of the ten fixed slots are currently used by external adapters. The following list details these adapters:

Memory Controller	Slot 0
Up to three MASSBUS Adapters	Slots 4 through 6
UNIBUS Adapter	Slot 8

The last six slots are reserved for adapters with configuration registers and are called floating slots.

Each slot has four SCB vectors in the first SCB page assigned to it, one for each IPL value from 20 to 23. As shown in Figure 5-2, the first 16 vectors are assigned to IPL 20. The second SCB page on the VAX-11/750 is used for directly vectored UNIBUS device interrupts. Each SCB vector corresponds to a UNIBUS vector in the range from 0 to 774 (octal). The third SCB page on a VAX-11/750 in a two-UNIBUS configuration is used for directly vectored UNIBUS device interrupts on the second UNIBUS.

5.1.2.3   **VAX-11/780 External Adapters.** On the VAX-11/780, the Synchronous Back-plane Interconnect (SBI) connects the CPU, memory controllers (including MA780s), DR780s, CI780s, and UNIBUS or MASSBUS adapters. Each connection to the SBI is assigned a transfer request (TR) number that identifies its SBI priority. TR numbers range from 0 (highest priority) to 15 (lowest priority). There is a limit of 15 connections to the SBI (see Table 5-1). TR number 14 is reserved for the CI780; TR number 0 is used for a special purpose on the SBI and has no corresponding external adapter. The TR number defines the physical address space through which the device's registers are accessed and through which vectors the device will interrupt.

An adapter is not restricted to having a specific TR number. However, the relative priorities of the various adapters may not change. That is, a system cannot have an MBA with a higher priority (lower TR number) than a UBA. For instance, if a system has two local memory controllers and an MA780

Table 5-1: Standard SBI Adapter Assignments on the VAX-11/780

External Adapter Type	VAX-11/780 Assignment	Comments
	TR 0	Hold Line for next cycle. TR 0 is the highest TR level and is not assigned to a device.
First Memory Controller	TR 1	
Second Memory Controller	TR 2	
First MA780 Shared Memory		
Second MA780 Shared Memory		
First UNIBUS Adapter	TR 3	
Second UNIBUS Adapter	TR 4	
Third UNIBUS Adapter	TR 5	
Fourth UNIBUS Adapter	TR 6	
	TR 7	Reserved
First MASSBUS Adapter	TR 8	
Second MASSBUS Adapter	TR 9	
Third MASSBUS Adapter	TR 10	
Fourth MASSBUS Adapter	TR 11	
DR780 SBI Interface	TR 12	
	TR 13	Reserved
CI	TR 14	
	TR 15	Reserved
	TR 16	The CPU has implicit TR 16. Level 16 is the lowest TR level.

shared memory controller, the first UNIBUS adapter on that system could have TR number 4, with the MA780 having TR number 3, and the memory controllers having TR numbers 1 and 2.

5.1.2.4 **Adapter Configuration.** On the VAX-11/750 and VAX-11/780, the presence of an adapter at a particular slot or TR number is checked by testing the first longword in the adapter's I/O register space, and checking for nonexistent memory. The presence or absence of an external adapter is determined by the primary bootstrap program VMB (see Chapter 24) as part of that program's memory sizing operation. Specifically, VMB loads the machine check vector in the SCB with the address of a special routine while it is sizing memory and determining which external adapters are present. If a nonexistent memory machine check occurs, there is no connected adapter at the location being tested. The result of this testing is stored in a 16-byte array in a data structure called a restart parameter block (RPB). The later stages of system initialization use the information obtained by VMB and stored in the RPB when they configure specific adapters into the system.

On the VAX-11/730, VAX-11/750, and VAX-11/780, only IPL levels 20 through 23 are used for device interrupts. Within the SCB, vectors are reserved for each IPL level available to each adapter (see Figure 5-2). Whenever an adapter generates an interrupt for a device connected to it, the slot number or TR number of the adapter and the device IPL are used by the hardware to index into the SCB for the appropriate interrupt service routine. Some adapters such as local memory controllers do not generate interrupts.

5.2 **VAX/VMS INTERRUPT SERVICE ROUTINES**

The interrupt service routines used by the VMS operating system operate in the limited system context or interrupt context described in Chapter 1. These routines execute at elevated IPL on the interrupt stack outside the context of a process.

5.2.1 **Restrictions Imposed on Interrupt Service Routines**

There are several restrictions imposed on interrupt service routines either by the VAX architecture or by synchronization techniques used by the VMS operating system. These restrictions result from the limited context that is available to any routine that executes outside the context of a process. The following list of items indicates some of the specific operations and data references that cannot occur in an interrupt service routine. The description of interrupt context in Chapter 1 contains a more general list of these and other restrictions.

- Interrupt service routines should be very short and do as little processing as possible at elevated IPL.
- Any registers used by an interrupt service routine must first be saved.
- Although an interrupt service routine can elevate IPL, it cannot lower IPL below the level at which the original interrupt occurred.
- The size of the interrupt stack, the stack used by all hardware interrupt service routines, is controlled by the SYSBOOT parameter INTSTKPAGES (which has a default value of two pages). This parameter determines the amount of stack storage available to interrupt service routines.
- Any elements pushed onto the stack by an interrupt service routine must be removed before the interrupt is dismissed in order that REI works correctly.
- Because the low two bits of interrupt service routine addresses in the system control block are used for stack selection, interrupt service routines called directly by the hardware must be longword aligned.
- No pageable routines or data structures can be referenced above IPL 2.
- Data structures that are synchronized by either IPL$_SYNCH or by mutexes cannot be referenced by interrupt service routines without destroying the synchronization (unless the interrupt service routine is executing at IPL$_SYNCH with the express purpose of accessing the data structure).
- No references to per-process address space (P0 space or P1 space) are allowed.

5.2.2   Servicing UNIBUS Interrupts

Each device on the UNIBUS has one (or more) vector number(s) to identify the device, and a bus request (BR) priority to allow the UNIBUS to arbitrate among devices when multiple interrupts occur. There are 4 BR levels, called BR4, BR5, BR6, and BR7. BR7 has the highest priority. If multiple interrupts occur for devices with the same BR level, the device electrically closest to the UNIBUS interface has the highest priority. The device IPL used equals the BR priority + 16. For example, BR4 corresponds to IPL 20.

5.2.2.1   VAX-11/730 and VAX-11/750 UNIBUS Interrupt Service Routines. UNIBUS
interrupts on the VAX-11/730 and VAX-11/750 are directly vectored through the second page of the system control block. The system control block contains separate addresses for the interrupt service routines for all of the UNIBUS interrupt vector locations. When a unit is connected (using SYSGEN), the appropriate fields in the SCB are initialized to point to the interrupt service routines for the device vectors. The interrupt service routines eventually transfer control to the appropriate device driver interrupt service routines. The *VAX/VMS Guide to Writing a Device Driver* describes the data struc-

tures in the I/O database, and contains a more complete discussion of driver interrupt service routines than that presented here.

When a UNIBUS device generates an interrupt on the VAX-11/730 or VAX-11/750, the interrupt is vectored directly through the SCB, and control is immediately transferred to the following instruction in the appropriate device controller's channel request block (CRB).

```
PUSHR    #^M<R0,R1,R2,R3,R4,R5>
```

The next instruction in the CRB is a JSB to the driver interrupt service routine (see Figure 5-3). The longword following the JSB instruction contains the address of another data structure (the IDB, interrupt dispatch block). This address is pushed onto the stack (as the return PC for the JSB instruction). However, control is never returned there because that address is removed from the stack by the driver interrupt service routine.

After the JSB instruction in the CRB transfers control to the driver interrupt service routine, the following events take place.

1. The driver interrupt service routine removes the IDB pointer from the stack and uses it to obtain both the address of the device controller's control/status register (CSR) and the address of the UCB for the device generating the interrupt.
2. Having found the UCB, the interrupt service routine determines whether the interrupt was expected or not, and, if expected, restores the driver context stored in the UCB and transfers control to the saved PC.
3. When the driver finishes processing the interrupt, it issues an RSB.
4. Control is transferred back to the driver interrupt service routine, which restores the registers (R0 through R5) saved by the PUSHR instruction and dismisses the interrupt with an REI.

If the interrupt was unsolicited, the driver may either take some appropriate action or simply dismiss the interrupt by restoring R0 through R5 and issuing an REI.

5.2.2.2   **VAX-11/780 UNIBUS Interrupt Service Routines.** When a device on the UNIBUS requests an interrupt, the UBA converts that request into an interrupt on the SBI. The SBI interrupt is vectored through the SCB to a UNIBUS adapter interrupt service routine. In the case of interrupts generated by a UNIBUS device on the VAX-11/780, the corresponding adapter receives device interrupt requests, determines which has the highest priority, and generates an interrupt of its own for the CPU (on behalf of the interrupting device). It is actually the adapter interrupt that is vectored through the SCB (using the interrupting device's IPL and the adapter's TR number), to an adapter interrupt service routine. The adapter interrupt service routine saves registers R0

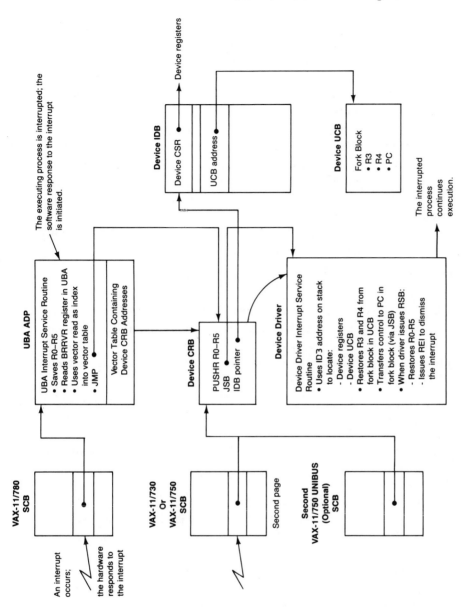

Figure 5-3
Control Flow in Servicing a UNIBUS Interrupt

through R5, determines which device actually requested the interrupt, and then passes control to an interrupt service routine in the device driver for the interrupting device. The driver interrupt service routine can then respond to the interrupt in a device-dependent fashion. After servicing the interrupt, the registers saved by the adapter interrupt service routine must be restored, and an REI instruction issued to dismiss the interrupt.

There are four interrupt service routines for each UBA, one for each BR level at which UNIBUS devices request interrupts. They differ only in which internal UBA register they read to determine which device requested the interrupt. These interrupt service routines are found in a data structure describing the UBA (the adapter control block) that is created when the system is bootstrapped (from module INITADP).

UNIBUS interrupt servicing on the VAX-11/780 begins in one of four UNIBUS adapter interrupt service routines.

1. The UBA interrupt service routines (see Figure 5-3) save registers R0 through R5.
2. A UBA internal register (BRRVR) is read to determine the identity of the interrupting device. Each BRRVR register contains either the vector number corresponding to the device interrupt or an indication that the UBA is interrupting on behalf of itself, not for some device. (There are four BRRVRs in the UBA, one for each BR level.)
3. If the UBA is interrupting on behalf of itself, it is normally indicating an adapter error condition. These errors usually result when a reference is made to a nonexistent address in UNIBUS I/O space. They may indicate only a transient hardware error or a bug in a device driver. These errors are logged, up to a maximum of 3 in any given 15-minute period, and the interrupt is dismissed.
4. For a device interrupt, the vector number is used as an index into a vector table. The vector table contains a pointer to the JSB instruction inside the CRB. Control is transferred to the JSB instruction by a JMP instruction in the adapter interrupt service routine.

    The vector table entry pointing to the CRB, as well as the address fields in the CRB, are filled in by SYSGEN at the time the device driver is loaded into the system with the SYSGEN command CONNECT.

The instruction inside the CRB is a JSB to the driver interrupt service routine. The longword following the JSB instruction contains the address of another data structure (the IDB, interrupt dispatch block). This address is pushed onto the stack (as the return PC for the JSB instruction). However, control is never returned there because that address is removed from the stack by the driver interrupt service routine.

After the JSB instruction in the CRB transfers control to the driver interrupt service routine, the following events take place:

108

1. The driver interrupt service routine removes the IDB pointer from the stack and uses it to obtain both the address of the device controller's control/status register (CSR) and the address of the UCB for the device generating the interrupt.
2. Having found the UCB, the interrupt service routine determines whether the interrupt was expected or not, and, if expected, restores the driver context stored in the UCB and transfers control to the saved PC.
3. When the driver process finishes processing the interrupt, it issues an RSB.
4. Control is transferred back to the driver interrupt service routine, which restores the registers (R0 through R5) saved by the UBA interrupt service routine and dismisses the interrupt with an REI.

If the interrupt was unsolicited, the driver may either take some appropriate action or simply dismiss the interrupt by restoring R0 through R5 and issuing an REI.

At this point, interrupt dispatching proceeds exactly as it does in the case of the VAX-11/750. Note that device drivers need not concern themselves with whether they are on a VAX-11/730, a VAX-11/750, or a VAX-11/780, because their interrupt service routines will be entered in a transparent manner.

5.2.3 MASSBUS Interrupt Service Routines

Unlike UNIBUS interrupt dispatching, the MASSBUS interrupt sequences for the VAX-11/750 and the VAX-11/780 MASSBUS are identical. The VAX-11/730 has no MASSBUS. When the system is bootstrapped, entries are made in the SCB to transfer control to locations in the CRB for the MASSBUS adapter. The instructions in the MBA CRB are a PUSHR for R2 to R5 and a JSB to the MBA interrupt service routine MBA$INT (which is part of module MBAINTDSP).

MBA interrupts are handled differently from UNIBUS interrupts, partly because one MBA interrupt may indicate that multiple devices on the adapter need servicing. The MBA interrupt service routine reads an attention summary register to determine what it must do to respond to an interrupt.

If the interrupt enable bit in the MBA is set, an MBA interrupt can be caused by any of the following operations.

- A data transfer completes.
- An attention line is asserted while the MBA is not busy.
- An MBA error occurs while the MBA is not busy.
- The power is turned on for the MBA.

Devices on the MASSBUS can assert the attention line under the following circumstances:

- If an error occurs, whether or not a transfer is taking place
- When a mechanical motion such as a disk seek or tape rewind completes
- When a device changes its state

In general, MASSBUS device drivers do not request ownership of the MBA until they need it to perform a transfer. The MBA interrupt service routine assumes that if the MBA owner is expecting an interrupt, then the interrupt currently being serviced indicates that a transfer has completed or been aborted. That is, when an MBA interrupt occurs and the current owner of the MBA is expecting an interrupt, MBA$INT dispatches immediately to the owner's driver. It then checks whether other devices on the MASSBUS need attention. The UCB list contained in the IDB allows MBA$INT to associate UCB addresses with devices that are requesting service.

   MBA$INT responds to an interrupt in one of three ways (see Figure 5-4). It may perform all three of these actions to service multiple attention requests in response to a single interrupt.

- For an expected interrupt for a single-unit controller (a disk), MBA$INT issues a JSB instruction that transfers control directly to the fork PC stored in the UCB of the interrupting device. The driver returns to MBA$INT when it has completed its work.
- For an unsolicited interrupt for a single-unit controller, MBA$INT issues a JSB instruction that transfers control to a driver-supplied unexpected interrupt service routine, which will return to MBA$INT.
- For a multidevice controller (a magtape), MBA$INT transfers control to the CRB for the device controller. The device controller CRB dispatches to a controller interrupt service routine that saves R2 to R5 and transfers control to the driver interrupt service routine. This service routine eventually returns control to MBA$INT.

The way MBA$INT decides whether an entry in the MBA IDB is a UCB address (single-unit controller), or a pointer into a CRB (multidevice controller) is by checking the low-order bit of the entry in the MBA IDB for the controller. If the bit is set, then the entry is for a multidevice controller. If the bit is clear, the entry represents the UCB address for the device on a single-device controller. UCBs, like CRBs, are always longword aligned (the low order two bits are clear). When a CRB is created for a multidevice controller, and its address stored in the MBA IDB, the address is incremented by 1 so the low order bit will be set. Control is actually transferred to the PUSHR instruction in the multidevice controller CRB using the following instruction (where R5 contains the MBA IDB entry) so that the low-order bit is cleared before control is actually transferred:

```
JSB    -(R5)
```

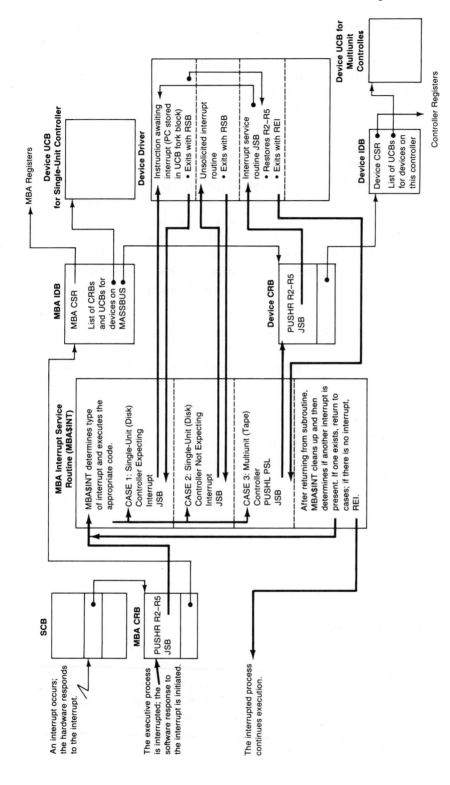

Figure 5-4
Control Flow in Servicing a MASSBUS Interrupt

Because data transfer functions block the interrupts from nontransfer functions until the data transfer completes, MBA$INT always checks the MBA attention summary register after a driver interrupt service routine returns control. This check is made to determine if another device on the MASSBUS requested an interrupt either while the MASSBUS owner was transferring data or while the current interrupt was being processed.

5.2.4   **DR32 Interrupt Service Routine**

DR32 (or DR750 and DR780) interrupt dispatching is handled similarly to MBA interrupt dispatching. When the system is bootstrapped, entries are made in the SCB to transfer control to locations in the CRB for the DR32. The instructions in the CRB are a PUSHR for R2 to R5, and a JSB. The DR32 IDB address follows the JSB instruction in the DR32 CRB (see Figure 5-5).

Initially, the JSB in the DR32 CRB transfers control to routine DR$INT in module DRINTHAND. This routine simply performs the following operations:

1. It clears the adapter power up and power down bits in a DR32 control register.
2. It calls a controller initialization routine to reset the DR32 (and disable DR32 interrupts).
3. It restores registers R2 to R5.
4. It issues an REI instruction.

When the DR32 driver (XFDRIVER) is loaded by SYSGEN (as part of AUTOCONFIGURE when the system is bootstrapped, or by an explicit CONNECT command), the JSB instruction is overwritten to point to the interrupt service routine in the driver. This routine performs the following operations:

1. It responds to the various types of DR32 interrupts.
2. It restores registers R2 to R5.
3. It issues an REI instruction.

5.2.5   **MA780 Interrupt Dispatching**

Although the standard MS780 memory controller does not generate interrupts, the shared memory (MA780) controller does. Interrupts are requested by a driver or the executive to interrupt another processor connected to the shared memory. Interrupts occur whenever a shared memory event flag is set or a shared memory mailbox message is written, or whenever there is interprocessor communication in the VAX-11/782. Note that this discussion describes MA780 used as shared memory among VAX-11/780s; interrupt han-

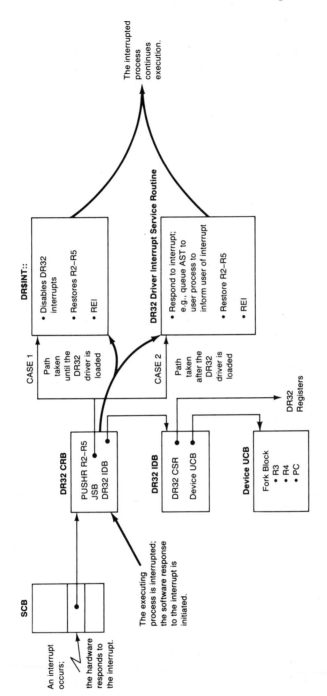

Figure 5-5
Control Flow in Servicing a DR32 Interrupt

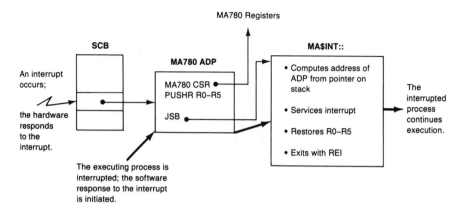

Figure 5-6
Control Flow in Servicing an MA780 Interrupt

dling in the VAX-11/782 is somewhat different and is briefly discussed in Section 5.2.6. Chapter 28 gives a more complete description of MA780 interrupts in the VAX-11/782.

When the system is bootstrapped, module INITADP places entries into the SCB to transfer control to locations in the MA780 ADP when MA780 interrupts occur (see Figure 5-6). The locations in the ADP contain a PUSHR instruction saving R0 to R5, and a JSB instruction that transfers control to routine MA$INT (in MAHANDLER).

1. When MA$INT obtains control, it removes the value pushed onto the stack by the JSB instruction in the ADP and uses it to determine the address of the MA780's ADP.
2. It uses fields in the ADP to locate adapter registers in the MA780 and to determine which port requested an interrupt (and what kind of interrupt was requested).
3. If the interrupt is for a processor being connected to the memory, the interrupt is dismissed by restoring R0 to R5 and issuing an REI.
4. Otherwise, MA$INT services the interrupt.
5. Finally, the interrupt is dismissed by restoring R0 to R5 and issuing an REI.

5.2.6   MA780 Interrupts on the VAX-11/782

The VAX-11/782 multiprocessing system uses interrupts from the MA780 to allow the processors to interrupt one another. Thus, the MA780 interrupts must be handled somewhat differently on the VAX-11/782.

When the multiprocessing code is loaded, the MA780 interprocessor interrupt vectors in the primary processor's SCB are redirected to point to a multiprocessing MA780 interrupt routine (only for the first MA780). The interrupt routine serves interrupts from the secondary processor. A new SCB is created in nonpaged pool for the secondary processor. The new SCB contains vectors that point to multiprocessing MA780 interrupt routines for the secondary processor. The interprocessor interrupt vector for the remaining MA780s is pointed to an unexpected interrupt handler.

When multiprocessing code is loaded, the operating system debugger (XDELTA) is moved from interrupt vector 5 to interrupt vector 15. Interrupt vector 5 is used for the multiprocessing rescheduling routine.

For more information on the VAX-11/782 multiprocessing system, see Chapter 28.

5.3 CONNECT-TO-INTERRUPT MECHANISM

The connect-to-interrupt mechanism allows a process to be notified of a UNIBUS device interrupt by the delivery of an AST, by the setting of an event flag, or both. The process can also specify an interrupt service routine that will respond to device interrupts.

A suitably privileged process (with CMKRNL and PFNMAP privileges) can respond to an interrupt by reading or writing device registers and, possibly, by initiating further device activity. However, in order to directly manipulate device registers, the process must first map the UNIBUS I/O page(s) containing the registers for the device into its own process space (P0 or P1). The *VAX/VMS Real-Time User's Guide* contains a discussion of mapping the UNIBUS I/O page and using the connect-to-interrupt capability. Chapter 16 of this book contains more detailed information on how the mapping is actually performed.

Note that the physical addresses of the UNIBUS I/O page differ among the VAX-11/730, VAX-11/750, and VAX-11/780. Therefore, different PFNs must be used when mapping the UNIBUS I/O page. The details of mapping to the I/O page are described in the *VAX/VMS Real-Time User's Guide*. Appendix B contains a list of symbols defined by the $IO730DEF, $IO750DEF, and $IO780DEF macros to make this mapping as symbolic as possible.

The connect-to-interrupt facility is an extension of the interrupt dispatching scheme. In order to use it, the connect-to-interrupt driver (CONINTERR) must be associated with the interrupt vector. The association is made using the SYSGEN command CONNECT, specifying all of the following:

- A name for the device (to be used by the process that connects to the interrupt)
- The address of the device
- The interrupt vector at which the device generates interrupts
- The CONINTERR driver, which initially responds to the device interrupts

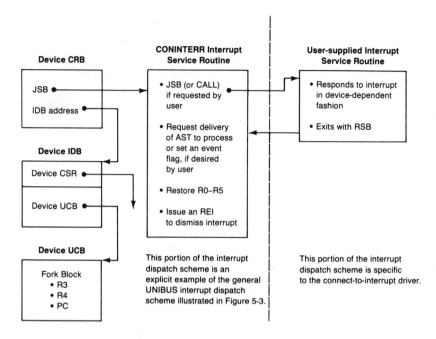

Figure 5-7
Extending Interrupt Dispatch Mechanism with the
Connect-to-Interrupt Facility

When the device generates an interrupt, the normal UNIBUS interrupt dispatching sequence is followed, as discussed in Sections 5.2.1 and 5.2.2. However, the CONINTERR interrupt service routine transfers control to the
user-supplied interrupt service routine (if one was supplied) using a JSB or
CALL instruction (as requested by the user). This transfer is illustrated in
Figure 5-7. When the user-supplied interrupt service routine issues an RSB (or
RET), the CONINTERR interrupt service routine regains control. Before restoring R0 to R5 and issuing an REI, the CONINTERR interrupt service routine queues an AST to the process (if requested) to notify the process that an
interrupt has occurred (via the AST, or by setting an event flag).

In order for the process-supplied interrupt service routine to be accessible
to the CONINTERR interrupt service routine, the CONINTERR driver dou-
ble-maps the user routine into system address space. The double mapping
requires enough system page table entries (reserved by the REALTIME_SPTS
SYSBOOT parameter) to map the user-supplied routines (other driver routines besides an interrupt service routine may be specified when connecting
to an interrupt). When the process disconnects from the interrupt, the SPTEs
used to map the routines for that process are made available for later use by
other processes.

6 Software Interrupts

Noise is the most impertinent of all forms of interruption. It is
not only an interruption, but also a disruption of thought.
—Schopenhauer, *Studies in Pessimism: On Noise*

The software interrupt mechanism that is provided as an integral part of the
VAX architecture is relied on heavily by the VAX/VMS operating system for
several purposes. The scheduler is invoked as a software interrupt service
routine. Software interrupts provide device drivers a clean method for lowering IPL. Several I/O completion routines run as software interrupt service
routines. This chapter first describes the general software interrupt mechanism and then lists several uses of software interrupts in the VAX/VMS operating system.

6.1 THE SOFTWARE INTERRUPT

A software interrupt is actually a hardware mechanism, similar to an interrupt generated by an external device. It causes a PC/PSL pair to be pushed
onto an appropriate stack (usually the interrupt stack) and passes control to
an interrupt service routine whose address is stored in the system control
block. Like hardware interrupts, the VMS operating system interprets software interrupts as system-wide events that are serviced independently of the
context of a specific process. The AST interrupt, discussed briefly at the end
of this chapter and in greater detail in Chapter 7, is the only variation from
this sequence of events.

The big difference between software interrupts and hardware interrupts,
and the reason for the name, is that software interrupts are generated by an
explicit request from software. The typical software interrupt request occurs
as the result of a hardware interrupt or within another software interrupt
service routine. However, there are examples within the VMS operating system of software interrupts being issued from code executing in process context.

6.1.1 Hardware Mechanism of Software Interrupts

The VAX architecture provides 15 software interrupt levels, from IPL 15
down to IPL 1. There are 15 entries in the system control block (SCB) for
addresses of software interrupt service routines, one for each IPL level. A
software routine (usually a hardware or software interrupt service routine)

requests a software interrupt at a given IPL level by writing the desired IPL value into the privileged register Software Interrupt Request Register (PR$_SIRR). Writing to this register causes a bit in the Software Interrupt Summary Register (PR$_SISR) to be set. The bit in the SISR is cleared when the interrupt is finally taken. The layout of these two processor registers is pictured in Figure 6-1. All software interrupt requests in the VMS operating system use the SOFTINT macro to write the SIRR. This macro expands into the following instruction:

```
.MACRO    SOFTINT IPL
MTPR      IPL,S^#PR$_SIRR
.ENDM     SOFTINT
```

The usual situation in the VMS operating system is that the requested IPL level is less than or equal to the current IPL (as determined by PSL>20:16<). In this case, the interrupt is deferred until the IPL drops below the requested level. The deferral of pending software interrupts based on current IPL is exactly the way that pending hardware interrupts are treated. This lowering of IPL usually occurs as the result of an REI instruction but could also occur if privileged code directly altered the current IPL by writing to the PR$_IPL register (with the SETIPL or the ENBINT macros, described in Chapter 2).

If the requested IPL value is higher than the level at which the processor is currently running, then the interrupt service routine whose address is in the selected slot in the SCB is entered immediately. (This is the same way that pending hardware interrupts are treated.)

There are a few occurrences in the VMS operating system of a software interrupt request at an IPL level greater than that at which the processor is

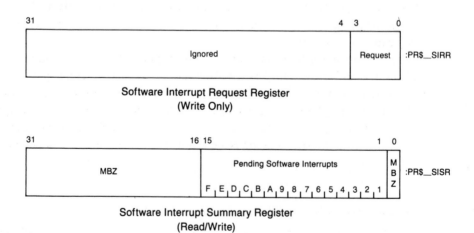

Software Interrupt Request Register
(Write Only)

Software Interrupt Summary Register
(Read/Write)

Figure 6-1
Content of Software Interrupt Request Register and Software Interrupt Summary Register

currently running. For example, device driver FDT routines may signal completion by calling the routines EXE$FINISHIO or EXE$FINISHIOC. These routines execute at IPL 2 and terminate by requesting the I/O postprocessing software interrupt at IPL 4. In this case, the interrupt is taken immediately. The file system ACP uses the same technique to signal I/O completion for requests in which it was involved.

6.1.2   **Software Interrupt Service Routines**

There are several features about the use of software interrupts in the VMS operating system that are independent of the purposes of individual interrupt service routines. Some of these are dictated by the particular way that software interrupts are treated in the hardware.

Because the VAX architecture supplies no mechanism for determining how many times a software interrupt has been requested before it is taken, software must supply some protocol for determining this number. The VMS operating system uses queues (doubly linked lists manipulated by the INSQUE and REMQUE instructions) for this purpose. In general, each queue element represents a specific operation that must be performed. The use of queues, particularly the use of the INSQUE and REMQUE instructions, allows other optimizations to be made.

- The software interrupt service routine can use the information provided by condition code settings, this time as the result of executing a REMQUE instruction. That instruction returns the V-bit set if the queue was empty before the instruction began execution, an indication that the work of this particular interrupt service routine is complete.
- By coding software interrupt service routines so that they keep removing work list elements from a queue until there is no more work to do, it is possible to simply ignore spurious software interrupt requests. In fact, all of the software interrupt service routines in the VMS operating system, including those that do not use queues, handle interrupts, even in the event of spurious interrupts requests.

6.2   **SOFTWARE INTERRUPT LEVELS IN THE VAX/VMS OPERATING SYSTEM**

The VMS operating system uses the software interrupt mechanism for several purposes.

- Mount verification cancellation executes above driver fork IPL and below device IPL so that DMA operations will work, yet drivers cannot interfere with the device data structures.
- Device drivers use forks in order to execute at an IPL below device IPL.

Table 6-1: Software Interrupt Levels Used by the Executive

IPL	Use	Stack
15	XDELTA on VAX-11/782	Interrupt
14-13	Unused	Interrupt
12	Mount Verification Cancellation	Interrupt
11	IPL=11 Fork Dispatching	Interrupt
10	IPL=10 Fork Dispatching	Interrupt
9	IPL=9 Fork Dispatching	Interrupt
8	IPL=8 Fork Dispatching	Interrupt
7	Software Timer Service Routine	Interrupt
6	IPL=6 Fork Dispatching	Interrupt
5	Used to Enter XDELTA, also Scheduling on VAX-11/782	Interrupt
4	I/O Postprocessing	Interrupt
3	Rescheduling Interrupt	Kernel
2	AST Delivery Interrupt	Kernel
1	Unused	na

- The software timer service routine performs timer operations that would bog the system down (because I/O device interrupts are blocked) if they were performed at IPL 24, the level at which the hardware clock interrupts.
- The need for I/O postprocessing can be flagged by device driver interrupt service routines but the actual processing deferred while another pending I/O request is started.
- Rescheduling, the removal of the current process from execution and the selection of a new process for execution, is implemented as a software interrupt service routine.
- The AST delivery interrupt is the only software interrupt that is treated as a process-specific interrupt rather than a system-wide event.

Table 6-1 lists all the software interrupt levels used by the VAX/VMS operating system.

6.2.1 Mount Verification Cancellation

If a Files-11 volume is mounted in a drive, and the corresponding device driver generates one of a select set of errors, mount verification is invoked. Mount verification allows the system to recover gracefully from certain errors, rather than wait indefinitely or report a bugcheck. While mount verification is in progress on a particular device, no other requests will be serviced by the ACP associated with that device.

If the device undergoing mount verification uses the same ACP as the system disk, mount verification can effectively stall the system until the mount verification either completes or times out. This stall can occur because the ACP will not service any other requests.

In order to abort mount verification, an IPL 12 interrupt must be requested from the console terminal. The interrupt service routine that serves the IPL 12 interrupt prompts with the following prompt:

```
IPC>
```

At this point, commands can be issued to cancel mount verification or enter XDELTA. More information about canceling mount verification can be found in the *VAX/VMS System Management and Operations Guide*.

6.2.2 Fork Processing

Another use of software interrupts is found in the mechanism called fork processing employed by device drivers. The interrupt nesting scheme defined by the VAX architecture will not work correctly if an interrupt service routine lowers IPL below the level at which the interrupt occurred. However, device driver interrupt service routines, initially entered or invoked at device IPL (typically 20 to 23 decimal), often must perform lengthy processing that does not require device interrupts to be blocked, the usual reason for maintaining high IPL. Some mechanism is required to allow device drivers to lower IPL without destroying the interrupt nesting scheme.

Several IPL values (6, and 8 to 11) and their associated SCB slots are used by device drivers to allow them to continue their execution at lower IPL, as so-called fork processes. There are also six quadword listheads associated with the fork IPLs. (Because IPL 7 software interrupts are used by the software timer, this listhead is not used by the fork processor but merely serves as a place saver so that context indexed addressing can be used by the fork processor and the fork dispatcher with the IPL value as an index.) The queue elements that describe each individual operation that must be performed at lower IPL are called fork blocks and are used to pass context between driver interrupt service routines and the fork level software interrupt service routines. A fork block (pictured in Figure 6-2) is often part of a larger structure such as a unit control block.

When a driver must lower its IPL (by creating a fork process), it calls routine EXE$FORK with R5 containing the address of the fork block. That routine saves the driver context (R3, R4, and saved PC) in the fork block, inserts the fork block into the appropriate fork queue, and requests a software interrupt at the requested IPL level. The actual instructions in routine EXE$FORK that perform these functions are listed here to illustrate how work queues and software interrupt requests are managed.

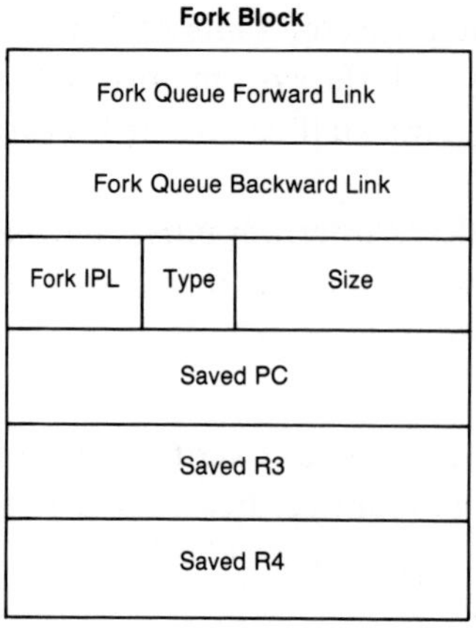

Fork Block

Fork Queue Forward Link
Fork Queue Backward Link

Fork IPL	Type	Size

Saved PC
Saved R3
Saved R4

Figure 6-2
Layout of Fork Block

```
EXE$FORK::
           MOVQ      R3,FKB$L_FR3(R5)
           POPL      FKB$L_FPC(R5)
           MOVZBL    FKB$B_FIPL(R5),R4
           MOVAQ     W^SWI$GL_FQFL-<6*8>[R4],R3
           INSQUE    (R5),@4(R3)
           SOFTINT   R4
           RSB
```

The fork dispatcher, which is the software interrupt service routine that executes in response to the requested interrupt, executes the following sequence
of instructions (or a sequence much like it), which removes each queue element in turn from the associated queue and processes it. This processing
continues until the queue is empty, at which time the software interrupt is
dismissed with an REI. R6 is loaded with the address of the fork queue listhead before this sequence is executed.

```
           .ALIGN    LONG
EXE$FORKDSPTH::
           PUSHL     R5
           PUSHL     R4
           PUSHL     R3
           PUSHL     R2
           PUSHL     R1
           PUSHL     R0
           REMQUE    @(R6),R5
           BVS       20$

10$:       MOVQ      FKB$L_FR3(R5),R3
           JSB       @FKB$L_FPC(R5),
           REMQUE    @(R6),R5
           BVC       10$
```

```
20$:    POPR    #^M<R0,R1,R2,R3,R4,R5,R6>
        REI

        .END
```

6.2.3   Software Timer

Most of the timer operations in the VMS operating system execute in response to a software interrupt at IPL 7. These operations are described in
detail in Chapter 11. The use of software interrupts by the timer support
routines is described here.

When the hardware clock interrupt service routine (executing at IPL 24)
determines that further service is required (due to quantum expiration or
because the first element in the timer queue has come due), it requests a
software interrupt at IPL 7 (IPL$_TIMER). Unlike the fork queue described in
the previous section, timer queue elements (TQEs) are not placed into the
timer queue by an interrupt service routine. Rather, they are usually placed
there by one of the timer-related system services (such as $SETIMR or
$SCHDWK). The key to the timer queue is that the queue elements are or-
dered by expiration time so that only the first TQE has to be examined by the
hardware clock service routine.

The software interrupt service routine rechecks for quantum expiration
and takes action if necessary. After any required quantum end processing has
occurred, the software timer service routine examines the timer queue for
any timer requests that have expired. Any timer queue element that has an
expiration time earlier than the current system time is then removed from
the timer queue and serviced. Because of the time ordering of the timer
queue, this removal takes place from the beginning of the list. When no more
expired timer queue elements remain (the expiration time of the first TQE in
the queue is later than the current system time), the software interrupt is
dismissed. Note that a second difference between this software interrupt
service routine and fork processing is that the software timer service routine
may leave timer queue elements (the ones that have not yet expired) in the
queue when it dismisses the interrupt. For more information on timers and
timer queues, see Chapter 11.

6.2.4   I/O Postprocessing

When a device driver or FDT routine detects that a particular I/O request is
complete, it calls a routine that places the I/O request packet (pointed to by
R3) at the tail of the I/O postprocessing queue (located through global pointer
IOC$GL_PSBL) and requests a software interrupt at IPL 4 (IPL$_IOPOST) if
the queue was previously empty. The following instructions (from routine

IOC$REQCOM in module IOSUBNPAG) show the similarities between the software interrupt requests for fork processing and I/O postprocessing. (Other routines that request an IPL$_IOPOST software interrupt, $QIO completion code and ACP routines, execute similar instructions.)

```
          .
          .
          .
    INSQUE      (R3),@W^IOC$GL_PSBL
    SOFTINT     #IPL$_IOPOST
          .
          .
          .
```

The I/O postprocessing software interrupt service routine removes each IRP in turn from the beginning of the queue (located through global pointer IOC$GL_PSFL) and processes it. When the queue is empty, the IPL 4 software interrupt is dismissed. The similarities between fork processing and I/O postprocessing are also found in their respective software interrupt service routines. The following instructions from module IOCIOPOST illustrate these similarities.

```
IOC$IOPOST::
            MOVQ      R4,-(SP)
            MOVQ      R2,-(SP)
            MOVQ      R0,-(SP)
IOPOST:     REMQUE    @W^IOC$GL_PSFL,R5
            BVC       10$
            MOVQ      (SP)+,R0
            MOVQ      (SP)+,R2
            MOVQ      (SP)+,R4
            REI

10$:
            .                           ;Complete processing of
            .                           ; this request
            .
            BRx       IOPOST
```

6.2.5   Rescheduling Interrupt

The routine that removes a process from execution and selects the highest priority process for execution is invoked as a software interrupt service routine at IPL 3 (IPL$_SCHED) by the routine that makes a process computable. Whenever the state of a resident process becomes computable and its priority is greater than or equal to the priority of the current process, this software interrupt is requested. Because several processes could all become computable at effectively the same time, there could be multiple requests for this software interrupt service routine.

The rescheduling interrupt is not totally independent of process context like the fork processing and I/O postprocessing interrupts. The SCB entry for this interrupt indicates that it should be serviced on the kernel stack (see Table 6-1). In fact, its first operation is to remove the current process from execution with a SVPCTX instruction. However, that instruction performs a stack switch from the kernel stack to the interrupt stack so the rest of the rescheduling interrupt service routine is performed in system context. The operation of the scheduler, including a detailed description of the rescheduling interrupt, is discussed in Chapter 10.

Unlike fork processing or I/O postprocessing requests, there is no need to count requests for the rescheduling interrupt, because only one process can become current at a given time. The software priorities of the computable processes determine which of them is chosen for execution. The scheduler will select the process with the highest software priority. The rest of the processes will remain in the computable state until some system event occurs that alters the scheduling balance of the system and causes one of these processes to be selected for execution. For example, if a higher priority process were to become computable, an IPL 3 software interrupt would be requested. (If the current process were to enter a wait state, a different path is taken through the scheduler, one that bypasses the software interrupt request and executes the code contained in the second half of the rescheduling interrupt service routine.)

6.2.6   AST Delivery Interrupt

The software interrupt that indicates that there is an AST to deliver differs in several respects from the other software interrupts.

- The AST delivery interrupt is associated with a specific process and is serviced on the kernel stack of that process.
- The interrupt request is made in two steps. Routines that recognize that there is an AST that can be delivered to a process indicate that by writing the access mode associated with the AST into a per-process privileged register called the AST level register (PR$_ASTLVL). The REI instruction compares the contents of this register with the access mode that it is restoring to determine whether to request an IPL 2 software interrupt.
- As this mechanism suggests, IPL 2 software interrupts have a second dimension associated with them, namely access mode.

The use of ASTs in the VMS operating system is so important and complex that it is described in a separate chapter (Chapter 7).

7 AST Delivery

There's absolutely no reason for being rushed along with the
rush. Everybody should be free to go very slow. . . . What you
want, what you're hanging around in the world waiting for, is for
something to occur to you.

—Robert Frost

Asynchronous system traps (ASTs) are a mechanism for signaling asynchronous events to a process. Specifically, a procedure (or routine) designated by either the process or the system executes in the context of the process. ASTs are created in response to system services such as $QIO, $SETIMR, and $DCLAST. Additionally, unrequested ASTs occur as implicit results of other operations such as I/O completion, process suspension, and obtaining information about another process with the Get Job/Process Information ($GETJPI) system service. The reason that ASTs are used for these operations is that it is necessary for code to execute in the context of a specific process. ASTs fulfill this need.

AST enqueuing is a system event that may result in a rescheduling interrupt. AST delivery occurs in the context of the process that is to actually receive the AST. This chapter discusses how ASTs are enqueued and delivered to a process. Several examples of how ASTs are used by the VMS operating system are also included.

7.1 HARDWARE ASSISTANCE TO AST DELIVERY

The delivery of ASTs is an example of the VAX hardware providing assistance to the VMS operating system. Three hardware components or mechanisms contribute to AST delivery:

- The REI instruction
- The PR$_ASTLVL processor register
- The IPL 2 software interrupt

The first two features are discussed in this section. The IPL 2 interrupt service routine, ASTDEL, is discussed in Section 7.3.

7.1.1 REI Instruction

The return from exception or interrupt routine instruction, REI, provides the initial step in the delivery of an AST to a process. Among the operations performed by the REI microcode are the following.

1. A check is made to determine which stack will be active after the return. No ASTs are delivered if the interrupt stack is active.
2. The value in the AST level processor register, PR$_ASTLVL, is compared with the access mode to which control is being passed. If the destination access mode number is less than the value in PR$_ASTLVL (that is, more privileged), no ASTs can be delivered.
3. If the interrupt stack is not going to be used and the access mode number is greater than or equal to the PR$_ASTLVL value, then an AST can be delivered. The REI instruction microcode requests a software interrupt at IPL 2. (Note that the requested IPL 2 interrupt will not actually be granted until the IPL drops below 2.) The IPL 2 software interrupt service routine is found at global location SCH$ASTDEL (see Section 7.3).

7.1.2   ASTLVL Processor Register (PR$_ASTLVL)

The processor register, PR$_ASTLVL, is a per-process hardware register indicating the deliverability of ASTs to the current process. PR$_ASTLVL is part of the hardware context of the process (loaded by LDPCTX) and is recorded in the hardware process control block (see Chapter 10). PR$_ASTLVL can contain the following values:

0	A kernel mode AST is deliverable.
1	An executive mode AST is deliverable.
2	A supervisor mode AST is deliverable.
3	A user mode AST is deliverable.
4	No AST is deliverable.

Thus, if multiple ASTs are deliverable, PR$_ASTLVL contains the access mode value for the AST that has the innermost access mode. The null value of four is chosen so that the REI test, described above, will fail, regardless of the destination access mode of the REI instruction. If the access mode of the deliverable AST is at least as privileged as the destination access mode of the REI instruction, the AST delivery interrupt will be requested.

7.2   QUEUING AN AST TO A PROCESS

ASTs are queued to a process as the corresponding events (I/O completion, timer expiration, and so on) occur. The AST queue is maintained as a list structure of AST control blocks (ACBs) with the listhead contained in the software process control block (PCB) (see Figure 7-1).

7.2.1   AST Control Block

The AST control block (ACB) contains the following information necessary to deliver an AST to a process:

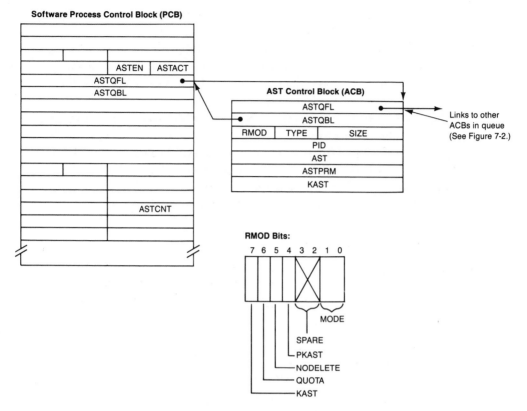

Figure 7-1
AST Control Block and AST Queue in Software PCB

- The process identification and AST routine address
- The correct access mode
- The appropriate parameter to pass to the routine

The ACB is allocated from nonpaged dynamic memory before the queuing of an AST to a process is requested.

Figure 7-1 shows the format of an AST control block and the relevant software PCB fields. ACB$L_ASTQFL and ACB$L_ASTQBL link the ACB into the AST queue for the process. The listhead of this queue is the pair of longwords PCB$L_ASTQFL and PCB$L_ASTQBL. The field ACB$B_RMOD provides five types of information.

1. Bits <0:1> (ACB$V_RMOD) contain the value corresponding to the access mode in which the AST routine is to execute.
2. Bit <4> (ACB$V_PKAST) indicates the presence of a piggyback special kernel mode AST (see Section 7.2.4).

3. Bit <5> (ACB$V_NODELETE) indicates that the ACB should not be deallocated after the AST is delivered. Typically this bit indicates that the ACB is a portion of a larger structure.
4. Bit <6> (ACB$V_QUOTA) indicates whether the allocation of the data structure is accounted for in the process AST quota, PCB$W_ASTCNT.
5. Bit <7> (ACB$V_KAST) indicates the presence of a special kernel mode AST (see Sections 7.2.3 and 7.4).

ACB$L_PID identifies which process is to receive the AST. ACB$L_AST and ACB$L_ASTPRM are the entry point of the designated AST routine and the AST parameter, respectively. ACB$L_KAST contains the entry point of a system-requested special kernel mode AST routine if the ACB$V_PKAST or ACB$V_KAST bit of ACB$B_RMOD is set (items 2 and 5 above).

ACBs can be created by three types of action.

1. The process explicitly declares an AST. The $DCLAST system service simply allocates an ACB, fills in the ACB information from its argument list, and requests the queuing of the ACB. The following checks are made before the ACB is queued:

   • The AST quota for the process is checked to make sure it is not exceeded by the request.
   • The access mode in which the AST routine is to execute is checked to make sure that it is no more privileged than the access mode from which the system service was called.

   The ACB$V_QUOTA bit is set to indicate that this AST is counted against the process AST quota, PCB$W_ASTCNT.

2. The process requests an AST to be associated with an event such as the completion of a request (I/O or update section, lock management, or timer requests). System services such as these have arguments that include an AST routine entry point and an AST parameter. The delivery of an AST is accounted for in the PCB$W_ASTCNT field. The control block (ACB) is actually a reuse of the I/O request packet (IRP), lock block (LKB), or timer queue element (TQE) used in the initial operation. (Compare the ACB format pictured in Figure 7-1 with the TQE format shown in Figure 11-1, the LKB format shown in Figure 13-1, or the IRP layout shown in the *VAX/VMS Guide to Writing a Device Driver.*)

3. The system, or another process, can request an AST to execute code in the context of the selected process. Examples of this type of action include I/O completion, Get Job/Process Information system service executed from another process, Forced Exit system service, expiration of CPU time quota, and working set adjustment as part of the quantum end event (see

Chapter 10). AST control blocks used in these situations are not deducted from the AST quota of the target process because of their involuntary nature.

7.2.2 Access Mode and AST Queuing

The ACB$V_RMOD bits of the ACB$B_RMOD field determine the insertion position of an AST control block when it is queued to a process. The AST queue is maintained as a first-in/first-out (FIFO) list for each access mode. ASTs of different access modes are placed into the queue in ascending access mode order, that is, kernel mode ASTs first and user mode ASTs last. Special kernel mode ASTs precede normal kernel mode ASTs.

When the subroutine SCH$QAST (in module ASTDEL) is invoked, the preallocated and preinitialized AST control block is inserted into the AST queue of the appropriate process at IPL$_SYNCH. The following steps are then performed.

1. If the process is nonexistent, the ACB is deallocated and the AST event is ignored. An error status code is returned.
2. If the AST queue is empty (the contents of PCB$L_ASTQFL are equal to its address), the ACB is inserted as the first element in the AST queue.
3. Otherwise, the queue elements (ACBs) are scanned until either the end of the queue is reached or an ACB is found with an access mode less privileged than the one being inserted (that is, the ACB$V_RMOD value is higher). The new AST control block is inserted at this point. Thus, ASTs are first-in/first-out within an access mode and grouped by access mode in decreasing amount of privilege. User mode ASTs are always placed at the tail of the queue.

7.2.3 Special Kernel Mode ASTs

Special kernel mode ASTs represent a fifth type of AST. They are maintained as a separate group in the AST queue. Special kernel mode ASTs are indicated by the ACB$V_KAST bit of the ACB$B_RMOD field. Insertion of a special kernel mode AST will occur after any previous special kernel mode ASTs, but before any normal ASTs of any access mode (including kernel). The organization of the AST queue is shown in Figure 7-2.

Section 7.4 discusses special kernel mode ASTs more fully and provides several examples.

7.2.4 Piggyback Special Kernel Mode ASTs

Piggyback special kernel mode ASTs (PKASTs) are a new form of AST delivery used in VAX/VMS Version 3. PKASTs allow a special kernel mode AST to

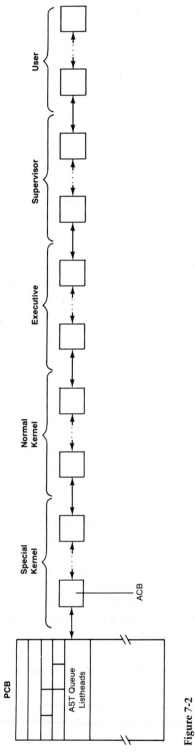

Figure 7-2
Organization of the AST Queue

ride piggyback in the ACB$L_KAST field of a normal mode AST. Piggyback special kernel mode ASTs are inserted in the AST queue according to the mode of the normal mode AST on which they ride.

When the normal AST becomes deliverable, the information in the ACB is saved and the special kernel mode AST is delivered first. When the special kernel mode AST returns, the normal mode AST is called.

There are reasons for using piggyback special kernel mode ASTs:

1. It is faster to deliver two ASTs from one interrupt than to deliver two ASTs separately.
2. There are times when delivering an AST requires some additional work in kernel mode in the context of the calling process. Piggyback special kernel mode ASTs reduce the work involved in this operation.

    The lock manager uses piggyback special kernel mode ASTs to load the fields of the caller's lock status block and lock value block. In order to copy the information from the lock manager's database to the caller's process space, a piggyback special kernel mode AST is required.
3. A piggyback special kernel AST can be used to queue other normal mode ASTs to a process. The lock manager uses this feature to deliver both blocking and completion ASTs to one process. The terminal driver uses piggyback special kernel mode ASTs to requeue out-of-band ASTs (thus making them repeating).

7.2.5 Computation of a New Value for ASTLVL

An AST can be enqueued to a process at any time, because the software PCB and the AST control blocks are neither paged nor swapped. Each time an AST control block is inserted into the queue, the assignment of a value to ASTLVL (processor register and hardware PCB field) is attempted. However, the process can be in any one of three possible situations that determine to what degree the state of the AST queue can be updated.

- If a process is outswapped, the ASTLVL cannot be updated because the process header (including the hardware process control block) is not available. When the process becomes resident and computable at a later time, ASTLVL will be calculated by the swapper (by invoking SCH$NEWLVL in module ASTDEL).
- If the process is memory resident but not currently executing, the new value for ASTLVL will be recorded in the hardware PCB field but not in the processor register.
- If the process is currently executing, the new ASTLVL value will be stored in both the hardware PCB field and the processor register, PR$_ASTLVL.

The ASTLVL value indicates the deliverability and access mode of the first pending AST in the queue. There is no indication of the deliverability of any other pending ASTs. ASTLVL is calculated in the following steps:

- If the AST queue is empty, ASTLVL is set to 4.
- If the AST queue is not empty and the first ACB is for a special kernel mode AST (see Sections 7.2.3 and 7.4), then ASTLVL is set to 0.
- If the AST queue is not empty and the first ACB is for a normal mode AST, ASTLVL is set to the access mode of that ACB (the value contained in RMOD).

7.3 DELIVERING AN AST TO A PROCESS

An AST is delivered to a process when an REI instruction determines (from the destination access mode and the PR$_ASTLVL register) that a pending AST is deliverable (see Sections 7.1 and 7.2). A software interrupt is requested at IPL 2. The amount of time before the AST is actually delivered is dependent upon the interrupt activity of the system. When IPL finally drops below two, the AST delivery interrupt service routine will be executed.

Note that a rescheduling interrupt at IPL 3 may be requested and granted, prior to the granting of the IPL 2 AST delivery interrupt request. Thus, it is possible for a spurious AST delivery interrupt to be granted in the context of a different process than was originally requested. Such spurious AST interrupts are detected and ignored.

7.3.1 AST Delivery Interrupt

Routine SCH$ASTDEL (in module ASTDEL) is the IPL 2 interrupt service routine. Its function is to remove the first pending AST from the queue and execute the appropriate AST routine in the correct access mode.

SCH$ASTDEL performs the following operations:

1. After raising the IPL to SYNCH, the first AST control block is removed from the AST queue of the process. If the queue was empty, the routine sets ASTLVL to 4 and exits with an REI instruction. This test detects spurious AST delivery interrupts.
2. The removed ACB is tested for a special kernel mode AST (using ACB$V_KAST in ACB$B_RMOD). If the AST is a special kernel mode AST, a shortened sequence of steps occurs:

   a. IPL is dropped from SYNCH to IPL$_ASTDEL (IPL 2).
   b. The special kernel mode routine is executed by a JSB instruction with the ACB address in R5 and the PCB address in R4.
   c. On return from the special kernel mode routine, SCH$ASTDEL returns to step 1.

3. If the AST removed from the queue is not a special kernel mode AST, then a check is made to confirm that the mode of the AST is at least as privileged as the destination of the REI instruction that initiated AST delivery. This test is accomplished by checking the saved PSL on the kernel stack. If the mode of the AST is not correct, the ACB is reinserted at the head of the queue and the routine exits through the REI instruction, setting the new ASTLVL; these tests detect spurious AST delivery interrupts. Similar checks are made for already active ASTs (PCB$B_ASTACT, which insures that an AST is not interrupted by another AST at the same access mode) and for disabled access modes (cleared bits in PCB$B_ASTEN indicate that the access mode that corresponds to the bit cannot receive ASTs).

4. If the AST is deliverable, then the following operations are performed before dispatching to the AST routine.

   a. The bit corresponding to the current access mode in PCB$B_ASTACT is unconditionally set.

   b. If the ACB is accounted for in the PCB$W_ASTCNT quota, then the count is incremented to show delivery of the AST and deallocation of the ACB to nonpaged pool.

   c. ASTLVL is recomputed because the removal of the first ACB alters the state of the AST queue. The new value of ASTLVL is the access mode of the current process plus one (the next outer mode). The access mode is calculated in this manner in order to prevent another AST interrupt when SCH$ASTDEL executes its REI to EXE$ASTDEL. ASTLVL is computed more precisely when the AST procedure is done, based on the access mode of the first ACB in the queue.

   d. IPL is dropped to ASTDEL.

   e. A kernel mode AST does not require changing access mode, and the appropriate stack is already active. For executive, supervisor, and user mode ASTs, however, the inactive stack pointer is obtained.

   f. An argument list (described in the next section) is built on the stack of the AST's access mode.

   g. For ASTs for the outer three access modes, a PC/PSL pair of longwords is built on the kernel stack. The stored PC is the location EXE$ASTDEL, the AST dispatcher. The stored PSL contains the access mode in which the AST is to be delivered in both its current mode and previous mode fields.

   h. If a piggyback special kernel mode AST is associated with the current AST, the special kernel mode AST routine is dispatched through a JSB instruction with the ACB address in R5 and the PCB address in R4. When the AST routine returns, processing continues with the next step.

   i. If a piggyback special kernel mode AST does not exist, the bit

ACB$V_NODELETE is tested. If the bit is set, processing continues with the previous step; if the bit is not set, the ACB is deallocated and returned to nonpaged dynamic memory.

j. EXE$ASTDEL executes in the access mode of the AST. For kernel mode, this merely requires dropping the IPL to zero. For the other access modes, transfer of control and change of access mode is accomplished through an REI instruction, the only way to reach a less privileged access mode (see Figure 1-4). (The PC and PSL used by the REI instruction are described above in item 4g.) A CALLG instruction is executed, transferring control to the AST procedure, with the argument pointer (AP) pointing to the argument list.

7.3.2   Argument List

User-written ASTs are procedures, which means that they can be written in any language. The procedures must begin with an entry mask and return control to their caller (the AST dispatcher) with a RET instruction.

Figure 7-3 shows the argument list passed to an AST procedure by the interrupt service routine, ASTDEL. The AST parameter is obtained from the ACB where it was initially stored by a system service such as $QIO, $SETIMR, or $DCLAST. The parameter was originally an argument to that system service. The interpretation of the AST parameter is dependent on the application.

The general purpose registers, R0 and R1, are saved in the argument list because the procedure calling convention does not require that they be saved. The asynchronous nature of ASTs implies that the R0 and R1 contents are unpredictable and cannot be destroyed. The registers are saved and restored by the AST delivery mechanism.

The saved PC and PSL values are the register contents originally saved when the IPL 2 interrupt was initiated by the hardware. The values are nor-

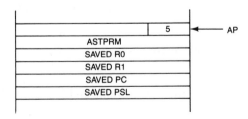

Figure 7-3
Argument List Passed to AST by Dispatcher

mally the pair that was about to be used by the original REI instruction requesting the AST delivery.

7.3.3   AST Exit Path

When the AST routine issues the RET instruction, control is returned to the location EXE$ASTRET in the access mode of the AST. The call frame, but not the argument list, was removed from the current stack by the RET instruction. The argument list remains because a CALLG rather than a CALLS instruction was used to execute the AST routine. The following steps then occur.

1. The argument count and the AST parameter are removed from the stack, leaving the R0, R1, PC, and PSL values.
2. The following instruction is executed:

    CHMK   #ASTEXIT

    This instruction invokes the change-mode-to-kernel system service dispatcher, CMODSSDSP (described in Chapter 9). The service code of zero (ASTEXIT = 0) causes the normal kernel mode dispatching mechanism to be bypassed.
3. In place of the kernel mode dispatching mechanism, the following actions are performed while in kernel mode:

    - The IPL is raised to SYNCH.
    - The appropriate PCB$B_ASTACT bit is cleared to signal AST completion.
    - The ASTLVL value is recomputed.

    These fields can only be written from kernel mode. Thus, it is necessary for the AST dispatcher to reenter kernel mode after the AST returns control to the dispatcher and before the AST delivery interrupt is dismissed.
4. An REI instruction, still in module CMODSSDSP, drops the IPL to zero, and returns the access mode to that of the AST.
5. Code in the module ASTDEL resumes at the previous access mode and IPL 0 with the following steps:

    - The saved values in R0 and R1 are restored.
    - Another REI instruction is issued.

The REI instruction returns control to the access mode and location originally interrupted by AST delivery.

Note that the REI instructions in CMODSSDSP and ASTDEL may cause another IPL 2 interrupt to occur, depending upon the ASTLVL value and the access mode transitions.

7.4   **SPECIAL KERNEL MODE ASTs**

Special kernel mode ASTs are different from normal ASTs in several ways:

1. The ASTs represent system actions that must occur in the context of the process. These actions are frequently requested when the process is not currently executing.
2. The special kernel mode AST routines are dispatched at IPL 2 and execute at that level or higher. Synchronization is provided by the interrupt mechanism itself, rather than requiring additional PCB$B_ASTACT and PCB$B_ASTEN bits. Only one special kernel mode AST can be active at any moment because the AST delivery interrupt is blocked.
3. The special kernel mode AST routines are invoked by a JSB instruction rather than a CALLG instruction. There is no argument list (the PCB address is in R4 and the ACB address is in R5). When the special kernel mode AST routine executes its RSB instruction, the stack must be in its original state (when the special kernel mode AST routine was called). The routine must also save and restore general registers R6 through R11.
4. The AST routine is responsible for the deallocation of the ACB (to non-paged pool). (For normal ASTs, this deallocation is done by the AST delivery routine.)
5. On return from the AST routine (with an RSB instruction), the AST queue is checked once more (in case a special kernel mode AST queued a normal AST to the process). If the queue is empty, an REI instruction is executed. This instruction attempts to pass control to the originally interrupted PC/PSL pair. IPL will drop from two to zero at the same time.

The next five sections briefly describe five examples of the special kernel mode AST mechanism.

7.4.1   **I/O Postprocessing in Process Context**

Part of the sequence of completing an I/O request involves the delivery of a special kernel mode AST to the requesting process. I/O postprocessing is described in the *VAX/VMS Guide to Writing a Device Driver*. This request is made by the IPL 4 (I/O postprocessing) interrupt service routine by queuing the former I/O request packet as an ACB. The operations performed by the I/O completion AST routine are those that must execute in process context, particularly those that reference process virtual addresses. The primary operations (executed at IPL 2) are the following.

1. For buffered read I/O operations only, the data is moved from the system buffer to the user buffer, and the system buffer is deallocated to nonpaged dynamic memory.
2. The buffered or direct I/O count field of the process header is incremented for accounting information.

3. If a user diagnostic buffer was specified, the diagnostic information is moved from the system diagnostic buffer before it is deallocated.
4. The channel control block (in the control region) is updated to show I/O completion. Updating the CCB may make the channel idle.
5. The event flag associated with the I/O request is set.
6. If an I/O status block (IOSB) was specified, the IOSB is written using information in the I/O request packet.
7. If an AST was specified with the $QIO request, then the ACB$V_QUOTA bit was set in the IRP. The AST procedure address and the optional AST parameter were originally stored in the IRP (now an ACB). The former IRP is queued to the process once again in the access mode of the requesting process.
8. Otherwise, the IRP/ACB is deallocated to nonpaged dynamic memory.

7.4.2 Process Suspension

When a $SUSPND system service request specifies a process other than the requesting process, the suspend mechanism requires a special kernel mode AST to enter the context of the target process.

When the special kernel mode AST is delivered, the following actions are performed:

1. The ACB is deallocated to nonpaged dynamic memory.
2. After raising IPL from ASTDEL (IPL 2) to SYNCH, the PCB$V_RESPEN bit is cleared. If a request to resume from the $RESUME system service was pending, then the resume request has precedence. That is, the AST routine exits without suspending the process (after dropping IPL back to ASTDEL).
3. If no resume request was pending, then the process is placed into the SUSP wait state. The process hardware context is saved with a SVPCTX instruction (described in detail in Chapter 10). The process quantum field in the process header is charged with a voluntary wait interval (determined by the special system parameter IOTA, described in Chapter 10). The time at which the process enters the wait state is stored in the process header at offset PHD$W_WAITIME. Control is passed to the scheduler at SCH$SCHED to select the next process for execution.

When the process finally executes again (after a $RESUME system service call), the PCB$V_SUSPEN bit is unconditionally cleared and the process is made computable.

7.4.3 Process Deletion

The major portion of the steps involved in process deletion occur in a special kernel mode AST routine queued in response to a $DELPRC system service call. A detailed explanation of process deletion is provided in Chapter 22. The use of the special kernel mode AST mechanism provides the following:

- Execution as the current process is accomplished by AST delivery. Almost all waiting processes are made computable by AST delivery (see Chapter 10), with the exception of suspended processes. The $DELPRC service ensures the deletion of a suspended process by issuing a $RESUME first.

  Execution as the current process is required for process virtual address translation and other operations that require process context (particularly in obtaining the information contained in the control region).
- The delivery of deletion ASTs cannot be prevented by the $SETAST system service. A process can only avoid deletion by raising IPL to ASTDEL (IPL 2) or above to prevent all AST deliveries. Because IPL can only be elevated while in kernel mode, only privileged processes, or the system acting on behalf of some process, can explicitly prevent process deletion.

7.4.4   **$GETJPI System Service**

The $GETJPI system service is described in Chapter 30. When information is requested for a process other than the requesting process, the target process must execute to establish process context. In addition, if the target process is outswapped, the enqueuing of the special kernel mode AST will make the process an inswap candidate. This action brings in both the working set and the process header (where much of the accounting information is maintained).

In general terms, the $GETJPI AST activity is as follows.

1. An ACB is constructed for a special kernel AST. A system buffer is also allocated and a pointer to it is placed in the ACB.
2. When the special kernel mode AST routine executes in the context of the target process, the requested information is moved into the system buffer. (The requests had been encoded in the ACB.) The ACB is then reset to deliver a special kernel mode AST back to the requesting process.
3. The second special kernel mode AST moves data from the system buffer into a user buffer in the requesting process. Other actions include the following:

   - Deallocating the system buffer
   - Setting an event flag
   - Delivering an AST in the access mode of the caller, if requested

4. If an AST is delivered, the ACB is used for the third time. If no AST is delivered, then the ACB is deallocated.

7.4.5 Power Recovery ASTs

Another example of the use of special kernel mode ASTs occurs in the implementation of power recovery ASTs, a tool that enables processes to receive notification that a power failure and successful restart have occurred. (Power failure and power recovery are described in Chapter 27.)

When a successful power recovery occurs, all processes that have established a power recovery AST are notified first with a special kernel mode AST. This AST retrieves information from the P1 pointer page that allows the user-requested AST to be delivered. The AST is required because P1 space information is only available from process context.

7.4.6 Other System Use of ASTs

Three other features within the executive are implemented through ASTs, but these ASTs are not special kernel mode ASTs. The automatic working set adjustment that takes place at quantum end is implemented with normal kernel ASTs. (See Chapter 10 for information on quantum end activities and Chapter 16 for detailed description of of automatic working set adjustment.) CPU time limit expiration is implemented with potentially multiple ASTs. Beginning with user mode, the AST procedure calls the $EXIT system service. If the process is not deleted, a supervisor mode time expiration AST is queued. This loop continues with higher access modes until the process is deleted. The Force Exit system service (see Chapters 12 and 21) causes a user mode AST to be delivered to the target process.

7.5 ATTENTION AND OUT-OF-BAND ASTs

Two other categories of AST use are the mechanisms for serving attention and out-of-band ASTs. Attention ASTs and out-of-band ASTs are used in association with I/O operation to notify processes or routines that an unsolicited event has occurred on a device. Out-of-band ASTs are described in Section 7.5.5.

7.5.1 Set Attention Mechanism

In order to establish an attention AST for a particular device (whose driver supports this function), the user must issue a $QIO system service request with the I/O function IO$_SETMODE (or IO$_SETCHAR for some devices). The kind of attention AST requested is indicated by a function modifier.

The following steps are provided by the routine COM$SETATTNAST in module COMDRVSUB. (This routine requires process context and so is called only from device driver FDT routines.)

1. If the user AST routine address (the $QIO P1 parameter) is zero, the request is interpreted as a flush attention AST list request (see Section 7.5.3).
2. An expanded ACB is allocated from nonpaged dynamic memory. The ACB is deducted from the process quota, PCB$W_ASTCNT.
3. Information from the I/O request packet (such as the AST routine entry point, AST parameter, device channel number, and process ID) is moved into the ACB.
4. IPL is raised to UCB$B_DIPL, the IPL at which this list is synchronized. The ACB is linked to the unit control block (UCB) of the associated device in a singly linked, last-in/first-out (LIFO) list.

7.5.2   Delivery of Attention ASTs

The occurrence of a situation for which attention ASTs have been defined causes the delivery of all such attention ASTs. The mechanism of delivery is implemented in the routine COM$DELATTNAST of module COM-DRVSUB. COM$DELATTNAST is usually invoked by a device driver at device IPL (IPL 20 through 23), after specifying which list of attention AST fork blocks/ACBs is to be used.

Each ACB is originally formatted as a fork block with the AST information located at different offsets. Figure 6-2 shows the layout of a fork block. The control block contains relevant additional information such as saved PC, R3, and R4 values, the channel number for the device, and the IPL value for processing the AST (IPL$_QUEUEAST = IPL 6). During fork processing, the control block is reformatted into a standard ACB.

When COM$DELATTNAST begins execution, the CPU is usually executing at device IPL. The queuing of ASTs is an operation using IPL$_SYNCH as a synchronization mechanism (see Chapter 2). Specifically, IPL must be raised to SYNCH. To accomplish correct synchronization, the IPL 6 fork dispatcher is used.

The following steps summarize the delivery of attention ASTs:

1. At IPL 20 through 23, each attention AST fork control block/ACB is removed from the appropriate list in the reverse order of declaration.
2. The routine invokes the FORK system macro to dispatch to EXE$FORK. EXE$FORK queues the fork block to the listhead defined by the fork IPL field and requests an interrupt at that IPL.
3. As the interrupt priority level of the CPU drops below six, the fork interrupt is taken. The IPL$_QUEUEAST fork dispatcher removes each fork control block from its queue and passes the control block back to a location in COM$DELATTNAST at IPL 6.
4. At IPL 6, the fork control block is then reformatted into an ACB, representing an AST in the access mode of the original requesting process.

5. The ACB is then queued to the process through SCH$QAST (which will immediately raise IPL to IPL$_SYNCH in order to synchronize access to the ACB listhead and the scheduler database).

7.5.3   Flushing an Attention AST List

The list of attention ASTs is flushed as the result of an explicit user request, a cancel I/O request, or a deassign channel request for the associated device.

An explicit user request to flush the attention AST list is performed as the result of a set attention AST request with an AST routine address of zero (see Section 7.5.1). COM$SETATTNAST then branches to COM$FLUSHATTNS.

Device drivers can request the flushing of the attention AST list by either invoking COM$SETATTNAST with an AST routine address of zero or by directly invoking COM$FLUSHATTNS with the channel number of the device in R6.

COM$FLUSHATTNS performs the following operations.

1. The IPL is raised to the hardware IPL of the device (IPL 20 through 23).
2. As each control block in the attention AST list is found, the process ID of the process requesting the flushing operation is compared with the process ID stored in the control block. An AST control block is retained in the attention AST list if the process IDs do not match.
3. If the process IDs match, then the channel numbers must match. One channel number is passed in R6 from the flush request, and the other is in the control block from the declaration of the AST. If the channel numbers do not match, then the control block is retained in the attention AST list. Otherwise, the control block is removed from the attention AST list. Control blocks are therefore removed for a specific process on a specific channel.
4. IPL is dropped from device interrupt level (IPL 20 through 23).
5. The ASTCNT quota is incremented to indicate deallocation of the control block.
6. The control block is deallocated to nonpaged dynamic memory. This operation requires execution through the fork dispatcher at IPL$_QUEUEAST to insure proper synchronization with IPL. (Actual deallocation is done at IPL 11 as described in Chapter 3.)
7. Processing continues until the entire attention AST list has been scanned.

7.5.4   Examples in the VAX/VMS Executive

Two devices that commonly have attention ASTs associated with them are terminals and mailboxes. Brief descriptions of the support for attention ASTs in these device drivers are given here.

7.5.4.1   **Terminal Driver and CTRL/Y Notification.** The terminal IO$_SETMODE and IO$_SETCHAR functions may take either IO$M_CTRLCAST or IO$M_CTRLYAST function modifiers. When a CTRL/C is typed on a terminal, the CTRL/C attention AST list is emptied by delivering each CTRL/C AST associated with the terminal. If no CTRL/C attention AST is declared, then the CTRL/C is interpreted as a CTRL/Y and the CTRL/Y AST list is searched instead. If a CTRL/Y is typed, only the CTRL/Y attention AST list is emptied.

Because the list is emptied each time a CTRL/Y or a CTRL/C is typed, both CTRL/C and CTRL/Y attention ASTs must be reenabled each time they are delivered to a process. In contrast, out-of-band ASTs are repeating. That is, once declared, out-of-band ASTs can be delivered to the process for the life of the process, or until the Cancel system service is called to flush the AST list.

7.5.4.2   **Mailbox Driver.** The IO$M_READATTN and IO$M_WRTATTN function modifiers provide notification of mailbox requests from other processes. IO$M_WRTATTN provides notification of unsolicited input to a mailbox. IO$M_READATTN notifies the enabling process when any process issues a read to a mailbox when no message is available.

Multiple attention ASTs of each type may be declared by processes for the same mailbox. When a condition corresponding to an attention AST occurs in a mailbox, all ASTs of the appropriate type are delivered. Only the first process to issue a responding I/O request will be able to complete the transfer of data signaled by the attention ASTs.

Read and write attention ASTs must be reenabled after delivery because the entire attention AST list is delivered (and removed) after each occurrence of the specified condition.

7.5.5   **Out-of-Band ASTs**

In VAX/VMS Version 3.0 a new form of AST mechanism was introduced specifically for the terminal driver. Routines establish out-of-band ASTs in order to intercept control characters received from the terminal (ASCII codes 00 through 20 [hex]) and to perform special processing as a result of the control character being typed. This mechanism is intended to supplement the attention AST mechanism described in Section 7.5, which applies only to the characters CTRL/C and CTRL/Y (ASCII codes 03 and 19 [hex]) in the terminal driver.

7.5.5.1   **Set Out-of-Band AST Mechanism.** The mechanism of out-of-band ASTs is similar in many ways to that of attention ASTs. Out-of-band ASTs are established by issuing the $QIO system service, specifying IO$_SETMODE (or IO$_SETCHAR) with the function modifier IO$M_OUTBAND. Like attention ASTs, the list of out-of-band ASTs is linked to the unit control block (UCB) of the associated terminal.

The following steps are performed by the routine COM$SETCTRLAST in module COMDRVSUB. (This routine requires process context, so it can be called from device driver FDT routines only.)

- If the user AST routine address (the $QIO P1 parameter) is zero, or if the character mask (the $QIO P2 parameter) is zero, the request is interpreted as a flush out-of-band AST list request (see Section 7.5.5.3).
- The list of out-of-band ASTs is scanned, searching for an out-of-band AST control block with the same characteristics as the caller. The following items are checked:

   —The process ID (PID). Out-of-band ASTs can be issued to the same terminal device from a process and its subprocesses (which will have different PIDs).
   —The channel number.
   —The character mask.

If an out-of-band AST control block is found with the same characteristics, the request is interpreted as a request to modify the existing out-of-band AST control block. If a similar out-of-band AST control block is not found, a new control block is allocated from nonpaged dynamic memory. The ACB in the out-of-band AST control block is deducted from the process AST quota, PCB$W_ASTCNT.

- Information from the I/O request packet (such as the AST routine entry point, AST parameter, device channel number, and process ID) is moved into the out-of-band AST control block.
- The out-of-band AST control block is placed on the tail of the control block list.
- The character mask is ORed into the out-of-band AST summary mask.

7.5.5.2   **Delivery of Out-of-Band ASTs.** When a control key is typed at a terminal, a check must be made to see if an out-of-band AST has been enabled for that key. The character typed is compared with the out-of-band AST summary mask. If the bit in the summary mask is set, an out-of-band AST has been declared for that control character and the AST is delivered. The mechanism of delivery is implemented in the routine COM$DELCTRLAST of module COMDRVSUB. COM$DELCTRLAST is invoked by the terminal driver at device IPL.

Each out-of-band AST control block is originally formatted as a fork block with the AST fields located at different offsets. (The first six longwords of the unit control block pictured in the *VAX/VMS Guide to Writing a Device Driver* are the most common example of a fork block.) The control block contains relevant additional information, such as: the saved PC, R3, and R4 values; the channel number for the device; and the IPL value for processing the AST (IPL$_QUEUEAST = IPL 6). During fork processing, the out-of-band AST control block is reformatted into a standard ACB.

When COM$DELCTRLAST begins execution, the CPU is executing at device IPL. ASTs are queued using IPL$_SYNCH as a synchronization mechanism (see Chapter 2). Specifically, IPL must be raised to SYNCH. To accomplish correct synchronization, the IPL 6 fork dispatcher is used.

The following steps summarize the delivery of out-of-band ASTs.

1. At device IPL, the list of out-of-band AST control blocks is searched for a block whose character mask contains the character typed at the terminal. When a match is found, a bit in the out-of-band AST control block is checked to see if the control block is already in use. If the block is in use, it is skipped; if the block is not in use, it is marked in-use, the control block is modified to act as a fork block, and the block is queued to the IPL6 fork queue listhead.
2. The routine invokes the FORK system macro to notify the fork dispatcher through the IPL 6 software interrupt.
3. As the interrupt priority level of the CPU drops below six, the fork interrupt is taken. The IPL$_QUEUEAST fork dispatcher removes each fork control block from its queue and passes the control block back to a location in COM$DELCTRLAST at IPL 6.
4. At IPL 6 the fork control block is then reformatted into an ACB, representing an AST in the access mode of the original requesting process. The no delete and piggyback special kernel mode AST flags are set in the ACB, and the special kernel mode AST field is loaded with the address of the piggyback special kernel mode AST.
5. The ACB is then queued to the process through SCH$QUAST (which will immediately raise IPL to IPL$_SYNCH).
6. When the process receives the ASTs, the piggyback special kernel mode AST is delivered first. The piggyback special kernel mode AST performs two functions:

   - It clears the busy bit.
   - If the out-of-band AST is marked as "lost," it is deallocated. "Lost" control blocks occur when a request to flush the AST list cannot deallocate a control block because the busy bit is set (see Section 7.5.5.3). Once the AST is delivered and the busy bit is clear, the control block is no longer needed and can be deallocated.

7.5.5.3   **Flushing an Out-of-Band AST List.** The list of out-of-band ASTs is flushed as the result of an explicit user request, a cancel I/O request, or a deassign channel request for the associated device.

An explicit user request to flush the out-of-band AST list is performed as the result of a set out-of-band AST request with an AST routine addresss of zero or a character mask of zero (see Section 7.5.5.1). COM$SETCTRLAST then branches to COM$FLUSHCTRLS.

Device drivers can request the flushing of the out-of-band AST list by either invoking COM$SETCTRLAST with an AST routine address of zero (or a character mask of zero) or by directly invoking COM$FLUSHCNTRLS with the channel number of the device in R6.

COM$FLUSHCTRLS performs the following operations.

1. The IPL is raised to the device IPL for the terminal.
2. The list of out-of-band AST control blocks is scanned. As each control block is found, the process ID of the process requesting the flushing operation is compared with the process ID stored in the control block. An AST control block is retained in the out-of-band AST list if the process IDs do not match.
3. If the process IDs match, then the channel numbers must match. One channel number is passed in R6 from the flush request; the other is in the control block from the declaration of the AST. If the channel numbers do not match, then the control block is retained in the out-of-band AST list.
4. If the channel numbers match, the busy bit is checked. If the busy bit is set, the "lost" bit is set so that the control block will be deallocated once its AST is delivered. Otherwise, the control block is removed from the out-of-band AST list.
5. IPL is dropped from device interrupt level.
6. The ASTCNT quota is incremented to indicate deallocation of the control block.
7. The control block is deallocated to nonpaged dynamic memory. This operation requires execution through the fork dispatcher at IPL$_QUEUEAST to insure proper synchronization with IPL. (The actual deallocation is done at IPL 11 as described in Chapter 3.)
8. Processing continues until the entire out-of-band AST list has been scanned.

8   Error Handling

There is always something to upset the most careful of human
calculations.

—Ihara Saikaku, *The Japanese Family Storehouse*

There are several levels for reporting system-wide errors in the VMS operating system. (Process-specific and image-specific errors are handled by the exception mechanism described in Chapter 4.)

- The error logging subsystem allows device drivers and other system components to record errors and other events for later inclusion in an error log report.
- The BUGCHECK mechanism is used by the VMS operating system to shut down the system in an orderly fashion when internal inconsistencies or other irrecoverable errors are detected.
- A machine check is an exception that indicates that the processor has detected some CPU-specific error.

8.1   ERROR LOGGING

The error logging subsystem is used to record device errors, processor-detected conditions, and other noteworthy events, such as volume mounts and system startups.

8.1.1   Overview of the Error Logging Subsystem

Error logging occurs in three steps.

1. Components such as device drivers that wish to log an error call routines in the executive that write error messages into one of two buffers permanently allocated in the executive image.
2. When the buffer allocation routine detects that a buffer is full, it awakens the ERRFMT process so that the buffer contents can be written to the error log file SYS$ERRORLOG:ERRLOG.SYS.
3. The contents of this file can be assembled into a report by the report generator utility SYE.

8.1.2   Device Driver Errors

There are two routines in the error log subsystem used by device drivers. ERL$DEVICERR is used to report device-specific errors. ERL$DEVICTMO

147

can be called by a driver to report a device timeout. In either case, the following action is performed by the routines:

1. An error message buffer is allocated.
2. The buffer is loaded with information obtained from the unit control block and from the current I/O request packet.
3. The driver is called at its register dump routine entry point to store device-specific information into the error message buffer.

8.1.3   Other Error Log Messages

The VMS operating system uses the error log subsystem to record other information besides device errors. The kinds of items written to the error log include the following:

- Warm start entries. These entries record successful recoveries from power failure.
- Cold start entries. These entries record all successful system bootstrap attempts.
- All bugchecks, fatal and otherwise. Bugchecks are described in the next section.
- Machine check occurrences.
- Volume mounts and dismounts.
- Any messages written to the error message buffer by the Send Message to Error Logger system service. The use of this system service requires BUGCHK privilege.

8.1.4   Operation of the Error Logger Routines

Error message buffer allocation occurs at IPL 31. This high IPL allows the allocation routine (ERL$ALLOCEMB) to be called from anywhere in the system (including machine check handlers, which execute at IPL 31) without causing IPL problems. IPL is restored to the caller's IPL before control is passed back to the caller.

There are two 512-byte buffers used for holding messages. A flip-flop switch (ERL$GB_BUFIND) indicates which of the two buffers is currently active. Allocation involves finding enough free space in the buffer indicated by ERL$GB_BUFIND to hold a message. When the current buffer is filled, the switch is thrown to activate the other buffer and the ERRFMT process is awakened to write the filled buffer to the error log file.

After a message buffer is successfully allocated, its address is returned to the caller of the allocation routine, which loads the buffer with information specific to the message being logged. Once the information has been stored, a second routine (ERL$RELEASEMB) is called to write more information into the message header, indicating that the message is valid.

8.1.4.1   **Waking the ERRFMT Process.** The routine ERL$WAKE is called at least once a second from EXE$TIMEOUT (see Chapter 11). This routine is also called when one of the two log buffers is filled. The routine does not automatically wake the ERRFMT process. Rather, it decrements a counter (ERL$GB_BUFTIM) and only wakes ERRFMT if the counter goes to zero.

If the counter goes to zero, it is also reset. The current starting value for the error log timer is 30. (This value is an assembly-time parameter, not adjustable with SYSGEN.) That is, the routine can be called a maximum of 30 times before ERRFMT is awakened. Thus, a maximum of thirty seconds can elapse without ERRFMT's becoming computable, forcing error messages to be written to the error log file at reasonable intervals, even on systems that have very few errors occurring.

This timing mechanism is exploited by the allocation and deallocation routines if they wish to force an awakening of ERRFMT. Either of these routines simply loads a 1 into ERL$GB_BUFTIM. The next call to ERL$WAKE (which must be done at IPL 7 and, thus, cannot be done directly either by the allocation or deallocation routine) is guaranteed to wake ERRFMT.

The allocation routine forces a wake whenever it is forced to switch buffers because the current buffer is full. The buffer release routine forces a wake if the current message buffer contains ten or more messages.

8.1.5   **Cursory Overview of the ERRFMT Process**

The ERRFMT process copies a previously filled error message buffer to the error log file SYS$ERRORLOG:ERRLOG.SYS, as described by the following steps:

- The contents of the message buffer are copied into the P0 space of ERRFMT. This copying occurs at IPL 31 to synchronize with the allocation subroutine.
- Once the message buffer contents are accessible in ERRFMT's address space, they can be put into a format acceptable to SYE, the error log report generator. The reformatted error messages are written to SYS$ERRORLOG: ERRLOG.SYS.
- If a process has declared an error log mailbox, each message in the error log buffer is also sent to that mailbox.
- If ERRFMT detects volume mounted or volume dismounted messages within the message buffer, it will send volume mounted or volume dismounted message to terminals enabled as disk or tape operators.

After ERRFMT has completed its output operations, it reenters the hibernate (HIB) state.

8.1.6   Error Log Mailbox

The error logging subsystem provides the capability (currently available for internal use by DIGITAL) for a process to monitor error logging activity as it is happening rather than wait for offline processing with the formatting program SYE. This capability is provided through an unsupported system service called Declare Error Log Mailbox (SYS$DERLMB).

8.1.6.1   System Service Call.

A process that has DIAGNOSE privilege can call the $DERLMB system service with a single argument, the unit number of the mailbox to receive error log messages. If the error log mailbox is not in use (the error log mailbox descriptor EXE$GQ_ERLMBX contains a zero), the unit number is stored in the first word of the mailbox descriptor and the PID of the requesting process is stored in the second longword.

Note that the Declare Error Log Mailbox ($DERLMB) system service is not supported by DIGITAL, and is not documented in the *VAX/VMS System Services Reference Manual*.

If this service is called with a unit number of zero, the descriptor is cleared, disabling the error log mailbox feature. The descriptor is also unconditionally cleared by the image rundown routine (see Chapter 21).

8.1.6.2   Action of the ERRFMT Process.

If the ERRFMT process detects that the error log mailbox feature is enabled, it sends each message that it extracts from the error log buffer to that established mailbox. Thus a process can monitor messages that the ERRFMT process is writing to the error log file.

8.2   SYSTEM CRASHES (BUGCHECKS)

When the VMS operating system detects an internal inconsistency, such as a corrupted data structure or an unexpected exception, it declares a bugcheck. If the system can continue running, a nonfatal bugcheck is declared, which results in an error log entry. Serious errors result in fatal bugchecks, through which the system is shut down in a controlled fashion.

1. The contents of physical memory are written to the system dump file (unless inhibited by a SYSBOOT flag, DUMPBUG).
2. After the system is halted, it may restart itself (again according to the setting of a SYSBOOT flag, BUGREBOOT).

8.2.1   Bugcheck Mechanism

The path into the bugcheck routine appears in source code as the invocation of the BUG_CHECK macro. This macro expands into opcode ^XFF, a byte containing ^XFE, and a word containing the particular bugcheck code.

The execution of opcode ^XFF results in a reserved instruction exception (SS$_OPCDEC, opcode reserved to DIGITAL), causing control to be transferred through the system control block to an exception-specific service routine. This routine checks for both of the following:

- If the opcode is ^XFF.
- If the byte following the reserved opcode is either ^XFE or ^XFD. (A ^XFE indicates that the bugcheck code is contained in the next word. A ^XFD indicates that the bugcheck code is contained in the next longword. The VMS operating system does not currently use longword bugcheck codes.)

If both of these checks succeed, the VMS operating system interprets this exception as a bugcheck and transfers control to routine EXE$BUG_CHECK. Otherwise, the illegal opcode exception is treated in the usual manner described in Chapter 4.

8.2.2 Operation of Bugcheck Routine

The bugcheck routine performs several steps, depending on the access mode in which the bugcheck occurred and whether the bugcheck was fatal. (The fatality of the bugcheck is determined by the severity field, bits <2:0> in the bugcheck code. If the BUG_CHECK macro call includes the parameter FATAL, a code of STS$K_SEVERE [value of 4] is placed into this field. Otherwise, a zero is placed there.) If the SYSBOOT flag BUGCHECKFATAL is set, all bugchecks are treated as fatal, independent of the severity code in the low-order three bits of the bugcheck code. The BUGCHECKFATAL flag is clear by default, which means that nonfatal bugchecks do not cause the system to crash.

8.2.2.1 Bugchecks from User and Supervisor Mode.
If a bugcheck is generated from either user or supervisor mode, and the process has BUGCHECK privilege, a message (of type user-generated bugcheck) is written to the error log buffer.

- If the bugcheck is fatal, the $EXIT system service is called with the code SS$_BUGCHECK as the final image status. What happens as a result of this call depends on whether the process is executing a single image (no supervisor mode termination handler has been established) or the process is an interactive or batch job.

  —If the process is executing a single image, a fatal bugcheck from user or supervisor mode results in process deletion.
  —With the current use of supervisor mode termination handlers, a fatal bugcheck issued from an interactive or batch job causes the currently executing image to exit and control to be passed to the CLI to receive the next command.

In either case, the only difference between user and supervisor mode is that user mode termination handlers are not called if a fatal bugcheck is issued from supervisor mode.

- If the bugcheck code is not fatal, the exception (the initial path into the bugcheck code) is dismissed, and execution continues with the instruction following the BUG_CHECK macro.

The BUGCHECKFATAL flag has no effect on bugchecks issued from user or supervisor mode. The severity field in the bugcheck code is used to determine whether a given bugcheck is fatal. In addition, neither user nor supervisor mode bugchecks cause the system to shut down.

8.2.2.2 **VMS Use of Bugchecks.** The bugchecks that the VMS operating system uses for its own purposes are issued from executive or kernel mode. If the bugcheck is not fatal and the SYSBOOT parameter flag BUGCHECKFATAL was turned off, the bugcheck routine proceeds as it does for nonfatal bugchecks for the outer two access modes. A message is sent to the error logger and the exception is dismissed, passing control back to the caller at the instruction following the bugcheck invocation.

A fatal bugcheck results in an orderly shutdown of the system. Rather than describe each step that the bugcheck routine takes to accomplish this shutdown, several items of general interest in the operation of the orderly shutdown are described.

- All disk I/O performed by the bugcheck routine uses the bootstrap disk driver used by the initialization programs VMB and SYSBOOT (see Chapter 24) and loaded into nonpaged pool by INIT (see Chapter 25). The use of this driver allows a dump file to be written even if the system disk driver is corrupted.

- Most of the bugcheck routine and all the bugcheck codes and associated text are not resident. They are stored in the executive image SYS.EXE and read into memory (by the boot driver).

  This code and data are read into system space on top of a read-only portion of the executive. Global label BUG$FATAL defines the beginning of the buffer into which the bugcheck code and data will be read. This label immediately precedes the blank program section (named ". BLANK ." and located at address 80007A6E in VAX/VMS Version 3.0).

  The code and data that are read into memory at this time include the following:

  —The bulk of the bugcheck service routine
  —A template for the message that is typed on the console terminal
  —Some primitive console terminal output routines
  —The textual description of all possible bugcheck messages

There are two implications of reading code into memory on top of existing code.

—None of the routines destroyed by BUGCHECK is available for use by the bugcheck code. This requirement is most important in deciding how the nonpaged executive is laid out.

—Portions of the dump may look strange when inspected by SDA. For example, it is impossible to determine if a portion of the instruction stream is corrupted because SDA displays bugcheck code and data instead of the original instructions and read-only data.

• A header block for the dump file is constructed in the 512 bytes immediately preceding the area into which the bugcheck code and data were written. This area contains more read-only portions of the nonpaged executive. (The system virtual address range whose contents are altered by the operation of bugcheck, including the 512-byte dump file header block, extends from 8000786E to 8000A26E. These numbers are valid for VAX/VMS Version 3.0 but are almost certain to change with the next major release of the system.)

The contents of the dump file header block are listed in Table 8-1. Note that the error log entry associated with this bugcheck is written into the header to avoid loss of information if the error log buffers were full when

---

Table 8-1: Contents of the Dump File Header Block

Description	Size
Last error log sequence number (unused)	Longword
Dump file flag	Word
(Low bit set if dump file analyzed)	
Dump file version	Word
(Contains 1 if Version 2.0 format)	
Contents of SBR, SLR, KSP, ESP, SSP, USP, ISP	7 Longwords
Quadword memory descriptors for up to eight memory controllers (each quadword is broken down as follows:	8 Quadwords
Page count	24 Bits
TR number for this controller	8 Bits
Base PFN for this controller	32 Bits
System version number	Longword
One's complement of previous longword	Longword
Error log entry for crash/restart	125 Words
(See Table 8-2)	
Contents of software PCB of current process	156 Bytes
(See Table B-2)	

---

the bugcheck occurred. This error log entry will be written into one of the error log buffers by SYSINIT (see Chapter 25) when the rest of the error log messages (blocks 2 and 3 in the dump file) are put back into the buffers. (If there is no room in the error log buffers, the bugcheck entry will never be written to the error log file, although it is preserved in the dump file.)

- A small amount of information describing the bugcheck is written to the console terminal. This information includes the contents of general registers, the kernel and executive stacks, the contents of processor internal registers, and a summary of the reason for the bugcheck. This output occurs before the dump file is written and should not be interrupted by halting the VAX processor from the console terminal. Such an interruption would prevent the dump file from being written.
- The dump header, the contents of the two error log buffers, and the contents of physical memory are written to the system dump file. This step can be inhibited by clearing the SYSBOOT parameter flag DUMPBUG. The system dump file is described in some detail in the next section.
- The last step in the bugcheck routine reboots the system. This is accomplished by writing a special code (^XF02) into the console transmit data buffer (PR$_TXDB). (The special uses of the console registers are described in Chapter 19.) After the bootstrap code is written, a HALT instruction is executed that allows console microcode to gain control and process the bootstrap command.

    —On a VAX-11/730 processor, the AUTO RESTART/BOOT switch must be in the AUTO RESTART ON position in order for the system to automatically reboot following a bugcheck.
    —On a VAX-11/750 processor, the bootstrap device selector switch must be properly set and the system disk must be unit 0 in order for the system to automatically reboot following a bugcheck.
    —On a VAX-11/780 processor, the contents of the file DEFBOO.CMD on the console floppy must contain commands to direct a reboot from the system disk.

The automatic reboot following a bugcheck can be prevented by clearing the SYSBOOT parameter flag BUGREBOOT. This flag is also manually cleared by OPCCRASH, the program that executes as part of the orderly shutdown procedure SHUTDOWN.COM. When automatic rebooting is inhibited, the system loops at IPL 31, waiting for a command to be entered at the console terminal.

8.2.3 System Dump File

The most important operation that is performed by the bugcheck routine is writing the contents of physical memory and other important information to

Table 8-2: Contents of Error Message Buffer for Crash/Restart Entry

Description	Size
Error message buffer header	Longword
Size in bytes of buffer	Word
Allocation buffer indicator	Byte
Error message valid indicator	Byte
Entry type (contains EMB$K_CR = 37 decimal)	Word
System time when crash occurred (from EXE$GQ_SYSTIME)	Quadword
Error log sequence number (low order word of ERL$GL_SEQUENCE)	Word
Contents of KSP, ESP, SSP, USP, ISP	5 Longwords
Contents of R0 to R11, AP, FP, SP, PC, PSL	17 Longwords
Contents of P0BR, P0LR, P1BR, P1LR, SBR, SLR, PCBB, SCBB, ASTLVL, SISR, ICCS, ICR, TODR, ACCS	14 Longwords
Contents of CPU-specific registers	21 Longwords
There are no CPU-specific registers saved for the VAX-11/730.	
For the VAX-11/750 this area contains the following:	
Translation buffer disable register (PR$_TBDR)	Longword
Cache disable register (PR$_CADR)	Longword
Machine check error summary (PR$_MCESR)	Longword
Cache error register (PR$_CAER)	Longword
CMI error summary register (PR$_CMIERR)	Longword
For the VAX-11/780 this area contains the following:	
SBI fault status (PR$_SBIFS)	Longword
SBI comparator register (PR$_SBISC)	Longword
SBI maintenance register (PR$_SBIMT)	Longword
SBI error register (PR$_SBITA)	Longword
SBI timeout address register (PR$_SBIS)	Longword
Bugcheck crash code	Longword
Length in bytes of software PCB	Word

NOTE. The error log entry for a nonfatal bugcheck contains the same information as the entry for a fatal bugcheck except for the 35 longwords set aside for architectural and CPU-specific processor registers.

the dump file. In the case of system crashes, the dump file can be examined by the System Dump Analyzer (SDA) to determine the reason for the crash. SDA is invoked by the DCL command ANALYZE/CRASH_DUMP. The dump file contains three distinct pieces.

1. The previously constructed dump header (see Table 8-1) is written to the first block in the file.
2. The two error log buffers are written to the next two blocks. These buffers

will be copied back into the error log buffers in memory from the dump file by SYSINIT (see Chapter 25) as part of the initialization code. In this way, no error log information is lost across a system crash or an operator-requested shutdown.

3. The rest of the dump file is filled with the current contents of physical memory. Bugcheck uses the memory descriptors in the restart parameter block (RPB) constructed by VMB (see Chapter 24) to provide an accurate layout of physical address space. If a MA780 shared memory adapter is present on the system, its contents are also written to the dump file.

The size of the dump file must be four blocks larger then the number of physical pages in the system. (The fourth block is not currently used.) In order to insure that a crash dump can be analyzed with SDA, it is important that the dump file be large enough. If a dump file is too small, only the physical pages that fit into the underconfigured dump file will be written. In a typical VMS configuration, the most crucial contents of physical memory, the system page table, are located at the largest physical addresses (see Chapter 24) and will not be written, making a partial dump useless. That is, SDA cannot be used to examine a dump file that does not contain all of physical memory.

8.3   MACHINE CHECK MECHANISM

A machine check is an exception that is reported when the CPU or an external adapter detects an internal error. The initial processing of a machine check exception is CPU specific. This section contains an overview of machine check handling. Consult the *VAX Hardware Handbook* or other hardware-related literature for information about a specific type of machine check.

The basic philosophy of any of the machine check handlers is to keep as much of the system running as possible. There are two important pieces of information that determine how serious a particular machine check is: the nature of the machine check itself and the access mode in which the machine check occurred.

- If the machine check is recoverable, the simple action is to log an error. This step is taken no matter what access mode was active when machine check occurred. In addition, the error time is recorded. If machine checks start occurring too quickly (more than one machine check per 10-millisecond interval), then the handler assumes that something is seriously wrong and treats a recoverable machine check in the same way that it treats an abort. The distinction between recoverable machine checks and aborts is CPU specific. The *VAX Hardware Handbook* or the module MCHECKxxx (where xxx represents the processor number) contains information about the machine checks that can occur on a particular processor.

- If the machine check has put the system into a state from which it cannot recover, the action taken by the machine check handler depends on the access mode in which the machine check occurred. If the previous mode was supervisor or user, a machine check exception is reported to that access mode. (Unless the process has taken special action, this step will result in image exit.) If the previous mode was executive or kernel, an irrecoverable machine check causes a fatal bugcheck (with the bugcheck code BUG$_MACHINECHK).

8.3.1 VAX-11/730 Machine Check

When a machine check occurs on a VAX-11/730, IPL is elevated to 31 and the interrupt stack contains the following information.

- The length in bytes of the exception-specific information pushed on the stack. (This count does not include either the PC/PSL pair or the count longword itself.) There are currently 3 longwords in this list, which result in a value of 0C hex onto the stack.
- Machine check error code.
- Two parameters, the contents of which depend on the machine check error code. The machine check codes and the information passed in these two parameters are detailed in Table 8-3.
- PC of aborted opcode.
- PSL at the time of the abort.

The machine check error code (the second item on the stack) determines the specific action of the machine check handler. If the machine check is an abort (PC left in an indeterminate state), then recovery is impossible. In addition, a subset of the VAX-11 instruction opcodes on the VAX-11/730 cannot be restarted. (The list of these instructions can be found in module MCHECK730.)

In addition to the VAX-11/730 machine checks that appear as exceptions (through the SCB vector at offset 4), one type of machine check can appear as an interrupt through a dedicated SCB vector. When this machine check occurs, only the PC and PSL are pushed onto the interrupt stack.

This machine check is a corrected memory data condition (CRD) and will interrupt at IPL 26 through SCB vector 54 (hex). This exception simply causes an error log entry (indicating a soft memory error) to be written. (If errors occur too quickly, the CRD interrupt bit in the memory controller is turned off by the machine check handler.)

8.3.2 VAX-11/750 Machine Check

When a machine check occurs on a VAX-11/750, IPL is elevated to 31 and the interrupt stack contains the following information.

Table 8-3: VAX-11/730 Machine Check Codes and Their Associated Parameters

Code	Explanation	MC$L_P1	MC$L_P2
MICRO_ERRORS	Microcode detected errors	0: No information available 2: Unable to set PTE modify bit 3: Bad microprocessor interrupt	zero
TB_PARITY	Translation Buffer Parity Error	PTE in error	VA of PTE in TB
BAD_MEM_CSR	Illegal format for memory CSR	VA referenced	Bad CSR value
NO_FAST_INT	Fast interrupts with no IDC present	zero	zero
FPA_PARITY	Floating Point Accelerator Parity Error	FPA parity information	zero
SPTE_READCHK	Hard Memory Error on SPTE read	Physical Address of SPTE	Memory Controller Diagnostics
RDATASUBS	Uncorrectable ECC Errors Read Data Substitute	Physical Address Referenced	Memory Controller Diagnostics
NX_MEM	Nonexistent Memory	Physical Address Referenced	zero
UNALIGNED_IO	Unaligned or non-longword reference to I/O space	Physical Address Referenced	zero
UNK_IO_ADDR	Illegal I/O space address	Physical Address Referenced	zero
BAD_UB_ADDR	Illegal UNIBUS reference	Physical Address Referenced	zero

- The length in bytes of the exception-specific information pushed on the stack. (This count does not include either the PC/PSL pair or the count longword itself.) There are currently 10 longwords in this list, which result in a value of 28 hex on the stack.
- Machine check error code.
- Virtual address of the last fetch or store operation.
- Program counter at the time of the error.
- Memory data of the last fetch or store operation.
- Saved mode register.
- Read lock timeout register.
- Translation buffer parity error register.
- Cache error register.
- Bus error register.
- Error summary register.
- PC of aborted opcode.
- PSL at the time of the abort.

The machine check error code (the second item on the stack) determines the specific action of the machine check handler. If the machine check is an abort (PC left in an indeterminate state), then recovery is impossible. In addition, a subset of the VAX-11 instruction opcodes on the VAX-11/750 cannot be restarted. (The list of these instructions can be found in module MCHECK750.)

In addition to the VAX-11/750 machine checks that appear as exceptions (through the SCB vector at offset 4) there are two machine checks that appear as interrupts through dedicated SCB vectors. When either of these occurs, only the PC and PSL are pushed onto the interrupt stack.

- A corrected memory data condition (CRD) will interrupt at IPL 26 through SCB vector 54 (hex). This exception simply causes an error log entry (indicating a soft memory error) to be written. (If errors occur too quickly, the CRD interrupt bit in the memory controller is turned off by the machine check handler.)
- A write bus error condition will interrupt at IPL 29 through SCB vector 60 (hex). This error is treated as an irrecoverable error and further processing depends on the previous access mode.

8.3.3   VAX-11/780 Machine Check

When a machine check occurs on a VAX-11/780, IPL is elevated to 31 and the interrupt stack contains the following information.

- The length in bytes of the exception-specific information pushed on the stack. (This count does not include either the PC/PSL pair or the count longword itself.) There are currently 10 longwords in this list, which result in a value of 28 hex on the stack.

- Machine check summary parameter.
- CPU error status.
- Trapped micro PC, the microcode error location.
- Virtual address at fault time.
- CPU D register at fault time.
- Translation buffer status register 0.
- Translation buffer status register 1.
- Physical address causing SBI timeout.
- Cache parity error status register.
- SBI error register.
- PC of instruction that caused the machine check.
- PSL of machine at fault time.

The machine check summary parameter determines the specific action of the machine check handler. If the machine check is an abort (PC left in an indeterminate state), then recovery is impossible. In addition, a subset of the VAX-11 instruction opcodes on the VAX-11/780 cannot be restarted. (The list of these instructions can be found in module MCHECK780.)

There are also several error conditions on the VAX-11/780 that generate interrupts instead of machine check exceptions.

- A corrected read data condition or a read data substitute condition interrupts through SCB vector 54 (hex) and raises IPL to 26.
- An SBI alert interrupts through vector 58 at IPL 27.
- An SBI fault interrupts through vector 5C at IPL 28.
- An asynchronous write error is reported through SCB vector 60 at IPL 29.

The first three of these errors result in error log entries. An attempt is made to continue from the error. The asynchronous write error causes a fatal bugcheck if it occurred in kernel or executive mode or if an error occurred while updating a page table.

8.3.4   Machine Check Recovery Blocks

The VMS operating system provides a capability for a block of kernel mode code to protect itself from machine checks while the protected code is executing. For example, the VMS operating system uses this feature if an interrupt is generated from a previously unconfigured adapter. If the code that read the configuration register were not protected and the interrupt were spurious, then the configuration register would not exist and the reference to a nonexistent I/O space address would crash the system.

There are several restrictions on the protected code.

1. It must be executing in kernel mode.
2. The stack cannot be used across the entry into or the exit out of the protected code block. This restriction exists because a coroutine mechanism is used to pass control between the protected block and the VMS routines that establish the protected code.
3. VMS elevates IPL to 31 so a limited number of instructions should be included in the block.
4. R0 is destroyed by the mechanism.

8.3.4.1   **Using the Recovery Mechanism.** Several macros are provided in the macro library SYS$LIBRARY:LIB.MLB to use this protection mechanism. The following macro defines the beginning of the block:

```
$PRTCTINI   LABEL,MASK
```

The label argument is identical to the label argument associated with the following macro, which defines the end of the block:

```
$PRTCTEND   LABEL
```

If no error occurred while the protected code was executing, R0 contains the success code SS$_NORMAL. Otherwise, the low bit of R0 is clear.

The mask argument allows the block of code to protect itself from different classes of errors. The following list describes the specific types of protection that are defined by the $MCHKDEF macro:

MCHK$M_LOG	Inhibit error logging for the error
MCHK$M_MCK	Protect against machine checks
MCHK$M_NEXM	Protect against nonexistent memory
MCHK$M_UBA	Protect against UNIBUS adapter error interrupts

Two other features used by the VMS operating system are a part of this protection mechanism. The following macro allows the VMS system to determine whether a recovery block is in effect and take action accordingly:

```
$PRTCTEST   ADDRESS,MASK
```

The status is returned in R0. The low bit set indicates that a recovery block is in effect and that the specified mask is being used.

The following macro is used by the machine check handlers for the VAX-11/730, the VAX-11/750, and the VAX-11/780 before issuing a fatal bugcheck.

```
$BUGPRTCT
```

If no recovery block is in effect, control is passed back to the location where this macro was invoked, where a bugcheck is usually issued. If a recovery block is in effect, control is passed to the end of the protected block with R0 containing an error code of SS$_MCHECK.

9 System Service Dispatching

Between the idea
And the reality
Between the motion
And the act
Falls the Shadow.

—T.S. Eliot, *The Hollow Men*

Many of the operations that the VMS operating system performs on behalf of the user are implemented as procedures called system services. Most of these procedures are linked as part of the executive and reside in system space; others are contained in privileged libraries. System services have global entry point names of the form EXE$service and typically execute in kernel or executive access mode so that they can read or write data structures protected from access by less privileged access modes. Some services are invoked directly by application programs. Others are called on behalf of the user by components such as RMS. This chapter describes how control is passed from a user program to the procedures in the executive that execute service-specific code.

9.1 SYSTEM SERVICE VECTORS

The addresses 7FFEDE00 to 7FFEE5FF (four pages of P1 space) are reserved for entry points to the system services and to RMS service routines. The global entry point name of each system service vector is SYS$service, as distinguished from EXE$service, the global name of the procedure in the executive image that performs the actual work of the system service.

Previous to Version 3.0, the system service entry points were maintained in the the lowest four pages of system virtual address space (addresses 80000000 to 800005FF). These entry points still exist in this location, in order that programs that were linked before VAX/VMS Version 3.0 will still refer to the correct entry points. The vectors were moved to process space so that system services could be intercepted on a per-process basis.

As new services are added to future releases of the VAX/VMS operating system, the vector area will grow to make room for new entry points. In addition, the absolute locations of the SYS$service entry points of existing services will remain fixed forever, so that existing user programs will not have to be relinked each time there is a new release of the VMS operating system.

Each service entry point contains eight bytes of code and data called a system service vector. Each vector consists of a global entry point named

SYS$service, a register save mask, a single instruction that transfers control eventually to a service-specific procedure in the executive, and an instruction (usually a RET) that passes control back to the caller.

Note that the vectors for the "composite" system services ($QIOW and $ENQW) contain the number of bytes required to execute the service, test return conditions, conditionally execute the $WAITFR service, and pass control back to the caller.

Most of the system services execute in kernel mode and the vectors for these services contain a CHMK instruction. A few system services and all of the RMS services contain a CHME instruction. Some services such as the text formatting services execute in the access mode of the caller and dispatch directly to the service-specific code in the VMS operating system with a JMP instruction. The following examples illustrate the three sets of instructions found in the system service vector area. The entry mask in each system service vector is identical to the entry mask found at location EXE$service. Table 9-1 lists the VMS system services that use each of the three illustrated methods of initial dispatch.

Vectors for system services that change mode to kernel contain the following code:

```
SYS$service::                                   ;Entry point
        .WORD       entry-mask
        CHMK        I^#service-specific-code
        RET                                     ;Return to caller
        .BLKB       1                           ;Spare byte
```

The extra byte here and in the vector for executive mode is used to keep the entry points on quadword boundaries.

Vectors for system services that change mode to executive contain the following code:

```
SYS$service::                                   ;Entry point
        .WORD       entry-mask
        CHME        I^#service-specific-code
        RET                                     ;Return to caller
        .BLKB       1                           ;Spare byte
```

Most vectors for RMS service calls replace these last two bytes with a branch to an RMS synchronization routine.

Vectors for system services that do not change mode contain the following code:

```
SYS$service::                           ;Entry point
        .WORD   entry-mask              ; of the caller
        JMP     @#EXE$service + 2       ;Transfer control to
                                        ; first instruction after
                                        ; the entry mask at
                                        ; EXE$service
```

This JMP instruction transfers control to the first instruction after the entry mask at EXE$service.

Table 9-1: System Services and RMS Services That Use Each Form of System Service Vector

The following system services execute initially in kernel mode:

$ADJSTK	$CREMBX	$DEQ	$GETPTI	$SETAST	$SETSSF
$ADJWSL	$CREPRC	$DERLMB	$GETSYI	$SETEF	$SETSTK
$ALLOC	$CRETVA	$DGBLSC	$HIBER	$SETEXV	$SETSWM
$ASCEFC	$CRMPSC	$DLCEFC	$LCKPAG	$SETIME	$SNDERR
$ASSIGN	$DACEFC	$ENQ	$LKWSET	$SETIMR	$SUSPND
$BRDCST	$DALLOC	$ENQW	$MGBLSC	$SETPFM	$TRNLOG
$CANCEL	$DASSGN	$EXIT	$PURGWS	$SETPRA	$ULKPAG
$CANEXH	$DCLAST	$EXPREG	$QIO	$SETPRI	$ULWSET
$CANTIM	$DCLCMH	$FORCEX	$QIOW	$SETPRN	$UPDSEC
$CANWAK	$DCLEXH	$GETCHN	$READEF	$SETPRT	$WAITFR
$CLREF	$DELLOG	$GETDEV	$RESUME	$SETPRV	$WAKE
$CMKRNL	$DELMBX	$GETDVI	$RUNDWN	$SETRWM	$WFLAND
$CNTREG	$DELPRC	$GETJPI	$SCHDWK	$SETSFM	$WFLOR
$CRELOG	$DELTVA				

The following system services execute initially in executive mode:

$CMEXEC	$NUMTIM	$SNDOPR
$GETTIM	$SNDACC	$SNDSMB
$IMGACT		

The following system services execute in the access mode of the caller. The services marked with a (1) can be called from any access mode; the services marked with a (2) can be called from executive and outer access modes. Those not marked can only be called from supervisor and user mode.

$ASCTIM (1)	$FAOL (1)	$IMGSTA
$BINTIM (1)	$GETMSG (2)	$PUTMSG
$EXCMSG (2)	$IMGFIX	$UNWIND
$FAO (1)		

The following RMS services execute in executive mode and branch to a synchronization routine before returning to the caller:

$CLOSE	$EXTEND	$OPEN	$REWIND
$CONNECT	$FIND	$PARSE	$SEARCH
$CREATE	$FLUSH	$PUT	$SPACE
$DELETE	$FREE	$READ	$TRUNCATE
$DISCONNECT	$GET	$RELEASE	$UPDATE
$DISPLAY	$MODIFY	$REMOVE	$WAIT
$ENTER	$NXTVOL	$RENAME	$WRITE
$ERASE			

The following RMS services execute in executive mode. The vectors for these RMS services contain RET instructions rather than a branch to an RMS synchronization routine.

$RMSRUNDWN	$SETDDIR	$SETDFPROT	$SSVEXC

9.2   **CHANGE MODE INSTRUCTIONS**

When a change mode instruction is executed, an exception is generated that pushes the PSL, the PC of the next instruction, and the code that is the single operand of the change mode instruction onto the stack indicated in the instruction. (As pointed out in Chapter 4, the actual access mode is the minimum of the access mode indicated by the instruction and the current access mode contained in the PSL.) For example, the execution of a CHME #5 instruction will push a PSL, the PC of the instruction following the CHME instruction, and a 5 onto the executive stack. Control is then passed to the exception service routine whose address is located in the appropriate entry in the system control block (SCB).

9.2.1   **The CHMK and CHME Instructions**

At initialization time, the VMS operating system fills in the SCB entries for CHMK and CHME with the addresses of change mode dispatchers that pass control to the procedures that perform service-specific code. The action of these two dispatchers is discussed in the next section.

9.2.2   **The CHMS and CHMU Instructions**

The SCB entries for CHMS and CHMU are filled in with the addresses of exception service routines that usually pass control to the general exception dispatcher described in Chapter 4. In this case, a CHMS or CHMU exception would be reported to a process through the normal signal and mechanism arrays. The particular exception names are SS$_CMODSUPR and SS$_CMODUSER respectively.

However, a user can short circuit the normal exception dispatching in the case of either of these exceptions by using the $DCLCMH system service to establish a per-process change-mode-to-supervisor or change-mode-to-user exception handler. This service fills location CTL$GL_CMSUPR or CTL$GL_CMUSER in the P1 pointer page with the address of the user-written change mode dispatcher. The exception service routines for the CHMS and CHMU exceptions check these locations for nonzero contents and dispatch accordingly.

The DCL and MCR command language interpreters use this service to create a special change-mode-to-supervisor handler. This handler is used when it is necessary to get to supervisor mode from user mode when an image is interrupted with a CTRL/Y. The use of the change-mode-to-supervisor handler is discussed in Chapter 23. The job controller uses a change-mode-to-user dispatcher for its processing of error messages.

165

9.3   **CHANGE MODE DISPATCHING IN THE VMS EXECUTIVE**

The change mode dispatcher that receives control from the CHMK or CHME instruction in the system service vector must dispatch to the procedure indicated by the code that is found on the top of the stack. In addition, because the service routines are written as procedures, the dispatcher must construct a call frame on the stack. Building the call frame could be accomplished by using a CALLx instruction and a dispatch table of service entry points.

However, the call frame that must be built is identical for each service. In addition, the registers that the service-specific procedure will modify have already been saved because the register save mask in the vector area (at global location SYS$service) is the same as the register save mask at location EXE$service. So the dispatcher avoids the overhead of the general purpose CALLx instruction and builds its call frame by hand.

Further speed improvement is achieved in this commonly executed code

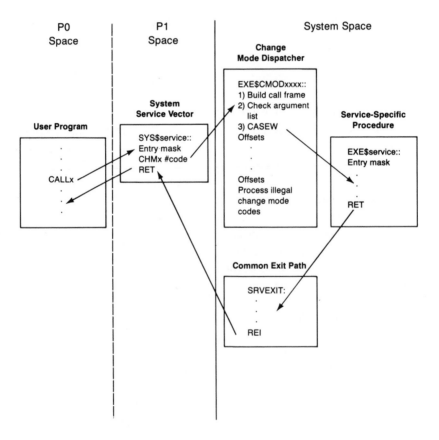

Figure 9-1
Control Flow of System Services That Change Mode

path by overlapping memory write operations (building the call frame) with register-to-register operations and instruction stream references. The actual dispatch to the service-specific procedure is then accomplished with a CASEW instruction that uses the CHMx code as its index into the case table. Figure 9-1 pictures the control flow from the user program all the way to the service-specific procedure. This flow is illustrated for both kernel and executive access modes. Figure 9-2 shows the corresponding flow for those services that do not change mode.

9.3.1 Operation of the Change Mode Dispatcher

The operation of the change mode dispatchers is almost identical for kernel and executive modes. This section discusses the common points of the dispatchers for kernel and executive modes. The next sections point out the only differences between the dispatchers for the two access modes.

The first instruction of the dispatcher pops the exception code, unique for each service, from the stack into R0. In both the kernel mode dispatcher and the executive mode dispatcher, the call frame is built on the stack by the following four instructions.

```
PUSHAB    B^SRVEXIT
PUSHL     FP
PUSHL     AP
CLRQ      -(SP)
```

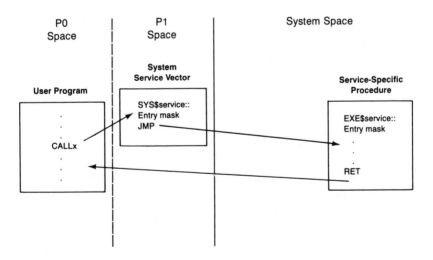

Figure 9-2
Control Flow of System Services That Do Not Change
Mode

While the call frame is being built, two checks are performed on the argument list. The number of arguments actually passed (found in the first byte of the argument list) is compared to a service-specific entry in a prebuilt table to determine whether the required number of arguments for this service have been passed. Read accessibility of the argument list is checked (with the PROBER instruction generated by the IFNORD macro). If either of these checks fails, control is passed back to the caller, with an error indication in R0.

Finally, a CASEW instruction is executed, using the unique code in R0 as an index into the case table. The case table has been set up at assembly time to contain the addresses of the first instruction of each service-specific routine. Because each service is written as a procedure with a global entry point named EXE$service pointing to a register save mask, the case table contains addresses of the form EXE$service + 2. This structure is illustrated in the following examples of dispatchers. If control is passed to the end of the case table, then a CHMx instruction was executed with an improper code and the error processing described in the next section is performed.

Code Example 9-1 compares the code for the two dispatchers, copied from the module CMODSSDSP. The entries containing the string "*******" indicate places where the change mode dispatchers differ. The instructions are not listed in exactly the same order that they appear in the source module. Rather, the instructions are shown in the order that they are found when all the PSECTs have been sorted out at link time.

The examples shown in Code Example 9-2 contain the error routines to which the change mode dispatchers branch. These routines are invoked if the argument list is inaccessible or if an insufficient number of arguments was passed to the service.

The routine in Code Example 9-3 is the common exit path for all system service and RMS service calls. The usual exit path is the REI instruction. The alternate exit path is to report a SS$_SSFAIL exception.

9.3.2 Change-Mode-to-Kernel Dispatcher

There are two steps performed by the change-mode-to-kernel dispatcher that are not performed by the change-mode-to-executive dispatcher. Before control is passed to those services that execute in kernel mode, the address of the PCB for the current process (found at global location SCH$GL_CURPCB) is placed into R4. The second difference is that CHMK #0 is a special entry path into kernel mode that is used by the AST delivery routine following the call to the AST procedure. If the CHMK code removed from the stack is a zero, control is passed to a routine called ASTEXIT. The action of this routine is described in Chapter 7.

Code Example 9-1

Change Mode to Kernel Dispatcher   Change Mode to Executive Dispatcher

```
EXE$CMODKRNL::                            EXE$CMODEXEC::
        POPL     RO                               POPL     RO
        BEQL     ASTEXIT                          ******
        PUSHAB   B^SRVEXIT                        PUSHAB   B^SRVEXIT
        MOVZBL   RO,R1                            MOVZBL   RO,R1
        PUSHL    FP                               PUSHL    FP
        MOVZBL   W^B_KRNLARG[R1],R1               MOVZBL   W^B_EXECNARG[R1],R1
        PUSHL    AP                               PUSHL    AP
        MOVAL    @#4[R1],FP                       MOVAL    @#4[R1],FP
        CLRQ     -(SP)                            CLRQ     -(SP)
        IFNORD   FP,(AP),ACCVIO                   IFNORD   FP,(AP),EXACCVIO
                 prober  #0,fp,(ap)                        prober  #0,fp,(ap)
                 beql    accvio                            beql    exaccvio
        MOVL     SP,FP                            MOVL     SP,FP
        CMPB     (AP),R1                          CMPB     (AP),R1
        BLSSU    KINSARG                          BLSSU    EXINSARG
KERDSP:                                   EXEDSP:
        MOVL     SCH$GL_CURPCB,R4                 ******
        CASEW    RO,#1,#KCASMAX                   CASEW    RO,#0,S^ECASMAX
          .                                         .
          .                                         .
          .                                         .
        offset to EXE$service + 2                offset to EXE$service + 2
          .                                         .
          .                                         .
                                                 JSB      @CTL$GL_RMSBASE
        *****                                      .
          .                                         .
          .                                         .
        check inhibit bits                       check inhibit bits
          .                                         .
          .                                         .
          .                                         .
        BSBW     CHECKARGLIST                     BSBW     CHECKARGLIST
        MOVL     @#CTL$GL_USRCHMK,R1              MOVL     @#CTL$GL_USRCHME,R1
        BEQL     10$                              BEQL     10$
        JSB      (R1)                             JSB      (R1)
10$:    MOVL     L^EXE$GL_USRCHMK,R1      10$:     MOVL     L^EXE$GL_USRCHME,R1
        BEQL     20$                              BEQL     20$
        JSB      (R1)                             JSB      (R1)
20$:    NOP                              20$:     BRW      ILLSER
        NOP
ILLSER: MOVZWL   #SS$_ILLSER,RO
        RET
```

Code Example 9-2

```
EXACCVIO:                                  ;From EXE$CMODEXEC
        MOVL     SP,FP                     ;Point FP to call frame
                                           ; so that RET works
        CMPW     R0,#RCASCTR               ;Only report INSARG for RMS
                                           ; and built-in functions
        BGEQU    EXEDSP                    ;Otherwise, get back in line
        BRW      ACCVIO_RET


EXINSARG:
        CMPW     R0,#RCASCTR               ;Only report INSARG for RMS
                                           ; and built-in functions
        BGEQU    EXEDSP                    ;Otherwise, get back in line
        BRW      INSARG                    ;Report error to caller


CHECKARGLIST:                              ;Check argument list for
                                           ; read accessibility
        IFNORD   #4,(AP),ACCVIO_RET        ;First check count
        CVTBL    (AP),R1                   ;Then get count
        BLSS     10$                       ;Branch if more than 128 arguments
        ASHL     #2,R1,R1                  ;Convert to byte count
        IFNORD   R1,4(AP),ACCVIO_RET       ;Now check rest of list
        RSB
10$:    MOVZBL   R1,R1                     ;Clear high three bytes
        ASHL     #2,R1,R1                  ;Convert to byte count
        PUSHL    R0
        PUSHL    R2
        PUSHL    R3
        MOVAL    4(AP),R0                  ;Get beginning of list
        CLRL     R3                        ;Kernel mode
        JSB      EXE$PROBER                ;Can addresses be read?
        POPL     R3                        ;restore registers
        POPL     R2                        ;
        BLBC     R0,20$                    ;Address could not be read,
                                           ; return access violation
        POPL     R0                        ;Address could be read,
        RSB                                ;Return
20$:    POPL     R0
        BRB      ACCVIO_RET


ACCVIO:
        MOVL     SP,FP                     ;Set FP so that RET works
ACCVIO_RET:
        MOVZWL   #SS$_ACCVIO,R0
        RET


KINSARG:
        CMPW     R0,#KCASCTR               ;Is this a recognized code?
        BGEQU    KERDSP                    ;No. Get back in line

INSARG:
        MOVZWL   #SS$_INSFARG,R0
        RET
```

Code Example 9-3

```
SRVEXIT:
        BLBC         RO,SSFAIL
SRVREI:
        REI


SSFAIL:
        BITL         #7,RO                          ;Check for mere warning
        BEQL         SRVREI                         ;If so, do not generate
                                                    ; exception
        BRW          SSFAILMAIN                     ;Go to SSFAIL logic

SSFAILMAIN:
        MOVL         G^CTL$GL_PCB,R1
        TSTW         PCB$W_MTXCNT                   ;Check for ownership of a mutex
        BNEQ         20$                            ;If so, BUGCHECK
        EXTZV        #PSL$V_CURMOD,#PSL$S_CURMOD,4(SP),-(SP)
        ADDL         #PCB$V_SSFEXC,(SP)             ;Are system service
                                                    ; failure exceptions enabled
                                                    ; for caller's access mode
        BBC          (SP+),PCB$L_STS(R1),10$        ;If not, dismiss the
                                                    ; exception
        MOVPSL       -(SP)                          ;Get current PSL
        EXTZV        #PSL$V_CURMOD,#PSL$S_CURMOD,(SP),(SP)+
                                                    ;If the current mode is kernel
        BNEQ         5$
        SETIPL       #0                             ;IPL must be lowered to 0
5$:     JMP          EXE$SSFAIL                     ;Pass control to the
                                                    ;general exception dispatcher
10$:    REI                                         ;Return from service with
                                                    ; error status
20$:    BUG_CHECK    MTXCNTNONZ,FATAL
```

9.3.3   Change-Mode-to-Executive Dispatcher

The change-mode-to-executive dispatcher performs one step unique to executive mode. If the CHME code is not a recognized system service, the CASEW instruction passes control to the end of the case table. At that point, the change-mode-to-executive dispatcher transfers control to the RMS dispatcher to determine whether this was a valid RMS call before dropping into the error processing described in the next section.

9.3.4   RMS Dispatching

The RMS dispatcher, illustrated in Figure 9-3, consists of two instructions. The CASEW instruction will dispatch to RMS service-specific procedures for legitimate RMS service codes. These procedures will exit with a RET back to SRVEXIT. If an illegal code (that is, a code not recognized as an RMS service call) was issued, the RSB instruction following the CASEW instruction will pass control back to EXE$CMODEXEC for normal error processing.

171

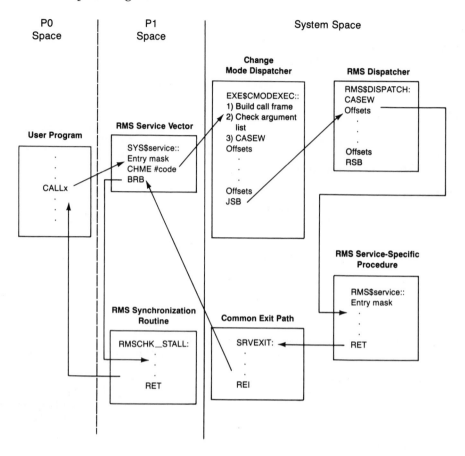

Figure 9-3
Control Flow of RMS Dispatching

9.3.5 Return Path for System Services

When the service-specific procedure has completed its operation, it places a status code in R0 and issues a RET instruction. This instruction returns control to the code at label SRVEXIT (shown in the examples in Section 9.3.1) because this address was put into the saved PC area of the call frame built by the change mode dispatcher. The routine SRVEXIT first checks whether an error occurred. If no error occurred or if the error was merely a warning (R0>2:0<=0), the CHMx exception is dismissed with an REI instruction that passes control to the instruction following the CHMx in the vector area. This instruction is a RET which finally returns control to the user program following the call to SYS$service (see the code examples in Section 9.1).

One additional step is taken by routine SRVEXIT when it is executed in kernel mode: IPL is explicitly lowered to zero. This step is unnecessary unless the process has enabled system service failure exceptions because the

REI instruction that dismisses the CHMK exception will lower IPL. However, if a system service failure exception is to be generated, the exception code must be entered with IPL set to zero. (A similar check is not needed for executive mode services because only kernel mode code can execute at elevated IPL.)

If an error or severe error occurred, a check is made to see whether the process owns any mutex. If so, the system service has not released all of its mutexes on exit (an erroneous error path) and a fatal bugcheck is generated. (Chapter 8 describes bugcheck processing. Mutexes are described in Chapter 2.) If the mutex check succeeds, a check is made to determine whether this process has enabled system service exceptions for the calling access mode. If it has, control is passed to the exception dispatcher at global label EXE$SSFAIL. The exception that will be reported to the caller in the signal array is SS$_SSFAIL. Otherwise, control is passed back to the caller with R0 containing the error status code.

9.3.6   Return Path for RMS Services

The return path for RMS services is slightly more complicated than the return path for system services. The last two bytes of the vector contain a branch (BRB) to an RMS synchronization routine (contained in module CMODSSDSP). This routine first checks whether the caller of the RMS service wishes to wait. This is the usual case, but RMS does allow asynchronous I/O operations. (The return status code is set to RMS$_STALL by RMS in the usual state, where the process must wait until the completion of the RMS operation.)

9.3.6.1   Wait State Associated with RMS Requests.
If a stall is indicated, the caller is put into an event flag wait state, waiting for the event flag associated with the I/O request that RMS has just issued. The crucial point in this implementation is that the caller is waiting at the access mode associated with the original call to RMS and not in executive access mode, thus allowing AST delivery for all access modes at least as privileged as the caller of RMS. (In the usual case where RMS is called from user mode, the access mode of the wait state allows both user and supervisor ASTs as well as executive and kernel ASTs to be delivered while waiting for the RMS operation to complete.)

When the original I/O request completes, RMS gains control first in an executive mode AST that it associated with its $QIO request. If it determines that the original request is complete, it sets final status in the data structure (FAB or RAB) associated with the operation and returns from its AST. The caller now drops through the event flag wait in the synchronization routine (because the I/O completion routine set the event flag). The synchronization routine determines that the RMS operation is complete (because the FAB or

RAB status field contains nonzero), and executes a RET, passing control back to the point where the initial call to RMS was issued.

If the RMS executive mode AST determines that more I/O is required to complete the original request (such as occurs when reading a large record from a sequential file with small internal buffers or when operating on an ISAM file), RMS issues the next $QIO and returns from its AST. Because the previous I/O completion set the associated event flag, the process is now computable. However, the RMS operation is not yet complete. For this reason, the RMS synchronization routine (executing in the caller's access mode) checks the status field in the RAB or FAB for zero, indicating that RMS has more to do. In this case, the caller is again placed into the LEF state by the RMS synchronization routine. In other words, at a primitive level, the process is placed into a LEF state by RMS one or more times. However, the actual indication that the RMS operation has completed is nonzero contents in the status field of the FAB or RAB.

9.3.6.2 **RMS Error Detection.** When the RMS synchronization routine finally decides that RMS has completed its work, it checks the final status. If this status indicates either success or warning, a RET is executed. If either an error or a severe error occurred, a special RMS call ($SSVEXC) is issued. This service simply reports the error status through the normal VMS service exit path (SRVEXIT) that determines whether the process has enabled system service failure exceptions. Because RMS errors are reported through the system service dispatcher, they are treated in exactly the same manner as system service errors.

9.4 **USER-WRITTEN SYSTEM SERVICE DISPATCHING**

The VAX architecture reserves CHMx instructions with negative codes for customer use. VMS system service dispatching acknowledges this in its dispatch scheme and contains hooks that allow a privileged user to write his own system services. The method for doing this is described in the *VAX/VMS Real-Time User's Guide*. This section merely describes how control is passed to user-written system services.

The code examples in Section 9.3.1 illustrate the error processing code that follows the case table for the change-mode-to-kernel or change-mode-to-executive dispatcher. The only differences between these two routines are the names of the global pointers that are referenced.

9.4.1 **Per-Process User-Written Dispatcher**

If the index into the case table is too large, the CHMK or CHME instruction was executed with an invalid code (control is passed to the end of the case

174

table). The VMS operating system attempts to pass control to a user-written change mode dispatcher. First, a location in P1 space (CTL$GL_USRCHMK or CTL$GL_USRCHME) is checked to see whether a per-process dispatcher exists. Nonzero contents of this location are interpreted as the address of a user-written dispatcher and control is passed to it with the stack as shown in Figure 9-4. The assumption being made by the VMS operating system at this point is that a valid change mode code will result in the eventual transfer of control to SRVEXIT with a RET instruction. If the per-process dispatcher rejects the code, it returns control to the code listed in Section 9.3.1 with an RSB instruction.

9.4.2 Privileged Shareable Images

The usual contents of CTL$GL_USRCHMK and CTL$GL_USRCHME are addresses within the two pages in P1 space set aside by the VMS operating system for user-written system services and image-specific message processing. Kernel mode and executive mode each have one half page (256 bytes) devoted to system service dispatching. The initial content of the first byte of each dispatch area (set up by PROCSTRT) is an RSB instruction. With the dispatch scheme described in the previous section, there is effectively no per-process change mode dispatching.

However, if an image executes that was previously linked with a privileged shareable image (linked with the /PROTECT and /SHAREABLE options and installed with the /PROTECTED and /SHARED options), the image activator replaces the RSB instruction with a JSB to the user-written change mode dispatcher specified as a part of the privileged shareable image (see Figure 9-5). The VMS operating system allows multiple privileged shareable images to be linked into the same executable image. (There is a limit of 42 user-writ-

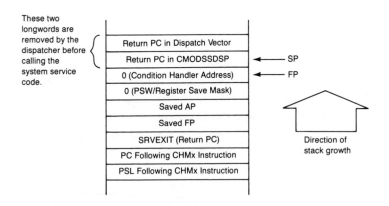

These two longwords are removed by the dispatcher before calling the system service code.

Return PC in Dispatch Vector	
Return PC in CMODSSDSP	◄—— SP
0 (Condition Handler Address)	◄—— FP
0 (PSW/Register Save Mask)	
Saved AP	
Saved FP	
SRVEXIT (Return PC)	
PC Following CHMx Instruction	
PSL Following CHMx Instruction	

Direction of stack growth

Figure 9-4
State of the Stack within a User-Written Dispatcher

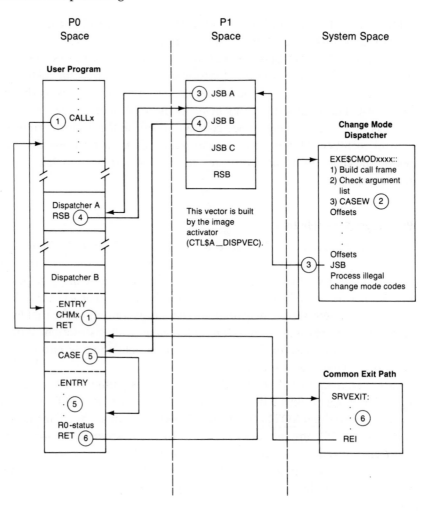

Figure 9-5
Dispatching to User-Written System Services

ten dispatchers of each type. How these dispatchers are collected into privileged shareable images determines the number of privileged shareable images that can be included in a single executable image.) An RSB instruction follows the last JSB instruction in the dispatch area. The example pictured in Figure 9-5 shows three privileged shareable images.

When the image activator (see Chapter 21) encounters a privileged shareable image as a part of the executable image it is activating, it maps the section(s) containing the user-written system services in the usual manner. However, it also uses information stored in a protected image section or in the first eight longwords of the image (a privileged library vector pictured in

Figure 9-6) to modify the P1 space dispatch area. For example, if a privileged shareable image contained a change-mode-to-kernel dispatcher, the image activator would insert a JSB instruction in P1 space that transferred control to the dispatcher specified by the PLV$L_KERNEL longword in the privileged library vector. Once the image containing user-written system services is ˙activated, execution proceeds normally until one of the services is invoked. Dispatching proceeds as follows (see Figure 9-5).

① A CALLx instruction transfers control to a service-specific entry mask in P0 space. The CHMx (CHMK or CHME) instruction located there transfers control to the VMS change mode dispatcher.

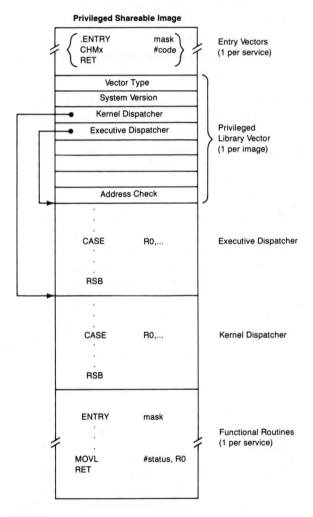

Figure 9-6
Structure of Privileged Shareable Image

② Execution proceeds as if a VMS service was invoked except that the change mode code is not recognized by the VMS dispatcher and control passes to the end of the case table (see the code examples in Section 9.3.1).

③ The JSB instruction in CMODSSDSP passes control to the P1 space dispatch area where another JSB instruction passes control to the first dispatcher.

④ The change mode code is rejected by the first dispatcher by simply executing an RSB back to the P1 space vector where a second JSB is executed.

⑤ The second dispatcher recognizes the change mode code as valid and dispatches (probably with a CASEx instruction) to a service-specific procedure that is also a part of the second privileged shareable image.

⑥ When the service completes (successfully or unsuccessfully), it loads a final status into R0 and exits with a RET which passes control to SRVEXIT. At this point, user-written system service dispatching merges with VMS system service dispatching.

If each dispatcher rejected the change mode code (by executing an RSB), control would eventually reach the RSB instruction in the P1 space vector. This RSB instruction passes control back to the VMS change mode dispatcher in CMODSSDSP where a system-wide dispatcher is checked for next.

9.4.3 System-Wide User-Written Dispatcher

If the P1 space location contains a zero, or if no per-process dispatchers are invoked, or if the last per-process user-written dispatcher returns to the routine in CMODSSDSP with an RSB, a location in system space (EXE$GL_USRCHMK or EXE$GL_USRCHME) is checked for the existence of a system-wide user-written dispatcher. If none exists (contents are zero, its usual contents in a VMS system), or if this dispatcher passes control back with an RSB, an illegal system service call (SS$_ILLSER) is reported back to the user in R0. This scheme assumes that user-written system services that complete successfully will exit with a RET back to SRVEXIT, where an REI instruction will dismiss the CHMK or CHME exception. Note that there is no standard documented way to add a system-wide user-written dispatcher to the system.

9.5 RELATED SYSTEM SERVICES

There are five system services in the VMS operating system that are closely related to system service dispatching and the change mode instructions. The $DCLCMH system service was briefly described in Section 9.2.2. This section describes the $SETSFM service, the $SETSSF service, and the change mode system services.

178

9.5.1 Setting System Service Failure Exceptions

The $SETSFM system service either enables or disables the generation of exceptions when an error is detected by the system service common exit path. The service itself simply sets (to enable) or clears (to disable) the bit in the process status longword (at offset PCB$L_STS in the software PCB) for the access mode from which the system service was called.

9.5.2 Change Mode System Services

The $CMKRNL and $CMEXEC system services provide a simple path for privileged processes to execute code in kernel or executive mode. These services check for the appropriate privilege (CMKRNL or CMEXEC) and then dispatch (with a CALLG instruction) to the procedure whose address is supplied as an argument to the service. (Note that if $CMKRNL is called from executive mode, no privilege check is made.)

The procedure that executes in kernel or executive mode must load a return status code into R0. If not, the previous contents of R0 will be used to determine whether an error occurred.

9.5.3 System Service Filtering

In some applications, especially user-written CLIs, it is desirable to deny access to system services that can be called from user mode. The Set System Service Filter ($SETSSF) system service was provided for this purpose.

When the module CMODSSDSP is assembled, in order to create the system service vectors, two tables of bytes are created, one for kernel mode system services (at the symbol B_KMASK), and one for executive mode system services (at the symbol B_EMASK). Each entry in these tables contains a mask that indicates whether or not the system service can be disabled by $SETSSF. If the service can be disabled by $SETSSF, the mask also indicates the system service filter groups for which the service is disabled. Group 0 specifies all services, except $EXIT; group 1 specifies most services, with the exception of $EXIT and those services required for condition handling or image rundown. The *VAX/VMS System Services Reference Manual* lists the services that are not disabled by $SETSSF.

The byte at offset CTL$GB_SSFILTER in the per-process control region contains the system service filter mask for a particular process. Usually this mask contains the value zero. When $SETSSF is called, the mask value specified in the call to $SETSSF is written into this mask.

When the system is bootstrapped, module INIT checks the bit EXE$V_SSINHIBIT at global location EXE$GL_DEFFLAGS. This bit corresponds to the SYSBOOT paramter SSINHIBIT. If the bit is set, the entry points in the change mode dispatcher for CHME and CHMK are revectored to the entry points EXE$CMODEXECX and EXE$CMODKRNLX, respectively.

When control is passed to these alternate entry points (from a CHME or CHMK instuction), the value in CTL$GB_SSFILTER is ANDed with the value in the system service filter tables (found at locations B_EMASK or B_KMASK). The CHMx code is used as an index into these tables. If the result of the AND is zero, processing continues and control is passed to the system service; if the result of the AND is nonzero, the call to the system service fails with the exit status SS$_INHCHME or SS$_INCHMK, depending on whether the system service was an executive mode or kernel mode service.

PART III/Scheduling and Timer Support

10 Scheduling

It is equally bad when one speeds on the guest unwilling to go,
and when he holds back one who is hastening. Rather one should
befriend the guest who is there, but speed him when he wishes.

—Homer, *The Odyssey*

Scheduling is concerned with the order of execution of processes and the occurrence of events over time. The scheduler identifies and executes the highest priority, memory-resident process. Processes may or may not be scheduled, depending on the scheduling state of the process and the nature of the event or resource for which the process is waiting. Transitions from one state to another occur as the result of system events such as the setting of an event flag, enqueuing an AST, calling the $WAKE system service, and so forth. This chapter describes the interactions of software priorities, process states, and system events, as well as the operation of the scheduler.

10.1 PROCESS STATES

The state of a process defines the readiness of the process to be scheduled for execution. In addition, the process state may indicate whether the process is memory resident or outswapped. If a process is waiting for the availability of a system resource or the occurrence of an event, then the process state is one of several distinct wait states. The wait state reflects the particular condition that must be satisfied for the process to become computable again.

10.1.1 Process Control Block

The major data structure describing the state and priority of a process is the software process control block (PCB). Figure 10-1 illustrates the fields of the software PCB that are particularly important to scheduling. The field PCB$W_STATE contains a numeric value associated with a particular process state. The process state is established by moving the appropriate value into PCB$W_STATE and inserting the PCB into the corresponding state queue by means of the state queue link fields, PCB$L_SQFL and PCB$L_SQBL. Appendix B contains a complete description of the software PCB. Table 10-1 lists the process state names and the corresponding PCB$W_STATE values. Other software PCB fields define the scheduling or software priority of the process and indicate whether the process is in mem-

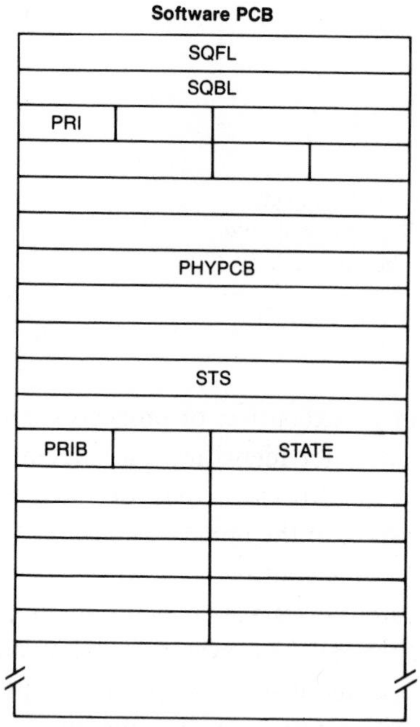

Software PCB

SQFL	
SQBL	

PRI			

PHYPCB	

STS	

PRIB		STATE

Figure 10-1
Process Control Block Fields Used in Scheduling

ory or outswapped. The location of a data structure containing the hardware context of the process is also stored in the software PCB (PCB$L_PHYPCB).

10.1.2   Software Priority

Software priority (as distinct from interrupt priority, a hardware mechanism) is used in determining the relative precedence of processes for execution and memory residence. Software priority is a value in the range from 0 to 31. The null process executes at software priority level 0, and the highest priority real-time process executes at software priority level 31. The range of 32 software priority levels is divided evenly between the normal process levels of 0 to 15 and the real-time process levels of 16 to 31. The execution behavior of a process is significantly affected by the type of process (normal or real time) and the assigned software priority level.

Two fields of the software process control block directly describe the scheduling or software priority of the process. The field PCB$B_PRI (see Figure 10-1) defines the current software priority of the process, which is used to make scheduling decisions. PCB$B_PRIB defines the base priority of the process, from which the current priority is calculated. For normal or time-sharing processes, these priority values are sometimes different, while real-

Table 10-1: Process Scheduling States

State Name	Mnemonic	Value
Collided Page Wait	COLPG	1
Miscellaneous Wait	MWAIT	2
Mutex Wait		
Resource Wait		
Common Event Flag Wait CEF		3
Page Fault Wait	PFW	4
Local Event Flag Wait (Resident)	LEF	5
Local Event Flag Wait (Outswapped)	LEFO	6
Hibernate Wait (Resident)	HIB	7
Hibernate Wait (Outswapped)	HIBO	8
Suspend Wait (Resident)	SUSP	9
Suspend Wait (Outswapped)	SUSPO	10
Free Page Wait	FPG	11
Computable (Resident)	COM	12
Computable (Outswapped)	COMO	13
Currently Executing Process	CUR	14

time processes always have identical current and base priority values. Each field may have a value from 0 to 31.

However, the values in these fields are stored internally in an inverted order. That is, the base and current priorities of 0 for the null process are stored internally in the PCB fields as 31. The highest priority process possible would have internally stored software priority values of 0. Thus, the internal field values are stored as 31 minus the software priority value. This inverted value causes priority promotions or boosts to be implemented through subtract or decrement instructions. System utilities such as SDA, MONITOR, and the DCL command SHOW SYSTEM interpret these inverted values and display external values, where 0 is the lowest priority and 31 is the highest. External values are also returned by the $GETJPI system service when a process priority is requested.

Note that all discussions in this book treat software priority as an increasing entity from 0 (for the null process) to 31 (for the highest priority real-time process). Please take this convention into account when relating descriptions in this book to the actual routines in the listings, where inverted priorities are used.

10.1.2.1   Real-Time Priority Range. Processes with software priority levels 16 through 31 are considered real-time processes. There are two scheduling characteristics that distinguish real-time processes.

1. The software priority of a real-time process does not change over time, unless there is a direct program or operator request to change it (with a Set

Priority system service or a SET PROCESS/PRIORITY command). The fact that the priority does not change implies that the base priority and the current priority of a real-time process are identical, and no dynamic priority adjustment (see Section 10.1.2.3) is applied by the operating system.

2. A real-time process executes until it is either preempted by a higher or equal priority process or it enters one of the wait states (see Section 10.1.3.2). Thus, a real-time process is not susceptible to quantum end events (see Section 10.1.2.4) and is not removed from execution (rescheduled) because some interval of execution time has expired.

Taken in isolation, the real-time range of VMS software priorities provides a scheduling environment like traditional real-time systems: preemptive, priority-driven scheduling without time slices or quanta.

10.1.2.2 **Normal Priority Range.** Normal processes include interactive terminal sessions, batch jobs, and all system processes except the swapper. The scheduling behavior of a normal process is different from that of a real-time process.

1. The current software priority of the process varies over time while the base priority remains constant (unless altered by the Set Priority system service or by a SET PROCESS/PRIORITY command). This behavior is the result of dynamic priority adjustment applied by the VMS system to favor I/O-bound and interactive processes at the expense of compute-bound (and frequently also batch) processes. The mechanism of priority adjustment is discussed in the following section. Priority adjustment can also occur as a result of locking a mutex (see Section 2.3.1) or as a result of action by the routine EXE$TIMEOUT (see Section 11.3.5).

2. Normal processes run in a time-sharing environment that allocates CPU time slices (or quanta) to processes in turn. Therefore, an executing normal process will control the CPU until one of the following events occurs:

   • It is preempted by a higher or equal priority, computable process (see Figure 10-2, event 5, for example).
   • It enters a resource or event wait state (see Figure 10-2, event 7, for example).
   • The current quantum or time slice has been used (see Figure 10-2, event 17, for example).

3. Processes with identical current priorities are scheduled on a round robin basis. That is, each process at a given software priority level executes in turn before any other process at that level executes again. Although this mechanism applies to real-time processes as well, it generally has no effect because real-time processes are usually assigned to unique software priority levels and their priorities do not change. Normal processes do experience round robin scheduling both because there are usually more of them

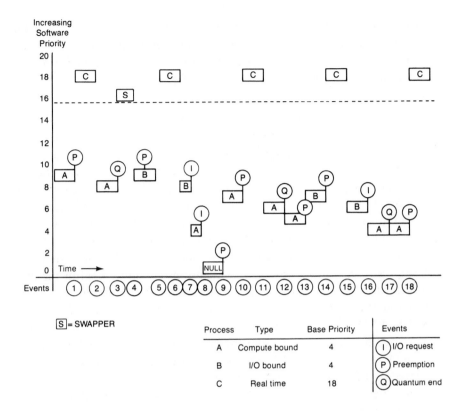

Figure 10-2
Software Priorities and Priority Adjustments

on a given system and because the default behavior (from Create Process system service arguments or from the user authorization file) is to assign a base priority of four to all user processes. Thus software priority levels four through nine tend to be occupied by several processes simultaneously.

10.1.2.3   Priority Adjustment. Normal processes do not generally execute at a single software priority level. Rather, a process software priority changes over time in a range of zero to six software priority levels above the base process priority. Two mechanisms provide this priority adjustment. As a condition for which the process has been waiting is satisfied or a needed resource becomes available, a boost or priority increment may be applied to the base priority to improve the scheduling response for the process (see Section 10.2.4). Each time the process executes without further system events (see Section 10.2) or quantum expiration (see the next section) occurring, the current priority is moved toward the base priority (or demoted) by one priority level (see Section 10.3). Over time, compute-bound process priorities tend to remain at their

187

base priority levels, while I/O-bound and interactive processes tend to have average current priorities somewhat higher than their base priority. An example of priority adjustment that occurs over time for several processes is illustrated in Figure 10-2.

10.1.2.4 **Quantum Expiration.** The SYSBOOT parameter QUANTUM determines, for most process states, the minimum amount of time a process can remain in memory after an inswap operation, but it is not an absolute guarantee of memory residence. (The swapper's use of the initial quantum flag is described in Chapter 17.) The quantum also defines the size of the time slice for the round robin scheduling of normal processes. The value of QUANTUM is the number of 10-millisecond intervals (clock ticks) in the quantum. The default QUANTUM value of 30 therefore produces a scheduling interval of 300 milliseconds. After each 10-millisecond interval, the hardware clock interrupt service routine updates the quantum-remaining field in the process header of the current process. When this value becomes zero, the software timer routine signals a quantum end event by invoking the subroutine SCH$QEND in module RSE.

An additional deduction from the QUANTUM is governed by the special SYSBOOT parameter IOTA. This value (in units of 10 milliseconds) is deducted from the remaining quantum value each time a process enters a wait state. Therefore, the default IOTA value of 2 charges 20 milliseconds against the quantum of the process. This mechanism is provided to insure that all processes experience quantum end events with some regularity. Processes that are compute bound experience quantum end as a result of using a certain amount of CPU time. Processes that are I/O bound experience quantum end as a result of performing a reasonable number of I/O requests. This scheme guarantees that processes that spend most of their time in some wait state can also accomplish useful work before they are outswapped.

The routine SCH$QEND is executed at the end of every quantum, regardless of the software priority of the current process. For real-time processes, however, the only action performed is to reset the process header quantum field to the full quantum value and to clear the initial quantum bit in the PCB status vector (bit PCB$V_INQUAN in the field PCB$L_STS, pictured in Figure 10-1). The cleared initial quantum bit makes a process more likely to be outswapped, if process swap mode has not been disabled.

The following notes relate to the numbers at the bottom of Figure 10-2:

① Process C becomes computable. Process A is preempted.
② C hibernates. A executes again, one priority level lower.
③ A experiences quantum end and is rescheduled at its base priority. B is computable outswapped.
④ The Swapper process executes to inswap B. B is scheduled for execution.

⑤ B is preempted by C.

⑥ B executes again, one priority level lower.

⑦ B requests an I/O operation (not terminal I/O). A executes at its base priority.

⑧ A requests a terminal output operation. The Null process executes.

⑨ A executes following I/O completion at its base priority + 3. (The applied boost was 4.)

⑩ A is preempted by C.

⑪ A executes again, one priority level lower.

⑫ A experiences quantum end and is rescheduled at one priority level lower.

⑬ A is preempted by B. A priority boost of 2 is not applied to B because the result would be less than the current priority.

⑭ B is preempted by C.

⑮ B executes again, one priority level lower.

⑯ B requests an I/O operation. A executes at its base priority.

⑰ A experiences quantum end and is rescheduled at the same priority (its base priority).

⑱ A is preempted by C.

For normal processes, however, the occurrence of quantum expiration involves several different operations.

1. As with real-time processes, normal processes have the process header quantum field reset and the initial quantum bit cleared.

2. If there are any inswap candidates (SCH$GL_COMOQS is nonzero, indicating at least one nonempty COMO state queue), the current priority of the process is set to its base priority. (If SCH$GL_COMOQS contains a zero, the priority is left alone.)

3. Routine SCH$SWPWAKE is called to determine whether swapper activity is required. The swapper process is awakened if any of the following are true:

   • There is at least one computable outswapped process.
   • Modified page writing is required as indicated by the upper and lower limit thresholds for the free and modified page lists.
   • There is at least one process header of a deleted process still in the balance slots.
   • A powerfail recovery has just occurred.

These checks avoid needless awakening of the swapper, with the associated context switch overhead, only to determine that the swapper has no useful work to do.

The swapper process does not execute immediately but must be scheduled for execution. As a computable (after waking), resident, real-time process of software priority 16, the swapper is very likely to be the next process scheduled.

4. The CPU limit field of the process header is next checked to determine if a CPU limit has been imposed and if that limit has expired. If the CPU limit has expired, each access mode will have an interval of time to clean up or run down before the image exits and the process is deleted. The size of the warning interval given to each access mode is defined by the SYSBOOT parameter EXTRACPU. (This parameter has a default value of one second.)

5. If no CPU limit expiration has occurred, then the automatic working set adjustment calculations take place if they are enabled. The size of the process working set may be expanded or contracted by amounts specified by the SYSBOOT parameters WSINC or WSDEC. Five SYSBOOT parameters determine threshold values to be applied to the automatic adjustments:

- For a new adjustment to take place, this process must have accumulated AWSTIME units of CPU time (each clock tick accounts for 10 milliseconds) since the last test for adjustment.
- The page fault rate must be larger than PFRATH faults per 10 seconds or less than PFRATL faults per 10 seconds.
- The working set cannot be contracted through automatic working set adjustment below AWSMIN nor expand above a process-specific maximum number of pages (see the next item).
- If there are more than BORROWLIM free pages, the working set list can grow up to WSEXTENT. If there are fewer than BORROWLIM free pages, the working set list can only grow to WSQUOTA. Note that this growth affects the working set list, not the actual working set size. Pages can be added to the extended working set list when a page fault occurs and there are more than GROWLIM pages on the free page list.

There are two possible courses of action that will disable automatic working set adjustment, and a third method is available to keep working set size less than or equal to WSQUOTA (disable borrowing) on a per-process basis:

- Use the DCL command SET WORKING_SET/NOADJUST to disable it on a per-process basis.
- Set the SYSBOOT parameter WSINC to zero to disable it on a system-wide basis.
- Set WSEXTENT equal to WSQUOTA, or set BORROWLIM to −1, to disable borrowing on a per-process basis.

Automatic working set adjustment is discussed from the memory management point of view in Section 16.4.1.3.

6. Finally, a scheduling interrupt at IPL 3 will be requested to remove the current process from execution and schedule the highest priority, memory-resident, computable process for execution. Note that on a quiet system, the currently executing process may be selected for execution again.

10.1.3   State Queues

With the exception of the single process executing at a given moment, all processes in the system are in a process wait state, the computable resident state, or the computable outswapped state. The process state is indicated by the PCB$W_STATE field and the linking of the process control block into a queue of similar PCBs. The listheads for all wait queues, computable resident (COM) queues, and computable outswapped (COMO) queues, as well as the pointer to the PCB of the current (CUR) process, are defined in the module SDAT.

10.1.3.1   Computable States. Processes in the computable or executable state are not waiting for events or resources, other than acquiring control of the CPU for execution. Computable resident (COM) processes are placed in one of 32 priority queues, with the queue chosen by the internal value for the current software priority of the process (see Figure 10-3). There is a similar set of 32 quadword listheads for the computable outswapped (COMO) state. Processes in the computable outswapped state are waiting for the swapper process to bring them into memory. As computable resident processes, they can then be scheduled for execution. Processes must be in the computable resident state to be considered for scheduling. Processes are created in the computable outswapped (COMO) state. Deletion of processes occurs from the current (CUR) state.

10.1.3.2   Wait States. The listheads for the process control block queues corresponding to all process wait states except the common event flag wait state (CEF) look like Figure 10-4. (Common event flag wait queues are described in Chapter 12.) The first two longwords are the longword links to the PCBs in this queue. The STATE field of the queue header contains the numerical value corresponding to the process state. All PCBs in a state queue have PCB$W_STATE values identical to the STATE value of the wait state queue header. Recognized STATE values and the corresponding state names are summarized in Table 10-1. The COUNT field of the wait state queue header is simply the number of process control blocks currently in this state and queue.

10.1.3.2.1   *Voluntary Wait States.* There are two process states associated with local event flag waits. Resident processes waiting for local event flags are placed into the LEF state, while outswapped processes occupy the LEFO state. There

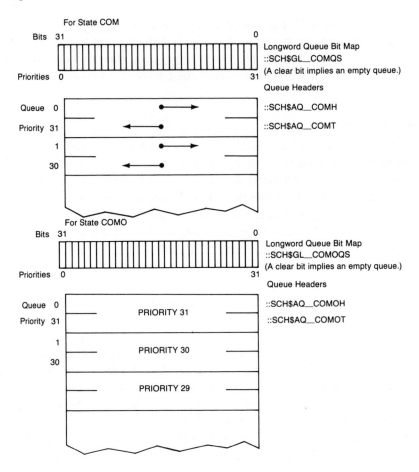

Figure 10-3
Computable (Executable) State Queues

are separate queues maintained for these states, and an LEF state process being outswapped must be removed from the LEF queue and placed into the LEFO state queue. Processes enter the LEF state as a result of issuing $WAITFR, $WFLOR, and $WFLAND system services directly or indirectly (for example, with a $QIOW or $ENQW system service call, issued either by the user or on his behalf by some system component such as RMS). Removal from the LEF or LEFO states to the computable (COM) or computable outswapped (COMO) states can occur as a result of matching the event flag wait mask, enqueuing an asynchronous system trap (AST), or process deletion.

Similarly, there are separate resident and outswapped states and queues for hibernating and suspended processes. The Hibernate and Suspend system services cause processes to enter the resident wait states. Hibernating proc-

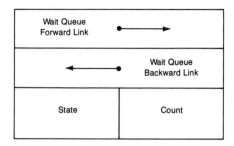

Figure 10-4
Format of Wait State Queue Headers

esses can leave the HIB and HIBO states and enter the COM and COMO states as a result of $WAKE system services, AST enqueuing, or process deletion. Suspended processes are sensitive only to $RESUME system services and process deletion (because ASTs cannot be delivered to processes while they are suspended). The transitions between states are diagrammed in Figure 10-5.

10.1.3.2.2 *Memory Management Wait States.* Three process wait states are associated with memory management. Each state is represented by a single queue and listhead of the form shown in Figure 10-4. Differentiation of resident and outswapped processes in these states is accomplished only by means of the PCB$V_RES bit of the PCB$L_STS field. The outswapping of processes in these states does not involve removal from and insertion into queues. The PCB$V_RES bit is simply cleared in the process control block. (Memory management wait states are discussed from another point of view in Chapter 15.)

The page fault wait state (PFW) is entered when a process refers to a page that is not in physical memory. While the page read is in progress, the process is placed into the PFW state. Completion of the page read, AST enqueuing, or process deletion can cause the process to become computable (COM) or computable outswapped (COMO), depending upon its PCB$V_RES bit value when the satisfying condition occurs.

The free page wait state (FPG) is entered when a process requests a page to be added to its working set, but there are no free pages to be allocated from the free page list. This state is essentially a resource wait until the supply of free pages is replenished through modified page writing, process outswapping, or virtual address space deletion.

The collided page wait state (COLPG) usually occurs when several processes cause page faults on the same shared page at the same time. The initial faulting process enters the PFW state, while the second and succeeding proc-

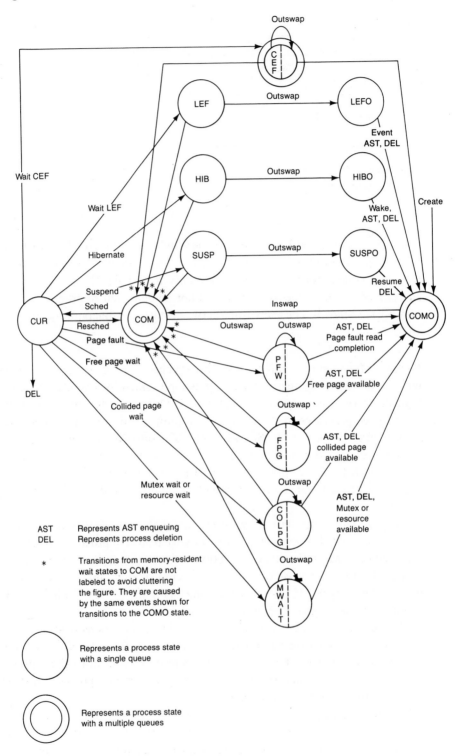

Figure 10-5
State Transition Diagram

esses enter the COLPG state. The COLPG state can also be entered when a process refers to a private page that is already in transition from the disk. All COLPG processes are made computable or computable outswapped when the read operation completes. (A more detailed discussion of collided pages is contained in Chapter 15.)

10.1.3.2.3   *Miscellaneous Wait State (MWAIT).* The miscellaneous wait state (MWAIT) is used to indicate processes waiting for resources not managed by any of the other process wait states. There is a single MWAIT queue for memory-resident and outswapped processes. Table 10-2 lists the resources associated with the two forms of the MWAIT state.

The miscellaneous resource wait state is used to wait for the availability of a depleted or locked resource. A process may enter a resource wait if the resource requested has already been allocated. Common examples are the depletion of nonpaged dynamic memory or no room in mailboxes. The process will become computable when the resource becomes available again. The number of the resource (a small integer defined by the $RSNDEF macro) is stored in the PCB$L_EFWM field (see Table 10-2), and the PCB$W_STATE is changed to MWAIT to indicate a miscellaneous resource wait. Whether a process can be made executable by the enqueuing of an AST to the process is dependent upon the interrupt priority level of the caller of the routine declaring the resource wait. If the IPL in the saved PSL in the hardware process control block is two or larger, the process will reexecute the resource wait code and be placed back into the MWAIT state immediately. If the saved IPL is smaller than two, an AST delivery interrupt will occur, resulting in the execution of the previously enqueued AST.

The Set Resource Wait Mode system service ($SETRWM) can force the immediate return of an error status code rather than placing the process in the MWAIT state. $SETRWM does this by setting the PCB$V_SSRWAIT bit of the PCB$L_STS field. Disabling resource waits affects many directly requested operations (such as I/O requests or timer requests) but has no effect on allocation requests by the system on behalf of the user. An example of this situation is the pager requiring an I/O request packet to perform a page read operation. If nonpaged dynamic memory is depleted, the process will enter the MWAIT state, even if $SETRWM had been used to disable resource waits. The reason for this distinction is that a process can respond to a depleted resource error from a system service call or an RMS request but has no means of reacting to a similar error in the event of an unexpected event such as a page fault.

System routines that access data structures protected by mutexes will place a process in the MWAIT state if the requested mutex ownership cannot be granted (see Chapter 2). Thus, the mutex wait state indicates a locked resource and not necessarily a depleted one. The logical name system serv-

Table 10-2: Types of MWAIT State

Reason for Wait	Contents of PCB$L_EFWM (1)	
Mutex Waits	*Symbolic*	*Numeric (hex)*
System Logical Name Table	LOG$AL_MUTEX	80002750
Group Logical Name Table		80002754
I/O Database	IOC$GL_MUTEX	800028C0
Common Event Block List	EXE$GL_CEBMTX	800028C4
Paged Dynamic Memory	EXE$GL_PGDYNMTX	800028C8
Global Section Descriptor List	EXE$GL_GSDMTX	800028CC
Shared Memory Global Section Descriptor Table	EXE$GL_SHMGSMTX	800028D0
Shared Memory Mailboxes	EXE$GL_SHMMBMTX	800028D4
(Not used)	EXE$GL_ENQMTX	800028D8
Known File Entry Table	EXE$GL_KFIMTX	800028DC
Line Printer Unit Control Block (2)	UCB$L_LP_MUTEX	(Note 2)
Resource Waits	*Symbolic*	*Numeric (hex)*
AST Wait (Wait for system or special kernel AST)	RSN$_ASTWAIT	00000001
Mailbox Full	RSN$_MAILBOX	00000002
Nonpaged Dynamic Memory	RSN$_NPDYNMEM	00000003
Page File Full	RSN$_PGFILE	00000004
Paged Dynamic Memory	RSN$_PGDYNMEM	00000005
Breakthrough (Wait for broadcast message)	RSN$_BRKTHRU	00000006
Image Activation Lock	RSN$_IACLOCK	00000007
Job Pooled Quota (Not currently used)	RSN$_JQUOTA	00000008
Lock Identification Database	RSN$_LOCKID	00000009
Swap File Space	RSN$_SWPFILE	0000000A
Modified Page List Empty	RSN$_MPLEMPTY	0000000B
Modified Page Writer Busy	RSN$_MPWBUSY	0000000C

(1) The symbolic contents of PCB$L_EFWM will probably remain the same from release to release. The numeric contents for mutex waits are almost certain to change with each major release of the operating system.

(2) The mutex associated with each line printer unit does not have a fixed address like the other mutexes. Its value depends on where the UCB for that unit is allocated.

ices operating on the system and group logical name tables are one example of this type of operation. When the owner of the requested mutex releases it, the requesting process becomes resident computable (COM), or computable outswapped (COMO) if it has been outswapped, and requests ownership of the mutex again. AST enqueuing cannot make a mutex-waiting process computable for long because the IPL in the stored PSL is IPL$_ASTDEL (IPL 2), blocking the AST delivery interrupt.

The mutex wait state is distinguished from the resource wait state by storing the system virtual address of the requested mutex in the PCB$L_EFWM field. (When treated as a signed integer, the contents of this field are positive and small when the process is waiting for a resource. When the process is waiting for a mutex, the contents are negative, as listed in Table 10-2.) For example, if a process wishes to allocate a block of paged dynamic memory, it must first acquire the paged pool mutex to allow it to search the linked list of available blocks (see Chapter 3). If another process is already looking at paged pool, this process is put into a mutex wait state (with 800028C8, the address of the paged pool mutex, stored in PCB$L_EFWM). Once the mutex is available and then owned by this process, paged pool is searched for a block of the requested size. If there is no block large enough to satisfy the allocation request, the process is placed into a resource wait state (with 00000005, the value of RSN$_PGDYNMEM, stored in PCB$L_EFWM). The process remains in this state until a block of paged pool is deallocated.

10.1.3.3 **Common Event Blocks.** Processes waiting for one or more common event flags are enqueued to wait queues in data structures called common event blocks (CEBs). These data structures are allocated from nonpaged dynamic memory when processes create common event flag clusters. The contents of a CEB include three longwords that exactly correspond to a wait state queue header (see Figure 10-4). The entire format of the common event block is shown in Chapter 12.

The number of CEF state queues depends upon the number of common event flag clusters that exist on a particular system at any given time. (Additional processes associating with existing common event flag clusters do not create further CEBs or CEF queues.) Outswapped processes waiting for common event flags are differentiated from similar memory resident processes by the PCB$V_1RES bit of the PCB$L_STS field only. In addition to satisfying the event flag wait mask, the system can also make a CEF process computable by AST enqueueing or process deletion.

10.2 **SYSTEM EVENTS**

System events are occurrences of operations that change the states of processes. A system event may make a process computable, memory resident, or outswapped. System events provide the transitions among the process states diagrammed in Figure 10-5.

A process initially enters a wait state from the current state (CUR). That is, a process either directly or indirectly executes a request for a system operation for which it must wait. Direct requests such as $QIOW, $HIBER, $SUSPND, and $WAITFR place the process in the voluntary wait states LEF, CEF, HIB, and SUSP. Subsequent outswapping (from the process viewpoint an unrequested system operation) may move a process to the LEFO, HIBO, or SUSPO states.

197

10.2.1 Process State Changes

Indirect wait requests occur as a result of paging or contention for system resources. A process does not request PFW, FPG, COLPG, or MWAIT transitions. Rather, the transitions to these wait states occur because direct service requests to the system cannot be completed or satisfied at the moment.

A process can become computable for a variety of reasons. The availability of a requested resource or the satisfaction of a wait condition (such as an event flag setting or a $WAKE system service call) will make the process computable. In all process states except SUSP and SUSPO, the enqueuing of an AST will make a process computable even if the wait condition is not satisfied. (Because processes are usually put into the MWAIT state at IPL 2, the AST is not able to be delivered until the miscellaneous wait is satisfied. Thus, the typical process in an MWAIT state will not become computable for long, due to the enqueuing of an AST. In particular, processes waiting for resources or mutexes typically cannot be deleted.) Process deletion, implemented with a special kernel mode AST, will make all processes that are being deleted computable (including processes in the SUSP or SUSPO states) because the target process is resumed before the AST is queued.

Exchanges of processes between the current executing state (CUR) and the computable, memory-resident state (COM) are performed by the scheduler routine (see Section 10.3). The movement of a process into and out of the balance set is the responsibility of the swapper process (see Chapter 17).

10.2.2 Wait States and AST Delivery

One of the responsibilities of the routines that place processes into wait states is to insure that these processes will correctly enter their appropriate wait states after successful delivery of an AST. There are three different techniques used, depending on the particular wait state being entered.

10.2.2.1 System Service Wait States.
In the case where a process is entering a wait state as a result of executing a system service (HIB, LEF, or CEF), the wait routine is entered with the PC and PSL of the the system service CHMK exception (see Chapter 9) on the top of the stack. The first implication of this arrangement is that the process will wait in the access mode in which the system service was issued. Because ASTs are enqueued and delivered based on access mode, a supervisor mode AST can be delivered to a process waiting on an event flag as a result of a $QIOW call issued from user or supervisor mode.

In addition, the wait code backs up the saved PC by four so that it points to the CHMx instruction in the system service vector (see the code examples in Section 9.1). If a process receives an AST while in such a wait state, the AST is delivered and executes. When the AST delivery routine releases its interrupt through an REI instruction, the system service executes again, typically placing the process right back into the wait state it was in before the AST was delivered.

10.2.2.2 **Memory Management Wait States.** The page fault handler (see Chapter 15) is solely responsible for placing processes into the three wait states associated with memory management. This routine places a process into a wait state with the PC and PSL associated with the page fault as the saved process context. Once again, because the PSL reflects the access mode in which the fault occurred, ASTs can be delivered for that and all inner access modes. (Note that this routine does not need to change the PC that it finds on the stack because page fault exceptions are faults and not traps. Faults, discussed in full in Chapter 4, cause the PC of the faulting instruction and not the PC of the next instruction to be pushed onto the exception stack.)

If an AST is delivered to and executes in such a process, the process will execute the faulting instruction again. If the reason for the fault has been removed (a free page became available or the page read completed) while the AST was being delivered or was executing, the process will simply continue with its execution. If, on the other hand, the situation that caused the process to wait still exists, the process will reincur the page fault and be placed back into one of the memory management wait states. (Note that a process that was initially in a PFW state would be placed into a COLPG state by such a sequence of events.)

10.2.2.3 **Special Cases.** The two remaining wait states (SUSP and MWAIT) are handled in a special way by the wait routine. A process suspension occurs as a result of executing a special kernel AST. ASTs cannot be delivered to suspended processes. That is, an AST queued to a suspended process has its AST control block inserted into the AST queue in the software PCB. However, the AST event is ignored by the scheduler. (In fact, while a process is suspended, the saved PC is an address in the special kernel AST that caused the process to enter the suspend state. The saved PSL indicates kernel mode and IPL 2.)

When a process is placed into a wait state waiting for a mutex (see Chapter 2), its saved PC is either SCH$LOCKR or SCH$LOCKW, depending on whether it is attempting to lock the mutex for read access or write access. The saved PSL indicates kernel mode and IPL 2, which implies that processes in an MWAIT state waiting for a mutex cannot receive ASTs.

A process can also be placed into an MWAIT state while waiting for an arbitrary system resource. In this case, the caller of SCH$RWAIT controls the PC and PSL that are saved when the process is placed into the MWAIT state. In particular, the current access mode and IPL in the saved PSL determine whether any ASTs can be delivered to a process that is waiting for a resource.

10.2.3 Event Reporting

Events are reported to the scheduler from many system routines through the RPTEVT macro, which generates the following code:

```
JSB     SCH$RSE
.BYTE   EVT$_event-name
```

The byte value stored depends upon the event being declared by the system routine. The address of the value will be pushed on to the stack by the BSBW instruction. Additional parameters (priority increment class and PCB address of the affected process) are passed in registers.

The routine SCH$RSE (in module RSE) performs the following operations:

1. The event number is loaded into a register and the return PC value (on the stack as a result of the BSBW instruction) is adjusted to point to the address after the stored byte event value.
2. The state and the event are checked for a significant transition. Each event (or state transition) has a bit mask defining which states this event can affect. The state of the process is obtained from the PCB$W_STATE field.

   - For example, a wake event is only significant for processes that are hibernating (HIB or HIBO states).
   - An outswap event is only significant for the four states (COM, HIB, LEF, and SUSP) where a wait queue change is required.
   - The enqueuing of an AST is significant to some process states. If the process is in a SUSP or SUSPO, COM or COMO, or CUR state, the enqueuing of an AST is ignored by SCH$RSE. If the event is not significant for the current process state, the event is ignored (and SCH$RSE simply issues an RSB).

3. For significant events, one of the following actions is taken:

   - An outswap event producing an LEF to LEFO, HIB to HIBO, or SUSP to SUSPO transition simply removes the PCB of the process from the resident wait queue and inserts it in the corresponding outswapped wait queue. The corresponding wait queue header count fields and the process state (PCB$W_STATE) are also adjusted.
   - An outswap event producing a COM to COMO transition removes the PCB from the COM priority queue corresponding to PCB$B_PRI and inserts it into the corresponding COMO priority queue. The value in PCB$W_STATE is changed to the value SCH$C_COMO. The SCH$GL_COMQS status bit vector is also modified if the COM queue is now empty. The appropriate SCH$GL_COMOQS bit is unconditionally set.
   - For transitions from the LEF (implied resident) or CEF resident state to the COM state, the saved PC in the hardware PCB stored in the process

header is incremented by four to point past the CHMx instruction. Saving the PC value allows the process to begin execution immediately following the system service call rather than going through a Wait for Event Flag system service for a flag that is already set. The residence check is necessary because the saved PC of nonresident processes is usually not available. (The saved PC is stored in the hardware PCB in the process header, which may be outswapped if the process is not resident.)

- For the remaining transitions (all of which make a process computable), the process is removed from the wait queue and the wait queue header count is decremented. The PCB is inserted into a COM or COMO state queue depending upon whether the process is memory resident or outswapped, and the state field in the PCB is altered. The particular priority queue of the COM or COMO state is selected for insertion after a priority adjustment is attempted (see the following section). The SCH$GL_COMQS or SCH$GL_COMOQS summary bit corresponding to the selected priority queue is unconditionally set.

4. Subsequent scheduling or swapping activity is necessary to execute or inswap the now computable process. The swapper is awakened (routine SCH$SWPWAKE is called) if the now computable process is presently outswapped (see Section 10.1.2.4, item 3).

   The scheduler is requested, through an IPL 3 software interrupt, if the now computable process is memory resident and has a priority greater than or equal to that of the currently executing process. This priority check avoids needless context switches with their associated overhead, only to have the previously executing process again execute.

10.2.4   System Events and Associated Priority Boosts

System routines that report events to the scheduler not only describe the event and the process that is responsible, but also specify one of five classes of priority increments or boosts that may be applied to the base priority of the process. Table 10-3 lists the events, the priority class, and the potential amount of priority increment applied to the process. The table does not show AST enqueuing because system routines enqueuing ASTs to a process can select any of the priority increment classes to be associated with the enqueuing of an AST.

The actual software priority of the process is determined by the following steps:

1. The priority increment for the event class (see Table 10-3) is added to the base priority of the process (PCB$B_PRIB).

Table 10-3: System Events and Associated Priority Boosts

Event	Priority Class (1)	Priority Boost
Page Fault Read Complete	0 (PRI$_NULL)	0
Quantum End	0	0
Other Events with No Boost	0	0
Direct I/O Completion	1 (PRI$_IOCOM)	2
Nonterminal Buffered I/O Completion	1	2
Update Section Write Completion	1	2
Set Priority	Priority	2
Resource Available	2 (PRI$_RESAVL)	3
Wake a Process	2	3
Resume a Process	2	3
Delete a Process	2	3
Timer Request Expiration	2 (PRI$_TIMER)	3
Terminal Output Completion	3 (PRI$_TOCOM)	4
Terminal Input Completion	4 (PRI$_TICOM)	6
Process Creation	4	6

(1) Routines that report system events pass an increment class to the scheduler. The scheduler uses this class as a byte index into a table of values (local label B_PINC in module RSE) to compute the actual boost.

2. If the process has a current priority higher than the result of step one, the current priority will be retained (such as occurs in Figure 10-2, event 13).
3. If the higher priority of steps one and two is above 15, then the base priority of the process is used. (Note that this test accomplishes two checks at the same time. First, all real-time processes fit this criterion, with the result that real-time processes do not have their priorities adjusted in response to system events. Second, priority boosts cannot move a normal process into the real-time priority range.)

A side effect of step three is that real-time processes always execute at their base priorities. Further, note that normal processes with base priorities from 10 to 15 will not always receive priority increments as events occur. As the base priority of a normal process is moved closer to 15, the process will spend a greater amount of time at its base priority. Priority 14 and 15 processes experience no priority boosts. Thus, this strategy benefits those processes that most need it, I/O-bound and interactive processes with base priorities of 4 through 9. Processes with elevated base priorities do not require this assistance as they are always at these levels.

10.3 RESCHEDULING INTERRUPT

The IPL 3 interrupt service routine, SCHED, schedules processes for execution. The actual work of the scheduler is performed at IPL$_SYNCH to block concurrent access and modification of the scheduler's database by other system components. The principal purpose of this interrupt service routine is to remove the currently executing process by storing the contents of the process private processor (hardware) registers and replacing the register contents with those of the highest priority computable resident process. This operation, known as context switching, is accompanied by modifications to the affected processes in terms of process state, current priority, and state queue.

10.3.1   Hardware Context

The definition of a process from the viewpoint of the hardware is contained in the hardware context. This collection of data is the set of hardware processor registers whose contents are unique to the process. These include the following categories of information:

- The general purpose registers, R0 through R11, the argument pointer (AP), the frame pointer (FP), and the program counter (PC).
- The per-process access mode stack pointers for kernel, executive, supervisor, and user stacks. One of these four registers contains the current stack pointer for the process, as indicated by the current mode field in the saved PSL.
- The processor status longword (PSL).
- The AST level processor register (ASTLVL).
- The process page table registers for the program and control regions (P0BR, P0LR, P1BR, and P1LR).

With the exceptions of the ASTLVL register value and the contents of the memory management registers for the program and control regions, the current values for the various registers forming the hardware context of the current process are maintained only in the processor registers. When a process is not executing, the complete hardware context is contained in a portion of the process header called the hardware process control block.

The hardware process control block (see Figure 10-6) is a part of the fixed portion of the process header for each process. It is resident in memory whenever the corresponding process is in the balance set. Access by the operating system occurs normally through offsets from the starting address of the particular process header. However, during context switching operations, the hardware must access this data structure directly without address translation. This access is accomplished by using the current value in the process control block base register (PR$_PCBB). This register contains the physical address of the hardware process control block for the currently executing process. The VMS operating system stores the physical address of the hardware process control block for each resident process (calculated when the process is swapped into memory) in the PCB$L_PHYPCB field of the corresponding software process control block (see Figure 10-1).

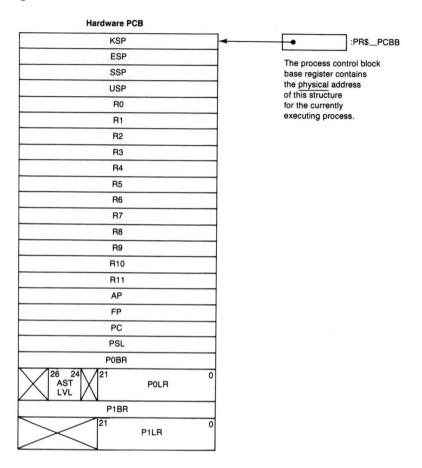

Figure 10-6
Hardware Process Control Block

10.3.2   Removal of Current Process from Execution

The entry point SCH$RESCHED in the module SCHED performs the operations of rescheduling, preserving the hardware context of the currently executing process, and removing it from execution. Rescheduling is accomplished by the following steps:

1. The hardware context of the current process is saved by the SVPCTX instruction. The destination of the data is the hardware process control block whose physical address is contained in the process control block base register, PR$_PCBB. Additional operations of the SVPCTX instruction are described in Section 10.3.5.1.
2. The address of the software process control block for the current process is obtained from the pointer SCH$GL_CURPCB in the module SDAT. (A

single longword pointer is required for the current state (CUR), rather than a quadword listhead, because there is only one current process and not a queue of several such processes.)

3. The current priority of the process is determined from the PCB$B_PRI field. The current priority is used to determine which of the resident computable state queues is to include this PCB. The process is inserted at the tail of the corresponding priority queue.
4. The state of the process is changed to computable (COM) by updating the PCB$W_STATE field.

At this point, there is no current process, and the search for the next process to execute begins.

10.3.3   Selection of Next Process for Execution

The entry point SCH$SCHED begins the portion of code that searches for the next process to be scheduled for execution. Under some circumstances (such as system initialization, placing the previous process into a wait state, or deletion of the previous process) there may not be a current process to be saved by SCH$RESCHED. In these cases, system routines transfer control directly to SCH$SCHED for process selection. (The difference between the two entry points is determined by whether the previous process is still computable. Typically, a process entering a wait state will cause entry at SCH$SCHED, while a higher priority process becoming computable will cause entry, through a software interrupt, at SCH$RESCHED.)

The SCH$RESCHED logic flows directly into SCH$SCHED. As with rescheduling, the search for and modification of the next process to be executed must be performed at IPL$_SYNCH to block other potential system operations on the scheduler database.

The following operations are involved in selecting and executing the next process:

1. The first software process control block (PCB) in the highest priority, nonempty, computable resident (COM) state queue is removed from the queue and pointed to by SCH$GL_CURPCB as the current process. Consistency checks are made to insure that the queue really had at least one PCB and that the data structure removed was actually a PCB. Failure of either of these tests results in a fatal bugcheck (BUG$_QUEUEMPTY).
2. The state of the process is made current by inserting the appropriate value (SCH$C_CUR) into the PCB$W_STATE field.
3. The current process priority is examined and potentially modified. If the process is a real-time process or if it is a normal process already at its base priority, then the process is scheduled at its current or base priority (they are the same). If the current process is a normal process above its base

priority, then a decrease of one software priority level is performed before scheduling. Thus, priority "demotions" always occur before execution, and a process executes at the priority of the queue to which it will be returned (and not the priority of the queue from which it was removed). See Figure 10-2, event 2 for an example

4. The physical address of the hardware process control block for the scheduled process is loaded into the PR$_PCBB register from the software process control block PCB$L_PHYPCB field, and a load process context, LDPCTX, instruction is executed (see Section 10.3.5.2).

5. Control is passed to the scheduled process by executing an REI instruction. This transfer of control is possible because the LDPCTX instruction left the PC and PSL of the scheduled process on the kernel stack. When control is passed to the process through the REI instruction, the following operations are performed:

   • The interrupt priority level is dropped from IPL$_SYNCH.
   • The access mode is typically changed from kernel to a less privileged one.
   • If ASTs are queued to the process control block, they are likely to be delivered at this time, depending on their access mode and the access mode at which the process is reentered (see Chapter 7).

10.3.4   Summary Longword and Computable State Queues

The search for the highest priority computable resident process and the removal of its PCB from the computable state (COM) queue is achieved in three instructions (see Figure 10-7). The efficiency of this operation is due to the instruction set and the design of the scheduler database for the computable (COM) and computable outswapped (COMO) states (see Figure 10-3).

① A find first set (FFS) instruction will locate the least significant set bit in the longword SCH$GL_COMQS. The located bit position indicates the highest priority nonempty computable resident state queue. The swapper's search for the first PCB in the highest priority nonempty computable outswapped (COMO) queue uses the same operations (see Chapter 17).

One reason for storing the software priority in inverted or 31-complement form is the following. By making bit 0 correspond to software priority 31, and so on, the highest priority queues will be scanned first. Conversion in the various user interfaces occurs because systems and users generally associate higher priority numbers with higher priority jobs, tasks, or processes.

② The listhead of the selected computable resident queue is found by using

the nonempty queue bit position as an index into the contiguous listheads.

③ The first PCB in the selected queue is removed by indirect reference
through the forward link of the listhead.

④ If the removed PCB was the only one in the queue, the corresponding
SCH$GL_COMQS bit must now be cleared because the queue is now
empty.

10.3.5   Hardware Assistance in Context Switching

The VAX architecture was designed to assist the software in performing critical, commonly performed operations. One example is the delivery of asynchronous system traps through the REI instruction (see Chapter 7). The
mechanism of replacing the hardware context of the current process with the
context of the highest priority resident process is another example of hardware assistance to the operating system. The switching of hardware context
is performed by two special purpose instructions, SVPCTX and LDPCTX.

10.3.5.1   SVPCTX Instruction.
The save process context instruction, SVPCTX, per-
forms several operations and assumes a special set of initial and final conditions. The following initial conditions are assumed:

- The current access mode must be kernel.
- The program counter (PC) and processor status longword (PSL) are on the
current stack (either kernel or interrupt stack). If the SVPCTX instruction
that executes is the one in the rescheduling interrupt service routine, both
the PC and PSL are on the kernel stack as a result of the IPL 3 software
interrupt.
- The process control block base register (PR$_PCBB) contains the physical
address of the hardware PCB for the current process.
- The current values of ASTLVL, P0BR, P0LR, P1BR, and P1LR are already
stored in the hardware PCB.

When the SVPCTX instruction is executed, the following operations are
performed by the VAX hardware:

1. The per-process stack pointers for the four access mode stacks are moved
to the hardware PCB.
2. The general purpose registers, R0 through R11, the argument pointer (AP),
and the frame pointer (FP) to the hardware PCB are moved to the hardware
PCB.
3. The program counter (PC) and the process status longword (PSL) are
popped from the current stack and moved to the hardware PCB.

```
                                .SBTTL  SCH$RESCHED RESCHEDULING INTERRUPT HANDLER
0000                    43
0000                    44  ;++
0000                    45  ; SCH$RESCHED - RESCHEDULING INTERRUPT HANDLER
0000                    46  ;
0000                    47  ; THIS ROUTINE IS ENTERED VIA THE IPL 3 RESCHEDULING INTERRUPT.
0000                    48  ; THE VECTOR FOR THIS INTERRUPT IS CODED TO CAUSE EXECUTION
0000                    49  ; ON THE KERNEL STACK.
0000                    50  ;
0000                    51  ; ENVIRONMENT:
0000                    52  ;     IPL=3 MODE=KERNEL IS=0
0000                    53  ; INPUT:
0000                    54  ;     00(SP)=PC AT RESCHEDULE INTERRUPT
0000                    55  ;     04(SP)=PSL AT INTERRUPT.
0000                    56  ;--
0000                    57          .ALIGN  LONG
0000                    58  MPH$RESCHED::                    ;MULTI-PROCESSING CODE HOOKS IN HERE
0000                    59  SCH$RESCHED::                    ;RESCHEDULE INTERRUPT HANDLER
0000                    60          SETIPL  #IPL$_SYNCH       ;SYNCHRONIZE SCHEDULER WITH EVENT REPORTING
0003            07      61          SVPCTX                    ;SAVE CONTEXT OF PROCESS
0004 51 0000'CF D0      62          MOVL    W^SCH$GL_CURPCB,R1     ;GET ADDRESS OF CURRENT PCB
0009 52    0B A1 9A     63          MOVZBL  PCB$B_PRI(R1),R2      ;CURRENT PRIORITY
000D 00 0000'CF 52 E2   64          BBSS    R2,W^SCH$GL_COMQS,10$ ;MARK QUEUE NON-EMPTY
0013    2C A1 0C B0     65  10$:    MOVW    #SCH$C_COM,PCB$W_STATE(R1) ;SET STATE TO RES COMPUTE
0017 53 0000'CF42 7E    66          MOVAQ   W^SCH$AQ_COMT[R2],R3  ;COMPUTE ADDRESS OF QUEUE
001D    93    61 DE     67          INSQUE  (R1),@(R3)+          ;INSERT AT TAIL OF QUEUE
0020                    68  ;+
0020                    69  ; SCH$SCHED - SCHEDULE NEW PROCESS FOR EXECUTION
0020                    70  ;
0020                    71  ; THIS ROUTINE SELECTS THE HIGHEST PRIORITY EXECUTABLE PROCESS
0020                    72  ; AND PLACES IT IN EXECUTION.
0020                    73  ;
0020                    74  ;-
0020                    75  MPH$SCHED::                      ;MULTI-PROCESSING CODE HOOKS IN HERE
0020                    76  SCH$SCHED::                      ;SCHEDULE FOR EXECUTION
0020                    77          SETIPL  #IPL$_SYNCH      ;SYNCHRONIZE SCHEDULER WITH EVENT REPORTING
```

```
52  0000'CF 20  00  EA  0023         FFS     #0,#32,W^SCH$GL_COMQS,R2    ;FIND FIRST FULL STATE
53              3D  13  002A         BEQL    SCH$IDLE                    ;NO EXECUTABLE PROCESS??
    0000'CF42   7E  0F  002C         MOVAQ   W^SCH$AQ_COMH[R2],R3        ;COMPUTE QUEUE HEAD ADDRESS
54          53      3C  1D  0032     REMQUE  @(R3)+,R4                   ;GET HEAD OF QUEUE
                    06  12  0037     BVS     QEMPTY                      ;BR IF QUEUE WAS EMPTY (BUG CHECK)
    00  0000'CF 52  E5  0039         BNEQ    20$                         ;QUEUE NOT EMPTY
                                     BBCC    R2,W^SCH$GL_COMQS,20$       ;SET QUEUE EMPTY
                                20$:
        0A A4   0C  91  003F         CMPB    #DYN$C_PCB,PCB$B_TYPE(R4)   ;MUST BE A PROCESS CONTROL BLOCK
        2C A4   2E  12  0043         BNEQ    QEMPTY                      ;OTHERWISE FATAL ERROR
        0000'GF 0E  B0  0045         MOVW    #SCH$C_CUR,PCB$W_STATE(R4)  ;SET STATE TO CURRENT
        0B A4   54  D0  0049         MOVL    R4,W^SCH$GL_CURPCB          ;NOTE CURRENT PCB LOC
                2F A4   91  004E     CMPB    PCB$B_PRIB(R4),PCB$B_PRI(R4);CHECK FOR BASE
                            0053                                         ;PRIORITY=CURRENT
        03 0B A4    08  13  0053     BEQL    30$                         ;YES, DONT FLOAT PRIORITY
            0B A4   04  E1  0055     BBC     #4,PCB$B_PRI(R4),30$        ;DONT FLOAT REAL TIME PRIORITY
    0000'CF 0B A4   90  96  005A     INCB    PCB$B_PRI(R4)               ;MOVE TOWARD BASE PRIO
        10  18 A4   DA  90  005D     MOVB    PCB$B_PRI(R4),W^SCH$GB_PRI  ;SET GLOBAL PRIORITY
                            0063     MTPR    PCB$L_PHYPCB(R4),#PR$_PCBB  ;SET PCB BASE PHYS ADDR
                        06  0067 30$: LDPCTX                             ;RESTORE CONTEXT
                        02  0068     REI                                 ;NORMAL RETURN
                            0069
                            0069 SCH$IDLE:
    0000'CF 20  90  006C             SETIPL  #IPL$_SCHED                 ;NO ACTIVE, EXECUTABLE PROCESS
                                                                         ;DROP IPL TO SCHEDULING LEVEL
            AD  11  0071             MOVB    #32,W^SCH$GB_PRI            ;SET PRIORITY TO -1(32) TO SIGNAL IDLE
                    0073             BRB     SCH$SCHED                   ;AND TRY AGAIN
                    0073
                    0077 QEMPTY:     BUG_CHECK QUEUEMPTY,FATAL           ;SCHEDULING QUEUE EMPTY
                    0077
                                     .END
```

Figure 10-7
Scheduler Routine That Selects Next Execution Candidate

Finally, if the current stack is the kernel stack, the SVPCTX instruction saves the current stack pointer (SP) in the kernel stack field of the hardware process control block and switches to the interrupt stack (by setting the PSL$V_IS bit and copying the PR$_ISP register contents into the SP register). Switching to the system-wide interrupt stack is essential because there is no current process once the instruction completes.

The ASTLVL, P0BR, P0LR, P1BR, and P1LR fields of the hardware process control block are not changed. It is the responsibility of the various system components that alter these fields to always update both the hardware process control block fields and the per-process processor registers. ASTLVL is unusual in that it can be altered even when the process is not current. In that case, only the hardware PCB field is altered. The processor register is not altered because the process does not own that register when it is not the current process. These fields do not change frequently compared to the frequency of context switching. The overhead of storing these fields in the hardware process control block is incurred only when the field values change.

The SVPCTX instruction occurs in several locations in the executive:

- The rescheduling interrupt service routine contains an instance of this instruction when the current process remains computable after it is removed from execution.
- Module SYSWAIT contains another example of the instruction when the current process is being placed into a scheduling wait state.
- The pager (module PAGEFAULT) issues a SVPCTX instruction directly when it places a process into one of the memory management wait states (PFW, FPG, COLPG).
- One of the last steps of process deletion involves removing the process being deleted from execution with a SVPCTX instruction.

10.3.5.2 **LDPCTX Instruction.** The load process context instruction, LDPCTX, performs the operations required in establishing the hardware context of the process. As with the SVPCTX instruction, assumptions are made about the initial and final conditions of the instruction. The following initial conditions are assumed:

- The processor must be in kernel mode, using either the kernel or the interrupt stack. (The processor is always on the interrupt stack for the one occurrence of the LDPCTX instruction in the VMS executive.)
- The process control block base register (PR$_PCBB) must contain the physical address of the hardware process control block to be used (from the PCB$L_PHYPCB field of the software process control block).

When the LDPCTX instruction is executed, the following operations are performed by the VAX hardware:

1. The per-process half of the translation buffer is invalidated. All of the previous translation buffer entries belonged to the previous process. They are invalidated to prevent mistranslation of virtual addresses and to protect the data of the previous process.
2. The per-process access mode stack pointers (KSP, ESP, SSP, and USP) are loaded from the hardware process control block.
3. The general purpose registers, R0 through R11, the argument pointer (AP), and the frame pointer (FP) are loaded into the corresponding processor registers.
4. The memory management mapping registers (P0BR, P0LR, P1BR, and P1LR) are checked for legal values and loaded from the hardware process control block. Note that although the SVPCTX instruction does not save these registers, the LDPCTX must load them. Until they are loaded, the values in the registers belong to the previous process.
5. The ASTLVL register is loaded. This register was also not saved by the SVPCTX instruction.
6. If the instruction began execution using the interrupt stack, then the following operations are performed:

    - The contents of the current stack pointer register (SP) are saved in the interrupt stack pointer register (ISP).
    - The PSL$V_IS bit is cleared to indicate the switch to the kernel stack.
    - The current stack pointer is updated with the contents of the kernel stack pointer register (KSP).

7. Finally, the saved program counter (PC) and processor status longword (PSL) are pushed onto the kernel stack from the hardware process control block. These values are not stored into the appropriate registers. This particular operation occurs because the next instruction (in the scheduler routine) is expected to be an REI instruction. The REI pops the two longwords, verifies the PSL format, and inserts the two longwords into the appropriate registers.

The only occurrence of a LDPCTX instruction in the entire VMS system is the one shown in Figure 10-7, the second half of the rescheduling interrupt service routine.

11 Timer Support

Love, all alike, no season knows, nor clime,
Nor hours, days, months, which are the rags of time.
—John Donne, *The Sun Rising*

Support for time-related activities that require either the time of day and date or the measurement of an interval of time is implemented both in the VAX-11 hardware and in the VAX/VMS operating system.

11.1 TIMEKEEPING IN THE VAX/VMS OPERATING SYSTEM

Two hardware clocks are updated at regular intervals, the interval clock and the time-of-day clock. These clocks are used by the VMS system to manage two different times, the system time and the time since the system was last bootstrapped. Additionally, the software timer interrupt service routine provides timer services, such as scheduled wakeups, by maintaining a time-ordered queue of requests and delivering them as the expiration times occur.

11.1.1 Hardware Clocks

The hardware clocks are a set of processor registers that are used or updated regularly by timing circuitry. Initialization, calibration, and interpretation of the registers are performed by VMS routines during system initialization and normal operations.

The processor registers that implement the hardware clocks are summarized in Table 11-1, along with the memory locations that implement the various software time values.

11.1.1.1 Interval Clock.
The interval clock is implemented as a set of three 32-bit processor registers. The clock "ticks" at one microsecond intervals with an accuracy of at least 0.01 percent (an error of less than nine seconds per day). The frequency at which the interval clock causes an interrupt is determined by the value in one of the processor registers, PR$_NICR.

The three interval clock registers (see Table 11-1) are used as follows.

1. The interval clock control/status register (PR$_ICCS) controls the interrupt status of the interval clock. This register is set by the CPU hardware and then reset by the hardware clock interrupt service routine (see Section 11.2) each time the interval clock interrupts.

Table 11-1: VAX/VMS Hardware Clocks and Software Timers

Name	Use	Size (bits)	Units	Frequency	Updated by
PR$_ICR	Interval clock	32	1 microsecond	1 microsecond	CPU hardware
PR$_NICR	Next interval	32	1 microsecond	(1)	System initialization
PR$_ICCS	Interval clock control/status	32	control/status bits	10 milliseconds	Hardware clock interrupt service routine
PR$_TODR	Time-of-day clock	32	10 milliseconds	10 milliseconds	CPU hardware, $SETIME system service
EXE$GQ_SYSTIME	System time	64	100 nanoseconds	10 milliseconds	Hardware clock interrupt service routine, $SETIME system service
EXE$GL_ABSTIM	System absolute time	32	1 second	1 second	System initialization, EXE$TIMEOUT repeating system subroutine
EXE$GL_TODR	Time-of-year base value	32	10 milliseconds	(2)	$SETIME system service
EXE$GQ_TODCBASE	Time-of-year base value (in system time format)	64	100 nanoseconds	(2)	$SETIME system service

(1) PR$_NICR is written only at system initialization time and after powerfail recovery.
(2) EXE$GL_TODR and EXE$GQ_TODCBASE are modified only when one of the following is true:
- The time-of-day value is changed by a $SETIME system service request (either explicitly or as an integral part of the system bootstrap operation).
- The PR$_TODR has been lost due to a prolonged power failure.

213

2. The next interval count register (PR$_NICR) defines how often the interval clock will cause a hardware interrupt. During system initialization, the routine INIT loads this processor register with a value of -10000. This value defines the hardware clock interrupt interval to be 10 milliseconds (10000 microseconds).

3. The interval count register (PR$_ICR) is incremented every microsecond from the PR$_NICR value toward zero. When PR$_ICR becomes zero, the register overflows, causing the following actions:

   a. The PR$_NICR value is copied into PR$_ICR to define the next interval.

   b. The PR$_ICCS register is set to indicate the overflow condition. This operation causes a hardware interrupt (IPL 24) to occur, serviced by the hardware clock interrupt service routine.

The PR$_ICCS is reset by the hardware clock interrupt service routine to indicate servicing of the interrupt and reenabling of the hardware clock.

11.1.1.2 **Time-of-Day Clock.** The time-of-day clock is a hardware component consisting of one 32-bit processor register and a battery backup supply for at least 100 hours of operation (the battery backup is not a standard feature on the VAX-11/730). The time-of-day clock has an accuracy of at least 0.0025 percent (an error of about 65 seconds per month) and a resolution of 10 milliseconds. The base time for the time-of-day clock is 00:00:00.00 hours on January first of the current year. The time-of-day clock overflows after 497 days.

Values in PR$_TODR are biased by 10000000 [hex]. Values smaller than this indicate loss of power or time-of-day overflow, conditions causing the system to prompt the operator to reset the time (through the $SETIME system service).

The validity of the time-of-day clock is determined at system initialization time. If the contents of the time-of-day clock are valid, the initialization process, SYSINIT, will not prompt the operator for the time. If the contents of the time-of-day clock are not valid (the value is less than 10000000 [hex]), the value of the SYSBOOT parameter TIMEPROMPTWAIT determines the processor action on recovery from a power failure (see Section 27.2.2).

Because the time-of-day clock has a better accuracy than the interval clock, the time-of-day clock is used for recalibrating the system time (EXE$GQ_SYSTIME) at system initialization and at other times when the $SETIME system service is called (see Section 11.1.3). In addition, because the time-of-day clock has battery backup (except on the VAX-11/730), it is used to reset the system time after a power failure or after the machine has been turned off.

11.1.2   Software Time

Software time is managed by VMS routines as a result of changes in the hardware clocks. The system time is defined by a quadword value measuring the number of 100-nanosecond intervals since 00:00 hours, November 17, 1858 (the time base for the Smithsonian Institution astronomical calendar). EXE$GQ_SYSTIME (see Table 11-1) is updated every 10 milliseconds by the hardware clock interrupt service routine (see Section 11.2). This quadword is the reference for nearly all time-related software activities in the system. For example, the $GETTIM system service simply writes this quadword value into a user-defined buffer.

EXE$GL_ABSTIM measures the number of one-second intervals that have elapsed since the system was last bootstrapped. This absolute time is used to periodically check for I/O device and lock request timeouts. The absolute time is also the value for "system uptime" interpreted and displayed by the DCL command SHOW SYSTEM.

EXE$GL_TODR contains the base 32-bit time value. EXE$GQ_TODCBASE contains the base quadword system time value. These base time values represent the more recent of the following times:

- 00:00 hours on January 1 of the current year
- The last time that the time-of-day was redefined by $SETIME

PR$_TODR (and EXE$GL_TODR) are biased by a factor of 10000000 (hex). If a power failure occurs, the value in PR$_TODR will be zeroed and the clock will start to count from there. If the value in PR$_TODR is less than 1000000 (hex), it can safely be assumed that a power failure has occurred.

Both the values in EXE$GQ_TODCBASE and EXE$GL_TODR are maintained in the system image file as a semipermanent record of the base system time on which the contents of the time-of-year clock (PR$_TODR) are based. Both represent the same time (the last time they were adjusted), in different formats. EXE$GQ_TODCBASE represents the time of last adjustment in standard 64-bit time; EXE$GL_TODR represents the time of last adjustment in the same 32-bit format as the time-of-year clock (PR$_TODR). PR$_TODR cannot be set to zero (because of the 10000000 hex bias), rather it is initialized to the contents of EXE$GL_TODR.

When a new system time is specified, EXE$GQ_TODCBASE, EXE$GL_TODR, and PR$_TODR are modified, and the new base values are written to the system image file. When the system time (EXE$GQ_SYSTIME) is recalibrated, the values are modified only when more than a year has passed since the last recalibration.

11.1.3   Set Time System Service

The $SETIME system service allows a system manager or operator to change the system time while the operating system is running. This may be necessary because of a power failure longer than the battery backup time of the time-of-day clock or because of changes between standard and daylight saving time, for example. The new system time (absolute time, not relative time) is passed as the optional single argument of the system service. The $SETIME system service is also invoked during system initialization to reset the system time (and possibly the time-of-day clock).

If the requesting process does not have the process privileges OPER and LOG_IO, the routine returns with an SS$_NOPRIV error status code. If the input quadword cannot be read, the routine returns with an SS$_ACCVIO error status code.

11.1.3.1 $SETIME System Time Recalibration Requests. If no argument was passed to the system service or the time argument is a zero value, then the request is considered a request to recalibrate the system time (EXE$GQ_SYSTIME). The following actions take place.

1. The new system time, EXE$GQ_SYSTIME, is computed by the following equation:

$$\text{EXE\$GQ\_SYSTIME} = \text{EXE\$GQ\_TODCBASE} + ((\text{PR\$\_TODR} - \text{EXE\$GL\_TODR}) \times 100000)$$

EXE$GQ_SYSTIME and EXE$GQ_TODCBASE are quadword system times in units of 100 nanoseconds. PR$_TODR and EXE$GL_TODR are longword time-of-day times in units of 10 milliseconds. The multiplier of 100000 is the number of 100-nanosecond intervals in 10 milliseconds.

2. The values in PR$_TODR, EXE$GL_TODR, and EXE$GQ_TODCBASE are corrected if more than one year has passed since the system time was recalibrated (in order to prevent PR$_TODR from overflowing its 497-day limit).

3. Each element in the timer queue (see Section 11.3.2) that specified a delta time has its expiration time adjusted by the difference between the previous system time and the new system time. This modification prevents the actual delta time value from being changed by a modification to system time. TQEs containing absolute times are not adjusted so that the TQE will come due at the time that was specified by the user.

4. The entire collection of system parameters, including EXE$GQ_TODCBASE and EXE$GL_TODR, is written back to the system image file.

11.1.3.2 $SETIME Time-of-Day Readjustment Requests. If a nonzero time value is supplied as an argument to $SETIME, then the following operations occur.

1. The input argument, specified in system time units of 100 nanoseconds, is converted into time-of-day units (the number of 10-millisecond intervals after 00:00 hours on January 1 of the base year).

2. The converted specified time is written into PR$_TODR and EXE$GL_TODR.
3. The unconverted specified time is written into EXE$GQ_TODCBASE and EXE$GQ_SYSTIME.
4. Finally, the timer queue is updated and the new values for the time-of-day clock base are written to the system image file (along with the system parameters). (See steps 3 and 4 described above in Section 11.1.3.1).

11.2   HARDWARE CLOCK INTERRUPT SERVICE ROUTINE

The hardware clock interrupt service routine, EXE$HWCLKINT in module TIMESCHDL, services the IPL 24 hardware interrupt signaled when the interval clock, PR$_ICR, reaches zero. The interval clock is set (through PR$_NICR) to interrupt every 10 milliseconds.

The hardware clock interrupt service routine has two major functions.

• Updating the system time (and possibly process accounting)
• Checking the timer queue for timer events that have timed out

11.2.1   System Time Updating

The updating of the system time and the potential updating of process accounting fields requires several distinct actions.

1. The PR$_ICCS register is reset to indicate the servicing of the interrupt and the reenabling of the hardware clock.
2. The system time, EXE$GQ_SYSTIME, is updated by adding the equivalent of 10 milliseconds to the quadword value.
3. If the hardware clock interrupts while a process is executing (the former current stack was not the interrupt stack), then the accumulated CPU utilization and quantum value are incremented in the process header. The quantum value is used to determine quantum end (see Section 11.3.1 and Chapter 10). If the quantum value reaches zero, an IPL 7 software interrupt, serviced by the software timer routine, is requested. The check for whether the interrupt occurred while already on the interrupt stack prevents a process from being charged for CPU time that the system was using to service interrupts.

11.2.2   Timer Queue Testing

The timer queue is discussed with the software timer in the next section. The hardware clock interrupt service routine has the responsibility to determine if the software timer must be requested to service the timer queue. If the first timer queue element has an expiration time less than or equal to the newly updated system time, then the timer event is due. The software timer routine is requested through the IPL 7 interrupt.

11.3 SOFTWARE TIMER INTERRUPT SERVICE ROUTINE

The software timer interrupt service routine, EXE$SWTIMINT in module TIMESCHDL, is invoked through the IPL 7 software interrupt. The software timer is requested because either the current process has reached quantum end or the first timer queue element must be serviced.

11.3.1 Quantum Expiration

The expiration of the quantum interval for the current process is determined by testing the PHD$W_QUANT field. This field is incremented by the hardware clock service routine. A zero quantum value indicates quantum expiration. The processing of the quantum end event is performed by the scheduler in routine SCH$QEND, which is described in Chapter 10.

11.3.2 Timer Queue and Timer Queue Elements

If the system time, EXE$GQ_SYSTIME, is greater than or equal to the expiration time of the first element in the timer queue, then the timer event is due. The comparison with the system time must be performed at IPL 24 to block the hardware clock interrupt.

If a timer request is due, then the TQE is removed from the timer queue, the IPL dropped back to IPL$_TIMER (IPL 7), and one of three sequences of code is performed (depending upon the type of request).

Timer requests are maintained in a doubly linked list that is ordered by the expiration time of the requests. EXE$GL_TQFL and EXE$GL_TQBL are a pair of longwords (defined in the module SYSCOMMON) that form the list-head of the timer queue. Elements in the timer queue are data structures that are generally allocated from nonpaged dynamic memory and initialized as a result of $SETIMR system service calls (see Section 11.4.1). The allocation of timer queue elements (TQEs) is governed by the pooled job quota JIB$W_TQCNT.

The format of the timer queue element is shown in Figure 11-1. The link fields (TQE$L_TQFL and TQE$L_TQBL), the TQE$W_SIZE field, and the TQE$B_TYPE field are characteristic of system data structures allocated from dynamic memory. The TQE$B_RQTYPE field defines the type of timer request (process timer request, periodic system routine request, or process wake request) and whether the request is a one-time or repeating request (see the list of TQE request types in Figure 11-1). Bit <6> of TQE$B_RMOD is set if an AST is to be delivered when the timer event occurs. This bit is

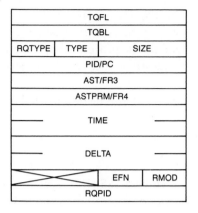

TQFL		
TQBL		
RQTYPE	TYPE	SIZE
PID/PC		
AST/FR3		
ASTPRM/FR4		
— TIME —		
— DELTA —		
	EFN	RMOD
RQPID		

RQTYPE Bits:

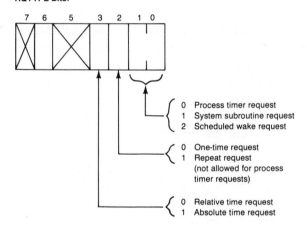

Figure 11-1
Layout of a Timer Queue Element

equivalent to the ACB$V_QUOTA bit of the AST control block described in Chapter 7.

The interpretation of the next three longword fields depends upon whether the request is from a system subroutine or a user process. For system subroutine requests, the fields contain the PC, R3, and R4 register values to be loaded before passing control to the subroutine. For process timer requests, the fields define the process ID of the process to report the event, the address of an AST routine to execute (if requested), and an optional AST parameter.

TQE$Q_TIME is the quadword absolute system time at which a particular timer event is to occur. TQE$Q_DELTA is the quadword delta time for repeating requests. The access mode of the requesting process is stored in TQE$B_RMOD. The event flag to set when the timer event occurs is defined by TQE$B_EFN. The TQE$L_RQPID contains the process ID of the process that made the initial timer request. (The requesting process is not necessarily the same as the target process.)

If an AST is requested, the timer queue element will be reformatted into an AST control block (ACB) when the event occurs.

11.3.3   Timer Request Servicing

If the TQE is a process timer request (created by a $SETIMR system service call and indicated by a TQE$B_RQTYPE value of zero), then the following operations are performed:

1. The event flag associated with this timer event is set by using the TQE$L_PID and TQE$B_EFN fields and invoking the SCH$POSTEF routine. A software priority increment of three may be applied when the process next executes (see Chapter 10).
2. If the target process is no longer in the system, the TQE is simply deallocated without further action.
3. Otherwise, the JIB$W_TQCNT quota is incremented to indicate the delivery of the timer event and the impending deallocation of the TQE.
4. If an AST was requested (indicated by bit <6> of TQE$B_RQTYPE), then the TQE$B_RMOD field is moved to TQE$B_RQTYPE to reformat the TQE into an AST control block (ACB). The ACB is then queued to the target process, in the access mode of the original timer request, by calling the routine SCH$QAST (see Chapter 7).

When the processing of this timer queue element has been completed, the software timer routine checks to see if another TQE element can be removed from the queue.

Note that process timer requests are strictly one-time requests. Any repetition of timer requests must be implemented within the requesting process.

11.3.4   Scheduled Wakeup

The second type of timer queue element is associated with a request for a scheduled $WAKE to a hibernating process. This type of request may be either one-time or repeating and may be requested by a process other than the target process.

The following operations are performed for scheduled wake TQEs.

1. The target process (indicated by TQE$L_PID) is awakened by executing the routine SCH$WAKE. If the target process is no longer in the system, the PCB$W_ASTCNT quota of the requesting process (TQE$L_RQPID) is

incremented and the control block is deallocated to nonpaged dynamic memory.

2. If the request is a one-time request (indicated by a cleared TQE$V_ REPEAT bit in the TQE$B_RQTYPE field), then the deallocation operation is the same as that described in item 1.

3. If the request is a repeating type, then the repeat interval (TQE$Q_ DELTA) is added to the request time (TQE$Q_TIME), and the timer queue element is reinserted in the timer queue.

The software timer routine then checks to see if the next timer request can also be performed at this time.

11.3.5   Periodic System Procedures

The third type of timer queue element defines a system subroutine request. A request of this type is not the result of any process request, but is a system-requested time-dependent event. The software timer interrupt service routine handles this type of TQE by the following action:

- Loading R3 and R4 from the TQE$L_FR3 and TQE$L_FR4 fields (normally defined as the TQE$L_AST and TQE$L_ASTPRM fields)
- Executing a JSB instruction using the TQE$L_FPC field (normally defined as the TQE$L_PID field)

On return from the system subroutine, the TQE$V_REPEAT bit is tested. If the bit is set, then the TQE is reinserted in the timer queue using the TQE$Q_DELTA time field. If the request was a nonrepeating one, then the timer routine immediately checks the timer queue for further TQEs to service. The TQE is not deallocated because these requests do not use dynamic memory. This type of TQE is defined in static nonpaged portions of system space, such as the module SYSCOMMON in the case of the EXE$TIMEOUT subroutine.

One example of this type of request, a repeating system subroutine request, is the once-per-second execution of the subroutine EXE$TIMEOUT.

1. The routine SCH$SWPWAKE is called to possibly awaken the swapper process (see Chapter 17).

2. The EXE$TIMEOUT subroutine updates the EXE$GL_ABSTIM field to indicate the passing of one second of system uptime.

3. The routine ERL$WAKE is called to possibly awaken the ERRFMT process (see Chapter 8).

4. This subroutine scans the I/O database for devices that have exceeded their timeout intervals. Drivers for such devices are called at their timeout entry points at device IPL. A path through this subroutine checks for terminal timed reads that have expired.

5. The first entry on the lock manager time out queue is checked to see if it has expired. If it has, a deadlock search is initiated.

6. The PCB pointer list is searched for normal-priority (priority less than 16) processes in the COM or COMO state, whose priority is less than that of the current process (or the highest priority computable process). The current priority of these lower priority processes is boosted so that they become the highest priority COM or CUR process. This feature was implemented to prevent a high-priority, compute-intensive job from causing other processes to be unable to release system (or other) resources. The number of processes that can receive this boost is determined by the special SYSBOOT parameter PIXSCAN. The PCB pointer list is searched in a circular fashion, in order that all processes will eventually receive the priority boost.

The TQE for this subroutine is permanently defined in the module SYS-COMMON, and the timer queue is initialized at bootstrap time with this data structure as the first element in the queue.

The terminal driver also uses a repeating system timer routine to implement its modem polling. The controller initialization routine in the terminal driver loads the expiration time field in a TQE in the terminal driver with the current system time, sets the repeat bit, and loads the repeat interval with the SYSBOOT parameter TTY_SCANDELTA. When the timer routine expires, it polls each modem looking for state changes.

11.4   TIMER SYSTEM SERVICES

Two system services are used to insert entries in the timer queue, Schedule Wakeup request ($SCHDWK) and Set Timer request ($SETIMR). Both of these services are contained in the module SYSSCHEVT. Two complementary services delete entries from the timer queue, $CANWAK and $CANTIM. These system service routines are in the module SYSCANEVT.

11.4.1 $SETIMR Requests

The $SETIMR system service calls produce timer queue entries of the single process request type, TQE$C_TMSNGL. The following steps are performed:

1. The event flag specified as an argument to the system service is cleared in preparation for subsequent setting at expiration time.
2. The request is checked to make sure that the following are true:

   • The delta time location is accessible by the requesting process.
   • The PCB$W_ASTCNT of the requesting process is not exceeded (if an AST is to be associated with this timer request).
   • The JIB$W_TQCNT of the requesting job is not exceeded

3. A timer queue element is allocated from nonpaged dynamic memory and the TQE is initialized from the system service arguments (delta time, request type, and process ID).
4. If the expiration time was expressed as an interval (a negative argument), then the absolute expiration time of the request is calculated by adding the delta time of the request to the current system time, EXE$GQ_SYSTIME. The absolute expiration time is stored in the TQE$Q_TIME field.
5. The JIB$W_TQCNT field of the pooled job quotas is decremented to indicate the allocation of the TQE.
6. The access mode of the system service caller is stored in the TQE$B_RMOD field. If an AST routine was specified as an argument to the $SETIMR call, then the process PCB$W_ASTCNT is decremented to indicate the future AST delivery and bit <6> of TQE$B_RMOD is set to indicate the AST accounting.
7. The AST parameter (request identification) and event flag number arguments are copied to the TQE.
8. The TQE is then inserted into the timer queue and the routine returns.

The $CANTIM system service removes one or more timer queue elements before expiration. Two arguments, the request identification parameter and the access mode, control the actions taken by this routine.

1. The access mode requested is maximized with that of the caller. (That is, no requests can be deleted for access modes more privileged than the caller.)
2. Each TQE in the timer queue that meets all of the following criteria is removed and deallocated:

   - The process ID of the $CANTIM system service caller is the same as the process ID stored in the TQE.
   - The access mode of the caller is at least as privileged as the access mode stored in the TQE.
   - The request identification parameter argument is the same as that stored in the TQE. If the argument value is zero, then all TQEs meeting the first two criteria are removed.

11.4.2 Scheduled Wakeup Operations

The logic for managing scheduled wakeup requests is similar to that for $SETIMR requests. Two differences are the ability to specify repeating scheduled wakeup requests and the ability to schedule wakeup requests for another process. The following steps create a scheduled wakeup request.

1. The target process ID is verified from a system service argument. If the target process is not in the system, the scheduled wakeup request is ignored.

2. If the target process exists, and if the current process is suitably privileged (GROUP or WORLD) with respect to it, then the repeat time is tested to determine whether the request is a one-time or repeating scheduled wakeup, TQE$C_WKSNGL or TQE$C_WKREPT of the TQE$B_RQTYPE field.

3. The requested repeat time is formatted for insertion in the TQE. If the repeat time is less than 10 milliseconds, it is increased to that value (the resolution of the hardware clock interrupt).

4. A TQE is allocated from nonpaged dynamic memory.

5. The repeat time, request type, and target process ID are inserted into the TQE.

6. If the initial scheduled wakeup time is expressed as an interval, then the initial absolute expiration time is calculated as in $SETIMR from the initial delta time and the current system time.

7. The ASTCNT quota of the requesting process is decremented to account for the allocation of the TQE.

8. The TQE is inserted into the timer queue.

When the expiration time is reached, a process wakeup is set to the target process (see Section 11.3.4). Deallocation of the TQE occurs after delivery of a one-time scheduled wakeup request or as a result of a $CANWAK system service call.

The $CANWAK system service cancels all one-time and repeat scheduled wakeup requests for a target process. Each canceled TQE is deallocated to nonpaged dynamic memory and the PCB$W_ASTCNT of the initial requesting process is incremented to indicate the deallocation.

12 Process Control and Communication

I claim not to have controlled events, but confess plainly that
events have controlled me.
—Abraham Lincoln, letter to A.G. Hodges, April 4, 1864

The VMS operating system provides many services that allow processes to communicate with one another and allow one process to control the execution of another. Event flags are the most primitive control and communication tool available (in terms of amount of information). Other communication techniques include logical names, mailboxes, the VAX/VMS lock management system services (lock manager), global shared data sections, and shared files. (The lock manager is discussed only briefly here; for a full description, see Chapter 13.) System services allow a process to alter some of its parameters (such as name or priority). Other services allow a process to affect its own scheduling state or that of another process. A summary of process control system services is listed in Table 12-1.

12.1 EVENT FLAG SERVICES

Event flags are used within a single process for synchronization of I/O requests, enqueue lock requests, $GETJPI system service calls, and timer requests. They can also be used either within a single process or among several processes in the same group as application-specific synchronization tools. System services are provided to read, set, or clear collections of event flags. Other services allow a process to wait for one event flag or a collection of event flags.

12.1.1 Local Event Flags

Each process has available to it 64 local (process-specific) event flags and 64 shareable event flags (among processes in the same group). The 64 local event flags are stored directly in the software PCB, at offsets PCB$L_EFCS and PCB$L_EFCU (see Figure 12-1). Local event flags 0 to 31 are located in longword PCB$L_EFCS. Local event flags 32 to 63 are located in longword PCB$L_EFCU.

225

Table 12-1: Summary of Process Control System Services

Service Name	Affect Other Processes	Privilege Checks
Create Common Event Flag Cluster	Same group only	PRMCEB (for permanent clusters only)
Delete Common Event Flag Cluster	Same group only	PRMCEB
Wait for Single Event Flag		
Wait for Logical AND of Event Flags		
Wait for Logical OR of Event Flags		
Hibernate	No (1)	None
Wake	YES	GROUP or WORLD
Schedule Wakeup	YES	GROUP or WORLD
Cancel Wakeup	YES	GROUP or WORLD
Suspend	YES	GROUP or WORLD
Resume	YES	GROUP or WORLD
Exit	No	None
Forced Exit	YES	GROUP or WORLD
Create Process	YES	DETACH for other than subprocesses
Delete Process	YES	GROUP or WORLD
Set AST Enable	No	Access Mode Check
Set Power Recovery AST	No	Access Mode Check
Set Priority	YES	ALTPRI and GROUP or WORLD
Set Process Name	No	None
Set Resource Wait Mode	No (2)	None
Set Swap Mode	No (2)	PSWAPM
Set System Failure Mode	No (2)	Access Mode Check
Get Job/Process Information	YES	GROUP or WORLD

(1) As part of the Create Process system service, a process can specify that the process being created hibernate before a specified image executes.

(2) These three features can each be specified as a part of the Create Process system service.

12.1.2 Common Event Flags

Common event flag clusters do not initially exist. They must be created by the first process that calls the Associate Event Flag Cluster system service for a given cluster. This service allocates a structure called a common event block (see Figure 12-2) from nonpaged pool and loads its address into the PCB pointer field (either PCB$L_EFC2P or PCB$L_EFC3P). The common event block is linked into a system-wide list of common event blocks located by global listhead SCH$GQ_CEBHD (see Figure 12-3).

As additional processes associate with this cluster, the CEB list is searched in order to locate the CEB, the event flag cluster pointers in their PCBs are updated, and the reference count for that cluster is updated. As processes

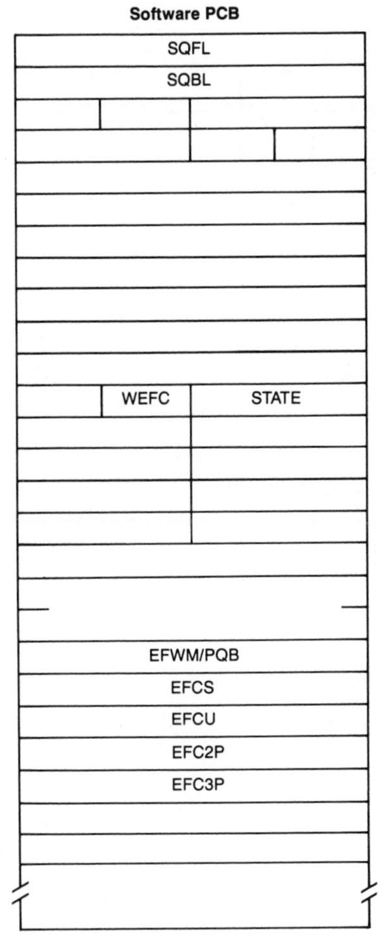

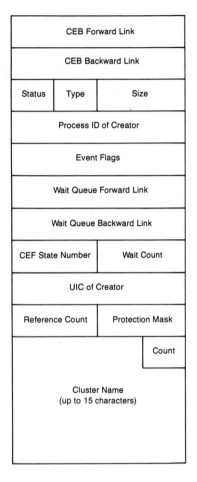

Software PCB

SQFL

SQBL

WEFC | STATE

EFWM/PQB

EFCS

EFCU

EFC2P

EFC3P

Figure 12-1
Software PCB Fields That Support
Event Flags

CEB Forward Link

CEB Backward Link

Status | Type | Size

Process ID of Creator

Event Flags

Wait Queue Forward Link

Wait Queue Backward Link

CEF State Number | Wait Count

UIC of Creator

Reference Count | Protection Mask

Count

Cluster Name
(up to 15 characters)

Figure 12-2
Layout of Common Event Block

disassociate from a cluster (with the $DACEFC system service), the reference
count is decremented. When the reference count for a temporary cluster goes
to zero, the cluster is automatically deleted and the CEB deallocated.

Permanent clusters must be explicitly deleted (using the $DLCEFC system
service) in order to cause the CEB to be deallocated when the reference count
goes to zero. Alternatively, permanent clusters can continue to exist without
requiring that they be associated with any processes. In fact, the only operation performed by the Delete Common Event Flag Cluster system service is
to turn off the CEB$V_PERM bit. (If the reference count of the cluster is zero
when the permanent bit is turned off, the cluster is deleted.)

227

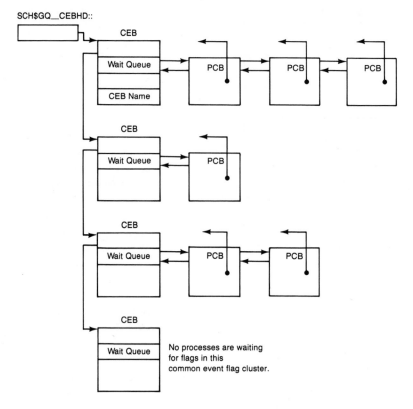

Figure 12-3
Common Event Flag Wait Queues

12.1.3 Event Flag Wait States

Processes are placed into event flag wait states implicitly when any of the following actions are performed:

- Executing a $QIOW or $ENQW system service
- Using the RMS services as synchronous operations (the usual way they are called)
- Executing one of the three event flag wait services ($WAITFR, $WFLOR, $WFLAND)

If the flag or flags in question are already set, the system service immediately returns successfully to its caller. Otherwise, the process is placed into either a local or common event flag wait state. The saved PC in the hardware PCB is backed up by 4 (see Chapter 10) to allow ASTs to be delivered to the process while it is waiting for the flag(s) to be set. The event flag cluster number (0 or 1 for local clusters and 2 or 3 for global clusters), indicating which flags are being waited for, is stored in the PCB (at offset

PCB$B_WEFC). The list (mask) of event flags being waited for is stored (in one's complement form) in PCB$L_EFWM.

- If the process is waiting for a single event flag (SYS$WAITFR), the PCB$L_EFWM mask contains a 1 in every bit except the bit number corresponding to the specified flag.
- If the process is waiting for any one of several flags to be set (SYS$WFLOR), the PCB$L_EFWM mask contains the one's complement of the mask passed to the $WFLOR system service. (The $WAITFR mask is thus a special case of a wait for any one of a group of flags to be set.) If any of the flags in the requested mask is set when $WFLOR is called, the process is not placed into a wait state. Instead, the service immediately returns a success code to its caller.
- If a process calls the $WFLAND system service, indicating a wait for all flags in a given mask to be set, the wait mask is modified so that event flags that are set when the service is called are not represented in the wait mask. In addition, a bit in the process status longword (PCB$V_WALL in PCB$L_STS) is set, indicating that all flags represented by the mask must be set before the wait is satisfied.

There exist two local event flag wait states (LEF and LEFO) and two corresponding wait queue listheads (SCH$GQ_LEFWQ and SCH$GQ_LEFOWQ) for the entire system. On the other hand, there exists one common event flag wait queue listhead for each common event cluster that currently exists. Each common event flag wait queue listhead is located in the corresponding common event block (see Figure 12-2) and has the same overall structure as any other wait queue listhead (see Figure 12-3).

12.1.4 Setting and Clearing Event Flags

Event flags can be set directly by a process by calling the Set Event Flag system service. A process could use this service at AST level to communicate with its mainline code. It can also set common event flags to communicate with other processes. Event flags are also set in response to I/O completion, timer expiration, the granting of a lock request, and delivery of a $GETDVI, $GETJPI, or $GETSYI request.

It should be noted here that when the VAX/VMS operating system uses shared event flags to communicate information between processes, a strict set of ownership rules is used. When a controlling process is getting ready to set an event flag, it owns the flag. When the process has set the flag (thereby allowing waiting processes to become computable), it relinquishes its ownership of the flag to the other processes. It is then the responsibility of the other processes to clear the flag and notify the controlling process that it has regained ownership of the flag. In this scheme, ownership is maintained by convention alone; it is not enforced by the software. DIGITAL recommends that applications that use shared event flags as a communications tool adhere to these same conventions.

Both the system service and the special paths call the same routine (SCH$POSTEF) to perform the actual event flag setting and check for possible scheduling implications.

The operation of SCH$POSTEF depends on what kind of event flag is being set.

- If the event flag that is being set is local, a check is made to determine whether this flag satisfies the process's wait request. In a $WFLOR wait, this flag merely has to match one of the flags being waited for. In a $WFLAND wait, all of the flags being waited for must be set in order to satisfy the process's wait request and report an event to the scheduler.

- When a common event flag is set, the list of PCBs in the common event block wait queue is scanned to determine if any of the processes waiting for flags in this cluster satisfy its wait request as a result of setting this flag. A system event is reported for each such process.

  All such processes are made computable. If the priority of any one of them is greater than the priority of the currently executing process, a re-scheduling interrupt is requested. As with all other cases in the system where several processes become computable as a result of the same system-wide event, the process with the highest software priority will be selected for execution.

- For common event flags located in shared memory, there is one more level of complication. The event flag must be set in the master CEB located in shared memory, and other processors connected to this shared memory unit must be notified that a shared memory common event flag was just set. (Shared memory common event flag data structures are discussed at the end of this chapter. Other shared memory data structures are described in Chapter 14.)

  Any other processor connected to the same global event flag cluster receives initial notification through an MA780 interrupt. The interrupt service routine determines that the interrupt was due to an event flag in shared memory being set, copies the entire set of event flags from the master CEB to the slave CEB, and checks whether any of the processes waiting for flags in this cluster are now computable.

12.1.4.1 Other Event Flag Services. The Clear Event Flag system service simply clears the specified event flag. Note that when clearing a flag in common event flag clusters in shared memory, only the event flag in the master CEB is cleared. It is not necessary to copy the set of flags from the master CEB to the slave CEBs on other processors when an event flag is cleared for the following two reasons:

- The event flag wait services only use the master CEB when checking whether to place a process into a wait state or return immediate success.
- The event flag posting routine copies the master set of flags to the local slave CEB before testing whether any process wait requests are satisfied. The master set of flags is copied into all other slave CEBs as a result of notifying other processors that a flag has been set.

The Read Event Flag system service is simply informational. It has no effect on the computability of any process on any processor. The event flag cluster is read from the same destinations as those affected by the Clear Event Flag system service.

- Local event flag clusters are read from the software PCB.
- Regular common event flag clusters are read from the CEB.
- Common event flag clusters located in shared memory are read from the master CEB located in shared memory.

12.2 AFFECTING THE COMPUTABILITY OF ANOTHER PROCESS

In any multiprocessing application, it is necessary for one process to control whether and when other processes in the application can execute. The VMS operating system contains several services that provide this control.

12.2.1 Common Event Flags

Common event flags described in the previous section are one method of synchronization control. One process can reach a critical point in its execution and wait on a global event flag. Another process can allow this process to continue its execution by setting the flag in question.

Common event flags are also used as semaphores for more complicated forms of interprocess communication that use logical names or global sections.

12.2.2 Process Control Services

Several system services allow one process to directly alter the scheduling state of another process.

12.2.2.1 Privilege Checks. All system services that permit one process to directly affect another allow the process to be specified either by process name or by process identification (PID). In either case, the VMS operating system must determine whether the specified process exists and whether the caller has the proper privilege (GROUP, WORLD) or is part of the same process tree and can thus affect the other process. This work is centralized in a routine called EXE$NAMPID that is called by all such system services.

If the specified process exists, and the caller can affect the specified process, EXE$NAMPID returns successfully (at IPL 7) with the PCB address of the specified process in R4. Note that this return condition alters the contents of R4, which usually contains the caller's PCB address. If the specified process is a part of the same process tree as the caller (the JIB address is identical), EXE$NAMPID will return successfully. A second important use of EXE$NAMPID is in obtaining a PID when the process name is known. If a process name is specified and the PID address argument points to a zero longword, the PID of the named specified process is returned to the caller at the designated location.

12.2.2.2   **Process Creation and Deletion.** A first step in a multiprocess application requires that a controlling process create other processes for designated work. These processes may be deleted when they have completed their work or they may exist in some wait state in anticipation of additional work. The detailed operation of process creation is described in Chapter 20. Process deletion is described in Chapter 22.

12.2.2.3   **Hibernate/Wake.** There are two different ways that a process can be temporarily halted, called hibernation and suspension. The differences between these two wait states are described in the *VAX/VMS System Services Reference Manual*.

A process can only put itself into the hibernate state. (That is, a process cannot put another process into the HIB state.) If the wake pending flag is not set (this flag check also clears the flag), indicating that an associated wake has not preceded the hibernate call, the process is placed into the hibernate wait state. As described in Chapter 10, the saved PC is backed up by 4 so that the process will be put back into the hibernate state in case it receives ASTs while it is hibernating. (Note that the check of the wake pending flag by the Hibernate system service includes the case where a process first hibernates and then is awakened by a wake call issued from an AST.)

The $WAKE system service is the complementary service to Hibernate. A process may awaken itself (by calling $WAKE from an AST) or it may be awakened when another process calls $WAKE with the target process specified either by name (if the target process is in the same group, and the caller has GROUP privilege) or by process ID (if the caller has GROUP or WORLD privilege). This service sets the wake pending flag in the software PCB and reports the awakening event to the scheduler. The process is removed from the HIB or HIBO queue and placed into the COM or COMO state in the queue corresponding to its updated priority. (A wake event results in a priority boost class of PRI$_RESAVL, which is equivalent to a boost of 3.)

The next time the process executes, the hibernate service executes again (because the PC was backed up by 4). Because the wake pending flag is now set, the process returns immediately from the hibernate call (with the wake pending flag now clear). Notice that if the process is in any state other than HIB or HIBO when it is awakened, the net result is to leave the wake pending flag set with no other change in its scheduling state.

12.2.2.4 **Suspend/Resume.** Process suspension is slightly more complicated internally than hibernation because a process can be placed into the SUSP state by other processes. The scheduling philosophy of the VMS operating system, illustrated in Figure 10-5, assumes that processes enter various wait states from the state of being the current process and in no other way. This assumption requires that the process being suspended (the target) become current, replacing the currently executing process, the caller of the Suspend system service.

The VMS operating system accommodates this scheduling constraint by using a special kernel AST, the same tool that it uses when it needs access to a portion of process address space. In this case, it is not the process address space that is so important. Rather, the process must first be made current before it is placed into the SUSP state.

12.2.2.4.1 *Process Suspension.* Process suspension occurs in two pieces. The portion of the service that executes in the context of the caller sets the suspend pending bit in the software PCB of the target process and queues the special kernel AST (the routine that performs the actual suspension) to that process. This implementation includes the special case where a process suspends itself.

Through the normal scheduling selection process, the target process eventually executes. The special kernel AST that performs the suspension executes first unless there are previously queued special kernel ASTs. This AST first checks (and clears) the resume pending flag in PCB$L_STS. (This check avoids the deadlock that could otherwise occur if the associated call to the $RESUME service preceded the call to $SUSPEND.) If the resume pending flag is set, the process simply clears the suspend pending bit, returns from the AST, and continues with its execution.

Otherwise, it is placed into the SUSP wait state. The saved PSL contains IPL 2, preventing delivery of ASTs while a process is suspended. (In addition, the AST system event is ignored for processes in either the SUSP or the SUSPO state.) The saved PC is an address within the suspend special kernel AST. When the process is resumed (the only way that a suspended process can continue with its execution), it reexecutes the check of the resume pending flag, which is now set, causing the process to return successfully from the special AST.

12.2.2.4.2 *Operation of the Resume System Service.* The Resume system service is very simple. The resume pending flag in PCB$L_STS of the target process is set and (if the target process of the resume request is in either the SUSP or

SUSPO state) a resume event is reported to the scheduler. As with all other system events, this report may result in a rescheduling pass, a request to wake the swapper process, or nothing at all.

12.2.2.5   Exit and Forced Exit. The Exit system service terminates the currently executing image. If the process is executing a single image (it is neither an interactive nor batch job), image exit usually results in process deletion. A detailed discussion of the Exit system service, including the calling sequence of termination handlers, is given in Chapter 21.

The Force Exit system service is a tool that allows one process to execute the Exit system service on behalf of another process. The service simply sets the force exit pending flag in PCB$L_STS and queues a user mode AST to the target process. This AST, executing in user mode, calls the Exit system service after clearing the AST active flag by executing the following instruction:

```
CHMK    #ASTEXIT
```

(For more information on this instruction, see Chapter 7). The call to Exit is executed in the context of the target process. Execution proceeds in exactly the same manner as it would if the target process had called Exit itself.

12.2.3   Miscellaneous Process Attribute Changes

Finally, there are several system services that allow a process to alter its characteristics, such as its response to system service failures, its software priority, and its process name. Some of these changes (such as priority elevation or swap disabling) require privilege. The Set Priority system service is the only service described in this section that can be issued for a process other than the caller.

12.2.3.1   Set Priority. The Set Priority system service allows a process to alter its own software priority or the priority of other processes that it is allowed (through GROUP or WORLD privileges) to affect. If a process has the ALTPRI privilege, it can change priority to any value between 0 and 31. A process without this privilege is restricted to the range between 0 and its own base priority. In VAX/VMS Version 3.0, the cell PHD$B_AUTHPRI was added to the process header. Storing a process's base priority in this cell allows the process to lower its priority below its base priority and raise it again up to its base priority.

For most scheduling states (everything except COM, COMO, and CUR), the Set Priority system service simply changes the base software priority in the software PCB (at offset PCB$B_PRIB). If a process alters its own priority, not only its base but also its current priority (at offset PCB$B_PRI) is changed. When the priority of a computable process (either COM or COMO) is altered, the process is removed from the COM or COMO queue corresponding to its current priority and placed into a COM or COMO queue corresponding to its new priority (the new base with a boost of 2). In addition, a scheduling event is reported. If the new process priority (new base plus a boost of 2) is greater than or equal to the current priority of the current process, a rescheduling interrupt is requested.

12.2.3.2   **Set Process Name.** Both the Set Process Name system service and the DCL command SET PROCESS/NAME= allows a process to change its process name. The new name cannot contain more than 15 characters. If no other process in the same group has the same name, the new name is placed into the software PCB (at offset PCB$T_LNAME). (Note that this service allows more flexibility in establishing a process name than is available from the usual channels, such as the authorization file or a $JOB card, because there are no restrictions imposed by the service on characters that can make up the process name. Even the DCL command is limited by characters that are unacceptable to DCL.)

12.2.3.3   **Process Mode Services.** There are several miscellaneous system services whose only action is to set or clear a bit in some field in the software PCB. In particular, the software PCB contains a status longword (not to be confused with the hardware entity, the PSL or processor status longword) that records the current software status of the process. Table 12-2 lists each of the flags in this longword, and the direct or indirect ways that these flags can be set or cleared.

The Set Resource Wait Mode, Set System Service Failure Exception Mode, and Set Swap Mode system services all set (or clear) bits in this status longword. The ability to disable swapping is protected by the PSWAPM privilege. The other two services require no privilege. Several other system services (such as $DELPRC, $FORCEX, $RESUME, or $SUSPND) set or clear bits in the status longword as an indication of their primary operation.

The Set AST system service sets or clears (enables or disables) delivery of ASTs for a given access mode. The AST enable flags are stored at offset PCB$B_ASTEN within the PCB. These flags are discussed in Chapter 7.

12.3   **INTERPROCESS COMMUNICATION**

In any application involving more than one process, it is necessary for data to be shared among the several processes or for information to be sent from one process to another. The VMS operating system provides several services that accomplish this information exchange. The services vary in the amount of information that can be transmitted, the transparency of the transmission, and the amount of synchronization provided by the VMS operating system.

Table 12-2: Meanings of Flags in PCB Status Longword (PCB$LSTS)

Symbolic Name	Meaning of Flag if Set	Flag Set by	Flag Cleared by
PCB$V_RES	Process is resident (in the balance set)	Swapper	Swapper
PCB$V_DELPEN	Process deletion is pending	$DELPRC	
PCB$V_FORCPEN	Forced exit is pending	$FORCEX	Image and process rundown
PCB$V_INQUAN	Process is in its initial quantum (following inswap)	Swapper	Quantum end routine
PCB$V_PSWAPM	Process swapping is disabled	$SETSWM, $CREPRC	$SETSWM
PCB$V_RESPEN	Resume is pending (skip suspend)	$RESUME	Suspend special AST
PCB$V_SSFEXC	Enable system service exceptions for kernel mode	$SETSFM	$SETSFM, process rundown
PCB$V_SSFEXCE	Enable system service exceptions for executive mode	$SETSFM	$SETSFM, process rundown
PCB$V_SSFEXCS	Enable system service exceptions for supervisor mode	$SETSFM	$SETSFM, process rundown
PCB$V_SSFEXCU	Enable system service exceptions for user mode	$SETSFM, $CREPRC	$SETSFM, image and process rundown
PCB$V_SSRWAIT	Disable resource wait mode	$SETRWM, $CREPRC	$SETRWM
PCB$V_SUSPEN	Suspend is pending	$SUSPND	Suspend special AST

Table 12-2: Meanings of Flags in PCB Status Longword (PCB$LSTS) (continued)

Symbolic Name	Meaning of Flag if Set	Flag Set by	Flag Cleared by
PCB$V_WAKEPEN	Wake is pending (skip hibernate)	$WAKE, expiration of scheduled wakeup	$HIBER
PCB$V_WALL	Wait for all event flags in mask	$WFLAND	Next $WFLOR or $WAITFR
PCB$V_BATCH	Process is a batch job	$CREPRC	
PCB$V_NOACNT	Do not write an accounting record for this process	$CREPRC	
PCB$V_SWPVBN	Modified page write to the swap file is in progress	Modified page writer	Modified page writer
PCB$V_ASTPEN	AST is pending (No longer used)		
PCB$V_PHDRES	Process header is resident	Swapper	Swapper
PCB$V_HIBER	Hibernate after initial image activation	$CREPRC	
PCB$V_LOGIN	Login without reading the authorization file	$CREPRC	
PCB$V_NETWRK	Process is a network job	$CREPRC	
PCB$V_PWRAST	Process has declared a power recovery AST	$SETPRA	Routine that queues recovery ASTs, image and process rundown
PCB$V_NODELET	Do not delete this process (not used)		
PCB$V_DISAWS	Do not perform automatic working set adjustment on this process	SET WORKING_SET/NOADJUST $CREPRC	SET WORKING_SET/ADJUST

12.3.1 Event Flags

Global or common event flags can be treated as a method for several processes to share single bits of information. In fact, the typical use of common event flags is as a synchronization tool for other more complicated communication techniques. The internal operations of common event flags are described in the beginning of this chapter.

12.3.2 VAX/VMS Lock Management System Services

The lock management system services allow processes to name a shared resource and request locks on that resource. If access to a resource cannot be immediately granted to a lock, a queuing mechanism is provided for a process to wait until it can be granted access to the resource. The lock manager provides a number of lock modes to control how the resource is to be shared with other processes. Blocking ASTs and a lock value block are also provided to pass information about, or synchronize access to, a resource. The internals of the lock manager are described in Chapter 13.

12.3.3 Mailboxes

Mailboxes are I/O devices in that they are written to and read from by the normal VMS I/O system, either through RMS or with the $QIO interface. Although process-specific or system-wide parameters may control the amount of data that can be written to a mailbox in one operation, there is no limit to the total amount of information that can be passed through a mailbox with a series of reads and writes.

There are two forms of synchronization provided for mailbox I/O. Because mailboxes are I/O devices, a simple but restrictive technique would have the receiving process issue a read from the mailbox and wait until the read completes. Of course, the read could not complete until the process writing to the mailbox completed its transmission of data. The limitation of this technique is that the receiving process cannot do anything else while it is waiting for data. Even if the process issues asynchronous I/O requests, an I/O request must be outstanding at all times in order to receive notification when some other process writes to the mailbox. In some applications, these limitations may be acceptable and so this technique can be used.

Other applications may have a receiving process that can perform different tasks, depending on the information available to it. Putting such a process into a wait state for one task prevents it from servicing any of its other tasks. For such applications, the VMS operating system provides a special $QIO request called Set Attention AST that allows a process to receive notification through an AST when anyone writes into its mailbox. This technique allows a process to continue its mainline processing and handle requests from other processes only when such work is needed, without having an I/O request outstanding at all times.

12.3.4   Logical Names

Logical names (see Chapter 29) are used extensively by the VMS operating system to provide total device independence in the I/O system. However, logical names can be used for many other purposes as well. Specifically, one process can pass information to another process by creating a logical name (in the group or system table) with information stored in the equivalence string. The receiving process simply translates the name to retrieve the data.

   Although some form of synchronization is provided by an error return (SS$_NOTRAN) from the Translate Logical Name system service, processes using such a technique should use event flags (or an equivalent method) to synchronize this communication technique. One use of this technique where synchronization is not required occurs when a process creates a subprocess or detached process and passes the new process data in the equivalence strings for SYS$INPUT, SYS$OUTPUT, or SYS$ERROR. Using this method, there is no possibility for the translation to occur before the creation.

12.3.5   Global Sections

Global sections provide the fastest method for one process to pass information to another process. Because the two processes have the data area mapped into their address space, no movement of data takes place. Instead, the method provides for a sharing of the data. The method is not transparent because each process must map the global section that will be used to share data. In addition, the processes must use event flags, the lock management system services, or their own synchronization to prevent the receiver from reading data before it has been made available by the sender.

12.3.6   Interprocessor Communication with the MA780

VMS support for the MA780 shared memory unit provides a transparent communication path for interprocess communication even when processes are located on different processors connected through a shared memory unit (MA780). The three communication paths provided are common event flags, mailboxes, and global sections.

   Each of these entities is described by a name. When a process connects to one of them (with the Associate Common Event Flag Cluster system service, the Create Mailbox system service, or the Create and Map Section or Map Global Section system services), a logical name translation is performed on the name of the object. If the equivalence name is of the following form, the service makes the appropriate connection between the process and the data structure describing the object that exists in shared memory.

```
shared-memory-name:object-name
```

If the shared memory data structure does not exist, it is created (except that the Map Global Section system service does not create global sections that do not exist). The data structures that the VMS operating system uses to describe shared memory are pictured in Chapter 14. In addition, memory management data structures, including those structures that describe shared memory global sections, are found in that chapter.

- For a common event flag cluster in shared memory, the event flag cluster in the software PCB (PCB$L_EFC2P or PCB$L_EFC3P) points to the slave CEB for the local processor. The slave CEB contains information that describes the master CEB that is located in the shared memory (see Figure 12-4). The following procedures are used to identify the slave PCB:

  —If the slave CEB already exists, the system service simply points the PCB to the CEB.
  —If the slave CEB does not exist but the master does (there are currently no references to this cluster on this CPU), then a slave CEB is created; the address of the master is stored in the slave; and the address of the slave is stored in the PCB.
  —If the master CEB does not exist either, it is created first in the shared memory. Then the slave is created and execution proceeds as described in the previous case.

  The way in which common event flags are set and cleared is described in the beginning of this chapter. The differences between shared memory common event blocks (master and slave) and local memory common event blocks are pictured in Figure 12-5. (A local memory common event block is pictured in Figure 12-2).

- For a mailbox in shared memory, there are also three cases.

  —If the mailbox already exists on this port, the Create Mailbox system service simply assigns a channel to it. (The UCB pointer in an available channel control block is loaded with the address of the UCB describing the shared memory mailbox.)
  —If the mailbox is being created on this node for the first time, a UCB is allocated and loaded with parameters that describe the mailbox. A bit is set in a mailbox-dependent field indicating that this mailbox UCB describes a mailbox in shared memory. Finally, the address of the shared memory mailbox control block is loaded into the UCB.

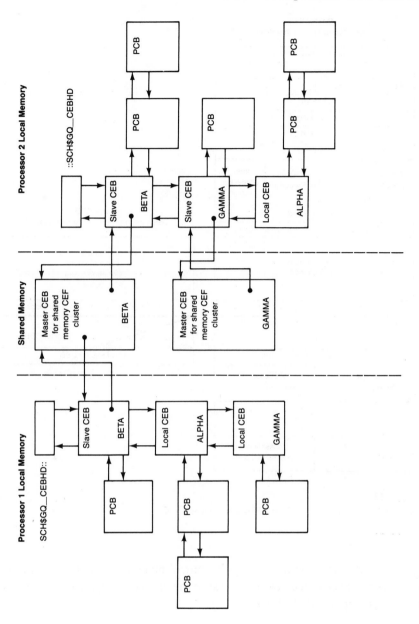

Figure 12-4
Relationship between Master and Slave CEB

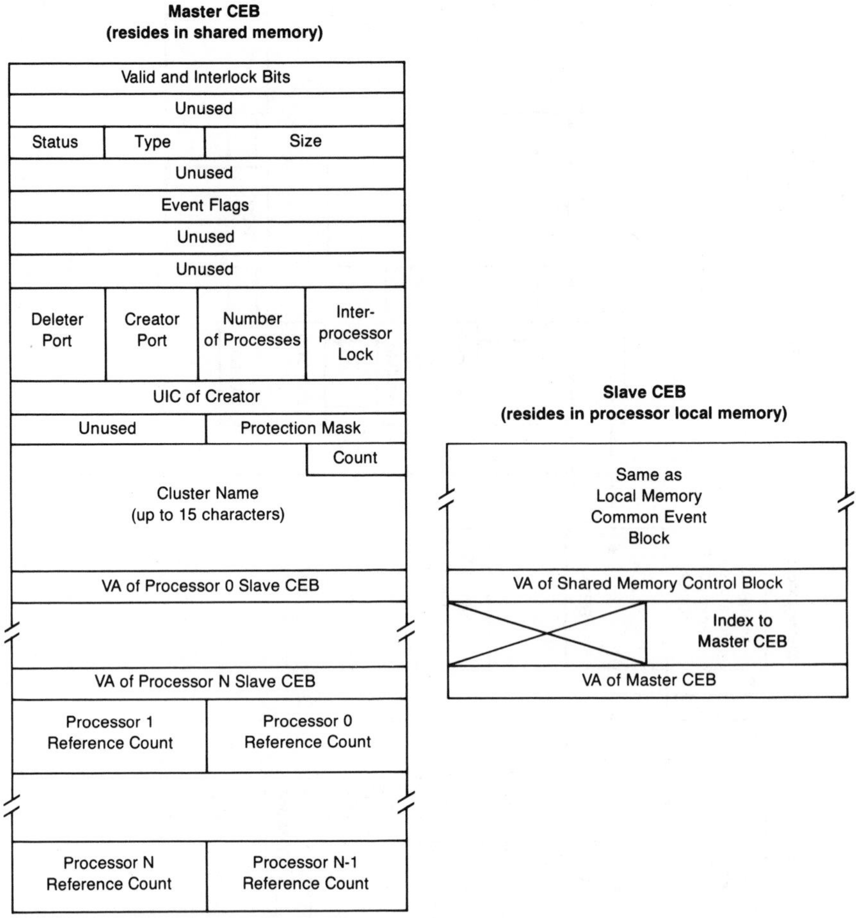

Master CEB
(resides in shared memory)

Valid and Interlock Bits

Unused

Status	Type	Size

Unused

Event Flags

Unused

Unused

Deleter Port	Creator Port	Number of Processes	Inter-processor Lock

UIC of Creator

Unused	Protection Mask

Slave CEB
(resides in processor local memory)

	Count

Cluster Name (up to 15 characters)

Same as Local Memory Common Event Block

VA of Processor 0 Slave CEB

VA of Shared Memory Control Block

	Index to Master CEB

VA of Processor N Slave CEB

VA of Master CEB

Processor 1 Reference Count	Processor 0 Reference Count

Processor N Reference Count	Processor N-1 Reference Count

Figure 12-5
Shared Memory Common Event Flag Data Structures

—If the shared memory mailbox control block (see Figure 18-2) does not exist, it is created before the rest of the operations described in the previous step are performed.

Shared memory mailbox data structures are pictured in Figures 18-2 and 18-3. Mailbox creation is described in more detail in Chapter 18.

- For a global section in shared memory, a special global section descriptor is allocated that describes the global section in shared memory. Unlike global sections that exist in local memory, there are no global page table entries set up for global sections in shared memory.

When a process maps to the shared memory global section, its process page tables are set up to contain the PFNs of the shared memory pages and marked as valid. Such pages are not counted against the process working set. That is, pages in shared memory do not incur page faults. They are always valid, and therefore they can be described with a simple descriptor that is contained in the global section descriptor, rather than a set of global page table entries required for global pages that exist in local memory. Memory management data structures are described in Chapter 14. The memory management system services are discussed in Chapter 16.

13 VAX/VMS Lock Manager

'Tis in my memory lock'd,
And you yourself shall keep the key of it.
—*Hamlet* 1, 3

The VAX/VMS lock manager provides semaphores that cooperating processes can use to synchronize access to shared resources. The lock manager allows callers to specify one of six degrees of shareability (lock modes) ranging from no access to exclusive access. Once the lock is granted, the owning process can request a lock conversion to change the lock mode. The lock manager provides a queuing mechanism by which processes can wait in turn until a shared resource becomes available. Two queues are available: a waiting queue for new locks and a conversion queue for lock conversions.

The lock modes are:

NL   Null lock. Owner can neither read nor write; compatible with all other locks.

CR   Concurrent read. Read access and sharing with other readers and writers.

CW   Concurrent write. Write access and sharing with other readers and writers.

PR   Protected read. Read access and sharing with other readers; no writers allowed.

PW   Protected write. Write access and sharing with CR mode readers; no other writers allowed.

EX   Exclusive access. Write access; denies access to any other readers or writers.

This chapter first discusses the data structures used by the lock manager. The action of the lock manager when locks are queued and dequeued is then described. The last section in this chapter describes deadlock detection. The treatment in this chapter assumes that the reader is familiar with the description of the VAX/VMS lock management system services found in the *VAX/ VMS System Services Reference Manual*.

13.1 LOCK MANAGER DATA STRUCTURES

Essentially the lock database consists of the following four structures:

• Lock blocks that describe the locks requested by processes

- Resource blocks that describe the resource names for which locks have been requested
- The lock ID table that locates the lock blocks
- The resource hash table that locates the resource blocks

13.1.1   Lock Blocks

Figure 13-1 shows the structure of the lock block (LKB). The lock block is allocated from nonpaged pool, and is composed of two overlaying structures. The first structure in the lock block contains an AST control block (ACB). When a lock is granted, the ACB is used to queue a kernel mode AST to perform kernel mode operations in the context of the caller; the ACB is also used to queue completion ASTs. When a blocking AST is required, the ACB is used to queue the blocking AST.

The second part of the lock block describes the information specific to the lock request (for example, a blocking AST address, the event flag number, and the address of the lock status block) and the current state of the lock (for example, the lock mode and the queue links used to locate the lock). The

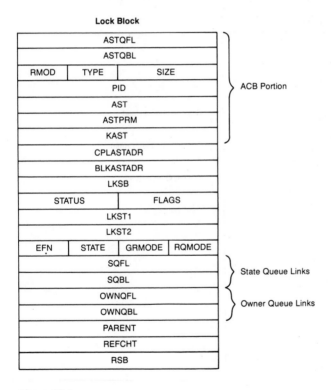

Figure 13-1
Layout of a Lock Block

state queue links in the lock block are used to link the LKB into a resource's state queue.

The lock block is created when a process requests a new lock and is owned only by that process. When a process dequeues a lock, the lock block is deallocated.

13.1.2   Resource Blocks

A resource block describes a resource and contains listheads for the granted, conversion, and waiting queues for the resource. The state queue links in the lock block (LKB$L_SQFL and LKB$L_SQBL) link the lock blocks to these queues. Note that the conversion and waiting queues are ordered first-in/first-out; the granted queue has no order. Figure 13-2 shows the structure of the resource block. The resource blocks are allocated from nonpaged pool. In addition to queue heads, a resource block contains the lock value block for the resource, the address of the resource's parent resource block (if any), and

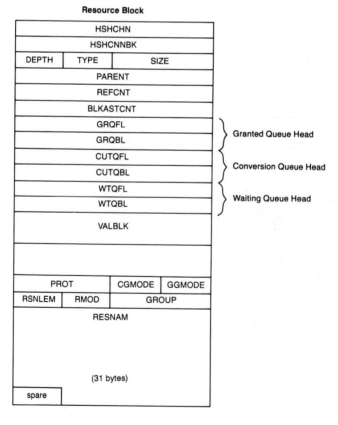

Figure 13-2
Layout of a Resource Block

the number of sublocks owned by the resource. Only one resource block will exist for each resource being locked.

Resource blocks are deallocated when there are no locks associated with the resource (the state queues in the resource block are empty).

13.1.3   Accessing the Lock and Resource Blocks

The VAX/VMS lock manager has two ways in which information in the lock management database can be located, the lock ID table and the resource hash table. The lock ID table is used to locate lock blocks; the resource hash table is used to locate resource blocks. Both of these structures are allocated from nonpaged pool.

Once a resource block has been located through the resource hash table, the lock blocks associated with the resource can be found through the state queue pointers. Conversely, once a lock block has been located through the lock ID table, the name of the resource that is locked can be located by the resource block address field in the lock block. (A third way to locate information in the lock management database using process control blocks is discussed in Section 13.1.4.)

13.1.3.1   **The Lock ID Table.** The lock ID table is used to locate locks when the lock ID is known. When a caller requests a new lock, the $ENQ system service returns a lock ID to the caller. The lock ID is actually an index into the lock ID table. The caller can then use the lock ID to identify a specific lock when performing conversions or dequeuing locks. The lock ID table is located by the global symbol LCK$GL_IDTBL. Figure 13-3 shows the structure of the lock ID table.

When an entry in the lock ID table is in use, it contains the address of the lock block that is associated with the lock ID. When an entry in the lock ID table is not used, the low-order word contains an index to the next unused entry in the lock ID table. When the VAX/VMS operating system is initialized, the module INIT loads each entry in the lock ID table with the index of the subsequent entry in the table. The first entry in the table is initialized to zero and is not used. A zero entry indicates an unusable lock ID table entry.

The global symbol LCK$GL_NXTID contains a lock ID table index that points to the first free lock ID table entry. When a caller requests a new lock, LCK$GL_NXTID is used to locate the new lock ID table entry. The low-order word of LCK$GL_NXTID is returned to the caller as the new lock ID. Two actions are then performed on the new lock ID table entry.

- The contents of the new lock ID table entry (which contains a pointer to the next free lock ID table entry) are copied into LCK$GL_NXTID.
- The address of the new lock block is written into the lock ID table entry.

Because it is possible that an error in a calling routine could pass an errone-

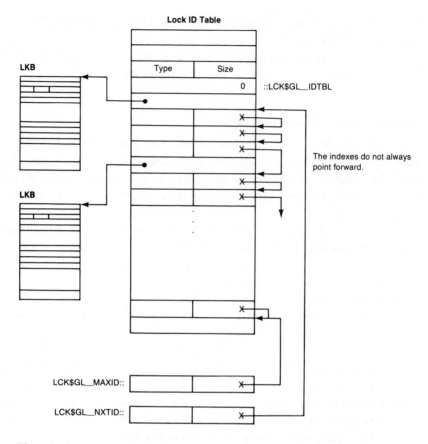

Figure 13-3
Structure of the Lock ID Table

ous value as the lock ID, the lock manager compares the caller's process identification and access mode with the process identification and access mode stored in the lock block. If the comparison fails, the lock manager exits with the return status code SS$_IVLOCKID.

When a lock block is deallocated, the lock ID table entry is located by its lock ID. The contents of LCK$GL_NXTID are written into the lock ID table entry (replacing the address of the deallocated lock block) and the lock ID is written into LCK$GL_NXTID.

The global symbol LCK$GL_MAXID contains the index to the last entry in the lock ID table. The lock ID table entry at that location always contains a zero. The size of the lock ID table is controlled by the SYSBOOT parameter LOCKIDTBL.

13.1.3.2 **The Resource Hash Table.** The resource hash table is used to locate resource blocks. The resource name is hashed and the result of the hash is used as an index into the resource hash table. Note that the entries in the resource hash table are longword addresses, not quadword queue heads; the resource hash table contains only forward pointers to the lists. The table is located by the global symbol LCK$GL_HASHTBL. The size of the hash table is determined by the SYSBOOT parameter RESHASHTBL. The hashing algorithm is similar to the algorithm used for hashing logical names (see Section 29.1.4).

Each longword entry in the resource hash table points to the first resource block in a resource hash chain. Because the resource blocks are maintained in a list that is doubly linked, but not circular (the resource hash table contains no backward pointers), the list of resource blocks is termed a chain. The first two longwords in each resource block contain the forward and backward pointers for the resource hash chain. The last block in the chain has a zero forward pointer. If a longword entry in the resource hash table contains a zero, there are no resource blocks associated with that hash table entry.

Figure 13-4 shows the structure of the resource hash table and its relationships to hash chains.

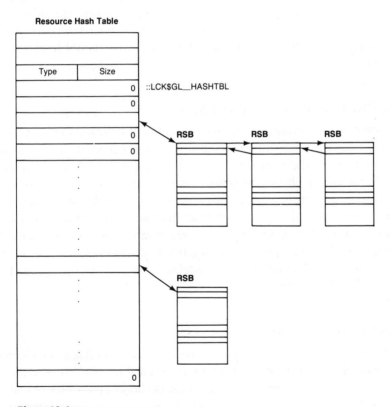

Figure 13-4
Resource Hash Table and Hash Chains

13.1.4 Relationships in the Lock Database

There are three ways in which the lock manager can access the lock database.

- Given a resource name, the lock manager can locate the RSB through the resource hash table. Using the state queue heads, all locks associated with the resource can be located.
- Given a lock ID, the lock manager can locate the lock block through the lock ID table. Using the resource address field in the lock block, the resource associated with the lock can be located.
- Given a process control block, the lock manager can locate the lock queue header (at offsets PCB$L_LOCKQFL and PCB$L_LOCKQBL). Using the lock queue links, all locks owned by a specific process can be located.

A lock with a parent lock and resource is termed a sublock. When a sublock is requested, the new lock block will contain the address of the parent lock block (at offset LKB$L_PARENT); the resource block associated with the sublock will point to the parent resource (at offset RSB$L_PARENT). This relationship is shown in Figure 13-5. When a sublock is created, the reference count fields in the parent lock block and resource block are incremented to account for the sublocks. A lock block or resource block cannot be deallocated unless the reference count equals zero. By the reference count, parent locks can tell the number of sublocks they own; they do not have a list of their sublocks.

13.2 QUEUING AND DEQUEUING LOCKS

The lock manager becomes active only when calls are made to the $ENQ or $DEQ system services. When the $ENQ service is called, the lock manager attempts to grant the requested new lock or the lock conversion immediately. If the new lock or conversion cannot be granted, the lock block is placed on the waiting or conversion queue. When the $DEQ service is called, the lock manager dequeues the lock from the resource and then searches the resource's state queues for locks that are compatible with the currently granted locks. Lock compatibility is described fully in the *VAX/VMS System Services Reference Manual*. The following sections describe the action of the $ENQ and $DEQ services.

13.2.1 The $ENQ System Service

When a process calls the $ENQ system service, the event flag and lock mode are validated and the lock status block is checked for read/write access. If these checks are successful, the request type is checked (new lock or conversion). Section 13.2.2 discusses in detail the action of the lock manager for lock conversions.

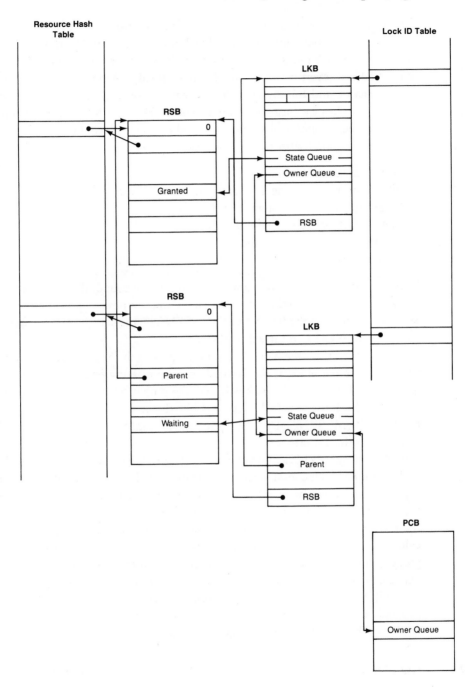

Figure 13-5
Relationships between Locks and Sublocks

If a new lock is requested, a lock block and a resource block are allocated. The fields of the lock block are initialized, including the fields in the ACB at the top of the lock block. A new resource block for the resource is allocated and initialized (even if the resource exists already). After hashing the new resource name and finding an index into the resource hash table, the lock manager searches the hash chain for a resource block with the same resource name. For each resource block encountered on the hash chain, the following fields are compared with the new resource block:

- Parent resource block address
- UIC group number (the UIC group number is zero for system locks)
- Access mode (user through kernel mode)
- Name space (system or group wide)
- Length of the resource name string
- Resource name string

If the resource block for the named resource is not found, the new resource block is added to the end of the hash chain and the new lock is granted (see Section 13.2.1.1). If the flag bit LKB$M_SYNCSTS is set, the success status code SS$_SYNCH is returned to the caller.

If the named resource block is found in the search for the resource name, the new resource block is deallocated and the existing one is used. The requested mode in the lock block is tested for compatibility with the currently granted locks. If the new lock is compatible, the new lock is granted. Again, if the bit LKB$M_SYNCSTS is set, the success status code SS$_SYNCH is returned to the caller.

In order to speed checks for compatibility with the currently granted locks, each resource block contains a field indicating the highest granted lock mode of all locks in the granted and conversion queue for that resource. This field is termed the group grant mode. Note that locks on the conversion queue retain their granted mode; it is the granted mode of these locks that is used in calculating the group grant mode, not their requested mode. The value of the group grant mode is stored in the resource block at offset RSB$B_GGMODE. Because this value is calculated only when a new lock is granted and is maintained in the resource block, compatibility checking involves only one compare operation; the lock manager does not have to spend time comparing lock modes each time it attempts to grant a lock.

13.2.1.1   Granting a Lock. The action of granting a lock involves five steps:

1. The compatibility of the locks (group grant mode) is recomputed.
2. The lock block is placed on the granted queue.
3. The event flag is set.

4. If a completion AST was specified, it is queued.

5. If a blocking AST was specified and the lock is blocking another lock request, the blocking AST is queued.

To place a lock on the granted queue, the listheads for the granted queue are located in the resource block at offsets RSB$L_GRQFL and RSB$L_GRQBL. The lock block is then linked into the granted queue. The order in which locks are placed on the queue is unimportant. The only time that the granted queue is traversed is when the group grant mode is computed, and, in that case, no particular order is required.

The event flag number is stored in the lock block at offset LKB$B_EFN. The global routine SCH$POSTEF is called to set the event flag.

13.2.1.2   **ASTs and the Lock Manager.** Because the lock manager must modify information in per-process space, a special kernel mode AST routine is required to perform some actions when granting a lock. The following operations are performed by the special kernel mode AST routine.

- The contents of the lock status block (and optionally the contents of the lock value block) are copied to the caller's lock status block.
- If a completion AST has been queued and if a blocking AST is required at this time, the blocking AST is queued.
- If the NODELETE bit is clear in the ACB, the ACB is deallocated.

If no completion AST or blocking AST routine is specified by the caller, a special kernel mode AST is used to perform these actions. However, if an AST routine was specified by the caller, the special kernel AST is queued as a piggyback special kernel AST in the caller's ACB (see Section 7.2.4).

Because the ACB can contain the address of only one AST routine, special treatment is required when a the lock manager must signal both a completion AST and a blocking AST. When the lock is granted, the AST routine field in the lock block ACB (offset LKB$L_AST) is loaded with the the address of the completion AST routine (stored at offset LKB$L_CPLASTADR). When the completion AST is delivered, the contents of the ACB are saved on the stack and the piggyback special kernel AST is delivered. Because the contents of the ACB were saved, it can be modified now to contain the address of the blocking AST. The special kernel mode AST routine loads offset LKB$L_AST with the address of the blocking AST routine (stored at offset LKB$L_BLKASTADR) and requeues the AST. When the special kernel mode AST routine exits, the completion AST routine is executed.

13.2.1.3   **Waiting Locks.** Before an incompatible lock can be placed on the waiting queue, the flag LKB$M_NOQUEUE is checked. If the flag is set, the lock is not queued and the failure return status SS$_NOTQUEUED is returned to the caller. If the flag is not set, the lock block is queued to the end of the waiting queue for the resource. The queue headers for the waiting queue are found at offsets RSB$L_WTQFL and RSB$L_WTQBL.

13.2.2   Lock Conversions

When a caller requests a lock conversion, the lock manager is passed the lock ID of the lock to be converted and the new lock mode for the conversion. The new lock mode is compared with the value of the group grant mode. If the new lock mode is compatible with the current granted locks, the lock is granted (see Section 13.2.1.1).

If the requested mode of the conversion is not compatible with the group grant mode, the requested lock mode is compared to the value of the conversion grant mode (stored at offset RSB$B_CGMODE). If the lock is compatible with the conversion grant mode, the lock is granted. If the lock is incompatible, it is placed at the tail of the conversion queue.

Most of the time the conversion grant mode contains the same value as the group grant mode. The only time the conversion grant mode is different from the group grant mode is when both of the following are true:

- The current lock mode of the lock at the head of the conversion queue is the most restrictive lock mode for the resource.
- That lock is the only lock at the current mode.

If both of these conditions are true, the granted lock mode of the lock on the conversion queue is omitted from the calculation of the conversion grant mode. The use of the conversion grant mode insures that lock conversions between incompatible lock modes will not block themselves.

Suppose that a resource has one lock in its granted queue at null (NL) mode. If a lock request is issued for the resource at protected write (PW) mode, the group grant mode is NL mode, so the PW mode lock is granted. When the new lock is granted, the group grant and conversion grant modes are recalculated; both equal PW mode.

Now the PW mode lock requests a conversion to exclusive (EX) mode. If the group grant mode was used to determine compatibility, the conversion to EX mode could not be granted, because the PW mode lock is actually blocking its own conversion (remember that group grant mode includes both the granted and conversion queues). However, the lock at the head of the conversion queue has the most restrictive lock mode currently granted. In calculating the conversion grant mode, the lock at the head of the conversion queue is omitted. Thus, the conversion grant mode is NL mode, and the conversion can be granted.

13.2.3   The $DEQ System Service

When making a call to the $DEQ system service, the caller passes the lock ID of the lock to be dequeued to the lock manager. The $DEQ system service uses the lock ID to locate the lock block and then verifies that the caller has the correct access mode and PID to access the lock. The resource block address in the lock block is used to locate the resource block. If the reference count in the lock block is zero, the lock block is dequeued from its current state queue and is deallocated. The lock manager then checks the state queue headers in the resource block to which the lock was queued. If all of the state queues in the resource block are empty and the reference count is zero, the resource block is removed from the hash chain and is deallocated.

If the resource block reference count is nonzero, the lock manager attempts to grant locks waiting on the conversion or waiting queues.

- The lock mode of the first lock in the conversion queue is compared with the conversion grant mode.

  —If the lock is incompatible, the $DEQ system service exits and returns control to the user.
  —If the lock is compatible, it is dequeued from the conversion queue and is granted.
  —When the lock is dequeued from the conversion queue, a new lock takes its place as the first lock on the conversion queue.

  This step is repeated for the new first entry in the conversion queue until either the conversion queue is emptied or an incompatible lock is found and the lock manager exits.

- If the conversion queue is emptied, the lock mode of the first lock in the waiting queue is compared against the group grant mode.

  —If the lock is incompatible, the $DEQ system service exits and returns control to the user.
  —If the lock is compatible, it is dequeued from the waiting queue and granted.
  —When the lock is dequeued from the waiting queue, a new lock takes its place as the first lock on the waiting queue.

  This step is repeated on the new first entry in the waiting queue until either the waiting queue is emptied, or an incompatible lock is found.

13.3   HANDLING DEADLOCKS

A deadlock occurs when several locks are waiting for each other in a circular fashion. The VAX/VMS lock manager resolves deadlocks by choosing a participant in the deadlock cycle (a lock request that is waiting on the conversion or waiting queue) and refusing that participant's lock request. The participant that is chosen to break the deadlock is termed the victim. The victim's lock or conversion request fails and the error status code SS$_DEADLOCK is returned in the victim's lock status block.

There are three parts to deadlock handling in the VAX/VMS lock manager.

- The lock manager suspects that a deadlock exists.
- A deadlock search proves that a deadlock actually exists.
- The victim is chosen.

13.3.1 Initiating a Deadlock Search

Because deadlock detection is a time-consuming task, it is not desirable to search for deadlocks every time a lock or conversion is requested. It is far better to search for a deadlock only when the system suspects that a deadlock exists. The VAX/VMS lock manager searches for a deadlock only when a process has been waiting for a resource for a specified amount of time. The SYSBOOT parameter DEADLOCK_WAIT specifies the amount of time to wait before initiating a deadlock search.

Whenever a lock is placed in the conversion or waiting queue, the lock block is also queued to the lock manager timeout queue (located by the global symbol LCK$GL_TIMOUTQ). The AST queue fields in the lock block are used to link the lock block into the timeout queue. When a lock must wait on the conversion or waiting queue, the value in DEADLOCK_WAIT is added to the current absolute system time (EXE$GL_ABSTIM), and the result is stored in the lock block at offset LKB$L_DUETIME. (LKB$L_DUETIME is actually a double use of the special kernel AST routine address field, LKB$L_KAST.)

Once every second, the VAX/VMS operating system executes the routine EXE$TIMEOUT. In addition to checking for device timeouts, this routine checks to see if the the first entry in the lock manager timeout queue has timed out. The value in LKB$L_DUETIME is compared with the absolute system time. If the due time has not been reached, the routine exits. However, if the due time has passed, a deadlock search is initiated.

13.3.2 Deadlock Detection

There are two separate forms of deadlock that can occur in the VAX/VMS lock manager. Each requires a different form of detection. One form (a conversion deadlock) is easily detected, because it is restricted to a single resource. Multiple resource deadlocks require a more complex search to locate.

13.3.2.1 Conversion Deadlocks. Conversion deadlocks occur when there are at least two locks in the conversion queue for a resource. When the requested mode

of the first lock in the conversion queue is incompatible with the granted mode of the second lock in the conversion queue, a deadlock exists.

For example, assume that there are two protected read (PR) mode locks on a resource. One PR mode lock requests a conversion to exclusive (EX) mode. Because PR mode is incompatible with EX mode, the conversion request must wait. While the first conversion request is waiting, the second PR mode lock also requests a conversion to EX mode. Now, the first lock will never get granted because its requested mode (EX) is incompatible with the second lock's granted mode (PR). The second conversion request will never get granted because it is waiting behind the first.

In detecting a conversion deadlock, the search begins with the lock block indicated by the lock manager timeout queue. The state queue backward link is used to locate the previous lock in the conversion queue. The granted mode of the previous lock is compared with the requested mode of the lock that timed out. If the modes are compatible, the previous lock in the conversion queue is located using the state queue backward link. The test is repeated until an incompatible lock is found or the beginning of the queue is found.

If an incompatible lock is found, a deadlock exists and a victim is selected (see Section 13.3.3). If the beginning of the queue is reached, a conversion deadlock does not exist, and a search for a multiple resource deadlock is initiated.

13.3.2.2 **Multiple Resource Deadlocks.** Multiple resource deadlocks occur when a circular list of processes are each waiting for one another on two or more resources.

For example, assume Process A locks Resource 1 and Process B locks Resource 2. Process A then requests a lock on Resource 2 that is incompatible with B's lock on resource 2, and thus, Process A must wait. Note that at this point, a circular list does not exist. When Process B then requests a lock on Resource 1 that is incompatible with A's lock on Resource 1, it must wait. A multiple resource deadlock now exists. Processes A and B are both waiting for each other to release different resources. These steps are shown in Figure 13-6. In the figure, locks that are blocking a resource (incompatible with waiting locks) are shown beneath the resource block; locks that are waiting on a resource are shown above the resource block.

This type of deadlock normally involves two or more resources, unless one process locks the same resource twice. (Usually a process will not lock the same resource twice; however, if the process is multithreaded, double locking may occur. Double locking also represents a multiple resource deadlock.)

To verify that a multiple resource deadlock exists, a recursive algorithm is used. The approach is summarized as follows:

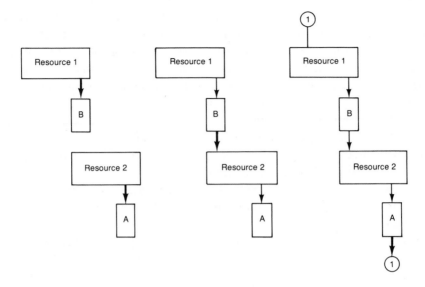

Figure 13-6
Example of a Deadlock Occurring

- A waiting lock will be waiting for locks owned by other processes.
- Any of the other processes might themselves have waiting locks.
- Those waiting locks will be waiting for locks owned by other blocking processes.

In implementation, the lock manager starts with the lock that timed out on the lock manager timeout queue. The address of the PCB associated with the lock that timed out is saved and the multiple resource deadlock routine (SEARCH_RESDLCK) is called. If a lock with the same owner PCB can be found blocking a resource, a deadlock exists.

Each time SEARCH_RESDLCK is called, a stack frame is pushed onto the stack. Each stack frame contains information on the current position in the search. Figure 13-7 shows the the contents of the stack frame.

Each call to SEARCH_RESDLCK specifies the address of a waiting lock block. The resource associated with the lock block is located and the resource state queues are searched for lock blocks whose granted or requested lock mode is incompatible with that of the waiting lock block. If an incompatible lock block is found, that lock is considered to be blocking the waiting lock block.

When a blocking lock is found, the owner PCB of the blocking lock is located. If the owner PCB is the same as the PCB of the lock that initiated the deadlock search, the list is proven to be circular and a deadlock exists. A victim is chosen (see Section 13.3.3 for details on victim selection), and dead-

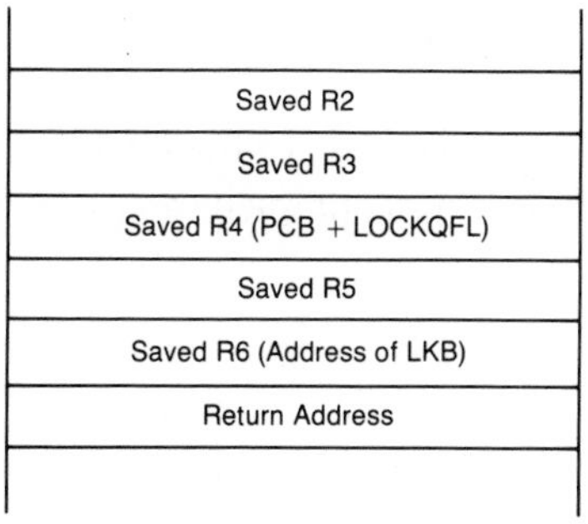

Saved R2
Saved R3
Saved R4 (PCB + LOCKQFL)
Saved R5
Saved R6 (Address of LKB)
Return Address

Figure 13-7
Stack Frame Built by the Lock Manager

lock detection returns control to EXE$TIMEOUT. If the PCB of the blocking lock is not the same as the saved PCB, another call is made to SEARCH_RESDLCK, specifying the address of the new blocking lock block.

Each time SEARCH_RESDLCK is called, it searches the state queues associated with the specified lock block, to see if the lock block is waiting on a resource.

When all the state queues for a given resource have been searched and no blocking lock has been found for that lock block, the routine removes the stack frame and returns control to its caller. If the caller itself was SEARCH_RESDLCK, the previous search for blocked locks on the resource can now be resumed.

A process bitmap is maintained by the VAX/VMS lock manager in order to reduce the number of repeated searches for blocking locks on a particular process. Each time a new blocking PCB is located, a bit corresponding to that process is set. If the bit for the PCB is set already, the search for locks blocking that process is terminated, because its locks have been searched already.

13.3.2.3   Unsuspected Deadlocks. Note that the use of the process bitmap speeds the location of the suspected deadlock, but prevents the accidental detection of unsuspected deadlocks. An unsuspected deadlock is one that exists within the lock management database, but has not been detected so far, because none of its locks have timed out on the lock manager timeout queue. This behavior is acceptable in the VAX/VMS lock manager for the following reasons:

- Deadlocks should be rare.
- Finding a process a second time in a deadlock search does not necessarily indicate that an unsuspected deadlock exists.
- The occurrence of unsuspected deadlocks should be rarer still.

- Any deadlock search that does not find a deadlock is a waste of processor time.
- The unsuspected deadlock will become a suspected deadlock when one of its own locks times out on the lock manager timeout queue and a deadlock search is initiated on its behalf.

Figure 13-8 shows two deadlocks. One deadlock is suspected and a search is in progress (the path with the heavy arrows); the other is unsuspected. This figure is an extension of the deadlock cycle shown in Figure 13-6. In this case, the deadlock search was initiated as a search for the locks blocking Process A. Because Process C is the first process found granted for Resource 2, it was the first lock that is investigated for participation in the deadlock cycle. Process C is waiting for Resource 3. The bit corresponding to Process C is set in the process bitmap. The context of the search is saved on the stack and SEARCH_RESDLCK is called to search for processes blocking Process C's lock.

Process D has a blocking lock on Resource 3. Process D is also waiting for Resource 2. The bit corresponding to Process D is set in the process bitmap. The context of the search is saved on the stack and SEARCH_RESDLCK is called to search for processes blocking Process D's lock. Process C has a blocking lock on Resource 2. This situation is a deadlock. However, because the bit corresponding to Process C was set in the process bitmap, the deadlock search for Process C is abandoned. One by one the stack frames are removed and the search whose context was saved continues. Eventually the

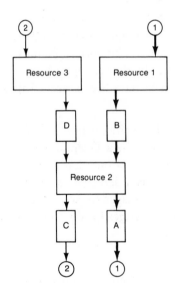

Figure 13-8
Suspected and Unsuspected Deadlocks

deadlock search will continue with locks blocking Resource 2 and the deadlock cycle of Processes A and B will be discovered.

Eventually one of the locks requested by Processes C and D will time out,
and a deadlock search will be initiated for that deadlock.

13.3.2.4   **Example of a Search for a Multiple Resource Deadlock.** Figure 13-9 shows a
series of locks that result in a deadlock. The heavy arrows in the figure show
the path of the deadlock cycle.

Assume that the lock owned by Process A timed out on the resource timer
queue. Process A is waiting for a lock on Resource 1. The deadlock search
routine saves Process A's PCB and calls SEARCH_RESDLCK, passing the
address of Process A's LKB.

The incompatible lock on Resource 1 is owned by Process C. Process C has
no other waiting locks, so SEARCH_RESDLCK moves on to the next incompatible lock. This lock is owned by Process D. When SEARCH_RESDLCK
follows the PCB queue for Process D, it finds that this process is waiting for a
lock on Resource 3.

SEARCH_RESDLCK calls itself, passing the address of the lock block
owned by process D. The new invocation of SEARCH_RESDLCK pushes a
stack frame detailing the position of the search on Resource 1, and
SEARCH_RESDLCK starts to search for locks on Resource 3 that are incompatible with Process D's lock. Resource 3 has two incompatible locks, owned

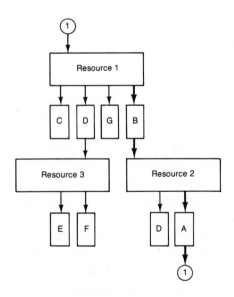

Figure 13-9
Example of a Multiple Resource Deadlock

261

by Processes E and F. Neither of these processes is waiting for a lock, so the search on Resource 3 terminates. The contents of the stack frame are restored and SEARCH_RESDLCK returns to its previous invocation. The search for processes blocking Process A resumes.

The next incompatible lock found on Resource 1 is owned by Process G. Process G has no waiting locks, so the search continues with Process B. The PCB queue for Process B shows that it is waiting for a lock on Resource 2.

Again, SEARCH_RESDLCK calls itself, passing the address of the lock block owned by Process B. The new invocation of SEARCH_RESDLCK pushes a new stack frame onto the stack, and SEARCH_RESDLCK finds that Process D owns a lock that is incompatible with the lock owned by process B. However, because locks owned by Process D have been searched already (the bit for Process D is set in the lock manager process bitmap), the search moves on to the next process.

The next incompatible lock is owned by Process A. Because the PCB address of Process A matches the PCB address that was saved initially, the list is proven to be circular and a deadlock exists. Now a victim must be chosen.

13.3.3   Victim Selection

Because conversion deadlocks involve only two processes, the victim selection routine simply chooses the process with the lower deadlock priority (stored in the PCB at offset PCB$L_DLCKPRI).

For multiple resource deadlocks, the victim selection routine is only slightly more complicated. The frames that were pushed onto the stack in each recursion into the deadlock location routine are searched for the lowest deadlock priority. Each time a lower deadlock priority value is found, the priority and the owner PCB are noted. If a deadlock priority of zero is found, that process is immediately chosen as the victim. When all frames have been searched, or a deadlock priority of zero is found, the stack pointer is restored and the process whose PCB had the lowest deadlock priority is chosen as the victim.

Note that the current implementation of the VAX/VMS operating system initializes the deadlock priority of all new processes to zero. Thus, it is not possible to assume which process will be chosen as the victim. With the current implementation, victim selection depends primarily on timing. However, other applications or implementations of the VAX/VMS operating system may use the deadlock priority to determine victim selection. If other applications need to use the deadlock priority scheme, they must write a privileged shareable image that accesses the PCB and loads a value into the deadlock priority field (PCB$L_DLCKPRI).

A last note on victim selection may be of interest to users intending to implement a binary victim selection. In this search, specific processes are always victims (their deadlock priority is zero); other processes are never selected as victims (their deadlock priority is always set to a predetermined value). If this victim selection scheme is used, the implementation must make sure that at least one process exists in a deadlock cycle that can be chosen as the victim to break the deadlock. Otherwise, the victim will be chosen at random.

PART IV/Memory Management

14 Memory Management Data Structures

> . . . but there's one great advantage in it, that one's memory
> works both ways.
> —The Queen in Lewis Carroll, *Through the Looking Glass*

Virtual memory support in the VAX/VMS operating system is implemented by several distinct pieces of the executive. The translation-not-valid fault handler (pager) is the exception service routine that responds to page faults and brings process virtual pages into memory on behalf of a process. The swapper process keeps the highest-priority computable processes in physical memory. In order to keep processes in memory, the swapper is responsible for shrinking process working set sizes and removing processes that are blocked for some reason in order to gain more pages of memory. Several system services allow a program to exercise some control over its behavior in memory while it is executing.

The system maintains many tables, some process-specific and others system-wide, that must be manipulated by the major components of the memory management subsystem. Before these components are described in the following chapters of this section, this chapter will describe the tables used by the components. The following structures are presented and described in this chapter:

- The process-specific data, found mostly in the process header.
- The data that is used to account for physical memory, the so-called PFN database.
- The special structures that are used for system and global pages.
- The structures that are required to keep track of processes in memory.
- The structures that are required to swap processes out of memory.
- The structures that are required to describe the page and swap files.
- The structures that support the MA780 shared memory.

14.1 PROCESS DATA STRUCTURES (PROCESS HEADER)

The most important process-specific data structures used by the memory management subsystem are contained in the process header (Figure 14-1). The process header contains all of the process-specific data that can be removed from memory when a process is outswapped. The address of the process header is stored in the software PCB.

267

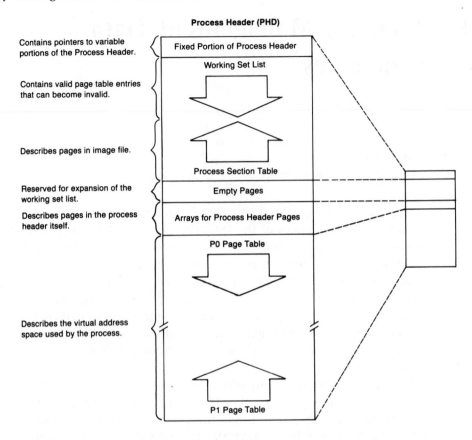

Process Header (PHD)

Contains pointers to variable portions of the Process Header.

Fixed Portion of Process Header

Working Set List

Contains valid page table entries that can become invalid.

Describes pages in image file.

Process Section Table

Reserved for expansion of the working set list.

Empty Pages

Describes pages in the process header itself.

Arrays for Process Header Pages

P0 Page Table

Describes the virtual address space used by the process.

P1 Page Table

Figure 14-1
Discrete Portions of the Process Header

Figure 14-1 shows the portions of the process header that are of special interest to memory management. Chapter 26 describes how the sizes of the pieces of the process header are related to SYSBOOT parameters. The smaller figure to the right of the process header shows the relative sizes of the portions of the process header on a typical system. The following pieces of the process header are of interest to this discussion:

- The P0 and P1 page tables are the largest contributors to the size of the process header and contain the complete description of the virtual address space currently being used by the process.
- The working set list describes the subset of process page table entries that are currently valid but can become invalid in the future. PFN-mapped pages and pages in shared memory are valid for the entire time that they are mapped and do not appear in the working set list.
- The process section table contains information used by the pager when a page resides in an image file.

- Because the sizes of the different pieces of the process header vary from system to system, there must be some method of determining where each piece is located. Pointers or indexes in the fixed portion of the process header serve this purpose. Process accounting information, some of which is used by the pager or the swapper, is also located in this area.
- There are several arrays that contain information about each process header page. This information is used by the swapper when it is necessary to outswap the process header.

14.1.1   Process Page Tables

The process page tables are the first memory management data structures encountered by either hardware or software. The contents of the page table entries are used by the hardware to translate a virtual address to its physical counterpart. When translation fails to determine the physical location of a page, the page table entries are used by the page fault handler to locate the invalid page.

Figure 14-2 shows the portion of the process header devoted to the P0 and P1 page tables. The figure also shows those fields in the fixed portion that are used to locate different pieces of the P0 or P1 page table.

- The P0 page table contains page table entries for all pages currently defined in P0 space. The number of pages in P0 space is stored in offset PHD$L_P0LR (and moved into PR$_P0LR by LDPCTX when the process is selected for execution). The virtual page number of the first unmapped page in P0 space (the index of the first nonexistent P0PTE) is stored at offset PHD$L_FREP0VA.
- In a similar manner, the P1 page table contains page table entries for the pages currently defined in P1 space. Like P1 space itself, the P1 page table grows toward smaller addresses. To simplify the address translation logic, the P1 base register contains the virtual address of the page table entry that would map virtual address 40000000. The P1 length register contains the number of P1 page table entries that do not exist. The virtual page number of the high address end of the unmapped portion of P1 space (Figure 14-2) is stored at offset PHD$L_FREP1VA.
- The number of page table entries available for the expansion of either P0 space or P1 space is stored in offset PHD$L_FREPTECNT. The number of entries here depends on the SYSBOOT parameter VIRTUALPAGECNT, minus the current sizes of the P0 and P1 page tables.

When a process references a virtual address that is not valid, it incurs a page fault, an exception that transfers control to the page fault handler. One of the exception-specific parameters pushed onto the stack by the page fault handler is the invalid virtual address. This address enables the pager to retrieve the

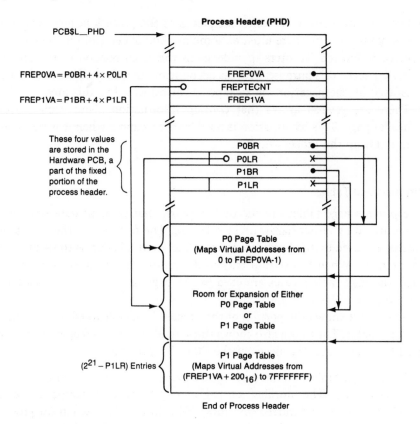

Figure 14-2
Process Page Tables

page table entry for the invalid page in order to determine where the page is located.

The page table entries for invalid pages are set up in such a way that they contain either the location of the page or a pointer to further information about the page. Figure 14-3 shows the different forms that an invalid page table entry can take. A valid page table entry is included for comparison. Notice that bits <31> (valid bit), <30:27> (protection code), and <24:23> (owner access mode) have the same meaning in all possible forms of page table entry. Table 14-1 lists the symbolic and numeric forms of possible protection codes.

The pager uses bits <26> and <22> in the invalid page table entry to distinguish the different PTE forms. (Because protection checks are made before the valid bit is checked, PTE <30:27> must contain a protection code, even when the valid bit is clear.) The various forms are described in the following paragraphs, starting with the entry at the bottom of the figure.

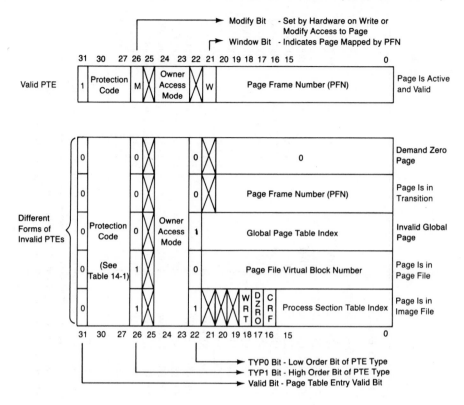

Figure 14-3
Different Forms of Page Table Entry

14.1.1.1   **Process Section Table Index.** When a page is located in an image file, the page table entry contains an index into the process section table. This index locates a process section table entry, which contains information about where the image file is located and which block in the image file contains the faulting page. Control bits in the process section table entry indicate whether the section is a global section <0> (process section table entries always have this bit clear), whether it is writeable <3>, and whether the section is copy on reference <1>. Process section tables are discussed in Section 14.1.3 and further in Chapter 15.

14.1.1.2   **Page File Virtual Block Number.** When a virtual page resides in a page file, its associated page table entry contains the virtual block number within the page file where the page is located. The page file that is used by this process is indicated by the field PHD$B_PAGFIL in the process header. PHD$L_ PAGFIL, a longword field that contains zero in its low-order three bytes and overlaps PHD$B_PAGFIL in the high-order byte, is a skeleton for any page table entry that acquires a page file backing store address. A virtual block

271

Table 14-1: Memory Access Protection Codes in Page Table Entries

Protection	SYMBOL = binary value	Protection Mask
No Access Allowed	PRT$C_NA = 0000	PTE$C_NA = 00000000
Reserved	PRT$C_RESERVED = 0001	
Kernel Write (Kernel Read)	PRT$C_KW = 0010	PTE$C_KW = 10000000
Kernel Read (No Write)	PRT$C_KR = 0011	PTE$C_KR = 18000000
User Write (User Read)	PRT$C_UW = 0100	PTE$C_UW = 20000000
Executive Write (Executive Read)	PRT$C_EW = 0101	PTE$C_EW = 28000000
Executive Read, Kernel Write	PRT$C_ERKW = 0110	PTE$C_ERKW = 30000000
Executive Read (No Write)	PRT$C_ER = 0111	PTE$C_ER = 38000000
Supervisor Write (Supervisor Read)	PRT$C_SW = 1000	PTE$C_SW = 40000000
Supervisor Read, Executive Write	PRT$C_SREW = 1001	PTE$C_SREW = 48000000
Supervisor Read, Kernel Write	PRT$C_SRKW = 1010	PTE$C_SRKW = 50000000
Supervisor Read (No Write)	PRT$C_SR = 1011	PTE$C_SR = 58000000
User Read, Supervisor Write	PRT$C_URSW = 1100	PTE$C_URSW = 60000000
User Read, Executive Write	PRT$C_UREW = 1101	PTE$C_UREW = 68000000
User Read, Kernel Write	PRT$C_URKW = 1110	PTE$C_URKW = 70000000
User Read (No Write)	PRT$C_UR = 1111	PTE$C_UR = 78000000

Note that the following rules govern memory access protection:

- If a given access mode has write access to a specific page, then that access mode also has read access to that page.
- If a given access mode can read a specific page, then all more privileged access modes can read the same page.
- If a given access mode can write a specific page, then all more privileged access modes can write the same page.

Access that is implied (rather than explicitly a part of the symbolic protection name) is included in parentheses.

number of zero indicates that a block in the page file will exist for the page, but has not yet been reserved.

14.1.1.3   **Global Page Table Index.** An invalid process page mapped to a global page contains an index into the global page table, where an associated global page table entry contains further information used to locate the page. The global page table is described in Section 14.3. Page faults involving global pages are discussed in Chapter 17.

14.1.1.4   **Page in Transition.** There are several different situations where a virtual page can be associated with a physical page, and yet the page is not valid, not in the process working set. For example, when a page is removed from a process working set, it is not discarded but put on the free page list or modified page list. Such a page is called a transition page. The process page table entry contains a PFN, but the valid bit is clear. The two type bits (PTE<26> and PTE<22>) are also clear.

Transition pages are described by the entries for the physical page found in the PFN database (see Section 14.2). In particular, the PFN STATE array designates the particular transition state the physical page is in.

14.1.1.5   **Demand Zero Pages.** A special form of the transition page table entry format has a zero in the PFN field. This zero indicates a special form of page called a demand-allocate zero-fill page or demand zero page for short. When a page fault occurs for such a page, the pager allocates a physical page, fills the page with zeros, inserts the PFN into the PTE, sets the valid bit, and dismisses the exception. (For this reason, and a second reason explained in Section 14.2.5, physical page zero cannot be used by memory management.)

14.1.2   **Working Set List**

The working set list contains the subset of a process's page table entries that are currently valid. The working set list is used by the pager and swapper to determine which virtual page to discard (to mark invalid) when it is necessary to take a physical page away from the process. The swapper also uses the working set list to determine which virtual pages need to be written to the swap file when the process is outswapped.

Figure 14-4 shows the working set list in the process header and the various fields in the fixed portion that locate different pieces of the list. Each of these fields, including the quota fields, contains a longword index (multiply contents by four or use context index addressing) to the working set list entry in question.

14.1.2.1   **Division of the Working Set List.** The working set list consists of three pieces: the permanently locked portion of the working set list, the pages that are

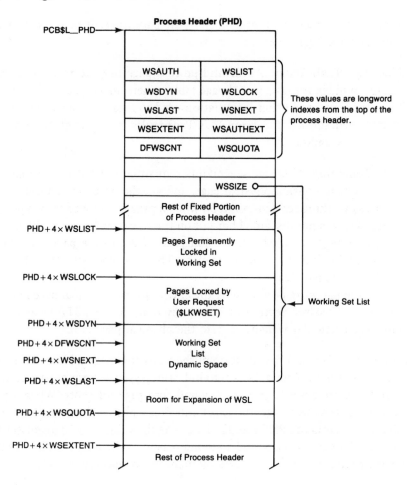

Figure 14-4
Working Set List

locked by user request, and the dynamic portion of the working set. The quota fields in the fixed portion of the process header determine how large the working set list may grow in response to different working set size adjustments. The contents of the three pieces are as follows:

- The permanently locked portion of the working set list (from WSLIST to WSLOCK) contains the pages that are forever a part of the process working set. These include the following structures:

  —The kernel stack.
  —The P1 pointer page.
  —The P1 page table page that maps the kernel stack and the P1 pointer page.
  —The P1 page table page that maps the P1 window to the process header.
  —The process header pages that are not page table pages. These include

274

the fixed portion, the working set list, the process section table, and the process header page arrays.

- The portion of the working set list between WSLOCK and WSDYN contains all pages that are locked by user request, specifically with the Lock Pages in Working Set or Lock Pages in Memory system services.
- The dynamic portion of the working set list is the portion that is used for page replacement. It is delimited by WSDYN and WSEXTENT. The entry that was just put into the table is pointed to by WSNEXT. The replacement algorithm, explained in detail in Chapter 15, is a modified first-in/first-out scheme.

The current size of the working set list is WSSIZE. The actual number of pages that a process is currently occupying is the sum of the process private page count (PCB$W_PPGCNT) and the global page count (PCB$W_GPGCNT).

Normally, the maximum size to which the working set can grow is WSQUOTA. However, if there are more than BORROWLIM pages on the free page list, the working set list can be extended up to WSEXTENT (at quantum end). If there are more than GROWLIM pages on the free page list, pages can be added to a process's working set above WSQUOTA (on resolution of a page fault). WSQUOTA can be altered in interactive and batch jobs by the SET WORKING_SET/QUOTA command. Part of the image reset logic, invoked at image exit, resets the end of the working set list to DFWSCNT. The meanings of the various working set list quotas and limits are summarized in Table 16-1.

The format of a working set list entry (WSLE) is shown in Figure 14-5. Notice that the virtual page number is contained in the upper 23 bits, in the same location that virtual page numbers are found in virtual addresses. The placement of the virtual page number allows the WSLE to be passed to several utility routines as a virtual address, where the byte offset bits (WSLE control bits) are not looked at. The meanings of the various control bits are as follows:

<0>   When the WSL Entry Valid bit is clear, the working set list entry can be used without removing a page from the working set.

<1:3>   The Page Type field (a duplicate of the contents of the PFN TYPE array) distinguishes pages that require different action when removed from a process working set.

<4>   The Page Locked in Memory bit indicates that this page is locked into physical memory with the Lock Pages in Memory system service. Such pages are also locked into the process working set. (The working set lock bit is not set but the WSLEs are moved into the portion of the working set list that contains pages locked by user request.)

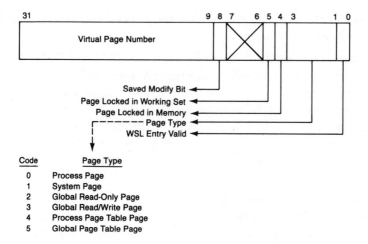

Figure 14-5
Format of Working Set List Entry

<5>   The Page Locked in Working Set bit indicates those pages
that are permanently or dynamically locked into the process
working set. The only pages that can be dynamically locked
are page table pages that map currently valid pages. (Pages
that are permanently locked or locked into the working set
by user request also have this bit set in their working set list
entries.)

<8>   The Saved Modify bit in the WSLE is used when the process
is outswapped to record the logical OR of the modify bit in
the page table entry and the saved modify bit in the PFN
STATE array.

14.1.3   Process Section Table

The process section table contains process section table entries (PSTEs).
PSTEs are data structures used to locate image sections within image files.
The location of the process section table within the process header is pictured in Figure 14-6. Offset PHD$L_PSTBASOFF contains the byte offset to
the bottom of the process section table. All process section table entries
within the table are then located through negative longword indexes from the
bottom of the PST.

The PSTEs are maintained in two doubly linked lists. One list of PSTEs
contains those that are in use. The negative index PHD$W_PSTLAST points
to the most recent addition to the in-use list. Figure 14-6 shows a hypotheti-
cal list of free and allocated PSTEs; the allocated PSTEs are shaded. When a
section is deallocated, the PSTE that mapped the section is placed on a free
list so that it can be reused. The negative index PHD$W_PSTFREE points to

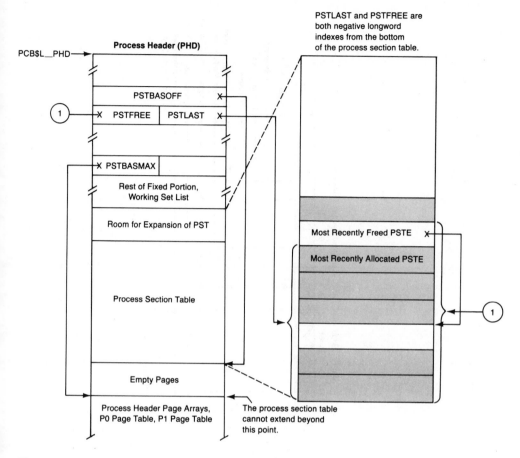

Figure 14-6
Process Section Table

the most recent addition to the free list. The first longword in the PSTEs on the free list contains a negative index that can be used to find the previous element on the free list. When sections are created, the allocation routine for PSTEs first checks the free list. If there are no free PSTEs, a new PSTE is created from the expansion region between the working set list and the PST.

When it is necessary to expand the working set list into the area already occupied by the process section table, space is allocated from the empty page area (if it exists). Then the entire PST is moved into the allocated space and a new value of PSTBASOFF is inserted into the fixed portion of the process header. All other references to individual process section table entries are unaffected by this change. For more information on expansion of the working set list see Chapter 15.

The format of a process section table entry is pictured in Figure 14-7. The following steps are used to locate a block in an image file:

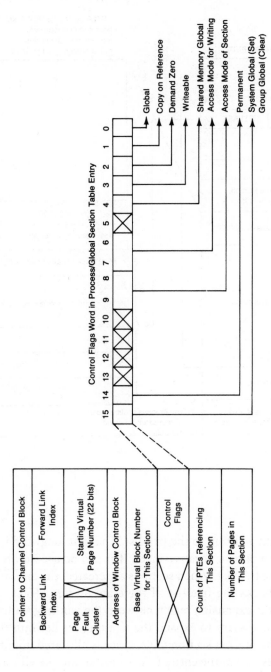

Figure 14-7
Layout of Process Section Table Entry

1. The WCB address points to the window control block for the image file. The WCB contains the mapping information that relates virtual block numbers in a file to logical block numbers on a volume.
2. The starting virtual page number for the section, when subtracted from the virtual page number of the faulting page, gives the page offset into the section.
3. The starting virtual block number of the section is added to the difference computed in step 2 to give the virtual block number of the faulting page within the image file.

14.1.4   Process Header Page Arrays

When a process header is outswapped, some information about each process header page must be stored in the outswapped process header. The process header page array portion of the process header provides an area where this information can be stored (Figure 14-8). Two of the arrays, the BAK array and the WSLX array, save information from the PFN database about each process header page in the working set. The other two arrays (locked WSLE count and valid WSLE count) keep statistics about each page table page. These four arrays are described in greater detail in Chapter 17.

14.2   PFN DATABASE

The memory management data structures include information about the available pages of physical memory. The fact that this information must be available while the page is being used prevents this information from being stored in the page itself. In addition, the caching strategy of the free page list and modified page list requires physical page information to be available even when pages are not currently active and valid. A portion of the nonpaged executive is set aside for this accounting data, called the PFN database.

The PFN database, unlike many of the other executive data structures, is not a table-oriented structure. Rather, the same item of information about all physical pages is stored in successive elements of an array (see Figure 14-9). The page frame number is then used as an index into each array. Table 14-2 lists each item of information in the PFN database, including the global name of the pointer to the beginning of each array.

14.2.1   PTE Array

When a physical page is assigned to another use, the pager must be able to find the PTE that maps the page. The PFN PTE longword array contains the system virtual address of the page table entry that maps each physical page.

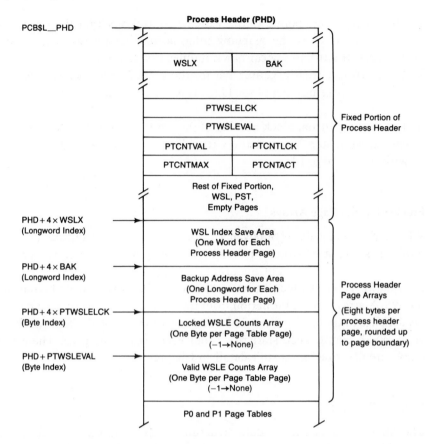

Figure 14-8
Process Header Page Arrays

PFN PTE array elements for global pages point to the global page table entries.

14.2.2   BAK Array

The PFN BAK longword array stores the original contents of the PTEs. When a physical page is assigned to another use, all links with the PTE that currently maps the page must be broken. The PTE is set to indicate where the contents of the page can be obtained the next time that they are needed. The BAK array element contains the information that goes back into the PTE. The PFN PTE array element is used to locate the PTE that must be altered. Figure 14-10 shows the possible contents of a PFN BAK array element. In terms of page table entry contents (see Figure 14-3), the only forms of PTE that can go into the BAK array are a process section table index or a page file virtual block number.

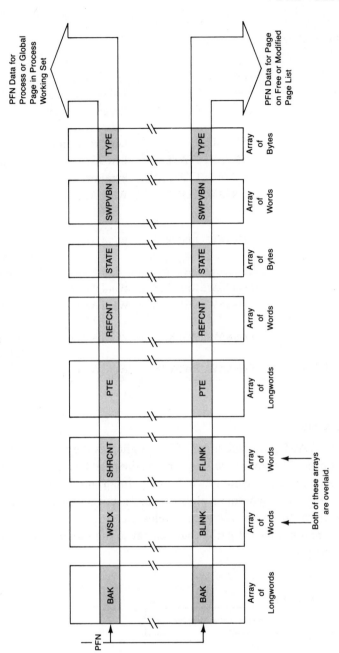

Figure 14-9
PFN Database Arrays

281

Table 14-2: PFN Database Arrays

Array Element Contents	*Global Address of Pointer to Start of Array*	*Size of Array Element*	*Comment*
System Virtual Address of Page Table Entry	PFN$AL_PTE	Longword Array	
Backing Store Address	PFN$AL_BAK	Longword Array	(Figure 14-10)
Physical Page State	PFN$AB_STATE	Byte Array	(Figure 14-11)
Page Type	PFN$AB_TYPE	Byte Array	(Figure 14-12)
Forward Link	PFN$AW_FLINK	Word Array	(Figure 14-13) Overlays the SHRCNT array
Backward Link	PFN$AW_BLINK	Word Array	(Figure 14-13) Overlays the WSLX Array
Reference Count	PFN$AW_REFCNT	Word Array	
Global Share Count	PFN$AW_SHRCNT	Word Array	Overlays the FLINK Array
Working Set List Index	PFN$AW_WSLX	Word Array	Overlays the BLINK Array
Swap File Virtual Block Number	PFN$AW_SWPVBN	Word Array	

14.2.3   STATE Array

The PFN STATE array (see Figure 14-11) indicates the physical state of each physical page. The low three bits contain the page location code. The upper bit in a STATE array element is extremely important. It is the setting of this bit that determines whether a physical page is put on the free page list or the modified page list when the page is released.

There are a number of paths that can cause the modify bit in the STATE array to be set.

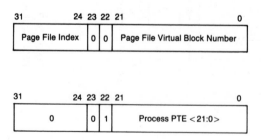

Figure 14-10
Possible Contents of PFN BAK Array Element

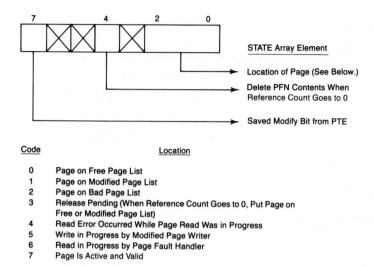

Figure 14-11
Contents of PFN STATE Array Element

- When a page is removed from a process working set, the modify bit in the page table entry is logically ORed into the saved modify bit in the STATE array.
- When pages are to be used as read buffers in direct I/O, the executive routine that locks down pages (IOLOCK) sets the modify bit in the PTE. When the page is removed from the process's working set, the OR operation will cause the bit to be set in the PFN STATE array.
- When copy-on-reference pages are faulted into a process's working set, the modify bit in the STATE array is set. The set bit forces a write to the page file when the page is removed from the process working set.

The delete bit in the PFN STATE array element affects physical page contents. When the reference count of a physical page goes to zero, all ties with a virtual page (PFN PTE array contents) are destroyed. The physical page is then put at the front of the free page list where it will be reused as quickly as possible.

14.2.4   TYPE Array

The PFN TYPE array (see Figure 14-12) distinguishes the different types of valid pages. The reason for this distinction is that either the pager or swapper must take different action depending on what type of page is being acted on. The collided page bit in the TYPE array element is set when a page fault occurs while the page is already being read in from its backing store address. Collided pages are described briefly in Chapter 17.

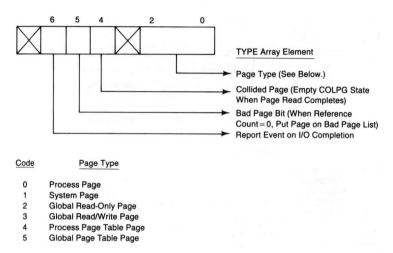

Code	Page Type
0	Process Page
1	System Page
2	Global Read-Only Page
3	Global Read/Write Page
4	Process Page Table Page
5	Global Page Table Page

Figure 14-12
Contents of PFN TYPE Array Element

14.2.5 Forward and Backward Links

The three page lists (free page list, modified page list, and bad page list) must all be doubly linked lists because an arbitrary page is often removed from the middle of the list. However, the links cannot exist in the pages themselves because the original contents of each page must be preserved. Two word arrays, the FLINK array and the BLINK array, contain elements that are interpreted as the physical page numbers of the successor and predecessor to a given physical page.

A zero in one of the link fields indicates the end of the list (and is not a pointer to physical page zero). For this reason, physical page zero cannot be used in any dynamic function by the VMS operating system but may be mapped by some system virtual page that is always resident. The usual contents of physical page zero are the restart parameter block (see Chapter 24).

Figure 14-13 shows an example of pages on the free list, along with the corresponding FLINK and BLINK array elements. The STATE array elements for all of these pages contain zero, indicating that the physical pages are on the free page list.

14.2.6 REFCNT Array

The PFN REFCNT array counts the number of reasons why a page should not be put on the free or modified page list. One reason for incrementing the reference count is that a page is in a process working set. Pages are locked down for direct I/O by incrementing the reference count.

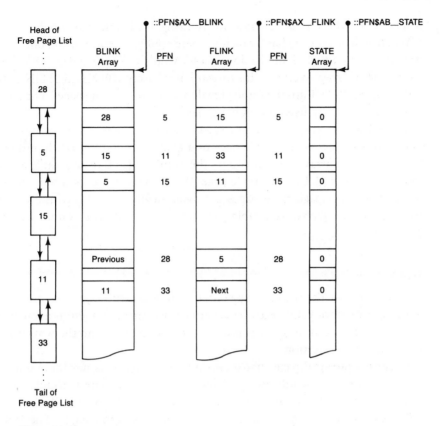

Figure 14-13
Example of Free Page List Showing Linkage Method

I/O completion and working set replacement use the same routine to dec-rement the reference count. If the reference count goes to zero, the physical page is released to the free or modified page list as indicated by the saved modify bit in the PFN STATE array. Manipulations of the reference count are illustrated in the discussion of paging dynamics in Chapter 17.

14.2.7   SHRCNT Array

A second form of reference count is kept for global pages. The PFN SHRCNT array counts the number of process page table entries that are mapped to a particular global page. When the SHRCNT for a particular page goes from zero to one, the reference count is incremented. Further additions to the share count do not affect the reference count.

As the global page is removed from the working set of each process mapped to the page, the share count is decremented. When the share count finally

285

reaches zero, the reference count for the page is also decremented.

When a physical page has a nonzero share count, it cannot be on one of the page lists. The forward and backward link words are not needed. The global share count array overlays the forward link array. (PFN$AX_FLINK and PFN$AX_SHRCNT are the same global location in system space.) The global share count is only used for global pages.

The SHRCNT array is used for a second purpose when the physical page in question is a process page table page or a global page table page. In either of these cases, the array element counts the number of active page table entries in the process or global page table page. When this value passes from zero to nonzero, process page table pages are dynamically locked into the process working set and global page table pages are locked into the system working set.

14.2.8   WSLX Array

The working set list index array contains an index into a process or system working set list for valid pages. The content of an array element is a longword index from the beginning of the process (or system) header to the working set list element in question.

Because a physical page that is in some working set is not on one of the page lists, the link words are available for other uses. The working set list index array overlays the backward link array. (PFN$AX_BLINK and PFN$AX_WSLX are the same global location in system space.) The WSLX array is not used for global pages.

14.2.9   SWPVBN Array

The swap virtual block number array is used to support the outswap of a process with I/O in progress. When such an outswap occurs, the virtual block number in the swap file where the locked-down page would go is recorded in the SWPVBN array. The modified page writer checks this array for nonzero contents and, if they are nonzero, diverts the page from its normal backing store address to the designated block in the swap file.

14.3   DATA STRUCTURES FOR GLOBAL PAGES

The treatment of global pages is not much different from that of process private pages. However, the system is required to keep some system-wide database of the various global pages in the system.

14.3.1   Global Section Descriptor

When a global section is created, a structure called a global section descriptor (GSD) is allocated from paged dynamic memory and loaded with information

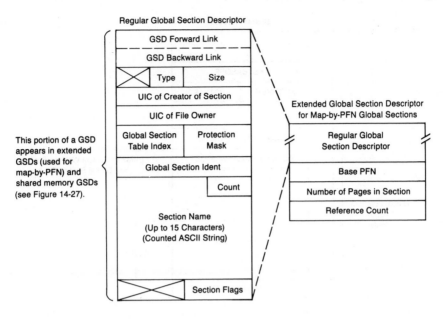

Figure 14-14
Layout of Global Section Descriptor

that describes the section (see Figure 14-14). The information about the section stored in the GSD is only used when the section is created or deleted, or when some process attempts to map to the section. The pager does not use this data structure.

The GSD is linked into one of two GSD lists maintained by the system. All system global sections are put into one list; group global sections (independent of group number) are put into the other list. The global section table index field of the GSD contains an index that allows a second structure (called a global section table entry) to be located.

14.3.2   The System Header and Global Section Table Entries

The system maintains two data structures for itself that parallel structures maintained for each process in the system. The system PCB and system header are used by the pager to allow page faults of system pages to be treated almost identically to page faults for process pages.

The system header (see Figure 14-15) contains the working set list that governs page replacement for system pages. The section table area in the system header contains section table entries for the image files that contain pageable system pages. These include the executive image (SYS.EXE), the record management services image (RMS.EXE), and the system message file (SYSMSG.EXE).

287

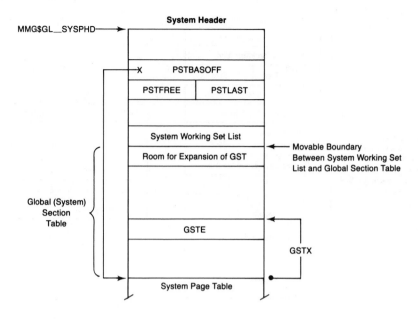

Figure 14-15
The System Header Containing the System Working Set
List and the Global Section Table

The section table area in the system header serves a second purpose. When a global section is created, a section table entry that describes the global image file is created. The new section table entry is placed into an area of the system header called the global section table. The format of a global section table entry (see Figure 14-16) is nearly identical to the format of a process section table entry. The only difference is that the first longword points to the global section descriptor (instead of the channel control block).

Global section table entries are accessed in exactly the same way as process section table entries, with a negative longword index from the bottom of the global section table. The global section table index in the global section descriptor is such an index, associating a GSTE with a GSD.

14.3.3 Global Page Table Entries

A third set of data is also created for each global section. Each page in the global section is described by a global page table entry in the global page table (see Figure 14-17). The pager uses global page table entries just like process page table entries to locate global pages.

Global page table entries are restricted to a subset of the forms illustrated in Figure 14-3.

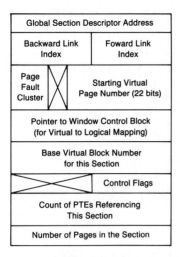

Figure 14-16
Layout of Global or System Section Table Entry (Global
Page Table Entries)

- The global page table entry can be valid, indicating that the global page is in at least one process working set.
- The global page table entry can indicate a demand zero page. Global demand zero pages are used to initialize global page file sections.
- The global page table entry can indicate some transition state. The PFN STATE array indicates which transition state is involved in the usual way.
- The global page can be in a global image file, in which case the global page table entry contains a global section table index.

14.3.4   Global Page Table and System Page Table

Global page table entries are located in exactly the same manner as process or system page table entries. Location MMG$GL_GPTBASE contains the address of the base of the global page table. All references to global page table entries use what can be thought of as a virtual page number as an index into the global page table.

The interesting thing to note about this approach is that the base of the global page table coincides with the base of the system page table. Further, the virtual page numbers that are used as indexes into the global page table are system virtual page numbers. In fact, when looking at system virtual address space, the global page table simply appears as an extension to the system page table. The global page table index associated with the first global

289

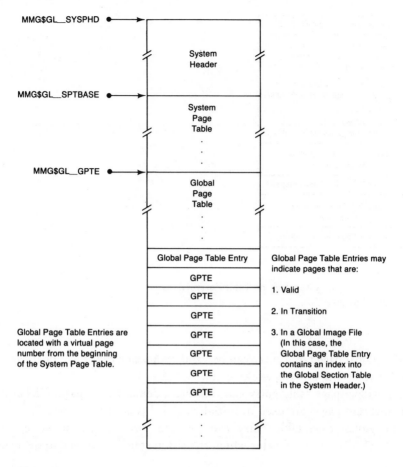

Figure 14-17
Location of Global Page Table at Virtual End of System
Page Table

page is one greater than the largest system virtual page number for a given configuration.

This logical extension of the system page table exists only when looking at system virtual address space. The global page table does not exist in physical pages adjacent to the system page table. The system length register only records the number of real system page table entries, not the logical extensions. In other words, global pages are not mapped into system virtual address space and are not accessible through system virtual addresses. This pseudoextension to the system page table is only available to the software routines in the memory management subsystem.

Figure 14-18 shows how the global page table relates to the system page

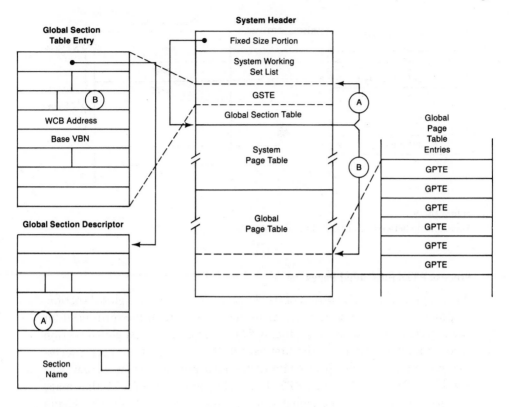

Figure 14-18
Relationships among Global Section Data Structures

table. It also shows the relationship among the global section descriptor, the global section table entry, and the global page table entries for a given section. There are several relationships among these three structures.

- The central structure is the global section table entry (see Figure 14-16 The first longword in the GSTE points to the global section descriptor.
- The virtual page number field (labeled (B) in Figure 14-18) contains the pseudo system virtual page number that serves as a longword index to the first global page table entry that maps this section.
- The global section descriptor contains a global section table index (labeled (A) in the figure) that allows the GSTE to be located from the GSD.
- The original form of each global page table entry is a section table index (identical to the GSTX found in the global section descriptor), effectively pointing to the GSTE. When any given GPTE is either valid or in transition, the GSTX is stored in the PFN BAK array. Note that GPTEs for global page file sections contain the page file backing store address.

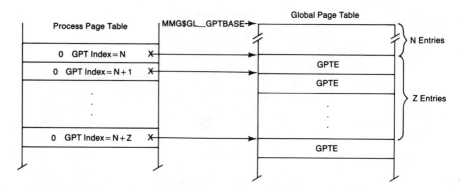

Figure 14-19
Relationship between Process PTEs and Global PTEs

14.3.5   Process PTEs for Global Pages

When a process maps a portion of its virtual address space to a global section, its process page table entries that map the section are in the form used for global page table indexes. The process PTE that maps the first global section page contains the GPTX of the first page in the global section. Each successive process page table entry contains the next pseudo system virtual page number (GPTX), so that each PTE effectively points to the GPTE that maps that particular page in the global section. This concept is shown in Figure 14-19. Assume that the section shown in the figure contains Z number of pages.

Figure 14-3 shows the possible forms for process page table entries.

All of the data structures associated with global sections will be described in detail in Chapter 17 where page faults for global pages are discussed. The initial allocation of these structures is briefly described along with the Create and Map Section and Map Global Section system services in Section 16.3.1.

14.4   SWAPPING DATA STRUCTURES

There are three data structures that are used primarily by the swapper but indirectly by the pager. The SYSBOOT parameter BALSETCNT determines the maximum number of concurrently resident processes. In particular, it determines the amount of system address space set aside for process headers.

14.4.1   Balance Slots

When the system is initialized, an amount of virtual address space equal to the size of a process header times BALSETCNT is allocated exclusively for process headers (see Figure 14-20). Each of these process header areas is called

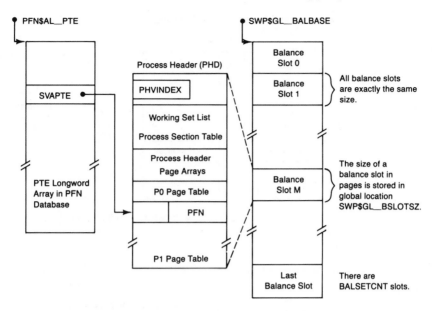

Figure 14-20
Balance Slots Contain Process Headers

a balance slot. The location of the first balance slot is stored in global location SWP$GL_BALBASE. The size of a process header (in pages) is stored in global location SWP$GL_BSLOTSZ. The calculations that are performed by SYSBOOT to determine the size of the process header are described in Chapter 26.

14.4.2 Balance Slot Arrays

The system maintains two word arrays describing each process with a process header stored in a balance slot (see Figure 14-21). Both of the word arrays are indexed by the balance slot number occupied by the resident process. The balance slot number is stored in the fixed portion of the process header at offset PHD$W_PHVINDEX. Entries in the first array contain the number of references to each process header; entries in the second array contain an index into a longword array that points to the process control block for each process header.

The entries in the reference count array (based at the global pointer PHV$GL_REFCBAS) count the number of reasons why the process header cannot be removed from memory. Specifically, this array element counts the number of page table pages that contain either valid or transition PTEs.

The entries in the process index array (based at the global pointer PHV$GL_PIXBAS) contain an index into the longword array based at the

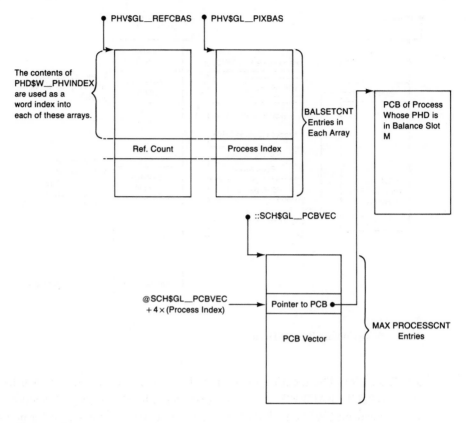

Figure 14-21
Process Header Vector Arrays

global pointer SCH$GL_PCBVEC. The entries in the longword array contain pointers to the process control blocks of the processes with a process header in a balance slot. Figure 14-21 illustrates how the executive turns the address of a process header into the address of the PCB for that process, using the entry in the process index array.

If the process header address is known, the balance slot index can be calculated (as described in the next section). By using this as a word index into the process index array, the longword index into the PCB vector is found. The array element in the PCB vector is the address of the PCB (whose PCB$L_PHD entry points back to the process header). A more detailed description of the PCB vector can be found in Chapter 20, where its use by the Create Process system service is discussed.

14.4.3 Comment on Equal-Size Balance Slots

The choice of equal-size balance slots, at first sight seemingly inefficient, has some subtle benefits to portions of the memory management subsystem.

There are several instances, most notably within the modified page writer, when it is necessary to obtain a process header address from a physical page's page frame number (PFN). With fixed size balance slots, this operation is straightforward.

The contents of the PFN PTE array point to a page table entry somewhere in the balance slot area. Subtracting the contents of SWP$GL_BALBASE from the PFN PTE array contents and dividing the result by the size of a balance slot (the size of a process header) in bytes produces the balance slot index. If this index is multiplied by the size of the process header in bytes and added to the contents of SWP$GL_BALBASE, the final result is the address of the process header that contains the page table entry that maps the physical page in question.

14.5   DATA STRUCTURES THAT DESCRIBE THE PAGE AND SWAP FILES

Page and swap files are used by the memory management subsystem to save physical page contents or process working sets. Page files are used to save the contents of modified pages that are not in physical memory. Both the swap and page files are used to save the working sets of processes that are not in the balance set.

14.5.1   Structure of Page and Swap Files

Figure 14-22 illustrates the data structures used to access page and swap files. Location MMG$GL_PAGSWPVC contains the address of an array of long-word pointers, called the page and swap file vector. The number of pointers in the array is the maximum number of page and swap files allowed on the system (SYSGEN parameters SWPFILCNT and PAGFILCNT) plus one.

INIT initializes the page and swap file vector and loads the pointers with the address of a null page file control block. The first pointer in the array is loaded with the address of the page file control block for the shell process. When SYSINIT initializes the primary page file control blocks, the pointer located by the index SWPFILCNT+1 is redirected to the control block for the primary page file (SYS$SYSTEM:PAGEFILE.SYS).

The second pointer in the page and swap file vector is redirected to point to the control block for the primary swap file (SYS$SYSTEM:SWAPFILE.SYS). If there is no swap file, or if the value of the SYSGEN parameter SWPFILCNT equals zero, this pointer is not redirected. In this case all swap operations are performed to the primary page file.

The page file control blocks and pointers for the alternate page and swap files are created by SYSGEN.

Page file control blocks are used to describe both page and swap files. When

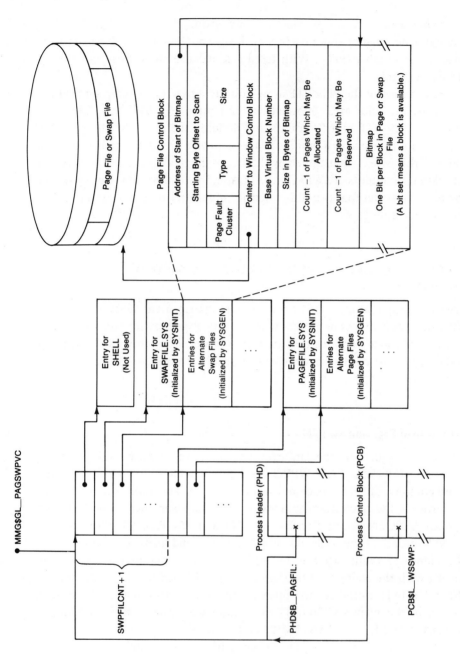

Figure 14-22
Page and Swap File Database

the SYSINIT process initializes the page file control blocks for the primary page and swap files, the following operations are performed:

1. The file is opened.
2. The address of the window control block is stored in the control block.
3. The page file bitmap is allocated from nonpaged pool and initialized to all bits set.
4. The address of the control block is stored in the appropriate location in the page and swap file vector.

The SYSINIT process is described in more detail in Chapter 25.

Note that the locations of the window control block field, the virtual block number field, and the page fault cluster factor field are in the same relative offsets in these structures as they are in a section table entry. Because the offsets are the same, I/O requests can be processed by common code, independent of the data structure that describes the file being read or written.

When any page or swap file is opened, all mapping information for the file is copied into the window control block. These so-called cathedral windows insure that the memory management subsystem does not have to take a window turn (see Section 19.1.4), which could lead to system deadlock.

14.5.2   The Shell Process

The first longword in the page and swap file vector points to the control block for the shell process. This control block is initialized by the module INIT (see Chapter 25) and contains the starting VBN of the shell process and the system window control block. This information is used in process creation to read copies of the shell process into the system. When INIT initializes the shell control block, it adds one to the value of the SYSGEN parameter SWPFILCNT and stores the result in the global location SGN$GW_SWPFILCT. For more information on the shell process, see Chapter 20.

14.5.3   Structure of Swap Files

When a process is created, it is assigned a swap space within the swap or page file. This swap space contains room for the process header and the process body (the P0 and P1 pages belonging to the process). The initial size of the swap space is equal to the value of the SYSGEN parameter MPW_WRTCLUSTER. If the value of MPW_WRTCLUSTER is less than the size of the shell process, the initial size of the swap space is set to the size of the shell (16 pages). This initial swap space size insures that a system being bootstrapped can create processes. The structure of swap spaces is illustrated by Figure 14-23.

If a process's working set list grows so that it no longer fits its swap space,

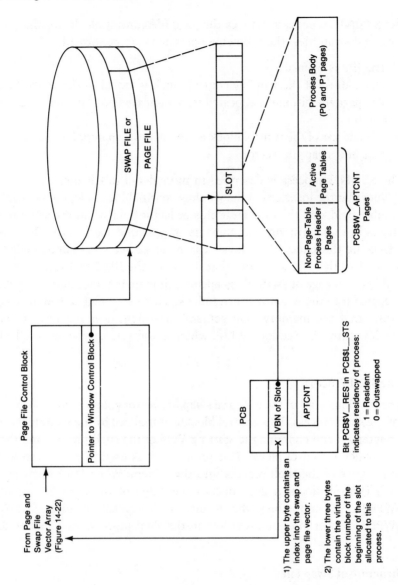

Figure 14-23
Swap File Database

the process is reassigned to a new swap space, which is MPW_WRTCLUSTER pages bigger. In this manner, the process's swap space is increased in multiples of MPW_WRTCLUSTER. A process's swap space can grow up to WSQUOTA pages. At image exit, the process's working set is reduced back to PHD$W_DFWSCNT, and the process is reassigned to an initial size swap space.

Dynamically allocated swap spaces represent a significant change from previous versions of the VAX/VMS operating system. Previously, swap files were composed of a number of fixed size areas known as swap slots. These swap slots were permanently allocated. The size of the swap slots was tied directly to the SYSGEN parameter WSMAX. This rigidity placed some restrictions on the system. The fixed size of the swap slots limited the possible growth of process working sets; because each swap slot was the maximum required size (for WSMAX), this limited the number of processes that could be created. VAX/VMS Version 3.0 decoupled the link with WSMAX, in part to accommodate the new working set expansion provided with the new system. Now the size of the swap spaces is limited only by WSQUOTA.

14.5.4   Alternate Page and Swap Files

Alternate page and swap files can be created by the SYSGEN commands INSTALL/PAGEFILE and INSTALL/SWAPFILE. A system with alternate swap files can support a greater number of processes or processes with larger working sets. In a system with alternate page files, newly created processs are assigned to the page file that contains the most free pages. The assignment lasts for the life of the process. Thus, adding alternate page files enhances system performance by reducing paging activity to the existing page files (and again, making more space available for swap spaces).

14.6   SWAPPER AND MODIFIED PAGE WRITER PAGE TABLE ARRAYS

The VAX/VMS I/O subsystem allows direct I/O requests (DMA transfers) to virtually contiguous buffers. There is no requirement that pages in the buffer be physically contiguous or even have any relationship to each other.

14.6.1   Direct I/O and Scatter/Gather

The I/O locking mechanism invoked at the FDT level brings each page into the working set of the requesting process, makes it valid, and increments that page's reference count (in PFN REFCNT array) to reflect the pending read or write. The buffer is generally described in the I/O request packet through three fields.

- IRP$L_SVAPTE contains the system virtual address of the first PTE that maps the buffer.
- IRP$W_BOFF and IRP$W_BCNT together describe the buffer size that is used to calculate how many PTEs are required to map the buffer.

When a driver processes this I/O request, it allocates the required number of MBA or UBA mapping registers and loads them with the page frame numbers found in the page table entries. The adapter hardware handles the mapping from its address space to VAX physical addresses. The ability to transfer to discontiguous physical pages (the so-called scatter-read/gather-write capability) is a beneficial side effect of this mapping.

14.6.2   Swapper I/O

The swapper is presented with a more difficult problem. It must write a collection of pages to disk that are not even virtually contiguous. It solves this problem elegantly.

When the system is initialized, an array of WSMAX longwords is allocated from nonpaged pool for use as the swapper's I/O table. The starting address of this array is stored in global pointer SWP$GL_MAP. (The address is also stored in the saved P0 base register in the swapper's process header so the pages mapped by this array are effectively the swapper's P0 space. This use is discussed in Chapter 20.)

When the swapper scans the working set list of the process being outswapped, the page frame numbers in each valid PTE are moved to successive entries in the swapper's I/O table. The address of the base of the table is put into the SVAPTE field of the IRP by the swapper before the IRP is passed on to the driver. (The swapper can exercise this control because it builds a portion of its own IRP, rather than using the entire $QIO mechanism.) The I/O table looks just like any other page table to the mapping register subroutines called by the driver. The PFNs are extracted from this array and loaded into adapter mapping registers.

What the swapper has succeeded in doing is making pages that are not virtually contiguous appear to be virtually contiguous to the I/O subsystem. (A different interpretation is that the pages are virtually contiguous in the P0 space of the swapper, the process that is actually performing the I/O.) At the same time that each PTE is being processed, any special actions based on the type of page are also taken care of. The whole operation of outswap and the complementary steps taken when the process is swapped back into memory are discussed in Chapter 17.

14.6.3   Modified Page Writer PTE Array

The modified page writer, in its attempt to write many pages to backing store with a single write request (so-called modified page write clustering), is faced

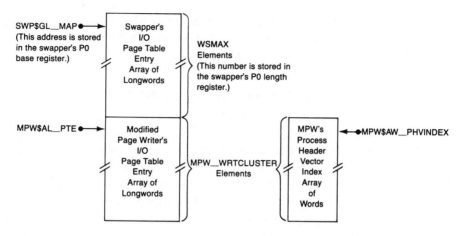

Figure 14-24
Swapper and Modified Page Writer PTE Arrays

with a problem similar to the swapper's problem, with one additional twist. When the modified page writer is building an I/O request, there are three forms of page that it can encounter. Pages that are bound for the swap file (SWPVBN nonzero) are written individually. Pages that are bound for an image file are not necessarily virtually contiguous, these pages will be written as a group only if they are contiguous. Pages on the modified page list that are to be written to a page file may be not only discontiguous within a process address space but may also belong to several processes. The modified page writer builds a table of PTEs in a manner similar to the swapper.

At initialization time (in module INIT), two arrays are allocated from nonpaged pool for the modified page writer (see Figure 14-24). Each array contains MPW_WRTCLUSTER elements. The longword array will be filled with page table entries containing PFNs analogous to the swapper map. The word array contains an index into the process header vector for each page in the map. In this way, each page that is put into the map and written to its backing store location is related to the process header containing the PTE that maps this page. The operation of the modified page writer, including its clustered writes to a page file, is discussed in detail in Chapter 17.

14.6.4   Nonreentrancy of Swapper and Modified Page Writer

The use of these arrays to hold page table entries for the I/O subsystem makes the swapper and the modified page writer not reentrant. That is, the swapper process can perform only the following simultaneous operations:

- An inswap or outswap operation that uses the swapper map. This action is recorded by setting the swap in progress flag (SCH$V_SIP) in location SCH$GB_SIP.

301

- A modified page write to a page file, an image file, or a swap file VBN. The modified page write in progress flag (SCH$V_MPW) in the same global location (SCH$GB_SIP) records this action.

14.7   DATA STRUCTURES USED WITH SHARED MEMORY

The MA780 shared memory unit can be used as an interprocessor communication path with common event flags, mailboxes, or global sections. This VMS support requires data structures located in the shared memory that describe the shared memory itself and the shared memory common event flag clusters, mailboxes, or global sections used. In addition, each processor connected to the shared memory requires data structures located in local memory that describe processor-specific information (such as the starting PFN or port number). Information common to both processors (for example, the size of the global section descriptor tables) is maintained in the shared memory data structures.

Note that the shared memory described in this section differs significantly from the MA780 shared memory used in the VAX-11/782. In the VAX-11/780, shared memory is used as a common data area or communications path between two processors; in the VAX-11/782, the MA780 is used as main memory.

14.7.1   Shared Memory Control Structures

The shared memory unit consists of a series of pages of physical memory. The bootstrap sequence records the presence of the shared memory unit but does not configure the physical pages into the system (unless the processor is a VAX-11/782), allowing the user to include shared memory in a site-specific way (for example, whether to reinitialize the MA780 shared memory after each reboot or not). In either case, the physical memory pages must be virtually mapped so that they are accessible to program code (because memory management is enabled).

The virtual mapping used by one processor to access shared memory pages may be different from the virtual mapping used by another processor. For this reason, some of the data structures that the VMS operating system uses to manipulate its data structures located in shared memory are self-relative queue elements. (Self-relative queue elements are described in the *VAX-11 Architecture Reference Manual*.)

Note that the VMS operating system cannot use one of its usual synchronization techniques, elevated IPL, to control access to shared memory data structures. Elevated IPL blocks interrupts, but only on one processor. Instead, all accesses to shared memory data that must be synchronized are done with one of the interlocked instructions provided for just this purpose in the VAX architecture. These instructions are:

INSQHI	Insert Entry into Queue at Head, Interlocked
INSQTI	Insert Entry into Queue at Tail, Interlocked
REMQHI	Remove Entry from Queue at Head, Interlocked
REMQTI	Remove Entry from Queue at Tail, Interlocked
BBSSI	Branch on Bit Set and Set Interlocked
BBCCI	Branch on Bit Clear and Clear Interlocked
ADAWI	Add Aligned Word Interlocked

The four instructions that manipulate self-relative queues actually provide two levels of interlocking. Because self-relative queue elements must be quadword aligned, the low three address bits (all zero) are available for other uses. The low-order bit in the forward link is used as a secondary interlock. When this bit is set, interlocked access to the head or tail of the queue is denied. This interlock bit is read in a interlocked fashion that is used by the other three inteructions in the list (BBSSI, BBCCI, and ADAWI).

14.7.1.1 **Physical Layout of Shared Memory.** If the shared memory is to be supported by the VMS operating system, it must be configured into the system with the SYSGEN utility. This installation step is described in the *VAX/VMS System Management and Operations Guide.* The resulting physical layout of shared memory is illustrated in Figure 14-25. The VMS data areas are initialized when the first processor (port) connects the shared memory unit. As other ports make their connection, their local memory data structures are simply initialized to point to the shared structures.

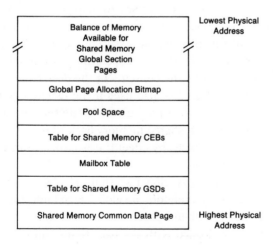

Figure 14-25
Physical Layout of Shared Memory

14.7.1.2 **Shared Memory Common Data Page.** The shared memory page with the highest physical address is used by the VMS operating system to contain the information that describes this shared memory unit. This page is called the common data page. Because this page may be virtually mapped in different ways on each port (and may not even exist at the same physical address), each pointer in the common data page is a relative pointer from the base virtual address of the common data page. The contents of the common data page are listed in Table 14-3.

14.7.1.3 **Processor-Specific Control.** As each processor connects itself to the shared memory unit, a data structure in processor local memory is initialized that allows that processor to locate the common data page. That structure also contains physical page information that allows the shared physical memory to be virtually mapped on that processor. The layout of the shared memory control block is pictured in Figure 14-26.

14.7.2 **Global Sections in Shared Memory**

The creation and mapping of a global section in shared memory are slightly different from the corresponding actions for local memory global sections. The global section is recognized as a shared memory global section because its name translates to an equivalence name of the form:

```
shared-memory-name:section-name
```

The Create and Map Section system service then creates the data structures necessary to describe this section.

- The global section descriptor for such a section (see Figure 14-27) is located in shared memory and contains information used to map the section.
- Only the port that creates the global section has a global section table entry (in the local memory of the creating processor) describing the section. This section table entry is used by the VMS operating system to load the physical pages of the section with the contents of the designated file when the section is created. The GSTE is also used if the Delete Global Section or Update Section system services are called to write the contents of a writeable global section located in shared memory back to its original file. (Either system service will not have any effect if it is issued from any port other than the creator port.)
- Because the pages of a shared memory global section are always valid, there is no need to page those pages; therefore, no global page table entries are created for the section. Instead, when a process maps to such a section, its process page table entries are loaded with the page frame numbers of the shared memory section pages and marked valid. These pages are not charged against the process's working set.

Table 14-3: Contents of Shared Memory Common Data Page

Mnemonic	Item	Size
SHD$L_MBXPTR	Relative Pointer to Mailbox Table	Longword
SHD$L_GSDPTR	Relative Pointer to GSD Table	Longword
SHD$L_CEFPTR	Relative Pointer to CEB Table	Longword
SHD$L_GSBITMAP	Relative Pointer to Global Page Bitmap	Longword
SHD$L_GSPAGCNT	Total Count of Pages for Global Sections	Longword
SHD$L_GSPFN	Relative PFN of First Global Section Page	Longword
SHD$W_GSDMAX	Number of entries in GSD Table	Word
SHD$W_MBXMAX	Number of entries in MBX Table	Word
SHD$W_CEFMAX	Number of entries in CEB Table	Word
	(spare word for alignment)	Word
SHD$T_NAME	Name of Shared Memory	16 Bytes
	(counted ASCII string)	
SHD$Q_INITTIME	Initialization Time	Quadword

This is the end of the constant area of the shared memory common data page.

Mnemonic	Item	Size
SHD$L_CRC	CRC of Fields in Constant Area	Longword
SHD$W_GSDQUOTA	Count of GSDs Created (one word per port)	16 Words
SHD$W_MBXQUOTA	Count of Mailboxes Created (one word per port)	16 Words
SHD$W_CEFQUOTA	Count of CEBs Created (one word per port)	16 Words
SHD$B_PORTS	Number of Ports	Byte
SHD$B_INITLCK	Owner of Initialization Lock	Byte
SHD$B_BITMAPLCK	Owner of Global Page Bitmap Lock	Byte
SHD$B_FLAGS	Flags for Locking Data Structures	Byte
SHD$B_GSDLOCK	Owner of GSD Table Lock	Byte
SHD$B_MBXLOCK	Owner of MBX Table Lock	Byte
SHD$B_CEFLOCK	Owner of CEF Table Lock	Byte
	(spare byte for alignment)	
SHD$W_PRQWAIT	Ports Waiting for Interprocessor Request Blocks (one bit per port)	Word
SHD$W_POLL	Ports Actively Using the Memory (one bit per port)	Word
SHD$W_RESWAIT	Ports Waiting for a Resource (one bit per port) (one word mask per resource)	16 Words
SHD$W_RESAVAIL	Ports Needing to Report Resource Available (one bit per port) (one word mask per resource)	16 Words
SHD$W_RESSUM	Ports with Resources to Report (one bit per port)	Word
	(three spare words for alignment)	3 Words
SHD$Q_PRQ	Free Interprocessor Request Block Listhead	Quadword
SHD$Q_POOL	Free Pool Block Listhead	Quadword
SHD$Q_PRQWRK	Interprocessor Request Work Queue Listheads (one listhead per port)	16 Quadwords

Shared Memory Control Block

Link to Next SHB		
VA of Common Data Page		
Flags	Type	Size
Reference Count		
Base PFN for Global Section Pages		
⨯	Port Number	TR Number of Memory
Address Past Last Byte of Shared Memory Pool		
Address of Adapter Control Block		

Figure 14-26
Contents of Shared Memory Control Block

Because of the way in which the VMS operating system uses shared memory for global sections, putting global sections into shared memory, even when the memory unit is not connected to another processor, improves system utilization. Each process using the shared sections is getting a free extension to its working set. There is no demand placed on the global page table. The local physical memory that would otherwise be required to contain such

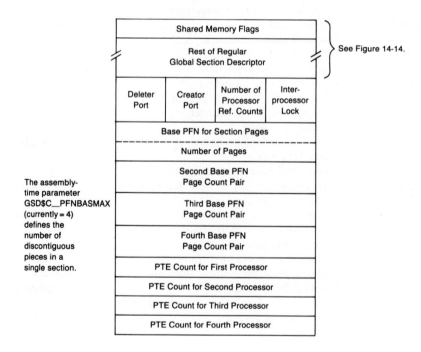

The assembly-time parameter GSD$C_PFNBASMAX (currently = 4) defines the number of discontiguous pieces in a single section.

Figure 14-27
Contents of Shared Memory Global Section Descriptor

entities as DCL or the Run-Time Library is available for other uses such as an expanded physical page cache (free page list).

14.7.3   Mailboxes in Shared Memory

When a mailbox is created in shared memory, it is described by a shared memory mailbox descriptor block (MBX) located in the shared memory (see Figure 18-2). In addition, each port connected to the shared memory mailbox has a unit control block (UCB) in its local memory I/O database that makes the connection between the local I/O system and the shared memory mailbox. The relationships of shared memory mailbox data structures are pictured in Figure 18-3.

14.7.4   Common Event Flag Clusters in Shared Memory

As with global sections and mailboxes (and the shared memory itself), there are data structures in shared memory and other structures in local memory required to fully describe a common event flag cluster located in shared memory. The shared memory data structure is called a master CEB (common event block) and contains the only valid set of event flags. Each port connected to this common event flag cluster has a slave CEB that locates the master. The relationship between the master CEB and the slave CEBs is pictured in Figure 12-4. The layouts of the master and slave common event blocks are pictured in Figure 12-5.

15 Paging Dynamics

I consider that a man's brain originally is like a little empty attic,
and you have to stock it with such furniture as you choose. . . .
Now, the skillful workman is very careful indeed as to what he
takes into his brain-attic. He will have nothing but the tools
which may help him in doing his work, but of these he has a large
assortment, and all in the most perfect order. It is a mistake to
think that the little room has elastic walls and can distend to any
extent. Depend upon it, there comes a time when for every
addition of knowledge you forget something that you knew
before. It is of highest importance, therefore, not to have useless
facts elbowing out the useful ones.

—Sir Arthur Conan Doyle, *A Study in Scarlet*

In the previous chapter, the various data structures that are maintained by
memory management were described apart from the context in which they
are used. This chapter shows how the various structures are manipulated by
the pager in response to different forms of page faults.

Although pager action is described here, it is not presented in a flowchart
or decision fashion. Rather, the actions are described in terms of modifications to data structures.

15.1   OVERVIEW OF PAGER OPERATION

Before discussing how the pager reacts to different forms of page faults, this
chapter will briefly describe the overall operation of the pager.

15.1.1   Hardware Action

All program references generated by the CPU are virtual addresses. Each address must be translated to a physical address before a reference to memory
(or an I/O space page) can be made. The virtual address (see Figure 15-1) is
used by the address translation mechanism to find the page table entry that
will be used to translate the address.

If the page table entry is valid, its contents are used to translate the virtual
address to a physical address and execution continues. If the page table entry
is invalid (PTE<31> = 0), then a translation-not-valid fault is generated.
Figure 15-2 shows the state of the kernel stack following a page fault.

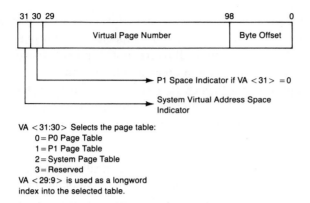

VA <31:30> Selects the page table:
   0 = P0 Page Table
   1 = P1 Page Table
   2 = System Page Table
   3 = Reserved
VA <29:9> is used as a longword
index into the selected table.

Figure 15-1
Format of Virtual Address Showing Fields Used
to Locate Page Table Entry That Maps the Page

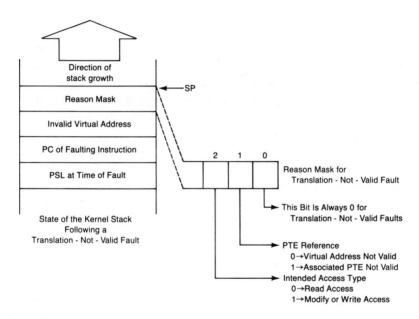

Figure 15-2
State of the Kernel Stack Following
Translation-Not-Valid Fault

15.1.2   Initial Pager Action

Before the pager does any work, it performs a consistency check by demanding that the IPL be no higher than 2. If the IPL is higher than 2, a fatal bugcheck is generated. This check is made for the following two reasons:

309

- Code that is executing at a higher IPL needs to perform a series of instructions without being interrupted. If a page fault happens, the faulting process might be removed from execution, allowing another process to execute the same routine or access the same protected data structure.
- Page faults are exceptions that happen to a process. When the system is executing at IPL higher than 2, it is often on the interrupt stack, acting in response to an external trigger. There is not necessarily a process that can be charged for the page fault.

The next step that the pager takes is to retrieve the invalid virtual address from the kernel stack. It uses this address to locate the page table entry that maps this page by performing the same operations that the address translation mechanism uses.

1. The upper two bits of the virtual address (VA<31:30>) select which page table (or which base register) to use.
2. The virtual address field (VA<29:9>) is used as a longword index into the page table.

Before the page table entry is examined, the pager determines whether the system virtual page containing the page table entry is itself valid. (This check avoids the necessity of making the pager recursive.) If not, the page table page is made valid first. Note that the pager does not perform this check using the page table valid bit in the exception parameter; rather, it checks the valid bit in the page table entry for the system virtual page.

Once the page table entry is available, the pager takes different actions depending on the nature of the invalid page table entry. (See Figure 14-3 for the different forms of invalid page table entry.) The next several sections describe some of the major paths through the pager. Extraordinary conditions such as read and write errors are only mentioned in passing.

15.2   PAGE FAULTS FOR PROCESS PRIVATE PAGES

The first set of page faults concern process private pages. The different path through the pager when sharing is involved is discussed in the next section. There are four cases that must be described.

- Two of the cases involve a page that is originally faulted from an image file. The two cases are distinguished by whether or not the section is copy on reference.
- A third private section can consist of a series of demand zero pages.
- Finally, an intermediate state that can result from both copy-on-reference pages and demand zero pages has the faulting page residing in a page file.

15.2.1   Page Located in an Image File

There are two different types of page that can initially reside in a private image file, pages that are copy-on-reference, and those that are not. The page table entry for either page contains a process section table index. The only initial difference between the two pages is the setting of the copy-on-reference bit in the page table entry (see Figure 14-3).

15.2.1.1   Image Page That Is Not Copy on Reference. The first type of page fault involves a page in an image file that is not copy on reference. The various transitions that such a page can possibly make are illustrated in Figure 15-3. The numbers in circles are keyed to explanations of each transition listed below. (For simplicity, clustered reads and writes are ignored in the discussion that follows. Section 15.5 discusses all aspects of paging I/O.) The page table entry is initially set to the form illustrated at the top of Figure 15-3. It contains a process section table index (PSTX) with the copy-on-reference bit (PTE<16>) clear.

① A page fault occurs. The pager uses the virtual address exception parameter to locate the page table entry. The page table entry contains a process section table index. Information contained in the process section table entry indicates which virtual block in the image file should be read. The pager allocates a physical page from the head of the free page list. The page is added to the process working set. This step may require the pager to remove another page from the working set in order to make room for the page currently being added.

   The PFN arrays are initialized. The STATE array element indicates that a read is in progress. The PTE array element points to the process page table entry. The working set list index array element locates the working list entry just set up. The BAK array element is loaded with the initial contents of the page table entry, the process section table index. The reference count array element contains a two, one for being in the working set and one for the read in progress.

   The pager builds an I/O request packet (see Section 15.5) that describes the read that is being done. The process is placed into a page fault wait state.

② Because most of the work was done in response to the initial fault, there is little left to do when the page read completes. The reference count is decremented (but stays above zero, so nothing special happens). The state of the page is changed to active and valid. Finally, the valid bit is set in the process page table entry and the process is removed from the page fault wait state. The next time that the process is selected for execution, it will execute the same instruction that caused the initial page fault.

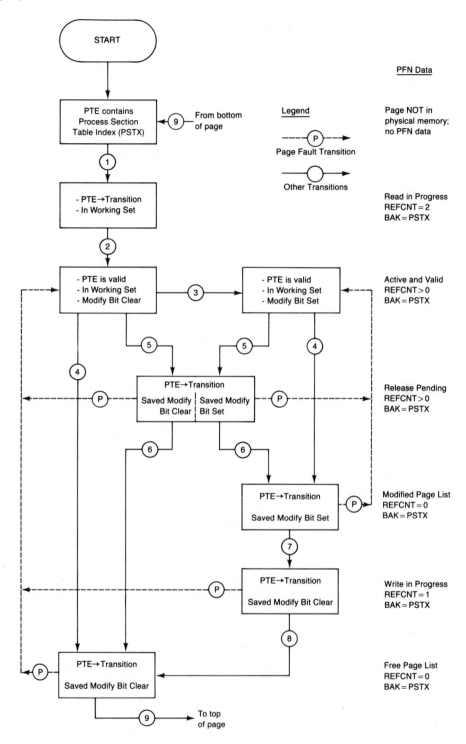

Figure 15-3
State Diagram Showing Page Transitions for Private
Section Page That Is Not Copy on Reference

③ One transition that a valid page can undergo (and still remain valid) occurs when the page is modified as a result of instruction execution. The hardware sets the modify bit in the page table entry. The change is not noted at this time in the PFN database.

④ When the page is removed from the process working set, several things happen.

    a. The working set list entry is made available.

    b. The WSLX array element is cleared.

    c. The modify bit in the page table entry is logically ORed into the PFN state array element.

    d. The VALID, TYP0, and TYP1 bits in the PTE are all cleared. The PFN field is left alone.

    e. The REFCNT array element is decremented. If the reference count goes to zero, the page is put the free or modified page list, according to the setting of the saved modify bit in the PFN STATE array element. The new location of the page is inserted into the STATE array.

    Note that pages are not removed from the working set until room is required for other pages, until the virtual pages are deleted, or in response to a $PURGWS system service call.

⑤ If the reference count does not go to zero, there is outstanding I/O for this page. The state is changed to release pending. The ultimate destination for the page (free or modified list) is recorded in the saved modify bit in the STATE array.

⑥ The I/O completion routine decrements reference counts for pages that are locked down. When this routine detects that the count has gone to zero, it places the page on either the free list or the modified list as appropriate. The STATE array element is changed.

    If the page is placed on the modified list and if it has a backing store address already, the page file index is cleared and the page file deallocation routine is called to release the page in the page file. Because the page has been modifed, it is assumed that the contents at its backing store address are now invalid.

⑦ The modified page writer will eventually write this physical page to its backing store address, which is located in the PFN BAK array. Writeable pages that are not copy on reference are written back to the image file from which they originally came.

    The state of the page is set to write in progress. The saved modify bit is cleared. The reference count of one reflects this outstanding output operation.

    It is worth noting at this time that writeable private pages that are not copy on reference are not usual products of the linker. Such sections must be created with the Create and Map (Private) Section system service.

⑧ When the modified page write completes, the page is placed on the free page list. The same routine decrements the reference count, notes that the reference count went to zero, and notes that the saved modify bit is clear.

⑨ While the physical page has remained attached to the process, the page table entry has always contained a PFN and the PFN PTE array has always contained the address of the process page table entry.

When the physical page is reused for another purpose, several steps must be taken to break the ties between the process virtual page and the physical page that is about to be reused.

The process PTE must be altered to reflect the backing store address of the page. (The PFN PTE array is used to locate the page table entry.) In this case, the PTE is reset so that it contains a process section table index (PSTX), the same contents that it had before the initial page fault.

The PFN array elements for this physical page are all cleared before the page is passed on to the new owner of the physical page. In particular, the PTE array element, the only connection from the PFN database to the process page table, is cleared.

15.2.1.2 **Page Faults Out of Transition States.** Figure 15-3 also shows the transitions that a page makes when a page fault occurs while the physical page is in the transition state. While the changes back to the active state are somewhat straightforward, there are details about each fault that should be mentioned. Note that each of these page faults requires that a new working set list entry be acquired, and the acquisition may involve the removal of some other page from the process working set.

1. A page fault from the free page list is resolved by placing the page back into the active and valid state, resetting the PTE, and incrementing the reference count.

2. A page fault from the modified list has exactly the same effect. The fact that the page was previously modified but never written to its backing store address is shown in the figure by putting the page back into its modified state.

   In fact, the modify bit in the PTE is not actually turned on by the pager. Rather, the saved modify bit in the PFN STATE array records the fact that the page has not been backed up.

3. A page fault from the release pending state has no special effects. Again, the state is changed to active, the valid bit in the PTE is turned on, and the reference count is incremented.

   Artistic license is taken in the figure to differentiate physical pages that were modified from pages that were not. Again, the only difference between the two pages is the setting of the saved modify bit in the PFN STATE array, not the setting of the modify bit in the PTE.

4. The transition that deserves special comment is a page fault that occurs while the modified page writer is writing the page to its backing store address. The saved modify bit is cleared before the write begins so that the page will be placed on the free list when the write completes. Although the page has not yet been completely backed up, the assumption is made that the write will complete successfully. Page faults can thus put the page into the active but unmodified state. The only difficulty occurs in the event of a write error. The I/O completion routine detects this state of affairs and turns the saved modify bit back on.

15.2.1.3   Copy-on-Reference Page. A more common type of writeable process private page is called copy on reference. Figure 15-4 illustrates the transitions that such a page makes from its initial page fault until it is written to some backing store address.

Many of the transitions that occur here are no different from the case just described. This section will note each transition but only elaborate on those areas that are different.

① The initial setting of the page table entry (START1 in the figure) is again the process section table index, but the copy-on-reference bit (PTE>16<) is now set. When a page fault occurs, the pager again allocates a physical page, sets its PFN into the PTE, and initiates the read. Two important steps are taken at this time that differ from the previous case.

First, the saved modify bit in the PFN STATE array is turned on. Setting the bit guarantees that the page will be written to its backing store address when removed from the process working set, regardless of what instructions or I/O operations the process chooses to execute.

Second, the BAK array element is set to point to the page file, with an indication that no block has yet been allocated. At this time, all ties to the original image file are broken. When the modified page writer wants to write this page to its backing store address (as it certainly will because the saved modify bit was just turned on), it will allocate a block in the page file and write the contents of the physical page there.

② When the read completes, the page is marked as active and valid (and effectively modified).

③ When the page is removed from the process working set (and the reference count is zero), the page is unconditionally placed on the modified page list.

④ If the reference count did not go to zero when the page was removed from the process working set, the physical page is placed into the release pending state until the I/O completes.

⑤ At that time, the page is placed on the modified page list.

A page fault from either the release pending state or from the modified page list puts the page back into the active (but effectively modified) state. That is,

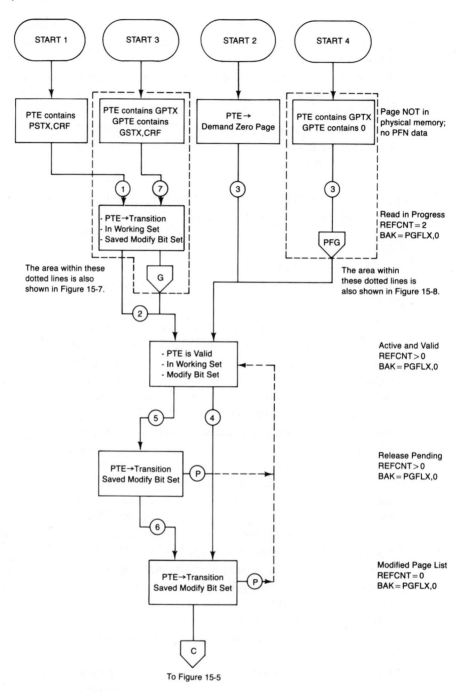

Figure 15-4
State Diagram Showing Page Transitions for Private
and Global Copy-on-Reference Pages and for Demand Zero
Pages

the saved modify bit in the PFN STATE array remains set, causing the page to be put back on the modified page list when it is removed from the working set again.

The transition from the modified page list that is taken when the modified page writer writes the page to its backing store address (in the page file) fits into the transition diagram for faults from the page file (see Figure 15-5). The connection between Figure 15-4 and Figure 15-5 is indicated by path C in the two figures.

15.2.2   Demand Zero Pages

The initial setting of a page table entry can be set to demand zero as a result of a Create Virtual Address Region system service. One of these services can be issued explicitly by the process or on its behalf by the system (as part of image activation or in the LIB$GET_VM Run-Time Library procedure).

When the pager detects a page fault for a demand zero page, it takes the following steps.

1. A physical page is allocated from the beginning of the free page list.
2. The PFN array elements are initialized. The PTE array element points to the process page table entry.
3. The BAK array element denotes a not-yet-allocated block in the page file.
4. The page is filled with zeros. This is done with a MOVC5 instruction that uses a zero-length source string and a null fill character.
5. The reference count is incremented; the page is added to the process working set; and the state is set to active.
6. Finally, the fault is dismissed and control is passed back to the user process without interruption.

These steps all take place along path 3 in the upper righthand portion of Figure 15-4.

15.2.3   Global Copy-on-Reference and Page-File Pages

There are two forms of pages that merge into the same set of state transitions as private copy-on-reference sections and demand zero pages. These forms are global copy-on-reference pages and global page-file backing-store pages. The details of global page fault resolution are discussed in Section 15.3.

Suffice it to say here that that global copy-on-reference pages are initially faulted from a global image file but, from that time on, are indistinguishable from other global writeable pages. Global page-file backing-store pages are initially faulted as global demand zero pages and from then on are indistinguishable from private demand zero pages.

Paging Dynamics

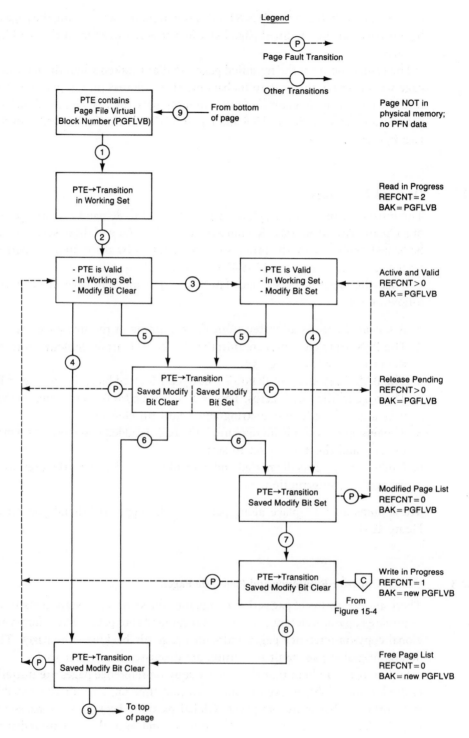

Figure 15-5
Transitions for Pages Located in a Page File

15.2.4   **Page Located in the Page File**

The transitions that a page faulted from the page file goes through (see Figure 15-5) are no different from the transitions described for pages that are not copy on reference (see Figure 15-3). The only difference in the PFN data between the two figures is that the BAK array element in Figure 15-5 indicates that the page belongs in the page file. The BAK array element in Figure 15-3 contains a process section table index.

The other difference between the two figures is the entry point into the transition diagram. Pages can start out in an image file (PTE contains PSTX) but pages can never start out in a page file. The entry into Figure 15-5 is from Figure 15-4, from one of three initial states that eventually result in the physical page contents being written to the page file.

15.3   **PAGE FAULTS FOR GLOBAL PAGES**

The page fault resolution for global pages can be described in exactly the same way as process private pages are described. Following the transition of a global page table entry and its associated PFN database entries adds nothing to the information already presented in Figure 15-3.

A more interesting approach is to look at the interaction of the process page table entries and the global page table entries that they point to. The following discussion uses a specific example rather than a general case, to allow specific numbers to be used.

15.3.1   **Page Fault for Global Read-Only Page**

Figure 15-6 illustrates the transitions that occur for a global read-only page that is mapped by two processes. The mapping is shown separately from the operation of section creation to simplify the figure. A second simplification in the figure is that the page is assumed to be read only. The implications of a read/write global page are described in the next section without the benefit of a figure.

(START)
   When the global section is initially created, the data structures described in the previous chapter are all set up. The global page table entry for the page we will follow contains a global section table index, which locates the global section table entry containing information about the global image file.

① When Process A maps to the section, the process page table entry contains a global page table index, effectively a pointer to the global page table entry.

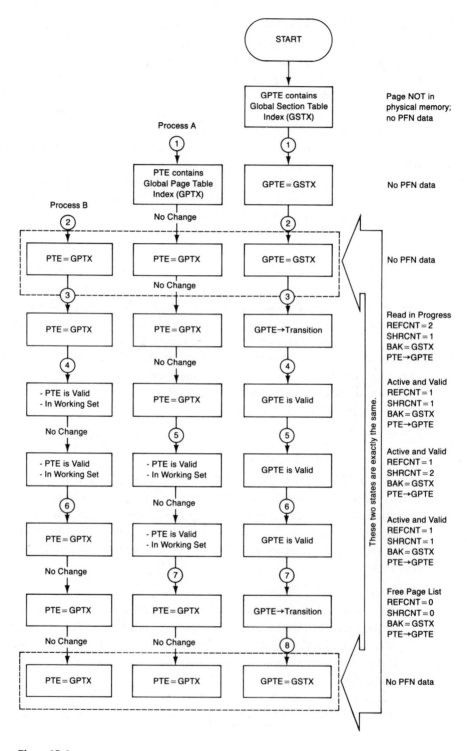

Figure 15-6
Example of Page Transitions Made by a Global Page
Mapped by Two Processes

② When Process B maps to the section, its page table entry contains exactly the same global page table index as found in Process A's PTE.

③ Process B happens to incur a page fault on this global page first. Several things happen.

  a. The pager notes that the process PTE contains a global page table index (GPTX). This index is used to locate the global page table entry (GPTE).

  b. The GPTE contains a global section table index (GSTX), indicating that the global page resides on disk somewhere. Exactly the same things are done to initiate the read here as in the case of a process private page.

  c. A physical page is allocated.

  d. The state of that page is set to read in progress.

  e. The reference count is incremented.

  f. The BAK array element is loaded with the GSTX.

  g. Note that the PFN PTE array element is loaded with the address of the GPTE, not the address of the process PTE. Note also that, while the read is in progress, the GPTE contains the transition PTE but the process PTE still contains the GPTX.

  h. The reference count is two, one for the read in progress and one for recording the fact that the page is in some process working set (the global share count is nonzero). The global share count array element contains a one while the read is in progress.

④ Several steps are taken when the read completes.

  a. The state of the page is changed to active and valid.

  b. The global page table entry is set to valid, to record the fact that this page is in some process working set.

  c. The process page table entry, located through its address stored in the I/O request packet, is set up to contain the low-order 21 bits from the global page table entry, with the valid bit set and bits 21 and 26 cleared.

  d. The reference count and share count are both one at this point.

⑤ When Process A faults the same global page, the initial pager action is the same as it was in Step 3, because the page table entry is again a global page table index. Now, however, the pager finds a valid GPTE. Resolution of this page fault is simple.

   A working set list is created for Process A. The global page table entry is simply copied to Process A's page table. The share count is incremented, and the fault is dismissed.

⑥ When the global page is removed from Process B's working set, the share count is decremented. Because the share count is still positive, nothing dramatic happens to the physical page.

At this time, Process B's page table entry must be restored to its previous state. (The page table entry does not assume some transition form.) The PTE array element contains the address of the global page table entry so the global page table index must be recalculated.

The calculation is straightforward. The contents of MMG$GL_ GPTBASE are subtracted from the PTE array element, the result is divided by four (to create a longword index), and the quotient stored in the process page table entry in the GPTX field.

(7) When the global page is removed from Process A's working set, the process page table entry is restored as described in Step 6.

The share count is decremented. Now the share count reaches zero, so the reference count is also decremented. If the page is unmodified and there is no outstanding I/O, the physical page is placed on the free page list.

The GPTE contains a transition PTE. The STATE array element indicates the free page list. The other PFN array elements are unchanged.

(8) When the physical page is reused, the ties must be broken between the physical page and, in this case, the global page table entry. (None of the processes mapped to this page are affected in any way by this step.)

The contents of the BAK array element (a GSTX) are inserted into the GPTE located by the contents of the PFN PTE array element. The PFN PTE array element is then cleared, breaking the connection between the physical page and the global page table.

These steps put the process and global page tables back to the state they were in following Step 2 (although it is pictured here as a different state to make the figure simpler).

15.3.2   Global Read/Write Pages

The transitions that occur for global writeable pages are no different from the transitions for a process private page that is not copy on reference. The only difference between such transitions and the transitions illustrated in Figure 15-3 is that the global page table entry, not the process page table entry, is affected by the transitions of the physical page.

The process page table entry for global pages contains a global page table index up until the time that the page is made valid. Only then is a PFN inserted into the process PTE. As soon as the page is removed from the process working set, the GPTX is placed back into the process PTE. All ties to the PFN database are made through the global page table entry, which retains the PFN while the physical page is in the various transition states.

15.3.3   Global Copy-on-Reference Pages

The global pages previously described are all shared pages. One form of global page is shared only in its initial state. As soon as the fault occurs, the page is treated exactly like a process private page.

These pages are global copy-on-reference pages and commonly occur in shareable images that contain impure data areas. For example, all of the local variables in a FORTRAN shareable image would be in a global copy-on-reference section. Each process that uses the image would get its own private copy of the local variables, but all processes would get the same initial values for the variables.

Figure 15-7 illustrates the transitions that occur for a global copy-on-reference page.

① The initial conditions are identical to those used in Figure 15-6. The section is created and the GPTEs contain a GSTX, although here the copy-on-reference bit is set.

② Process A maps the page and has its PTE set to contain a GPTX.

③ Process B maps the page and gets the same GPTX in its PTE. Up to this point nothing is different from Figure 15-6.

④ Now when Process B incurs a page fault, the pager follows the GPTX to the GPTE, noting that the page is located in a global image file and is copy on reference. A read is initiated and the following modifications are made to the process PTE and the PFN database.

  a. The global page table entry is not touched. It retains its GSTX contents.
  b. The process page table entry is set to a transition PTE.
  c. The state of the physical page is set to read in progress.
  d. The BAK array element contains a page file index (with no block allocated yet).
  e. The PTE array element contains the address of Process B's PTE.

Note that all ties between Process B and the global section are broken. The page is now treated exactly like a private copy-on-reference page. The two boxes outlined for Process B in Figure 15-7 are the boxes within the dashed outline in Figure 15-4.

⑤ When Process A faults the same page, exactly the same steps are taken, this time with a totally different physical page.

Thus, both Process A and Process B get exactly the same initial copy of the global page from the global image file, but, from that point on, each process has its own private copy of the page to modify as it wishes.

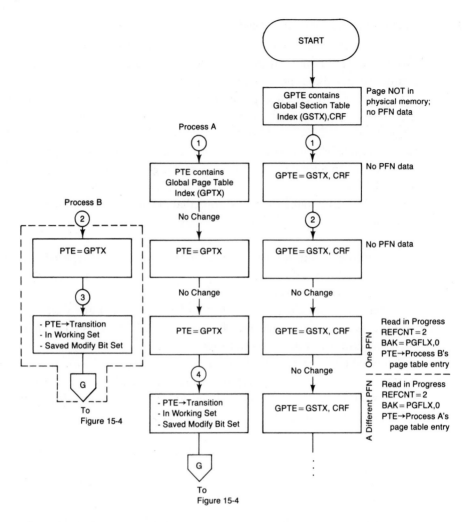

Figure 15-7
Example of Page Transitions for Global
Copy-on-Reference Pages

15.3.4   Global Page-File Backing-Store Pages

Global page-file backing-store pages provide a means by which processes can share global pages without requiring a file for backing store. By their nature these pages have no initial contents, and are thus initialized as demand zero pages.

Figure 15-8 illustrates the transitions that occur for a global page-file backing-store page.

(1) The initial conditions are identical to those used in Figure 15-6. The section is created and the GPTEs contain a zero in the PFN field.

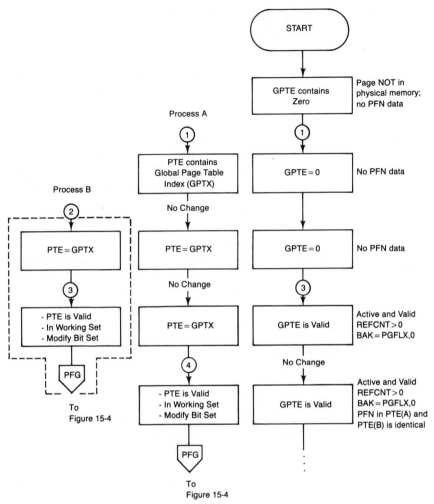

Figure 15-8
Example of Page Transitions for Global
Page-File Backing-Store Pages

② Process A maps the page and has its PTE set to contain a GPTX.
③ Process B maps the page and has its PTE set to contain a GPTX.
④ When Process B incurs a page fault, the pager follows the GPTX to the
  GPTE and notes that the GPTE is demand zero. The following modifications are made to the PTEs and to the PFN database.

  a. An entry in the PFN database is allocated.
  b. The PTE array element in the PFN database points to the GPTE.
  c. The BAK array element in the PFN database contains the system page
     file index (with no block allocated).

     d. The new PFN is stored in the GPTE.

     e. The valid bit is set in the GPTE.

     f. The PFN in inserted into Process B's PTE and the valid bit is set.

(5) When Process A incurs a fault on the page, the pager follows the GPTX to the GPTE and finds that the GPTE is valid. The valid GPTE is copied to Process A's PTE.

Transitions for a global page-file backing-store page are no different from the transitions for a page located in a page file (see Figure 15-5). However, in global page-file backing store pages, the GPTE, not the process PTE, is affected by the transitions that the physical page makes. Once the global page is removed from the working set, the process PTE reverts to the GPTX form.

15.4   WORKING SET REPLACEMENT

The working set list replacement algorithm that the VMS executive uses is a modified first-in/first-out scheme. The page that has been in the working set list for the longest time is the one first considered for replacement.

15.4.1   Scan of Working Set List

When the pager needs an empty working set list entry, it calls routine MMG$FREWSLE. This routine manipulates the working set list (see Figure 14-4) in the following fashion:

1. If the WSLE indexed by PHD$W_WSNEXT is already available (contents are zero), that entry is used. (For details on checks that are made before a page is used, see Section 15.4.3.)
2. If not, the WSNEXT pointer is incremented. If the WSNEXT pointer exceeds the end of the list (WSLAST), it is reset to the beginning of the dynamic working set list (WSDYN), thus implementing the working set list as a circular buffer.
3. If the newly indexed WSLE is available, then it is simply used. (Again, see the checks made before it can be used.)
4. If the new WSLE is locked into the dynamic portion of the working set list, that entry is skipped (which means going back to Step 2.) Only process page table pages can be locked into the dynamic portion of the working set list. Pages locked by user request result in a shuffling of the working set list (see Chapters 14 and Chapter 16).

15.4.2   Reusing Working Set List Entries

Dropping through the previous checks indicates that the virtual page indicated by the WSLE must be removed before this WSLE can be reused. If working set list skipping (described in Section 15.4.4) is disabled, the working set list entry is reused, whatever its state.

For global pages, the share count is decremented. If the share count goes to zero, the reference count is decremented.

For process private pages, the reference count is decremented. If the page is placed into a transition state, the balance slot reference count for this process header is incremented to prevent the outswap of the process header.

15.4.3   Using an Available Entry in the Working Set List

If an available WSLE is found, checks must be made to see if the page can be added to the working set. If there are fewer pages in the working set than are indicated by WSQUOTA, a new physical page can always be added to the working set. It may also be possible to add physical pages to the working set list above WSQUOTA (up to WSEXTENT), depending on the size of the free page list.

The following checks are made before an available working set entry can be used:

1. If the size of the working set (process page count plus global page count) equals the size of the working set list (WSSIZE), the next WSLE is reused. (In other words, the working set is full.)
2. If the WSNEXT pointer exceeds the end of the list (WSLAST), WSNEXT is reset to the beginning of the dynamic working set list. If an available WSLE is found at the end of the list, and if the working set is full, WSLAST is reset to point to the last unavailable (nonzero) WSLE in the working set list. In other words, the working set list is shrunk if it contains more entries than the size of the working set will allow.
3. If the working set is not full, the size of the working set is compared to WSQUOTA. If the size of the working set is less than WSQUOTA, a new page is allowed in the working set.
4. If there are more than WSQUOTA pages in use, the number of pages on the free page list is compared to the SYSBOOT parameter GROWLIM. If there are more than GROWLIM pages on the free page list, a new page is allowed in the working set.

   Note that in order to extend the working set above WSQUOTA, the working set list itself must have been extended above WSQUOTA. To extend the working set list above WSQUOTA, the free page list must contain more than the SYSBOOT parameter BORROWLIM pages. For more information on BORROWLIM and automatic working set adjustment, see Section 16.4.1.3.
5. If there are fewer than GROWLIM pages on the free page list, the next WSLE in the working set list is reused. Again, if the WSNEXT pointer

exceeds the end of the list, the pointer is reset to the beginning of the list and WSLAST is shrunk back over available entries at the end of the list (as in Step 2).

15.4.4 Skipping Working Set List Entries

The special SYSBOOT parameter TBSKIPWSL (which has a default value of eight) is used by the working set removal routine to permit frequently referenced pages to remain in the working set, thereby allowing the operating system to modify its strict first-in/first-out page replacement algorithm with some frequency of use information.

The modified algorithm works in the following manner. Before a WSLE can be reused, a check is made to see if the virtual address contained in that WSLE is still valid in the translation buffer. If the virtual address is valid, the search for an available WSLE starts again with the next WSLE. After TBSKIPWSL WSLEs have been skipped in this manner, the translation buffer checks are abandoned and the next WSLE is simply reused. If the value of TBSKIPWSL is set to zero, no entries are checked in the translation buffer and the scheme is defeated.

The following pages in the working set are skipped over in this scan:

* Pages that are valid in the translation buffer
* Pages that are locked in the working set

15.5 INPUT AND OUTPUT THAT SUPPORT PAGING

There is very little special-purpose code in the I/O subsystem to support pager I/O and swapper I/O. The pager and swapper each build their own I/O request packets, but these packets are queued to the device driver in the normal fashion. These are the only differences.

* Module SYSQIOREQ contains special entry points for pager and swapper I/O that insert special I/O function codes into the I/O request packet.
* These codes are detected by the I/O postprocessing service routine. There are special completion paths for page read (the process is removed from PFW state and made computable) and for other forms of I/O (the address of a special kernel mode AST stored in IRP$L_ASTPRM field is used to notify modified page writer or swapper that I/O has completed).

   In order to make reading and writing as efficient as possible, the pager supports a feature called clustering, where it checks to see whether pages adjacent to the virtual page that it is reading are located in the same file in adjacent virtual blocks. If so, a multiple block read is issued and several pages are brought into the working set at one time.

   The modified page writer and the Update Section system service also cluster their write operations, both to make their writes as efficient as possible and to allow subsequent clustered reads for the pages that are being written.

15.5.1   Page Reads and Clustering

When the pager determines that a read is required to satisfy a page fault, it allocates an I/O request packet and fills it with parameters that describe the read. Table 15-1 lists those fields that are used for special purposes by the pager.

The pager attempts to create a cluster of pages to read. The manner in which this cluster is formed depends on the initial state of the faulting page table entry.

15.5.1.1   Terminating Condition for Clustered Reads.

The pager scans PTEs that map larger virtual addresses, checking for more virtual pages that are located in the same backing-store location, until the desired cluster size is reached or until one of the following other terminating conditions is reached:

- A page table entry different from the original faulting PTE is encountered.
- The page table page is itself not valid. (Satisfying this fault would offset the benefits gained by clustering.)
- No more working set list entries are available. (Each page in the cluster is added to the working set.)
- No physical page is available.

If, after scanning the adjacent page table entries toward higher virtual addresses, no pages have been clustered, the process is repeated toward lower virtual addresses with the same terminating conditions. The scan is made initially toward higher virtual addresses because programs typically execute sequentially toward higher virtual addresses and these pages are likely to be needed soon. If the forward attempt fails, the pager attempts to read pages adjacent to the faulting page on the assumption that even pages at lower virtual addresses but near the faulting page are likely to be needed soon.

15.5.1.2   Matching Conditions While Scanning Page Table.

The match that is looked for when scanning the adjacent page table entries depends on the form of the initial page table entry.

- If the original PTE contains a process section table index, successive PTEs must contain exactly the same PSTX.
- If the original PTE contains a page file virtual block number, successive PTEs must contain PTEs with successively increasing (or decreasing) virtual block numbers.

Table 15-1
Description of I/O Requests Issued by Memory Management

Type of/Description of I/O Request	Priority	Process ID	System Virtual Address of PTE	AST Address
	IRP$B_PRI	*IRP$L_PID*	*IRP$L_SVAPTE*	*IRP$L_AST*
Process Page Read	Priority of Faulting	PID of Faulting		
1. Page in Image File(1)	Process	Process	1. P0PT/P1PT	1. 0
2. Page in Page File			2. P0PT/P1PT	2. 0
3. Page Table Page			3. SPT	3. 0
System Page Read	Priority of "System"	PID of "System"		
1. System Page(2)	Process 16	Process	1. SPT	1. 0
2. Global Page			2. GPT	2. Slave PTE Address(<0)
3. Global CRF Page			3. Process Page Table	3. Master PTE Contents(>0)
4. Global Page Table Page			4. SPT	4. 0
Modified Page Write	MPW_PRIO	PID of Modified	Points to Modified	0
1. To Page File			Page Writer	
2. To Image File(3)		(PID of Map Swapper)		Page Writer's
3. To Swap File (SWPVBN=0)				
Update Section Page Write(4)	Priority of Caller	PID of Caller	a. Process Page Table b. Global Page Table	AST Address (if specified)
Swapper I/O	SWP_PRIO	PID of Swapper	Points to Swapper Map	0

(1) One field in the I/O request packet (IRP$L_ASTPRM) for page reads from a private section is sensitive to whether the section is copy on reference. These two cases are distinguished as:
   a. Not Copy on Reference
   b. Copy on Reference
(2) Pageable executive routines originate in one of three image files (SYS.EXE, RMS.EXE, and SYSMSG.EXE) described by three system section table entries (SSTE) located in the system header.
   The static executive data is all located in the nonpaged executive. The only pageable writeable data is the paged pool area, which starts out as a series of demand zero pages. Paged pool pages are written to and subsequently faulted from the page file.
   These two cases are distinguished as:
   a. Pageable executive routines
   b. Paged pool pages
(3) The modified page writer takes special note of whether pages that are written back to an image file are part of a
   a. Private section
   b. Global section

Table 15-1 *(continued)*
Description of I/O Requests Issued by Memory Management

AST Parameter	Address of Window Control Block	Cluster Factor	Priority Boost at I/O Completion
IRP$L_ASTPRM	IRP$L_WIND	—	—
1a. 0	1. From PSTE	1. pfc/PFCDEFAULT(6)	Class=0
1b. PSTX			Boost=0
2. 0	2. From PFL	2. PFCDEFAULT	
3. 0	3. From PFL(5)	3. PAGTBLPFC	
			Class=0
			Boost=0
1. 0	1a. From SSTE	1a. SYSPFC	
	1b. From PFL	1b. PFCDEFAULT	
2. 0	2. From GSTE	2. pfc/PFCDEFAULT(6)	
3. GSTX (PFN$V_GBLBAK is set)	3. From GSTE	3. pfc/PFCDEFAULT(6)	
4. 0	4. From PFL(5)	4. 1	
Address of MPW's special			None(7)
kernel AST (WRITEDONE)	1. From PFL	1. MPW_WRTCLUSTER	
	2a. From PSTE	2. MPW_WRTCLUSTER	
	2b. From GSTE		
	3. From SFTE	3. 1	
AST Parameter (if specified)	a. PSTE	MPW_WRTCLUSTER	Class=1
	b. GSTE		Boost=2
Swapper's KAST (IODONE)	SFTE	Not Applicable	None(7)

(4) In a similar manner, the Update Section system service behaves differently depending on whether the pages are part of a
   a. Private section
   b. Global section

(5) Process page tables and global page tables originate as demand zero pages that are written to and faulted from the page file.

(6) The cluster factor for a private section or a global section can be specified at link time or when the section is mapped by explicitly declaring a cluster factor (pfc). In the absence of such a specification, the pager uses the default system cluster factor determined by the SYSBOOT parameter PFCDEFAULT.

(7) The swapper (and by implication the modified page writer) is a real-time process and is therefore not subject to priority boosts.

- If the original page table entry contains a global page table index, successive PTEs must contain successively increasing (or decreasing) indexes. In addition, the global page table entries must all contain exactly the same global section table index.

15.5.1.3 **Maximum Cluster Size for Page Read.** The maximum number of pages that can be in a cluster is determined in several ways, depending on the type of page being read.

- Global page table pages are not clustered.
- The cluster factor for process page table pages is taken from offset PHD$B_PGTBPFC in the fixed portion of the process header. Unless some user-written kernel mode routine has modified this field, the value of this field is taken from the special SYSBOOT parameter PAGTBLPFC for all processes in the system. The default value for this parameter is two. This value is chosen to avoid an artificial end to building a cluster when the page table page also had to be faulted. Two page table pages are guaranteed to span 127 pages, regardless of the initial faulting virtual address. Decreasing this value may defeat clustered reads. Increasing it above two is likely to have negligible effect in most systems.
- The cluster factor for page file pages is taken from the PFL$B_PFC field of the page file control block (see Figure 14-22). The usual contents of this field are zero. In that case the cluster factor is taken from the PHD$B_DFPFC field of the process header. In the absence of user-written modification, the value placed into this field is the SYSBOOT parameter PFCDEFAULT.
- The cluster factor for process or global sections is taken from the SEC$B_PFC field of the process or global section table entry (see Figures 14-7 and 14-16). These fields usually contain values of zero, in which case the default page fault cluster is used. (Just as for clustered reads from the page file, this default is taken from the PHD$B_DFPFC field in the process header. The value of this field is usually equal to the PFCDEFAULT SYSBOOT parameter.)

  There are two methods available to the user to control the cluster factor of process or global sections. By including the following line in the linker options file, the page fault cluster factor in the image section descriptor can be set to nonzero contents:

  ```
  CLUSTER = cluster-name,[base-address],[pfc],[file-spec,...]
  ```

  Sections that are mapped by the user (with a Create and Map [Private or Global] Section system service) can have their page fault cluster factor specified by including the optional PFC argument in the system service call.

15.5.1.4 **Page Read Completion.** The page read completion is detected by the I/O postprocessing routine (IPL 4 software interrupt service routine) by the special code inserted in the IRP before the request was queued.

Page read completion is not reported to the faulting process in the normal fashion with a special kernel mode AST because none of the postprocessing has to be performed in the context of the faulting process. Instead, the work is done by this service routine and the process made computable by reporting a page read completion event to the scheduler.

The details that the service routine takes care of when a page read successfully completes include the following steps for each page:

1. The reference count is decremented, indicating that the read in progress has completed.
2. The physical page state is set to active and valid.
3. The valid bit in the page table entry is set.
4. If the page is a global page, the valid bit set in Step 3 was in the global page table entry. In this case, the process (slave) PTE must be loaded with the PFN and made valid.

After the individual pages have been tended to, the scheduler is notified that a page read has completed (by reporting a page fault completion event with a null priority increment) so that the process that was put into a page fault wait state when the read was initiated can be made computable. (If any of the pages just read were collided pages, the collided page wait queue is also emptied. That is, all processes in that state are made computable. Collided pages are discussed in Section 15.6.3.)

15.5.2 Modified Page Writing

The modified page writer (a subroutine of the SWAPPER process) also attempts to cluster when writing modified pages to their backing store addresses. There are not so many special cases here as there are in the page read situation. The three different cases encountered by the modified page writer depend on the three possible backing store locations that pages on the modified page list can have.

15.5.2.1 Operation of the Modified Page Writer. The modified page writer proceeds in approximately the following fashion:

1. The first page is removed from the modified page list. Its page table entry address is retrieved from the PFN PTE array.
2. Adjacent page table entries are scanned (first toward lower virtual addresses and then toward higher virtual addresses) to look for transition page table entries that map pages on the modified page list either until the desired cluster size is reached or until one of the other terminating conditions is reached.

   This scan begins first toward smaller virtual addresses for the same reason that the read cluster routine begins toward larger addresses. If the program is more likely to reference higher addresses, the modified page writer does not want to initiate a write operation, only to have the page immediately faulted (and likely modified again). The modified page writer chooses to first write those pages with a smaller likelihood of being referenced in the near future.

3. The write is initiated, the state of all of the pages is changed to write in progress, and their reference counts are incremented.

4. The modified page writer returns to the SWAPPER process until notified by its special kernel mode AST that the modified page write has completed.

15.5.2.2 Modified Page Write Clustering. The terminating conditions for the scan of the page table include the following:

- The page table page is not valid, implying that there are no transition pages in this page table page. The special check is made to avoid an unnecessary page fault.
- The page table entry does not indicate a transition format.
- The page table entry indicates a page in transition, but the physical page is not on the modified page list.
- The physical page number is greater than the contents of global location MMG$GL_MAXPFN. This check avoids pages in shared memory, which have no PFN data associated with them.
- The SWPVBN array element must be zero. Pages with nonzero SWPVBN contents are treated in a special way by the modified page writer.
- If the contents of the BAK array indicate that the backing store location for the page is a (private or global) image file, the section index must be the same for all pages in the cluster.
- If the BAK array element indicates that the pages are to be written to the page file, the contents of the virtual block number field are ignored. However, all pages must contain the same page file index in their BAK array elements.

15.5.2.3 Backing Store Addresses for Modified Pages. There are three different kinds of backing store address that the modified page writer encounters as the modified page writer removes pages from the modified page list.

- If the SWPVBN array element is nonzero, this indicates that the process is outswapped and this page remained behind, probably due to an outstanding read request. The modified page writer does not attempt to cluster. Instead, a write of a single page to the designated block in the swap file is issued. A description of how the SWPVBN array element can be loaded is found in Chapter 17, where the entire outswap operation is discussed.
- If the backing store address is a section, the modified page writer creates a

cluster (up to the value of the SYSBOOT parameter MPW_WRTCLUSTER). Any of the terminating conditions listed in the previous section will limit the size of the cluster.

- If the backing store address is a page file, adjacent pages bound for the same page file are also written at the same time.

    The modified page writer attempts to allocate a number of blocks in the page file equal to MPW_WRTCLUSTER. The desired cluster factor is reduced to the number of blocks actually allocated. Section 15.5.2.4 describes allocation of space within the page file.

    The actual cluster created for a write to the page file consists of several smaller clusters, each one representing a series of virtually contiguous pages (see Figure 15-9).

    —The modified page writer creates a cluster of virtually contiguous pages, all bound for the same page file.

    —If the desired cluster size has not yet been reached, the modified page list is searched until another physical page bound for the same page file is found.

    —Pages virtually contiguous to this page form the second minicluster that is added to the eventual cluster to be written to the page file.

    —This process continues until either the cluster size is reached or no more pages on the modified page list have the designated page file as their backing store address. The modified page writer is building a large cluster that consists of a series of smaller clusters. The large cluster terminates only when the desired size is reached or the modified page list contains no more pages bound to the page file in question. Each smaller cluster can terminate on any of the conditions listed in the previous section, or on the two terminating conditions for the large cluster.

15.5.2.4 **Page File Space Allocation.** Before the modified page writer searches for pages to write, it must first determine the size of the write cluster. To do this, it must determine the number of contiguous blocks in the page file that can be allocated.

When the modified page writer attempts to allocate blocks in the page file, it looks for a cluster of blocks that is the current allocation size in length (the current allocation size is stored in the page file control block at the offset PFL$L_ALLOCSIZ and is usually equal to MPW_WRTCLUSTER). If the desired number of blocks is not available, the allocation size is reduced by 16 blocks and the search for contiguous blocks starts again at the beginning of the page file. If the page file deallocation routine determines that it has freed a large enough cluster, it increases the allocation size by 8 (up to MPW_WRTCLUSTER).

When the allocation size for the page file is less than or equal to 16, a special-case allocation routine is called. This special-case allocation routine

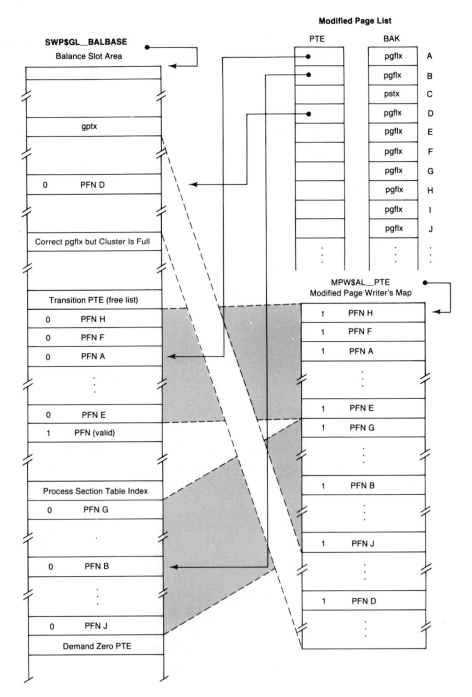

Figure 15-9
Example of Clustered Write to a Page File

searches for and allocates the first available cluster of blocks that it encounters. The routine can allocate between 1 and 16 contiguous blocks. If the special-case allocation routine determines that more than 65 percent of the page file is in use, the following message is issued on the console terminal:

```
SYSTEM-W-PAGEFRAG, Page file 65 full, system continuing
```

If the allocation routine determines that more than 90 percent of the page file is in use, the following message is issued on the console terminal:

```
SYSTEM-W-PAGECRIT, Page file 90 full, system trying to continue
```

If you see either of these messages on the console terminal, it is a good indication that the system requires an(other) alternate page file.

15.5.2.5   **Example of Modified Page Write to a Page File.** Figure 15-9 illustrates a sample cluster for writing to a page file. The modified page list (pictured in the upper right-hand corner of the figure) is shown as a sequential array to simplify the figure.

1. The first page on the modified page list is PFN A. By scanning backward, first PFN F and then PFN H are located. The PTE preceding the one that contains PFN H is also a transition PTE, but the page is on the free page list. This page terminates the backward search.
2. The modified page writer map begins with PFN H, PFN F, and PFN A. The search now goes in the forward direction, with each page bound for the page file added to the map up to and including PFN E. The next page table entry is valid so the first minicluster is terminated.
3. The next page on the modified page list, PFN B, leads to the addition of a second cluster to the map. This cluster begins with PFN G and ends with PFN J. The backward search was terminated with a PTE containing a section table index. The forward search terminated with a demand zero PTE.

   Note that this second cluster consists of pages belonging to a different process from the first cluster. The difference is reflected in the word array element for each PTE in the map that contains a process header vector index for each page (see Figure 14-24).
4. The next page on the modified page list is PFN C. This page belongs in a global image file and is skipped over during the current write attempt.
5. PFN D leads to a third cluster that was terminated in the backward direction with a page table entry that contains a global page table index. The search in the forward direction terminated when the desired cluster size was reached, even though the next PTE was bound to the same page file. This size is either MPW_WRTCLUSTER or a number of virtually contiguous blocks available in the page file, whichever is smaller. In any case, this cluster will be written with a single write request.
6. Note that reaching the desired size resulted in leaving some pages on the modified page list bound for the same page file, such as PFN I in the figure.

15.5.2.6 **Modified Page Write Completion.** The modified page writer is notified that the write is complete by a special kernel mode AST (whose address was stored in the ASTPRM field of the IRP while the write was in progress). Modified page writing is recorded in the IRP as a swap write to allow this completion method to be used. For the purposes of the I/O postprocessing routine, the only form of page write request is the one issued by the Update Section system service.

This kernel mode AST decrements various reference counts that indicated the write in progress. If the reference count is now zero, the pages are placed on the free page list. If the number of pages on the modified page list (SCH$GL_MFYCNT) is still above the low limit threshold for the modified page list (SCH$GL_MFYLOLIM), then the modified page writer removes the new first page from the modified page list and starts all over.

15.5.3 **Update Section System Service**

The Update Section system service allows a process to write pages in a section to their backing store addresses in a controlled fashion, without waiting for the modified page writer to do the backup. This system service is especially useful for frequently accessed pages that may never be written by the modified page writer, because they are always being faulted from the modified page list back into the working set before they are backed up.

This system service is a cross between modified page writing and a normal write request. Like any Queued I/O request, this service can receive completion notification with an event flag, an AST, or through an I/O status block. The number of pages written is specified by the address range passed as an input parameter to the service. The cluster factor is the minimum of MPW_WRTCLUSTER and the number of pages in the input range. The direction of search for modified pages is determined by the order that the address range is specified to the service.

15.5.3.1 **Page Selection.** If the section that is being backed up is a process private section, only those pages that have the modified bit set in the page table entry (or in the PFN state array for transition pages) are written out.

If the section is a global section, then information about whether the page is modified is found in both the PFN database and the page table entries of all processes mapped to this global page. (The modify bit in the global page table entry is inaccessible to hardware and contains no useful information.) Because there are no back pointers for valid global pages, this information is unavailable. Therefore, all pages in a global section are written to their backing store location, regardless of whether the pages have been modified.

If the flags parameter passed to Update Section has its low bit set, the set bit indicates that the caller is the only process capable of modifying the section. In that case, the process page table entries (and the PFN database) are used to select candidate pages for backing up, and only modified pages are written.

15.5.3.2   **Write Completion.** The process that issued the Update Section system service is first notified about write completion with a special kernel mode AST. This AST first checks whether all the pages requested by the original call have been written or whether another write is required. If more pages have to be written, another cluster is set up and queued. If all requested pages have been written, the normal I/O completion path involving event flags, I/O status blocks, and user-requested ASTs is entered, and the process is notified.

15.6   **PAGING AND SCHEDULING**

Page fault handling can influence the scheduling state of processes in several different ways. If a read is required to satisfy a page fault, the faulting process is placed into a page fault wait state. If a resource such as physical memory or page file space is not available, the process is placed into an appropriate wait state. There are several other wait states that a process may be placed into as a result of a page fault.

15.6.1   **Page Fault Wait State**

The most obvious wait state is page fault wait (PFW), which is required if a read is required to resolve the fault. The process that requires the read to resolve its page fault is placed into a page fault wait state. The I/O completion routine detects that a page read has completed and reports a page fault completion event to the scheduler. The scheduler removes the process from the page fault wait state and makes it computable. There is no priority increment due to page fault read completion so the scheduling decision is made based on the process's current priority.

15.6.2   **Free Page Wait State**

If there is not enough physical memory available to satisfy the page fault, the process is placed into a free page wait state (FPG). The physical page manager (module ALLOCPFN) checks for processes in this state whenever pages are added to an empty list. If the free page wait state is not empty, all processes in the state are made computable.

The physical page manager makes no scheduling decision about which process will get the page. There is no first-in/first-out approach to the free page wait state. Rather, all processes waiting for the page are made computable. The next process to execute will be chosen by the scheduler, using the normal algorithm that the highest priority resident computable process executes next.

15.6.3   Collided Page Wait State

It is possible for a page fault to occur for a page which is already being read from disk. Such a page is referred to as a collided page. The collided bit (in the PFN TYPE array) is set and the process placed into the collided page (COLPG) wait state.

One of the details that the page read completion routine checks is the collided bit in the TYPE array element for the page. If the collided bit is set, the collided page wait state is emptied. There is no check for the page that is being waited for by each process as it is made computable.

This lack of check has two advantages.

- As was the case for free page availability, there is no special code to determine which process will get the page first. All processes are made computable, and the normal scheduling algorithm selects the process that executes next.
- The probability of a collided page is small. The probability of two different collided pages is even smaller. If a process waiting for another collided page is selected for execution, that process will incur a page fault and get put right back into the collided wait state. Nothing unusual occurs and the operating system avoids a lot of special-case code to handle a situation that rarely, if ever, occurs.

16 Memory Management System Services

Confusion now hath made his masterpiece!
—Macbeth 2,3

The previous two chapters discussed the data structures used by the memory management subsystem to describe physical and virtual memory and the action of the page fault handler when a page was referenced in which the valid bit was not set. This chapter describes the system services available to the user (and also used internally by the operating system) to allocate these structures and initialize their contents.

1. Some system services create or delete virtual address space within the limitations imposed by process quotas and limits and SYSBOOT parameters.
2. Private and global sections can be created that allow the blocks of a file to be mapped as a portion of a process address space. Although the section services are also associated with the layout of virtual address space, they are treated separately because of their added level of complexity.
3. System services allow users to lock portions of their working sets into memory, avoiding the overhead of page faults or allowing portions of code to execute at elevated IPL. A process can also disable swapping, preventing itself from being removed from memory.
4. There are other miscellaneous operations associated with the memory management available to a process. For example, a process may force the contents of all modified pages to be written to their backing store addresses (Update Section system service) or purge some or all pages from its working set (Purge Working Set system service).

16.1 DISPATCH METHOD FOR MEMORY MANAGEMENT SYSTEM SERVICES

Almost all of the memory management system services specify a desired address range as an input parameter. The page table entries associated with these addresses contain an owner field (see Figure 14-3), indicating whether the caller of each service can manipulate the pages in the desired fashion. Another peculiarity of the memory management system services is that many of the services can partially succeed (because they are done on a page-by-page basis). This partial success is indicated by returning an error code combined with the address range over which the operation was completed (in the **retadr** argument).

A common dispatch method is used by most of the memory management system services to reflect the similarity of the services:

- Information about the specific service, including the input parameters, is placed on the stack for later retrieval.
- Page ownership is checked to insure that a less privileged access mode is not attempting to alter the properties of some pages owned by a more privileged access mode.
- The address of a page-by-page routine to accomplish the desired action of the original service is placed into R6.
- A common routine is called that performs general page processing and calls the single page service-specific routine for each page in the desired range.
- The address range actually operated on is returned to the caller (if it is requested).

16.2   VIRTUAL ADDRESS CREATION AND DELETION

The first level of memory management available to a process is the creation or deletion of virtual address space. These services are also used by the system when an image first begins executing (the image activator calls several services to create process address space) and as part of image exit (the image reset routine deletes all of P0 space and a small part of P1 space). The memory management performed by the system as part of image activation or process deletion is described in Chapter 21.

16.2.1   Address Space Creation

Address space creation is essentially a simple operation. A series of demand zero pages is created, either at the end of the designated address space (the Expand Region [$EXPREG] system service) or in the specified address range (the Create Virtual Address Space [$CRETVA] system service). If any pages already exist in the requested range, they must be deleted first.

These two system services can partially succeed. That is, a number of pages smaller than the number originally requested may be created. Once the specified address range is determined, the demand zero pages are created one at a time. It is possible to run into one of the limits on the number of pages that can be created after several pages have already been successfully created. For this reason, it is especially important for the caller of either $CRETVA or $EXPREG to look at the **retadr** argument to determine whether the service ($CRETVA or $EXPREG) was partially successful.

16.2.1.1   Limits on Virtual Address Space Creation. There are three limitations on the amount of virtual address space that can be created.

- The SYSBOOT parameter VIRTUALPAGECNT controls the total number of page table entries (P0PTEs plus P1PTEs) that any process can have in its process header. The division of these pages between P0 space and P1 space is totally arbitrary and process specific. It is only the sum of P0 and P1 pages that is limited by the SYSBOOT parameter.
- The size of a process working set also controls the size of that process's address space. When a process page is valid, the page table page for that page is not only valid but also dynamically locked into the working set. For small address spaces, the set of valid process pages can be represented by a small number of page table pages.

    As the address space grows, the probability that a given page table page maps more than one valid process page decreases. (The limiting case, one that can usually be reached only with very large process address spaces, requires two working set list entries for each valid process page.) In any case, there is an implicit limit to the process address space imposed by the process working set quotas.

    The specific check that is made is whether the size of the dynamic working set list can lock down all the page table pages necessary to map the process address space and still leave enough fluid working set (PHD$W_FLUID), plus the worst case number of page table pages required to map PHD$W_FLUID pages, in order to allow the process to perform useful work. The number of page table pages that results is the minimum of PHD$W_FLUID and the number of page table pages not already locked down. If this check fails, the working set list is expanded. If the working set is at its limit, the virtual address creation fails with the status of SS$_INSFWSL.
- The third constraint on the total size of the process address space is the page file quota. Each demand zero page and each copy-on-reference section page is charged against the job's page file quota (JIB$L_PGFLCNT).

16.2.1.2   Expand Region System Service. The Expand Region system service is a special case of the Create Virtual Address Space system service. The requested number of pages is simply converted into a P0 or P1 page range and control is passed to a page creation routine that is common between the two services.

16.2.1.3   Automatic User Stack Expansion. A special form of P1 space expansion occurs when a request for user stack space exceeds the remaining size of the user stack. Such a request can be reported by the hardware as an access violation exception or by software when insufficient user stack space is detected. (Software detection is done by the AST delivery routine and the Adjust Stack system service if the request is for user mode stack space.)

The routine EXE$EXPANDSTK is called directly by the two software routines and invoked by the access violation exception handler if the access violation occurred in user mode. This routine checks that a length violation (as opposed to a protection violation) occurred and that the inaccessible address is in P1 space. If so, P1 space is expanded from its current low address end to the specified inaccessible address. For the usual case, one in which a program requires more user stack space than requested at link time, the expansion typically occurs one page at a time.

Because this automatic expansion cannot be disabled on a process-specific or system-wide basis, a runaway program (one that is using stack space without returning it) will not be aborted until it exceeds the virtual address size determined by the SYSBOOT parameter VIRTUALPAGECNT (a quota violation which is indicated by $CRETVA returning an error status of SS$_VASFULL). In addition, a program that makes a random (and probably incorrect) reference to an arbitrary P1 address smaller than the top of the user stack will probably continue to execute (after the creation of many demand zero pages) rather than exiting with some error status.

If the stack expansion fails for whatever reason (the Create Virtual Address system service can fail for several reasons), the process is notified in a way that depends on who originally called EXE$EXPANDSTK.

- The Adjust Stack system service for user mode can fail with several of the error codes returned by $CRETVA.
- An attempt to deliver an AST to a process with insufficient user stack space results in an AST delivery stack fault exception being reported to the process. (Enough information is removed from the stack by the error routine that the exception dispatcher can at least get started in reporting the exception.)
- If the user stack cannot be expanded in response to a P1 space length violation, then an access violation fault is reported to the process. If there is not enough user stack to report the exception, the normal condition handler search is bypassed and the exception is reported directly to the last chance handler (see Chapter 4). In the default case, this handler causes the currently executing image to terminate.

16.2.2 Address Space Deletion

For a couple of reasons, page deletion is more complicated than page creation.

- Creation involves taking the process from one known state (address space does not yet exist) to another known state (the page table entries contain demand zero PTEs). Page deletion must deal with initial conditions that include all the possible states that a virtual page can be in.
- Page creation may first require that the specified pages be deleted in order

to put the process page tables into their known state. That is, page deletion is often an integral part of page creation.

16.2.2.1 **Delete Virtual Address Space System Service.** When a page is deleted, all process and system resources associated with the page must be returned. These include the following forms:

- A page frame for valid and transition pages
- A page file virtual block for pages whose backing store address indicates an already allocated block
- A working set list entry for a page in the process working set list
- Page file quota for all pages with a page file backing store address, including pages that have not yet allocated a block in the page file

Private section pages that are deleted cause the reference count in the process section table entry (see Figure 14-7) to be decremented. If the reference count goes to zero, the PSTE itself can be released.

In addition, valid or modified pages with a section backing store address (as opposed to a page file backing store address) must have their latest contents written back to the section file. (The contents of pages with a page file backing store address are unimportant after the virtual page is deleted and do not have to be saved before the physical page is reused.)

16.2.2.2 **Page Deletion and Scheduling.** Pages that have I/O in progress cannot be deleted until the I/O completes. Such processes are placed into a page fault wait state (requesting that a system event be reported when I/O completes) until the page read or write completes. Pages in the write-in-progress transition state will cause the same effect. Pages in the read-in-progress transition state are faulted, with the immediate result that the process is placed into the collided page wait state. Special action must be taken for global pages with I/O in progress because there is no way to determine if the process deleting the page is also responsible for the I/O. In such cases, the process is placed into a miscellaneous wait state (MWAIT) until its direct I/O completes. (If the process has no direct I/O in progress, the problem does not arise in the first place, and the deletion is allowed to proceed.)

Once all reasons for keeping the page around have been taken care of, the page is deleted. Deletion of a physical page means that the contents of the PFN PTE array are cleared, destroying all ties between the physical page and any process virtual address. In addition, the page is placed at the head of the free page list, causing it to be used before other pages whose contents are still useful.

16.2.2.3 **Contract Region System Service.** The Contract Region system service is a special case of the Delete Virtual Address Space system service. The requested number of pages is simply converted into a P0 or P1 page range and control is passed to a page deletion routine that is common between the two services.

16.2.3 Controlled Allocation of Virtual Memory

There is a second level of memory management available to a process. The Run-Time Library procedures LIB$GET_VM and LIB$FREE_VM provide a mechanism for allocating small blocks of virtual memory in a controlled fashion. Allocation from the free memory pool is performed in much the same way as pool space is allocated by the VMS operating system (see Chapter 3). If there is not a block of memory in the pool large enough to satisfy the request, P0 space is expanded (by calling $EXPREG), and the pool is extended to include the newly created virtual address space.

16.3 PRIVATE AND GLOBAL SECTIONS

A second method of creating address space is available. The Create and Map Section system service allows a process to associate a portion of its address space with a specified portion of a file. The section may be specific to a process (private section) or shared among several processes (global section). The Map Global Section system service allows a process to map a portion of its virtual address space to an already existing global section. These two services are used by the image activator (see Chapter 21) to map portions of process address space to either the image file or previously installed global sections.

The Create and Map Section system service also provides two special options. Rather than mapping a portion of process address space to a file, a suitably privileged process (with PFNMAP privilege) can associate (map) virtual addresses to specific physical addresses. Global sections can be created and mapped in shared memory as well as in local memory.

16.3.1 Create and Map Section System Service

The Create and Map Section system service is the system service that performs all of these operations. (In a sense, the Map Global Section system service is a special case of $CRMPSC where the section does not have to be created.) The particular path that is taken through the service is determined by the contents of the flags argument passed to the service. (The *VAX/VMS System Services Reference Manual* lists those flags that can be used together and those that are incompatible.) One way of looking at the action of this service is to examine the data structures that are created as a result of exercising one of the several options available to it.

16.3.1.1   **Private Section Creation.** When a process private section is created, a process section table entry (see Figure 14-7) is allocated from the area of the process header set aside for PSTEs. The information that associates the virtual address range with virtual blocks in the file is loaded into the PSTE. (When the private section is being created as a part of image activation as described in Chapter 21, the original source for much of the data stored in the PSTE is an image section descriptor contained in the image file.) In addition, each process page table entry in the designated address range is loaded with identical contents, namely a process section table index (see Figure 14-3).

The memory management subsystem cannot take a window turn on pages within a section (see Section 19.1.4). Therefore, it requires that all the mapping information for the newly mapped file be available in the window control block. If the Create and Map Section system service determines that not all mapping information is available, its operations are temporarily suspended while a request is made to the ACP for all mapping information for the file. Because the window control block occupies nonpaged pool, the extension of the window control block is charged against the process's BYTLM quota.

Because of the way space is allocated in the process header (see Chapter 26), it is possible that the space to hold a section table entry may extend into the working set list. When this occurs, the entire process section table can slide down into one of the empty pages set aside in the process header for exactly this purpose. All references to process section table entries are relative to the bottom (high address end) of the table that is located through offset PHD$L_PSTBASOFF. That is, the entire structure is position independent. Header expansion involves mapping the first empty page, moving the entire structure down one page, and changing PHD$L_PSTBASOFF to locate the new bottom of the table.

16.3.1.2   **Global Section Creation.** The creation of a global section (located in local memory) is similar to the creation of a private section except that the data structures are located in the system header (see Figures 14-15 and 14-18) instead of the process header:

1. A global section descriptor (see Figure 14-14) is allocated from paged dynamic memory and loaded with information that describes the name and protection attributes of the section. This data structure is used by subsequent Map Global Section system service calls to determine whether the named section exists and to locate the global section table entry in the system header that more fully describes the section.
2. A global section table entry (see Figure 14-16) in the system header (see Figure 14-15) is the analogous structure to the process section table entry.
3. A series of global page table entries are created in a virtual extension to the

system header (see Figure 14-17). These page table entries contain information that describes the current state of each global page in the section. They are not available to the memory management hardware but are used by the page fault handler when a process incurs a page fault for a global page.

4. A global section can be created and mapped by a single system service call. Alternatively, the section can be created in one step and mapped later on by either the creating process or by any other process allowed to map the section. In any case, mapping to a global section results in no changes to the global database. Rather, the process page table has a series of page table entries that contain a global page table index (see Figure 14-19) added to describe the designated address range. The process page table entries for global pages can be in one of two states, either valid or containing the appropriate global page table index.

16.3.1.3 **Global Sections in Shared Memory.** Global sections that are located in shared memory are treated in a slightly different fashion from local memory global sections. The sections are created by the Install Utility (INSTALL) after shared memory has been initialized. (See Chapter 14 for a description of the data structures that describe global sections in shared memory.) Global sections in shared memory have the following characteristics:

1. A special global section descriptor (see Figure 14-27) is created that contains, among other things, a list of the physical pages in shared memory that will contain the section. The section is temporarily mapped by INSTALL and each page of the section is loaded from the image file.

2. A global section table entry is created only on the CPU that originally creates the section. This GSTE allows the initial read to be performed and allows subsequent section updates (with SYS$UPDSEC) for writeable sections. Pages are also written back to the image file on the creating CPU when the section is deleted.

3. No global page table entries are needed for global sections in shared memory because the state of each page is known to be valid. The PFN information necessary to allow processes to map into this section is contained in the shared memory GSD.

4. When a process maps to the shared memory global section, the process page table entries are set to valid with the appropriate page frame numbers loaded into the PTEs. These pages are not counted against the process working set.

16.3.1.4 **Map by PFN.** The Create and Map Section system service allows a privileged process (one with PFNMAP privilege) to map a portion of its virtual address space to specific physical addresses. Although the primary intention of this service is to allow process address space to be mapped to I/O addresses, it can also be used to map specific physical memory pages.

When a private PFN-mapped section is created, the only effect is to add a series of valid PTEs to the process page table. The PFN fields in these PTEs contain the requested physical page numbers. The PTE$V_WINDOW bit in the PTE (see Figure 14-3) is set in each PTE to indicate that each of these virtual pages is PFN mapped. These pages are not counted against the process working set. In addition, no record is maintained in the PFN database that such pages are PFN mapped.

When a global PFN mapped section is created, the only data structure created to describe such a mapping request is a special form of global section descriptor (see Figure 14-14). There are no global page table entries nor is there a global section table entry. When a process maps to such a section, its process page table entries are set to valid, mapped by PFN (PFN$V_WINDOW is set), and the PFN fields are filled in according to the contents of the extended GSD (see Figure 14-14).

16.3.2   Map Global Section System Service

The Map Global Section system service can be considered a special case of the Create and Map (Global) Section system service, where the global section already exists. This service usually has no effect on the global database (other than to include the latest mapping in various reference counts). Rather, this service allows a range of process addresses to become mapped to the named global section.

The actual effect of this service is to load each of the designated process PTEs with a global page table index (see Figures 14-3 and 14-19). These global page table indexes are effectively pointers to global page table entries in the system header, where the current state of each global page is actually recorded.

When a process maps to a global section in shared memory or to a section that is PFN-mapped, there are no global page table entries to be pointed to. Instead, each process page table entry is set to valid with the PFN field containing a physical page number either in shared memory (for shared memory global sections) or anywhere in physical address space (as indicated by the extended GSD for PFN-mapped global sections).

16.3.3   Delete Global Section System Service

Like the Delete Virtual Address Space system service, the Delete Global Section system service is more complicated than global section creation because the section must be reduced from one of many states to nothing. In addition, global writeable pages must be written to their backing store addresses before a global section can be fully deleted. For these reasons, the global section deletion is often separated in time from the system service call.

When the Delete Global Section system service is called, the named section is marked for deletion, which means that the GSD is moved from the normal doubly linked GSD list to the delete pending list. The delete pending bit in the GSD is set. In addition, the permanent indicator in the GSD is turned off. However, the actual section deletion cannot occur until the reference in the global section table entry, the count of process page table entries mapped to the section, goes to zero. Although it is possible for the reference count to be zero when the section is marked for deletion, the more typical global section deletion occurs as a side effect of virtual address deletion (which itself might occur as a result of image exit or process deletion).

A reference count of zero indicates that no more process page table entries are mapped to the section. At that time, the following data structures that describe the system can be deallocated:

- The global page table entries in the system header are freed for further use. If an entire page of global page table entries is freed, that page can be unlocked from the system working set.
- The global section table entry in the system header is removed from the active list and placed on the free list of system section table entries for possible later use.
- The global section descriptor is placed on the free list of GSDs. When a global section is later created, this list is checked for a GSD before a new structure is allocated from paged dynamic memory.

Global sections in shared memory and PFN-mapped global sections exercise some of the same logic when the sections are deleted, but the effects are different because not all of the global data structures exist for these special global sections. A PFN-mapped section is described entirely by an extended global section descriptor (see Figure 14-14). In addition, no reference counts are kept for such sections, so the GSD can be placed on the free list of GSDs immediately.

When a shared memory global section is deleted, there are no global page table entries to delete. In addition, a global section table entry only exists on the port from which the section was created (to allow the section to be loaded when it was initially created and to allow the Update Section system service or Delete Global Section system service to preserve its contents).

16.3.4   Update Section System Service

The Update Section system service requests that a specified range of process private or global pages be written to their backing store addresses. When a private section is being updated, only those pages that have been modified (as indicated either by the PTE$V_MODIFY bit in the PTE or by the PFN$V_MODIFY bit in the PFN STATE array) are written. With global pages, the modify state of a physical page is the logical OR of the PFN STATE array modify bit and the modify bits in all of the process page table entries mapped to the section. Because there are no back pointers to all of these PTEs, this information is not available. Instead, when a global section is updated, all pages in the designated address range are written back to the global image file. (When the "exclusive writer" flag is passed to the Update Section system service, only those pages modified by the caller are written.) The interaction between the Update Section system service and the I/O subsystem is described in Chapter 17.

16.4   RELATED SYSTEM SERVICES

Other memory management system services allow a process to control its working set, alter page protection, and lock pages into the working set or into physical memory.

16.4.1   Working Set Size Adjustment

It is possible to make the process working set either larger or smaller, either manually with the Adjust Working Set Limit system service or automatically as a part of the quantum end routine. When the working set is expanded, new pages can be added to the working set without removing already valid entries. Adding pages to a process's working set decreases the probability that the process will incur a page fault.

It is unlikely that a program will voluntarily reduce its working set limit, unless it has a good understanding of its paging behavior. The system reduces a process working set as a part of the automatic working set adjustment. The swapper process can shrink a process's working set in an attempt to gain more pages, before resorting to swapping a process out of the working set. In addition, a process working set limit is reset to its default value as a part of the image rundown procedure (see Chapter 21) that is invoked when an image exits. Table 16-1 lists the process-specific and system-wide working set list parameters.

16.4.1.1   Adjust Working Set Size System Service. The effective result of altering the process working set size is to change the value of the WSSIZE working set list counter (see Figure 14-4).

In the case of working set list expansion, the working set size is limited by the maximum working set size (PHD$W_WSEXTENT). If the expanded working set extends into the process section table (see Figure 14-1), the process section table is moved down in exactly the same manner as is done to

Table 16-1: Working Set Lists: Limits and Quotas

Description	Location or Name	Comments
Beginning of Working Set List	PHD$W_WSLIST	Always has the value 60 (hex) (This is PHD$K_LENGTH / 4)
Size of the entire working set	PHD$W_WSSIZE	Set by LOGINOUT, altered by call to SYS$ADJWSL or by automatic working set adjustment
Beginning of list of permanently locked entries	PHD$W_WSLOCK	The same for all processes in a given system
Beginning of dynamic portion of working set list	PHD$W_WSDYN	Identical to WSLOCK unless this process has called SYS$LKWSET or SYS$LCKPAG
Index of most recently inserted working set list entry	PHD$W_WSNEXT	Updated each time an entry is added to the working set
End of current working set list	PHD$W_WSLAST	Updated by calling SYS$ADJWSL, by image exit, by pager, or by automatic working set adjustment
Default working set size	PHD$_DFWSCNT	Set by LOGINOUT, altered by SET WORKING_SET/LIMIT command
Normal limit to working set size	PHD$W_WSQUOTA	Set by LOGINOUT, altered by SET WORKING_SET/QUOTA command
Maximum limit to working set size	PHD$W_WSEXTENT	Set by LOGINOUT, altered by SET WORKING_SET/EXTENT command
Upper limit to working set quota	PHD$W_WSAUTH	Set by LOGINOUT, cannot be altered
Upper limit to working set extent	PHD$W_WSAUTHEXT	Set by LOGINOUT, cannot be altered
Lower limit to size of dynamic working set size	PHD$W_WSFLUID	Set up by SHELL, equal to the value of MINWSCNT SYSBOOT parameter

Table 16-1: Working Set Lists: Limits and Quotas (continued)

Description	Location or Name	Comments
Size of dynamic working set after allowing room for PHD$W_WSFLUID process page entries and a reasonable number of page table pages	PHD$W_EXTDYNWS	Updated each time size of dynamic working set is changed
Number of pages in use by process	PCB$W_PPGCNT + PCB$W_GPGCNT	Updated each time a page is added to or removed from the working set
Authorized default working set size	UAF$W_DFWSCNT	Loaded into PHD$W_DFWSCNT
Authorized default working set limit	UAF$W_WSQUOTA	Loaded into both PHD$W_WSQUOTA and PHD$W_WSAUTH
Authorized default working set maximum	UAF$W_WSEXTENT	Loaded into both PHD$W_WSEXTENT and PHD$W_WSAUTHEXT
System-wide minimum working set size	MINWSCNT	SYSBOOT parameter
System-wide maximum working set size	WSMAX	SYSBOOT parameter
Working set size for system paging	SYSMWCNT	SYSBOOT parameter
Default value for working set size default (used by SYS$CREPRC)	PQL_DWSDEFAULT	SYSBOOT parameter
Minimum value for working set size default (used by SYS$CREPRC)	PQL_MWSDEFAULT	SYSBOOT parameter
Default value for working set quota (used by SYS$CREPRC)	PQL_DWSQUOTA	SYSBOOT parameter
Minimum value for working set quota SYSBOOT parameter (used by SYS$CREPRC)	PQL_MWSQUOTA	

accommodate process section table expansion. However, there is not always enough room in the process header to accommodate the expanded working set list. The process header size is determined by WSMAX (and PROCSECTCNT) and the working set parameters (PHD$W_WSEXTENT and PHD$W_WSAUTHEXT) are minimized with WSMAX. (The calculation of the size of each piece of the process header is described in Chapter 26.) Note that there is no check to determine how many process section table entries in the process header are allocated; thus, the process section table can grow so large that there is not enough working set list area available.

In the case of working set list contraction, the working set cannot be contracted below MINWSCNT. In addition, the extra dynamic working set size (PHD$W_EXTDYNWS) cannot be reduced below zero. If the PHD$W_WSNEXT pointer locates an entry beyond the new end of the list, it is reset to point to the new end. The contracted list can have holes in it; the PHD$W_WSLAST pointer is only moved back as a side effect of freeing excess working set list entries (above the new limit).

16.4.1.2   SET WORKING_SET Command. The SET WORKING_SET command allows the default working set size (PHD$W_DFWSCNT) or the working set maximum (PHD$W_WSEXTENT) to be altered at the command level. Neither the default size nor the maximum can be set to a value larger than the authorized upper limit (PHD$W_WSAUTHEXT).

If the working set maximum is altered, it changes the upper limit for future calls to the Adjust Working Set Limit system service. If the limit (default size) is altered, it affects the working set list reset operation performed by the routine MMG$IMGRESET invoked as a result of image exit. If the limit is set to a value larger than the current quota, both the quota and the limit are altered to the new value. (Note that automatic working set adjustment is disabled for any process that has its quota and default (limit) set to the same value.)

16.4.1.3   Automatic Working Set Size Adjustment. In addition to working set adjustment as a result of explicit calls to SYS$ADJWSL or as a side effect of image exit, the operating system also provides automatic working set adjustment to keep a process's page fault rate within limits set by one of several SYSBOOT parameters (see Table 16-2). All of the SYSBOOT parameters listed in this table are dynamic and can be altered without rebooting the system.

The automatic working set adjustment takes place as part of the quantum end routine (see Chapter 10), because a process that cannot execute for even a single quantum will not benefit from an increased working set size. (Note that no adjustment takes place for real-time processes.) The adjustment takes place in several steps:

Table 16-2: Automatic Working Set Size Adjustments: Process and System Parameters

Description	Location or Name	Comments
Total amount of CPU time charged to this process	PHD$L_CPUTIM	Updated by hardware clock service routine
Amount of CPU time when last adjustment took place	PHD$L_TIMREF	Updated by quantum end routine when adjustment check is made
Total number of page faults for this process	PHD$L_PAGEFLTS	Updated each time this process incurs a page fault
Number of page faults when last adjustment took place	PHD$L_PFLREF	Updated by quantum end routine when adjustment check is made
Most recent page fault rate for this process	PHD$L_PFLTRATE	Recorded but not used each time an adjustment check is made
Amount of CPU time that process must accumulate before a page fault rate check is made	AWSTIME (S)	
Lower limit page fault rate	PFRATL (S)	
Amount by which to decrease working set list size	WSDEC (S)	
Lower bound for decreasing working set list size	AWSMIN (S)	Do not adjust if PCB$W_PPGCNT is less than or equal to this value
Upper limit page fault rate	PFRATH (S)	
Amount by which to increase working set list size	WSINC (S)	Disables automatic adjustment for entire system if zero
Free page list size to allow growth of working set	GROWLIM (S)	Do not adjust working set size if @SCH$GL_FREECNT is less than or equal to this value
Free page list size to allow extension of working set list	BORROWLIM (S)	Do not adjust working set list size if @SCH$GL_FREECNT is less than or equal to this value

(S) These values are SYSBOOT parameters.

1. If the WSINC parameter is set to zero, the adjustment is disabled on a system-wide basis, so nothing is done. If automatic working set adjustment has been turned off by the DCL command SET WORKING_SET/ NOADJUST, the adjustment is disabled for the process, and, again, nothing is done.

2. If the process default working set size (PHD$W_DFWSCNT) is equal to its quota (PHD$W_WSQUOTA), then adjustment is disabled for this process, so, again, nothing is done.

3. If the process has not been executing long enough since the last adjustment (the difference between accumulated CPU time, PHD$L_CPUTIM, and the time of the last adjustment attempt, PHD$L_TIMREF, is less than the SYSBOOT parameter AWSTIME), no adjustment is done at this time.

If the process has accumulated enough CPU time, the reference time is updated (PHD$L_CPUTIM is loaded into PHD$L_TIMREF), and the rate checks are made.

4. The current page fault rate is calculated. The philosophy for automatic working set adjustment consists of two premises. If the page fault rate is too low, the system can benefit from a smaller working set size (because more physical pages become available) without harming the process (by causing it to incur many page faults). If the page fault rate is too high, the process can benefit from a larger working set size (by incurring fewer faults), without degrading the system.

   • If the current page fault rate is too high (greater than or equal to PFRATH), a determination is made to see if the working set list can be extended. If the size of the working set list is below WSQUOTA, the working set list is extended by WSINC. If the size of the working set list is greater than or equal to WSQUOTA, the number of pages on the free page list is compared to the SYSBOOT parameter BORROWLIM. If there are more than BORROWLIM pages on the free page list, the working set list is increased by WSINC. However, if there are fewer than BORROWLIM pages on the free page list, the working set list is not extended. The working set list can only be extended up to WSEXTENT.

      Note the adjustment taking place here affects only the working set list, not the working set itself. Once the working set list has been extended, newly faulted pages can be added to the working set. The page fault exception handler will add pages to the working set above WSQUOTA only when there are more than the SYSBOOT parameter GROWLIM pages on the free page list (see Section 15.4.3).

   • If the current page fault rate is too low (strictly, less than PFRATL), the working set is decreased (by WSDEC). However, if the contents of PCB$W_PPGCNT are less than or equal to AWSMIN, no adjustment takes place. This decision is based on the assumption that many of the pages in the working set are global pages and that therefore the system will not benefit (and the process may suffer) if the working set is decreased. Note that in the update for VAX/VMS Version 3.1, PFRATL was set to zero, effectively turning off this method of working set reduction in favor of swapper working set trimming. The rationale for this change is explained at the end of this list.

5. The actual working set adjustment is accomplished by a regular kernel mode AST that executes an Adjust Working Set system service. The AST parameter passed to this AST is the amount of previously determined increase or decrease. This step is required because the system service must be called from process context (at IPL 0) and the quantum end routine is executing in response to the IPL 7 software timer interrupt.

Two other pieces of the executive control the size of a process's working set: the page fault routines and the swapper. As described in the previous list, the page fault handler can add a page to a process's working set if the size of the free page list is greater than GROWLIM. In an effort to gain pages, the swapper will reduce the working sets of processes in the balance set before actually removing processes from the balance set. This working set reduction is known as swapper trimming or working set shrinking. Process selection is performed by a table-driven, prioritized scheme (see Section 17.2.2).

Two problems are inherent in using the quantum end scheme of automatic working set adjustment: processes that are compute-intensive will reach quantum end many times and images that have been written to be efficient with respect to page faults (a low page fault rate) will qualify for working set reduction, because their page fault rate is lower than PFRATL. In both of these cases, working set reduction is not desirable. By contrast, swapper trimming selects its processes starting with those that are least likely to need large working sets.

In what can be seen as an evolutionary change to the operating system, working set reduction at quantum end was turned off in the VAX/VMS Version 3.1 update. The default value of PFRATL has been set to zero. In this manner, swapper trimming and the image exit reset are the only methods used to reduce working set size.

16.4.1.4   **Purge Working Set System Service.** The Purge Working Set system service requests that all virtual pages in the specified address range that happen to be in the working set be removed from the working set. A program could use this service if it recognized that a certain set of routines or data was no longer required. By voluntarily removing entries from the working set, a process can exercise a little control over the working set list replacement algorithm, increasing the chances for frequently used pages to remain in the working set. The VMS executive uses this service as part of the image startup sequence (see Chapter 21) to insure that a program starts its execution without unnecessary pages (such as CLI command processing routines in its working set).

16.4.2   **Locking and Unlocking Pages**

For time-critical applications and other situations where a program wishes to access code or data without incurring a page fault, system services are provided to lock pages into the process working set or into memory.

16.4.2.1   **Locking Pages in the Working Set.** A set of virtual pages can be locked into the process working set to prevent page faults from occurring on references to these pages. Locking pages in the working set guarantees that when this process is executing (is the current process), the locked pages are always in the process working set. In addition to the obvious benefit of this service, it can also be used by routines that execute at elevated IPL (above IPL 2), because the operating system does not allow page faults to occur above IPL 2. There is no implication that these pages remain resident when the process is not current because the entire working set can be outswapped. (Residency is guaranteed by either a combination of this system service and the Set Swap Mode system service or by using the Lock Pages in Memory system service.)

All pages in the specified range are faulted into the working set if they are not already valid. The working set list (see Figure 14-4) must be reorganized so that the locked pages appear in the list following the WSLOCK pointer. This reorganization is accomplished by exchanging the locked WSLE with the entry pointed to by WSDYN, and then incrementing WSDYN to point to the next element in the list. The WSLX PFN array elements for the two valid pages must also be exchanged. In addition, the WSL$V_WSLOCK bit is set in the working set list entry.

A check is made to insure that the process will be left with enough dynamic working set after the specified number of pages are locked. Enough dynamic working set means that the extra dynamic working set size, the size of the dynamic working set after space has been allocated for page table pages and a minimum working set size, is greater than zero. (Like most of the memory management system services, this service can partially succeed. In this case, the address range that is actually locked is returned to the caller by means of the **retadr** argument.)

When a process is being outswapped, global read/write pages are dropped from the process working set (see Chapter 17) to avoid cumbersome accounting problems about whether the outswapped page contains the most up-to-date information. For this reason, global read/write pages cannot be locked into the process working set. (Such pages can be locked into memory because the Lock Pages in Memory system service prevents outswap of either the process header or the locked pages, avoiding the swapping situation altogether.) The swapper also performs an optimization with global read-only pages by dropping them from the working set on outswap if the global share count is larger than one. If such pages are locked into the working set, they are not dropped from the working set, regardless of the contents of the PFN SHRCNT array.

16.4.2.2 **Locking Pages in Memory.** The Lock Page in Memory system service is similar to the Lock Page in the Working Set service except that the WSL$V_PFNLOCK bit in the WSLE is set and the process header is locked into memory. This service performs an implicit working set lock in addition to guaranteeing permanent residency to the specified virtual address range. Because this operation is permanently allocating a system resource, physical memory, it requires a privilege (PSWAPM).

16.4.2.3 **Unlocking Pages.** The converse of either of the two locking services unlocks pages from either the working set or physical memory. In addition, the working set list entries may have to be exchanged with other locked entries to place the unlocked entries back into the dynamic portion of the list. As with the exchange associated with locking pages, the WSLX PFN array elements must also be exchanged. Finally, the appropriate bit in the WSLE (WSL$V_WSLOCK or WSL$V_PFNLOCK) is cleared.

16.4.3 **Process Swap Mode**

A process with PSWAPM privilege can prevent itself from being removed from memory. The set process swap mode ($SETSWM) system service simply sets the PCB$V_PSWAPM bit in the status longword (PCB$L_STS) in the software PCB. When the swapper is searching for suitable outswap candidates, processes with this bit set are passed over.

16.4.4 **Altering Page Protection**

It is possible for a process to alter the page protection of a set of pages in its address range with the Set Protection on Pages system service ($SETPRT). In general, the operation of this service is straightforward. However, there is one interesting side effect. If a section page for a read-only section has its protection set to writeable, the copy-on-reference bit is set. This set bit will force the page to have its backing store address changed to the page file when the page is faulted, preventing a later attempt to write the modified section pages back to a file to which the process may be denied write access.

The symbolic debugger uses this service to implement its watchpoint facility. The page containing the data element in question is set to no write access for user mode. When the program attempts to access the page, an access violation occurs, which is fielded by the debugger's condition handler. This handler performs the following actions:

1. Checks whether the inaccessible address is the one being watched and reports the modification if it is
2. Sets the page protection to PRT$C_UW to allow the modification
3. Sets the TBIT in the PSL to give the debugger control after the instruction completes
4. Dismisses the exception

When the instruction completes, the debugger's TBIT handler gains control, sets the page protection back to no write access for user mode, and allows the program to continue its execution.

17 Swapping

A time to cast away stones and a time to gather stones
together. . .
—Ecclesiastes 3:5

The VAX/VMS operating system does not allow the amount of physical
memory to limit totally the number of processes allowed in the system.
Physical memory is effectively extended by keeping only a subset of the total
number of active processes resident at a given time. This number is kept at a
maximum by controling the number of pages that any one process has in
memory at any given time. The remaining processes work with reduced
working sets or reside in backing store locations. The reduction in size of low
priority working sets, movement of low priority processes to backing store,
and the subsequent filling of memory with high priority computable processes is the responsibility of the swapper. In fact, the swapper process can be
viewed as the system-wide memory manager.

In VAX/VMS Version 3.0 the responsiblities of the swapper changed con-
siderably. Previous to Version 3.0, the swapper was solely responsible for
moving processes in and out of physical memory. The swapper in Version 3.0
attempts not to swap processes out of physical memory. Rather it will shrink
process working sets in order to gain free pages.

17.1 SWAPPING OVERVIEW

Before discussing the details of swapper operation (moving a process into or
out of memory), some basic swapper concepts will be reviewed. The specific
uses of each of the memory management data structures manipulated by the
swapper will be pointed out.

17.1.1 Swapper Responsibilities

The swapper has two main responsibilities:

- The subset of processes that are currently resident should represent the
  highest priority executable processes in the system. When nonresident
  processes become computable, the swapper must bring them back into
  memory.
- The swapper is also responsible for keeping the number of pages on the free
  page list above the low limit threshold established by the SYSBOOT parameters FREELIM and FREEGOAL. Requests for physical pages come

from several sources. One request comes from the pager in resolving a page fault for a page that is not currently in memory. Another originates with an attempt by the swapper to acquire enough physical pages to inswap a computable but outswapped process. There are four operations that the swapper performs to keep pages on the free page list.

1. Process headers of previously outswapped process bodies may be eligible for outswap. If so, they will be outswapped. (Process headers for already deleted processes are simply deleted.)
2. The swapper will write modified pages until the number of pages on the modified list falls below the low limit threshold stored in global location SCH$GL_MFYLOLIM. However, the swapper will not write modified pages if there are fewer than the SYSBOOT parameter MPW_THRESH pages on the modified list. The value of SCH$GL_MFYLOLIM ensures that a certain number of pages will be available on the modified list for page faults; MPW_THRESH simply sets a lower bound to be met before the swapper can write the modified page list to gain pages.
3. In an attempt not to outswap processes, the swapper will shrink working set sizes. The table used to determine outswap selection is also used to determine the order by which working sets will be reduced. See Section 17.2.2 for more information on outswap selection.
4. As a last resort to maintaining the size of the free page list, the swapper will select an eligible process for outswap and remove that process from memory. The table used to determine outswap selection is also used in reducing working set sizes.

17.1.2   Swapper Implementation

The swapper is a separate process in the operating system. As such, it can be selected for execution just like any other process in the system. It also has its own resources and quotas that are charged when the swapper does I/O.

By making the swapper a separate process, the pieces of the system that detect a need for one of the swapper's duties simply have to wake the swapper up (by issuing a JSB to routine SCH$SWPWAKE). As already noted in Chapter 10, this routine does not simply wake the swapper. Instead, it performs a series of checks to determine whether there is a need for swapper activity. If so, the swapper process is awakened. If not, the routine simply returns. By performing these checks in this routine rather than in the swapper process itself, the overhead of two needless context switches is avoided.

When the swapper is the current process, it executes entirely in kernel mode. All of the swapper code resides in system space. (The swapper makes use of its P0 space when it creates a new proces by using the module SHELL in the executive image. This operation is described in Chapter 20.)

17.1.3 Comparison of Paging and Swapping

The VMS operating system uses two different techniques to make efficient use of available physical memory. The ability to support programs with virtual address spaces larger than physical memory is the responsibility of the pager. The swapper allows a running system to support more active processes than can fit into physical memory at one time. The swapper's responsibilities are more global or system wide than the pager's. Table 17-1 compares and contrasts the pager and swapper in several details.

17.2 SWAP SCHEDULING

The swapper is a part of the system that performs both memory management and scheduling functions. The scheduling aspects of the swapper are here discussed from two points of view. First, the actions that the swapper takes to determine whether to inswap, outswap, or shrink a particular process are discussed. Then, those system events that trigger swapper activity are briefly described.

17.2.1 Selection of Inswap Candidate

The scheduler maintains 32 quadword listheads for outswapped computable (COMO) processes, one for each software priority (see Figure 10-3). These queues are identical to the 32 queues maintained for the computable resident (COM) processes. The steps that the swapper takes to locate an inswap candidate (once it has decided that an inswap can be performed) exactly parallel the steps that the rescheduling interrupt service routine takes (see Chapter 10) to select the next candidate for execution.

1. A FFS instruction on the COMO queue summary longword (SCH$GL_ COMOQS) locates the highest priority nonempty COMO queue.
2. The first process in this queue is removed and prepared for being swapped into memory.

Figure 17-1 shows the parallel between the inswap candidate selection and the operation of the rescheduling interrupt service routine. The key instructions in the two routines are identical. The only differences are in the global data items referenced by the instructions.

After a process has been chosen for inswap, the swapper checks if there are enough pages on the free page list to hold the inswap candidate and leave at least FREELIM pages remaining on the list. If so, the inswap proceeds. If not, the swapper attempts to make more pages available by shrinking working sets, outswapping one or more processes, writing modified pages, or deleting process headers of already deleted process bodies.

Table 17-1: Comparison of Paging and Swapping

Differences

Paging	*Swapping*
The pager is a process-wide component of the executive that moves pages into and out of process working sets.	The swapper is a system-wide component of the executive that moves entire processes into and out of physical memory.
The page fault handler is an exception service routine that executes in the context of the process that incurred the page fault.	The swapper is a separate process that is awakened from its hibernating state by components that detect a need for swapper activity.
The unit of paging is the page, although the pager attempts to read more than one page with a single disk read.	The unit of swapping is the process (or more accurately, the process working set).
Page read requests for process pages are queued to the driver according to the base priority of the process incurring the page fault. Modified page write requests are queued according to the SYSBOOT parameter MPW_PRIO.	Swapper I/O requests are queued according to the value of the SYSBOOT parameter SWP_PRIO.
Paging supports programs with very large address spaces.	Swapping supports a large number of concurrently active processes.

Similarities

1. The pager and swapper work from a common database. The most important structures that are used for both paging and swapping are the process page tables, the working set list, and the PFN database.
2. The pager and swapper do conventional I/O. There are only slight differences in detail between pager I/O and swapper I/O on the one hand and normal Queued I/O requests on the other.
3. Both components attempt to maximize the number of blocks read or written with a given I/O request. The pager accomplishes this with read and write clustering. The swapper attempts to inswap or outswap the entire working set in one (or a small number of) I/O request(s).

The routine SCH$SCHED, that selects the next execution candidate has an exact parallel in the swapper. The first half of the parallel shows the swapper's selection of the next inswap candidate and the nearly identical instructions in the scheduler.

Swapper's Selection of Inswap Candidate	Notes	Scheduler's Selection of Execution Candidate

```
QEMPTY: BUG-CHECK QUEUEMPTY, FATAL           SCH$IDLE:
                                                 SETIPL  #IPL$_SCHED
                                                 MOVB    #32,W^SCH$GB_PRI
                                                 BRB     SCH$SCHED

SWAPSCHED:                                   SCH$SCHED::
    DSBINT  #IPL$_SYNCH              (1)          SETIPL  #IPL$_SYNCH
    BBSS    S^#SCH$V_SIP,W^SCH$GB_SIP,5$
    FFS     #0,#32,W^SCH$GL_COMOQS,R2  (2)        FFS     #0,#32,W^SCH$GL_COMQS,R2
    BNEQ    10$                                   BEQL    SCH$IDLE
    BBCC    S^#SCH$V_SIP,W^SCH$GB_SIP,5$
5$: ENBINT
    RSB

10$: PUSHR   #^M<R6,R7,R8,R9,R10,R11,AP,FP>
     MOVAQ   W^SCH$AQ_COMOH[R2],R3   (3)          MOVAQ   W^SCH$AQ_COMOH[R2],R3
     MOVL    (R3),R4                (4)          REMQUE  @(R3)+,R4
     CMPB    #DYN$C_PCB,PCB$B_TYPE(R4)
     BNEQ    QEMPTY
       .
       .
       .
```

At this point, the swapper has found an inswap candidate. It then takes the steps necessary to bring this process into memory. The scheduler, on the other hand, continues execution. The REMQUE instruction shown above for the scheduler is duplicated below to emphasize that, while a long time elapses between inswap candidate selection and completion of the inswap, there is no time lapse for execution selection.

Some time later, the inswap operation completes. The swapper rebuilds the working set list and the process page tables. The parallel resumes when the swapper calls the scheduler to make the newly inswapped process computable.

(1) IPL is raised to synchronize access to the scheduler's database.
(2) The highest priority (COMO/COM) queue is selected.

(3) The address of its forward pointer is loaded into R3.
(4) The address of the selected PCB is loaded into R4.

State Change from COMO to COM	Notes	State Change from Computable to Current
`SCH$SCHEP:`		
`    REMQUE  (R4),R1`	(5)	`    REMQUE  @(R3)+,R4`
		`    BVS     QEMPTY`
		`    BNEQ    20$`
`    BNEQ    10$`		
`    MOVZWL  PCB$W_STATE(R4),R1`		
`    BBC     R1,EXESTATE,10$`		
`    MOVZBL  PCB$B_PRI(R4),R1`		
`    BLBC    PCB$W_STATE(R4),5$`		
`    ADDL    #32,R1`	(6)	
`5$: BBCC    R1,W^SCH$GL_COMQS,10$`	(7)	`    BBCC    R2,W^SCH$GL_COMQS,20$`
`10$: MOVB   R0,PCB$B_PRI(R4)`		
`    MOVL    #SCH$C_COM,R1`		
`      .`	`20$:`	
`      .`		
`30$: MOVW   R1,PCB$W_STATE(R4)`	(8)	`    CMPB    #DYN$C_PCB,PCB$B_TYPE(R4)`
`    MOVAQ   L^SCH$AQ_COMT[R0],R1`		`    BNEQ    QEMPTY`
`    BBSS    R0,W^SCHGL_COMQS,40$`		`    MOVW    #SCH$C_CUR,PCB$W_STATE(R4)`
`40$: INSQUE (R4),@(R1)+`	(9)	`    MOVL    R4,W^SCH$GL_CURPCB`
`    RSB`		

At this point, the parallel ends. If the process just made computable is of higher priority than the swapper, that process will be scheduled as soon as the IPL is lowered below 3 and the rescheduling interrupt occurs. In other cases, the process will not execute until it becomes the highest priority computable process. The scheduler's service routine continues its operation, placing the selected process into execution.

(5) Remove the selected PCB from former state (COMO/COM).

(6) Bias R1 so that it points to SCH$GL_COMOQS, the summary longword for the COMO state. (This is noted so the BBCC instruction makes sense.)

(7) If the removal of the PCB emptied the queue, clear the associated priority bit in the summary longword.

(8) Load the STATE field in the PCB with the new state (COM/CUR) of the process.

(9) Finally, place the PCB into its new scheduling queue.

Figure 17-1
Parallels between Inswap Candidate Selection by the Swapper and Execution Candidate Selection by the Scheduler

365

There is one optimization that the swapper performs that may prevent an eventual outswap. The swapper only inswaps compute-bound low priority processes at a rate determined by the special SYSBOOT parameter SWPRATE. (The definition of such a process is one whose current priority is equal to its base priority, which priority is less than or equal to the SYSBOOT parameter DEFPRI.) The inswap is abandoned if all of the following are true:

- The swapper is attempting to inswap such a process.
- The process will not fit.
- The SWPRATE interval has not yet expired.

Each time that the swapper successfully inswaps one of these so-called cruncher processes, it resets its inswap clock to contain the current time plus SWPRATE.

17.2.2 Selection of Shrink or Outswap Candidates

When the swapper must resort to shrinking or swapping resident processes to make room for a computable (but outswapped) process, it must determine which process to select first. The examination order for potential outswap candidates attempts to modify last those processes that would suffer the most from a working set reduction or an outswap. Note that this algorithm is not altogether straightforward; some processes benefit from being swapped, rather than having their working sets reduced.

Any time that free pages are gained by action of the swapper, a check is made to see if there are enough pages on the free and modified page lists to satisfy the deficit. If enough pages are available, the swapper completes its actions and hibernates.

The swapper maintains a table (in module OSWPSCHED) that determines the order and conditions for which the various resident scheduling states are examined. When the swapper searches for candidates, it starts at the first section in its table and evaluates all the processes indicated by that section. For each section in the table, the swapper makes three passes looking for candidates. On each pass, the criteria for a process to remain inswapped increase in severity. When all three passes have been completed for all the processes represented by the section, the swapper evaluates the next section in the table.

The selection table is shown in Table 17-2. Note that the table may have more than one scheduling state in each section of the table. These states are viewed by the determination algorithm as being more or less equivalent in their requirements. Processes cannot be outswapped if they have locked themselves into the balance set.

In addition to the process's scheduling state, the following characteristics can be used to select processes:

Table 17-2: Selection of Shrink and Outswap Candidates

| | *Selection dependent on:* | | | *FLAGS* | | |
Process State	*Direct I/O?*	*Priority?*	*Initial Quantum?*	*LONGWAIT*	*SWAPASAP*	*SWPOGOAL*
SUSP	No	No	No	0	0	0
LEF	No	No	No	1	0	1
HIB	No	No	No	1	0	1
CEF	No	No	No	0	0	1
LEF	No	No	No	0	0	1
HIB	No	No	No	0	0	1
FPG	No	Yes	No	0	1	0
COLPG	No	Yes	No	0	1	0
MWAIT	No	No	No	0	1	0
CEF	Yes	Yes	Yes	0	0	0
LEF	Yes	Yes	Yes	0	0	0
PFW	No	Yes	Yes	0	1	0
COM	No	Yes	Yes	0	1	0

- In some entries, processes that have not completed their initial quantum (those that have the initial quantum flag PCB$V_INQUAN set in PCB$L_STS) are not considered as candidates for outswap. There are two circumstances under which the swapper does not make the initial quantum check: a real-time process (a process whose priority is greater than or equal to 16) must be swapped in, or the swapper has failed to swap out a process on the SYSBOOT parameter SWPFAIL number of tries.

    The swapper maintains a failure counter that records the number of times that it attempted to locate an outswap candidate and failed. When this count reaches a value equal to SWPFAIL, the swapper ignores the setting of the initial quantum flag. The counter is reset each time that an outswap candidate is successfully located.
- In some entries, processes can be considered for swapper action if their priority is less than or equal to that of the potential inswap process (stored in global location SWP$GB_ISWPRI).
- Processes that are performing direct I/O are selected later than those that are not. If a process is doing direct I/O and is waiting on an event flag, the swapper assumes that the event flag wait is associated with the direct I/O. The motivation behind delaying direct I/O process selection is the desire to avoid the overhead of swapping the process, only to have the process's state change to COM, even before the outswap completes.
- The following three flags are used in the selection of processes. The flags are maintained for table entries and direct the swapper to include specific processes in the table entry or to take specific action on one of the passes through the table entry.

LONGWAIT | When this flag is set, processes can be included in the table entry if they have been waiting in a scheduling state for longer than the SYSBOOT parameter LONGWAIT. This flag is only applicable to processes in the LEF or HIB scheduling states.

The effect of the LONGWAIT flag is to subdivide the processes in LEF and HIB scheduling states into processes that have been waiting a long time to become computable and those that have been waiting a short time. The philosophy here is that processes that have been waiting a long time will probably wait longer still, whereas those that have only been waiting a short time could become computable rather quickly.

SWAPASAP | This flag indicates that the swapper must swap out processes indicated by this state, after reducing their working set to WSQUOTA. The processes indicated by a table entry with SWAPASAP set are computable or are likely to become computable very soon. If the system needs memory badly enough, one of these processes will be swapped out at its current size. When the outswapped process becomes computable again, it will not have to waste compute time rebuilding its working set.

SWPOGOAL | This flag indicates that the swapper must shrink the working set size of processes indicated by the table entry to SWPOUTPGCNT.

The three passes made on each table section are as follows:

1. The first pass reduces extended working sets to WSQUOTA. If the SWAPASAP flag is set for the table section, processes are shrunk and then outswapped as they are processed.
2. If the current section of the selection table is affected by the SWPOGOAL flag, the second pass reduces the working set size of processes indicated by this section. Working sets are reduced to the SYSBOOT parameter SWPOUTPGCNT.
3. In the third pass, processes selected by this section are swapped out of physical memory.

When the swapper scans a series of processes queued to a particular priority within a scheduling state, the scan begins with the most recently queued entry (at the tail of the queue). This starting point insures that the longer a process has been waiting in a queue, the less chance it has of being shrunk or swapped.

Table 17-3: Events That Cause the Swapper or Modified Page Writer to Be Awakened

Event	Module	Additional Comments
Process that is outswapped becomes computable	RSE	The swapper will attempt to make this process resident.
Quantum End	RSE	An outswap previously blocked by initial quantum flag setting may now be possible.
CPU Time Expiration	RSE	The process may be deleted, allowing a previously blocked inswap to occur.
Process Enters Wait State	SYSWAIT	The process that entered a wait state may be a suitable outswap candidate. (For example, priority may not be important for this wait state.)
Modified Page List Exceeds Upper Limit Threshold	ALLOCPFN	Modified page writing is performed by swapper.
Free Page List Drops Below Low Limit Threshold	ALLOCPFN	The swapper must balance free page count by: 1. Writing modified pages 2. Swapping headers of previously outswapped process bodies 3. Swapping more processes
Free Page Limit Exceeds Upper Limit Threshold	ALLOCPFN	A process that could not be inswapped due to lack of physical pages may now fit.
Balance Slot of Deleted Process Becomes Available	SYSDELPRC	A previously blocked inswap may now be possible.
Process Header Reference Count Goes to Zero	PAGEFAULT	A process header can now be outswapped to join a previously outswapped process body.
System Timer Subroutine Executes	TIMESCHDL	The swapper is awakened every second to check if there is any work to be done.

17.2.3   System Events that Trigger Swapper Activity

The swapper spends its idle time in a hibernating state. Those components that detect a need for swapper activity wake the swapper (by calling routine SCH$SWPWAKE). Table 17-3 lists the system events that trigger a need for swapper activity, the module that contains the routine that detects each need, and the reason why the swapper needs to be informed about these system events.

The swapper does not worry about why it was awakened. Every time that it is awakened, it tends to all of its responsibilities. The main loop of the swapper performs the following steps:

1. If the free page count is too low, the list is replenished, which might result in an outswap of a process if modified page writing (Step 2) will not free enough physical pages.

2. Modified pages are written. Every time the swapper is awakened, the modified page writer is called. If the size of the modified page list exceeds its upper limit threshold (SCH$GL_MFYLIM), modified pages will be written until the size of the list falls below the low limit threshold (SCH$GL_MFYLOLIM).

   There are times when the swapper wants to flush the entire modified page list. The logic of the modified page writer requires that both of these threshold parameters be zeroed for the list to be flushed. The last step that the modified page writer takes before exiting is to restore the two modified page list thresholds to the values described by the SYSBOOT parameters MPW_HILIMIT and MPW_LOLIMIT.

3. The swapper attempts to inswap a process in the COMO state (if one exists). This attempt can fail if there are not enough physical pages to accommodate the outswapped process and none of the resident processes are suitable outswap candidates.

4. The fact that the swapper is a separate process that executes fairly frequently (at least once a second) makes it a convenient vehicle for testing whether a powerfail recovery has occurred and, if so, notifying all processes that have requested power recovery AST notification (with the Set Powerfail Recovery AST system service). The details of this delivery mechanism are described in Chapter 27.

5. Finally, the swapper puts itself into the hibernate state, after checking its wake pending flag. If anyone (including the swapper itself in one of its three main subroutines) has requested swapper activity since the swapper began execution, the hibernate is skipped and the swapper goes back to Step 1.

17.3 SWAPPER'S USE OF MEMORY MANAGEMENT DATA STRUCTURES

In Chapter 16, the memory management data structures that are used by both the pager and the swapper were described. The discussion here will review those structures and add descriptions of those structures that are used exclusively by the swapper.

17.3.1 Process Header

The bulk of information that the swapper uses in managing the details of either inswapping or outswapping is contained in the process header. The process page tables contain a complete description of the address space for a given process.

The working set list describes those PTEs that are valid. This list is crucial for the swapper because it is only the process working set that will be written to backing store when the process is outswapped. In a similar fashion, when it is time for a process to be inswapped, the working set list in the process header in an outswapped process describes what the rest of the process looks like in the swap file.

17.3.1.1 **Working Set List.** The working set list describes the portion of a process virtual address space that must be written to the swap file when the process is outswapped. A page in the process working set can be in one of the following three states:

1. The page is valid.
2. The page is currently being read into memory. The swapper treats page reads like any other I/O in progress when swapping a process. This treatment is described in Section 17.4.
3. The process page table contains a global page table index and the indexed global page table entry indicates a transition state. The swapper handles global pages in a special manner when outswapping a process. This treatment is also described in Section 17.4.

The operation of the swapper's scan of the process working set list at outswap is discussed in Section 17.4.

17.3.1.2 **Process Page Tables.** The working set list does not supply the swapper with all the information necessary to outswap a process. Other information is contained in either the valid (or transition) PTE or in one of the PFN array elements associated with the physical page. Each working set list entry effectively points to a different process (or system) page table entry that contains a page frame number. The PTE is copied to the swapper's I/O map and then the contents of the BAK array element for this physical page are put back into the process PTE. These actions eliminate any ties between an outswapped process's page tables and physical memory.

17.3.1.3 **Process Header Page Arrays.** The breaking of ties between process PTEs and physical memory is straightforward for process pages. The contents of the BAK array element are simply merged into the PTE. However, process header pages are also a part of the process working set. These pages reside in system space and are mapped by system page table entries that map the balance slot in which the process header resides.

The relinquishing of the balance slot implies that these SPTEs must also be surrendered. There is no analogous way to store the BAK array contents for process header pages. For this reason, the process header page arrays (see Figure 14-8) exist in the process header. There exists an array element for each page in the process header. When a process is outswapped, those process header pages currently in the working set have their BAK addresses put into the corresponding array elements in the process header page BAK array. When the process is swapped back into memory, the process header pages can be scanned and the BAK contents copied from the array back into the PFN BAK array elements for the physical pages that contain the process header.

In a similar manner, it is necessary to remember where each process header page fits into the working set. This record keeping is done by storing the WSLX PFN array element into the corresponding process header page WSLX array element. The use of this array while the process header is being rebuilt following inswap prevents a prohibitively long search of the working set list for each process header page.

17.3.2 Swapper I/O Data Structures

Like the pager, the swapper uses the conventional VMS I/O subsystem. It allocates its own I/O request packet and fills in some of the fields that will be interpreted in a special manner by the I/O postprocessing routine. After these fields have been filled in, it jumps to one of the swapper I/O entry points in module SYSQIOREQ (EXE$BLDPKTSWPR or EXE$BLDPKTSWPW) that fills in an appropriate function code and queues the packet to the appropriate disk driver. Table 15-1 shows how the I/O request packet is used by the swapper for its I/O activities.

Two other structures are used by the swapper. The system maintains a page file control block for each page and swap file in the system. The swapper uses a special I/O array that allows it to read or write a process working set, a collection of virtually discontiguous pages, in one or a small number of I/O requests.

17.3.2.1 **Page File Control Blocks Used by the Swapper.** Figure 14-23 shows the layout of a page file control block, the structure that allows a page or swap file to be located on disk. Notice that the window control block pointer and virtual block number field are located at the same offsets in page file control blocks and in process or global section table entries, which allow these data structures to be used by common routines that need not distinguish the type of structure being used to describe a memory management I/O request.

17.3.2.2 **Swap File Initialization.** When the system is initialized, the SYSINIT process initializes the swap file SYS$SYSTEM:SWAPFILE.SYS. If alternate swap files are installed (with the SYSGEN command INSTALL), the page file control block for the new swap file is initialized by SYSGEN.

17.3.2.3 **Allocation of Swap Space.** For each process, the indication of which page file control block to use is contained in the software PCB in field PCB$L_

WSSWP. The page file control block then indicates the file in which swapping space is assigned to the process. The upper byte is a longword index into the array of pointers to page file control blocks (see Figure 14-22).

When a process is first created, its initial swap space is allocated for the process in a call to the Create Process ($CREPRC) system service. The initial size of the swap space is the SYSBOOT parameter MPW_WRTCLUSTER (minimized by the size of the SHELL process). The page file index and the virtual block number of the beginning of the space are recorded in the process control block as negative values. A negative value indicates to the swapper that this PCB requires an inswap from the SHELL. After the SHELL has been swapped in, the values are restored to their positive form.

If a process control block contains a zero at location PCB$L_WSSWP, the swapping and paging systems assume that the process is permanently memory resident. Only the processes that are created before the page and swap files are located (NULL process, SWAPPER process, and SYSINIT process) are permanently memory resident.

When a process's working set list is extended, a check is made to see if the new working set will fit in the currently allocated swap space. If the new sized working set list will not fit in the current swap space, a new swap space (that is MPW_WRTCLUSTER pages larger) is allocated. The old swap space is deallocated.

17.3.2.4   **Swapper PTE Array.** The need for the swapper PTE array that allows it to write pages that are virtually discontiguous in the context of the process being swapped was described in Chapter 16. This array contains WSMAX longwords and is used for both outswap and inswap operations.

At outswap, the PFN of each page that will be written to the swap file is loaded into the array. This array is then passed on to the I/O system to perform the write. At inswap, the swapper allocates a number of PFNs to hold the process and reads the swap image into these pages. Each PFN is then placed into the appropriate page table as the working set list and process page tables are rebuilt.

17.4   **OUTSWAP OPERATION**

Outswap is described before inswap because it is easier to explain inswap in terms of what the swapper put into the swap file. The swapper does not remove processes from the balance set indiscriminately. In fact, the swapper tries hard not to swap. Processes are only removed if there is a need for physical pages that cannot be satisfied by shrinking working sets and flushing the modified page list.

17.4.1 Selection of Outswap Candidate

As is mentioned in Section 17.2, the outswap selection is driven by tables that contain a weight for each resident scheduling state. The swapper selects the process that it judges will benefit the least from remaining in memory. Once a candidate is selected, the swapper prepares the working set of that process for outswap.

17.4.2 Outswap of the Process Body

The swapper outswaps the process body (P0 and P1 pages) separately from the process header. There are two reasons for doing this:

- Fields in the process header (most notably working set list entries and process page table entries) are modified as the working set list is processed.
- The process header may not be swappable at this time due to outstanding I/O, pages on the modified page list, or some other reason.

17.4.2.1 Scanning the Working Set List.
The process body is prepared for outswap by scanning the working set list. Each page in the working set list must be looked at to determine if any special action is required. The swapper looks at a combination of the page type (found in the working set list entry as well as the PFN TYPE array) and the valid bit. Table 17-4 lists all combinations of page type and valid bit setting that the swapper encounters and the action that it takes for each. Several cases are discussed further here.

The basic step that the swapper must take as it scans the working set list is to move each swappable page into the swapper's I/O map. This causes the virtually discontiguous pages in the process's working set to appear virtually contiguous to the I/O system (see Figures 17-3 and 17-6). For each page, the swapper performs the following steps:

1. Locates the page table entry from the virtual page number field in the working set list entry.
2. Determines any special action based on page validity and page type.
3. Moves the PFN from the page table entry to the swapper map.
4. Records the modify bit (logical OR or PTE modify bit and PFN STATE array saved modify bit) in the working set list entry.
5. Sets the Delete Contents bit in the PFN STATE array element. This set bit will cause the page to be placed at the head of the free page list when its reference count goes to zero (which in normal circumstances will be when the swap write completes).

Note that the swapper does not have to explicitly put the contents of the PFN BAK array into each PTE. The contents are replaced when the page is released (after the swap write completes and all other references to the page have been eliminated).

Table 17-4: Scan of Working Set List of Outswap

The scan of the working set list on outswap is determined by a combination of the physical page type (WSL<3:1>) and the valid bit (PTE<31>).

Type of Page	Valid Bit	Action of Swapper for This Page
1. Process Page	Transition	a. (STATE = Read in Progress) Treat as page with I/O in progress. Special action may be taken at inswap or by modified page writer.
		b. (STATE = Active) Outswap. The page will be put back into active transition state at inswap time.
		c. (STATE = Read Error) Drop from working set.
		d. No other transition states are possible for a page in the working set.
2. Process Page	Valid	Outswap page.
		If there is outstanding I/O and the page is modified, load SWPVBN array element with block in swap file where the updated page contents should be written when the I/O completes.
3. System Page		It is impossible for a system page to be in process working set. The swapper generates an error.
4. Global Read Only	Transition	a. If the process page table entry still contains a PFN, this page is in active transition page. Outswap the page.
		b. If the process page table entry contains a global page table index, then the global page table must contain a transition PTE. The page is dropped from the process working set.
5. Global Read Only	Valid	a. If SHRCNT = 1, then outswap.
		b. If SHRCNT > 1, drop from working set. It is highly likely that a process can fault a page later without I/O. This check avoids multiple copies of same page in swap file.
6. Global Read/Write		Drop from working set. It is extremely difficult to determine whether the page in memory was modified after this copy was written to the swap file.
7. Page Table Page		Not part of the process body. However, while the swapper is scanning the process body, the VPN field in the WSL is modified to reflect the offset from the beginning of the process header because page table pages will probably be located at different virtual addresses following inswap.

17.4.2.2 **Pages with Direct I/O in Progress.** If a (modified) page has outstanding I/O while the process is being outswapped, the swapper takes note of this by loading the SWPVBN PFN array element with the virtual block number in the swap file where the page is being written to. The page is nevertheless swapped at this time to reserve a place for it in the swap file.

If the I/O operation is a read (or it is a write and some other action has caused the page to be modified), the physical page will be placed on the modified page list when the I/O completes. MMG$RELPFN, the routine that releases the page, puts pages on the modified page list either if the modify bit in the PFN STATE array is set or if the PFN SWPVBN array has nonzero contents.

The modified page writer takes special action for modified pages with nonzero contents in the SWPVBN array. That is, it writes each page to the designated block in the swap file rather than to its normal backing store address.

If the I/O operation is a write (from memory to mass storage) and the page was not otherwise modified, the contents that are currently being written to the swap file are good. The page will be placed on the free list when the write completes.

17.4.2.3 **Global Pages.** Global pages are also given special treatment at outswap. If the global page is writeable, it is dropped from the process working set before the process is swapped to disk. The task of recording whether the contents that are swapped are up to date when the process is brought back into memory is more complicated than simply refaulting the page (often without I/O) when the process is swapped back into memory.

Global read-only pages are only swapped if the global share count (PFN SHRCNT array) is one. In all other cases, the page is dropped from the working set and must be refaulted (most likely without I/O) when the process is inswapped. (Global pages that are explicitly or implicitly locked into the process working set are not dropped from the working set.) Global transition pages are also dropped from the process working set.

17.4.2.4 **Example of Process Body Outswap.** Figures 17-2 through 17-4 show some of the special cases encountered by the swapper while it is scanning the process working set list. As mentioned in connection with Table 17-4, the key information about each page is a combination of the PTE valid bit and the physical page type. The order of the scan is determined by the order defined by the working set list. Figure 17-2 shows the process working set, the process page tables, and the associated PFN database entries before the swapper begins its working set scan. Figure 17-3 shows the modified working set and the swapper map after the working set list scan but before the I/O request is initiated. Figure 17-4 shows the state of the page table entries after the swap write has completed and the physical pages have been released.

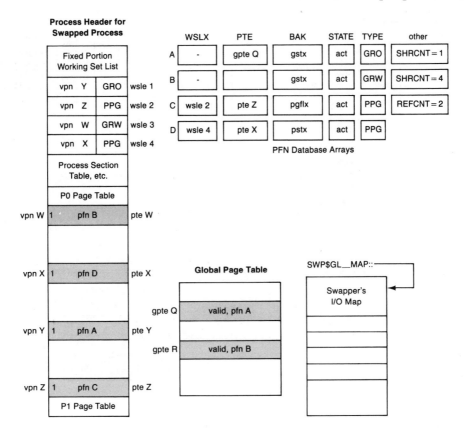

Figure 17-2
Example Working Set List before Outswap Scan

1. The first working set list entry is a global read-only page. The VPN field of the working set list entry locates the page table entry. The PFN field of the PTE locates the PFN data associated with this physical page. In particular, the global share count for this page is one. (This process is the only process that currently has this page in its working set.) The swapper will write this page out as part of the swap image for this process. Thus, PFN A is the first page in the swapper's PTE array (see Figure 17-3).

   When the swapper's write operation completes, the page will be deleted. That is, the PTE array element will be cleared and the page will be placed at the head of the free page list (see Figure 17-4).

2. The second working set list entry is a process page that also has I/O in progress (REFCNT = 2). This page will be swapped. This fact is illustrated by the inclusion of PFN C in the swapper map.

   If the page was previously modified (either the PTE modify bit or saved modify bit in the PFN STATE array was set), the virtual block number in

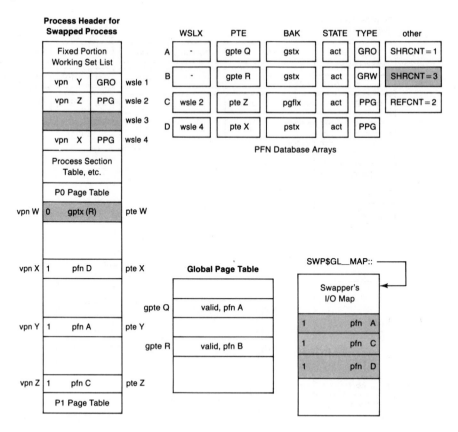

Figure 17-3
Example Working Set List after Outswap Scan

the swap file will be loaded into the SWPVBN array. Loading the SWPVBN array will force the page to the modified page list when it is released. If the process is still outswapped by the time that the modified page writer gets around to writing this page, the page will be written to the block reserved for it when the process is first outswapped.

The page is marked for deletion. That is, when the reference count for the page reaches zero (due to completion of both the outstanding I/O and the swapper's write), the page is placed at the head of the free page list and its PTE array element cleared.

3. The third working set list entry is a global read/write page. The page is dropped from the process working set (see Figure 17-3), meaning that the process page table entry is replaced with a global page table index (that locates global page table entry R) and the share count for PFN B is decremented. Notice that PFN B is not a part of the swapper map, which contains a list of the physical pages that will be written to the swap file.

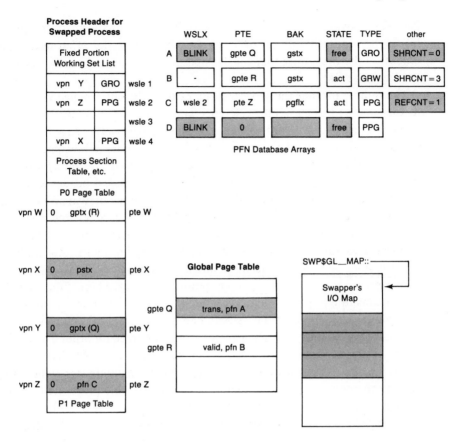

Figure 17-4
Process Page Table Changes after Swapper's Write
Completes

4. The last working set list entry in this example is a process page with nothing special about it. This page is added to the swapper map (PFN D) and its contents marked for deletion. The deletion will actually occur when the swapper's write operation completes.

17.4.3 Outswap of Process Header

The process header is not outswapped until after the process body has been successfully written to the swap file. The reason for this illustrates two other cases that can keep the process header in memory. Before the process header can be outswapped, all ties to physical memory that exist in the process page tables must be severed, including not only those pages that were in the process working set and written to the swap file but also those pages that are in some transition state, most notably pages on the free and modified page lists.

17.4.3.1 **Partial Outswap.** After the process body has been outswapped, the process header becomes eligible for outswap. In fact, the header of an outswapped process is the first thing that the swapper looks for in an attempt to balance the free page list.

    The indication that the process header cannot be outswapped yet is found in the process header vector reference count array (see Figure 14-21). This array counts the number of reasons (transition pages, active page table pages, and so on) that prevent the process header from being outswapped.

    Because the outswap of the header does not have to immediately follow the body outswap, it is possible (even probable) that a process header will not be swapped in the time between when a process body is outswapped and when that process is brought back into memory. Such a situation is referred to as a partial outswap. It has an obvious counterpart, a partial inswap, where the swapper does not have to allocate a balance slot and bring the process header into memory because the header is already resident.

    An important system management point is illustrated here. Process bodies, which consume physical memory, are relatively easy to remove from memory. Process headers consume a smaller amount of physical memory but they also occupy a balance slot. The balance slot is not freed for other use until the entire header is outswapped. If the SYSBOOT parameter BALSETCNT is set to too small a value, the system can reach the unfortunate state where there is more than enough physical memory, but computable processes cannot be brought into memory because the balance slots are still tied to already outswapped processes. This situation can be avoided by setting BALSETCNT to an adequate value. See the *VAX/VMS System Management and Operations Guide* for details on determining the correct value for SYSBOOT parameters.

17.4.3.2 **Scanning the Free Page List.** When the swapper locates a process header that can be removed from its balance slot, it takes whatever actions are required to remove the ties that bind the process header to physical memory. The first such step is to eliminate any transition PTEs where the physical page is on the free page list.

    Transition PTEs are located by scanning the entire free page list and looking for pages whose PTE array contents lie within the P0 or P1 page tables of the process header being examined. Whenever such a page is found, the process PTE is reset to the contents of the BAK array; the reference count and PTE array elements are cleared, and the page is moved from its current location to the head of the free page list.

17.4.3.3 **Flushing the Modified Page List.** Because the free page list is only one of several transition states, the scan of the free page list may not free the process header for removal. Pages may be in some other transition state. Transition states that represent some form of I/O in progress (release pending, read in progress, write in progress) are left alone because there is nothing that the swapper can do until the I/O completes.

However, the modified page list can be manipulated. The desired effect is removal of all pages from the modified page list, which is triggered by setting to zero both the lower and upper limit thresholds for the modified page list. Clearing the upper limit guarantees that a nonempty list has exceeded its threshold, initiating a request for modified page writing. Clearing the lower limit causes modified page writing to continue until the list is empty (below the low limit threshold).

17.4.3.4 **Outswap of the Process Header.** Once the reference count for the process header reaches zero, the header can be outswapped and the balance slot freed. The outswap of the process header is entirely analogous to the outswap of a process body. That is, the header pages that are not page table pages and the active page table pages are scanned and put into the swapper's PTE array to form a virtually contiguous block for the I/O subsystem.

There are several differences between the outswap of a process header and a process body. When a process body is outswapped, the header that maps that body is still resident. When the swapper's write completes and each physical page is deleted, the contents of the BAK array element for each page are put back into the process PTE.

Process header pages are mapped by system page table entries for that balance slot. The SPTEs are not available to hold the BAK array contents because they will be used by the next occupant of this balance slot. One of the process header page arrays (see Chapter 14) is set aside for exactly this purpose. As the process header is processed for outswap, the contents of the BAK array for each active header page are stored in the corresponding process header page array element.

At the same time, the location of each header page within the working set list is stored in the WSLX array. This array prevents a prohibitively long search to rebuild the process header when the process is swapped back into memory.

Once the header is successfully outswapped, the header resident bit (PCB$V_PHDRES) in the PCB is cleared and the balance slot is available for further use.

17.5 **INSWAP OPERATION**

The inswap is exactly the opposite of the outswap operation. The swapper brings the process header, including active page tables, and the process body back into physical memory. It then uses the contents of the working set list to rebuild the process page tables, an operation that primarily involves updating each valid PTE to reflect the new PFN used by that PTE. At the same time that each page is being processed, the swapper can resolve any special cases that existed when the process was outswapped.

17.5.1 Selection of an Inswap Candidate

As mentioned earlier in the chapter, the swapper selects a process for inswap exactly as the scheduler selects a candidate for execution. The following processes may be potential candidates for inswap:

- Newly created processes
- Processes in some outswapped wait state that were just made computable
- Processes that were outswapped while in the computable state

The highest priority process in this collection is the one selected for inswap.

17.5.2 Inswap of the Process Header

If the process header was outswapped when the body was outswapped, it must be brought back into memory before the process body can be reconstructed. Unlike the special operations that took place when the process was outswapped, an outswapped process header merely adds two details to the inswap operation.

1. If the header is resident, the number of header pages is subtracted from the size of the outswap image in the swap file. That is, whether the header is resident or not determines the total number of blocks that must be read from the swap file and the virtual block number where the read should begin.
2. If the header was swapped, those process parameters that are tied to a specific balance slot (that is, specific system virtual or physical addresses) must be adjusted to reflect the new locations in virtual or physical address space. These include the following:

   - Each SPTE must be loaded with the PFN that contains the contents of each process header page.
   - The virtual addresses of the P0 and P1 page tables must be calculated and loaded into their locations in the hardware PCB.
   - The physical address of the hardware PCB must be calculated and loaded into the software PCB (in field PCB$L_PHYPCB).
   - Finally, the P1 pages that double map the process header pages that are not page table pages must be loaded with the new page frame numbers that contain these pages.

17.5.2.1 Rebuilding the Process Header.
When a process header is read from the swap image into a new balance slot, the SPTEs that map each balance slot page

must be loaded with the PFNs from the swapper map that contain each header page. In addition, the PFN database must be set up for each of these physical pages. The swapper does all this work in a very simple loop that it executes for each header page.

The simplicity (and speed) of the loop results from the use of the two process header page arrays that exist in the process header. These arrays allow the PFN BAK and WSLX arrays to be loaded with their previous contents (because the two header arrays were loaded when the process was outswapped).

17.5.2.2   **P1 Window to the Process Header.** All of the process header pages except process page tables are double mapped with a range of P1 addresses. This double mapping is done for the following reason. When a process header is outswapped and subsequently inswapped, it probably resides in a different balance slot. Any routine that stores that process header address in a register and then references header locations with a displacement from this register might be referencing the header of another process if some scheduling and swapping occurred between obtaining the header base address and later references using it.

To avoid this problem, a range of P1 space is set up by the swapper to map these same header pages. The P1 pages are mapped in such a way that, even if an outswap and later inswap occur between two instructions, the P1 virtual addresses of the process header pages do not change. The conventions that the operating system observes about header references are these:

- Any reference to the process header should use the P1 address (CTL$GL_ PHD contents point to the P1 map of the process header).
- Any reference to the system space header must execute at IPL 7 (IPL$_ SYNCH) to prevent a swap.
- Any reference to process page tables must execute at IPL 7 because the page table pages are not double mapped.

There are two implications for the operating system here.

- These physical pages are not kept track of in any way through reference counts or any other technique. However, all of these header pages are a permanent part of the process working set.
- The P1 page table page that maps these pages must also be a permanent member of the process working set.

17.5.3   **Rebuilding the Process Body**

The process header must be put into a known state before the process body can be put back into the approximate shape it was in before the process was outswapped. If the header was never outswapped, there is very little that has to be done. If the header was outswapped, the steps just described are taken to put the process header back together again.

17.5.3.1   **Rebuilding the Working Set List and Process Page Tables.** The rebuilding of the process body involves a simple scan of both the swapper map and the process working set list. Recall that at outswap, the key to each special case was the combination of physical page type and the setting of the valid bit in the page table entry. On inswap, the key to each special case is the contents of the page table entry located by the virtual page number field in the working set list entry. An approximation of swapper activity for each page is as follows:

1. The page table entry is located from the VPN field of the WSLE.
2. In the usual case, the original contents of the PTE are put into the PFN BAK array and the PFN from the swapper map is loaded into the now valid PTE.
3. If for some reason a copy of the page already exists in memory, then that page is put into the process working set, and the duplicate page from the swapper map is released to the front of the free page list.

Table 17-5 contains a detailed list of the different cases that the swapper can encounter when rebuilding the process page tables. Three of the cases deserve special comment.

17.5.3.2   **Pages with I/O in Progress When Outswap Occurred.** Pages that had I/O in progress when the process was outswapped were written to the swap file anyway to reserve space. If the page was previously unmodified, then it would be put onto the free page list when both the swap write and the outstanding write operation completed. If the page was previously modified, then it would be put onto the modified page list when both the swap write and the outstanding write operation completed (because the contents of the SWPVBN array were nonzero).

In either case, it is possible for the process to be swapped back in before one of these physical pages was reused. The swapper uses the physical page that is already contained in the process PTE (as a transition page) and releases the duplicate physical page from the swapper map to the front of the free page list.

In the case of a page on the free page list, this decision is simply one of convenience. In the case of a page on the modified page list, the contents of the page in the swap image are out of date and the swapper has no choice but to use the physical page that is already in memory.

17.5.3.3   **Resolution of Global Read-Only Pages.** The only possible global page that could be in the swap file is a global read-only page that had a share count of one when the process was outswapped (or a page that was explicitly locked). All other global pages were dropped from the process working set before the process was outswapped.

Table 17-5: Rebuilding the Working Set List and the Process Page Tables at Inswap

At inswap time, the swapper uses the contents of the page table entry to determine what action to take for each particular page.

Type of Page Table Entry	*Action of Swapper for This Page*
1. PTE is valid.	Page is locked into memory and was never outswapped.
2. PTE indicates a transition page (probably due to outstanding I/O when process was outswapped).	Fault transition page into process working set. Release duplicate page that was just swapped in.
3. PTE contains a global page table index (GPTX). (Page must be global read-only because global read/write pages were dropped from the working set at outswap time.)	Swapper action is based on the contents of the global page table entry (GPTE) a. If the global page table entry is valid, add the PFN and the GPTE to the process working set and release the duplicate page. b. If the global page table entry indicates a transition page, make the global page table entry valid, add that physical page to the process working set, and release the duplicate page. c. If the global page table entry indicates a global section table index, then keep the page just swapped in, and make that the master page in the global page table entry as well as the slave page in the process page table entry.
4. PTE contains a page file index or a process section table index.	These are the usual contents for pages that did not have outstanding I/O or other page references when the process was outswapped. The PFN in the swapper map is inserted into the process page table. The PFN arrays are initialized for that page.

There are two different cases that the swapper will find when rebuilding the process page tables. In either case, the process page table entry contains a global page table index so the determining factor is the contents of the global page table entry.

1. The global page table entry contains a global section table index. In this case, the physical page from the swapper map is added to the global page table entry as well as the process page table entry.
2. It is possible that the global page was referenced by some other process while this process was outswapped. In that case, the global page table entry might contain a transition or valid PTE. In either case, the PFN that is already in the global page table entry is kept. (If the GPTE is in transi-

tion, it is made valid.) The duplicate PFN from the swapper map is re-leased to the front of the free page list.

17.5.3.4 **Example of an Inswap Operation.** To illustrate at least some of the special cases that the swapper encounters when a process body is swapped back into memory, Figures 17-5 through 17-7 contain an example of an inswap operation. Note that this example is not related to the outswap example used before (see Figures 17-2 to 17-4). This example is tailored to illustrate the interesting cases the swapper can encounter during an inswap operation.

Figure 17-5 shows the state of the process header after the process has been selected as an inswap candidate. Figure 17-6 shows that four physical pages have been allocated to contain the four working pages that the example is describing. Figure 17-7 shows the rebuilt process page tables and the PFN

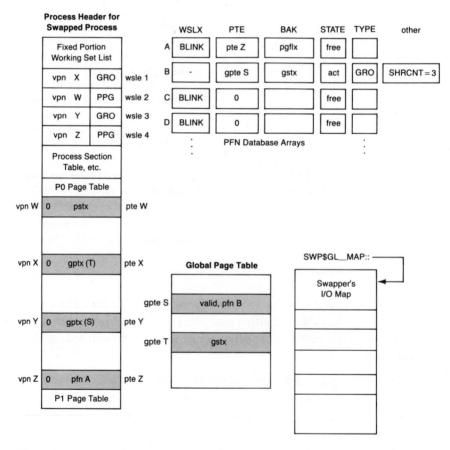

Figure 17-5
Working Set List and Swapper Map before Physical Page Allocation

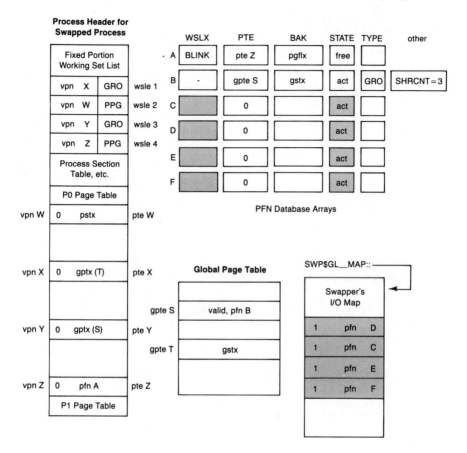

Figure 17-6
Working Set List and Swapper Map after Physical Page
Allocation

database changes that result from rebuilding the working set and process
page tables.

1. The first working set list entry locates virtual page number X. This PTE
   contains a global page table index. The referenced global page table entry
   (GPTE T) contains a global section table index, indicating that the global
   page table entry is not valid.

   The page frame number (PFN D) is put into the process page table. It is
   also added to the global page database by making the GPTE valid (see
   Figure 17-7), putting PFN D into the GPTE, and updating the PFN data for
   physical page D to reflect its new state.

2. The next working set list entry is a process page mapped by PTE W (see
   Figure 17-6). This PTE contains a process section table index. The PTE is

387

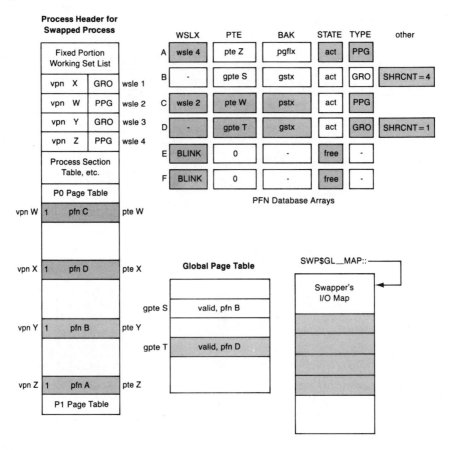

Figure 17-7
Working Set List and Rebuilt Page Tables

updated to contain PFN C and the PSTX is stored in the BAK array element for that page (see Figure 17-7). Other PFN arrays are updated accordingly.

3. The next working set list entry (that locates PTE Y) is exactly like the first, as far as the process data is concerned. However, the global page table entry (GPTE S) is valid, indicating that another copy of this page already exists. (This second copy could only have happened if another process faulted the page while this process was outswapped.)

   The duplicate page (PFN E) is released to the front of the free page list. The process page table entry is updated to contain the physical page that already exists (PFN B) and the share count for that page is incremented (from three to four).

4. The fourth working set list entry looks just like the second. However, the

process page table entry indicates a transition page. (This implies that the header in this example was never outswapped.)

The action taken here is similar to step 3, where a duplicate global page was discovered. The page just read (PFN F) is released to the head of the free list. The transition page (PFN A) is faulted back into the process working set by removing the page from the free list, setting its state to active, and turning the valid bit in the PTE back on.

17.5.3.5   **Final Processing of the Inswap Operation.** After the working set list has been scanned and the process page tables rebuilt, the process is ready to have its state changed from computable but outswapped to computable and resident. Several other scheduling details must be taken care of before the scheduler is notified.

1. A new value of ASTLVL is calculated and loaded into the hardware PCB in the process header. ASTs may have been enqueued to the process while it was outswapped. The hardware PCB, which contains a copy of the ASTLVL register, was not available while the header was not resident.
2. The resident bit and the initial quantum bit in the status longword in the software PCB are set.
3. A new quantum interval is loaded into the process header.
4. Finally, the scheduler is called to make the process computable.

PART V/Input/Output

18   I/O System Services

Delay not, Caesar. Read it instantly.
—*Julius Caesar* 3,1

Here is a letter, read it at your leisure.
—*Merchant of Venice* 5,1

All I/O operations performed on a device are requested using the I/O system services. Sometimes, in addition to being called directly by the user, the I/O system services are called on behalf of a user by system components, such as RMS.

This chapter describes the following topics:

- What must be done before an I/O request can be made (channel assignment and device allocation)
- How an I/O request is sent to a device driver
- How a user is notified of the completion of an I/O request
- How a user can obtain information about a particular device or I/O request

18.1   ASSIGNING AND DEASSIGNING CHANNELS

In order to request an I/O operation on a device, a process needs to identify the device to the system. The software mechanism used to link a process to a device is called a channel. Once a user establishes a channel to a device (using the $ASSIGN system service), the user may issue I/O requests (with the $QIO system service) for that device by specifying the channel number assigned to the device. If the user no longer wants to use the device, the $DASSGN system service can be used to deallocate the channel assigned to the device.

18.1.1   Channel Assignment

A channel is described by a channel control block (CCB) table, located in a dedicated portion of P1 space (see Figure 1-7 and Table 26-4). When a channel is assigned to certain nonshareable devices, the user may also associate a mailbox with that device to receive status information such as the arrival of unsolicited input from a terminal. It is up to the device driver for each device to either use or ignore this associated mailbox. The *VAX/VMS Guide to Writing a Device Driver* contains a complete description of the CCB.

The $ASSIGN system service calls on the system routines IOC$FFCHAN and IOC$SEARCHDEV (in IOSUBPAGD) to find a free I/O channel (CCB), and to find the unit control block (UCB) for the device that is being assigned. After that, one of the paths described in the following sections is taken, depending on whether the device is one of the following:

- A local device (not located on another node)
- A spooled device
- The network device NET
- A remote process or task (located on another node)

18.1.1.1 **Local Device Assignment.** This is the normal path through the Assign Channel system service.

1. A check is made to see if the device is allocated to another process that is not a parent process of the process assigning the channel.
2. The DEV$V_SHR bit in UCB$L_DEVCHAR is checked to see if the device is a shareable device. If the device is nonshareable and the volume protection and owner UIC allow it, the device is implicitly allocated to the process (by placing the process ID, from PCB$L_PID, into UCB$L_PID).

   The UCB address is stored in CCB$L_UCB. Whenever the user issues an I/O request, this pointer is used to locate the device.
3. If an associated mailbox was requested, it is identified by placing the UCB address (of the mailbox) in the UCB$L_AMB field of the UCB for the device to which the channel is being assigned. The UCB$W_REFC field of the associated mailbox is incremented, and the CCB$V_AMB flag is set in CCB$B_STS to indicate that an associated mailbox is present. Note that no association is made if one of the following is true:

   —The device is a file-oriented device (identified by the DEV$V_FOD bit in UCB$L_DEVCHAR).
   —The device is shareable (DEV$V_SHR in UCB$L_DEVCHAR).
   —The device already has an associated mailbox (the UCB$L_AMB field is nonzero).

4. The device reference count (UCB$W_REFC) is incremented.
5. The access mode (plus one) at which the channel is being assigned is stored in CCB$B_AMOD. IOC$FFCHAN identifies an unused CCB by looking in the CCB$B_AMOD field. If the value stored there is a zero, the CCB is not being used.
6. Any flags associated with the channel (such as CCB$V_AMB indicating that an associated mailbox is present) are stored in CCB$B_STS.
7. The channel number (really an index into the CCB table in process P1 space, provided by IOC$FFCHAN) is returned to the user at the address specified in the CHAN argument to $ASSIGN.
8. The normal successful completion code (SS$_NORMAL) is returned to the user.

18.1.1.2   **Special Action When Assigning A Spooled Device.** If the DEV$V_SPL bit in UCB$L_DEVCHAR is set, then the device being assigned is a spooled device. The only difference in channel assignment for spooled devices is that the status field in the channel control block (CCB$B_STS) is cleared. The device associated with the spooled device had its UCB address stored in the UCB$L_AMB field when the device was set to spooled. When an I/O request is passed to a spooled device, the $QIO system service recognizes that the device is spooled and actually performs the I/O request to the associated device.

18.1.1.3   **Assigning a Channel to the Network Device.** If the device being assigned is a network device (that is, the user is assigning a channel to the NET device, probably to perform task-to-task communication), the following steps are taken:

1. A check is made to see that the calling process has NETMBX privilege.
2. A network UCB is created by IOC$CREATE_UCB (in IOSUBPAGD).
3. The UCB is made to look like a mailbox UCB that is marked for deletion (the UCB$V_DELMBX bit in UCB$W_DEVSTS is set). When the user deassigns the channel, the UCB will be deleted.
4. The user's byte count quota and limit are reduced by the size of the UCB.
5. The NETDRIVER unit initialization routine is called.
6. Further processing proceeds as in the case of a local, nonshareable device.

18.1.2   **Channel Deassignment**

The $DASSGN system service deassigns a previously assigned I/O channel and clears the linkage and control information in the corresponding CCB. These tasks are accomplished with the following steps:

1. Any outstanding I/O is canceled.
2. If a file is open on the channel (indicated by CCB$L_WIND being non-zero), then that file is closed (by issuing a $QIOW with the IO$_DEACCESS function code, and specifying event flag number 30). This method is also used to dissolve logical links.
3. If any I/O is still outstanding (indicated by CCB$W_IOC being nonzero), the process is placed into an RSN$_ASTWAIT wait state (waiting for the I/O completion AST(s) to be delivered). Chapter 10 discusses wait states in detail.
4. The channel is actually deassigned by clearing the CCB$B_AMOD field.
5. If this was the last channel assigned to the device (UCB$W_REFC contains a 0), the device is implicitly deallocated (by clearing UCB$L_PID).
6. If the device is marked for dismount (the DEV$V_DMT bit in UCB$L_DEVCHAR is set) and it was not mounted with a VMS ACP (the foreign bit DEV$V_FOR is set), the dismount (DEV$V_DMT), mounted

(DEV\$V_MNT), read check (DEV\$V_RCK), write check (DEV\$V_WCK), and software write locked (DEV\$V_SWL) bits in UCB\$L_DEVCHAR are cleared. The UCB\$L_VCB field is cleared, and if that field was not zero, the volume control block pointed to by that field is deallocated. Also, the volume protection mask (UCB\$W_PROT) and the software volume valid bit (UCB\$V_VALID in UCB\$W_STS) are cleared.

7. If UCB\$W_REFC equals zero, or if the calling process has allocated the device, the associated device driver's cancel I/O routine is called to perform any device-dependent operations (see the *VAX/VMS Guide to Writing a Device Driver*). The reason code CAN\$C_DASSGN is passed to the cancel I/O routine.

8. If a mailbox was associated with the device when the channel was assigned (indicated by CCB\$V_AMB in CCB\$B_STS), then the linkage with the mailbox is cleared by taking these steps:

   a. Clearing UCB\$L_AMB
   b. Decrementing UCB\$W_REFC for the mailbox UCB
   c. Calling IOC\$DELMBX (in IOSUBNPAG) to see if the mailbox UCB should be deleted (in case this was the last process referencing a temporary mailbox)

9. If the device to which the channel was assigned was a mailbox (indicated by the DEV\$V_MBX bit in UCB\$L_DEVCHAR), IOC\$DELMBX is called to see if that mailbox should be deleted.

18.2   DEVICE ALLOCATION AND DEALLOCATION

A process allocates a device (using the \$ALLOC system service) to reserve that device for exclusive use. A process deallocates a device (using the \$DALLOC system service) to relinquish exclusive ownership. The code for the \$ALLOC and \$DALLOC is found in module SYSDEVALC.

18.2.1   Device Allocation

The following steps are taken by EXE\$ALLOC to allocate a device:

1. The generic allocation routine IOC\$SEARCHGEN is called to perform logical name translation and select a device, if generic allocation was requested.

2. The process ID (PCB\$L_PID) is stored in the device owner field (UCB\$L_PID).

3. The device allocated bit (DEV\$V_ALL in UCB\$L_DEVCHAR) is set.

4. The device reference count (UCB\$W_REFC) is incremented.

5. The access mode at which the device is allocated is placed in UCB\$B_AMOD.

Any of the following conditions will prevent device allocation:

- The device is already allocated by another process (UCB$L_PID is non-zero).
- The device reference count (UCB$W_REFC) is nonzero.
- The mounted bit (UCB$V_MNT in UCB$L_DEVCHAR) is set.
- The spooled bit (UCB$V_SPL in UCB$L_DEVCHAR) is set, and the process does not have ALLSPOOL privilege.
- The device is nonshareable, and the requesting process does not have access rights (located through PCB$L_ARB) allowing it to allocate the device, as determined by the device's owner UIC and volume protection (UCB$L_OWNUIC and UCB$W_VPROT).

18.2.2 Device Deallocation

A process may choose to deallocate a single device or all devices allocated to it. For each device that is to be deallocated, EXE$DALLOC finds its UCB address either directly, from the DEVNAM argument in the $DALLOC call, or by examining each UCB in the system. The routine IOC$SEARCHDEV is used to relate device names to UCB addresses and to perform logical name translations.

Each UCB in the system can be found by following a linked list of device data blocks (DDBs), that name each device controller in the system (the first DDB is pointed to by global symbol IOC$GL_DEVLIST). Each DDB contains a pointer to the first device UCB on the controller, and all of the UCBs for the devices on a given controller are linked together.

A device is deallocated when the following are true:

- The UCB$L_PID field matches the PCB$L_PID field of the process issuing the $DALLOC.
- The access mode at which the deallocate request is being made is at least as privileged as the access mode at which the device was allocated.
- The allocated bit (DEV$V_ALL in UCB$L_DEVCHAR) is set.
- The device mounted bit (DEV$V_MNT in UCB$L_DEVCHAR) is clear.
- The reference count (UCB$W_REFC) equals 1, indicating that no more channels are assigned to the device.

The device is deallocated by taking these steps:

1. Clearing the device allocated bit (DEV$V_ALL in UCB$L_DEVCHAR)
2. Clearing the device owner process id field (UCB$L_PID)
3. Decrementing the device reference count (UCB$W_REFC)
4. Calling the device driver's cancel I/O routine with the reason code CAN$C_CANCEL
5. Returning the normal successful completion code to the user in R0 (SS$_NORMAL)

18.3 $QIO SYSTEM SERVICE

The $QIO system service (in module SYSQIOREQ) allows a user to initiate an I/O operation by queuing a request to the device's associated driver. Once the I/O operation has been initiated, control will be returned to the user, who can synchronize I/O completion in one of three ways:

- The process can enter an event flag wait state until the I/O request completes, waiting for the specified event flag to be set.
- The address of an AST routine that will be executed when the I/O completes can be passed to $QIO. In this case, the process can continue executing or wait, depending on the particular method of synchronization.
- The I/O status block can be polled for a completion status. The status field in the IOSB is cleared by $QIO and set by the special kernel mode AST that completes an I/O request in process context. This last method is not recommended.

As an alternative to $QIO, the $QIOW system service may be used, which is equivalent to the $QIO system service followed by a $WAITFR system service. Using the $QIOW system service guarantees that the I/O operation will complete before control is transferred back to the user.

18.3.1   Device-Independent Preprocessing

EXE$QIO begins preprocessing an I/O request with the following steps:

1. Clearing the specified event flag (or event flag number 0 if no event flag was specified)
2. Validating the device-independent $QIO parameters (event flag number, channel number, I/O function code, and I/O status block)
3. Verifying that the device is online (UCB$V_ONLINE in UCB$W_STS must be set)
4. Clearing the I/O status block (if one was specified)

An I/O request packet (IRP) is allocated from nonpaged pool. If possible, this allocation is done from a queue of preallocated IRPs (pointed to by IOC$GL_IRPFL). Otherwise, routine EXE$ALLOCIRP in MEMORYALC is called to allocate an IRP from the general nonpaged pool area. Obtaining an IRP from the preallocated queue takes less time than calling the allocation routine.

The device-independent section of the IRP is initialized, including the following fields:

- The device-independent $QIO parameters
- The process base priority (from PCB$B_PRIB)

- The process ID
- The device UCB address
- The IRP$V_BUFIO flag in IRP$W_STS (which is set for a buffered I/O operation, and cleared for a direct I/O operation)

The process's privileges are checked to guarantee that it may perform the requested I/O function. In the course of checking process privileges, EXE$QIO converts a read or write virtual I/O request function code into the corresponding read or write logical function code (unless the virtual request is for a file-oriented device, DEV$V_FOD in UCB$L_DEVCHAR is set).

If an AST was requested, the AST quota (PCB$W_ASTCNT) is decremented, and the AST quota update flag (ACB$V_QUOTA) is set in IRP$B_RMOD.

Control is then transferred to a function decision table (FDT) routine (by a JSB) in the selected device driver. This routine is responsible for interpreting the device-dependent $QIO parameters (P1 to P6). If the FDT routine returns control to EXE$QIO (by issuing an RSB), EXE$QIO calls another FDT routine in the driver. Successive FDT routines are called until an FDT routine exits turning control over to a subroutine other than EXE$QIO (for example, EXE$QIODRVPKT, EXE$QIOACPPKT, or the user's routine).

18.3.2   FDT Routines

Function decision table (FDT) routines are device-specific extensions to $QIO. Their primary purpose is to validate the device-dependent $QIO parameters (P1 to P6). A device driver can include customized FDT routines or use some of the general purpose routines that are a part of the system image. Although some FDT routines are included in a driver image, they are logically device-dependent extensions of the $QIO system service.

FDT routines execute in the context of the process that issued the $QIO request. Therefore, they have access to data in the user's P0 and P1 address space. FDT routines communicate information about the I/O request to the driver by passing information in the device-dependent section of the IRP. FDT routines for direct I/O (I/O done directly to a user buffer) ensure that each buffer page is valid and locked into memory. (Buffer pages are locked into memory by incrementing the reference count in the PFN database for each physical page involved in the transfer.) FDT routines for buffered I/O operations must allocate a buffer from nonpaged pool that will be used by the driver for the actual transfer. If the operation is a buffered write, the data that is being written is copied into this buffer. System space buffers are required because the driver processes the I/O request in system context and only has access to system virtual address space. FDT routines are described in detail in the *VAX/VMS Guide to Writing a Device Driver*.

18.3.3   I/O Postprocessing

After a device driver completes an I/O operation, it invokes the REQCOM macro. This macro jumps to the routine IOC$REQCOM, which places the IRP on the I/O postprocessing queue and requests a software interrupt at IPL$_IOPOST (IPL 4). The I/O postprocessing routine (IOC$IOPOST, in IOCIOPOST) runs as a response to the software interrupt. It implements the device-independent facets of I/O completion, and handles paging I/O completion as well (see Chapter 15).

Some of the I/O postprocessing operations (for example, unlocking buffer pages, and deallocating buffers) are performed in the I/O postprocessing interrupt service routine (IOC$IOPOST), while other operations (such as writing the I/O status block and setting event flags) are performed by a special kernel mode AST routine (which executes in process context, and therefore has access to process address space).

When an IRP is removed from the I/O postprocessing queue (with list head IOC$GL_PSFL), IOC$IOPOST first determines if the I/O operation was a buffered or direct request.

18.3.3.1   Direct I/O Completion.

Portions of a direct I/O request can be completed in the IPL 4 I/O postprocessing interrupt service routine without the benefit of process context. The following steps are performed in the interrupt service routine:

1. The process direct I/O count in the software PCB (at offset PCB$W_DIOCNT) is incremented, indicating one less outstanding direct I/O request.
2. The buffer pointed to by IRP$L_SVAPTE is unlocked, using the IRP$L_BCNT and IRP$W_BOFF fields to determine the size of the locked buffer. Buffer pages are unlocked by decrementing their associated reference counts in the PFN database. This step may result in their being placed on the free or modified page list.
3. The IRP$V_EXTEND bit in IRP$W_STS is checked. If that bit is set, it indicates an IRP extension (IRPE) is pointed to by IRP$L_EXTEND. The IRPE may contain up to two locked buffers (pointed to by IRPE$L_SVAPTE1 and IRPE$L_SVAPTE2, with sizes determined by IRPE$W_BOFF1 and IRPE$L_BCNT1, and IRPE$W_BOFF2 and IRPE$L_BCNT2, respectively). These buffers, if present, are unlocked, and a check is made to see if the IRPE$V_EXTEND bit in IRPE$W_STS is set. If so, the same procedure is repeated, until the last IRPE in the linked list is found, and its buffers unlocked.
4. The direct I/O special kernel mode AST (DIRPOST in IOCIOPOST) is queued to the process (using the IRP$L_PID field to identify the process to which the AST should be queued). The IRP is used as the AST control block for routine SCH$QAST (as described in 7).

The remainder of I/O completion for a direct I/O request takes place in process context in the special kernel AST called DIRPOST, as follows:

1. The accumulated direct I/O count (stored in PHD$L_DIOCNT) is incremented. This count is an accounting statistic that is reported to the accounting manager (the job controller) when the process is deleted.
2. The I/O in progress counter in the channel control block (CCB$W_IOC) is decremented.
3. If this was the last I/O for the channel, and there is a deaccess request for the channel pending (CCB$L_DIRP does not equal zero), that deaccess request is queued to the ACP (so that a file can be properly closed or some similar operation performed), by calling routine IOC$WAKACP.
4. If an I/O status block was requested by the user, it is written using the quadword starting at IRP$L_IOST1 (same offset as IRP$L_MEDIA).
5. If any IRP extensions (IRPEs) were used, they are deallocated.
6. The event flag specified in the $QIO call is set (by calling routine SCH$POSTEF, whose operation is discussed in Chapter 12).
7. If the user requested an AST for the $QIO call, the IRP is again used as an AST control block, and is queued to the user (the IRP will be deallocated by the normal AST processing scheme, as discussed in Chapter 7).
8. If the user did not request an AST to be delivered upon the completion of the $QIO call, the IRP is deallocated.

18.3.3.2 **Buffered I/O Completion.** The portions of buffered I/O completion that take place in the IPL 4 interrupt service routine differ from the direct I/O case because of the differences in the way the two kinds of requests are processed. The following steps are accomplished by the IPL 4 interrupt service routine:

1. The process buffered I/O count (PCB$W_BIOCNT), the count of outstanding buffered I/O operations, is incremented.
2. The byte count quota that was allocated for the system buffer is given back by adding IRP$W_BOFF to JIB$L_BYTCNT.
3. If the I/O function was a read (bit IRP$V_FUNC in IRP$W_STS is set), the BUFPOST routine (in module IOCIOPOST) is used as the special kernel mode AST routine address.
4. Otherwise, DIRPOST is used as the special kernel mode AST routine address, and the buffer used to hold the data written to the device, if any, is deallocated (the buffer's address is found in IRP$L_SVAPTE).

The special kernel mode AST called BUFPOST is used for the case of a buffered read operation, because the data must be copied from the system buffer to the buffer specified in the original $QIO request. BUFPOST performs the following steps:

1. After the data is copied, the system buffer is no longer needed so it is deallocated to nonpaged pool.

2. The accumulated buffered I/O count accounting statistic (stored in PHD$L_BIOCNT) is incremented.

The remaining steps that this routine must perform are identical to the operations performed by DIRPOST. BUFPOST continues at step 2 in that routine.

18.4   I/O CANCELLATION

The $CANCEL system service cancels all I/O issued to a device from a specified channel by scanning all of the IRPs queued to the device UCB (starting at UCB$L_IOQFL). Several conditions must hold for an I/O request to be canceled.

- The request cannot be a virtual request (indicated by the setting of the IRP$V_VIRTUAL bit in IRP$W_STS). In general, I/O cannot be canceled on disk or tape devices. Drivers for these devices ensure that the IRP$V_VIRTUAL bit is set on all requests that cannot be canceled.
- The requesting process ID (PCB$L_PID) matches the stored process ID in IRP$L_PID.
- The requested channel number in the CHAN argument to $CANCEL matches the stored channel number in IRP$W_CHAN.

The I/O is canceled by taking the following steps:

1. Clearing the buffered read bit (IRP$V_FUNC in IRP$W_STS) for buffered I/O functions (identified by IRP$V_BUFIO in IRP$W_STS)
2. Placing the SS$_CANCEL function code in the low order word of and clearing the high-order word of IRP$L_IOST1
3. Placing the IRP in the I/O postprocessing queue, and requesting an I/O postprocessing software interrupt

The driver cancel I/O routine is called to allow the driver to perform any desired cleanup operations, and to cancel the I/O request currently in progress.

If there is a file open on the channel, EXE$CANCEL allocates and initializes an IRP on behalf of the user (and charges the user's buffered I/O quota, PCB$W_BIOCNT, for an I/O request). The IRP is queued to the ACP for further processing (using routine EXE$QIOACPPKT in SYSQIOREQ). The IRP specifies a function code of IO$_ACPCONTROL and uses event flag number 31 to indicate I/O completion.

18.5   MAILBOX CREATION AND DELETION

Mailboxes are virtual devices used for interprocess communication. They are created by the $CREMBX system service. There are two kinds of mailboxes, temporary and permanent. Temporary mailboxes are deleted automatically when no more processes have channels assigned to them, while permanent mailboxes must be explicitly marked for deletion using the $DELMBX system service. (After being marked for deletion, permanent mailboxes are deleted when no more processes have channels assigned to them).

18.5.1   Mailbox Creation

The $CREMBX system service (located in module SYSMAILBX) creates a virtual mailbox device named MBn: and assigns an I/O channel to it.

The routine EXE$CREMBX begins by translating the logical name specified by the user in the LOGNAM parameter (if any), and finding a free channel (CCB) to assign to the mailbox (using IOC$FFCHAN). It also verifies that the user has the appropriate privilege(s) for the type of mailbox being created:

* PRMMBX for a permanent mailbox
* TMPMBX for a temporary mailbox
* SHMEM for a mailbox in shared memory

If a logical name has been specified, EXE$CREMBX searches all existing mailbox UCBs to see if a mailbox with that name already exists. If a match is found and the caller has privilege to access the mailbox (or owns the mailbox), the reference count for that mailbox (UCB$W_REFC) is incremented, and a channel is assigned by taking the following steps:

1. Placing the mailbox UCB address in CCB$L_UCB
2. Placing the access mode at which the channel was assigned (plus one) in CCB$B_AMOD
3. Returning the channel number to the user in the CHAN parameter
4. Returning with an SS$_NORMAL completion status code

If the mailbox being created did not previously exist and is a temporary mailbox, the process buffered I/O byte count quota (JIB$L_BYTCNT) is checked to determine if the process has enough quota do the following:

* Support the creation of a mailbox UCB
* Buffer messages (according to the value specified in the BUFQUO parameter to $CREMBX)
* Allow for overhead (256 bytes) in case of process deletion

If the BUFQUO parameter is not specified, the SYSBOOT parameter DEFMBXBUFQUO (stored at IOC$GW_MBXBFQUO) is used for the amount of space reserved to buffer messages.

A logical name block is allocated, if required, which will contain the logical name specified for the mailbox by the user in the $CREMBX call. Routine IOC$CREATE_UCB (in IOSUBPAGD) is called to actually create the mailbox UCB. The routine allocates space for the UCB from nonpaged pool and initializes fields in the UCB (using a template UCB found through MB$UCB0 in DEVICEDAT). IOC$CREATE_UCB performs the following actions:

1. The mailbox is marked online (the UCB$V_ONLINE bit in set in UCB$W_STS).
2. The reference count (UCB$W_REFC) is set to 1.
3. The UIC of the creating process (PCB$L_UIC) is established as the owner of the mailbox (by loading UCB$L_OWNUIC).
4. The UCB is identified as being a shareable mailbox (the DEV$V_SHR and DEV$V_MBX bits are set in UCB$L_DEVCHAR).
5. The UCB is linked into the mailbox controller's device list (with UCB$L_LINK).
6. A unit number is assigned to the UCB (in UCB$W_UNIT). The number is in the range of 1 to 65535; when all unit numbers in the range have been used, the unit numbers start again at 1. Unit numbers that are still in use are skipped.
7. The mailbox controller's device count (CRB$W_REFC) is incremented.

After IOC$CREATE_UCB returns control, EXE$CREMBX performs the following steps:

1. It places the buffer quota calculated earlier in UCB$W_BUFQUO.
2. It places the protection mask specified by the user in the PROMSK parameter in UCB$W_VPROT.
3. It clears the device owner process ID field (UCB$L_PID).
4. The quota charge for the mailbox (UCB$W_CHARGE) is computed by the sum of UCB$W_BUFQUO and UCB$W_SIZE.
5. It places the buffer quota plus UCB size in UCB$W_CHARGE.
6. It places the maximum message size specified by the user in the MAXMSG parameter in UCB$W_DEVBUFSIZ. (If MAXMSG was not specified, the SYSBOOT parameter DEFMBXMXMSG, stored at IOC$GW_MBXMXMSG, is used).

If the mailbox being created is a permanent mailbox, the UCB$V_PRMMBX bit in UCB$W_DEVSTS is set. Three other steps are taken if the mailbox is a temporary mailbox:

- The UCB$V_DELMBX bit in UCB$W_DEVSTS is set to mark the mailbox for deletion. It will be deleted when the last channel assigned to it is deassigned.
- The process byte count limit (JIB$L_BYTLM) is reduced by UCB$W_CHARGE.
- The process byte count quota (JIB$L_BYTCNT) is reduced by UCB$W_CHARGE.

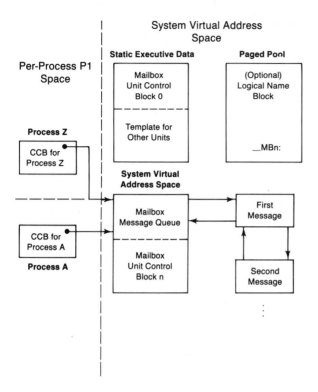

Figure 18-1
Data Structures Associated with Mailbox Creation

If a logical name was specified for the mailbox, a logical name is created using the logical name block allocated earlier. The association with the logical name is made through UCB$L_LOGADR. If no logical name was specified, UCB$L_LOGADR is cleared. Finally, a channel is assigned to the mailbox in the same way as if the mailbox had already existed. The relationships among the data structures associated with mailbox creation are pictured in Figure 18-1.

18.5.2   Mailbox Creation in Shared Memory

Note that although the format of a shared memory mailbox UCB is somewhat different from a local memory UCB, the general steps involved in the creation of the mailbox are the same. All of the logic is contained within the same module (SYSMAILBX).

One extra level of data structure is required to describe a shared memory mailbox. This structure, called a shared memory mailbox control block (Figure 18-2), is located in the shared memory. The UCBs on each port associated

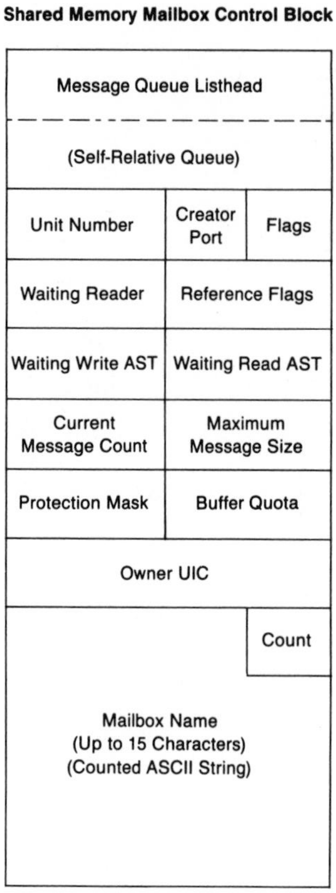

Shared Memory Mailbox Control Block

Message Queue Listhead		
(Self-Relative Queue)		
Unit Number	Creator Port	Flags
Waiting Reader	Reference Flags	
Waiting Write AST	Waiting Read AST	
Current Message Count	Maximum Message Size	
Protection Mask	Buffer Quota	
Owner UIC		
	Count	
Mailbox Name (Up to 15 Characters) (Counted ASCII String)		

Figure 18-2
Contents of a Shared Memory Mailbox Control Block

with the shared memory mailbox contain the (processor-specific) virtual address of the mailbox. There are three cases that the Create Mailbox system service can encounter when creating a mailbox in shared memory.

- If the shared memory mailbox control block (Figure 18-2) does not exist (if the mailbox does not already exist on this processor or another), it is created first. Then, the unit control block in local memory is created. A logical name block is allocated because shared memory structures always have a name associated with them. Finally, a channel is assigned for the creating process.
- If the mailbox is being created on this processor for the first time (but already exists on another), a UCB is allocated and loaded with parameters that describe the mailbox. A bit is set in a mailbox-dependent field indicating that this mailbox UCB describes a mailbox in shared memory. Finally, the address of the shared memory mailbox control block is loaded into the UCB.

- If the mailbox already exists on this processor, the Create Mailbox system service simply assigns a channel to it.

The data structures required to describe a shared memory mailbox are pictured in Figure 18-3.

18.5.3   Mailbox Deletion

The $DELMBX system service (located in module SYSMAILBX) is used to mark a permanent mailbox for deletion. The mailbox is actually deleted by IOC$DELMBX (in IOSUBNPAG) when its reference count (UCB$W_REFC) goes to zero (after the last channel assigned to it has been deassigned, as described in Section 18.1.2).

The mailbox to be marked for delete is identified by the CHAN argument in the $DELMBX call. The channel number is used to locate the CCB, from which the mailbox UCB address can be found (in CCB$L_UCB).

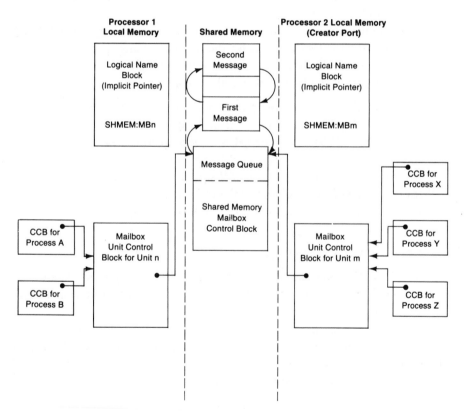

Figure 18-3
Shared Memory Mailbox Creation

The routine EXE$DELMBX verifies the following:

1. The UCB is for a mailbox (that the DEV$V_MBX bit is set in UCB$L_DEVCHAR).
2. The mailbox is a permanent mailbox (that the UCB$V_PRMMBX bit is set in UCB$W_DEVSTS).
3. The process has PRMMBX privilege.

If the above conditions are met, the mailbox is marked for deletion by setting the UCB$V_DELMBX bit in UCB$W_DEVSTS.

The routine IOC$DELMBX actually deletes a mailbox, whether it was temporary or originally permanent by taking the following steps:

1. Verifying that the device to be deleted is a mailbox (DEV$V_MBX is set in UCB$L_DEVCHAR), that the reference count (UCB$W_REFC) is zero, and that the mailbox has been marked for deletion (UCB$V_DELMBX is set in UCB$W_DEVSTS)
2. Unlinking this UCB from the other mailbox UCBs (using the UCB$L_LINK field) for this mailbox controller (because the UCBs for a controller are linked together)
3. Decrementing the controller's device reference count (CRB$W_REFC)
4. Removing the logical name for the mailbox (if any specified, using a non-zero value in UCB$L_LOGADR) from the logical name table
5. Deallocating the logical name block used for the mailbox

If the mailbox was a temporary mailbox (UCB$V_PRMMBX clear in UCB$W_DEVSTS), the byte count limit (JIB$L_BYTLM) and the byte count quota (JIB$L_BYTCNT) are updated (because the creation of a temporary mailbox required those resources). Any unprocessed messages that were queued to the mailbox (and are still stored in nonpaged pool) are deallocated (by calling EXE$DEANONPAGED in MEMORYALC). The UCB for the mailbox is deallocated (by calling EXE$DEANONPAGED).

18.6   BROADCAST SYSTEM SERVICE

The $BRDCST system service (EXE$BRDCST in SYSBRDCST) allows messages to be sent to one or more terminals (even if an I/O operation is currently in progress on the terminal).

After checking the buffer quota (to make sure enough quota is available to buffer the message), a broadcast descriptor block (BRD) is allocated from nonpaged pool and initialized. (See Figure 18-4 for the format of a BRD.)
If the message is to be sent to a single terminal, then EXE$BRDCST performs the following actions:

1. Locates the UCB address for the terminal (specified by the DEVNAM parameter) by calling IOC$SEARCHDEV

Broadcast Descriptor Block

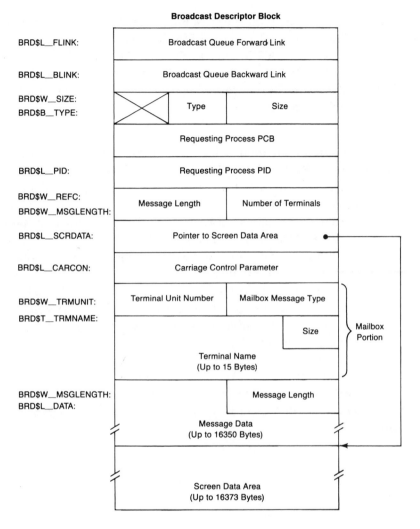

BRD$L__FLINK: Broadcast Queue Forward Link

BRD$L__BLINK: Broadcast Queue Backward Link

BRD$W__SIZE:
BRD$B__TYPE: Type   Size

Requesting Process PCB

BRD$L__PID: Requesting Process PID

BRD$W__REFC:
BRD$W__MSGLENGTH: Message Length   Number of Terminals

BRD$L__SCRDATA: Pointer to Screen Data Area

BRD$L__CARCON: Carriage Control Parameter

BRD$W__TRMUNIT: Terminal Unit Number   Mailbox Message Type

BRD$T__TRMNAME: Size   Mailbox Portion

Terminal Name
(Up to 15 Bytes)

BRD$W__MSGLENGTH: Message Length
BRD$L__DATA:

Message Data
(Up to 16350 Bytes)

Screen Data Area
(Up to 16373 Bytes)

Figure 18-4
Layout of a Broadcast Descriptor Block

2. Verifies that the process (or any parents of the process) either owns the terminal (UCB$L_PID equals PCB$L_PID) or has OPER privilege
3. Verifies that the UCB is for a terminal (DEV$V_TRM set in UCB$L_DEVCHAR), and that the terminal is online (UCB$V_ONLINE in UCB$W_STS)
4. Places the BRD in a queue of BRDs to be broadcast
5. Starts a broadcast

If the message is to be sent to all terminals, EXE$BRDCST first checks for OPER privilege and then performs steps 3 to 5 above for each terminal UCB.

Before the BRD is placed in the queue of BRDs (step 5) and if the terminal is unowned (UCB$W_REFCNT is zero), EXE$BRDCST verifies that the terminal is not set to AUTOBAUD (TT2$V_AUTOBAUD clear in UCB$L_TT_DEVDP2). The rational behind this step is to make sure that broadcast messages are not sent to terminals having an unknown baud rate (resulting in garbage on the screen).

Starting a broadcast involves several steps:

1. Mailbox-specific information is loaded into the mailbox portion of the BRD (BRD$W_TRMUNIT and BRD$T_TRMNAME).
2. If the specified terminal has enabled broadcast to mailbox (bit TT2$V_BRDCSTMBX set in UCB$L_TT_DEVDP1), the broadcast message is written to the mailbox associated with the terminal (by calling routine EXE$WRTMAILBOX in module MBDRIVER).
3. A write buffer packet that points to the BRD (see Figure 18-5) is allocated from nonpaged pool and initialized.
4. The write buffer packet is passed to the terminal driver's alternate start I/O entry point (by calling routine EXE$ALTQUEPKT in SYSQIOREQ). This routine activates the driver regardless of whether or not an I/O request is in progress for the device.
5. The terminal driver then accepts the broadcast message, or indicates that the message cannot be broadcast (because, for example, the user issued a SET TERMINAL/NOBROADCAST or /PASSALL command).
6. If the message is not accepted by the driver, the write buffer packet is deallocated.

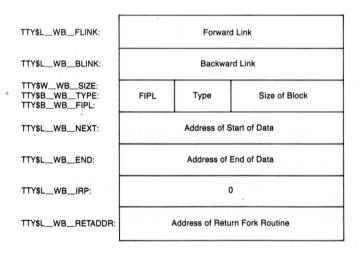

	Forward Link
TTY$L_WB_FLINK:	Forward Link
TTY$L_WB_BLINK:	Backward Link
TTY$W_WB_SIZE: TTY$B_WB_TYPE: TTY$B_WB_FIPL:	FIPL | Type | Size of Block
TTY$L_WB_NEXT:	Address of Start of Data
TTY$L_WB_END:	Address of End of Data
TTY$L_WB_IRP:	0
TTY$L_WB_RETADDR:	Address of Return Fork Routine

Figure 18-5
Layout of a Write Buffer Packet

7. If the message is accepted by the driver, the broadcast reference count is incremented (BRD$W_REFC).

While the driver is writing the message to the specified terminal(s), the process issuing the $BRDCST call is placed in an RSN$_BRKTHRU wait state. As soon as BRD$W_REFC goes to zero, indicating all of the broadcast messages have been sent to the specified terminal(s), the process is removed from the wait state; the BRD is deallocated, and the system service completes. The write buffer packet is deallocated after the message is output to the terminals.

18.7   INFORMATIONAL SERVICES

Application programs frequently require information about particular devices on the system. The VMS operating system allows a user to obtain specific information about a particular device using one of several system services ($QIO, $GETDVI, $GETDEV, and $GETCHN). The information obtained may be either common to all the devices on the system (device independent), or specific to a particular device type (device dependent).

18.7.1   Device-Independent Information

Device-independent information refers to information that is present for each device on the system (such as the device unit number, device characteristics, and the device type). It is obtained by reading fields in the UCB that have the same interpretation for all devices on the system.

18.7.1.1   Get Device/Volume Information.   The Get Device/Volume Information ($GETDVI) system service (located in SYSGETDEV) is provided to obtain device-independent information about a device (see the *VAX/VMS System Services Reference Manual* for a listing of the fields that can be returned). Support still exists for the older services $GETCHN and $GETDEV for upward compatibility. In the development of VAX/VMS Version 3.0, it was determined that the functions of $GETCHN and $GETDEV could not be extended without affecting users. $GETDVI was written to replace $GETCHN and $GETDEV, using the item list argument mechanism implemented in $GETJPI. In this way $GETDVI can be extended as much as necessary in the future.

Two sets of information, called the primary device characteristics and the secondary device characteristics, can be requested. These two sets of characteristics are identical unless one of the following conditions holds:

- The device has an associated mailbox (nonzero entry in UCB$L_AMB), in which case the primary characteristics are those of the device, and the secondary characteristics are those of the associated mailbox.

411

- The device is spooled (DEV$V_SPL is set in UCB$L_DEVCHAR), in which case the primary characteristics are those of the intermediate device, and the secondary characteristics are those of the spooled device.
- If the device represents a logical link in a network, the secondary characteristics contain information about the link.

Before it can locate the desired device's UCB address, $GETDVI must first determine whether it was passed a channel number or a device name. Once the source is determined, $GETDVI locates the UCB address in the same way that the UCB is located by $GETCHN and $GETDEV. The item list of requested information is then processed serially. The item codes are used to index a table that determines the location of the desired information within the UCB. If the low bit in the word containing the item code is clear, the primary UCB is used; if the bit is set, the secondary UCB is used. When an item is successfully located, it is copied into the user's buffer for that item.

The routines EXE$GETCHN and EXE$GETDEV differ only in how they initially find the desired device's UCB address. In the $GETCHN case, the CCB$L_UCB field for the CCB identified by the CHAN argument is used. In the $GETDEV case, routine IOC$SEARCHDEV is called to find the UCB address from the DEVNAM argument. Once the UCB address is found, the device-independent information is copied from the primary UCB to the user buffer (if a primary buffer was specified). After that, the device-dependent information is copied from the secondary UCB (located by UCB$L_AMB in the primary UCB, or, if that value is 0, the primary UCB is again used) into the user buffer (if a secondary buffer was specified).

18.7.2 Device-Dependent Information

Device-dependent information refers to information that is present for a particular device type on the system, but not for every device on the system. (For example, a unit control block for a card reader indicates whether that card reader is translating cards according to the 026 keypunch code or the 029 keypunch code.)

Device-dependent information can be made available to a user process by placing that information into the high-order longword of the I/O status block for a $QIO request. The information is placed there by the driver (by placing that information in R1 before issuing the REQCOM macro to complete the I/O request), and can be anything the driver writer feels is appropriate for a particular $QIO function code. That is, the information placed there can take on different meanings for different function codes.

Often, device drivers support special function codes that only return device-dependent information in the high-order longword of the I/O status block and that do not initiate any device activity. The function codes most frequently used in this way are IO$_SENSEMODE and IO$_SENSECHAR. For example, the magtape driver responds to the IO$_SENSEMODE $QIO by returning the tape characteristics in the I/O status block. Corresponding IO$_SETMODE and IO$_SETCHAR function codes are also usually provided so that the user can change the device mode or characteristics if the current ones are not acceptable.

In addition, the $GETDVI system service can return two longwords of device-dependent information (UCB$L_DEVDEPEND and UCB$L_DEVDEPND2), which can be used for different purposes by different devices. The *VAX/VMS I/O User's Guide* contains complete descriptions of how the information in that field should be interpreted for every supported device type. That manual also contains a detailed explanation of what information is returned by the IO$_SENSEMODE and IO$_SENSECHAR $QIOs for each device that supports those function codes.

19 VAX/VMS Device Drivers

"Open the pod-bay doors, HAL."
—Arthur C. Clarke, *2001: A Space Odyssey*

A VAX/VMS device driver is a collection of tables and routines used to control I/O operations on a peripheral device. The *VAX/VMS Guide to Writing a Device Driver* describes the general structure of a driver and introduces the system routines commonly called by device drivers. This chapter highlights various techniques used by selected system drivers and documents some of the device-specific processing performed by them. The intent is to present those techniques that are helpful in understanding the VAX/VMS I/O subsystem but are not described in the *VAX/VMS Guide to Writing a Device Driver*. No attempt is made to discuss each VAX/VMS device driver, nor is every feature of a particular driver described. For detailed descriptions of the features and capabilities provided by each supported device driver, see the *VAX/ VMS I/O User's Guide*.

19.1 DISK DRIVERS

Disks are random access mass storage devices placed either on the MASS-BUS, UNIBUS, UNIBUS through the UDA50, IDC (VAX-11/730 only), or CI through the HSC50. The drivers written for these devices are designed to do the following:

- Take advantage of the hardware error recovery and correction capabilities such as data checking, offset recovery, and error code correction (ECC)
- Optimize controller operations by overlapping seek and data transfer operations (although this is not true for all drivers)
- Perform dynamic bad block handling (in conjuction with the ACP)
- Support online diagnostics and error logging
- Support I/O requests at the logical and physical levels (non-DSA disks only), and cooperate with an ancillary control processor (ACP) to support virtual I/O requests

The *VAX/VMS I/O User's Guide* contains a general discussion of some of the disk driver characteristics listed above. The following sections supplement the information presented there.

19.1.1 ECC Error Recovery

ECC (error correcting code) errors occur only on read operations (read data, read header and data, write check data, and write check header and data).

They are corrected by applying a hardware-specified correction mask to the appropriate memory data. The transfer is then continued as if an error never occurred. Note that all RA-type disks have a different ECC scheme, which is implemented within their controllers (the UDA or the HSC).

The actual error correction code consists of the following:

- An 11-bit mask that must be XORed with the appropriate memory data
- A bit number within the sector that specifies the start of the error burst

Disk drivers call routine IOC$APPLYECC (in module IOSUBRAMS) to actually apply the ECC correction. IOC$APPLYECC requires the use of a system page table entry (SPTE). Device drivers that support ECC recovery specify the DPT$V_SVP flag in the flags argument to the DPTAB macro. When this flag is set, the SYSGEN command CONNECT allocates one SPTE for each unit and stores the system virtual page number in field UCB$L_SVPN in the unit control block. The system page table entry is used to double map a byte to be corrected. The driver must also specify the number of bytes that were transferred into memory (up to, but not including, the block to be corrected). This number can be calculated by adding the remaining byte count (loaded by the driver from a MASSBUS adapter control register, MBA$L_BCR, into the unit control block, in field UCB$W_BCR) to the transfer byte count (UCB$W_BCNT). The following steps are performed to apply the correction:

1. The transferred byte count is decremented and then ANDed with 1FF (hex) to calculate the byte offset from the start of the buffer to the block that contains the data to be corrected.
2. The starting bit number of the error burst (a number in the range from 1 to 4096, hex) is decremented to convert it to a relative bit number, and the result is separated into a byte offset within the block and a mask shift count.
3. The byte offset within the block is added to the byte offset from the buffer calculated in step 1. The result is the byte offset within the buffer to the start of the error burst.
4. The exclusive OR pattern mask is shifted left by the mask shift count calculated in step 2.

   At this point, the longword exclusive OR pattern and the byte offset within the buffer to the first byte to be corrected have been calculated. All that remains is to double map the data block to be corrected and XOR the pattern mask with memory. However, the following considerations must be accounted for.

a. The transfer may have been satisfied part way through the last block, and the error correction is outside the data of interest. For example, suppose the byte count terminated after 20 bytes into the sector, and the correctable data starts at byte 35.
b. The transfer may have been satisfied part way through the last block, and

and the error correction is partly inside and partly outside the data of interest. For example, the byte count terminated after 20 bytes into the sector, and the correctable data started at byte 19.

Thus, the correction must be applied one byte at a time. Steps 5 through 7 are repeated four times, if necessary.

5. The offset to the next byte to be corrected is compared with the transfer byte count. If the offset byte count is greater than or equal to the transfer byte count, remaining corrections are outside the area of interest. Step 8 is executed next.
6. The byte to be corrected is double mapped using the system virtual page number stored in UCB$L_SVPN, and the translation buffer is invalidated for that page.
7. The next byte (lowest) of the longword pattern mask is XORed with the memory data, the offset in the buffer is incremented, and the pattern mask is right shifted 8 bits. If all four correction bytes have not been applied, steps 5, 6, and 7 are repeated.
8. The transfer is continued by reexecuting the appropriate function after updating the current transfer parameters (byte count, disk address, and system virtual address of the next page table entry that maps the transfer).

19.1.2   Offset Recovery

Offset recovery is a technique whereby the drive read heads are moved in small increments (usually 200 to 400 microinches) from the track centerline in an attempt to pick up a stronger reading signal. The technique is performed only for read operations such as read header and data, write check data, and write check header and data. This technique is not implemented for RA-type disks, it is performed by the controllers (the UDA and the HSC).

Upon encountering an error that may be correctable using offset recovery, the following steps are taken by a disk driver:

1. The read heads are returned to the centerline.
2. Up to 16 attempts are made to read the data at the centerline.
3. The heads are offset an increment, and 2 retries are performed at that offset. This procedure is repeated up to 6 times.
4. If after 28 attempts (16 at the centerline, and 2 at each of 6 offset positions) the data still cannot be retrieved, a failure is returned.

19.1.3   Dynamic Bad Block Handling

Dynamic bad block handling is implemented as a cooperative effort between driver FDT routines, I/O postprocessing routines, and ACPs. FDT routines for IO$_READVBLK and IO$_WRITEVBLK construct an I/O packet (IRP),

416

and set the virtual bit in the IRP status word (IRP$V_VIRTUAL in IRP$W_STS). The I/O postprocessing routines (in module IOCIOPOST) discover transfer errors on virtual I/O functions and route the IRP to the appropriate ACP.

The ACP, using information in the IRP, calculates the bad block address and stores that information in [0,0]BADLOG.SYS. In addition, a bit is set in the file control block (FCB) and in the file's header. When the file is deleted, the ACP creates a process running the image BADBLOCK.EXE, which diagnoses the file. If the bad block is found, the image uses privileged ACP functions to mark the block as bad in the bad block file ([0,0]BADBLK.SYS;1).

Note that a bad block is not discovered until it is already part of a file and is not recorded in the bad block file until that file is deleted. When a bad block is discovered while writing a file, the bad block information is recorded; a bit is set in the FCB for the file, and an error indication is returned to the requesting process.

Bad block support is restricted to virtual I/O functions (that is, file I/O). Processes performing logical or physical I/O functions must provide their own bad block handling.

19.1.4   Multiple-Block Noncontiguous Virtual I/O

When a read or write virtual I/O function is processed by the $QIO system service (by routine EXE$QIO in module SYSQIOREQ), an attempt is made to perform the transfer without the intervention of an ACP. Conversion of virtual block numbers to logical block numbers is accomplished using mapping information contained in a data structure called a window control block (WCB) that was previously created by an ACP when the corresponding file was first accessed. If the WCB contains enough mapping information to convert the entire virtual range of the transfer into corresponding logical block numbers on the volume, then the virtual I/O transfer will be handled directly by the driver and I/O completion routines, even if the transfer consists of several noncontiguous pieces. If the WCB does not contain enough information to entirely map the virtual range of the transfer, the intervention of an ACP will be required at some time in order to complete the transfer. This intervention is known as a window turn. The number of window turns per unit of time can be displayed by the Monitor Utility with the DCL command MONITOR FCP.

Because a deadlock situation could occur when a page mapped by the memory management subsystem required a window turn, the memory management subsystem must avoid window turns. In order to do this, all files mapped by the memory management subsystem must have all their mapping information in the window control block. These large window control blocks are called cathedral windows.

19.1.4.1 **Mapping Information.** The WCB is pointed to by the channel control block (CCB), which is established by the $ASSIGN system service (as described in Chapter 18). The WCB contains a base virtual block number and a variable number of map entries (controlled by the /WINDOWS=n qualifier to the DCL command INITIALIZE, by the SYSBOOT parameter ACP_WINDOW for disks mounted with the /SYSTEM qualifier, and by the FAB field RTV at file open time). The map entries form a subset of the file retrieval information for the file. Each map entry consists of an extent size and a starting logical block number. The map entries represent a virtually contiguous set of blocks that are not necessarily physically contiguous on the disk.

When a virtual read or write request is specified, FDT routines initialize two fields in the IRP that will be used by the I/O postprocessing routines. The total byte count in the original request is stored in the original byte count field (IRP$L_OBCNT). The accumulated byte count field (IRP$L_ABCNT), a count of bytes actually transferred, is set to zero.

Routine IOC$MAPVBLK is then called to convert the virtual range specified in the transfer to a logical block range, using information in the WCB. There are three possible cases that can occur here:

- The virtual range is logically contiguous and mapping information is contained in the window control block.
- The window control block contains mapping information for the beginning of the virtual range, but the virtual range is not virtually contiguous.
- The mapping information that maps the first virtual block in the range to its logical counterpart is not in the WCB.

19.1.4.2 **No ACP Intervention.** In either of the first two cases, IOC$MAPVBLK returns a nonzero number of bytes mapped and a starting logical block number. These are loaded into the IRP (at fields IRP$L_BCNT and IRP$L_MEDIA respectively), and the I/O request packet is queued to the driver. Further processing of this request takes place in the I/O postprocessing routines. These routines (found in module IOCIOPOST) provide the additional processing necessary to effect the total transfer. They are responsible for accumulating the total number of bytes transferred and for propagating further processing of the request, if necessary.

Whenever the I/O postprocessing code encounters an I/O request packet (IRP) with the virtual bit set (IRP$V_VIRTUAL in IRP$W_STS), it updates the accumulated byte count (stored in IRP$L_ABCNT) by adding the number of bytes just transferred (IRP$L_BCNT). This updated accumulated byte count is then compared with the original byte count (stored in IRP$L_OBCNT). If the two numbers agree, the request is completed exactly like other direct I/O requests (as described in Chapter 18).

In the second case, the remaining byte count is placed into IRP$L_BCNT, and the segment starting virtual block number (IRP$L_SEGVBN) is retrieved. Routine IOC$MAPVBLK is again called to map the remaining virtual range. If the mapping is successful (a nonzero count of the number of bytes mapped is returned), the IRP$L_BCNT and IRP$L_MEDIA fields are updated, and the IRP is again queued to the driver. In this way, the virtual request continues until it completes or until a virtual range that cannot be mapped by information in the WCB is encountered.

19.1.4.3   ACP Intervention. If routine IOC$MAPVBLK cannot convert a virtual range to its logical counterpart, the files ACP associated with the volume involved in the transfer must be called upon to obtain the required mapping information. Note that this failure can be detected by FDT routines at the beginning of the transfer or by the I/O postprocessing routines after the request has been partially satisfied. In either case, the IRP is placed into a work queue and the associated ACP is awakened.

When the ACP processes this IRP, it reads the file header to obtain the mapping information necessary for the transfer in question. This information is stored in the WCB, perhaps replacing other mapping information already contained there. The ACP then updates the BCNT and MEDIA fields in the IRP in order to transfer the first piece of the remaining virtual range and queues the IRP to the driver to continue the transfer. When the I/O postprocessing routine receives this packet, it will usually find that the remaining virtual range can be mapped, allowing the request to complete without further ACP intervention (even though several discrete transfers may still be required). The only time that more than one window turn occurs is when a file is so badly fragmented that it cannot be mapped by the number of retrieval pointers established for this volume.

19.2   MAGNETIC TAPE DRIVERS

Magnetic tapes are sequential access mass storage devices placed either on the MASSBUS or the UNIBUS. In order to perform data transfer operations, the MASSBUS magnetic tape driver (in TMDRIVER or TFDRIVER) has to obtain ownership of both the TM03 or TM78 controller (primary channel) and the MASSBUS Adapter (secondary channel) by issuing the REQPCHAN and REQSCHAN macros, respectively. At times, the secondary channel may be released (using the RELSCHAN macro) so that other disks may use the MASSBUS. The *VAX/VMS Guide to Writing a Device Driver* contains information on how drivers are written for devices on the MASSBUS.

The *VAX/VMS I/O User's Guide* describes the features and capabilities provided by the magnetic tape drivers, and discusses the general error recovery and data check logic employed by them. The specific algorithm used to correct NRZI (non-return-to-zero-inverted) read errors is the following:

1. If the error occurred while reading in the forward direction, the tape is backspaced, and the record is read again.
2. If an error occurs while reading in the reverse direction (as the result of a read physical block reverse function), the following steps are taken:

   a. The record is read in the forward direction to set up the error correction in the hardware.
   b. The tape is backspaced over the record just read.
   c. The record is reread in the forward direction to apply the error correction.
   d. The tape is backspaced over the record to position the tape properly (because the initial request was for a read in the reverse direction).

A magnetic tape ACP is called from various driver FDT routines to perform functions like writing tape labels.

19.3 CLASS AND PORT DRIVERS

VAX/VMS Version 3.0 introduced a layered approach to device drivers and I/O. A number of drivers have been written (or rewritten) in two pieces: a class driver and a port driver. The reason for dividing the device drivers is to separate their functions into operations that depend on the protocol and hardware used to communicate with a device (the communications layer) and those operations that depend on the actual device (the function layer). The class and port strategy has been adopted by the terminal driver (see Section 19.4) and by the SCA-type drivers. SCA-type drivers are class and port drivers written for devices that communicate using a DIGITAL standard architecture known as systems communication architecture (SCA).

19.3.1 Implementation of SCA on the VAX/VMS Operating System

SCA defines a communications layer and the external interface to that layer. Systems communication services (SCS) are a VMS-specific implementation of SCA. SCA port drivers implement SCS on specific port devices. In VAX/VMS Version 3.0, SCA port drivers are provided for the CI (PADRIVER) and the UDA50 (PUDRIVER). SCA class drivers use SCS as a communications medium for some higher-level functions or protocols. The class drivers implement a function layer of the layered strategy and perform operations on a user-visible device without regard for the SCA communications medium used.

   Currently there are two protocols in the function layer that call SCS to communicate information: DECnet-VAX and mass storage control protocol (MSCP). DECnet-VAX uses SCS for communication over the CI; the CNDRIVER is the DECnet class driver. MSCP is a general mass storage pro-

420

Table 19-1: Names of SCA Class and Port Drivers

Type	Name	Application/Device
Class	CNDRIVER	DECnet on the CI
Drivers	DUDRIVER	MSCP Disks
Port	PADRIVER	CI port device
Drivers	PUDRIVER	UDA50 port device

tocol intended to be sufficient to describe all types of disk operation. MSCP is implemented by controllers for RA-type disks. The DUDRIVER is the MSCP class driver.

The class and port drivers supported in VAX/VMS Version 3.0 are shown in Table 19-1. Figure 19-1 shows a conceptual diagram of SCA.

The MSCP disk class driver (DUDRIVER) can use either the CI port driver

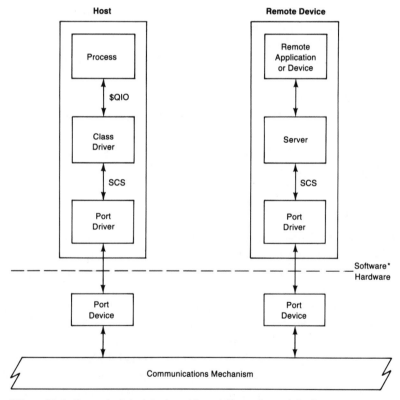

*It is possible for the remote device to implement the port driver and server in hardware.

Figure 19-1
Conceptual Diagram of SCA

421

(PADRIVER) or the UDA50 port driver (PUDRIVER). The DECnet class driver (CNDRIVER) uses the CI port driver (PADRIVER) exclusively.

19.3.2 I/O Processing

When a user application performs I/O through a class and port driver, a channel must be assigned to the class driver; $QIOs are issued to that channel.

The following sequence illustrates how class and port drivers are used to communicate information from a process on a host system to a remote device. The MSCP class driver is used as an example.

1. The process on the host system issues a $QIO to a class driver. The $QIO initializes an IRP and passes it to the class driver.
2. The class driver translates portions of the IRP to an MSCP request. The driver then builds an appropriate class driver request packet (CDRP). The CDRP contains information necessary for SCS to perform its operations (see Figure 19-2). As a convenience to the $QIO/class driver interface, CDRPs have been designed to be an extension of an IRP.
3. The class driver then calls SCS to transmit the MSCP request to the MSCP server (UDA50 or HSC50).
4. The SCS operations are interpreted by the port driver, which then communicates the I/O request to a remote port driver through the communications mechanism.
5. The remote port driver communicates the request to the MSCP server using SCS operations.
6. The server acts on the MSCP request and passes the I/O request to the remote application or device.

19.4 TERMINAL DRIVER

The terminal I/O subsystem is a collection of routines (in separate modules) that provide a flexible approach to terminal input and output (as described in the *VAX/VMS I/O User's Guide*). The terminal driver was rewritten in VAX/VMS Version 3.0 using the class and port driver strategy. Note that the terminal class and port drivers do not communicate using the SCS protocol, nor do the terminal port devices conform to the SCA standards. The terminal class driver (TTDRIVER.EXE) contains FDT routines and device-independent routines. The port drivers (DZDRIVER.EXE, YCDRIVER.EXE, and the routine CONINTDSP in SYS.EXE) contain interrupt service routines and controller-specific control subroutines for DZ-11, DZ-32, DMF-32, and the console terminal interface.

The logical components of the terminal I/O subsystem are illustrated in Figure 19-3. (The console interface is discussed in Section 19.6.)

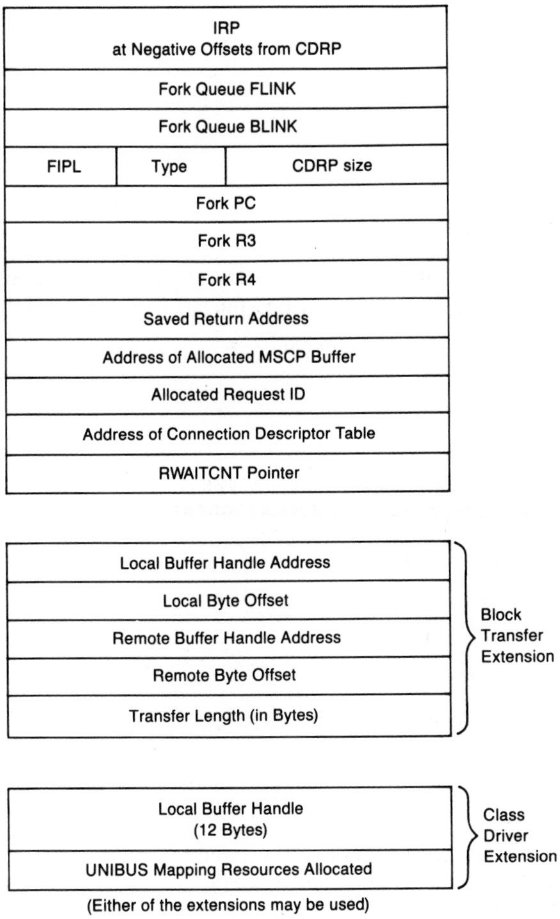

IRP at Negative Offsets from CDRP

Fork Queue FLINK

Fork Queue BLINK

FIPL	Type	CDRP size

Fork PC

Fork R3

Fork R4

Saved Return Address

Address of Allocated MSCP Buffer

Allocated Request ID

Address of Connection Descriptor Table

RWAITCNT Pointer

Local Buffer Handle Address
Local Byte Offset
Remote Buffer Handle Address
Remote Byte Offset
Transfer Length (in Bytes)

Block Transfer Extension

Local Buffer Handle (12 Bytes)
UNIBUS Mapping Resources Allocated

Class Driver Extension

(Either of the extensions may be used)

Figure 19-2
Portions of a Class Driver Request Packet

The class and port driver images are separate, loadable images. Therefore, changes can be made to the driver modules, and those modules can then be assembled and linked independently of the executive. The following steps are taken in assembling and linking the terminal driver.

- First the library for the terminal driver is created:

```
$ LIBRARY/CREATE/MACRO SYS$SYSTEM:TTYLIB SYS$SYSTEM:TTYUCBDEF.MAR
```

- Next, the modules in the terminal driver are assembled:

```
$ MACRO/LIST=SYS$SYSTEM:'module'/OBJECT=SYS$SYSTEM:'module'+-
SYS$SYSTEM:'module'+-
SYS$LIBRARY:LIB/LIBRARY
```

- This is done for each of the following modules:

```
$! TTYCHARI
$! TTYCHARO
$! TTYDRVDAT
$! TTYFDT
$! TTYSTRSTP
$! TTYSUB
$! DZDRIVER
$! YCDRIVER
```

- Finally, the object modules are linked into the terminal class driver (TTDRIVER) and the terminal port drivers (DZDRIVER and YCDRIVER).

```
$! In the link phase the file OPTIONS.OPT contains the single
line:
$! line:
$! BASE = 0
$!
$! Link the terminal class driver (TTDRIVER).
$ LINK/SHARE=SYS$SYSTEM:TTDRIVER/CONTIGUOUS-
    /MAP=SYS$SYSTEM:TTDRIVER/FULL/CROSS -
    SYS$SYSTEM:TTYDRVDAT,-
    TTYFDT,-
    TTYSTRSTP,-
    TTYCHARI,-
    TTYCHARO,-
    TTYSUB,-
    SYS$SYSTEM:SYS.STB/SELECTIVE_SEARCH,-
    SYS$SYSTEM:OPTIONS/OPTIONS
$!
$! Link port drivers. Done for DZDRIVER and YCDRIVER.
$!
$ LINK/SHARE=SYS$SYSTEM:'driver'/CONTIGUOUS-
    /MAP=SYS$SYSTEM:'driver'/FULL/CROSS-
    SYS$SYSTEM:'driver',-
    SYS$SYSTEM:SYS.STB/SELECTIVE_SEARCH,-
    SYS$SYSTEM:OPTIONS/OPTIONS
```

When the system is bootstrapped, the module SYSBOOT reads the terminal class driver (TTDRIVER.EXE) image into nonpaged pool. INIT later creates the necessary linkages between the class and port drivers by first linking the console port driver with the terminal class driver. The device-specific extension of a terminal UCB contains cells intended to contain pointers to the class and port vector dispatch tables. INIT locates the address of the dispatch tables for the terminal class driver and console port driver and loads these addresses into the console UCB. Later in system initialization, the SYSGEN command AUTOCONFIGURE determines the terminal controllers used by the system and loads the appropriate driver (DZDRIVER for DZ-11 and DZ-32 controllers, YCDRIVER for DMF-32 asynchronous lines). The controller and unit initialization routines of these port drivers initialize the UCB extensions.

The relationships among the terminal class driver, console port driver, and the console UCB are shown in Figure 19-4.

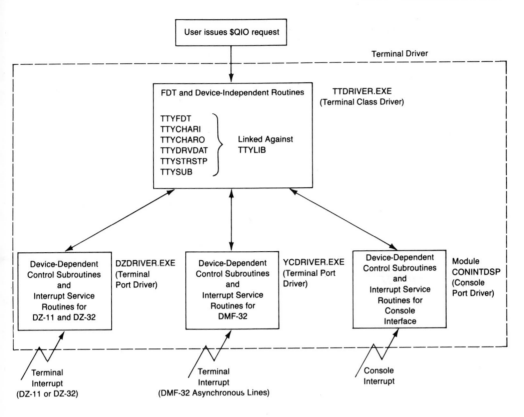

Figure 19-3
Terminal I/O System

The fact that the terminal driver class driver is loaded by SYSBOOT has implications for anyone who writes a new terminal class driver. It is a good idea to maintain a good copy of TTDRIVER in SYS$SYSTEM with a different name. In the event that the modified terminal driver contains errors that prevent the system from completing its initialization sequence, the SYS-BOOT parameter TTY_CLASSNAME can be set during a conversational bootstrap to contain the name of the good TTDRIVER.

Normally, the only module that will need to be altered (or replaced) is the terminal port driver, in order to provide the device-dependent processing for a specific device (such as a DL11).

To test a new terminal class driver on a system that has already autoconfigured the terminal devices, the system must be rebooted. A reboot is also necessary to use a new terminal port driver (for example, on autoconfigured DZ11s), because the SYSGEN command RELOAD will not reload terminal class or port drivers.

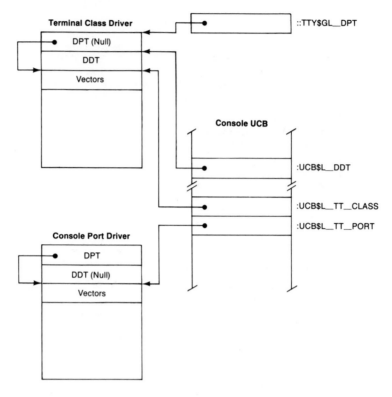

Figure 19-4
Terminal Driver Initialization

19.4.1 Full Duplex Operation

The terminal driver implements full duplex operation (unless specifically asked to operate in half duplex mode for a particular terminal) by utilizing an alternate start I/O entry point (specified as the ALTSTART parameter to the DDTAB macro). Whenever a write request is issued to a full duplex terminal, the write FDT routine (TTY$FDTWRITE in TTYFDT) allocates and initial- izes a write buffer packet to describe the write request, and calls routine EXE$ALTQUEPKT (in SYSQIOREQ) to enter the alternate start I/O routine of the driver. In the half duplex case, routine EXE$QIODRVPKT, also in SYSQIOREQ, is called.

Normally, FDT routines call on EXE$QIODRVPKT to invoke the start I/O routine of the driver, if the unit is not busy, or to queue the IRP to the UCB if the unit is busy. EXE$ALTQUEPKT differs from EXE$QIODRVPKT in the following respects:

1. No check is made to see if the UCB is busy (UCB$V_BSY set in UCB$W_STS). Therefore, EXE$ALTQUEPKT never queues the request to

the UCB. It is desirable not to check the UCB busy bit because a read request may be in progress; if the IRP waited on the UCB queue until the read request finished (and the busy bit was cleared), full duplex operation would not be possible.

2. The cancel and timeout bits in the UCB (UCB$V_CANCEL and UCB$V_TIMOUT in UCB$W_STS) are unaffected (not cleared) because they may be in use by the current IRP, if the UCB is busy.

3. The SVAPTE, BCNT, and BOFF fields are not copied from the IRP to the UCB because this would affect the current I/O operation if the UCB is busy.

4. The alternate start I/O routine in the driver is entered (rather than the regular start I/O routine).

TTY$WRTSTARTIO (in TTYSTRSTP) is the alternate start I/O routine entry point. This entry point is also used by the broadcast system service, as described in Chapter 18. This routine raises IPL to device IPL to block device interrupts from the current I/O operation, in case the device is busy, and processes the packet as follows:

1. If a write is currently in progress, the write buffer packet is queued.

2. If a read is occurring, but the buffer header specifies write breakthrough, the write is started.

3. If a read is occurring, but no read data has echoed yet, the write is started.

4. Otherwise, the write buffer is queued.

In order to complete write I/O requests for full duplex operation, the driver exits by calling routine COM$POST (in COMDRVSUB) rather than issuing the REQCOM macro. COM$POST places the I/O request packet in the postprocessing queue, requests an IPL$_IOPOST software interrupt (see Chapter 6), and returns. Routine IOC$REQCOM is avoided so that the next IRP queued to the UCB (which must be a read request) is not initiated (because the current read request, if any, has not yet terminated). Also, the status of the UCB busy bit is unaltered by COM$POST. However, all read requests (and half duplex writes) are terminated by invoking the REQCOM macro, so that the next request of this type may be processed in the normal fashion.

In full duplex operation, the device can be expecting more than one interrupt at a time (one for a read request, and one for a write request). Therefore, two fork PCs must be stored. (Usually drivers only expect one interrupt at a time, and store the fork PC in UCB$L_FPC.) The terminal driver stores more than one fork PC by altering the value of R5 (which normally points to the UCB), to point to the write buffer packet or the IRP before forking (by invoking the FORK macro). A fork block is therefore formed in the write buffer packet or in the IRP (containing R3, R4, and the fork PC). The fork block in the UCB is not used for read or write requests, although it is used at other times, such as when allocating a type-ahead buffer or when handling unsolicited data.

The technique of altering R5 before forking can easily be extended by any driver to allow more than one outstanding interrupt for a particular device, provided the driver can distinguish which interrupt is associated with which fork block. Therefore, any number of outstanding I/O requests may be handled by a driver entered at the alternate start I/O entry point. Of course, the driver must maintain queues for outstanding I/O requests and synchronize I/O operations. The driver should operate almost exclusively at device IPL (as the terminal port drivers do), to block out device interrupts in order to achieve synchronization with multiple I/O request processing.

19.4.2 Channels and Terminal Controllers

VMS terminal controllers have no controller channel concept. Therefore, the terminal driver never requests or releases a controller channel (with the REQCHAN and RELCHAN macros). The locations normally used in the CRB as list heads for the controller channel wait queue (CRB$L_WQFL and CRB$L_WQBL) are instead used to contain modem control status information.

19.4.3 Type-Ahead Buffer

A type-ahead buffer is allocated from nonpaged pool for each terminal. The size of the type-ahead buffer is determined by the SYSBOOT parameter TTY_TYPAHDSZ. Every character typed is placed into the buffer, even if a read request is active. If the buffer is within 8 characters (or the value of the SYSBOOT parameter TTY_ALTALARM) of being full and the terminal is in host-sync mode, the driver sends an XOFF character to the terminal to tell it to stop sending data. An XON character is not sent to the terminal to tell it to start sending data until the buffer is emptied. Using this technique prevents characters from being lost in block I/O transmissions from high-speed terminals.

19.5 PSEUDO DEVICE DRIVERS

The VMS operating system supports drivers for virtual devices (pseudo devices), including the null device (NL:), the network device (NET:), remote terminal devices (RT:), and mailboxes (MB:). Users can assign channels to these devices and issue I/O requests, just as though they were real devices. The following sections highlight some of the features of these pseudo device drivers.

428

19.5.1 Null Device Driver

The null device driver (in NLDRIVER) is assembled and linked with the system image (SYS.EXE). It is a very simple driver, consisting of two FDT routines (one to complete read requests, and one to complete write requests). The FDT routines in the null driver respond to read requests by returning an SS$_ENDOFFILE status code to the user, and they respond to write requests by returning an SS$_NORMAL status code. No data is transferred, nor are any privilege or quota checks made.

19.5.2 Network Device Driver

The network device (NET:) is best viewed as a mechanism for DECnet-VAX users to access network functions. When a process assigns a channel to NET, a network UCB is created and given a unique number, such as NET100. The channel number returned to the user points to the newly created UCB. This channel can then be used to perform access, control, and I/O operations on the network. When the user deassigns the last channel to the network UCB, the UCB is deleted.

The network device driver and the communication drivers support two I/O request interfaces: $QIOs and "internal" IRPs.

- When a user issues a $QIO, the executive and the driver's FDT routines cooperate to build an IRP. The driver then processes the IRP (normally by passing it to its own STARTIO routine).
- So-called internal IRPs are built by kernel mode modules (device drivers) and passed to another driver's alternate start I/O interface.

The remote terminal driver (RTTDRIVER) uses NETDRIVER's internal IRP interface in communication across the network.

NETDRIVER uses the internal IRP interface to pass I/O requests to communication device drivers.

There are actually two images that are used for network communication: the network device driver (NETDRIVER) and the network ACP (NETACP). NETDRIVER creates links to other CPUs, performs routing and switching functions, breaks user messages into manageable pieces on transmission, and reassembles the messages on reception. The actual I/O in network communication is performed by the communication device driver (for example, XMDRIVER performs network communication through DMC-11s).

NETACP performs the following tasks:

- Creates processes to accept inbound connects
- Parses network control blocks and supplies defaults when a user issues an IO$_ACCESS function code to create a logical link
- Transmits and receives routing messages to maintain a picture of the network
- Maintains the volatile network database

Figure 19-5 illustrates some network I/O functions. For more information on DECnet, see the *DECnet-VAX User's Guide* and the *DECnet-VAX System Manager's Guide*.

19.5.3 Remote Terminals

DECnet-VAX allows users to log in on a remote VAX/VMS processor and perform operations on that remote processor, just as they would at the local processor. The communication from the remote process to the controlling terminal is performed through a pseudo device on the remote processor called a remote terminal. The driver for remote terminals is RTTDRIVER.EXE. (Note that while DECnet-VAX can communicate with other DIGITAL operating systems running DECnet, the focus of this discussion is on DECnet communication between two VAX-11 processors running the VAX/VMS operating system.

In addition to DECnet, three images are required to support remote terminals: the local processor uses the image RTPAD.EXE; the remote processor uses the images REMACP.EXE and RTTDRIVER.EXE.

When a user on a local system issues the DCL command SET HOST, RTPAD uses DECnet-VAX to request a connection to a network object on the specified node. On remote processors running the VAX/VMS operating system, the object is REMACP. The image REMACP creates a UCB for the remote terminal and links the UCB into the driver tables by calling RTTDRIVER at its unsolicited input entry point. REMACP then returns information about the remote processor to RTPAD. RTPAD has routines for communicating with a number of different DIGITAL operating system (including RSTS, RSX-11M, TOPS-20, and VAX/VMS). The information returned from REMACP is used to determine which operating system is communicating with the local processor. In the VAX/VMS operating system, RTPAD sends unsolicited data to RTTDRIVER; sending this data to RTTDRIVER is equivalent to pressing the RETURN key on a terminal that is not logged in. RTTDRIVER creates a detached process running LOGINOUT. The user is now logged in to the remote system.

In communicating information across the network, RTTDRIVER receives $QIOs from the remote process, packs the information into a block, and uses the "internal" IRP interface to pass the request to NETDRIVER. RTPAD unpacks the information and reissues the $QIO for the local terminal. If the $QIO is a read, RTPAD packs the input information into a block and passes the packet(s) of information back to RTTDRIVER.

When the user logs off from the remote system, REMACP deletes the remote terminal UCB.

19.5.4 Mailbox Driver

Mailboxes are software-implemented devices that can be read and written to. Normally, mailboxes are used for communication between processes. Al-

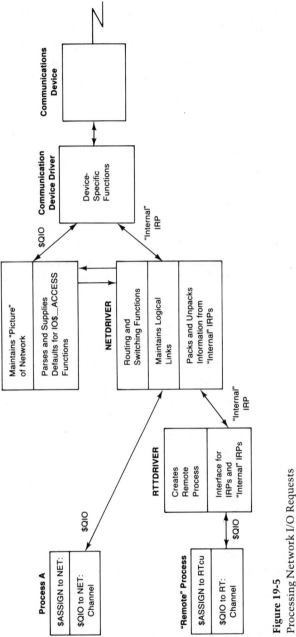

Figure 19-5
Processing Network I/O Requests

though mailboxes transfer information in much the same way that other I/O devices do, they are not actual devices. The following sections describe how the mailbox driver (in MBDRIVER, a module in the system image) buffers messages written to mailboxes and serializes mailbox read requests. Note that mailboxes in shared memory are supported by a separate, loadable driver, MBXDRIVER.

19.5.4.1   **Processing Set Mode Requests.** A process may request notification of a mailbox read or write request by issuing a $QIO request with an IO$_SETMODE function code (and an IO$_READATTN or IO$_WRTATTN function code modifier). See the *VAX/VMS I/O User's Guide* for details. The mailbox driver's FDT routines respond to these requests by taking the following steps:

1. Verifying that the process may access the mailbox.
2. Queuing the request to the appropriate list head (UCB$L_MB_W_AST for write requests, or UCB$L_MB_R_AST for read requests) by calling on routine COM$SETATTNAST in COMDRVSUB (which allocates, initializes, and queues an AST control block to the specified list head, as described in Chapter 7).
3. Raising IPL to IPL$_MAILBOX (IPL 11) and checking to see if the notification condition requested is present (current read or write request outstanding). If so, routine COM$DELATTNAST in COMDRVSUB is called to queue the attention AST to the requesting process (see Chapter 7). Otherwise, the attention AST request remains queued to the mailbox UCB, but the I/O request is completed by calling EXE$FINISHIOC. The attention AST will be queued to the process when a read or write request, as appropriate, is issued for the mailbox.

   Note that mailboxes use fork IPL$_MAILBOX (IPL 11, the highest fork IPL), to avoid possible synchronization problems with other drivers that reference mailboxes while at their respective fork IPLs (for example, to send a "device is off line" message to the operator's mailbox).

19.5.4.2   **Processing a Mailbox Read Request.** When a user issues a read mailbox $QIO, the mailbox driver FDT routines perform the following general functions:

1. The user request is validated to make sure the requesting process's UIC is given access to the mailbox, that the message size requested is allowed for the mailbox, and that the user has write access to the buffer specified (into which the mailbox message will be placed).
2. The address of the specified buffer, into which the mailbox message will be written, is saved in IRP$L_MEDIA.
3. The IRP$V_MBXIO bit in IRP$W_STS is set so that the I/O postprocessing routines will recognize a mailbox I/O request completion and announce the availability of the RSN$_MAILBOX resource.

4. If the IO$M_NOW function code modifier was not specified in the $QIO call, the request is queued to the driver's start I/O routine.

5. If the IO$M_NOW modifier was specified, IPL is raised to IPL$_MAILBOX (IPL 11), and, if any messages are available (UCB$W_MSGCNT is nonzero), the request is queued to the driver's start I/O routine. Otherwise, the SS$_ENDOFFILE message is returned to the user, and the I/O operation is completed.

The mailbox driver's start I/O routine performs the following steps:

1. It first tries to dequeue a message written to the mailbox (messages are queued to the UCB, with listhead at UCB$L_MB_MSGQ).

2. If no message is found, any pending read attention ASTs are queued to their process(es) (by passing the listhead address, UCB$L_MB_R_AST, to COM$DELATTNAST, as described in Chapter 7).

3. The mailbox UCB remains "busy" (the UCB$V_BSY bit is set in UCB$W_STS), although no further processing occurs until a write request is issued. Subsequent read requests will wait to enter the start I/O routine (although they will be preprocessed by FDT routines), because the busy bit is set. As soon as this read request terminates, the next read request will be processed by the start I/O routine.

4. If a message was found (or a write request occurs and a read request is outstanding, as discussed in step 3), then special action is taken.

   a. The address of the message block built by the write FDT routine (see Figure 19-6) is placed in IRP$L_SVAPTE in the read request's IRP so that the I/O postprocessing routines can locate the message and copy it into the user's buffer.

   b. The first two longwords in the message block are initialized to contain values expected by the I/O postprocessing routines. (The first longword points to the message data, stored in the message block, and the second longword points to the user buffer, where the data will be copied by the I/O completion special kernel mode AST.) The address of the user's buffer is retrieved from the IRP$L_MEDIA field in the read request's IRP.

   c. The outstanding message count (UCB$W_MSGCNT) for the mailbox is decremented.

   d. The process ID of the read request is placed in IRP$L_MEDIA+4 (so that it will become the high-order longword of the IOSB for the write request $QIO), and the SS$_NORMAL success code is placed in the low-order word of the IOSB (IRP$L_MEDIA).

   e. Routine COM$POST (in COMDRVSUB) is called to insert the write request's IRP on the I/O postprocessing queue. The driver calls this routine, rather than issuing the REQCOM macro, so that another IRP is

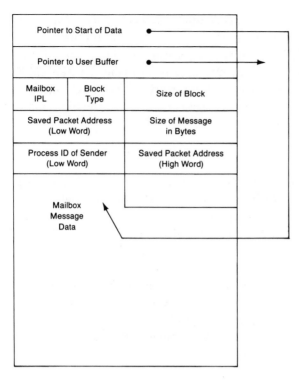

Figure 19-6
Layout of Mailbox Message Block

not dequeued (because only read request IRPs are queued to the UCB waiting to enter the start I/O routine). Also, the busy status of the unit is not changed (UCB$V_BSY in UCB$W_STS).

f. When COM$POST returns control, the process ID of the write request's IRP is placed in R1 (and will eventually become the high-order longword of the read request's IOSB), and the REQCOM macro is called to complete the read request. The next read request (if any) will automatically be dequeued and the start I/O sequence repeated. If no read request is outstanding, the busy bit will be cleared.

19.5.4.3 Processing a Mailbox Write Request. When a user issues a write mailbox $QIO, the mailbox driver FDT routines perform the following general functions.

1. The same validation checks that were made in steps 1 and 2 of the read $QIO FDT routines are performed here, except that the buffer containing the data to be written is checked for read access instead of write access.
2. A message block is allocated from nonpaged pool (by routine

EXE$ALONONPAGED), and initialized (as shown in Figure 19-6). The data to be written to the mailbox is copied into the message block. There are 22 bytes of overhead (not message data) in the message block.

3. IPL is raised to IPL$_MAILBOX, and the mailbox is examined to see if there is enough room for the message. If not, IPL is restored, the message block is deallocated, and the request is placed in a resource wait state (waiting for the RSN$_MAILBOX resource).

4. The message block is inserted at the tail of the queue of messages with list head UCB$L_MB_MSGQ (unless there is a read request outstanding, in which case control is transferred to step 4 in the start I/O routine, discussed in the previous section).

5. Any queued write attention ASTs are delivered (by passing the list head address, UCB$L_MB_W_AST, to COM$DELATTNAST, as described in Chapter 7).

6. IPL is lowered to what it was before step 3 was executed, and a check is made to see if the IO$M_NOW function code modifier was specified in the $QIO call.

7. If the IO$M_NOW function code modifier was specified, the write I/O request is completed (by calling EXE$FINISHIOC). Otherwise, the processing of the write I/O request is suspended (until a read request is issued), and control is passed to EXE$QIORETURN, so some other process in the system may resume execution.

19.6   CONSOLE INTERFACE

The console interface is the portion of the processor that initiates a bootstrap operation and permits microdiagnostics to execute. The console interface is not specified by the VAX architecture but is CPU specific. The *VAX Hardware Handbook* contains more details about the console interface for each CPU.

19.6.1   VAX-11/730 Console Interface

The console interface on the VAX-11/730 consists of a terminal, two TU58 cartridge devices, an optional remote diagnosis port, and a console microprocessor. The console program executes on the console microprocessor; when the console program has control (when the three-angle-bracket prompt appears on the console terminal), the VAX-11/730 cannot execute VAX-11 instructions.

There are eight processor internal registers on the VAX-11/730 for communicating with the three console devices. In addition, the VAX architecture specifies that the PR$_TXDB register is to be used for communication from code executing VAX-11 instructions to the console subsystem. The special uses of this register (some of which are not used by the VAX-11/730 and VAX-11/750) are listed in Table 19-2.

19.6.2   VAX-11/750 Console Interface

The console interface on the VAX-11/750 consists of a terminal, a TU58 cartridge device, an optional remote diagnosis port, and some microcode in the VAX-11/750 processor. When the console program has control (when the three-angle-bracket prompt appears on the console terminal), the VAX-11/750 processor is not executing user or system instructions but rather the console microcode.

There are eight processor internal registers on the VAX-11/750 for communicating with the the two console devices. As with the VAX-11/730, the PR$_TXDB register is also used for communication to the console program (see Table 19-2).

19.6.3   VAX-11/780 Console Interface

The VAX-11/780 console interface consists of an LSI-11 microcomputer, a floppy disk, the console terminal, and an optional remote diagnosis port (as described in the *VAX Hardware Handbook*). The console program executes on the LSI-11 (using the PDP-11 instruction set). Because the console program is executing on a separate processor, it is possible for the console subsystem to perform a limited set of functions without halting the VAX-11/780 CPU.

Table 19-2: Special Uses of the Console PR$¢TXDB Register

Register Contents	Meaning	Comments
F01	Software Done	This flag is used by the the VAX-11/780 Memory ROM program to notify console program that it has located 64K bytes of good memory.
F02	Reboot the CPU	This flag is used by the bugcheck routine to reboot the system after a fatal bugcheck.
F03	Clear Warm-Start Flag	This flag is maintained by the VAX-11/780 console program.
F04	Clear Cold-Start Flag	This flag is maintained by the console program on either processor to prevent nested bootstrap attempts.

The VAX-11/780 uses four processor internal registers to communicate to the two console devices. That is, unlike the VAX-11/730 and VAX-11/750, the same registers are used to communicate to two devices. The device ID is encoded into the control bits to allow the processor to distinguish between the two devices. All console data transfer operations are performed between the VAX-11/780 CPU and the LSI-11 CPU using these four internal processor registers. That is, no direct transfers are made between the VAX-11/780 CPU and the console terminal or floppy disk. As with the VAX-11/730 and VAX-11/750, the PR$_TXDB register is also used for communication to the console program (see Table 19-2).

19.6.4   Data Transfer between the VAX-11 CPU and Console Devices

The internal processor registers, PR$_TXCS and PR$_RXCS (and PR$_CSRS and PR$_CSTS on the VAX-11/730 and VAX-11/750), are used for control and status information (to enable interrupts and to indicate that a device is ready). The other two internal registers, PR$_RXDB and PR$_TXDB (and PR$_CSRD and PR$_CSTD on the VAX-11/730 and VAX-11/750), are used to transfer data. The TXxx (and CSTx) registers are used for transmit operations (with respect to the VAX-11 CPU), while the RXxx (and CSRx) registers are used for receive operations.

Most drivers treat device registers as if they were memory locations, using MOVB or MOVW instructions to read or write data in those registers. In the case of the console, the MTPR and MFPR instructions are used to transmit and receive data, respectively. For example, the following instructions on the VAX-11/780 transmit and receive data:

```
MTPR    data,#PR$_TXDB   ; Transmit data
MFPR    #PR$_RXDB,data   ; Receive data
```

The data is sent or received as a longword, with bits <7:0> containing the ASCII character, and bits <11:8> identifying which console device (terminal or floppy disk) is sending or receiving the data. On the VAX-11/730 and VAX-11/750, the distinction between devices is made by choice of register instead of by including a device code in a data buffer register. Note that all data is passed a character at a time, even to the floppy disk. Therefore, it is recommended that a separate files ACP be requested to service the console block storage device.

19.6.5   Console Interrupt Dispatching

As the previous discussion of processor registers indicates, the two console devices (terminal and block storage device) are treated slightly differently on the VAX-11/730 and VAX-11/750 and on the VAX-11/780. On the VAX-11/730 and VAX-11/750, the block storage device (a TU58 cartridge) has its own control registers and its own interrupt vectors. On the VAX-11/780, the two devices are handled more as a single entity, with common routines distinguishing terminal operations from floppy disk operations. This difference is also reflected in the different forms of interrupt dispatching on the two processors.

19.6.5.1 **Console Terminal Interrupts.** When the system is bootstrapped, the system control block (SCB) is initialized (from the SCB template in SCBVECTOR) so that the two vectors at offsets F8 and FC (hex) point to console interrupt service routines (CON$INTDISI for console input and CON$INTDISO for console output). Both routines respond to an interrupt by saving registers R0 through R5, and transferring control to routines in CONINTDSP (CON$INTINP for console input, CON$INTOUT for console output).

CON$INTINP reads the data and console device identification from the PR$_RXDB register and determines whether the interrupt was from the console terminal or block storage device. If the interrupt was from the console terminal, then the character read operation is handled by the terminal driver's character buffering routine whose address is stored in the console terminal UCB. The character is also echoed back to the console terminal by being placed in the PR$_TXDB register.

Routine CON$INTOUT transmits data to the console terminal through the PR$_TXDB register and determines whether the resulting interrupt is from the terminal or the console block storage device. If the interrupt was caused by the terminal, then the terminal output routine (whose address is stored in the console terminal UCB) is called to get the next character for output.

Note that the handling of console terminal I/O is done by the normal terminal driver routines. Only the initial fielding of interrupts and the device registers that are read or written distinguish console terminal I/O from operations through the regular terminal interface. Note also that the console terminal always interrupts at IPL 20 (the lowest device IPL used by drivers) on all three VAX processors.

19.6.5.2 **Console Block Storage Device I/O.** The device driver and associated database for the console block storage device are not loaded until an explicit CONNECT CONSOLE command is issued to SYSGEN. At that time, the device driver and data structures appropriate to the specific processor are loaded into memory and initialized.

A CONNECT CONSOLE command that is issued to SYSGEN on a VAX-11/730 or VAX-11/750 causes the TU58 driver (called DDDRIVER) to be loaded and data structures for a device called CSA1 to be built (on the VAX-11/730 a second set of structures for CSA2 is also created). In addition, two dedicated vectors in the SCB (at offsets F0 and F4 hex) are loaded to point to interrupt dispatch code contained in the CRB for CSA1.

The DDDRIVER thus responds to console TU58 interrupts in exactly the same way that it responds to interrupts generated by a TU58 on the UNIBUS. The only difference between the two interrupts is that console TU58 interrupts occur at IPL 23 while UNIBUS TU58 interrupts occur at IPL 20.

A CONNECT CONSOLE command that is issued to SYSGEN on a VAX-11/780 causes the console floppy disk driver (called DXDRIVER) to be loaded and data structures for a device called CSA1 to be built. Because the console floppy interrupts through the same vectors used by the console terminal, no further SCB modification is required at this time.

When a console device interrupt occurs, the interrupt service routine determines whether the interrupt was from the console terminal or from the block storage device. If the interrupt was from the block storage device, if the console has been connected (a UCB exists for device CSA1), and if the interrupt was expected (the UCB$V_INT bit is set in the status word in the UCB), then the driver context is restored from the UCB and the driver process is resumed at the saved PC (UCB$L_FPC). Otherwise, the interrupt is considered spurious and simply dismissed.

19.6.5.3 **Double Mapping of Buffer Pages.** One interesting feature of the TU58 driver and the floppy disk driver, drivers that transfer data one character at a time, is that they use the routines IOC$FILSPT, IOC$MOVFRUSER, and IOC$MOVTOUSER (in BUFFERCTL) to double map a page in the user's data buffer into system address space (so that data can be transferred directly to and from the user's buffer). User buffer pages are not normally accessible because device drivers execute in system context and do not have process address space available to them. By double mapping a buffer page into a system address range, the entire user buffer can be accessed by the device driver one page at a time. The system page table entry used to map the page is reserved in the driver by setting the DPT$V_SVP bit in the FLAGS argument to the DPTAB macro.

By making the user buffer accessible through system virtual addresses, these two drivers can use VMS direct I/O even though they are not DMA devices. This direct I/O allows them to issue virtual I/O requests, call existing ACP FDT routines, and use the virtual I/O completion routines in the I/O postprocessing code.

PART VI/Process Creation and Deletion

20 Process Creation

All things in the world come from being. And being comes from nonbeing.

—The Way of Lao Tzu

The creation of a new process requires the cooperation of several pieces of the executive:

- Creation begins in the context of an existing process that executes a Create Process system service call. The Create Process system service performs the following steps:

  a. It makes privilege and quota checks.
  b. It loads the PCB, possibly the JIB if creating a detached process, and the process quota block with explicit SYS$CREPRC arguments and implicit parameters taken from the context of the creator.
  c. It places the new process into the scheduler's data base.

- The initial scheduling state of the new process is COMO (computable but outswapped). Thus, execution of the shell process is suppressed until the swapper process moves the new process into the balance set. The following steps are performed in the context of the swapper process:

  a. The swapper inswaps the template process context from SHELL, a portion of the executive image SYS.EXE.
  b. The process header is built according to the values of SYSBOOT parameters for this configuration.

- The final steps of process initialization take place in the context of the new process in a routine called PROCSTRT. PROCSTRT performs the following steps:

  a. The arguments from the PQB are moved to their proper places in the process header and P1 space.
  b. The image activator is called to activate the image.
  c. The image is called at its entry point.

20.1 CREATE PROCESS SYSTEM SERVICE

The Create Process system service establishes the parameters of the new process. Some of these parameters are passed to the service by the caller. Others are taken from the context of the caller: the caller's process control

443

block (PCB), process header (PHD), job information block (JIB), and control region are all used (see Figure 20-1). The parameters that belong in the PCB or the JIB of the new process can be placed there by the Create Process system service. The parameters that belong in either the process header or the control region of the new process must be stored in a temporary structure until the new process comes into existence and has a virtual address space and process header that can be accessed. The process quota block (PQB) serves the purpose of this temporary data structure. Its contents are listed in Table 20-1.

20.1.1 Control Flow of Create Process

The Create Process system service allocates a PCB, a JIB (in creation of a detached process only), and a PQB. The service fills these three structures with the implicit and explicit parameters passed to it. The following list details the operation of the Create Process system service:

1. If the caller specified the UIC argument, the new process will be a detached process. The creating process must have DETACH privilege in

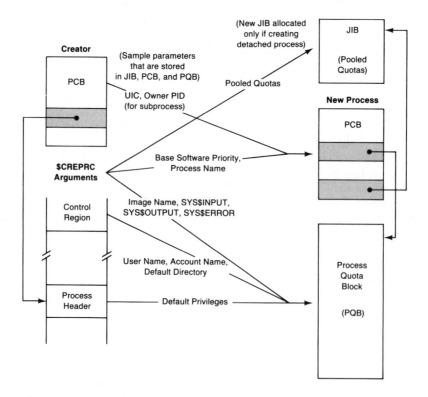

Figure 20-1
Sample Movement of Parameters in Process Creation

Table 20-1: Contents of the Process Quota Block

Item	Size (Bytes)
Privilege Mask	8
Size of PQB	2
Type Code	1
Status Flags	1
Image Name	64
Equivalence Name for SYS$ERROR	64
Equivalence Name for SYS$INPUT	64
Equivalence Name for SYS$OUTPUT	64
Equivalence Name for SYS$DISK	64
AST Limit	4
Buffered I/O Limit	4
Buffered I/O Byte Limit (Not Used [1])	4
CPU Time Limit	4
Direct I/O Limit	4
Open File Limit (Not Used [1])	4
Paging File Quota (Not Used [1])	4
Subprocess Limit (Not Used [1])	4
Timer Queue Entry Limit (Not Used [1])	4
Working Set Quota	4
Working Set Default	4
Process Lock Limit	4
Working Set Extent	4
Swap Space Allocation	4
User Name for Subprocess	12
Account Name for Subprocess	8
Default Directory String	84
Default File Protection	2
Default Message Flags	1

[1] The quotas and limits marked "Not Used" are now pooled in the JIB; hence, the PQB is no longer used to transfer these values.

order for the service to succeed. The DETACH privilege is also required when creating processes with the BATCH or NETWRK flags.

2. The PCB and PQB for the new process are allocated from nonpaged pool.
3. If a detached process is being created, a JIB must be allocated from nonpaged pool. The JIB pointer (PCB$L_JIB) in the new PCB points to the newly allocated JIB. The information fields (all but the 12 bytes of header) are cleared.

If a subprocess is being created, PCB$L_JIB points to the JIB of the creator (which is actually the JIB of the master process of the job). The relationship between the JIB and the PCBs of several processes in the same job is shown in Figure 20-2. The process count field in the JIB

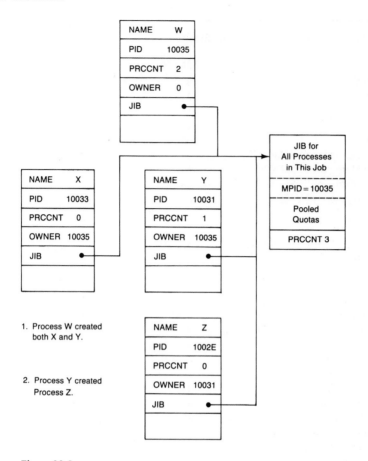

Figure 20-2
Relationship between the JIB and PCBs of Several
Processes in the Same Job

(JIB$W_PRCCNT) is incremented and a check is made to insure that the
count is still less than or equal to JIB$W_PRCLIM.

Note that the PRCCNT fields within each PCB (PCB$W_PRCCNT)
count the number of subprocesses created by that process. JIB$W_
PRCCNT counts the total number of subprocesses in the job.

4. Several fields in the PCB are initialized to nonzero values.

   a. The AST queue is set up as empty.
   b. ASTs are enabled for all access modes.
   c. The lock queue header is set up as empty.
   d. The pointer to the access rights block (ARB) is initialized to point to
      the PCB$Q_PRIV field of the PCB.

      The access rights block (ARB) is currently located within the PCB
      (see Figure B-24). However, routines such as ACPs and device drivers

446

that wish to check a process's access rights use the ARB pointer to locate the privilege mask and UIC. If, in the future, the ARB becomes an independent structure, the programs that use the ARB pointer will continue to work without modification.

e. The unit number of a termination mailbox is filled in. A unit number of zero will indicate to the process deletion routine that no termination message is to be sent back to the creator.

f. The process page count is initialized to the count of pages in the SHELL process.

5. The process name is loaded into the PCB.

6. The process privileges of the new process are determined and loaded into the PQB. If no privilege argument is present, the current privileges of the creator are used. (Table 21-1 summarizes the various privilege masks associated with a process.)

 If a privilege argument is present and the creator has SETPRV privilege, then the privilege argument is used with no modification.

 If a privilege argument is present and the creator does not have SETPRV privilege, then the privileges passed to the new process are the logical AND of the privileges of the creator and the privileges specified in the argument to Create Process. In short, a created process cannot receive privileges that its creator does not have.

7. The software priority of the new process is determined and loaded into the PCB in the base priority field, the initial priority field, and the current priority field. (Because this argument is passed by value, it is always present, with a default value determined by the treatment of missing arguments by the language processor.) If the creator has ALTPRI privilege, the priority specified in the argument list is used.

 If the creator does not have ALTPRI privilege, the smaller of his base priority and the priority in the argument list will be used.

8. The UIC of the new process is determined and loaded into the PCB. If a UIC argument is present, the new process is a detached process, and the argument is the UIC for that detached process.

 If a UIC argument is not present, then the new process is a subprocess. The UIC of the creator is used. In addition, the PID of the creator is put into the PCB$L_OWNER field of the PCB of the new process. The absence of the UIC argument will indicate to the process deletion routine that this is a subprocess for which special action must be taken.

9. A check is made to insure that the process name is unique within the group. This check is made by examining the process name fields of all PCBs in the system with the same group number. When calling the process control system services, a process can only refer to another process by name if the target process is in the same group (see the *VAX/VMS System Services Reference Manual*).

Table 20-2: Flags in the Status Longword in the PCB (PCB$L_STS) That Can Be Set at Process Creation

Flag in PCB$L_STS	Bit Number	Meaning (If Set)	Privilege Required
PCB$V_SSRWAIT	0	Disable System Service Resource Wait Mode	None
PCB$V_SSFEXCU	1	Enable System Service Exceptions for User Access Mode	None
PCB$V_PSWAPM	2	Inhibit Process Swapping	PSWAPM
PCB$V_NOACNT	3	Suppress Accounting	NOACNT
PCB$V_BATCH	4	Batch (Noninteractive) Process	DETACH
PCB$V_HIBER	5	Hibernate Process before Calling Image	None
PCB$V_LOGIN	6	Log In without Reading the Authorization File	DETACH
PCB$V_NETWRK	7	Process Is a Network Connect Object	DETACH
PCB$V_DISAWS	8	Disable System Initiated Working Set Adjustment	None

10. Several text strings are loaded into the PQB. The image name and the equivalence names for SYS$INPUT, SYS$OUTPUT, and SYS$ERROR are taken from the argument list to Create Process. The equivalence name for SYS$DISK is obtained from the Translate Logical Name system service. The user name, account name, and default directory string are obtained from the control region of the creator.

11. The default file protection and message flags are loaded into the PQB from the control region of the creator.

12. The status flags for the new process are extracted from the Create Process argument list and set in the PCB$L_STS field in the new PCB. Some of these flags require privileges (see Table 20-2). The privilege mask that is checked is that of the new process.

13. The quotas are determined for the new process and loaded into the PQB. Section 20.1.2 describes the several steps taken to determine the quota list for the new process.

14. The address of the PQB is stored in the PCB in the PCB$L_PQB field (see Figure 20-1). PCB$L_PQB uses the same longword as the event flag wait mask field, PCB$L_EFWM. This field is available because the process cannot yet be waiting for any event flags.

15. IPL is raised to IPL$_SYNCH (IPL 7) to prevent multiple accesses to the scheduler's database. Swap space is allocated for the process. Its address is stored in the PCB; the size of the swap space is stored in the PQB. The PCB vector (pictured in Figure 20-3 and described in Section 20.1.3) is searched for an empty slot.

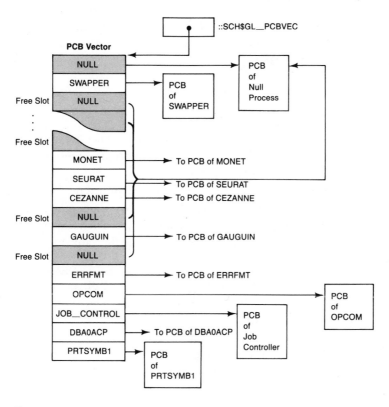

Figure 20-3
Sample PCB Vector

16. If the maximum process count has been exceeded (contents of SCH$GW_PROCCNT are larger than SCH$GW_PROCLIM), or if no swap space can be allocated, the process creation is aborted. Otherwise, a process ID is fabricated (see Section 20.1.4) and put into the PCB of the new process.

17. If a detached process is being created, its PID is loaded into the master PID field of the JIB (JIB$L_MPID).

18. The scheduler is called to make this process executable (and outswapped). A boost of 6 will be given to the base priority. It is this boosted priority that will determine when the new process is swapped in from SHELL.

19. If a subprocess is being created, the count of subprocesses owned by the creator (stored in field PCB$W_PRCCNT) is incremented. In addition, if the creator has a nonzero CPU time limit (there is a CPU time limit in effect), the amount of CPU time passed to the new process is deducted from the creator.

449

20. Finally, the PID of the new process is returned to the creator (if requested), IPL is restored to allow system event reporting, and control is passed back to the caller.

20.1.2 Establishing Quotas for the New Process

Two tables in the executive are used by the Create Process system service when quotas are set up for the new process: a minimum quota table and a default quota table. Each quota or limit in the system has an entry in both tables. The contents of the minimum table are determined by the SYSBOOT parameters whose names are of the form PQL_Mquota-name; the contents of the default table are of the form PQL_Dquota-name. The following list describes the steps that are taken in order to determine the value for each quota or limit that is passed to the new process.

1. The default values for each quota are put into the PQB as initial values.
2. Each quota that is included in the argument list to Create Process replaces the default value in the list.
3. Each quota is forced to at least its minimum value.
4. A check is made to insure that the creator possesses sufficient quota to cover the quotas that it is giving to the new process. This check is performed in the following way:

   a. If a detached process is being created, then no check is performed. Pooled quotas are placed directly into the newly allocated JIB.
   b. If a subprocess is being created and the quota is neither pooled nor deductible (the only deductible quota that is currently implemented is the CPU time quota), then the subprocess quota must be smaller than or equal to the creator's quota.
   c. Pooled quotas require no special action when a subprocess is being created because they already reside in the JIB, a structure that is shared by all processes in the job (see Figure 20-2).
   d. If a subprocess is being created and the quota in question is the CPU time limit quota, what happens depends on how much quota the creator process possesses. If the creator has infinite CPU time limit, then no check is performed. If the creator has a finite CPU time limit and specifies an infinite CPU time limit for the subprocess, half of the creator's CPU time limit is passed to the subprocess. If the creator has a finite CPU time limit and specifies a finite CPU time limit for the subprocess, the amount passed to the subprocess must be less than the creator's original quota, or the creation is aborted.

Table 20-3 lists the quotas that are passed to a new process when it is created, whether each quota is deductible or pooled, and where the limit is

Table 20-3: Storage Areas for Process Quotas

	Quota/Limit Name	Location of Active Count	Location of Process Limit	Count/Limit Stored by (1)
Nondeductible Quotas	AST Limit	PCB$W_ASTCNT	PHD$W_ASTLM	C/P
	Buffered I/O Limit	PCB$W_BIOCNT	PCB$W_BIOLM	C/C
	Direct I/O Limit	PCB$W_DIOCNT	PCB$W_DIOLM	C/C
	Working Set Quota	(2)	PHD$W_WSQUOTA	/P
	Working Set Default	(2)	PHD$W_DFWSCNT	/P
	Working Set Extent	(2)	PHD$W_WSEXTENT	/P
Deductible Quotas	CPU Time Limit	PHD$L_CPUTIM	PHD$L_CPULIM	(3)/P
	Buffered I/O Byte Limit	JIB$L_BYTCNT	JIB$L_BYTLM	(4)
	Open File Limit	JIB$W_FILCNT	JIB$W_FILLM	(4)
Pooled Quotas (Shared by all processes in the same job)	Page File Page Limit	JIB$L_PGFLCNT	JIB$L_PGFLQUOTA	(4)
	Subprocess Limit	JIB$W_PRCCNT	JIB$W_PRCLIM	(4)
	Timer Queue Entry Limit	JIB$W_TQCNT	JIB$W_TQLM	(4)
	Enqueue Limit	JIB$W_ENQCNT	JIB$W_ENQLM	(4)

With the exception of CPU time limit and subprocess count, all active counts start at their process limit values and decrement to zero. An active count of zero indicates no quota remaining. An active count equal to the corresponding process limit indicates no outstanding requests.

(1) The slash (/) separates the count from the limit.
   C/ indicates that the count value is stored by the Create Process system service.
   /C indicates that the limit value is stored by the Create Process system service.
   /P indicates that the limit value is stored by PROCSTRT.

(2) Working Set List quotas are handled differently from other quotas (see Chapter 15).

(3) CPU Time starts at zero and increments for each clock tick that the process is current. If limit checking is in effect (CPULIM nonzero), then CPUTIM may not exceed CPULIM.

(4) The contents of the JIB are loaded by Create Process when a detached process is created. Subprocess creation uses an existing JIB.

451

stored in the context of the new process. Further discussion of quotas can be found in the *VAX/VMS System Management and Operations Guide* and in the *VAX/VMS System Services Reference Manual*.

5. The quotas and working values that belong in the PCB are moved to the PCB (see Table 20-3).

20.1.3   The PCB Vector

When the system is initialized, an array of MAXPROCESSCNT longwords is allocated from nonpaged dynamic memory. This array will be used to locate the PCB of each process in the system at any given time. The first two entries in the table point to the PCBs of the null process and the swapper process. All other entries in the table initially point to the PCB of the null process. An entry that points to the PCB of the null process but has nonzero index is considered an empty slot. (The entry that locates the PCB of the null process that has an index of zero is the "real" pointer.) The scan for an empty slot begins at the bottom of the table so that those system processes that are created as a part of system initialization will have their PCB pointers located near the bottom of the table. An example of the contents of this table is shown in Figure 20-3.

20.1.4   Fabrication of Process IDs

The low-order word of the process ID contains the index into the PCB vector that locates the PCB of the identified process. The high-order word is taken from an array of words that is allocated from nonpaged pool at system initialization time. This array of words (termed sequence numbers) is initially set to zero and is used as a consistency check to determine that a number alleged to be a process ID corresponds to a real process in the system.

When an empty slot in the PCB vector is located, the corresponding entry in the sequence vector (see Figure 20-4) is incremented and used as the high-order 16 bits of the process ID. Sequence numbers cycle to 0 after reaching 32767; thus, process IDs, when they are interpreted as signed integers, are always positive.

Negative process IDs are used in a special form of I/O completion. The I/O postprocessing interrupt service routine interprets a negative PID in the IRP$L_PID field of an I/O request packet as the (system virtual) address of an internal I/O completion routine.

When a process is referenced by its process ID, the validity of the PID can be checked by using the low 16 bits as an index into the sequence vector and comparing the value found there with the high-order 16 bits of the PID. With this scheme, a second check must also be made. The entry in the PCB vector must be compared to the address of the null process. If the addresses are

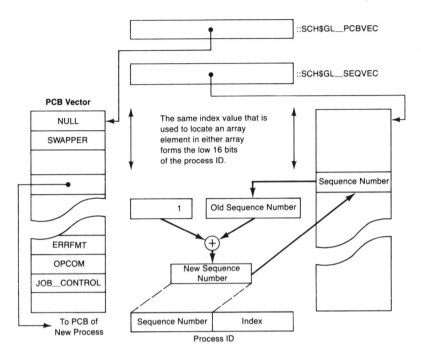

Figure 20-4
Fabrication of Process IDs

equal, the process has been deleted but no new process has been assigned to the empty slot.

The two checks described in the previous paragraph are actually performed in one step (in routine EXE$NAMPID) by using the low-order word of the PID as an index into the PCB vector. The PCB indexed by the PID contains its PID at offset PCB$L_PID. The PID in the PCB is compared to the PID that is being checked. If the process specified has been deleted (the PCB vector now points to the PCB of the null process) but the slot has not yet been reused (the sequence number is not yet incremented), the sequence number array element will match the high-order word in the process ID, but the full 32-bit PIDs will not match.

For example, suppose a process has been deleted, but its PCB vector slot has not yet been reused. Then the contents of the sequence array element match the high-order word of the process ID. But the indexed PCB pointer locates the PCB of the null process, which has a process ID of 00010000 and does not match the value of the PID in question. If, on the other hand, the slot has been reused, then the low-order word of the process ID indexes a process, but the high-order word in the PCB (or the contents of the sequence array element) is one larger than the sequence number field in the original process ID. Again, no match occurs.

20.2   THE SHELL PROCESS

A process comes into existence in the scheduling state COMO, computable but outswapped. However, the swap image of a newly created process does not reside in the swap file. Instead, a special swap image exists in the paged portion of the executive image file SYS$SYSTEM:SYS.EXE (see Figures 20-5 and 14-22). Table 26-2 shows the relative location of SHELL within the paged executive. This image contains a minimal process header and P1 space. The actual contents of the swap image found in SHELL are listed in Table 20-4.

20.2.1   Moving SHELL Into Process Context

The selection of a newly created process for inswap and the actual inswap operation are performed by the swapper. As a performance enhancement, the inswap from SHELL is not performed by a call to the I/O system (as the pages of normal processes are inswapped); rather, SHELL is moved into physical memory (and into the new process's P1 space) by a MOVC instruction. Because the SHELL resides in the paged portion of the executive, this optimization is especially effective in systems on which many processes are constantly being created.

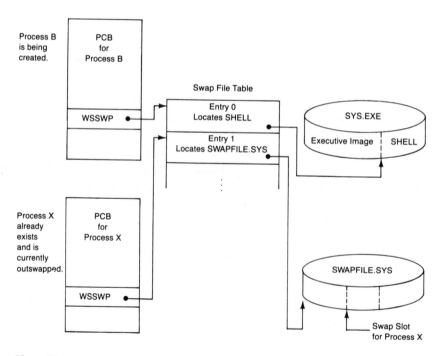

Figure 20-5
Location of Shell Process in the Executive Image File

Table 20-4: Contents of the Initial Swap Image in the Shell Process

Item	Size	Permanently Locked in Working Set?	Page Number in SHELL	Is Page Read from SHELL by SWAPPER Process?
Process Header (Fixed + WSL + PST)	Note 1	Yes	1	Yes, 1 Page only
P1 Page Table Pages	2	Yes	2,3	Yes, 2 Pages
P1 Pointer Page	1	Yes	4	Yes, 1 Page
Process I/O Segment	1	No	5	Yes, 1 Page
Process Allocation Region	1	No	6	Yes, 1 Page
Kernel Stack	3	Yes	7,8	Yes, First 2 Pages
Rest of Process Header	Note 1	Yes	—	No
Page Table Page Arrays	Note 2	Yes	—	No
TOTALS	Note 3	Note 4	8	

(1) The size of the top of the process header depends on the values of several SYSBOOT parameters. See Chapter 26 for details on how the size of the process header is calculated by SYSBOOT.

(2) There are eight bytes per process header page in these arrays. See Chapter 26 for details.

(3) There are six P1 pages, two P1 page table pages, and a variable number of process header pages (notes 1 and 2) that contribute to SHELL.

(4) The number of permanently locked pages is the result in Note 3 minus the two nonpermanent pages.

20.2.2   Configuration of the Process Header

When the executive image SYS.EXE was linked, the shell process was constructed to look exactly like an outswapped process. However, a process header cannot be entirely configured without taking into account several SYSBOOT parameters.

To accomplish the final configuration of the process header, the swapper makes one check (after the process has been read in, but before the working set is rebuilt) to determine whether this is a new process created from SHELL. If it is, a special subroutine is called to configure the process header before the final operations of inswap are completed.

This routine (SWP$SHELINIT), a subroutine of the swapper, does not execute very often, only as part of the creation of a new process. To avoid using up space in the resident executive, the routine is put into some of the pages that are read in from SHELL. Recall from Chapter 17 that the swapper's pseudo page table (as far as the I/O system is concerned) is also its P0 page table (as far as address translation routines are concerned). This special subroutine executes in P0 addresses in the context of the swapper process. When the new process page tables are set up, the physical pages that contain this code will become the kernel stack.

The routine SWP$SHELINIT performs the following actions:

1. Pages that are a part of SHELL (and also permanently locked into the working set), but are not read in from the copy of SHELL in the executive image, are filled with zeros. These pages are all but the first page of the beginning of the process header, one page of the kernel stack, and the page table page arrays (see Table 20-5). None of the information that will be put into these pages was assembled into the executive image. Their contents are determined dynamically and are loaded by PROCSTRT.

2. The system page table entries that map the fixed portion of the process header, the working set list, and the process section table are temporarily mapped so that this routine may access them. The initial contents of each SPTE are simply the contents of the swapper's I/O page table (Figure 14-24).

3. The system page table entries that map the empty pages of the process header (used for working set list expansion, see Chapter 14) are left as no access pages. The system page table entries that map the page table page arrays in the process header (see Chapters 14 and 17) are also temporarily mapped so that this routine may access them.

4. The translation buffer is invalidated.

5. The balance slot index is stored in the process header. This number is supplied to SHELL by the swapper, which records the number of the slot that has just been filled.

6. The SYSBOOT parameters that determine the default page fault cluster size and the default page table page fault cluster size are stored in the process header.

7. The page file with the most free space is selected as the page file for the new process. The page file number is recorded in the PHD at offset PHD$B_PAGFIL.

8. The index to the beginning of the working set list (PHD$W_WSLIST) and the pointer to the end of the process section table (PHD$L_PSTBASOFF) are calculated and stored.

9. The pointers to the four arrays in the page table page array portion of the process header (see Figure 14-8) are calculated and stored. The page table page arrays (that count valid and locked pages in each page of page table entries) are initialized to -1, indicating no valid or locked pages. The next to last page table page in P1 space has its entries corrected to reflect four locked pages and six valid pages. The four locked pages are the P1 pointer page and three pages of kernel stack. The two pages that are valid but not locked are one page of process allocation region and one page of process I/O segment.

10. The four counters in the fixed portion of the header that count page table pages with locked pages, valid pages, active page table pages, and those

PTEs with nonzero entries (see Figure 14-8) are initialized to the number of active P1 page table pages. There are two such pages for Version 3.0 of the VAX/VMS operating system.

11. Three working set list pointers (WSLOCK, WSDYN, WSNEXT) are adjusted from their initial values assembled into SHELL to reflect the additional pages from the top of the process header that are a permanent part of the working set. The working set list entries for the two pages that are valid but not locked (step 8) are slid down to make room for the WSLEs for the process header pages.

12. The pages that comprise the top of the process header (fixed portion, working set list, process section table, and page table page arrays) are added to the process working set list. In addition, the PFN arrays for the physical pages that are mapped are updated to indicate that these pages are page table pages (TYPE array), active (STATE array), and in the process working set (WSLX array).

13. The system page table entries that map the process page table entries are initialized to demand zero pages. The two P1 page table pages that are a permanent part of the working set are added to the working set list. The PFN arrays for the physical pages to which the P1 page table pages are mapped are updated as in step 11. Finally, the system page table entries that map these P1 page table pages are set up so that these pages are accessible.

14. The offsets from the beginning of the process header to the beginning of the P0 page table and the end of the P1 page table are calculated, reflecting the size of the beginning of the process header (see Chapters 14 and 26). The address of the first free virtual address in P1 space (stored in the process header at offset PHD$L_FREP1VA) and the contents of the copy of the P1 length register (stored in the hardware PCB in the process header) are also adjusted to reflect the size of the process header, which is mapped into P1 space.

15. The swapper I/O page table (see Figure 14-24) is adjusted to reflect the current state of the working set list. The address of the P1 window to the top of the process header is calculated and stored in location CTL$GL_PHD. (Although the swapper is the current process, it is able to access the P1 address of the newly created process because its pages are mapped as swapper P0 addresses in the swapper I/O page table.) When control is passed back to the swapper, the completion of the inswap operation will reflect the correct state of the working set list and the location of the P1 window to the process header.

16. The process header is marked resident (in field PCB$V_PHDRES in PCB$L_STS).

17. The WSQUOTA, WSAUTH, WSEXTENT, and WSAUTHEXTENT pointers are initialized to the value of the SYSBOOT parameter WSMAX. The

WSFLUID counter is initialized to the value of the SYSBOOT parameter MINWSCNT. The end of the working set list (WSLAST) and the default count (DFWSCNT) initially reflect the value of the SYSBOOT parameter PQL_DWSDEFAULT.

18. The P0 and P1 base registers are adjusted to reflect the virtual address of the process header. The calculations in step 14 adjusted the values of these two registers relative to the beginning of the process header. After this current step, the copies of these two registers contain the virtual addresses of the the beginning of the P0 and P1 page tables, exactly what is required for address translation.

19. The P1 PTEs that map the system service vectors are remapped with the SPTEs that map the system service vectors in system space. By doing this, system service vectors can be modified on a per-process basis, simply by modifying the process PTEs that map the system service vectors for the process.

20. Finally, the size of the initial swap space allocation is copied from the process quota block (at offset PQB$L_SWAPSIZE) to the process header (at offset PHD$L_SWAPSIZE).

SWP$SHELINIT returns control to the swapper's main inswap routine where the final steps of the inswap operation are completed. The operation of the swapper process is described in Chapter 17.

20.3 PROCESS CREATION IN THE CONTEXT OF THE NEW PROCESS

The final steps of process creation take place in the context of the newly created process. SHELL contains an initial hardware context for the process. In particular, the saved PC in the hardware PCB is the address of a routine called EXE$PROCSTRT. The saved PSL indicates kernel mode at IPL 2. Thus, the first code that executes in the context of a newly created process is the same for every process in the system.

20.3.1 Operation of PROCSTRT

By the time that PROCSTRT executes, the PCB and the process header have been properly configured. In addition, all information passed from the creator to the PCB has already been put there. PROCSTRT must take the information that is temporarily located in the process quota block and put it into its proper place in the process header and in P1 space (see Figure 20-6). PROCSTRT then prepares for execution the image whose name was passed by the creator and calls that image.

The steps that are performed by PROCSTRT are listed here. PROCSTRT

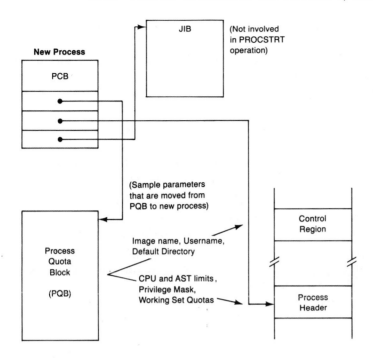

Figure 20-6
Removal of Process Parameters
from the Process Quota Block

begins execution in kernel mode at IPL 2 to prevent process deletion until the
PQB has been deallocated.

1. The address of the RMS dispatcher, and the address of the base of the
   control region (the address of the P1 map to the process header, which is
   the part of P1 space that is at the lowest virtual address) are put into the
   P1 pointer page.
2. The P1 space vectors for user-written system services and per-process or
   image-specific messages are initialized to point to RSB instructions. (The
   use of these vectors in dispatching to user-written system services is
   discussed in Chapter 9.)
3. The address of the process's PCB is stored in CTL$GL_PCB. The account
   name, user name, and default directory string are taken from the PQB and
   put into their proper places in P1 space.
4. Those quotas that are stored in the process header (currently only CPU
   time limit and AST limit) are moved from the PQB to their proper places
   in the process header (see Table 20-4).
5. The working set list pointers are initialized to reflect the quotas passed

from the creator (after minimization with the system-wide working set maximum).

6. The process's base priority is saved in the process header at offset PHD$B_AUTHPRI. Saving the base priority allows processes without ALPTRI privilege to lower their base priority and later raise it as high as their original base priority.

7. The process privilege mask is loaded into the first quadword of the process header (the working privilege mask), the permanent privilege mask (at location CTL$GQ_PROCPRIV in the P1 pointer page), and the authorized privilege mask (in field PHD$Q_AUTHPRIV). The use of each of these privilege masks is described in Chapter 21.

8. The default file protection and message flags are copied into P1 space.

9. At this point, the entire PQB is copied to the stack and the PQB deallocated to nonpaged pool. This step is taken to give back dynamic memory as quickly as possible, particularly before the time-consuming process of logical name creation.

10. The login time is saved.

11. The process logical name hash table is allocated from the process allocation region and is initialized.

    Once the PQB has been deallocated and the logical name hash table has been allocated, IPL can be lowered to zero, allowing the process to be deleted. By keeping IPL at 2 until the PQB has been given up, the need for special case code in Delete Process is avoided. There is no need to check in Delete Process whether the process being deleted is only partially created and still owns a process quota block from nonpaged pool.

    Another more philosophical interpretation is that at this point in the creation of a process, there exists something that is capable of being deleted, a full-fledged process.

12. Logical names are created for SYS$INPUT, SYS$OUTPUT, SYS$ERROR, TT, and SYS$DISK. The image name is moved to the image header buffer for subsequent use by the image activator.

13. The I/O channel table is created in P1 space (see Figure 1-7). The number of channels is determined by the special SYSBOOT parameter CHANNELCNT.

14. Access mode is changed to executive by fabricating a PSL on the stack and executing an REI instruction. The execution of an REI instruction is the only way to get to an outer (less privileged) access mode.

15. The shareable image list for the Address Relocation Fixup system service is initialized to point to a dummy element. (The Address Relocation Fixup system service is described in Chapter 21.) The PQB copy is removed from the stack.

    At this point, PROCSTRT has moved all the information from the creator to the context of the new process, and is now ready to activate the image that will execute in the context of the new process. The following steps accomplish the image activation.

16. The image activator is called to set up the page tables and perform the other steps necessary to activate the image. Image activation is described in Chapter 21.

17. An executive mode termination handler is declared that will call RMS$RUNDWN for each open file. This handler will be invoked when SYS$EXIT is called from executive access mode, which will usually happen when the process is deleted.

18. Access mode is changed to user by fabricating a PSL on the stack and executing an REI instruction.

19. The frame pointer (FP) is cleared, guaranteeing that the search of the stack for a condition handler by the exception dispatcher will terminate (see Chapter 4).

20. An initial call frame is set up on the stack by executing a CALLG instruction that refers to the next line of code.

```
        CALLG   (AP),B^15$

15$:    .WORD   0           ;Entry    Mask
        next instruction
```

The address of a catch-all condition handler is established in this frame and also in the last chance exception vector for user mode. The purpose and action of this handler are discussed in the next section. The Address Relocation Fixup system service ($IMGFIX) is called to perform fixups on the image.

21. An argument list that is nearly identical to the one used by one of the command language interpreters (see Chapter 23) is built on the stack. This argument list allows an image to execute with no concern over whether it was activated from PROCSTRT or from a CLI. The address of a dummy CLI call back routine is put into this argument list and also in location CTL$AL_CLICALBK. If an image that was activated from PROCSTRT attempts to communicate with a CLI (which does not exist), an error of CLI$_INVREQTYP will be returned.

22. Finally, the image is called at its initial transfer address. If the image terminates with a RET instruction (instead of calling the Exit system service, $EXIT, directly), PROCSTRT calls $EXIT itself. In general, there is no difference between an image terminating with a RET instruction or with a call to $EXIT.

    If the process was initially created with the hibernate flag, it is placed into hibernation before the image is called. When control is passed back to PROCSTRT following image termination, the hibernate flag is again checked. If no error occurred and the hibernate flag is set, the process is put back into the hibernate state.

In this instance, there is a difference between RET and SYS$EXIT. If a process is to be put into hibernation for future awakenings, it must use the RET instruction to return back to PROCSTRT rather than terminate with a call to SYS$EXIT.

20.3.2 Catch-All Condition Handler

This condition handler is established in the outermost call frame by PROCSTRT and by the command language interpreters before an image is called. Any condition that is resignaled (not properly handled) by other handlers (or unfielded because no other handlers have been established) will eventually be passed to this handler. The handler will issue a message using the SYS$PUTMSG service and, depending on the severity level of the condition, force image exit.

The catch-all condition handler performs the following actions:

1. If the condition is SS$_SSFAIL, then system service failure exception mode is disabled to avoid an infinite looping situation.

2. If the exception was generated by a call to LIB$SIGNAL (that is, the exception did not pass through the module EXCEPTION in the executive), then the argument list is adjusted to contain only those arguments passed to LIB$SIGNAL and not the PC and PSL fabricated into the signal array by that procedure (see Chapter 4).

3. Unless system services are inhibited for this process, SYS$PUTMSG is called to write an error message to SYS$OUTPUT (and to SYS$ERROR if different from SYS$OUTPUT). The service SYS$PUTMSG is described in the *VAX/VMS System Services Reference Manual* and in the *VAX-11 Run-Time Library Reference Manual*. The internal operation of the Put Message system service is discussed in Chapter 30 of this book.

4. If this handler was called through the last chance vector (indicated by a depth of -3), or if the error level is severe or greater (and if system services are not inhibited for this process), an exception summary is written to SYS$OUTPUT by the routine EXE$EXCMSG. This routine is described in Chapter 30.

In all other cases, the image is allowed to continue (by returning a status of SS$_CONTINUE to the exception dispatcher).

21 Image Activation and Termination

I would have you imagine, then, that there exists in the mind of
man a block of wax . . . and that we remember and know what is
imprinted as long as the image lasts; but when the image is
effaced, or cannot be taken, then we forget or do not know.

—Plato, *Dialogs, Theaetetus* 191.

Before an image can execute, the VMS operating system must take several
steps to prepare the image for execution. Process page tables and other data
structures must be set up to locate the correct image file on disk. Address
references between shareable images must be resolved. In addition, if the
debugger or traceback handler is expected to run when the image executes,
the correct hooks must be present to allow either or both of these images to
be invoked.

At image exit, termination handlers declared by the user or by the VMS
operating system must be called. If the image is executing in a batch or interactive environment, all traces of the image must be eliminated so that the
next image can begin execution with no side effects from the execution of the
previous image.

21.1 IMAGE INITIATION

The VMS operating system contains no special code to read images into
memory for initial execution. Instead, the paging mechanism that brings in
pages from an image file on demand is used when an image initially executes
as well as later on. In order for this scheme to work, the process page tables
must be properly setup to reflect the state of all the pages in the image file.
This setup is performed by the image activator.

Before control can be transferred to the image, .ADDRESS and G^ references that point to locations within shareable images must be resolved.
These address relocation fixups are delayed to activation time rather than
done at link time so that the size of the shareable images can change without
having to be relinked. However, because these fixups modify pointers within
the images themselves, they must be performed in the access mode from
which the main image will run. In this chapter, the term main image refers to
a main, controlling image that has been invoked by a user; although the
debugger or traceback handler could be viewed as a controlling image, this
discussion will name those images specifically when dealing with them.

The actual transfer of control to the image also takes place through the VMS operating system so that hooks can be inserted to allow later inclusion of either a debugger or the traceback facility. This path through the VMS operating system, called the debug bootstrap, always executes unless explicitly excluded at link time with a /NOTRACEBACK qualifier to the LINK command.

21.1.1 Image Activation

The module that contains the image activator (SYSIMGACT) is one of the largest modules in the executive. Although the concept of image activation is very simple, there are several alternate paths through the image activator that take into account the many special cases of image activation. Some of these cases will be discussed explicitly. Others will only be mentioned in passing.

The following types of image activation will be discussed explicitly:

- Activation of a "simple" image, one that contains no global sections.
  This is an artificial separation from the next case, simply to illustrate the difference in calls to the image activator.
- Activation of an image that contains global sections.
  Because almost every high-level language processor includes library routines, this case includes every image except those written entirely in VAX-11 MACRO with no explicit sharing of global sections.
- Initial activation of known images.
  When the Install Utility makes privileged or shareable images known to the system, the image activator is called with a noactivate option, to prepare the image for later activation.
- Later activation of known images.
  The activation of images that have been installed is streamlined by the data structures that were created when the image was initially installed.
- Activation of compatibility mode images.
  When the image activator is asked to activate a compatibility mode image, it actually activates the RSX-11M AME and passes the compatibility mode image name to the AME for further processing.

There are several other options that the image activator must check for. These will only be mentioned in the specific parts of image activation where they cause special action to be taken. Some specific parts that will be discussed are the following:

- Image activation at system initialization time.
  During initialization of the system, two image files must be opened without the support of either RMS or the disk ACP. These images are

SYSINIT and the system disk ACP itself. The image activator calls the special code in the executive that performs the simpler ACP operations without actually using the ACP. These routines are briefly described along with the rest of system initialization in Chapters 24 and 25.

- Merged image activation.

  Merged image activation is the technique that the executive uses for mapping a debugger, the traceback handler, a message file, or a command language interpreter into an unused area of P0 or P1 space. Rather than using the virtual address descriptors found in the image header of the merged image, the image activator simply uses the next available portion of P0 or P1 space. The user stack and image I/O segment are not mapped for a merged image. The RMS initialization routines are not called either because an image is already executing and has RMS context that cannot be destroyed.

- P0-only images.

  The linker can produce images that map all temporary structures including the user stack and the I/O segment in P0 space. The image activator must recognize this type of an image so that the two structures usually located in the lowest address portion of P1 space are correctly mapped.

  P0-only images are used whenever it is necessary to extend the permanent part of the low address end of P1 space. For example, the SET MESSAGE command causes a P0-only image called SETP0.EXE to execute. This image maps the indicated message section into the low address end of P1 space and alters location CTL$GL_CTLBASVA to reflect the new boundary between the temporary and permanent parts of P1 space. This last step is critical if the message section is to remain mapped when later images terminate.

- Privileged shareable images.

  Privileged shareable sections are used to implement user-written system services, as well as system service procedures that are not part of the system image (for example, $MOUNT and $DISMOU).

- Message sections.

  Message sections are used to add per-process or image-specific entries to the message facility.

- Images that do not reside on a random access mass storage device.

  The image activator can activate images from sequential devices (magnetic tape) and images that are located on another node of a network. An address space large enough to contain the entire image is first created. The image is then copied into this address space, thus causing all image pages, including read-only pages, to be set up as writeable.

21.1.1.1   Implementation of the Image Activator. The image activator is implemented as a system service, although it is not meant to be called directly by users.

The reason for this form of implementation is that the image activator will be indirectly called by users, both through a CLI, when running an image with some command, and through the Install Utility, when the system manager or some other privileged user is installing privileged or shareable images.

Thus, the image activator has its own slot in the system service vector area and is implemented as a procedure. The following eight arguments can be passed to the image activator:

name   String descriptor of image that is being activated.

dflnam   String descriptor for default file name.

hdrbuf   Address of 512-byte buffer in which the image header and image file descriptor are returned. The first two longwords in the buffer are the addresses (within the buffer) of the image header and the image file descriptor respectively.

imgctl   Image activation control flags. These flags control the form that the activation will take. The options are the following:

Flag	*Meaning*
IAC$V_NOACT	If set, the image activator is not to activate the image. This flag is used by the Install Utility to complete the installation of known file entries.
IAC$V_WRITABLE	If set, the image is writeable.
IAC$V_SHAREABLE	If set, the specified image is a shareable image that is being activated as a piece of an executable image. This flag can only be used in a recursive call to the image activator.
IAC$V_PRIVILEGE	If set, the executable image has amplified privileges. If this flag is set, the shareable image being activated must be installed as a known file. The flag IAC$V_SHAREABLE must also be set.
IAC$V_MERGE	If set, the image activator is directed to merge one executable image into the address space of another. When this flag is set, the user stack, the image I/O segment, and the privilege amplification flag are to be ignored. This flag must be set if the image activator is called from user mode.

IAC$V_EXPRG   If set, the **inadr** argument does not
                      give an actual address range, but
                      merely indicates the address space
                      (P0 space or P1 space) into which the
                      image is to be mapped. This flag is
                      only used during a merged image ac-
                      tivation.

inadr   Address of a two-longword array containing the virtual address
            range into which the image is to be mapped. This argument is
            usually omitted, in which case the address ranges designated by
            the image section descriptors in the image header are used.

retadr   Address of a two-longword array to receive the starting and end-
            ing addresses into which the image was actually mapped.

ident   Address of a quadword containing the version number and
            matching criteria for a shareable image.

The last three arguments are similar to the input arguments for various other
memory management system services that are described in Chapter 16.

21.1.1.2   Overview of Image Activation. There are essentially two steps that the image
activator performs each time that it activates an image. First, it opens the
image file, which allows the system to perform all of its file protection
checks. Then the image header is read and the image that is described there is
mapped into the user's virtual address space. The most important contents of
the image header are a series of image section descriptors, one for each section in the image. Each of these structures describes a portion of the image's
virtual address space, and their contents will be used by the image activator
as input parameters to other memory management system services. The
overall structure of an image header is pictured in Figure 21-1. The general
form of an image section descriptor is pictured in Figure 21-2.

21.1.1.3   Activation of an Image with No Global Sections. Most of the common operations that are performed by the image activator will be described in the activation of an image that does not contain any global sections. This section can
be interpreted as the general flow through the image activator. Other forms of
activation are explicitly described in later sections but are also mentioned in
this section when appropriate.

1. The image activator scratch area in P1 space is initialized.
2. The image file is opened as a process-permanent file.
3. If the image is being activated from a sequential device (magnetic tape or
   across a network), then the address range is created and the entire image
   read from the sequential file into virtual address space. All future page
   faults will be resolved from the page file.

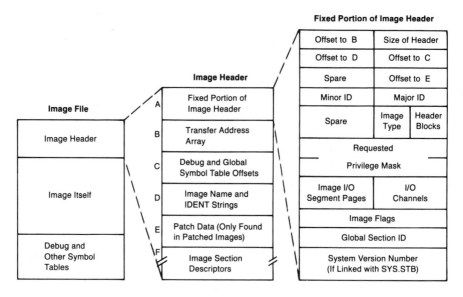

Figure 21-1
Contents of Image Header

4. The first block of the image header is read into memory. At this point, the check for a compatibility mode image is made. The contents of the last word of the first block of the image header indicate either an image produced by the VAX-11 Linker (−1) or an image produced by some other linker (0 or positive contents).

At present, only one type of compatibility mode image is supported. An image produced by the RSX-11M task builder has a zero in the code word and will cause the activation of SYS$SYSTEM:RSX.EXE. Further details about the activation of a compatibility mode image are found in Section 21.1.1.4.

5. At this point, the image activator begins its most important work, the setting up of the process page tables to reflect the address space produced by the linker. It performs this work by reading each image section descriptor contained in the image header (see Figure 21-2), determining the type of section that is being described, and calling the appropriate memory management system service to perform the actual mapping.

   a. The most common form of image section descriptor that occurs in a "simple" image describes a private section. This type of section may be either read only or read/write, depending on the attributes of the program sections that made up each such image section. Initial page faults for each page in this type of section will be satisfied from the appropriate blocks in the image file.

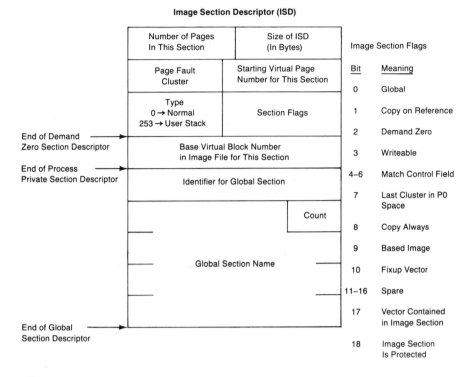

Image Section Descriptor (ISD)

Figure 21-2
General Form of an Image Section Descriptor

When the image activator encounters an image section descriptor that describes a private section, it uses the contents of the image section descriptor as input arguments to the Create and Map (Private) Section system service (see Figure 21-3), resulting in a series of page table entries that are process section table indexes. If the image has been installed as a shareable image by the Install Utility, the Map Global Section system service is called, rather than Create and Map Section. The number of PTEs is equal to the page count contained in the ISD. Notice that all of the PTEs index the same process section.

b. Another form of image section descriptor that may be found in an image is a demand zero section. The linker produces such a section whenever there are five—or some user-specified default number of—consecutive pages in the image file that contain all zeroes. The image file does not contain those pages, but merely an indication (in the ISD) that a certain range of virtual address space contains all zeroes.

When the image activator encounters such an image section descriptor, it uses the contents of the ISD as input arguments to the Create

469

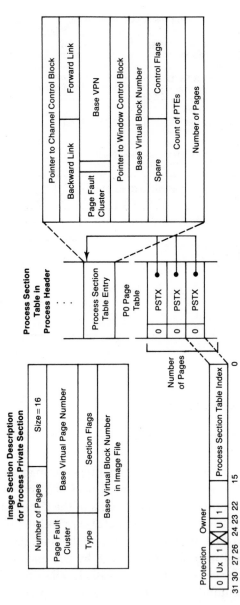

Figure 21-3
ISD and PTEs for Process Private Section

Virtual Address Space system service (see Figure 21-4), resulting in a series of page table entries that indicate demand zero pages. The number of PTEs is equal to the page count contained in the ISD. Note that one such section is the area in P1 space that contains the user stack. The linker differentiates this special demand zero section from others by a special code byte in the type designator in the ISD. The image activator puts off the mapping of the user stack until later in the activation.

c. The third form of image section descriptor that the image activator may find indicates that a range of virtual address space is to be mapped to an existing shareable image. When the image activator encounters such an image section descriptor, it calls itself recursively, requesting that the global image file containing the requested shareable image be activated as a part of the activation of a normal executable image. The details of this activation are described in the next section.

6. After the image activator has processed all the image section descriptors, it calls the Create Virtual Address Space system service to create the image I/O segment. The size of this area is determined by the special SYSBOOT parameter IMGIOCNT (default value of 32) but may be over-ridden with the following entry in the linker options file:

```
IOSEGMENT = n[,[NO]P0BUFS]
```

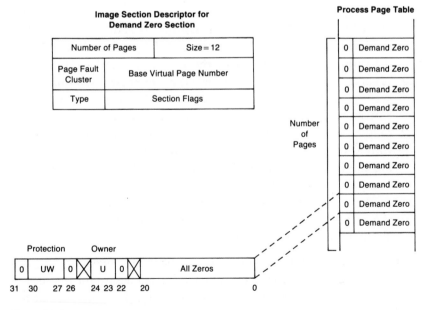

Figure 21-4
ISD and PTEs for Demand Zero Section

471

If a P0-only image is being activated, this area is located at the high address end of P0 space with the Expand Region system service.

7. Finally, the address space that is to contain the user stack is created (with an Expand Region system service). The usual location of the user stack is at the low address end of P1 space, where the automatic stack expansion facility of the exception dispatcher can add user stack space as needed. The location of the user stack in P0-only images is at the high address end of the P0 image.

 The default size of the user stack is 20 pages. This value can be overridden with the following line in the linker options file:

```
STACK = n
```

8. The initial value of the user stack pointer is stored in the P1 pointer page and loaded into the processor register PR$_USP. This value will be loaded into general register 14 (SP) when an REI instruction returns the process to user mode, which usually occurs following the return from the image activator.

9. The privileges that will be in effect while this image is executing are calculated. The logical AND of the privilege mask found in the image header (currently enabling all privileges and so effectively unused) with the process-permanent privilege mask (found at global location CTL$GQ_PROCPRIV in the P1 pointer page) is then ORed with the privilege enhancements for a privileged known image.

 The result is loaded into the process privilege mask in the PCB (PCB$Q_PRIV) and into two privilege masks in the process header, at offset PHD$Q_PRIVMSK (the mask that is actually checked by other routines in the system) and at offset PHD$Q_IMAGPRIV. The use of the various privilege masks by the system is described in Section 21.4.

10. A check is made to determine whether the image was linked with the system symbol table SYS$SYSTEM:SYS.STB. If so, a check is made to determine that the version of the symbol table agrees with the currently running system version. If the version numbers disagree, CMKRNL and CMEXEC privileges are turned off in the current privilege mask. Removing these privileges prevents many different spurious errors that can occur if the outdated, privileged image were to execute.

11. At this point, the image activator has finished its work. It loads a final status into R0 and returns to its caller (either PROCSTRT or a CLI) to allow the image itself to be called.

21.1.1.4 Activation of Shareable Images. As mentioned in the previous section, when the image activator encounters an image section descriptor that describes a shareable image, it calls itself recursively, although a different image file is indicated on the recursive call and different flags are set.

 Because the recursive call causes RMS to open the shareable image with the name stored in the image section descriptor, it is possible to use a logical name to cause a different image to be opened. In addition, the recursive call can prevent a nonprivileged user who has linked his image to a privileged shareable image from acquiring unauthorized privilege. Put simply, the VMS operating system does not trust the image section descriptors that it finds in the user's image file because the user can put almost anything he pleases there.

The image activator would like to read the original image section descriptor that is found in the shareable image file, presumably protected from write access by nonprivileged users. The simplest way to accomplish this is to have the image activator call itself, which will result in the shareable image file being opened, but with an implicit protection check being performed for the current user.

When the image activator processes the image section descriptors for each section in the shareable image, it maps each section into the user's address space with a Map Global Section system service (Figure 21-5) if the image has

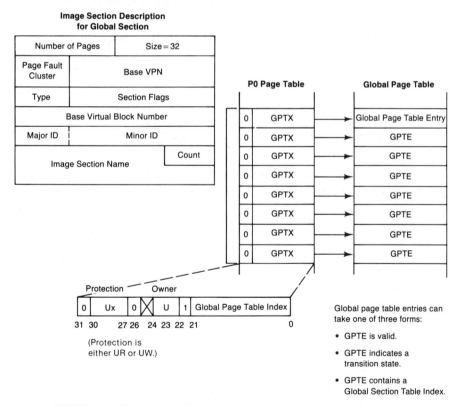

Figure 21-5
ISD and PTEs for Global Section

473

been installed as a shareable image (using the Install Utility). If the image has not been installed as a shareable image, the image activator will create a process private section with the Create and Map Section system service. Any version checking (to insure that the installed shareable image is compatible with the shareable image that was linked into the user's executable image) is performed by the Map Global Section system service and not directly by the image activator. If the Create and Map Section system service is called, version checking is not performed.

Note that any executable image that is installed shared is not really shared unless all users have read access to the image. If a user without read access attempts to activate the image, the image is activated and is usable; however, a process private section is mapped, rather than a global section. This is due to the restriction that only users who can read a file are allowed to map a global section to the file. Activation succeeds and the process private sections are mapped because the file is installed as a known file, and hence, file protection checks are bypassed by the image activator. However, the global section mapping checks are still in place.

One beneficial side effect of the recursive call to the image activator for shareable images is that they do not have to be installed. (In fact, read-only shareable images can be activated without their having been installed; writeable shareable images must be installed with the qualifiers /WRITE and /SHARE.) When the requested global section does not exist, the image activator performs a Create and Map (Private) Section system service. In the case of an installed shareable image, a Create Global Section system service (which does not map the section) was previously executed by the image activator as a part of the initial installation of a known shareable image.

21.1.1.5   **Initial Activation of a Known Image.** Known images exist for two main purposes in the VAX/VMS operating system:

- Images that require enhanced privileges but must execute in nonprivileged process context (such as MOUNT, SET, and SHOW) must have some method for acquiring their elevated privileges before the image executes and restoring process privileges when the image terminates.
- Shareable images (especially those that include privileged sections and those that exist in shared memory) must also be made known to the system.

The Install Utility is used to request the initial activation of known images. It calls the image activator with the NOACTIVATE flag set, telling the image activator to go through the motions of image activation but not to actually alter the address space of the process in which INSTALL is executing.

The crucial step that the image activator performs when it first activates a known image is the creation of a paged pool data structure called a known file entry in the known file entry list (see Figure 21-6). When this file is opened in the future, RMS will return the address of this structure to the image activator, indicating that a known image is being activated.

There is a third benefit to making images known to the system. Their activation may be facilitated by one of several options given when the image is installed:

- At the very least, the image activator saves the file ID and sequence number when it originally activates the image so that future open operations may be by file ID rather than by file name.
- The image file can be installed using the /OPEN qualifier, which will leave the file opened. In this case, the actual $OPEN call to RMS is essentially a null operation.

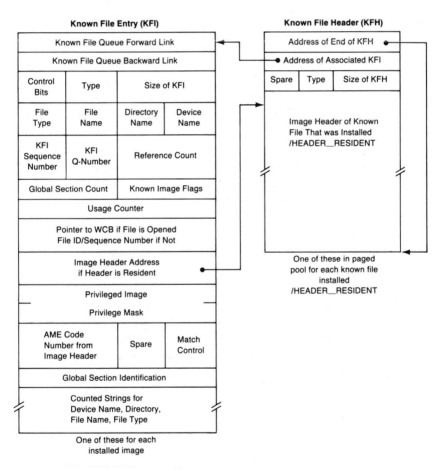

Figure 21-6
Format of a Known File Entry

- The image file can be installed using the /HEADER_RESIDENT qualifier, which directs the image activator to keep the entire image header resident in paged dynamic memory. Installing the image with the the header resident saves the additional read operations that are required to bring the header into memory each time that the image is activated.

21.1.1.6 **Later Activation of a Known Image.** When a known image is activated, the image activator is informed by RMS, which places the address of the known file entry in the CTX field of the FAB. Of course, the open operation may have been eased by one of the options mentioned in the previous section.

The activation of a known image proceeds in much the same way as a regular image, although some of the work that the image activator must perform in the regular case can be avoided here. In particular, a known image that has its header resident can be activated more quickly because the I/O overhead can be avoided.

In any case, the image section descriptors must still be processed and the page table entries set up so that the image can execute. In addition, the image activator must update the usage statistics for this known image (see Figure 21-6).

21.1.1.7 **Activation of Compatibility Mode Images.** When the image activator determines that it is attempting to activate a compatibility mode image, it does a change of course and activates an AME that is designated by the code word in the last word of the first block of the image header. At the present time, there is only one form of compatibility mode image and one AME supported. The RSX-11M AME (SYS$SYSTEM:RSX.EXE) will be activated whenever an image header contains a zero in the code word.

An AME is itself a native mode image that is responsible for mapping the compatibility mode image into the address range between 0 and 10000 (hex) (see Figure 1-8), passing control to that image while turning on the compatibility mode bit (with an REI instruction), and fielding all compatibility mode and other exceptions generated by the compatibility mode image.

From the point of view of image activation, once the image activator determines that it is activating a compatibility mode image, it continues with activation, but activation of the AME and not the compatibility mode image. The name of the compatibility mode image is stored in the compatibility mode page (at global location CTL$AG_CMEDATA) in P1 space where it is retrieved by the AME.

21.1.2 **The Address Relocation Fixup System Service**

The Address Relocation Fixup (EXE$IMGFIX) system service was implemented to postpone address assignment until image activation. By delaying address assignment, position independence can be maintained in images that are linked with shareable images, and within shareable images themselves.

There are two forms of addressing that are modified by EXE$IMGFIX: G^ references to addresses outside the main image, and .ADDRESS references to locations within nonbased images. Resolution of G^ references is deferred in order that the relative address will not be affected by a change in size of any of the intervening shareable images. The .ADDRESS directive references fixed addresses in virtual memory. Resolution of .ADDRESS locations in shareable images is deferred in order that the fixed address can be determined at run time, not link time. However, if the link options file specified a base address for an image, .ADDRESS references do not need to be deferred.

The *VAX-11 Linker Reference Manual* explains in more detail the motivation for the Address Relocation Fixup system service and the linker's action in preparing for image fixups.

When the Version 3.0 linker produces an image file, the last portion of the image contains a section called the fixup vector tables. These tables contain data that describe .ADDRESS references, data that describe G^ references, and a list of the shareable images referenced by the image. Figure 21-7 shows the layout of an image and its fixup vector tables.

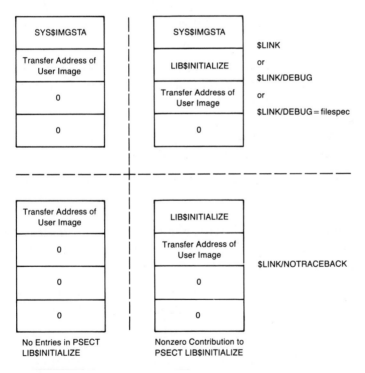

Figure 21-7
Image Layout with Fixup Vectors

21.1.2.1   **Shareable Image List.** There is one shareable image list element for each shareable image referenced by the image, plus one shareable image list element for the image itself. Each element in the shareable image list contains the base virtual address of the shareable image and the image name. The first shareable image list element (index 0) contains information used to resolve .ADDRESS locations.

21.1.2.2   **Resolution of G^ Locations.** When the image is linked, all G^ references are changed to @^L references (Longword Relative Deferred). The @^L address points to a location in the fixup vector tables reserved for G^ vectors. The G^ vector table contains a series of tables: one table for each shareable image linked with the main image. All references to a specific global label (within a specific shareable image) use the same G^ vector table entry. The linker loads the entries in the G^ vector tables with the location of the label, expressed as an offset from the base of its shareable image.

When resolving G^ references, each shareable image entry in the G^ vector table is located and the following action is performed:

- The index into the shareable image list is used to locate the appropriate shareable image list entry.
- Using this entry, the base virtual address of the shareable image is located.
- The base address is added to each offset contained in the G^ vector table and the resulting value is stored in the G^ vector table.

When the image is actually executed, the longword relative deferred address points to the cell within the G^ vector table. The cell in the G^ vector table will contain the correct virtual address of the reference.

21.1.2.3   **Resolution of .ADDRESS Locations.** When an image is linked, the following action takes place for each .ADDRESS directive:

- The offset of the specified location from the base of its image is determined. This offset is stored in the longword reserved by the .ADDRESS directive.
- The offset of the .ADDRESS directive from the base of its image is determined. This offset is stored in the .ADDRESS vector table portion of the fixup vector table.

Like G^ vector table entries, .ADDRESS vector table entries are separated into tables for each specific image. The .ADDRESS vector table also contains a table for entries in the image (if it is not a based image).

Figure 21-8 illustrates the resolution of .ADDRESS directives by the linker. The address of MTH$SQRT is within the shareable library VMSRTL. The .ADDRESS directive within MAIN.EXE contains the offset of the label MTH$SQRT from the base of VMSRTL.EXE. The entry in the .ADDRESS

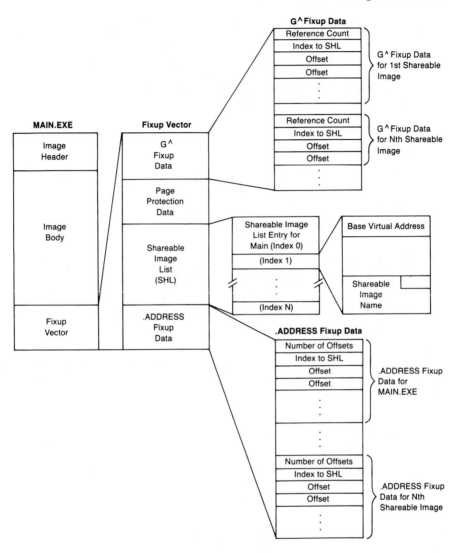

Figure 21-8
Resolution of the .ADDRESS Directive

vector table contains the offset of the .ADDRESS directive from the base of MAIN.

When EXE$IMGFIX resolves the .ADDRESS directives, it performs the following steps to obtain the actual address of the location:

- The offset to the .ADDRESS cell is added to the base address of the main image (using the previous example, the image MAIN). Separating the offset and base address in this fashion allows the main image to be a position-independent shareable image.

- The contents of the .ADDRESS cell (the offset to the label MTH$SQRT) are added to the base address of the shareable image (VMSRTL.EXE).
- The resulting address is loaded into the .ADDRESS cell.

This action is repeated for all .ADDRESS directives in all images in the image file, except in images that have a specified starting base address.

21.1.3   Image Startup

After the page tables have been set up by the image activator, the image is called at its transfer address. Depending on how the image was linked, the initial transfer of control may be to a debugger, to a user-supplied initialization procedure, or to the user image itself.

21.1.3.1   Transfer Vector Array.

In addition to the image section descriptors discussed in the previous section, the linker also includes a data structure called a transfer vector array in the image header. This array contains the user-supplied transfer address and also the means for including a debugger or a traceback handler in the user image.

The format of the transfer vector array is pictured in Figure 21-9. If a debug transfer address is specified or implied, it appears first in the list. An image-specific initialization procedure, if specified, occurs next. The last entry in

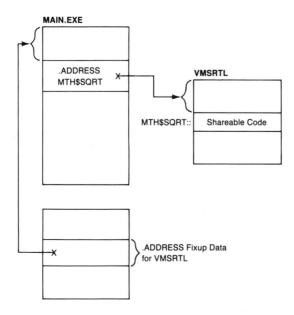

Figure 21-9
Transfer Vector Array

the list is the transfer address of the user image, either the argument of a
.END directive for a VAX-11 MACRO program or the first statement of the
main program written in a high-level language. A fourth slot containing a
zero is the end of list indication, no matter what options were passed to the
linker.

The initialization transfer address is described in the *VAX-11 Run-Time
Library Reference Manual* and will not be discussed here.

If the DCL command LINK/DEBUG=file-spec was used to link the file
(note the explicitly specified output file specification), the linker places the
transfer address found in the specified output file into the first element in the
transfer vector array. If the /NOTRACEBACK option is included (and not
overridden implicitly by including an explicit /DEBUG option), then there is
no debug transfer address. In all other cases (including the DCL command
LINK/DEBUG, which does not specify an output file), the linker places the
address of SYS$IMGSTA (found in the system service vector area) in the first
element of the transfer vector array.

21.1.3.2   **Image Startup System Service.** Unless explicitly suppressed (with the
/NOTRACEBACK qualifier), all images execute the Image Startup system
service, sometimes called the debugger bootstrap. This procedure examines
the various link and CLI flags and determines whether to start the user image
directly or map the debugger (specified by translating the logical name
LIB$DEBUG) into the user's P0 space and transfer control to it.

In any case, a condition handler is established in the current call frame that
will eventually gain control on signals that the user does not handle directly.
One option that this handler can exercise is to map the traceback facility that
will print a symbolic dump of the exception. The following steps are performed by the Image Startup system service:

1. The first step that Image Startup performs is a potential map of a debugger
   into P0 space. The mapping will be done under either one of two different
   conditions.

   - If the program was linked with the DCL command LINK/DEBUG and
     simply run (that is, not run with a RUN/NODEBUG command)
   - If the program was run with the DCL command RUN/DEBUG, inde-
     pendent of whether the debugger was requested at link time

     The debugger will not be mapped if the image is run with a RUN/
     NODEBUG command or if the /DEBUG option was omitted from both
     the LINK command and the RUN command.

2. Finally, a condition handler is established in the current call frame, the
   argument list is altered to point to the next address in the transfer vector
   array, and control is passed to the next transfer address. This will be either

the Run-Time Library procedure LIB$INITIALIZE or the transfer address of the user image.

21.1.3.3   Exception Handler for Traceback. The condition handler that was established before the image was called has two purposes:

- It invokes a debugger if a DEBUG command is typed after an image is interrupted with a CTRL/Y.
- It invokes the traceback handler to produce a symbolic stack dump if an unfielded condition occurs.

If a nonprivileged image is interrupted by typing CTRL/Y, and a DEBUG command is executed, the DCL (or MCR) command interpreter generates a signal of the form SS$_DEBUG. (Privileged images are simply run down in response to a CTRL/Y followed by the DCL command DEBUG.) Assuming that any handlers established by the image resignal the SS$_DEBUG exception, this handler will eventually gain control. Its response to a SS$_DEBUG signal is to map the debugger specified by the logical name LIB$DEBUG (if it is not already mapped) and transfer control to it. Notice that an image that was neither linked nor run with the debugger can still be debugged (albeit, without a debug symbol table) if the program reaches some undesirable state, such as an infinite loop.

The second purpose of the exception handler is to field any error conditions (where the severity level is WARNING, ERROR, or SEVERE) and pass them on to the traceback facility. In order to field the errors, the facility (denoted by the logical name LIB$TRACE) must be mapped into the user P0 space. Any conditions that have a severity level of either NORMAL or INFO are resignaled, which implies that they will be handled by the catch-all condition handler established by either PROCSTRT or the CLI that called the image.

21.2   IMAGE EXIT

When an image passes control back to the VMS operating system after it has completed its work, it calls SYS$EXIT either directly or by returning to its caller (either PROCSTRT or some command language interpreter), which executes the call to SYS$EXIT. The procedure SYS$EXIT simply calls whatever termination handlers have been declared by the process and then invokes $DELPRC. Usually, however, a CLI termination handler receives control and never returns to SYS$EXIT.

Termination handlers allow an image to perform image-specific cleanup operations before the image goes away. They also allow images to exert some control over whether and when they will terminate. The use of a supervisor mode termination handler by the VMS command language interpreters to prevent process deletion following image exit is discussed in Chapter 23.

21.2.1   Control Flow of the Exit System Service

The steps listed below show how the Exit system service, a procedure that executes in kernel mode, calls a succession of termination handlers for a given access mode and illustrates how termination handlers can be used to prevent image exit. The *VAX/VMS System Services Reference Manual* describes how termination handlers are declared and how the argument list will be passed to the handlers when they are called by the Exit system service.

1. The final status of the image (the single argument to the Exit system service) is stored in the P1 pointer page for possible insertion by the Delete Process system service into a termination mailbox. The force exit pending flag in the status longword (PCB$L_STS) in the PCB is cleared.
2. If SYS$EXIT was called from kernel mode, then the process is simply deleted. If SYS$EXIT was called from any other access mode, then the termination handler list (see Figure 21-10) is searched for handlers that have been declared, beginning with the access mode of the caller and proceeding toward inner (more privileged) access modes.
3. Once a nonzero list pointer is found, access mode is raised (privilege lowered) with an REI and the last termination handler that was declared is called. When (if) that handler returns to SYS$EXIT, the next handler in the list is called. This action continues until the list is exhausted.

   SYS$EXIT avoids an infinite loop by storing the list pointer in a register and clearing the list pointer itself. When this list pointer is next examined (step 4), the list will be empty.

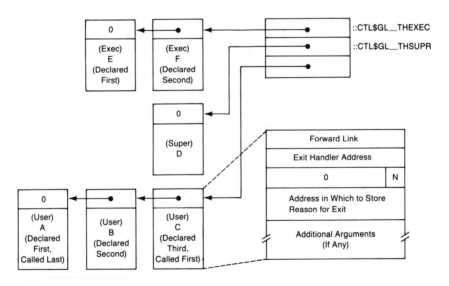

Figure 21-10
Sample Termination Handler Lists

4. Once all the termination handlers for a given access mode have been processed, SYS$EXIT must get back to a more privileged access mode. It accomplishes the access mode change by calling itself. If none of the exit handlers in the list just processed has done anything extraordinary (such as declaring another termination handler), then the logic described in step 3 will find the list empty and proceed to the next inner access mode in its search for more termination handlers.

21.2.2 Example of Termination Handler List Processing

To illustrate the processing of termination handlers, suppose that a process has its termination handler lists set up as shown in Figure 21-10. When the image calls SYS$EXIT from user mode, the following steps are taken:

1. The termination handler list is searched beginning with user mode. A nonzero listhead is found, pointing to the termination handler control block for procedure C, the last termination handler declared for user mode.
2. This address is stored in R0 and the listhead for user mode is cleared. Access mode is raised to user and procedure C is called. When C returns, procedure B and finally procedure A are called. When A returns, SYS$EXIT determines that the list for user mode is exhausted (because the forward pointer in the last termination handler contains a zero). SYS$EXIT is called again from user mode.
3. As in step 1, the search for termination handlers begins with user mode but this list is now empty. The search continues to supervisor mode where the single termination handler D has been declared. The supervisor listhead is cleared, access mode is raised to supervisor, and procedure D is called. When D returns, SYS$EXIT is again called, this time from supervisor mode.
4. Now the search for termination handlers begins with supervisor mode, whose list is empty. The list for executive mode contains two termination handlers, F and E, which will be called in turn from executive access mode. When they return, SYS$EXIT will again be called, this time from executive access mode. The search that now begins with the executive mode listhead will fail and the process will be deleted.

The logic illustrated here shows how a process can prevent image termination through the use of termination handlers. For example, if any of the handlers called in supervisor mode were to declare a termination handler (for supervisor mode), the search that is begun after SYS$EXIT is called from supervisor mode will locate the handler just declared, which when called, will declare another handler, and so on indefinitely. In fact, this use of termination handlers is just the mechanism used by DCL and MCR to allow multiple images to execute, one after another, in the same process. This mechanism is discussed in more detail in Chapter 23.

Note that a termination handler that is declared later (which implies that it will be called earlier) can prevent previously declared handlers for the same access mode from even being called by simply issuing a call to SYS$EXIT. In the example described above, procedure C could prevent termination handlers B and A from being called by calling SYS$EXIT itself.

21.3   IMAGE AND PROCESS RUNDOWN

In an interactive or batch environment that allows multiple images to execute one after another, several steps must be taken to prevent a later image from inheriting either enhancements (such as elevated privileges) or degradations (such as a reduced working set) from a previous image. In addition, when a process is deleted, all traces of it must be eliminated from the system tables and all reusable resources returned to the system.

The Rundown internal system service (SYS$RUNDWN) accomplishes much of the work for both of these purposes. It distinguishes between image rundown and process rundown by its single input parameter, access mode. (This flexibility requires that SYS$RUNDWN execute in kernel mode.) SYS$RUNDWN is called with an argument of user mode by both DCL and MCR (see Chapter 23) to clean up after an image that has just terminated and before the next image is activated. SYS$RUNDWN is also called from the Delete Process system service (see Chapter 22) with an argument of kernel mode to clean up after a process that is being deleted.

Much of the activity performed by Rundown is accomplished with system services. Rundown simply passes its input argument to these services to allow them to determine how much work to do. For example, the Delete Logical Name system service (see Chapter 29) can be called with an access mode argument and the implicit instruction to delete all logical names for this and outer access modes. If Rundown is called from user mode, the call to Delete Logical Name will only delete user mode (image-specific) logical names. If Rundown is called from kernel mode, then all process logical names will be deleted.

21.3.1   Control Flow of Rundown

The following steps detail the work performed by SYS$RUNDWN. The access mode argument is maximized with the access mode of the caller (by routine EXE$MAXACMODE). That is, the less privileged access mode is used. When used in the following list, the phrase "based on access mode" means "perform this operation for this access mode and all outer (less privileged) access modes." Those operations that are performed by system services have the name of the service included.

485

1. If a powerfail AST had been previously declared, it is eliminated.
2. Resource wait mode is enabled to make sure that the image rundown completes successfully.
3. The per-process and system wide user-written rundown routines are called.
4. If image accounting is enabled, an image deletion message is written to the accounting log file. The image count in the process header is incremented.
5. The four P1 space vectors for user-written system services and image-specific message sections (see Figure 9-5) are reset to contain RSB instructions.
6. All channels without open files are deassigned (SYS$DASSGN), based on access mode. The access mode check that is performed at the beginning of image rundown prevents process permanent files from being closed when an image is being run down (input argument is user mode). Other channels that will not be deassigned at this stage of image rundown include the image file and any other file that is mapped to a range of virtual addresses.
7. The image pages are reset (by calling MMG$IMGRESET). This routine performs all the image cleanup that is associated with memory management. The steps performed by this routine are listed here.

   a. All of P0 space is deleted. This will free the image file and any other file that is mapped. Physical pages will be released and blocks in the page file will be deallocated.
   b. The nonpermanent part of P1 space is deleted. The two parts of P1 space that are deleted by this operation are the user stack and the image I/O segment (see Figure 21-11). In addition, any expansions to

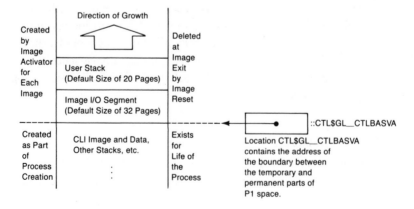

Figure 21-11
Low Address End of P1 Space
That Is Deleted at Image Exit

P1 space (at smaller virtual addresses than the user stack) that were performed by the user are also deleted.

   c. The working set is reset to its default value, undoing any expansion or contraction of the working set as a result of a call to SYS$ADJWSL (either explicitly or as a result of the automatic working set size adjustment). Working set size changes are described in Chapter 16.

   d. The process privilege masks in the first quadword of the process header and in the PCB are reset to their permanent value, found at location CTL$GQ_PROCPRIV. This step eliminates any privilege enhancements to the process due to the execution of an image that was installed with privilege.

   e. If any global sections were released as a result of releasing the process address space, the global sections are deleted.

   f. The pointer to the end of the active working set list (PHD$W_WSLAST) is reduced to point to the minimum size of the working set list.

   g. The process is allocated to a new, smaller swap space.

8. The same channel deassignment loop performed in step 6 is executed. However, because the image file and other mapped files have now been disassociated from virtual address space, the channels associated with those files will also be deassigned. As in step 6, this deassignment is based on access mode, implying that process-permanent files are unaffected by image rundown.

9. All devices are deallocated (SYS$DALLOC) for this and outer access modes.

10. All timer and wakeup requests are canceled (SYS$CANTIM and SYS$CANWAK) for this and outer access modes.

11. All remaining locks are dequeued (SYS$DEQ) for this and outer access modes.

12. Common event flag clusters 2 and 3 are disassociated, independent of access mode.

13. The next several steps must execute at IPL$_SYNCH (IPL 7) because system-wide data structures are being manipulated.

14. If this process has declared an error log mailbox, it is eliminated. The method for declaring an error log mailbox is described in Chapter 8.

15. All pending AST control blocks are removed from the list in the PCB, based on access mode. The blocks are then deallocated to nonpaged pool. This operation starts at the tail of the list and proceeds toward the head of the list until an AST control block is found with a more privileged (smaller) access mode than the Rundown argument, or until the AST pending queue is empty. (Recall from Chapter 7 that ASTs are enqueued in order of increasing access mode.)

16. Any change mode handlers for this and outer access modes are eliminated. Because change mode handlers only exist for user and supervisor modes, this step results in elimination of a change mode to user handler every time an image exits and the elimination of a change mode to supervisor handler when the process is deleted.

17. Any termination handlers for this and outer access modes are canceled. Termination handlers can exist for executive, supervisor, and user modes.

18. Exception handlers found in the primary, secondary, and last chance vectors are eliminated for this and outer access modes.

19. The AST active bits for this and outer access modes are cleared. The AST enable bits for this and outer access modes are set.

20. System service failure exceptions are disabled for this and outer access modes.

21. Any compatibility mode handler that has been declared is eliminated, regardless of the access mode argument to Rundown.

22. A new value of ASTLVL is calculated (by routine SCH$NEWLVL) to reflect the change in the AST queue resulting from step 15.

23. The force exit pending and wake pending flags in the PCB are cleared. Clearing these flags is the last step that must be performed at IPL$_SYNCH, so IPL is lowered to 0.

24. Rundown deletes all process logical names based on access mode. At image exit, all logical names created from within the image (with a call to SYS$CRELOG) and all logical names created with the ASSIGN/USER command will be eliminated. At process deletion, all process logical names will be deleted.

25. Resource wait mode is returned to its previous state, normal completion status is set, and control is returned to the caller.

21.4 PROCESS PRIVILEGES

One of the controls exercised by the VMS operating system to prevent unauthorized use of the system is the set of process privileges. One or more of these privileges is required to perform many of the system services, execute certain commands, or use privileged utilities.

21.4.1 Process Privilege Masks

The VMS operating system maintains several privilege masks for each process (see Table 21-1).

1. The first quadword of the process header (PHD$Q_PRIVMSK) contains the working privilege mask, the one checked by all VMS services that

Table 21-1: Process Privilege Masks

Symbolic Name	Location	Use of This Mask	Modified by	Referenced by
PHD$Q_PRIVMSK	Process Header	This is the working privilege mask that is tested by all system services that require privilege.	PROCSTRT LOGINOUT Image Activator $SETPRV	All system services that require privilege
PCB$Q_PRIV	Software PCB (Access Rights Block)	This mask is an exact duplicate of the process header mask.	Same as for PHD$Q_PRIVMSK	Device drivers and ACPs
CTL$GQ_PROCPRIV	P1 Pointer Page	This mask records the permanently enabled privileges for the process. The working privilege mask is reset to this value every time an image exits.	PROCSTRT LOGINOUT $SETPRV	Image Activator MMG$IMGRESET SET UIC command
PHD$Q_AUTHPRIV	Process Header	This mask records the privileges that this process is allowed to use according to its authorization record.	PROCSTRT LOGINOUT	$SETPRV
PHD$Q_IMAGPRIV	Process Header	This mask records the privilege mask for an image that is installed with enhanced privileges.	Image Activator	$SETPRV
UAF$Q_PRIV	Authorization Record	This mask records the privileges that this user is allowed to use.	AUTHORIZE	LOGINOUT
KFI$Q_PROCPRIV	Known File Entry for Privileged Installed Image	This mask records the additional privileges required by an image that is installed with privilege.	INSTALL	Image Activator
IHD$Q_PRIVREQS	Image Header of Any Image	This mask is currently unused. It contains all ones, enabling all privileges.	Linker	Image Activator

require privilege. This mask may be altered each time an image executes, can be altered by the Set Privilege system service, and is reset to the process-permanent privilege mask (CTL$GQ_PROCPRIV) as a part of image rundown.

2. The process privilege mask in the access rights block (ARB) (PCB$Q_PRIV) is always an exact duplicate of the privilege mask in the process header. The access rights block is currently a part of the software PCB.

3. The process-permanent privilege mask is located in the P1 pointer page at global location CTL$GQ_PROCPRIV. The contents of this location are written to the PHD privilege mask (and also to either the ARB or the PCB privilege mask) as a part of image exit by the image reset routine (MMG$IMGRESET). This field is initialized when the process is created.

4. The authorized privilege mask in the process header (PHD$Q_AUTHPRIV) is used by the Set Privilege system service to allow a nonprivileged process (a process without SETPRV privilege) to remove one of its permanent privileges and later regain that privilege. This field is also initialized when the process is created.

5. The image privilege mask in the process header (PHD$Q_IMAGPRIV) contains the privilege mask for a privileged known image while that image is executing. This mask is a convenient tool used by the Set Privilege system service that allows images installed with privilege to issue the Set Privilege system service without losing privileges.

21.4.2   Set Privilege System Service

The Set Privilege system service allows a process to alter its image-specific (PHD$Q_PRIVMSK and PCB$Q_PRIV) privilege masks or its process-permanent (CTL$GQ_PROCPRIV) privilege mask, gaining or losing privileges as a result. In addition, the service can return the previous settings of either the image-specific or process-permanent privileges, if requested.

The path through the code used to disable privileges requires no special privilege and clears the requested privilege bits in the image-specific (and optionally the process-permanent) privilege masks.

The path through the code used to enable privileges requires no privilege if the requested privilege is included in the list of privileges authorized for this process (PHD$Q_AUTHPRIV). If a process wishes a privilege that is not in its authorized list, one of two conditions must hold or the requested privilege is not granted.

- The process must have SETPRV privilege. A process with this privilege can acquire any other privilege with either the Set Privilege system service or the DCL command SET PROCESS/PRIVILEGES.

490

- The system service was called from executive or kernel mode. This mechanism is an escape that allows either VMS or user-written system services to acquire whatever privileges they need without regard for whether the calling process has SETPRV privilege. Such procedures must disable privileges granted in this fashion as part of their return path.

Note that the implementation of the Set Privilege system service does not return an error if a nonprivileged process attempts to add unauthorized privileges. In such a case, the service clears all unauthorized bits in the requested privilege mask, loads the modified privilege mask, and returns the alternate success status SS$_NOTALLPRIV.

22 Process Deletion

. . . for dust you are and to dust you shall return.
—Genesis 3:19

The Delete Process system service allows a process to delete itself or any other process in the system (provided that the process has GROUP or WORLD privilege). Process deletion is accomplished in two steps. The process is marked for deletion in the context of the process issuing the Delete Process system service and a special kernel mode AST is queued to the target process.

This AST executes in the context of the process being deleted and performs the actual deletion operation. Process deletion requires the following operations:

- All traces of the process must be removed from the system.
- All system resources must be returned.
- Accounting information must be passed to the accounting manager (the job controller).
- If the process being deleted is a subprocess, all quotas and limits taken from the creator when the process was created must be returned.
- Finally, if the creator requested notification of deletion through a termination mailbox, the deletion message must be sent.

22.1 PROCESS DELETION IN CONTEXT OF CALLER

The initial operation of the Delete Process system service takes place in the context of the process issuing the system service call. This part of the operation performs a simple set of privilege checks and then queues a special kernel mode AST that will cause the deletion to continue in the context of the process actually being deleted.

22.1.1 Delete Process System Service

The Delete Process system service ($DELPRC) initially calls the subroutine EXE$NAMPID to convert either a process name or a PID to the address of the PCB of the process being deleted. The subroutine checks that the name or PID corresponds to an actual process and verifies that the process calling the Delete Process system service has the privilege to delete the specified process. The Delete Process system service checks that the target process is neither the swapper nor the null process; neither of these may be deleted.

The Delete Process system service then performs the following steps:

1. The target process is marked for deletion. If it was already marked for deletion, the system service simply returns successfully to the caller.
2. If the target process is suspended (scheduling states SUSP or SUSPO), the process is resumed. If the process were to remain suspended, no AST (including the delete process special kernel mode AST) could be delivered to it.
3. An AST control block is allocated and initialized with the PID of the target process and the address of the special kernel AST (DELETE) that will perform the actual process deletion.
4. The AST is queued to the target process, with a potential boost of 3 to its software priority.

In other words, very little action, except the queuing of an AST to the target process, is performed in the context of the process that called $DELPRC.

22.2   PROCESS DELETION IN CONTEXT OF PROCESS BEING DELETED

Almost the entire operation of process deletion takes place in the context of the process being deleted. The queuing of the delete process special kernel mode AST to this process makes it computable; eventually the scheduler will select the process for exection. Assuming that the process has no other pending special kernel mode ASTs, the delete process special kernel mode AST will be the first code to execute in the context of the process being deleted.

By performing process deletion in process context, the target process's address space and process header are readily accessible. System services such as $DELTVA and $DELLOG and RMS calls such as SYS$RMSRUNDWN can also be used. Special cases, such as the deletion of a process that is outswapped, simply do not exist.

22.2.1   Special Kernel Mode AST for Process Deletion

The following steps are performed by the delete process special kernel mode AST:

1. Resource wait mode is enabled.
2. Any user-specified rundown routines are invoked to do image-specific cleanup.
3. RMS$RUNDWN is called for each open file. This procedure insures that

all RMS I/O activity is complete, closes all files, and resets the internal
FAB and RAB tables.

4. If the process owns any subprocesses, these subprocesses must be deleted
before deletion of the owner can continue. An example of process deletion when subprocesses are involved is found in the next section. The
following steps are performed to delete the subprocesses:

a. The PCB vector is scanned for all PCBs whose owner field specifies the
PID of the process being deleted. Each of these subprocesses is marked
for deletion. That is, a Delete Process system service call is made for
each of these processes, resulting in the queuing of the delete process
special kernel mode AST to each of them.

b. The count of subprocesses owned by the process currently being deleted (in field PCB$W_PRCCNT) is checked to see if it has reached zero.
If the count is greater than zero, the process is placed into the resource
wait state (MWAIT). The process will become computable again when
a special kernel mode AST is used to return quotas from one of the
subprocesses.

c. When the special kernel mode AST used to return quotas is delivered,
the subprocess count is checked. If the count is still nonzero, the process is put back in the MWAIT state until another AST is delivered.

5. The process is run down from kernel mode. The procedure followed by
SYS$RUNDWN is described in Chapter 21.

6. The virtual pages associated with any sections are deleted.

7. All process private volumes are dismounted.

8. All allocated devices are deallocated.

9. The process name string in the PCB is cleared by zeroing the count byte.

10. If the process is actually a subprocess (the PCB$L_OWNER field is non-
zero), all remaining quotas must be returned to the owner process. The
following steps are taken to return quotas to the subprocess's owner
process:

a. An I/O request packet is allocated for use as an AST control block. The
extra space at the bottom of the IRP will be used to hold the quotas
being returned to the owner.

b. The address of the return quota special AST (RETQUOTA) and the
PID of the owner are put into the AST control block.

c. The unused quotas are put into the bottom of the IRP. The only quota
that must be returned to the creator is unused CPU time. All other
quotas are either pooled or nondeductible (see Chapter 20).

d. Finally, the special AST is queued to the creator, giving it a priority
boost of 3.

11. If the creator of this process requested a termination mailbox message, a

termination message is constructed on the stack. The contents of the message are listed in Table 22-1.

12. Routine EXE$PRCDELMSG (in module ACCOUNT) is invoked to send an accounting message to the job controller. This message will be sent to the job controller, unless it was explicitly prevented by the NOACNT flag at process creation time, or unless process termination accounting has been disabled for the entire system. The contents of this message are used to fill in all relevant fields of the accounting identification and resource packets. (The data structures used by the Accounting Utility are described in the *VAX-11 Utilities Reference Manual.*)

13. The remainder of P1 space is deleted. (The actual parameters passed to $DELTVA are 40000000 to 7FFFFFFF.) Some of P1 space including the user stack might have already been deleted as a result of a previous image reset call.

14. At this point, the process must be removed from the scheduler's database. To synchronize access to this data, the rest of the code in the delete process special kernel mode AST executes at IPL$_SYNCH.

    The process is removed from execution (with a SVPCTX instruction).

15. The address of the PCB of the null process is put into global location

---

Table 22-1: Contents of the Termination Mailbox Message Sent to the Process Creator

Field in Message Block	Source of Information
Message Type	MSG$_DELPROC (1)
Final Exit Status	CTL$GL_FINALSTS
Process ID	PCB$L_PID (2)
Job ID	Not currently used
Logout Time	EXE$GQ_SYSTIME
Account Name	CTL$GT_ACCOUNT
User Name	CTL$GT_USERNAME
CPU Time	PHD$L_CPUTIM (3)
Number of Page Faults	PHD$L_PAGEFLTS (3)
Peak Paging File Usage	Not currently used
Peak Working Set Size	CTL$GL_WSPEAK
Buffered I/O Count	PHD$L_BIOCNT (3)
Direct I/O Count	PHD$L_DIOCNT (3)
Count of Mounted Volumes	CTL$GL_VOLUMES
Login Time	CTL$GQ_LOGIN
PID of Owner	PCB$L_OWNER (2)

Most of the information about the deleted process is found in the P1 pointer page at the global locations indicated in the second column. The exceptions are as follows:

(1) MSG$_DELPROC is a constant indicating that this is a process termination message.

(2) PCB$L_PID and PCB$L_OWNER are offsets into the PCB of the process being deleted.

(3) Names of the form PHD$L_name are offsets into the process header of the process being deleted.

SCH$GL_CURPCB (making the null process the current process) and also into the slot in the PCB vector formerly occupied by the process being deleted, thus freeing this slot for future use.

16. The pages in process space that were permanently locked into the working set (for example, the kernel stack and the P1 pointer page) are deleted and placed at the beginning of the free page list. The process header pages that are a permanent part of the working set will be deleted by the swapper when the process header is deleted.

17. Any remaining AST control blocks are removed from the PCB queue and deallocated to nonpaged pool.

18. The process swap space is deallocated.

19. The process count field in the job information block is decremented. If the process being deleted is a detached process (the PID of the process being deleted is equal to the master PID field in the JIB), the JIB is deallocated.

20. The owner process's subprocess count (PCB$W_PRCCNT) is decremented. If the owner process is also being deleted, the owner is currently in a wait state, waiting for the contents of this field to become zero. A resource available message is sent to the parent, causing it to check the value of PCB$W_PRCCNT. If the value is now zero, the parent can continue with its own deletion.

21. The PCB is deallocated to nonpaged pool.

22. The number of processes in the system and the number of processes in the balance set are decremented.

23. The swapper is awakened and informed that there is a process header to be removed from the balance slot area (see Chapter 17).

24. Finally, the delete process special kernel mode AST exits by jumping to the scheduler (at entry SCH$SCHED) to select the next process for execution (see Chapter 10).

22.2.2 Deletion of a Process That Owns Subprocesses

When a process owns subprocesses, the deletion of the owner process must be delayed until all the subprocesses that it owns are deleted. The prior deletion of subprocesses insures that all quotas taken from the creator are returned.

During the execution of the delete process special kernel mode AST, a check is made to see if the process being deleted owns any subprocesses. If it does, these processes must be located and marked for deletion. Marking a subprocess for deletion simply means issuing a Delete Process system service for the subprocess.

As Figure 22-1 shows, there are no forward pointers in the PCB of an owner process to indicate which subprocesses it has created. The only indication

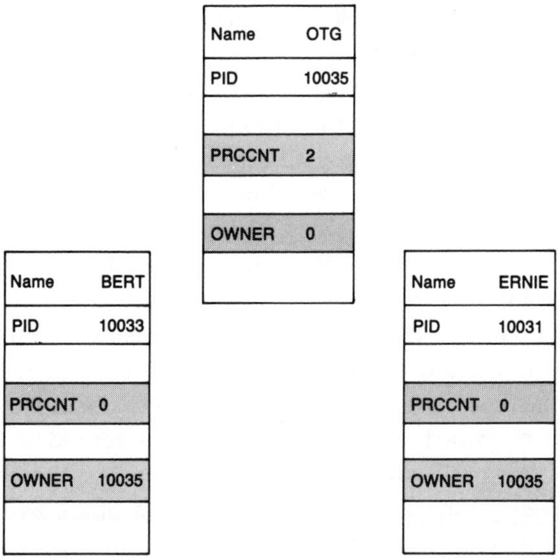

Name	OTG
PID	10035
PRCCNT	2
OWNER	0

Name	BERT
PID	10033
PRCCNT	0
OWNER	10035

Name	ERNIE
PID	10031
PRCCNT	0
OWNER	10035

Figure 22-1
Sample Job to Illustrate Process Deletion
with Subprocesses

that a process has created subprocesses is a nonzero entry in the
PCB$W_PRCCNT field. These processes can only be located by scanning all
the PCBs in the system until all PCBs are located that contain the PID of the
creator in their owner field.

22.2.3 Example of Process Deletion with Subprocesses

The details of this situation can be best illustrated with an example. Figure
22-1 shows a process whose process ID equals 10035 and whose name is
OTG. The process OTG owns two subprocesses: the first has a process ID of
10033 and the name BERT; the second has a process ID of 1003 and the name
ERNIE.

Neither of these subprocesses owns any further subprocesses. The following steps occur as a result of the process OTG being deleted. Assume that the
priorities are such that the processes execute in the order OTG, BERT, and
finally ERNIE.

1. The deletion of process OTG proceeds normally until it is determined that
   this process has created two subprocesses. The PCB vector is scanned until
   the two PCBs with 10035 in the owner field are located. These two processes are marked for deletion. This means that the delete process special

kernel mode AST is queued to the two subprocesses and they are made computable. Process OTG is placed into a wait state because the count of owned subprocesses is nonzero (actually 2 at this point).

2. The previous assumption about priorities implies that process BERT will execute next. Its deletion proceeds past the point where process OTG stopped because it owns no subprocesses. However, the next step in the delete process special kernel mode AST determines that process BERT is a subprocess and must return quotas to its owner. As listed above, the return of quotas is accomplished with the queuing of a special kernel mode AST (RETQUOTA) to process OTG, changing its state back to computable. When BERT has finished with all actions that require the presence of the JIB, it decrements the process count in OTG's PCB$W_PRCCNT. However, the count of owned subprocesses is still not zero (down to 1 now) so process OTG is put right back into the resource wait state.

3. The assumption about priorities indicates that process BERT will continue to execute until it disappears entirely from the system. Process ERNIE now begins execution of the delete process special kernel mode AST. Again, the check for owned subprocesses indicates none but the check that this is a subprocess indicates that it is. The RETQUOTA AST is again queued to process OTG and the count of owned subprocesses decremented (finally to zero).

4. Now process OTG will resume execution as a result of the delivery of the RETQUOTA AST and subsequently find that the count of owned subprocesses has gone to zero. In fact, process OTG will continue to be deleted at this point, even though process ERNIE has not been entirely deleted. This overlapping is simply a result of the timing in this example. The process ERNIE is well on the way to being deleted, and is no longer of any concern to process OTG. The important point is that the quotas given to process ERNIE have been returned to OTG. Once OTG's PCB$W_PRCCNT is equal to zero, it is irrelevant which process executes next; because ERNIE (and BERT) have finished work that depended on the presence of the JIB, OTG and the JIB can be deleted totally.

In the general case of a series of subprocesses arranged in a tree structure, if some arbitrary process is deleted, all subprocesses further down in the tree will be deleted first.

23 Interactive and Batch Jobs

In my end is my beginning.
—Motto of Mary Queen of Scots

The previous three chapters in this part describe the creation and deletion of a process that executes a single image. This chapter describes the special actions that must be taken to allow several images to execute consecutively in the context of the same process. Because this mode of operation occurs in all interactive and batch jobs, it merits special discussion. However, the total operation of a VAX/VMS command language interpreter will not be discussed.

23.1 THE JOB CONTROLLER AND UNSOLICITED INPUT

The job controller is the process that controls the creation of nearly all interactive and batch jobs. Interactive jobs are usually initiated by unsolicited terminal input. Batch jobs are usually initiated through the SUBMIT command, although unsolicited card reader input will also result in the creation of a batch job.

The crucial step that is performed by the job controller is the creation of a process that executes the image LOGINOUT. This image is activated and called exactly like any other image as described in Chapters 20 and 21. The actions that LOGINOUT takes, especially mapping a command language interpreter into P1 space, are what differentiate interactive and batch jobs from the single image process described in the previous three chapters. The creation of an interactive job is pictured schematically in Figure 23-1. The creation of a batch job is pictured in Figure 23-2.

23.1.1 Unsolicited Terminal Input

The terminal interrupt service routine performs special action when an unexpected interrupt occurs. A check is made to determine whether the device is owned. If the owner process has requested notification of unsolicited interrupts, it will be notified. Otherwise, the characters will be placed into a type-ahead buffer.

If the device is unowned, the job controller is notified through its mailbox that an unowned terminal has received an unexpected interrupt. In a sense, the job controller is the default owner of all otherwise unclaimed terminals.

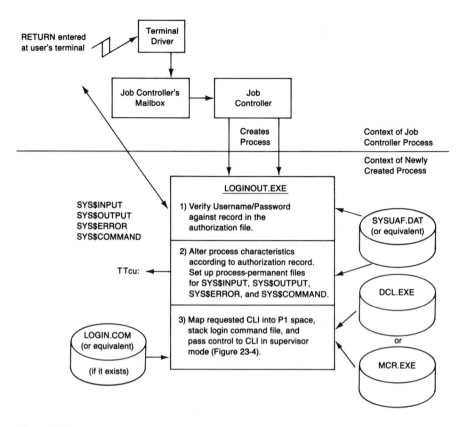

Figure 23-1
Steps Involved in Initiating an Interactive Job

The job controller routine that responds to unsolicited terminal input simply creates a process with the following parameters:

Process Name	_TTcu:
UIC	[1,4]
Image Name	SYS$SYSTEM:LOGINOUT.EXE
SYS$INPUT	_ _TTcu:
SYS$OUTPUT	_ _TTcu:
SYS$ERROR	_ _TTcu:
Base Priority	DEFPRI (SYSBOOT Parameter)
Privilege Mask	All Privileges

The string TTcu: indicates the controller/unit of the terminal where the unsolicited input was typed. Note that all interactive jobs begin with a name indicating their input/output device and the image LOGINOUT as the image that will be executed (see Figure 23-1).

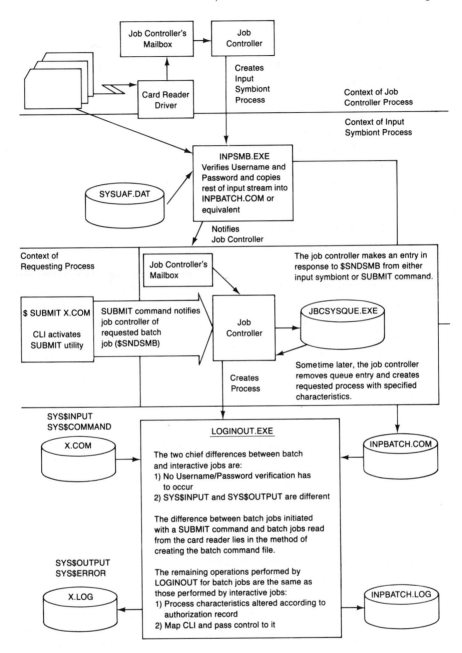

Figure 23-2
Steps Involved in Initiating a Batch Job

23.1.2   The SUBMIT Command

When the SUBMIT command is executed, a message is sent to the symbiont manager (the job controller), which places the requested job in one of its job queues. When the number of active jobs in one of the batch queues drops below its maximum value, the job controller selects the highest priority pending job from one of its queues and creates a process with the specified batch stream as SYS$INPUT and a log file in an appropriate directory as SYS$OUTPUT (see Figure 23-2). The image that will execute is LOGINOUT, which allows the language of the input stream to be a command language because LOGINOUT will map the appropriate CLI into the process P1 space.

23.1.3   Unsolicited Card Reader Input

An alternative method for starting batch jobs utilizes the so-called hot card reader feature that is a part of the card reader driver interrupt service routine. Like the terminal driver's interrupt service routine, the card reader driver informs the job controller that an unexpected interrupt has occurred on an unowned device. The job controller creates a process similar to the process created in response to unsolicited terminal input except that the image INPSMB.EXE, the input symbiont, executes in place of LOGINOUT. The following process parameters are passed by the job controller to the Create Process system service:

Process Name	_CRc0:
UIC	[1,4]
Image Name	SYS$SYSTEM:INPSMB.EXE
SYS$INPUT	_CRc0:
SYS$OUTPUT	_CRc0:
SYS$ERROR	_CRc0:
Base Priority	DEFPRI (SYSBOOT Parameter)
Privilege Mask	All Privileges

The letter c represents the controller number. The fact that this process has a card reader for its output device is irrelevant because it does no writing to either SYS$OUTPUT or SYS$ERROR.

The input symbiont reads the $JOB and $PASSWORD cards and performs a validation similar to the one performed by LOGINOUT. After determining the user's default directory from the authorization record, the input symbiont opens a file in that directory and reads the rest of the job cards into that file. Terminating conditions of this read are an end of file, an $EOJ card, or another $JOB card.

Once the input stream has been read into the user's directory, the input symbiont sends a message to the job controller, and the operation proceeds from this point in exactly the same manner as for the SUBMIT command.

That is, the job controller will eventually create a process with the card file as SYS$INPUT, some log file as SYS$OUTPUT, and LOGINOUT (which will map a CLI) as the image that will execute (see Figure 23-2).

23.2 THE LOGINOUT IMAGE

The LOGINOUT image is responsible for verifying that the user is authorized to use the system, reading his record in the authorization file, and altering the process characteristics to reflect what is found there. The most important step that this image performs in altering the process is to map a command language interpreter into its reserved place in P1 space (pictured in Figure 1-7 and listed in Table 26-4).

23.2.1 Interactive Jobs

When LOGINOUT executes in response to unsolicited terminal input, it must verify that the user has access to the system before it proceeds with the operations in interactive jobsrest of its operations. It does this by performing the following steps:

1. A user mode error handler is established to service any errors that occur while LOGINOUT is executing. When this handler is invoked, it checks the exit status code; if the code is valid, it is stored in P1 space in preparation for writing the code to the termination mailbox. The error handler then calls SYS$EXIT, which results in the eventual deletion of the process. When LOGINOUT executes executive mode code, the same error handler is declared in executive mode.

2. The logical names SYS$INPUT, SYS$OUTPUT, and SYS$ERROR are translated and the resultant strings are saved for later use.

3. The process I/O segment in P1 space is initialized. SYS$INPUT is opened. Because an interactive job is being created, SYS$OUTPUT and SYS$ERROR are already opened. RABs are connected to the FAB so that RMS operations may proceed.

4. The user name and password are prompted for and read from the requesting terminal. The record associated with this user is read from the authorization file and the password is verified.

5. If the password is correct, a number of other fields in the authorization file are checked; these fields include: the user or account job limit, the hourly restrictions, and the terminal types (dial-up or remote terminals).

6. If these checks are successful, and the interactive job count has not been exceeded, the login operation was a success. This success is indicated by the following announcement message:

```
Welcome to VAX/VMS Version V3.3
```

7. Process-permanent files are created for the input and output devices by calls to RMS (if the input and output devices are the same, only one file is created). The logical names SYS$INPUT and SYS$COMMAND are assigned to the input device; the logical names SYS$OUTPUT and SYS$ERROR are assigned to the output device. The equivalence names for these logical names are prefixed by four bytes consisting of: an escape (1B hex), a null character (00 hex), and a two-byte internal file identifier (IFI). When RMS receives such a string as a result of logical name translation, it uses the IFI as an index into one of its internal tables. Using the IFI allows extremely fast access to these commonly used files.

   The logical names SYS$LOGIN and SYS$SCRATCH are also created. The equivalence name for both of these logical names is the default disk and directory specified by the user's UAF record. The username qualifier /DISK=ddcu: (used with the username portion of the login sequence) can be used to override the default disk.

8. The command language interpreter is mapped into the low address end of P1 space (see Figure 1-7). This mapping is accomplished by a merged image activation of the selected CLI. (The procedure LIB$P1_MERGE first merges the CLI into P0 space to determine its size, deletes the P0 space, and maps the correct amount of P1 space. Global location CTL$GL_CTLBASVA is altered to reflect the new low address end of P1 space.)

   The default CLI is specified by the authorization file; however, it can be overridden with the username qualifier /CLI=cli at log in time (provided that the user is authorized to override the CLI).

9. The command-language-independent data area, including the symbol tables, is initialized. P1 space is expanded by a number of pages equal to the SYSBOOT parameter CLISYMTBL to accommodate the CLI symbol table.

10. Many of the process attributes extracted from the authorization file are put into their proper places, overwriting the attributes placed there when the process was created:

   • Default Disk and Directory String
   • User Name
   • Account Name
   • Default Privilege Mask
   • Process Quotas and Limits
   • Information about Primary and Secondary Day Restrictions (because this is a detached process)
   • Base Software Priority
   • UIC

LOGINOUT attempts to change the process name from _TTcu: to the username. This attempt will fail if another process in the same group already has the same name. (The most common occurrence of username duplication is when the same user is logged in at more than one terminal.) In the case of failure, the process will retain its name (_TTcu:), guaranteed to be unique for a given system.

11. LOGINOUT creates logical names PROC0 through PROC9, each equated to the file specification of a command procedure (or indirect command file) to be executed before the CLI enters its input loop. Currently, only PROC0 and PROC1 are used. PROC0 is equated to the translation of the logical name SYS$SYLOGIN; PROC1 is equated to the file specified by the LGICMD field of the user's UAF record or the file specified by the username qualifier /COMMAND at log in time (by an authorized user). If the contents of the LGICMD field are null, PROC1 is equated to the string LOGIN. The LGICMD field should indicate the null device (using the string NL:), if no login command file is to be executed.

   When the CLI is initialized, these logical names are translated and the command procedures (or indirect command files) are executed.

12. At this point, LOGINOUT has finished its work and must pass control to the CLI. In order to pass control to the CLI, LOGINOUT calls an executive mode routine, which performs the following:

   • The protection on pages containing the CLI data is changed so that the pages can only be accessed from supervisor and inner access modes.
   • The PSL in the call frame is modified so that the current and previous mode fields contain supervisor mode.
   • The transfer address of the CLI is written into the PC saved in the call frame.
   • The routine exits, and in order to return from executive mode, an REI is executed. The REI returns the process to supervisor mode with the PC pointing to the first instruction in the CLI.

23.2.2   LOGINOUT Operation for Batch Jobs

Many of the operations performed by LOGINOUT for interactive jobs must also occur when a batch job is being created. For example, it is still necessary to open the input and output streams and map the CLI. However, password verification is not necessary, either because the input symbiont already did it or because it is not necessary in the case of a SUBMIT command.

Rather than describing the steps performed by LOGINOUT again, the following list simply specified those differences for batch jobs:

1. The first indication that LOGINOUT has that it is creating a batch job is that the resultant strings for SYS$INPUT and SYS$OUTPUT are different. This means that it must open two files as process-permanent files rather than one and preserve two IFIs for later use.

2. The prompted read for user name and password and the announcement of the system are skipped because this step is unnecessary.

3. New logical names are again created for SYS$INPUT, SYS$OUTPUT, SYS$ERROR, and SYS$COMMAND. Because two files are involved, different IFIs will be added to the beginning of the resultant strings before Create Logical Name is called. One IFI is used for SYS$INPUT and SYS$COMMAND. The other IFI is used for SYS$OUTPUT and SYS$ERROR.

4. The process attributes are obtained from the authorization file, in order to supplement information not specified at batch queue creation or at job submission. These values are minimized by values supplied by the job controller.

5. The job parameters, P1 through P8, if present, are defined as user mode logical names in order that they can be passed to the CLI.

Mapping the CLI and transfering control to it happen in exactly the same way as they do for an interactive job. In both cases, if SYS$SYLOGIN is defined as a system logical name, the first commands that execute are the commands in the site-specific login command file. If the user authorization file does not specify a user login command file, the command file SYS$LOGIN:LOGIN-.COM is executed (if the CLI is DCL). Note that an authorized user can specify a different login command file, or none at all, by using the login command qualifier /COMMAND.

23.2.3 SPAWN and ATTACH

The DCL command SPAWN is used to create interactive subprocesses; the ATTACH command is used to transfer terminal control from one process to another within the same job. The real work involved in spawning a new subprocess is in copying process context information from the creating process to the subprocess. This information includes the process symbol table, process logical name tables, current privileges, out-of-band AST settings, verify flag settings, and the command line that was passed to SPAWN (if one exists).

When the DCL command SPAWN is issued, the following operations are performed:

- SPAWN disables the current process's out-of-band ASTs and saves the current event flags.
- A resource mailbox is created by the creating process. This mailbox will be used to pass process context information to the subprocess.
- The Create Process system service is called to create a subprocess. The image name argument specifies the image LOGINOUT. The **error** argument specifies the name of the newly created resource mailbox. If the creating process does not specify input and output files to the SPAWN

command, then the creating process's SYS$INPUT and SYS$OUTPUT file specifications are used. The call to Create Process also declares a termination mailbox for the subprocess.

- When LOGINOUT passes control to DCL in the context of the subprocess, DCL first translates the logical name SYS$ERROR. If the equivalence string contains the name of a mailbox, DCL recognizes that a SPAWN operation is in progress and that it must read the creating process's context information. The context information is passed in the following manner:

  —DCL issues read requests to the resource mailbox.
  —The creating process writes context information to the resource mailbox one record at a time. When the subprocess receives the information, it adds the information to its context.
  —The first records passed are the process header records, which contain the current privilege mask, out-of-band AST flag settings, and the verify flag setting.
  —Next, the SPAWN command string is passed (if one was specified).
  —The creating process then parses its process logical name table and passes user and supervisor mode logical name strings, their equivalence name strings, and their access mode to the subprocess. DCL receives the strings and fills in its own process logical name table.
  —Finally, the contents of the symbol table are then passed, one symbol at a time. Note that the DCL command tables are not passed to the subprocess.

- SPAWN creates a mailbox from the calling process and declares a write-attention AST for the mailbox. The DCL command ATTACH will use the mailbox to signal an attach request and communicate attach information.
- Once it has passed all information to the subprocess, SPAWN causes the calling process to hibernate.
- DCL, acting in the context of the new subprocess, deletes the resource mailbox, deassigns the logical name SYS$ERROR, and continues normal processing.

The DCL command ATTACH is used to transfers terminal control to a specified process (called the target process in this discussion). The operation of the DCL command ATTACH is a little simpler than SPAWN:

- ATTACH first checks that it is being executed from an interactive process, and then it checks that the target process is not itself.
- ATTACH creates an attach mailbox for the calling process. This attach mailbox will be used if a later ATTACH request names this process as its target. If an attach mailbox already exists, the write-attention AST is simply declared for the mailbox. The mailbox is created before the actual attach request is performed so that the ATTACH does not receive an affirm-

ative message from the target process only to find that it does not have the resources to create its own attach mailbox. At this point in time, AT-TACH also saves the event flags and disables out-of-band ASTs for the calling process.

- ATTACH locates the target process's attach mailbox and writes the name of its output stream (usually the equivalence name of SYS$INPUT) to the mailbox, thus triggering the write-attention AST that was declared when the target process spawned a subprocess. ATTACH then issues a read request on the target process's attach mailbox.
- The target process wakes to answer the write-attention AST. The AST routine compares the name of its output stream to the name in the mailbox. If the strings are the same, the target process writes an affirmative response to the attach mailbox.
- Once it receives the affirmation, ATTACH deassigns its channel to the target process's attach mailbox and causes the calling process to hibernate.
- The AST routine in the target process issues a wake request for the process, declares another write attention AST for its attach mailbox, and returns control to the target process.

When one of the subprocesses created by the SPAWN command is deleted, the termination AST is delivered. The termination AST simply performs cleanup work before the subprocess is deleted. The channels to the attach and termination mailboxes are deassigned, and the mailboxes are deleted. If the subprocess was created by a call to LIB$SPAWN and if an event flag or AST routine was specified in the call, then the event flag is set or the AST is delivered.

23.3 COMMAND LANGUAGE INTERPRETERS AND IMAGE EXECUTION

Once the command language interpreter gains control, it performs some initialization and then reads and processes successive records from SYS$INPUT. Several of these operations involve command language features. This discussion is concerned only with those commands that result in image execution, in order to contrast interactive and batch jobs with the simple processes described in previous chapters.

The VAX/VMS operating system supports two command language interpreters, DCL and MCR. The chief difference between these command languages lies in their treatment of indirect files, a topic that does not affect image execution. In fact, the steps taken by either CLI in activating an image are nearly identical. The operation of DCL will be described in detail; MCR will be mentioned only where it differs from DCL.

The most important step that the CLI performs is concerned is the declaration of a supervisor mode termination handler. It is this handler that will prevent process deletion following image exit and allow the successive execution of multiple images within the same process. A simplified flow of control through the CLI is pictured in Figure 23-3.

23.3.1   CLI Initialization

The first code that executes in DCL performs the following initialization steps before it enters the main command processing loop:

1. After translating the user mode logical names defined by LOGINOUT, DCL calls SYS$RUNDWN with an argument of user mode to run down the LOGINOUT image. Equivalence names for the parameters P0 through P8 are used to create symbols; equivalence names for PROC0 through PROC9 are used to specify the names of command procedures to be executed by DCL.
2. A change-mode-to-supervisor handler is established (by using the $DCLCMH system service). This handler allows DCL to get back to supervisor mode from user mode when it needs to write protected data structures. One instance where this is required is in symbol definition, because DCL's symbol tables are protected from write access by user mode.
3. A CTRL/Y AST is declared so that DCL always receives control when CTRL/Y is typed.
4. Finally, control is passed to the first instruction of the main command processing loop (at global label DCL$RESTART or MCR$RESTART).

23.3.2   Command Processing Loop

The main command processing loop reads a record from SYS$INPUT and takes whatever action is dictated by the command. Some actions can be performed directly by DCL (or MCR). Others require the execution of a separate image. Table 23-1 lists the general operations performed by DCL (or MCR) and indicates those actions that require an external image.

If the record that is read from the input stream is a recognized command, DCL (or MCR) must also determine whether it can perform the requested action itself or activate an external image. Table 23-2 lists the commands that can be executed by DCL or MCR without destroying a currently executing image. (Special commands used by the MCR indirect command file processor are not included in the table.) Any other command either requires an image in order to execute (such as COPY or LINK) or directly affects the currently executing image (such as STOP).

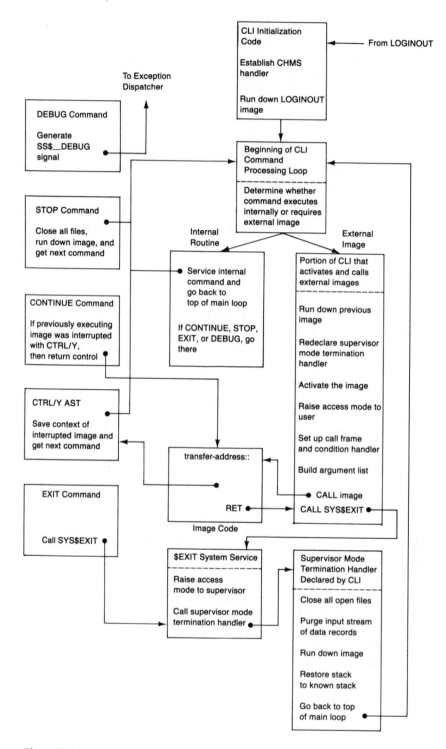

Figure 23-3
Simplified Control Flow

Table 23-1: General Actions Performed by a Command Language Interpreter

General CLI Operations	Sample Commands
Commands That Require External Images	COPY LINK Some SET Commands Some SHOW Commands
Commands That Require Internal Processing and an External Image	LOGOUT MCR RUN
Foreign Commands	string:=="$image-file-spec"
Other Operations That Destroy an Image	STOP EXIT Invoking a Command Procedure
Commands That CLI Can Execute Internally	EXAMINE, SET DEFAULT (See Table 23-2)
Other Internal Operations	Symbol Definition

23.3.3   Image Initiation by DCL

When an external image is required, DCL first performs some command-specific steps. It then enters a common routine to formally activate and call the image. The steps that it takes are nearly identical to the steps performed by PROCSTRT, described in Chapter 20.

1. The previous image (if any) is run down by calling SYS$RUNDWN. This call removes any traces of a previously executing image before another image is activated. In the case where the previous image terminated normally, this call is unnecessary. However, a CTRL/Y followed by an external command bypasses the normal image termination path, requiring this extra step to insure that a previous image is eliminated before another is activated.
2. The supervisor mode termination handler that will allow DCL to regain control at image exit is declared. Recall from Chapter 21 that an exit handler must be redeclared after each use.
3. The image is activated by calling SYS$IMGACT (see Chapter 21).
4. Access mode is raised to user.
5. The call frame chain is terminated by clearing FP.
6. An initial call frame is created on the user stack. The address of the catch-all condition handler is placed into this frame and also into the last chance exception vector.
7. Image addresses are relocated by calling the Address Relocation Fixup system service (SYS$IMGFIX).

Table 23-2: Command Handled by CLI Internal Procedures by PROCSTRT or a CLI

Command	*Description*
=	Create/Modify a symbol
ALLOCATE	Allocate a device
ASSIGN	Create a logical name
ATTACH (D)	Transfer control to another process in job
CLOSE (D)	Close a process-permanent file
CONTINUE	Resume interrupted image
DEALLOCATE	Deallocate a device
DEASSIGN (D)	Delete a logical name
DEBUG	Invoke the symbolic debugger
$DECK (D)	Delimit the beginning of an input stream
DEFINE (D)	Create a logical name
DELETE/SYMBOL (D)	Delete a symbol definition
DEPOSIT	Modify a memory location
$EOD (D)	Delimit the end of an input stream
EXAMINE	Examine a memory location
EXIT	Exit a command procedure
	Run down an image after invoking termination handlers
GOTO	Transfer control within a command procedure
IF (D)	Conditional command execution
INQUIRE (D)	Interactively assign a value to a symbol
ON	Define conditional action
OPEN (D)	Open a process-permanent file
READ (D)	Read a record into a symbol
SET CONTROL	Determine CTRL actions
SET DEFAULT	Define default directory string
SET [NO]ON	Determine error processing
SET PROTECTION	Define default file protection
SET UIC	Change process UIC and default directory string
SET [NO]VERIFY	Determine echoing of command procedure commands
SHOW DEFAULT	Display default directory string
SHOW PROTECTION	Display default file protection
SHOW QUOTA	Display current disk file usage
SHOW STATUS	Display status of currently executing image
SHOW SYMBOL	Display value of symbol(s)
SHOW TIME	Display current time
SHOW TRANSLATION	Show translation of single logical name
SPAWN (D)	Create a subprocess and transfer control to it

Table 23-2: Command Handled by CLI Internal Procedures *(continued)*

Command	Description
STOP	Run down an image bypassing termination handlers
WAIT (D)	Wait for specified interval to elapse
WRITE (D)	Write the value of a symbol to a file

(D) These commands are available in the DCL command interpreter but not in the MCR command interpreter.

8. The argument list (see Figure 23-4) that will be passed to the image (and to any intervening procedures such as SYS$IMGSTA) is built on the user stack.
9. The image is called at the first address in the transfer address array (described in Chapter 21). As mentioned in the discussion of image startup, the first transfer address will usually be the address of the debug bootstrap that will establish the traceback exception handler and map the debugger if requested.
10. The instruction following the call to the image results in a call to SYS$EXIT. Unlike the check made in PROCSTRT, the code path through DCL makes it irrelevant whether an image terminates with a RET or a call to SYS$EXIT. Other reasons, described in the *VAX-11 Run-Time Library Reference Manual*, still make the RET instruction the preferred method of image termination.

23.3.4   Image Termination

When an image in an interactive or batch job terminates, the Exit system service will eventually call the supervisor mode termination handler estab-

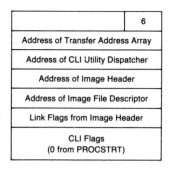

Figure 23-4
Argument List Passed to an Image by PROCSTRT or a CLI

lished by DCL before the image was called. This termination handler performs several cleanup steps before passing control to the beginning of the main command loop to allow DCL to process the next command.

1. Any files left open by the image are closed by calling SYS$RMSRUNDWN for each open file.
2. Any data records in the input stream (records that do not begin with a dollar sign for DCL or a right angle bracket for MCR) are discarded and a warning message issued.
3. The image that just terminated is run down by calling SYS$RUNDWN with an argument of user mode.
4. Finally, control is passed to the beginning of the main command loop so that DCL can read and process the next command. Control is passed by restoring the supervisor stack pointer to a known state (with the address of DCL$RESTART on the top of the stack) and issuing an RSB.

23.3.5 Abnormal Image Termination

When an image terminates normally, it is run down as a part of DCL's termination handler, and control is passed to DCL at the start of its command loop. An image can also be interrupted by typing CTRL/Y or by using the COBOL or FORTRAN pause capability. Further execution of the image depends on the sequence of commands that execute while the image is interrupted.

23.3.5.1 CTRL/Y Processing.

When CTRL/Y (or possibly CTRL/C) is typed at the terminal, the terminal driver passes control to the AST that was established by DCL as a part of its initialization. The first step performed by this AST is to redeclare itself. Redeclaring the AST causes future CTRL/Ys to be passed to the same AST. The previous mode of the PSL is then checked. If the previous mode was supervisor, DCL checks whether a SET NOCONTROL_Y command has been executed. If so, the interrupt is simply dismissed. If not, DCL is restored to its initial state (with no nesting of indirect levels) and control is passed to the beginning of the main command loop.

If the previous mode was user, then an image was interrupted. If the image was installed with enhanced privileges, the current privileges are saved and the process privileges are reset to those before the image was activated. A flag is set and DCL returns to DCL$RESTART. If, at this point, the user enters the DCL commands ATTACH, CONTINUE, or SPAWN, the appropriate action is taken and the image is not run down. Any other command will cause the privileged image to be run down before the next command is executed.

23.3.5.2 The Pause Capability.

The VAX-11 COBOL and VAX-11 FORTRAN languages provide the capability to interrupt an image under program control.

Either of the Run-Time Library procedures that implement this feature could also be called from any other language.

- The following COBOL statement generates a call to the Run-Time Library procedure COB$PAUSE, which sends the message "literal" to SYS$OUTPUT and passes control to the CLI at the beginning of its main command loop:

  ```
  STOP literal
  ```

- The following FORTRAN statement generates a call to the Run-Time Library procedure FOR$PAUSE, which sends the message "literal" to SYS$OUTPUT and passes control to the CLI at the beginning of its main command loop:

  ```
  PAUSE literal
  ```

  If the "literal" argument is omitted, FOR$PAUSE sends the following message to SYS$OUTPUT.

  ```
  FORTRAN PAUSE
  ```

23.3.5.3 **The State of Interrupted Images.** If a nonprivileged image was interrupted, the image context is saved and control is passed to the beginning of the main command loop to allow the user to execute commands. If DCL can perform the requested action internally (see Table 23-2), then the image can potentially be continued.

However, any command that requires an external image will destroy the context of the interrupted image. In addition, if the user executes an indirect command file while an image is interrupted, that image is destroyed, even though the commands in the indirect command file can be performed internally by DCL.

Six commands that the user can execute have special importance if an image has been interrupted by CTRL/Y. These commands are ATTACH, CONTINUE, DEBUG, EXIT, SPAWN, and STOP.

23.3.5.4 **CONTINUE Command.** If CONTINUE is entered while at CTRL/Y AST level and the previous mode was user, the AST is dismissed and control is passed back to the image at the point where it was interrupted.

23.3.5.5 **DEBUG Command.** As described in Chapter 21, a DEBUG command causes DCL to generate a SS$_DEBUG signal that will eventually be fielded by the condition handler established in image startup. This handler will respond to the SS$_DEBUG signal by mapping the debugger (if it is not already mapped) and transferring control to it. This technique allows the debugger to be used, even when the image was not linked with the /DEBUG qualifier. (In order for this capability to work, the image cannot be linked with the /NOTRACE-

BACK qualifier. That qualifier prevents image startup from executing, so that the handler that dynamically maps the debugger never is established.)

23.3.5.6 **The EXIT Command.** The EXIT command causes an Exit system service to be issued from user mode. Termination handlers are called and the image is run down.

23.3.5.7 **The STOP Command.** The STOP command performs essentially the same cleanup operations that occur for a normally terminating image. However, STOP does its own work and does not call SYS$EXIT. Thus, user mode termination handlers are not called when an image terminates with a CTRL/Y STOP sequence.

The STOP command processor first determines whether an image or a process is being stopped. (The various possible STOP commands are described in the *VAX/VMS Command Language User's Guide*.) If an image is being stopped, all open files are closed by calling SYS$RMSRUNDWN. The image itself is then run down (by calling SYS$RUNDWN). Finally, control is passed to the beginning of the main command loop.

Note that STOP performs nearly identical operations to the DCL termination handler invoked as a result of a call to SYS$EXIT or an EXIT command. The only difference between either EXIT sequence and the STOP command is that user mode termination handlers are not called first. Thus in most cases, the STOP and EXIT commands are interchangeable. One useful aspect of the STOP command is that it can be used to eliminate an image that contains a user mode termination handler that is preventing that image from completely going away, either intentionally or as a result of an error.

23.4 **THE LOGOUT OPERATION**

The same image that performs the initialization of an interactive or batch job is used to cause the eventual deletion of such a process. The indication that a logout is required is the existence of the process-permanent data region, used to communicate between LOGINOUT and the CLI. LOGINOUT takes whatever special action is required before calling the Delete Process system service, which will continue with those parts of process deletion that are independent of the kind of process that is being deleted.

1. The logout message is sent to SYS$OUTPUT, either the user's terminal for an interactive job or the batch log for a batch job.
2. SYS$OUTPUT is closed. If this is a batch job, then SYS$INPUT is different and must also be closed.
3. Finally, SYS$EXIT is called from executive mode. As was discussed in

Chapter 21, the search for termination handlers will only look at the executive mode list, bypassing the supervisor mode termination handler established by the CLI to prevent process deletion following image exit.

4. After the executive mode termination handler has performed its work, the Exit system service will call Delete Process, which will cause the logged-out process to disappear from the system.

PART VII/System Initialization

24 Bootstrap Procedures

ante mare et terras et quod tegit omnia caelum unus erat toto
naturae vultus in orbe, quem dixere Chaos

—Ovid, *Metamorphoses*

Before a VAX/VMS system can operate, some initialization programs (or bootstrap programs) must execute to configure the system and read the executive into memory. Parts of the bootstrap operation are specific to the type of VAX-11 processor. Others are common across all VAX family members. Figure 24-1 summarizes the steps that are taken to initialize a VAX/VMS system. Tables 24-2 through 24-5 summarize the programs that execute and the files that are referenced while initializing the system. This chapter describes all phases of the bootstrap operation that occur before code contained in the executive image (SYS.EXE) executes. Chapter 25 describes the initialization of the executive image.

24.1 PROCESSOR-SPECIFIC INITIALIZATION

The initial steps that occur in the initialization of a VAX/VMS system depend on the particular VAX processor that is being used. The next sections briefly describe the processor-specific steps that occur before the primary bootstrap program (VMB) gains control and begins execution. In all processors, the following steps occur:

- 64K bytes of error-free, page-aligned, contiguous memory are located.
- VMB is loaded into the 64K bytes of memory.
- The bootstrap device code and other boostrap flags are passed to VMB using registers R0 through R5.
- VMB is executed.

The way in which good memory is located and registers are loaded is CPU-dependent. The most obvious processor-specific item that affects the bootstrap operation is the console configuration. An overview of the console subsystem for a specific VAX-11 family member can be found in the *VAX Hardware Handbook*.

24.1.1 VAX-11/730 Initial Bootstrap Operation

The console subsystem on the VAX-11/730 consists of a separate microprocessor, two mass storage devices (TU58 cartridge tape drives), read-only mem-

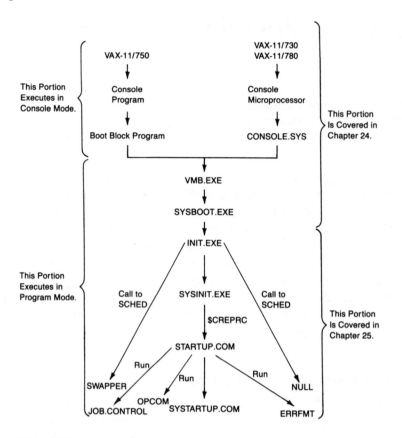

Figure 24-1
Sequence of Initialization Events

ory, and a terminal. When the CPU is in console mode, only the console program can execute; the CPU cannot execute any user code or even the VMS operating system itself.

There are five ways in which a bootstrap sequence may be initiated.

1. A power-on occurs (the boot switch is pressed, or the processor is turned on).
2. The console command B is typed while the processor is in console mode.
3. A HALT instruction is executed in kernel mode, and the Auto Restart switch is in the ON position.
4. The following instruction is executed, which invokes a bootstrap operation:

```
MTPR    #^XF02,#PR$_TXDB
```

5. An attempted restart fails and the Auto Restart switch is in the ON position.

Table 24-1: VAX-11/730 Bootstrap Command Files

Command File	Hardware Configuration
CODE00.CMD	No FPA, no IDC
CODE01.CMD	No FPA, with IDC
CODE02.CMD	With FPA, no IDC
CODE03.CMD	With FPA, with IDC

In the bootstrap sequence, the console subsystem must execute a series of programs in order to load and execute the primary bootstrap program (VMB). The initial bootstrap programs (listed in Table 24-2) are console microprocessor programs. The steps of initial bootstrap are as follows:

1. After performing a self test, the microprocessor locates the TU58 that contains the boot block, and loads blocks 0 through 5 from the tape into into microprocessor memory. The code in the boot block locates the main console microcode program CONSOL.EXE on the console TU58.
2. CONSOL.EXE then executes two indirect command files, POWER.CMD and CODE0n.CMD. POWER.CMD executes the routine POWER.CPU, which initializes the machine, searches for a page-aligned 64K byte block of good memory, and checks the configuration of the machine. When POWER.CPU exits, it returns an address 200 (hex) bytes beyond the beginning of the first good page. This address is loaded into SP. (In a typical system, one with no errors in the first 64K bytes, the contents of SP are 200.)

   Each possible configuration of the VAX-11/730 is assigned a value. The value returned from POWER.CPU is then substituted into the file name CODE0n.CMD. The CODE0n.CMD routines load the normal run-time microcode for the appropriate processor configuration. Table 24-1 lists the command files used with specific processor configurations.
3. The HALT/RESTART switch is checked. If it is set to HALT, the processor enters console mode and prints the console command prompt:

   >>>

   If the HALT/RESTART switch is set to RESTART, processing continues using the default bootstrap command file (DEFBOO.CMD).
4. There are many commands that the console command language understands. All three commands that cause a VMS system to be bootstrapped execute command files located on the console TU58.

   The commands and their associated command files are:

Command	Command File
B	DEFBOO.CMD
B dev	devBOO.CMD
@file-spec	file-spec

These command files identify the system disk and other characteristics of the bootstrap operation by loading general registers R0 through R5 with parameters that will be interpreted by the primary bootstrap program, VMB.

5. The following three commands in the bootstrap command files display the contents of SP (to identify the staring address in physical memory) and then load the primary bootstrap program, VMB, from the TU58 into the good 64K byte block of VAX memory, leaving the first page free:

```
E SP
LPS:@ VMB.EXE
S @
```

The free page will contain a data structure called a restart parameter block (RPB). The RPB is used by VMB and by the restart routines, in the event of a powerfail or other system failure. The third command, the START command, transfers control to the first byte of VMB.

VMB.EXE is described in greater detail in section 24.2.

24.1.2 VAX-11/750 Initial Bootstrap Operation

The console program on the VAX-11/750 resides in read-only memory within the CPU. When the CPU is in console mode, this program (and nothing else, such as a user program or the VMS operating system itself) is executing. When a VAX-11/750 system is initialized, the console program is the first in a series of programs that execute before the primary bootstrap program (VMB) executes. These programs include the following:

- The console subsystem, which initializes the CPU, locates a page-aligned 64K byte block of good memory, and passes control to a device-specific ROM program.
- A boot-device ROM, which reads logical block number 0 (LBN 0, the so-called boot block) from the bootstrap device into the first page of the good memory block.
- The boot block program, which reads a file from the bootstrap device into memory. When a VMS system is being bootstrapped, this file will always be VMB, the primary bootstrap program.

A list of the programs that execute during the initial CPU-dependent phase of initialization is contained in Table 24-3.

24.1.2.1 VAX-11/750 Console Program.
In the VAX-11/730 and VAX-11/780 the console program can execute indirect command files. Rather than using command files to pass information to VMB, the console program on the VAX-11/750 constructs the information from the device selected by the BOOT DEVICE switch and the bootstrap command itself. The console program on a

Table 24-2: Processor-Dependent Files Used to Bootstrap the VAX-11/730

Program Executing	Where Program Is Located	CPU Used by Program	Purpose of This Program
Console Microprocessor ROM Bootstrap	ROM in Console Subsystem	Console Microprocessor	Read TU58 boot block into memory and execute code contained there
TU58 Boot Block Program	Logical Block 0 on Console TU58	Console Microprocessor	Locate CONSOL.EXE, read it into memory, and pass control to it
CONSOL.EXE	Somewhere on Console TU58, An RT-11 Directory-Structured Device	Console Microprocessor	Put VAX-11/730 into known state, load general registers, and execute the next two indirect command files
POWER.CMD	Console TU58	Console Microprocessor	Locate 64K byte block of good memory, check configuration of the machine (1)
CODE0n.CMD	Console TU58	Console Microprocessor microcode (1)	Configuration-dependent
Bootstrap Indirect Command File (Usually DEFBOO.CMD)	Console TU58	Console Microprocessor	Load VMB into VAX memory and transfer control to it
VMB.EXE	Console TU58	VAX-11/730	(See Table 24-5)

(1) When POWER.CMD determines the configuration of the machine, it returns a value to CONSOL.EXE. This value is then used as n to determine which CODE0n.CMD to execute.

All programs execute in the VAX-11/750 CPU. There is no front-end processor performing any of the bootstrap operations.

Table 24-3: Processor-Dependent Files Used to Bootstrap the VAX-11/750

Program Executing	Where Program Is Located	Purpose of This Program
Console Program (Executes Microcode)	ROM in VAX-11/750 CPU	Locate block of good memory, determine action to be taken, and pass control to device-specific program
Device-Specific Program in ROM	ROM in I/O address space of VAX-11/750 CPU	Load boot block (LBN 0) of designated device into memory and pass control to it
Boot Block Program	Logical Block Number of System Device	Locate primary bootstrap program on system device (or console storage device) by logical block number and pass control to it
VMB.EXE	Specific Logical Block Number on Boot Device System Disk or TU58)	(See Table 24-5)
BOOT58 (Not Used During Bootstrap from System Disk)	Specific Logical Block Number on Console Block Storage Device	Use indirect command files or enhanced console commands

VAX-11/750 is stored in read-only memory within the CPU, allowing bootstrap operations on the VAX-11/750 to execute more quickly, at the price of some flexibility. The console program can initiate a bootstrap sequence for five different reasons:

- The system is powered on and the power-on selector switch is in the bootstrap position.
- The B (Boot) command is typed while the system is in console mode.
- A HALT instruction is executed and the power-on selector switch is in the bootstrap position.
- The following instruction is executed:

```
MTPR    #^XF02,#PR$_TXDB
```

The VMS bugcheck routine uses this mechanism on all CPUs to automatically reboot the system after a fatal software crash. (This automatic reboot capability can be inhibited by clearing the SYSBOOT flag BUGREBOOT.)
- An attempt to restart the system after a power failure recovery does not succeed, and the power-on selector switch is in the restart/bootstrap position.

Note that the implementation of the VAX-11/750 prevents unattended restarts (the last three reasons shown in the list above) unless the system device is unit 0 on the first controller of a given type such as the first MASSBUS adapter.

The important steps that are performed by the console program include the following:

- Locating 64K bytes of contiguous, error-free, page-aligned memory to be used by later stages of the bootstrap.
- Loading the first 128 map registers in the UNIBUS adapter to address this block of memory (a step not taken when using the console block storage device as a bootstrap device).
- Loading the general registers with parameters to be used by later stages of the bootstrap.
- Passing control to the device ROM selected by the bootstrap device selector switch.

24.1.2.2   Device-Specific ROM Program. The device ROM program consists of two main pieces, a control routine and a device-specific subroutine. This program simply reads the boot block (LBN 0) of the selected device into the first page of the good memory block and passes control to it (at an address 12 bytes past the beginning of the program).

24.1.2.3   Bootblock Program. This bootblock program has a single purpose, which depends on the type of bootstrap device specified to the console program. When a system bootstrap device is specified, the bootblock program loads the primary bootstrap program (VMB) into memory and passes control to it. When the console block storage device is selected, the bootblock program can pass control to an enhanced command processor called BOOT58. The bootblock program does not contain any I/O support. It uses the driver subroutine contained in the device ROM program.

There are three longwords of header information before the body of the bootblock program. These longwords contain the following:

1. The size of the primary bootstrap program
2. The starting logical block number of the primary bootstrap program
3. A relative offset into the block of good memory where this program is to be loaded

These longwords are loaded by the program WRITEBOOT when the boot block is written. Notice that the boot block has the LBN of the primary bootstrap program hard-coded into the block. If the position of the primary bootstrap program on the volume changes, WRITEBOOT must be executed to rewrite the boot block with new information.

Note that the location of VMB by the VAX-11/750 boot block program is the only situation in all of the VAX/VMS operating system where a file is located by a logical block number coded into another program. Thus, VMB on a VAX-11/750 system disk is the only file that is not free to move without external intervention (running WRITEBOOT) to preserve system integrity.

527

24.1.2.4 **BOOT58.** The console block storage device on the VAX-11/750 (TU58 cartridge) is not used during a normal bootstrap operation, in contrast to the VAX-11/730 bootstrap and VAX-11/780 bootstrap, which always read VMB and a command file from the console block storage device. However, the VAX-11/750 has an alternate bootstrap path that uses the TU58, which provides the following:

- Indirect command file capability
- An enhanced console command language
- The ability to bootstrap a system in the event that a boot block becomes corrupted

A stand-alone program called BOOT58 is an enhanced console command processor loaded from the TU58 that provides these features. BOOT58 is loaded by selecting the console block storage device (DDA0:) as the bootstrap device, either by the device selector switch or with the command:

```
>>>B DDA0:
```

Note that the drive DDA0: must contain the TU58 tape cartridge.

The boot block on the TU58 contains a program just like the boot block program on a system device. This program contains the LBN of BOOT58 (because it was put there by WRITEBOOT). Once BOOT58 prints its prompt, commands or indirect command file specifications can be entered.

24.1.3 **VAX-11/780 Initial Bootstrap Operation**

The console subsystem on the VAX-11/780 consists of a separate processor, an LSI-11 with its own mass storage device (RX01 floppy disk) and terminal. The fact that the console subsystem on a VAX-11/780 includes its own processor implies that the console system can perform certain (but not all) operations while the VAX-11/780 CPU is performing its own operations. Note that this is only true for the VAX-11/780.

The initial bootstrap programs that execute in order to initialize a VAX/VMS system on a VAX-11/780 are PDP-11 programs executing in the LSI-11. These programs (CONSOL.SYS and the boot block program) execute PDP-11 instructions as opposed to VAX-11 instructions (which are executed by the rest of the VMS operating system and also by the VAX-11/750 bootstrap programs).

1. The first program that executes in the LSI-11 is a bootstrap program located in read-only memory (ROM) that causes a program located on logical block number zero of the console floppy (sectors 1, 3, 5, and 7) to be loaded into LSI memory.
2. The program located at logical block number zero is a copy of the bootstrap program used by the RT-11 operating system. The RT-11 bootstrap, which understands the RT-11 file system, looks for a specific file (the

monitor), loads it into memory, and transfers control to it. (The RT-11 directory structure and bootstrap program are described in the *RT-11 Software Support Manual*.)

The bootstrap program that is found on the VAX-11/780 console floppy diskette looks for a program called CONSOL.SYS.

3. The console program loads the file WCSxxx.PAT from the floppy diskette into the VAX-11/780 diagnostic control store and then prints its prompt (>>>) on the console terminal. If there is a version mismatch between the WCS and either the PCS or the FPLA, an error message is displayed on the console terminal.

4. There are many commands that the console command language understands. The three commands that cause a VMS system to be bootstrapped execute command files located on the console floppy.

The commands and their associated command files are the following:

Command	Command File
BOOT	DEFBOO.CMD
BOOT dev	devBOO.CMD
@file-spec	filespec

These command files identify the system disk and other characteristics of the bootstrap operation by loading general registers R0 through R5 with parameters that will be interpreted by the primary bootstrap program (VMB).

The DEFBOO.CMD command file is also used to bootstrap the VAX-11/780 if any of the following conditions occur:

• A HALT instruction is executed and the AUTO RESTART switch is in the ON position.

• The following instruction is executed:

```
MTPR    #@XF02,#PR$_TXDB
```

This instruction tells the console subsystem to reboot the VMS operating system. The VMS bugcheck routine uses this mechanism on all CPUs to automatically reboot the system after a fatal software crash. (This automatic reboot capability can be inhibited by clearing the SYSBOOT parameter BUGREBOOT.)

• An attempt to restart the system after a power failure recovery does not succeed, and the AUTO RESTART switch is in the ON position.

Note that the DEFBOO.CMD command file used to bootstrap either processor on a VAX-11/782 multiprocessing system are not the same as the command files described here. The contents and operation of DEFBOO.CMD on a VAX-11/782 are described in Chapter 28.

5. The command files also contain the following commands:

```
START 20003000
WAIT
```

These two commands cause a program located in read-only memory in the first memory controller on the SBI to execute. The command file waits until the memory ROM program completes before executing its next command. (The memory ROM program signals the console program that it is done by writing the "software done" signal into one of the console registers with the instruction:

```
MTPR    #^XF01,#PR$_TXDB
```

The program in the memory controller ROM performs a primitive memory sizing operation in an effort to locate 64K bytes of error-free, page-aligned, contiguous physical memory that can be used by the remaining bootstrap programs.

The output of this program is an address 200 (hex) bytes beyond the beginning of the first good page. This address is loaded into SP. (In a typical system, one with no errors in the first 64K bytes, the contents of SP are 200.)

6. The following three commands cause the primary bootstrap program VMB to be loaded from the floppy disk into the good 64K byte block of VAX memory, leaving the first page free. This page will contain a data structure called a restart parameter block (RPB) that is used by both VMB and by the restart routines in the event of a powerfail or other system failure. The START command transfers control to VMB at its first location.

```
EXAMINE SP
LOAD VMB.EXESTART:@
START @
```

The initial bootstrap programs are listed in Table 24-4.

24.2 PRIMARY BOOTSTRAP PROGRAM

The first program that is common to all VMS systems, independent of CPU type, is the primary bootstrap program (VMB). The processor-independent files and programs used in bootstrap operations are listed in Table 24-5. The only differences between the initiation of VMB on a VAX-11/750 system and on VAX-11/730 and VAX-11/780 systems is the source of the program (the system disk on a 750 system versus the console block storage device on 730 and 780 systems), the method used to load R0 through R5, and the location of the program that passes control to VMB (the boot block VAX-11 program on a 750 versus the console microprocessor programs on the 730 and 780). VMB performs two major steps.

• It locates and determines the size of physical memory on the system.
• It locates the secondary bootstrap program, loads it into memory, and transfers control to it.

Table 24-4: Processor-Dependent Files Used to Bootstrap the VAX-11/780

Program Executing	Where Program Is Located	CPU Used by Program	Purpose of This Program
LSI-11 ROM Bootstrap	ROM in LSI-11 I/O Space	LSI-11	Read floppy boot block into memory and execute code contained there
Floppy Boot Block Program	Logical Block 0 on Console Floppy	LSI-11	Locate CONSOL.SYS, read it into memory, and pass control to it
CONSOL.SYS	Somewhere on Console Floppy, an RT-11 directory-structured device	LSI-11	Put VAX-11/780 into known state, load general registers, and invoke memory sizing program
Good Memory Locater	ROM in First Memory Controller on SBI	VAX-11/780	Locate 64K byte block of error-free memory
CONSOL.SYS (After Waiting for Memory ROM Program to Complete)		LSI-11	Load VMB into VAX memory and transfer control to it
VMB.EXE	Console Floppy	VAX-11/780	(See Table 24-5)

Table 24-5: Processor-Independent Bootstrap Files

Program Executing (process context)	Purpose of This Program	Files Used by This Program	Use of This File
VMB.EXE (1) (Stand-Alone program)	Primary Bootstrap Program	SYSBOOT.EXE (C)	Opened and Read into Memory
SYSBOOT.EXE (C) (Stand-Alone Program)	Secondary Bootstrap Program (Configures System and Reads Executive into Memory)	Parameter Files Created by SYSGEN (C)	Used to Configure System
		SYS.EXE	Opened and Read into Memory
		TTDRIVER.EXE	Opened and Read into Memory
		PAGEFILE.SYS	Opened and Read into Memory
		SYSLOAxxx.EXE	Opened and Read into Memory
		yyDRIVER.EXE	Opened and Read into Memory
		INILOA.EXE	Opened and Read into Memory
		SCSLOA.EXE	Opened and Read into Memory
SYS.EXE (Module INIT) (No Process Yet)	Executive Initialization	SCSLOA	
SYS.EXE (Module SWAPPER) (SWAPPER Process)	First Process Selected for Execution	SYSINIT.EXE	Image Specified to Create Process
SYSINIT.EXE (SYSINIT Process)	Continue Initialization in Process Context	RMS.EXE	Mapped as Pageable System Section
		SYS$MESSAGE:SYSMSG.EXE	Mapped as Pageable System Section
		SWAPFILE.SYS	Opened and Initialized
		DUMPFILE.SYS	Opened and Initialized
		F11zACP.EXE Process	Image That Executes in DxcuACP
		STARTUP.COM	SYS$INPUT for STARTUP Process
		LOGINOUT.EXE Process	Image Specified to Create STARTUP

Table 24-5: Processor-Independent Bootstrap Files *(continued)*

Program Executing (process context)	Purpose of This Program	Files Used by This Program	Use of This File
LOGINOUT.EXE (STARTUP Process)	Initial Image that Executes in Interactive Job	DCL.EXE (2) SYS$SHARE:DCLTABLES.EXE Activation	Mapped into P1 Space of STARTUP Process with Merged Image
INSTALL.EXE (STARTUP Process)	Install Privileged and Shareable Images	All Privileged, Shareable, and Installed Images	All Installed Images Are Set up as Known Images
SYSGEN.EXE (STARTUP Process)	Autoconfigure I/O Devices, Load Drivers, and Create I/O Data Base	All Device Drivers Loaded as a Result of AUTOCONFIGURE ALL	Drivers for All Configured Devices Are Loaded into Nonpaged Pool
RMSSHARE.EXE (STARTUP Process)	Allocate Block of Paged Pool for File Sharing	None	

(C) These files must be contiguous because they are loaded by the primitive ACP routines that are a part of the executive image.

(1) VMB must be contiguous because it is loaded by either the boot block program on the VAX-11/750 or the console program CONSOL.SYS on the VAX-11/730 and VAX-11/780.

(2) The authorization file is not used by LOGINOUT here because the STARTUP process is created with a flag that dictates that authorization should be skipped to allow totally automatic initialization and to eliminate the need for an initialization account in the authorization file.

24.2.1   Motivation for Two Bootstrap Programs

VMB and the secondary bootstrap program, SYSBOOT, are conceptually one program. The VAX-11/780 initialization (initially implemented for VAX/VMS Version 1.0) required that the initial bootstrap program reside on the console floppy. Rather than impose artificial restrictions on the size of the bootstrap program, it was divided into two pieces:

- A primary piece that resides on the floppy disk and whose only real purpose is to locate the secondary piece
- A secondary piece that resides on the system disk (with no real limits on its size) that performs the bulk of the bootstrap operation

Once this division was achieved, VMB became a more flexible tool that could be used to load programs other than the secondary bootstrap program SYSBOOT. In order to preserve this flexibility and maintain as much CPU independence as possible in the later stages of the bootstrap, the division of the bootstrap into primary and secondary pieces was preserved and enhanced in VAX/VMS Version 2.0.

In VAX/VMS Version 3.0 a number of enhancements were made to VMB. These enhancements included support for machines with more than eight megabytes of memory, support for new devices, and changes to the argument list passed to SYSBOOT. Because a user might attempt to bootstrap a Version 3.0 system using an earlier version of VMB, it is desirable to maintain backward compatibility between versions of VMB and SYSBOOT. Portions of SYSBOOT check the version of VMB being used and take appropriate action, depending on the relative versions. Backward compatibility is maintained by not removing functionality from VMB that is required by older versions of SYSBOOT.

VMB thus has become a general purpose bootstrap program that can be used for several options other than initializing a VMS system. There are three options currently available in addition to initializing a VAX/VMS system by loading SYSBOOT:

- The diagnostic supervisor [SYSMAINT]DIAGBOOT.EXE can be loaded in place of SYSBOOT.
- VMB can be directed to solicit for the name of any stand-alone program to be loaded into VAX memory. This program might be a stand-alone diagnostic program, an alternate secondary bootstrap, or even another operating system. The file system routines and control transfer mechanism used by VMB place some restrictions on this file.

  —The volume (the system disk) containing the file that VMB will load must be a Files-11 volume (Structure Level 1 or 2).
  —The file containing this program must be contiguous.

—Its transfer address must be the first byte in the first block of the program. (If the file is linked as a system image with a base address of zero, its transfer address must be at location zero.)

—The code in the program must be position independent.

- VMB can load the contents of a bootstrap block from the system disk and execute the program that it finds there. In general, this boot block is logical block number zero on the volume. The VAX-11/780 bootstrap sequences allow an alternate boot block number to be passed to VMB in R4.

  Passing control to a boot block program is the feature that makes VMB an extremely flexible tool. One possible use for a bootstrap program is support for a file system other than Files-11.

  The boot block option is only useful on a VAX-11/780. The VAX-11/730 and VAX-11/750 bootstrap sequence allows control to be passed directly from the console program to a boot block program without using VMB at all. That is, if a special bootstrap through a boot block program was required, the normal VAX-11/730 or VAX-11/750 sequence could be used but the special VAX-11/780 option would be required.

If none of these options is selected by setting the corresponding flags in R5, VMB enters its default path, which loads the VMS secondary bootstrap program SYSBOOT into memory and transfers control to it.

24.2.2   Operation of VMB

VMB determines the type of bootstrap that is being performed and the identity of the system disk, by the contents of registers R0 through R5. Tables 24-6 and 24-7 summarize the input parameters that are passed to VMB. These parameters are saved by VMB in a data structure called a restart parameter block (RPB) (see Table 24-8) and are used by later programs in the bootstrap sequence.

The steps that VMB takes to load SYSBOOT into memory are as follows:

1. VMB sets up a system control block with all interrupt and exception vectors (except TBIT and BPT exceptions) pointing to a single service routine. The vectors for TBIT and BPT exceptions are loaded with the addresses of exception service routines in XDELTA, linked as a part of the VMB image.

   Figure 24-2 illustrates the layout of physical memory once VMB has set up its SCB.

2. VMB then reads the processor ID register (PR$_SID) to determine the CPU type. VMB uses the CPU type as the basis of decisions about which piece of CPU-dependent code to execute. A similar step is performed later by SYSBOOT for the use of both SYSBOOT and the executive.

535

Table 24-6: Register Input to VMB (Primary Bootstrap Program)

Register	Contents
R0	Bootstrap Device Type Code

<31:16> Type-Specific Information
- MASSBUS: MBZ
- UNIBUS: Optional Vector Address
  - 0 => Use Default Vector

<15:8> MBZ

<7:0> Bootstrap Device Type Code

0	MASSBUS device (RM03/5,RP04/5/6,RM80)
1	RK06/7
2	RL01/2
3	IDC on VAX-11/730
4-16	Reserved for UNIBUS devices
17	UDA-50
18-31	Reserved
32	HSC on CI
33-63	Reserved for UNIBUS devices
64	Console block storage device

R1 Bootstrap Device's Bus Address

11/730 and	<31:4>	MBZ
11/780	<3:0>	TR number of adapter
11/750	<31:24>	MBZ
	<23:0>	Address of the I/O page for the boot device's UNIBUS

R2 Bootstrap Device Controller Information

UNIBUS:	<31:18>	MBZ
	<17:0>	UNIBUS address of the device's CSR
MASSBUS:	<31:4>	MBZ
	<3:0>	Adapter's controller/formatter number
CI:	<31:8>	MBZ
	<7:0>	HSC port number

R3 Boot Device Unit Number

R4 Logical Block Number of Boot Block (VAX-11/780 Only)

R5 Software Boot Control Flags

NOTE: The hardware or the CONSOLE program sets up the next three registers after a system crash or power failure. The halt code contained in AP is used by VMS on halt/restart to determine whether the powerfail recovery logic is to bugcheck or recover. These registers are not used by VMB.

R10 Halt PC
R11 Halt PSL
AP Halt code

NOTE: The memory ROM program returns information about a block of good memory in SP.

SP <base-address + ^X200> of 64Kb of good memory

Table 24-7: Bootstrap Control Flags to VMB (Contents of R5)

Bit Position	Symbolic Name	Meaning
0	RPB$V_CONV	Conversational boot. At various points in the system boot procedure, the bootstrap code solicits parameters and other input from the console terminal.
1	RPB$V_DEBUG	Debug. If this flag is set, VMS maps the code for the XDELTA debugger into the system page tables of the running system.
2	RPB$V_INIBPT	Initial breakpoint. If RPB$V_DEBUG is set, VMS executes a BPT instruction in module INIT immediately after enabling mapping.
3	RPB$V_BBLOCK	Secondary boot from boot block. Secondary bootstrap is a single 512-byte block, whose LBN is specified in R4.
4	RPB$V_DIAG	Diagnostic boot. Secondary bootstrap is image called [SYSMAINT]DIAGBOOT.EXE.
5	RPB$V_BOOBPT	Bootstrap breakpoint. Stops the primary and secondary bootstraps with breakpoint instructions before testing memory.
6	RPB$V_HEADER	Image header. Takes the transfer address of the secondary bootstrap image from that file's image header. If RPB$V_HEADER is not set, transfers control to the first byte of the secondary boot file.
7	RPB$V_NOTEST	Memory test inhibit. Sets a bit in the PFN bitmap for each page of memory present. Does not test the memory.
8	RPB$V_SOLICT	File name. VMB prompts for the name of a secondary bootstrap file.
9	RPB$V_HALT	Halt before transfer. Executes a HALT instruction before transferring control to the secondary bootstrap.
10	RPB$V_NOPFND	No PFN deletion (not currently used). Intended to tell VMB not to read a file from the boot device that identifies bad or reserved memory pages, so that VMB does not mark these pages as valid in the PFN bitmap.
11	RPB$V_MPM	Specifies that multiport memory is to be used for the total executive memory requirement; no local memory is to be used. This bit applies to the VAX-11/782 only. If the bit RPB$V_DIAG is set, the diagnostic supervisor enters AUTOTEST mode.
12	RPB$V_USEMPM	Specifies that multiport memory can be used in addition to local memory (as though both were one single pool of pages).
13	RPB$V_MEMTEST	Specifies that a more extensive algorithm is to be used when testing main memory for hardware uncorrectable (RDS) errors.
14	RPB$V_FINDMEM	Requests use of MA780 memory if MS780 memory is insufficient for bootstrap. This flag is used when performing software installations on a VAX-11/782.
<31:28>	RPB$V_TOPSYS	Specifies the top-level directory number for system disks with multiple systems.

Table 24-8: Contents of the Restart Parameter Block

Mnemonic	Item	Size in Bytes	Loaded by	Special Uses
RPB$L_BASE	Physical Base Address of 64K Block	4	VMB	Used to Locate RPB (Contents=Address)
RPB$L_RESTART	Physical Address of RESTART Routine	4	INIT	Used to Locate RESTART Routine
RPB$L_CHKSUM	Checksum of First 31 Longwords of RESTART Routine	4	INIT	Consistency Check on RPB and RESTART Routine
RPB$L_RSTSTFLG	Restart in Progress Flag	4	Set by Hardware Cleared by INIT Cleared by RESTART	Prevent Nested Restarts
RPB$L_HALTPC	PC at HALT/Restart	4	VMB	
RPB$L_HALTPSL	PSL at HALT/Restart	4	VMB	
RPB$L_HALTCODE	Code Describing Reason for Restart	4	VMB	
RPB$L_BOOTRx	Saved Bootstrap Parameters (R0 through R5)	24	VMB	
RPB$L_IOVEC	Address of $QIO Vector in Bootstrap Driver	4	VMB,INIT	Used by BUGCHECK to dump physical memory
RPB$L_IOVECSZ	Size (in bytes) of Bootstrap $QIO Routine	4	VMB	
RPB$L_FILLBN	Logical Block Number of Secondary Bootstrap File	4	VMB	
RPB$L_FILSIZ	Size (in blocks) of Secondary Bootstrap File	4	VMB	
RPB$Q_PFNMAP	Descriptor of PFN Bitmap	8	VMB	
	Size (in bytes) of PFN Bitmap	4	VMB	
	Physical Address of Start of PFN Bitmap	4	VMB	
RPB$L_PFNCNT	Count of Physical Pages	4	VMB	
RPB$L_SVASPT	System Virtual Address of System Page Table	4	INIT	Used by RESTART
RPB$L_CSRPHY	Physical Address of UBA Device CSR	4	VMB	
RPB$L_CSRVIR	Virtual Address of UBA Device CSR	4	INILOA	

Table 24-8: Contents of the Restart Parameter Block *(continued)*

Mnemonic	Item	Size in Bytes	Loaded by	Special Uses
RPB$L_ADPPHY	Physical Address of Adapter Configuration Register	4	VMB	
RPB$L_ADPVIR	Virtual Address of Adapter Configuration Register	4	INILOA	
	Descriptor of Bootstrap Device	4	VMB	
RPB$W_UNIT	Unit Number	2	VMB	
RPB$B_DEVTYP	Device Type Code	1	VMB	
RPB$B_SLAVE	Slave Unit Number	1	VMB	
RPB$T_FILE	Secondary Bootstrap File Name (Counted ASCII String)	40	VMB	
RPB$B_CONFREG	Byte Array of Adapter Types	16	VMB	
PB$B_HDRPGCNT	Count of Header Pages in Secondary Bootstrap Image	1	VMB	
RPB$B_BOOTNDT	Nexus Device Type of Boot Adapter	1		
	Spare (to Preserve Natural Alignment)	2	—	
RPB$L_ISP	Powerfail Interrupt Stack Pointer	4	Power Fail Routine	Restored by RESTART Routine
RPB$L_PCBB	Saved Process Control Block Base Register	4	Power Fail Routine	Restored by RESTART Routine
RPB$L_SBR	Saved System Base Register	4	INIT, Power Fail Routine	Restored by RESTART Routine
RPB$L_SCBB	Saved System Control Block Base Register	4	INIT, Power Fail Routine	Restored by RESTART Routine
RPB$L_SISR	Saved Software Interrupt Summary Register	4	Power Fail Routine	Restored by RESTART Routine
RPB$L_SLR	Saved System Length Register	4	INIT, Power Fail Routine	Restored by RESTART Routine
RPB$L_MEMDSC	Longword Array of Memory Descriptors	64	VMB	Used by BUGCHECK to dump physical memory
RPB$L_BUGCHK	Address of bugcheck loop for VAX-11/782 attached processor	4	VMB	
RPB$B_WAIT	Bugcheck loop code for VAX-11/782 attached processor	4	VMB,MP.EXE	Before MP.EXE is run, contains a jump to self

539

3. If the bootstrap breakpoint flag (RPB$V_BOOBPT, R5<5>) is set, VMB executes a BPT instruction, which transfers control to XDELTA, linked as a part of the VMB image. This breakpoint is useful in localizing hardware problems that are preventing a system from being started.

4. The input parameters to VMB are loaded into the restart parameter block (see Table 24-8).

5. A bitmap is set up to describe all physical memory that is to be used as main memory. This map includes a bit that is set for every physical memory page in the system that is free from errors. The routine that tests for memory errors is CPU specific.

   If the processor is the primary processor of a VAX-11/782, the flag RPB$V_MPM is used to indicate that only multiport memory should be used as main memory; local memory is to be ignored. If this flag is clear, multiport memory is ignored, and only local memory is used as main memory.

6. If the processor is a VAX-11/780, VMB looks for a CI780 port. If one is found, the CI microcode is located (file CI780.BIN on the console floppy) and loaded into memory and the flag VMB$V_LOAD_SCS in VMB_FLAGS is set, to indicate to SYSBOOT that the loadable SCS code is to be loaded.

7. The bus adapter for the bootstrap device is initialized (in a CPU-specific fashion). The bootstrap driver is initialized, if needed.

8. The secondary bootstrap image is identified (by flags and values in R5 and, optionally, information solicited from the console terminal). The order of precedence in choosing a secondary bootstrap image is the following:

   a. If the R5 flag called RPB$V_BBLOCK is set, a boot block program is read from the system disk. R4 contains the logical number of the disk block that contains the secondary bootstrap image. (This function is used only on the VAX-11/780 processor.)

   b. If the R5 flag called RPB$V_SOLICT is set, the name of the secondary bootstrap image is explicitly requested from the console terminal.

   c. If the R5 flag called RPB$V_DIAG is set, the diagnostic supervisor is loaded. This option causes a file called DIAGBOOT.EXE to be used as the secondary bootstrap image.

   d. The absence of any of the three options (a, b, or c) causes SYSBOOT.EXE to be used as the secondary bootstrap program. Before SYSBOOT.EXE can be located, the value in R5 at PRB$V_TOPSYS must be evaluated to determine which of the 16 systems on a multiple-system disk is being bootstrapped. By default, the high four bits of R5 are zero, and so, [SYS0.SYSEXE] is searched for SYSBOOT. For backward compatibility, if SYSBOOT is not found in [SYS0.SYSEXE], VMB looks in [SYSEXE].

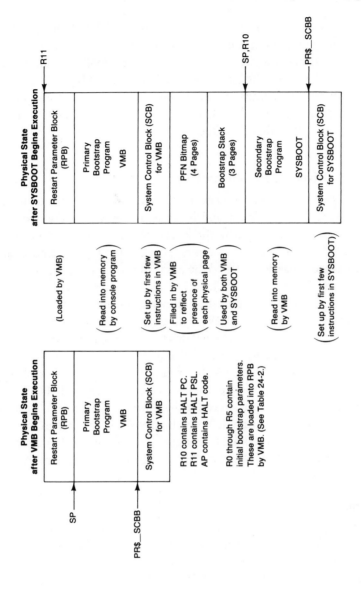

Figure 24-2
Physical Memory Layouts Used by VMB and SYSBOOT

9. If the system is not being booted with XDELTA, XDELTA is disabled.

10. The image is read into memory (see Figure 24-2) and control is passed to it at its transfer address. This address is normally the first byte in the image. However, setting the flag RPB$V_HEADER in R5 directs VMB to use the transfer address stored in the image header of the secondary bootstrap program, provided that the secondary bootstrap image was produced by the VAX-11 Linker.

24.2.3 Bootstrap Driver and I/O Subroutines

VMB contains a skeleton Queue I/O Request routine and device driver to perform its I/O. This driver and routine are loaded into nonpaged pool by INIT for possible later use by the bugcheck code (see Chapter 8).

The VMB image actually contains simple drivers for all possible system devices. Once it has determined the name of the bootstrap device (from register contents), VMB moves the driver code for the selected device so that it is adjacent to the $QIO routine, thus allowing the entire bootstrap I/O system to be moved with a single MOVC3 instruction. The location and the size of the $QIO routine plus the selected driver are loaded into the restart parameter block for later use by SYSBOOT and INIT.

This simple operation by VMB prevents nonpaged pool from being loaded with a set of bootstrap device drivers that are never used. That is, the only bootstrap driver that is preserved for the life of a VMS system is the bootstrap device driver for the system device, which is selected through input to VMB. All other bootstrap drivers are linked into the VMB image but disappear along with the rest of VMB when the VMS operating system is finally initialized.

24.2.4 File Operations

One of the problems that must be solved in any bootstrap operation involves location of files before the file system itself is in full operation. In a VMS system, the problem is faced with every file operation that must be performed before the system disk ACP (ancillary control process) is created.

The VMS operating system solves this problem by including two special object modules (FILEREAD and FILERWIO) in the executive image. The modules consist of a series of subroutines that can perform some primitive file operations on a Files-11 volume. The volumes can be either Structure Level 1 or 2. One of these modules (FILEREAD) is also linked into both the VMB and SYSBOOT images.

24.3 SECONDARY BOOTSTRAP PROGRAM (SYSBOOT)

The secondary bootstrap program, SYSBOOT, executes when VMB is directed to load a VMS system. Most of the operations that are performed by code that executes before the VMS operating system exists are performed by SYSBOOT. VMB has already tested main memory, read SYSBOOT into memory, and transferred control to it. SYSBOOT performs three major functions.

- The system is configured, which means that a set of adjustable SYSBOOT parameters (either the ones from the last system, which are contained in SYS.EXE, or a set of parameter explicitly selected through a conversational bootstrap) is loaded. Other system parameters whose values depend on the values of the adjustable parameters are calculated.
- A portion of system configuration that deserves separate mention involves the mapping of system virtual address space. The sizes of many of the pieces of system address space depend on the values of one or more SYSBOOT parameters. The calculations that SYSBOOT performs and the results of these calculations are detailed in Chapter 26.

  In addition to sizing the pieces of system space, SYSBOOT also sets up the system page table to map many of the pieces of the nonpaged and paged executive. In a related step, SYSBOOT prepares a P0 page table that allows memory management to be turned on. (This last step is described in Chapter 25.)
- The last major step that SYSBOOT performs is to read the various portions of the executive image (SYS.EXE) into the (physical) pages set aside when the system page table was set up. Other files (see Table 24-5) are also located and read into space allocated in nonpaged pool; their locations in pool are passed on to INIT in a bootstrap parameter block, defined by module BOOPARAM (see Table 24-9).

There is little CPU-dependent code in SYSBOOT. Most of the CPU dependencies have already been taken care of by VMB. However, SYSBOOT does load the CPU-dependent code used during normal VMS system execution.

24.3.1 Detailed Operation of SYSBOOT

SYSBOOT begins operation with the physical memory layout pictured in Figure 24-2. R11 points to the beginning of the restart parameter block. The following steps describe the operation of SYSBOOT.

1. SYSBOOT rewrites the system control block built by VMB with all vectors containing the address of a service routine in SYSBOOT. The vectors for TBIT and BPT are redirected to exception service routines in XDELTA, linked as a part of the SYSBOOT image. The machine check vector is modified to point to a customized exception service routine.
2. If the bootstrap breakpoint flag (RPB$V_BOOBPT, R5<5>) is set, SYSBOOT executes a BPT instruction, which transfers control to XDELTA, linked as a part of the SYSBOOT image.

   Note that the same flag controls breakpoint execution in both VMB

Table 24-9: Information passed from SYSBOOT to INIT

Global Location	Size	Description
BOO$GL_DSKDRV	Longword	Address of bootstrap device driver in nonpaged pool
BOO$GL_SYSLOA	Longword	Address of CPU-dependent image in nonpaged pool
BOO$GL_TRMDRV	Longword	Address of TTDRIVER.EXE in nonpaged pool
BOO$GQ_INILOA	Quadword	Pool descriptor for loadable initialization code
BOO$GL_NPAGEDYN	Longword	Size of nonpaged pool remaining (in bytes)
BOO$GL_SPLITADR	Longword	Address of bottom of IRP lookaside list
BOO$GL_LRPSIZE	Longword	Size of large request packets (in bytes)
BOO$GL_LRPMIN	Longword	Minimum size of request that can be allocated an LRP
BOO$GL_LRPSPLIT	Longword	Base address of LRP lookaside list
BOO$GL_SRPSPLIT	Longword	Base address of SRP lookaside list
BOO$GQ_FILCACHE	Quadword	Pool descriptor for FIL$OPENFILE cache
BOO$GL_BOOTCB	Longword	Address of boot control block in pool
BOO$GT_TOPSYS	10 Bytes	Top-level system directory (ASCIC string)
BOO$GB_SYSTEMID	6 Bytes	48-bit SCS system ID of remote port
BOO$GL_PRTDRV	Longword	Address of a port driver in pool
BOO$GL_UCODE	Longword	Address of port microcode in pool
BOO$GL_SCSLOA	Longword	Address of SCS loadable code in pool

and SYSBOOT. This flag can be used in locating a hardware problem or other problem that is preventing system initialization.

3. The version of VMB used to load SYSBOOT is checked. If an older version of VMB was used, SYSBOOT performs operations not performed by VMB. This step allows backward compatibility for versions of VMB. The following items are checked:

- Support for more than 8M bytes of memory
- Bootstrap nexus device type
- Contents of the SYSBOOT argument list

- Presence of the FIL$OPENFILE cache
- Memory descriptors in the RPB

4. The PR$_SID register is read to determine the CPU type. This type is stored for later use by code whose execution depends on the specific CPU type. This value, stored in global location EXE$GB_CPUTYPE, is used in several ways:

   - It will determine which pieces of CPU-dependent code within SYS-BOOT execute. For example, there is a check whether the hardware ECO status is at the level required to support a VAX/VMS system. On a VAX-11/730 and VAX-11/750, the hardware ECO level and microcode revision level are the values that are checked. On a VAX-11/780, this test requires communication with the console program to obtain the version numbers of the PCS, WCS, and FPLA.
   - The CPU type will determine the name of the separate image file (SYS-LOA730.EXE, SYSLOA750.EXE, or SYSLOA780.EXE) that contains CPU-dependent routines. This image is opened (located) and read into nonpaged pool by SYSBOOT.
   - Those portions of CPU-specific code that are selected at execution time (with suitable test and branch instructions) will use the CPU type as the object of the tests.
   - The size of the system control block, a part of the overall sizing effort of system address space described in step 9 and Chapter 26, depends on the CPU type.

   The different strategies that are used to handle CPU dependencies are described in the next chapter.

5. The executive image is opened and the portion containing system parameters is read into the SYSBOOT working table. Section 25.3 describes in more detail the movement of parameter information during the initialization sequence. The location of the executive image on the system disk (logical block number) is stored for later use.

6. The file SYSDUMP.DMP is opened. If the dump file is not found, the page file (PAGEFILE.SYS) is opened; the first blocks of the page file will be used as the dump file when the system bugchecks.

7. Several other files are opened and read into nonpaged pool; their locations in nonpaged pool are stored. These files include:

   - The system disk driver
   - The terminal driver
   - The image containing CPU-dependent initialization code
   - The image containing the CPU-dependent modules
   - The image containing the SCS-dependent modules (if required) by module SCSLOA

The addresses of these files are passed to INIT so that they can be stored in appropriate places in system address space after memory management is turned on.

8. At this point, SYSBOOT determines if the operator requested a conversational bootstrap by setting the RPB$V_CONV flag, R5<0>, as input to VMB. If so, SYSBOOT will prompt to allow interactive alteration of the parameter values. In any case, SYSBOOT enters the next phase with some set of adjustable parameters.

9. The size of the process header and the sizes of pieces of system address space, including the system control block, are calculated. In particular, the size of the system page table is calculated. The details of these calculations are described in Chapter 26. Pages of physical memory are allocated at the highest portion of physical memory for the system control block, the system page table, and the system header. The pages are filled with zeros and the SPTEs used to map the pages are filled in.

10. The first page of the system control block, is loaded with the contents of module SCBVECTOR, which contains the entry points for the interrupt and exception service routines located in SYS.EXE. The second and third pages of the SCB, if present, are loaded with the address of ERL$UNEXP, an unexpected interrupt handler.

11. The system header is configured. All entries in the system header whose contents depend on configuration parameters are filled in at this time. This step is analogous to the process header configuration that is performed by code in SHELL as a part of process creation (see Chapter 20).

12. Space for the interrupt stack is allocated and mapped. The SPTEs for the global page tables area filled in to indicate that they are demand zero pages. Physical memory is allocated for the initial sizes of the three lookaside lists, and the corresponding SPTEs are filled in. The size and address of each list is recorded.

13. The top of nonpaged pool is preallocated for the FIL$OPENFILE cache and a number of other loadable routines. The piece of pool used for FIL$OPENFILE cache will be deallocated later in the bootstrap operation. Allocating space here eliminates the problem of pool fragmentation when that piece is deallocated.

14. Pieces of the executive that are never paged (see Table 26-3) are mapped into the highest portion of physical memory. These include device drivers (for the null device and mailbox), the interrupt stack, the lookaside lists, and the boot driver. The physical pages to which the nonpaged portions of the executive are mapped will not be accounted for in the PFN database because their state will never change.

15. The pageable portions of SYS.EXE (the pageable executive routines) are also mapped to allow the executive to be read into memory.

16. The executive image is read into memory. Because memory management

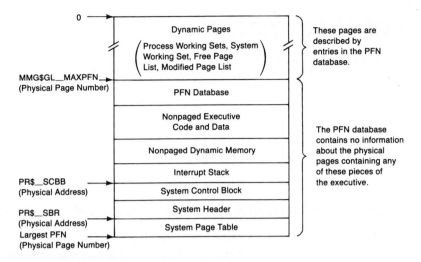

Figure 24-3
Physical Memory Layout Used by the Executive

has not yet been enabled, the complications of scattered reads into memory are not applicable here.

17. The contents of SYSBOOT's internal parameter table are copied to the portion of the memory image of the executive that contains all the adjustable parameters. This step preserves the current parameter settings (because SYSBOOT is going away) until they can be written back to the disk image of the executive by SYSINIT (see Chapter 25).

    The contents of the bootstrap parameter table are saved in the bootstrap parameter block (see Table 24-9).

18. SYSBOOT loads the base and length registers for the P0 and system page tables so that INIT can turn memory management on. Enabling memory management is described in more detail in Section 25.1.1.

19. Finally, SYSBOOT transfers control to module INIT in the executive. This transfer must be done to a physical location because memory management has not been enabled yet. The file descriptors and other information that SYSBOOT passes to INIT are stored in the bootstrap parameter block (see Table 24-9). The state of physical memory is pictured in Figure 24-3.

547

25 Operating System Initialization

Had I been present at the creation, I would have given some
useful hints for the better ordering of the universe.
—Alfonso the Wise

The second major phase of system initialization is performed in two phases:

- By code that is a part of the executive (module INIT)
- By a special process (SYSINIT) that is created to complete those pieces of initialization that require process context in order to execute

INIT turns on memory management and sets up those data structures whose size or contents depend on SYSBOOT parameters. SYSINIT opens system files, creates system processes, maps RMS and the message file, and creates the process that invokes the startup command file.

25.1 INITIAL EXECUTION OF THE EXECUTIVE (INIT)

The final instruction in SYSBOOT transfers control to (physical) address EXE$INIT, an address in module INIT. INIT turns on memory management, configures the I/O adapters, initializes several scheduling and memory management data structures, and finally releases the pages that it occupies so that code that executes only once during the life of the system does not consume system resources.

25.1.1 Turning On Memory Management

The first (and perhaps most important) step that INIT takes turns on memory management. Before SYSBOOT transfers control to INIT, it sets up the system page table to map the executive and dynamic data structures. In addition, a P0 page table is constructed so that the physical page containing EXE$INIT is mapped as a P0 virtual page where the virtual page number is identical to the physical page number. EXE$INIT can then be referenced as a P0 virtual address that is identically equal to the physical address of EXE$INIT. The reason that P0 space is used for this double mapping is that the P0 space address range from 0 to 40000000 is the same as the maximum physical address range permitted by the VAX architecture. That is, no matter how much physical memory is put on a VAX processor, there will always be a P0 address range with identical addresses.

25.1.1.1   **Double Mapping of INIT by SYSBOOT.** This P0 page table is constructed by loading the P0 base and length registers with values that access a portion of the system page table (see Figure 25-1). If we assume that EXE$INIT is located in PFN n, then P0LR is loaded with n+2 and P0BR is loaded with a system virtual address that is n longwords smaller than the system virtual address of the system page table entry that maps EXE$INIT.

The net result of all this mapping is that the physical page containing EXE$INIT can (and will) be accessed in three different ways (see Figure 25-2). These different mappings are listed here in order of mapping complication, and not in the order in which they are used. EXE$INIT can be accessed in the following ways:

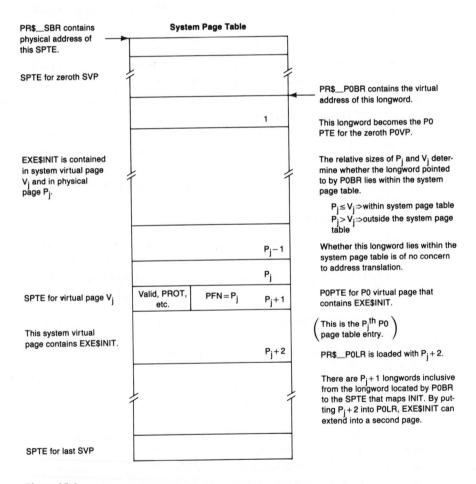

Figure 25-1
Double Use of System Page Table Entries by INIT

549

- As a physical address
- As a system virtual address (8001B06C in Version 3.0) that is mapped by the system page table
- As a P0 virtual address that is located by the subset of the system page table that is also used as a P0 page table

25.1.1.2 **Instructions that Turn On Memory Management.** When INIT begins execution, memory management is disabled. The PC contains the physical address of EXE$INIT.

① The first instruction executes in physical space:

```
MOVL    RPB$L_BOOTR5(R11),FP
```

Its effect is not related to turning memory management on.

② The second instruction actually turns memory management on:

```
MTPR    #1,S^#PR$_MAPEN
```

That is, all address references from that point on must be translated. Note that the instruction does not cause a transfer of control. The PC is simply incremented by three, the number of bytes in the instruction. However, the next PC reference will be translated because memory management has been enabled.

Because of the mapping set up by SYSBOOT, the incremented (physical) PC (the address of the JMP instruction), when translated using the P0 page table, yields the physical address of the JMP instruction.

③ The third instruction is the only instruction that executes with a P0 program counter:

```
JMP     @#10$
```

This instruction immediately transfers control to a system virtual address that was calculated when the executive was linked. When this system virtual address is translated, it results in the physical address of the next instruction in the physical page containing EXE$INIT.

The three instructions shown in Figure 25-2 execute in three different mapping contexts. The mapping that was set up by SYSBOOT results in a selection of successive instructions from the same physical page.

25.1.2 **Initialization of the Executive**

Once INIT has succeeded in turning on memory management, it is free to make references to system addresses. In particular, it is now possible to initialize dynamic data structures that have their listheads stored in static global locations in system space. Some of these steps involve allocation from nonpaged dynamic memory. (The nonpaged pool space allocated by INIT and the SYSBOOT parameters that control the amount of allocated space are

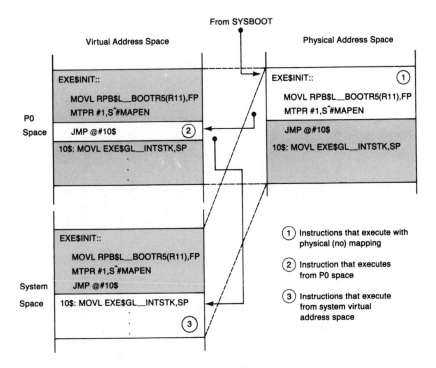

Figure 25-2
Address Space Changes as Memory Management
Is Enabled by INIT

listed in Table 25-1.) The detailed steps that INIT takes once memory management has been turned on are listed here.

1. The address of the interrupt stack is moved to the stack pointer.
2. If the SYSBOOT parameter SSINHIBIT is set, the CHMK and CHME vectors are redirected in order to enable system service filtering. System service filtering is described in the *VAX/VMS System Services Reference Manual*.
3. The system control block base register is loaded with the physical address of the SCB that contains the addresses of exception and interrupt service routines in the executive. This block was allocated and initialized by SYSBOOT.
4. Executive debugger support is either initialized or eliminated, according to the setting of the debug flag (RPB$V_DEBUG, R5<1>) on input to VMB.

   a. If debug support is selected, the BPT and TBIT exception vectors are loaded with the addresses of exception service routines within XDELTA.

Table 25-1: Use of Nonpaged Pool by Module INIT

Item	Global Address of Pointer	Factors That Affect Size
Real-Time Bitmap	EXE$GL_RTBITMAP	RBM$K_LENGTH + 4*REALTIME_SPTS (only present when REALTIME_SPTS nonzero)
Adapter Control Blocks for I/O Adapters	IOC$GL_ADPLIST	Number and Type of External Adapters (See Table 25-2)
PCB Vector and Sequence Vector	SCH$GL_PCBVEC SCH$GL_SEQVEC(1)	12 + (6*(MAXPROCESSCNT + 1))
Process Header Vectors	PHV$GL_PIXBAS PHV$GL_REFCBAS	12 + (4*(BALSETCNT + 1)) (2)
Page File Control Block Vector	MMG$GL_PAGSWPVC	4*(SWPFILCT + PAGFILCT) + 16
Swapper Map	SWP$GL_MAP	4*WSMAX + 4 + 12 (3)
Modified Page Writer Arrays	MPW$AL_PTE MPW$AW_PHVINDEX	12 + (6*MPW_WRTCLUSTER)
Bootstrap I/O Routines (NH)	RPB$L_IOVEC (4)	Size of Driver Itself
CPU-Dependent Code (NH)	EXE$AL_LOAVEC (5)	Size of Image SYSLOAxxx.EXE
Logical Name Blocks for SYS$DISK and SYS$SYSDEVICE	LOG$GL_SLTFL (6)	constant (6)

Table 25-1: Use of Nonpaged Pool by Module INIT (continued)

Item	Global Address of Pointer	Factors That Affect Size
Terminal Driver and Its Associated Data Structures	TTY$GL_DPT	Size of Image TTDRIVER.EXE
System Disk Driver and Its Associated Data Structures	(7)	Size of disk driver image
Lock ID Table	LCK$GL_IDTBL	12 + (4*LOCKIDTBL)
Resource Hash Table	LCK$GL_HASHTBL	12 + (4*RESHASHTBL)
Deadlock Detection Process Bitmap	LCK$GL_PRCMAP	13 + (MAXPROCESSCNT/8)

(NH) These structures are allocated without a 12-byte header that contains a size and type field. The lack of a header is not a problem because these structures are never deallocated. However, an interesting side effect of this absence of a header is that SDA interprets data as structure size and incorrectly dumps the beginning of nonpaged pool.

(1) There is one extra slot in each array for system PCB. The system process has a process index of MAXPROCESSCNT.

(2) There is one extra slot in each array for the system header. The system header has a balance slot index of BALSETCNT.

(3) The extra longword contains a zero, an end of list indicator.

(4) The bootstrap I/O routines are located through an offset in the restart parameter block.

(5) Loadable routines are connected to the executive through arguments to JMP instructions in module SYSLOADVEC (see Figure 25-3).

(6) The logical name blocks are constant because the sizes of both the logical name strings (SYS$DISK and SYS$SYSDEVICE) and the equivalence name strings (_DDcu:) are constant. The logical name blocks are linked into the system logical name table in the usual manner.

(7) Device drivers and their associated data structures are linked into the I/O database in several ways. See the *VAX/VMS Guide to Writing a Device Driver* for details.

    b. If debug support is not selected, the BPT instruction in INIT (at address INI$BRK) is converted to a NOP. In addition, the pages containing XDELTA (see Chapter 26) are included in the list of pages that INIT will release to the free page list as part of its exit routine.

5. The announcement message is printed on the console terminal. Note that this important milestone, while not very far into INIT, indicates that the executive has been read into memory and memory management turned on, both significant steps in initializing the executive.

6. The virtual page number of the boundary between the paged and nonpaged executive is loaded into the paged code arrays.

7. Nonpaged pool is initialized (see Chapter 3).

8. If the initial breakpoint flag (RPB$V_INIBPT, R5<2>) was set on input to VMB, then INIT executes a JSB to INI$BRK. If debug support has been selected, the instruction at INI$BRK contains a a BPT instruction, which will dispatch to XDELTA.

9. A tentative value for the maximum number of processes is established.

10. The values for the high and low thresholds of the modified page list are set.

11. If the system has more than 32M bytes of memory, PFN references in the nonpaged system image are modified to use longword context opcodes.

12. If the SYSPAGING system parameter flag is set, indicating that the pageable executive routines are going to page, then the SPTEs for these pages are set up to contain system section table indexes. In addition, the first section table entry in the system section table is initialized to point to the executive image SYS.EXE (Section 14.3.2 describes the system section table).

13. The fields in the restart parameter block used by the restart routine (see Section 27.2.2) are initialized.

14. The physical pages represented by the PFN bitmap set up by VMB are placed on the free page list. (Note that the pages that contain the PFN bitmap must be virtually mapped before they can be accessed.)

15. The system page table entries for paged dynamic memory are set up. If paged pool is going to page (the POOLPAGING system parameter flag is set), the SPTEs are set up to contain demand zero format PTEs. If pool paging is turned off, physical pages are allocated; their PFNs are loaded into the SPTEs; the protection codes (URKW) are loaded, and the valid bits are turned on.

16. The lookaside list packets are formatted and linked together. (The lookaside lists are described in Chapter 3.)

17. The minimum size of an IRP is calculated and loaded into IOC$GL_IRPMIN.

18. Preparations are made to connect configuration-dependent code. IPL is

set to 31 in order to allocate pool. The FIL$OPENFILE cache pointers and the top-level system directory name string are set up for FILEREAD. These global parameters were initialized by SYSBOOT.

19. Configuration-dependent routines are located in nonpaged pool and vectors are connected to these routines. The routines are the following:

    - SYSLOAxxx, the CPU-dependent loadable image
    - SCSLOA, Systems Communication Services loadable image
    - INILOA, loadable initialization code

    If the processor has a UDA50 or CI780, SCSLOA is called to initialize SCS data structures.

    INIT calls INILOA to locate, map, and initialize the external I/O adapters on the system. Once INILOA has executed, the nonpaged pool that it occupies is deallocated.

    Adapter initialization is discussed further in the next section.

20. If the SYSBOOT parameter REALTIME_SPTS is set to nonzero, that number of SPTEs is taken from the list of available SPTEs (see Chapter 26) and described in a real-time bitmap control block, allocated from nonpaged pool.

21. Lock manager data structures, including the lock ID table and the resource hash table, are initialized. If deadlock detection is enabled, a process bitmap is set up; the map has one bit for each possible process.

22. The PCB vector and sequence number vector (see Chapter 20) are allocated from nonpaged pool and initialized. All sequence numbers are initialized to zero. All PCB vector slots are set up to point to the PCB of the null process. Note that one extra entry is allocated at the end of each array. The extra entry in the PCB vector points to the system PCB. The system PCB is defined in module PDAT, and its dynamic contents are loaded by INIT. The system PCB is necessary for the pager to access its process address space and perform I/O.

23. The scheduler is called to make computable the two processes that are assembled as a part of the executive image, the swapper and the null process.

24. The process header vectors (see Chapter 14) are initialized for each balance slot. The reference count array is initialized to contain a negative one in each array element. The process index array is initialized to contain zeros, indicating free balance slots. (The null process is the process with a process index of zero. Because the null process does not swap, it does not require a balance slot. An index of zero can thus be used for another purpose, namely to indicate free balance slots.)

    As Chapter 26 illustrates, the system header and system page table immediately follow the balance slot area in system address space. In fact, portions of the memory management subsystem treat the system header as the occupant of an additional balance slot, one with a slot number equal to the SYSBOOT parameter BALSETCNT. The two process header vector arrays have one extra entry at the end to reflect this feature.

25. The swapper map is allocated from nonpaged pool (see Chapters 14 and 17). Its address is stored in global location SWP$GL_MAP and also in the swapper's P0 base register. Pages that appear in the swapper map are accessible as P0 virtual pages when the swapper is the current process.

26. The modified page writer arrays (Chapters 14 and 15) are allocated from nonpaged pool.

27. The page file control block vectors are initialized. Each vector contains a longword pointer to a data structure (called a page file block) for each page or swap file recognized by the system.

28. A number of miscellaneous initialization operations are performed here. The maximum depth of the lock manager resource name tree is calculated. The size of the tree is associated with the size of the interrupt stack. Space is reserved in the system working set for the shell. The address of the system header is moved into the appropriate cell in the system PCB and the process index for the system process is determined. The map of the file SYS.EXE, contained in the boot control block, is placed in a window control block.

29. The driver prolog tables (DPT) for the three devices (mailbox, null device, and console terminal) that are linked with SYS.EXE, and also the DPTs for the terminal driver and the system disk driver, are linked into the driver data base (located through listhead IOC$GL_DPTLIST).

30. Logical name blocks for SYS$DISK and SYS$SYSDEVICE are allocated from nonpaged pool, even though all other logical name blocks for system or group logical names are allocated from paged pool. Nonpaged pool is used because paged pool allocation is not possible above IPL 2. The two logical name blocks are linked into the system logical name table.

31. The terminal driver (SYS$SYSTEM:TTDRIVER.EXE) is located in nonpaged pool. The entry points of the driver are loaded into the device data block (DDB) for the console terminal (OPA0). The data structures for additional terminals will be established as a result of the AUTOCONFIGURE ALL command that is passed to SYSGEN as part of the command file STARTUP.COM.

32. The driver for the system device (and its port driver, if any) is located in nonpaged pool. Fields in its associated data structures (DDB, UCB, CRB, IDB, ADP) are loaded with information that depends on which specific unit and controller locate the system disk. All loaded drivers are then called at their controller and unit initialization points.

33. Once the system device controller and unit designators are determined, the equivalence names for SYS$DISK and SYS$SYSDEVICE are stored in their respective logical name blocks.

34. A page of physical memory (the so-called black hole page or rabbit hole page) is reserved for mount verification, MASSBUS adapter power fail, and UNIBUS adapter powerfail on the VAX-11/780. The cell EXE$GL_BLACK_HOLE contains the PFN of the black hole page. When power failure occurs on a UNIBUS, all virtual pages mapped to UBA registers or UNIBUS I/O space (24 pages in all) are remapped to this physical page. This remapping prevents drivers for UNIBUS devices from generating multiple machine checks while the power is off for the UBA. This same mechanism is used during MASSBUS Adapter powerfail. Powerfail operations are discussed in more detail in Chapter 27. Machine check operation is briefly discussed in Chapter 8.

35. The maximum allowable working set is readjusted (if necessary) to reflect the amount of available physical memory.

    Specifically, the number of physical pages used by the executive (see Chapter 26) is subtracted from available physical memory. System usage includes not only nonpaged code and data but also the system working set, MPW_LOLIM pages on the modified page list, and FREELIM pages on the free page list (but not the pages used by INIT). The value of WSMAX is then minimized with this difference.

36. Two flags used by the restart code (See Chapter 27) are cleared.

37. Finally, INIT frees up the pages that it occupied and jumps to the scheduler. The protection fields for these system virtual pages are set to No Access in the system page table and the physical pages are placed on the free page list. INIT accomplishes these steps by copying a small routine into nonpaged pool and transferring control to that routine. The routine itself vanishes as a result of the first allocation from pool, because the use of this block of pool was not recorded anywhere.

25.1.3   I/O Adapter Initialization

As shown in the description of INIT, the routine INILOA is used to determine the location of external adapters and initialize the adapters for later use by the SYSGEN configuration operations. (INILOA and the other routines called by INIT are found in source module INITADP, a logical extension of the code contained in module INIT.) Although some of the initialization that INILOA performs depends on the nature of the external I/O adapter, there are two general steps that are taken for each adapter, once it is located:

- An adapter control block that identifies the adapter and contains information about how the adapter's internal registers are mapped is allocated from nonpaged pool and loaded.
- System virtual space is set up to map to the I/O space addresses for internal adapter registers and other I/O space assignments.

Table 25-2 lists the differences in ADP size and mapping requirements for each of the possible external adapters.

INILOA also checks for the presence of UNIBUS memory. If UNIBUS memory is found, the UBA map registers are disabled.

25.1.4   CPU-Dependent Routines

There are two different types of CPU-dependent code that appear in the VAX/VMS operating system and two corresponding methods that the VMS operating system uses for incorporating the code.

- When there are one or two instructions or data references that depend on the specific type of CPU that is being used, the system usually includes the code or data sequence for all CPUs in line and uses the contents of location

Table 25-2: External Adapter Initialization

Adapter Type	Size of Adapter Control Block (bytes)	Number of System Virtual Pages Mapped for Adapter
Local Memory	None exists	1 Page
MA780 Shared Memory (VAX-11/780 only)	112 + 4*16 = 176 (1)	1 Page
UNIBUS Adapter (VAX-11/730) (VAX-11/750) (VAX-11/780)	580 580 580 + 148 + 4*128 = 1240 (2)	8 + 16 = 24 (3)
MASSBUS Adapter (VAX-11/750) (VAX-11/780)	28	8 Pages
DR32 Interface (VAX-11/750) (VAX-11/780)	28	4 Pages
CI Interface	28	8 Pages
Unoccupied Nexus Slot	None Exists	1 Page to Allow Access

(1) There are 112 bytes in the body of the ADP plus space for 16 longword vectors.
(2) The VAX-11/730 ADP contains 580 bytes of data. UNIBUS vectors are contained in the second page of the system control block.

    The VAX-11/750 ADP contains 580 bytes of data. The UNIBUS vectors are contained in the second page of the system control block; the vectors for a second UNIBUS (if one exists) are contained in the third page of the system control block.

    The VAX-11/780 ADP contains 580 bytes of data, the interrupt service routine for the UBA, which is 148 bytes long (in Version 3.0), and 128 longword vectors, corresponding to UNIBUS vectors from 0 to 774 (octal).
(3) Eight pages map the UBA internal registers such as mapping registers, datapath registers, and the like. There are 16 pages that map the UNIBUS I/O page to allow virtual access to device CSRs, data registers, and so on.

EXE$GB_CPUTYPE to determine which piece of the code or data to use. (This location was previously loaded by SYSBOOT from the contents of the PR$_SID register.)

• In the case of CPU-dependent routines (such as the purge datapath routine, IOC$PURGDATAP) or CPU-dependent modules (such as the machine check handler), a vectored entry point technique is used.

The vectored entry point method works in the following way. Each reference within the executive image to a CPU-dependent routine is dispatched to a JMP instruction in module SYSLOAVEC, which is linked with the executive image SYS.EXE. The CPU-dependent routines (one routine for each CPU) are linked together into a series of CPU-dependent images with names of the form SYSLOAxxx.EXE (currently SYSLOA730.EXE, SYSLOA750.EXE, or SYSLOA780.EXE). INIT uses the CPU type to load the correct CPU-dependent image SYSLOAxxx.EXE into nonpaged pool as a part of system initialization.

Another vector module called LOAVEC (actually the same module as SYSLOAVEC with a different setting of a conditional assembly flag), linked into each CPU-dependent image SYSLOAxxx.EXE, contains an offset into the loadable image for each of the CPU-dependent subroutines. INIT uses the information in this table to adjust the arguments of the JMP instructions (in module SYSLOAVEC) so that they point to the correct routines in the copy of SYSLOAxxx.EXE in nonpaged pool. The initial destination of all the JMP instructions is EXE$LOAD_ERROR, a global address of a HALT instruction within module SYSLOAVEC in SYS.EXE. If any of these CPU-dependent routines is referenced before INIT has completed its initialization, the system will halt.

The cost of separating out CPU-dependent routines from the system image, one extra level of indirection, is far outweighed by the benefits, which include fewer execution time decisions and no need for separate executive images for each CPU. The linkage that is established by INIT for CPU-dependent routines is illustrated in Figure 25-3.

25.2 INITIALIZATION IN PROCESS CONTEXT

Further steps in system initialization must be performed by a process. System services can only be called while executing in process context because the quota and privilege checks are made against process data structures. A command language interpreter can easily be mapped into P1 space, a per-process portion of virtual address space that is only available when executing in process context. The process phase of system initialization is divided into two parts, that performed by a special process called SYSINIT and the steps performed by the command file STARTUP.COM.

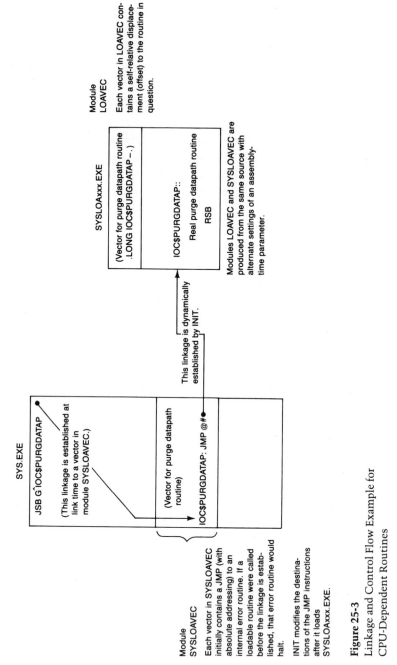

Figure 25-3
Linkage and Control Flow Example for
CPU-Dependent Routines

25.2.1   SYSINIT Process

When the scheduler executes, it selects the highest priority computable process for execution. Because there are only two processes in existence at this time, the swapper process is always selected (because it has an external priority of 16 and the null process has an external priority of 0). The swapper immediately creates another process, called SYSINIT, that performs those aspects of system initialization that require process context. The swapper initializes the paged pool listhead, which must be done from process context in order to handle page faults. The swapper then initializes the group and system logical name hash tables, which are allocated from paged pool.

In one sense, SYSINIT is an extension of the swapper process. However, the initialization code is isolated to prevent encumbering the swapper with code that only executes once during the life of a system. (This isolation is one of several techniques used during system initialization and process creation to cause seldom-used code to disappear after it is used. A list of such techniques appears in Chapter 31.)

The major functions that SYSINIT performs can be grouped into the following three categories:

- The swap file and page file are opened and their locations on disk stored in respective data structures.
- RMS.EXE and the system message file are mapped as system sections.
- The STARTUP process is created.

25.2.1.1   Pool Usage by SYSINIT. SYSINIT, like INIT, consumes large amounts of nonpaged pool and some paged pool. However, the sizes of various blocks are not directly related to SYSBOOT parameters. In addition, with one exception, all blocks allocated directly or indirectly by SYSINIT include a 12-byte header that contains a size field and unique identifier for each structure. Structures that are allocated from nonpaged pool as a result of the execution of SYSINIT include the following:

- Software PCBs and JIBs for system processes
- File control blocks and window control blocks for all opened files
- A volume control block for the system disk

25.2.1.2   Detailed Operation of SYSINIT. The detailed steps that SYSINIT takes are listed here.

1. System logical names are created for SYS$SYSTEM, SYS$SHARE, and SYS$MESSAGE. The creation of these names cannot be delayed until the creation of the STARTUP process because these names are needed as a part of the creation of that process.

   The name of the image that is passed to the STARTUP process is

SYS$SYSTEM:LOGINOUT. The LOGINOUT image performs a merged image activation (see Chapter 21) to map the DCL command language interpreter into P1 space. The image activator uses logical name SYS-$SHARE to locate the shareable image DCLTABLES.EXE that contains the command database for the DCL command language interpreter. The logical name SYS$MESSAGE is required for RMS to open the system message file.

2. The system time is calculated and stored.

If the SETTIME flag was passed to SYSBOOT, or if the contents of the time of day register (TODR) indicate that it contains a meaningless number (see Chapter 11), a new system time value must be determined. The value of the SYSBOOT parameter TIMEPROMPTWAIT determines the algorithm SYSINIT will use to find the new system time. If the value of TIMEPROMPTWAIT is 0, the system is booted with the last time value that was recorded in the system image (no operator is present).

If the value of TIMEPROMPTWAIT is greater than 0, SYSINIT prompts the operator for a new system time value. Then if TIMEPROMPTWAIT seconds pass and no response is given, SYSINIT assumes that no operator is present and boots the system using the last time value recorded in the system image.

If the value of TIMEPROMPTWAIT is less than 0, SYSINIT will prompt the operator for a time value and will wait indefinitely, until the operator responds.

In any case, the Set Time system service is called to calculate a new system time. In addition, that service copies the current parameter settings from their locations in memory to the disk image of the executive (SYS.EXE).

3. If the SYSBOOT parameter UAFALTERNATE is set, the logical name SYSUAF then translates to the equivalence name SYS$SYSTEM: SYSUAFALT.DAT. This feature allows an alternate authorization file to be used. If the alternate authorization file does not exist, all users are denied access to the system.

4. The following files are opened by the file I/O routines located in the executive:

```
SYS$SYSTEM:PAGEFILE.SYS
SYS$SYSTEM:SWAPFILE.SYS
SYS$SYSTEM:RMS.EXE
```

If the first part of the page file is being used as the dump file, SYSBOOT has already opened PAGEFILE.SYS; it does not need to be opened here.

5. The page file is initialized. This requires that the information obtained in SYSBOOT or in the previous step be loaded into a window control block that describes the page file. The address of that WCB is stored in the page file control block (see Figure 14-22) for the initial page file.

In addition, a bitmap that describes the availability of each block in the page file is allocated from nonpaged pool and initialized to all ones to indicate that all blocks are available. If the page file contains a valid dump, and the SYSBOOT paramter SAVEDUMP is set to 1, the blocks in the page file containing the dump are marked unavailable. When the dump is successfully copied to another file using the SDA command COPY, the blocks are marked available. If page file contains a valid dump, the second and third blocks of the dump file (error log buffers) are preserved before the page file is initialized.

6. If present, the swap file is initialized. As was done for the page file, a window control block is allocated from nonpaged pool. Its address is stored in the swap file table entry (see Chapter 14) for the first swap file.

   The swap file is divided into swap spaces, each space is a multiple of the SYSBOOT parameter MPW_WRTCLUSTER. The swap spaces are dynamically assigned. The number of spaces in the file (minimized with 128, the maximum number of spaces in a single swap file) is recorded in the SFTE. In addition, the maximum number of processes that the system can support (stored in global location SCH$GW_PROCLIM) is taken as the minimum of swap file space count and the initial MAXPROCESSCNT SYSBOOT parameter. (The contents of SCH$GW_PROCLIM can be increased later by installing additional swap files.)

7. RMS is set up as a pageable system section. The section table entries that describe this section are initialized, starting with the second section table entry in the system header. (The first system section table entry, the one that describes the executive image itself, was set up by INIT.)

8. The second and third blocks of the dump file contain the contents of the error log buffers if the system just crashed. These buffers were written to the dump file by the bugcheck code (see Chapter 8) so their contents would not be lost. If the system is rebooting after a crash, SYSINIT copies the second and third blocks of the dump file back to the error log buffers so their contents will eventually be written to SYS$ERRORLOG: ERRLOG.SYS.

   The bugcheck routine included the error log entry that describes the reason for the crash in the first block of the dump file as part of the dump file header block to avoid the loss of this data in the event that the two error log buffers·were full at the time of the crash. If this was the case when the system crashed, SYSINIT will be unable to copy this error log entry to one of the error log buffers. In that case, the error log entry that actually describes the crash will never appear in an error log report. However, in all cases including this rare occurrence of two full error log buffers, the reason for the system crash is contained in the dump file.

9. A cold start is logged in the error log.
10. The system disk is mounted. A direct result of this step is the creation of the disk ACP for the system disk.

    From this point on, the ACP is available for file operations. The primitive ACP routines that are a part of SYS.EXE are no longer required and will disappear in time due to system working set replacement. The FIL$OPENFILE cache can now be deallocated from nonpaged pool.
11. The logical name SYS$TOPSYS is created.
12. The system message file (SYS$MESSAGE:SYSMSG.EXE) is opened and mapped. The section table entries that describe the messages section are initialized following the section table entries for RMS in the system header.
13. Finally, a process called STARTUP is created. The important point about this process is that it executes the image LOGINOUT, which maps a command language interpreter (see Chapter 23).

25.2.2 The STARTUP Process

The STARTUP process created by SYSINIT completes system initialization. This process is the first process in the system that includes a command language interpreter. The inclusion of DCL allows the operation of this process to be directed by a DCL command procedure.

25.2.2.1 STARTUP.COM.
The steps performed by commands in this file can be divided into six major groups:

1. Several system logical names are created. These include:

   - VMS-specific names

     ```
     SYS$SYSROOT
     SYS$SYSDISK
     SYS$LIBRARY
     SYS$HELP
     ```

   - Other VMS-specific names that are reassigned to use SYS$SYSROOT in their equivalence names

     ```
     SYS$SYSTEM
     SYS$MESSAGE
     SYS$SHARE
     ```

   - Logical names for system management, installation, and testing
   - Logical names used by the symbolic debugger
   - Names required by language run-time systems for VAX-11 COBOL-74 and VAX-11 PASCAL
   - Logical names required by compatibility mode utilities

2. Three detached system processes are started.

```
Error Log Format (ERRFMT)
The Job Controller (JOB_CONTROL)
The Operator Communication Process (OPCOM)
```

3. The Install Utility is invoked to make privileged and shareable images known to the system.

4. The System Generation Utility (SYSGEN) is invoked to automatically configure external I/O devices. If a user-written driver must be loaded before normal VMS drivers, the driver should be written so that the SYSGEN command AUTOCONFIGURE will load and connect the driver (see the *VAX/VMS Guide to Writing a Device Driver*). Note that users must not modify the STARTUP.COM file, because doing so may cause SYS$UPDATE:VMSINSTAL.COM to produce inconsistent results.

5. The RMS Share Utility executes and allocates a block of paged pool (with a default of 20 pages) to contain the data structures for shared files.

6. If a secondary swap file is to be used, it is installed.

7. Finally, a site-specific command file called SYS$MANAGER: SYSTARTUP.COM is invoked.

25.2.2.2   **Site-Specific STARTUP Command File.** The site-specific command file, SYS$MANAGER:SYSTARTUP.COM, that is distributed with the VMS operating system is empty. This file can be used to do the following:

- Start batch and print queues
- Set terminal speeds and other device characteristics
- Create site-specific system logical names
- Install more privileged and shareable images
- Load user-written device drivers
- Mount volumes other than the system disk
- Load the console block storage driver (if desired) with a CONNECT CONSOLE command to SYSGEN and mount the console medium
- Issue the DCL command START/CPU to initialize the attached processor on a VAX-11/782.
- Start DECnet (if present on the system)
- Run SDA to preserve the previous dump file in case the system crashed
- Produce an error log report
- Announce system availability

25.3   **THE SYSTEM GENERATION UTILITY (SYSGEN)**

The System Generation Utility fits into the initialization sequence in two unrelated ways:

- It is invoked directly by STARTUP.COM to autoconfigure the external I/O devices.

- It interacts indirectly with system initialization by producing parameter files that may be used by SYSBOOT for future bootstrap operations.

The role of SYSGEN in autoconfiguring the I/O system is described in the *VAX/VMS Guide to Writing a Device Driver*. This section briefly compares and contrasts the operations that SYSBOOT and SYSGEN perform on parameter files. Table 25-3 summarizes this comparison.

25.3.1 Contents of Parameter Block

A common module called PARAMETER is linked into both the SYSBOOT and SYSGEN images. This module contains information about each adjustable parameter (see Table 25-4). This data never changes. In addition, each parameter occupies a cell in a table of working values. This table is manipulated with the following SYSBOOT and SYSGEN commands:

- Displayed by SHOW parameter-name commands
- Altered by SET parameter-name value commands
- Overwritten by a USE command

There is also a copy of the working table linked into the executive image, SYS.EXE. (This table is produced from the same source module as PARAMETER with a different setting of a conditional assembly parameter. The resultant module is called SYSPARAM.)

25.3.2 Use of Parameter Files by SYSBOOT

Figure 25-4 shows the flow of parameter value data during a bootstrap operation. The numbers in the figure describe the significant steps in setting values or moving data.

① The first step that SYSBOOT performs is to locate the executive image and read the parameter settings from the executive image into its working table. In the language of SYSBOOT and SYSGEN commands, this step is an implied command:

```
USE CURRENT
```

This operation causes the system to be initialized with the parameter settings used during the previous configuration of the system (due to step 5).

② If a conversational bootstrap was selected (R5<0> was set as input to VMB), then SYSBOOT will prompt for commands to alter current parameter settings. A USE command to SYSBOOT's prompt results in the working table being overwritten with an entire set of parameter values. There are three possible sources of these values.

Table 25-3: Comparison of SYSBOOT and SYSGEN

SYSBOOT	*SYSGEN*
Purpose	
SYSBOOT configures the system using parameters from the executive image or from a parameter file.	SYSGEN has four unrelated purposes: • It creates parameter files for use in future bootstrap operations. • It modifies dynamic parameters in the running system with the WRITE ACTIVE command. • It loads device drivers and their associated data structures. • It creates and installs additional page and swap files.
Use in System Initialization	
SYSBOOT is the secondary bootstrap program that executes after VMB but before control is passed to the executive.	The only place that SYSGEN occupies in the initialization sequence is related to its driver function. It is invoked to autoconfigure all I/O devices.
Environment	
SYSBOOT runs in a stand-alone environment with no file system, memory management, process context, or any other environment provided by VMS.	SYSGEN executes in the normal environment of a utility program. The driver and swap/page functions require privilege (CMKRNL). A WRITE ACTIVE command also requires CMKRNL privilege. The parameter file operations are protected through the file system.
Valid Commands	

USE
   USE file-spec
   USE CURRENT
   USE DEFAULT
   No Equivalent Command
SET
SHOW
CONTINUE (EXIT)
No Equivalent Command
No Equivalent Commands
No Equivalent Commands
	USE
	   USE file-spec
	   USE CURRENT
	   USE DEFAULT
	   USE ACTIVE
	SET
	SHOW
	EXIT (CONTINUE)
	WRITE
	Commands Associated with Device Drivers
	Commands Associated with Additional Page and Swap Files

Initial Conditions	

Implied
   USE CURRENT
	Implied
	   USE ACTIVE

Table 25-4: Information Stored for Each Adjustable Parameter by SYSBOOT and SYSGEN

(This structure is defined in both SYSBOOT and SYSGEN by invoking the $PRMDEF macro.)

Item			*Size of Item*
Address of Parameter (in SYS.EXE)			Longword
Default Value of Parameter			Longword
Minimum Value That Parameter Can Assume			Longword
Maximum Value That Parameter Can Assume			Longword
Parameter Flags			Word
DYNAMIC Parameter	SHOW /DYN		
STATIC Parameter			
SYSGEN Parameter	SHOW /GEN		
ACP Parameter	SHOW /ACP		
JBC Parameter	SHOW /JOB		
RMS Parameter	SHOW /RMS		
SCS Parameter	SHOW /SCS		
SYS Parameter	SHOW /SYS		
TTY Parameter	SHOW /TTY		
SPECIAL Parameter	SHOW /SPECIAL		
DISPLAY Parameter			
CONTROL Parameter			
MAJOR Parameter	SHOW /MAJOR		
PQL Parameter	SHOW /PQL		
NEG Parameter			
Size of This Parameter			Byte
Bit Position if Parameter Is Flag			Byte
Name String for Parameter			16 Bytes
Name String for Units			12 Bytes
Working Value of Parameter			Longword

NOTE. The working value of each parameter is found not only in internal tables in SYSBOOT and SYSGEN but also in the executive itself. In fact, the parameter address (first item) stored for each parameter locates the working value of each parameter in the memory image of the executive.

- USE file-spec directs SYSBOOT to the indicated parameter file for a new set of values.
- USE DEFAULT causes the working table in SYSBOOT to be filled with the default values for each parameter.
- USE CURRENT causes the parameter values in the executive image to be loaded into SYSBOOT's working table. (A USE CURRENT command is redundant if it is the first command passed to SYSBOOT.)

③ Once the initial conditions have been established, individual parameters can be altered with SET commands. The conversational phase of SYSBOOT is terminated with a CONTINUE (or EXIT) command.

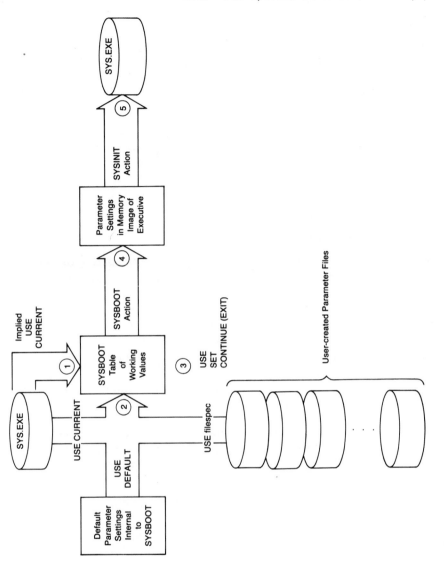

Figure 25-4
Movement of Parameter Data by SYSBOOT and SYSINIT

④ After SYSBOOT has calculated the sizes of the various pieces of system space, but before it transfers control to INIT, it copies the contents of its working table to the corresponding table in the memory image of the executive.

⑤ One of the first steps performed by the SYSINIT process copies the parameter table from the memory image of the executive to its disk image. Because SYSBOOT always does an implied USE CURRENT as its first step, this implied command guarantees that all subsequent bootstraps will use the latest parameter settings, even if no conversational bootstrap is selected.

25.3.3   Use of Parameter Files by SYSGEN

SYSGEN's interaction with parameter files is not an integral part of the bootstrap operation. However, its action, pictured in Figure 25-5, closely parallels that of SYSBOOT.

① The initial contents of SYSGEN's working table are the values taken from the memory image of the executive. The data movement pictured in Figure 25-5 is a movement from one memory area to another rather than the result of an I/O operation.

In any event, SYSGEN begins its execution with an implied command:

    USE ACTIVE

This set of initial conditions would differ from SYSBOOT's initial state only if someone had already run SYSGEN and written parameters to either CURRENT (the disk image of the executive) or ACTIVE (the memory image of the executive).

② SYSGEN can choose initial settings for its working table in exactly the same fashion as SYSBOOT.

There is an additional reserved file specification available to SYSGEN. A USE ACTIVE command causes the parameter table from the memory image of the executive to be copied into SYSGEN's working table.

③ SET commands can be used to alter individual parameter values. Typically, an EXIT (or CONTINUE) command would not be used until the final settings were preserved with a WRITE command.

④ This step preserves the contents of SYSGEN's working table in the following way:

- WRITE filespec creates a new parameter file that contains the contents of SYSGEN's working table.
- WRITE CURRENT alters the copy of the parameter table in the disk image of the executive. The next bootstrap operation will use these values automatically (even without a conversational bootstrap option).

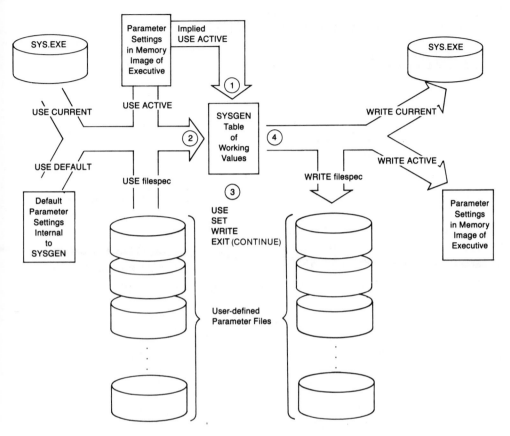

Figure 25-5
Movement of Parameter Data by SYSGEN

- Several parameters determine the size of portions of system address space. Other parameters determine the size of blocks of pool space allocated by INIT. These parameters cannot be changed in a running system. However, many parameters are not used in configuring the system. These parameters are designated as DYNAMIC (see Table 25-4).

A WRITE ACTIVE command to SYSGEN alters the settings of dynamic parameters only in the memory image of the executive.

A word of caution is in order here. Before one experiments with a new configuration, the parameters from a working system should be saved in a parameter file. If the new configuration creates a system that is unusable, the system can be restored to its previous state by directing SYSBOOT to use the saved parameters.

26   Size of System Virtual Address Space

A little inaccuracy sometimes saves tons of explanation.

—Saki, *The Comments of Moung Ka*

The executive image SYS$SYSTEM:SYS.EXE contains the operating system code for the VMS system but very little of the data. Many of the data structures that VMS uses are not created until the system is bootstrapped, so that the structure sizes can be determined from the appropriate SYSBOOT parameters. This chapter describes the relationships between these SYSBOOT parameters and the portions of system address space whose sizes they determine.

In the equations that appear in this chapter, two common features dominate. One feature is division by 512, the number of bytes in a page. This division is done whenever the input parameter is a number of bytes, such as the NPAGEDYN SYSBOOT parameter or an expression for the number of bytes in a process header. If 511 is added to an expression for a number of bytes before the integer division takes place, this represents a rounding up to the next highest page boundary.

The second feature is the number 128 that appears in expressions that count the number of pages for which system page table entries are needed. The significance of the number 128 is that a page table entry is four bytes long so that a page of page table entries maps 128 pages. In this case, the rounding factor that is added is 127.

26.1   SIZE OF PROCESS HEADER

Before the various portions of system address space are calculated, the size of the process header will be related to the SYSBOOT parameters that affect its size. Table 26-1 lists each portion of the process header, the SYSBOOT parameters that affect its size, and the global location where the size of that portion is stored. The table also introduces the notation used in the first set of equations to describe each piece of the process header. Figure 26-1 shows the actual layout of the process header and the relationship of the parts described in Table 26-1.

Table 26-1: Discrete Portions of the Process Header

Symbolic Name for Equations	Items Stored in This Part of the Process Header	Factors Affecting Size of This Part of Process Header	Global Location Where Size of This Part Is Stored
PHD(wsl_pst)	Fixed Portion Working Set List Process Section Table	PHD$K_LENGTH PROCSECTCNT WSMAX PQL_DWSDEFAULT	SWP$GW_WSLPTE
PHD(empty)	No Access Pages for Working Set List Expansion	WSMAX PQL_DWSDEFAULT	SWP$GW_EMPTPTE
PHD(bak)	Process Header Page Arrays and Page Table Page Arrays	Size of the Process Header	SWP$GW_BAKPTE
PHD(pte)	P0 and P1 Page Tables	VIRTUALPAGECNT	SGN$GL_PTPAGCNT

The following global locations contain sums of the sizes of several of the pieces listed above:

a. @SGN$GL_PHDAPCNT = PHD(wsl_pst) + PHD(bak)
b. @SGN$GL_PHDPAGCT = PHD(wsl_pst) + PHD(empty) + PHD(bak)
c. @SWP$GL_BSLOTSZ = PHD(wsl_pst) + PHD(empty) + PHD(bak) + PHD(page_tables)

26.1.1   Process Page Tables

Most of the process header is taken up by the P0 and P1 page tables. The total number of pages allocated for the process page tables depends on the parameter VIRTUALPAGECNT.

$$\text{PHD(page\_tables)} = \frac{\text{VIRTUALPAGECNT} + 127}{128} \qquad (26.1)$$

26.1.2   Working Set List and Process Section Table

The working set list and process section table are located at the low address end of the process header immediately after the fixed size area and grow toward each other. The size of the process section table depends on the parameter PROCSECTCNT. On first approach, one would assume that the working set list size depends on the parameter WSMAX. However, because the process header pages that are not page table pages are locked into the process working set, they always require physical pages. In most systems, many processes will have working sets that are much smaller than the allowed maximum. The initial working set list size is calculated to take this into account. The assumption is made that most processes will have working sets that are approximately equal to the parameter PQL_DWSDEFAULT.

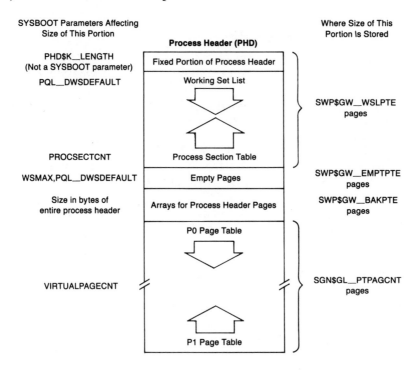

Figure 26-1
Process Header and SYSBOOT Parameters

Equation 26.2 calculates the maximum number of pages required for the fixed portion of the process header, the working set list, and the process section table. The extra space reserved for working set list expansion is calculated in Equation 26.3. The difference between these two numbers (Equation 26.4) is the number of pages initially available for the fixed portion, the working set list, and the process section table. The significance of the numbers 4 and 32 in Equation 26.2 is that a working set list element is a longword (or four bytes, WSL$C_LENGTH) and a process section table entry is 32 bytes long (SEC$K_LENGTH).

$$\text{PHD(temp)} = \frac{\left\{ \begin{array}{l} \text{PHD\$K\_LENGTH} + 4 \times \text{WSMAX} \\ + 32 \times \text{PROCSECTCNT} + 511 \end{array} \right\}}{512} \tag{26.2}$$

$$\text{PHD(empty)} = \frac{\text{WSMAX} - \text{PQL\_DWSDEFAULT}}{128} \tag{26.3}$$

$$\text{PHD(wsl\_pst)} = \text{PHD(temp)} - \text{PHD(empty)} \tag{26.4}$$

26.1.3   Process Header Page Arrays

The process header page arrays include two arrays that contain array elements for each page in the process header. (These two arrays are used by the swapper to store information about process header pages while the header is outswapped.) There are also two arrays of bytes in this portion of the process header that contain an array element for each page table page. To simplify the calculation of the size of this portion of the process header, space is allocated as if the last two arrays contained an element for each process header page. Because the page tables constitute approximately 90 percent of the process header in a typical system, this algorithm results in a very good approximation. Because the result is rounded up to the next page boundary, there is absolutely no difference in size for almost all combinations of SYSBOOT parameters.

Because the process header page arrays are located in the process header, the space allocated for this area depends on its own size. The calculation of this portion of the process header proceeds iteratively. An approximate size of the area is determined, based on the sizes of the other three areas. Then the estimates are refined until two successive calculations reach the same result.

Define the following:

$$\text{PHD(the\_rest)} = \text{PHD(wsl\_pst)} \\ + \text{PHD(empty)} \\ + \text{PHD(page\_tables)}$$
$$\text{PHD(bak,0)} = 0 \tag{26.5}$$

Perform the calculation shown in Equation 26.7 until the following equality exists:

$$\text{PHD(bak,N)} = \text{PHD(bak,N} - 1) \tag{26.6}$$

$$\text{PHD(bak,N)} = \frac{8 \times [\text{PHD(the\_rest)} + \text{PHD(bak,N} - 1)] + 511}{512} \tag{26.7}$$

Call the result of this calculation PHD(bak).

$$\text{PHD(bak)} = \text{PHD(bak,N)} \tag{26.8}$$

The sum of the four pieces of the process header yields its size in pages. The result of this calculation is stored in global location SWP$GL_BSLOTSZ.

$$\text{PHD(total)} = \text{PHD(wsl\_pst)} \\ + \text{PHD(empty)} \\ + \text{PHD(bak)} \\ + \text{PHD(page\_tables)} \tag{26.9}$$

26.2   SYSTEM VIRTUAL ADDRESS SPACE

Once the size of the process header has been calculated, the sizes of the dynamic pieces of system address space can be computed. Figure 26-2 pictures system address space and the nomenclature used to designate each piece. Table 26-2a–c lists each piece, the global location of the pointer to each piece, and the SYSBOOT parameters that determine its size.

26.2.1   System Virtual Address Space and SYSBOOT Parameters

The sizes of most of the pieces of system address space listed in Table 26-2 are either constant or simply related to one or two SYSBOOT parameters. Their sizes are computed in a straightforward manner by SYSBOOT. The sizes of the system page table and the PFN database are a little more complicated and a discussion of their sizes is postponed until the next section.

When SYSBOOT calculates the size of the system page table, it forms a sum of the sizes of the pieces of system virtual address space, and allocates an SPTE for each page. The calculation that is presented here considers each piece of system space in order of increasing virtual address, rather than in the order that SYSBOOT performs the calculation.

1. The first pages of system address space, containing the system service vectors and the FCP statistics blocks, have their size accounted for in the assembly-time parameter MMG$C_SPTSKEL defined in module SPTSKEL.

$$SVAS(sptskel) = 6 \tag{26.10}$$

    The FCP data area is less than two pages long. However, access protection is on a per-page basis. Part of the first page of the linked driver data structure area falls into the remaining part of the FCP data area and thus has a protection of UREW (the protection applied to the FCP data area); the remainder of the linked driver data structure area is URKW.

2. The area that will contain the linked executive, the RMS image, and the system message file has its size determined by the SYSBOOT parameter SPTREQ. In addition, there must be enough extra pages in this area to map the I/O adapters and to reserve a system virtual page for each device unit whose driver requests one.

    If there are any system page table entries required for mapping by PFN for real-time devices, the requested number (SYSBOOT parameter REALTIME_SPTS) is added to system virtual address requirements at this time.

$$SVAS(sptreq) = SPTREQ + REALTIME\_SPTS \tag{26.11}$$

576

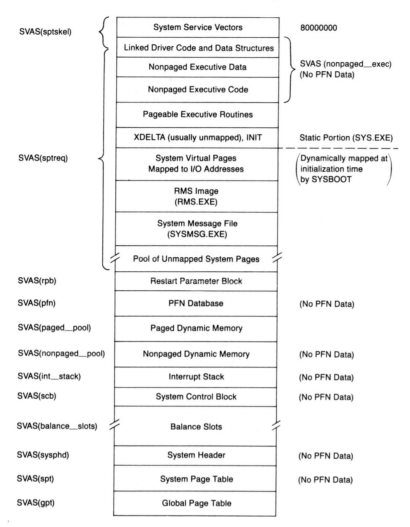

Figure 26-2
Layout of System Virtual Address Space

After the size of the system page table is calculated and rounded up to the next page boundary, any extra pages acquired are added to the pool of available system page table entries.

3. The restart parameter block is always one page long. In the notation of Figure 26-2, this is expressed by the following equation:

$$SVAS(rpb) = 1 \qquad (26.12)$$

The single page required for the restart parameter block is not counted when determining the initial size of the system page table. It is assumed that page rounding or one of the approximations will add the single SPTE required to map the RPB.

4. The number of pages in the PFN database is discussed in Section 26.2.2.

5. The space reserved for the paged dynamic memory area depends on the SYSBOOT parameter PAGEDYN. The parameter expresses the pool size in bytes and is truncated to the next smallest page boundary to give the pool size in pages. SYSBOOT modifies the parameter so that the next bootstrap operation will reflect the truncated pool size.

$$\text{SVAS(paged\_pool)} = \frac{\text{PAGEDYN}}{512} \qquad (26.13)$$

The pages in the middle of paged dynamic memory that have protection of EW are allocated by the utility program RMSSHARE to accommodate the data structures that RMS requires for shared files.

6. The space reserved for nonpaged pool is the sum of the size of nonpaged dynamic memory and the size of the the lookaside lists. The SYSBOOT parameter NPAGEDYN determines the size of nonpaged dynamic memory. The size of each portion of the lookaside list is determined by the size of the request packets and the number of packets in each list.

$$\text{SVAS(nonpaged\_pool)} = \frac{\text{NPAGEVIR}}{512}$$
$$+ \frac{\text{SRPSIZE} \times \text{SRPCOUNTV} + 511}{512}$$
$$+ \frac{\text{IRP\$C\_LENGTH} \times \text{IRPCOUNTV} + 511}{512}$$
$$+ \frac{(\text{LRPSIZE} + 64) \times \text{LRPCOUNTV} + 511}{512} \qquad (26.14)$$

Note that the size of nonpaged dynamic memory is truncated to the next smallest page boundary; the sizes of the lookaside lists are rounded up to the next page boundary.

7. The SYSBOOT parameter INTSTKPAGES gives the value of the interrupt stack in pages.

$$\text{SVAS(int\_stack)} = \text{INTSTKPAGES} \qquad (26.15)$$

In calculating the total size of the system page table, the guard pages (protection set to no access) at either end of the interrupt stack are not counted. These pages cause access violation exceptions (actually an interrupt stack not valid HALT) on both stack overflow and stack underflow.

8. The size of the system control block is CPU dependent. The VAX-11/730, the VAX-11/750, and the VAX-11/780 all contain the architectural system control block (see Figures 4-1 and 5-3). In addition the system control

Table 26-2a: Detailed Layout of System Virtual Address Space

The following pieces of the executive originate in the executive image file SYS$SYSTEM:SYS.EXE. The system addresses of each of these pieces remain unchanged until a new major release of the operating system.

Item	Global Address = Address (1)	Size	Protection	Owner	Pageable	Mapped by
System Service Vectors	VA$M_SYSTEM = 80000000	4 Pages	URKW	K	No	SYSBOOT
Nonpaged Executive Data	MMG$A_ENDVEC = 80000800	5 Pages + 288 Bytes	URKW	K	No	SYSBOOT
FCP Data Area	PMS$GL_FCP = 80000800	(1108 Bytes)	UREW (2)			
Linked Driver Data Structures	EXE$GL_BUGCHECK = 80000C54	(1740 Bytes)	URKW (2)			
Linked Driver Code	MMG$AL_BEGDRIVE = 80001320 DR$NT = 80001320	5 Pages + 84 Bytes	URKW	K	No	SYSBOOT
Nonpaged Executive Data	MMG$AL_ENDDRIVE = 80001DD8	12 Pages + 24 Bytes	URKW	K	No	SYSBOOT
Nonpaged Executive Routines	MMG$FRSTRONLY = 80003600 EXE$RESTART = 80003600	73 Pages (4)	UR	K	No	SYSBOOT
Pageable Executive Routines	@MMG$GL_PGDCOD = 8000C800 (4)	97 Pages	UR	K	Yes	SYSBOOT
Shell Process	SWP$GL_SHELLBAS = 80017A00	(8 Pages)	UR	K		
Usually Unmapped Pages	MMG$AL_PGDCODEN = 80018A00	48 Pages	NA	K	No (3)	SYSBOOT
XDELTA	(80018A00)	(18 Pages)	URKW (3)			
INIT	(8001AE00)	(10 Pages)				
BUGCHECK	(8001C200)	(20 Pages)				
End of Fixed Sized Portion of System Virtual Address Space	MMG$A_SYS_END = 8001EA00					

(1) Some global addresses listed here are only coincidentally at the beginning of the named region. Others, those whose names begin with MMG$, are defined in module MDAT solely as symbolic labels to delimit the portions of the linked executive.

(2) Although only 1108 bytes are used for file system statistics, the protection granularity defined by the VAX architecture is a page (512 bytes). For this reason, two entire pages (1024 bytes) are set to UREW protection. The remaining three pages in this area are set to URKW.

(3) The pages containing XDELTA only remain mapped if the R5 flag requesting the executive debugger is set when the system is initialized.

(4) The cell MMG$GL_PGDCOD points to the second page of the patch area that lies between the paged and nonpaged executive. Previous to Version 3.0, the end of the executive was established when the executive image was linked. This value is now determined when the module is assembled. If another patch page is required, the symbol will be changed to point to the next page.

Table 26-2b: Variable Size Portion—Mapped toward Increasing Virtual Addresses

The following pieces of the system are not a part of the executive image SYS.EXE. Their sizes are not fixed but rather depend on the values of specific SYSBOOT parameters or on the particular device and memory configuration. These pieces are located by storing their starting addresses in pointer fields, whose addresses are listed here.

The first items listed are mapped by INIT and SYSINIT. Items are mapped toward larger system virtual addresses. That is, the connect-to-interrupt pages are set aside first, I/O adapters are mapped next, and so on.

Item	Global Address of Pointer	Factors That Affect Size	Protection	Owner	Pageable	Mapped by
Beginning of Variable Sized Portion of System Virtual Address Space	MMG$A_SYS_END = 8001EA00					
System Virtual Pages for Connect-to-Interrupt	RBM$L_SPTFREL in Real-Time SPT Bitmap	REALTIME_SPTS	NA (1)	K	No	INIT
Mapping for I/O Addresses	MMG$GL_SBICONF (3)	Physical Configuration (Types of External Adapters)	KW	K	No (2)	INIT
System Virtual Page for System Disk Driver	UCB$L_SVPN in Unit Control Block for System Disk	Constant (1 Page)	KW	K	No	INIT
RMS Image	MMG$GL_RMSBASE	Size of RMS Image (168 Pages)	UR	K	Yes	SYSINIT
Null Page		Constant (1 Page)	NA	K		

Table 26-2b: Variable Size Portion—Mapped toward Increasing Virtual Addresses *(continued)*

Item	Global Address of Pointer	Factors That Affect Size	Protection	Owner	Pageable	Mapped by
System Message File	EXE$GL_SYSMSG	Size of System Message File (257 Pages)	UR	K	Yes	SYSINIT
Null Page			NA	K		
System Virtual Pages for Other Disk Drivers	UCB$L_SVPN in Unit Control Block for Each Unit	Number of Disk Units	KW	K	No (2)	SYSGEN in STARTUP.COM or When Driver Is Loaded
Pool of Available System Pages	BOO$GL_SPTFREL (4) BOO$GL_SPTFREH (4)	SPTREQ (Several Other Details)	NA	K		

(1) The pages set aside for connect-to-interrupt are only mapped No Access as part of initialization. These SPTEs are allocated in response to specific requests.

(2) It is meaningless to ask whether system virtual pages that are mapped to I/O addresses are pageable.

(3) MMG$GL_SBICONF is the address of a 16-longword array. Each longword array element contains the system virtual address of the first page that maps I/O addresses for that adapter.

(4) Locations BOO$GL_SPTFREL and BOO$GL_SPTFREH do not contain system virtual addresses. Rather, they contain the system virtual page numbers of the first and last pages in the pool of available SPTEs.

581

Table 26-2c: Variable Size Portion—Mapped toward Smaller Virtual Addresses

These pieces are also part of the dynamically configured portion of system virtual address space. Their sizes are determined by SYSBOOT parameters. These pieces are located by storing their starting addresses in pointer fields, whose addresses are listed here.

Item	Global Address of Pointer	Factors That Affect Size	Protection	Owner	Pageable	Mapped by
Restart Parameter Block	EXE$GL_RPB	Constant (1 Page)	URKW	K	No (1)	SYSBOOT
PFN Database	PFN$A_BASE PFN$AL_PTE	Everything	URKW	K	No	SYSBOOT
Paged Dynamic Memory	MMG$GL_PAGEDYN	PAGEDYN	URKW EW URKW	K	Yes	INIT
Nonpaged Dynamic Memory	MMG$GL_NPAGEDYN	NPAGEVIR	ERKW	K	No	SYSBOOT
Beginning of LRP list	IOC$GL_LRPSPLIT	LRPCOUNTV,LRPSIZE				
Beginning of IRP list	EXE$GL_SPLITADR	IRPCOUNTV				
Beginning of SRP list	IOC$GL_SRPSPLIT	SRPCOUNTV,SRPSIZE				
No Access Guard Page		Constant (1 Page)	NA	K		
Interrupt Stack	EXE$GL_INTSTK (S)	INTSTKPAGES	ERKW	K	No	SYSBOOT
No Access Guard Page		Constant (1 Page)	NA	K		
System Control Block	EXE$GL_SCB PR$_SCBB (P)	Constant (2) (1, 2, or 3 Pages)	ERKW	K	No	SYSBOOT
Balance Slot Area	SWP$GL_BALBASE	BALSETCNT Size of Process Header	ERKW	K	Yes (3)	SWAPPER
System Header	MMG$GL_SYSPHD	SYSMWCNT GBLSECTIONS	ERKW	K	No	SYSBOOT

Table 26-2c: Variable Size Portion—Mapped toward Smaller Virtual Addresses *(continued)*

Item	Global Address of Pointer	Factors That Affect Size	Protection	Owner	Pageable	Mapped by
System Page Table	MMG$GL_SPTBASE MMG$GL_GPTBASE MMG$GL_SBR (P) PR$_SBR (P)	Everything	ERKW	K	No	SYSBOOT
Global Page Table	MMG$GL_GPTE	GBLPAGES	URKW	K	Yes (4)	SYSBOOT
End of System Virtual Address Space	MMG$GL_MAXSYSVA MMG$GL_FRESVA MMG$GL_MAXGPTE					

(P) Global addresses or processor registers (PR$_name) whose names are followed by (P) contain physical addresses rather than system virtual addresses. The two physical addresses relevant to this table are the base of the system page table (in PR$_SBR) and the base of the system control block (in PR$_SCBB).

(S) The interrupt stack grows toward smaller virtual addresses. Thus, the contents of location EXE$GL_INTSTK point to the guard page that follows the interrupt stack.

(1) The restart parameter block does not page. However, it is not located in high physical memory as the rest of the nonpaged executive is. The restart parameter block is located in the first page of the the good 64K byte segment located by the memory bootstrap ROM. The page is not placed into the system working set so there is no way memory management can make the page invalid.

(2) The system control block on the VAX-11/730 and VAX-11/750 is two pages long. The system control block on a VAX-11/750 with a second UNIBUS is three pages long. The system control block on the VAX-11/780 is one page long.

(3) The process headers that reside in the balance slot area are a part of the process working set to which they are associated. Although portions of the process header do not page, the physical pages locked down in this manner are accounted for in process working sets and do not count toward the executive's use of memory.

(4) Global page tables are pageable. However, if a global page table page contains at least one valid global page table entry, then that page is locked into the system working set.

block in VAX-11/730 and VAX-11/750 processors has a second page devoted to UNIBUS interrupt dispatching (see Figure 5-3). If a VAX-11/750 has a second UNIBUS, it will have a third page in the system control block devoted to interrupt dispatching on that UNIBUS.

$$SVAS(scb) = \begin{cases} 2 \text{ (for the VAX-11/730)} \\ 2 \text{ or } 3 \text{ (for the VAX-11/750)} \\ 1 \text{ (for the VAX-11/780)} \end{cases} \tag{26.16}$$

9. The area devoted to balance slots constitutes more than half of system virtual address space in typical configurations. Its size depends on the SYSBOOT parameter BALSETCNT and the size of a process header in pages, calculated in Section 26.1. The constant size of balance slots makes this a trivial calculation.

$$SVAS(balance\_slots) = BALSETCNT \times PHD(pages) \tag{26.17}$$

The motivation behind constant size balance slots is explained in Chapter 14.

Because of the multiplicative nature of this relationship, it is necessary to reduce the BALSETCNT parameter in systems that must support a large process virtual address space. In a similar fashion, configurations that require a large number of concurrently resident processes should use a smaller value of VIRTUALPAGECNT.

10. The system header involves a calculation similar to the size of the process header, described in the last section. However, there is no optimization technique for empty pages because there is no large variation in working set sizes. There is also no need for the analog to process header page arrays because the system header does not describe an object that swaps. The size of the system page table, the system analog to process page tables, is calculated separately from the rest of the system header, which has a simple dependence on two SYSBOOT parameters.

The only system header components are the system equivalent to the working set list and the process section table in the process header. The system equivalents are the system working set list and the global section table. The SYSBOOT parameters that control their sizes are SYSMWCNT and GBLSECTIONS.

$$SVAS(sysphd) = \frac{\begin{cases} PHD\$K\_LENGTH + 4 \times SYSMWCNT \\ + 32 \times GBLSECTIONS + 511 \end{cases}}{512} \tag{26.18}$$

The system section table contains section table entries not only for all global sections but also for three system sections: the executive image itself, the RMS image, and the system message file.

11. The size of the system page table depends on the sizes of the other pieces of system address space. The calculation of its size is discussed in Section 26.2.2.
12. The last simple calculation of a portion of system virtual address space involves the size of the global page table, governed by the SYSBOOT parameter GBLPAGES.

$$SVAS(gpt) = \frac{GBLPAGES + 127}{128} \tag{26.19}$$

26.2.2   System Page Table and the PFN Database

The PFN database contains a description of each page of physical memory. However, it does not contain information about the nonpaged executive. Because the PFN database is part of the nonpaged executive, its size depends on itself. However, the situation is more complicated. The system page table, also nonpaged, maps the PFN database. Thus the size of the PFN database depends on its own size in two different ways.

The significance of the number 18 in the following equation is that there are 18 bytes of information stored for each page of physical memory. As explained in Chapter 14, each physical page is described by two byte arrays, six word arrays, and two longword arrays. Because the two link arrays overlap two other arrays, this amounts to a total of 18 bytes of information for each physical page. This value is represented by the global constant PFN$C_WORD_LEN defined by module SYSPARAM (or PARAMETER).

$$SVAS(pfn) = \frac{18 \times (PHYSICAL - NO\_PFN\_DATA) + 511}{512} \tag{26.20}$$

The value PHYSICAL represents the size of physical memory:

$$\begin{aligned}PHYSICAL = \text{minimum (size of physical memory,} \\ PHYSICALPAGES)\end{aligned} \tag{26.21}$$

NO_PFN_DATA represents the nonpaged portions of system space that are not accounted for in the PFN database.

$$\begin{aligned}NO\_PFN\_DATA = \; &SVAS(nonpaged\_exec) \\ &+ SVAS(pfn) \\ &+ SVAS(nonpaged\_pool) \\ &+ SVAS(int\_stack) \\ &+ SVAS(scb) \\ &+ SVAS(sysphd) \\ &+ SVAS(spt)\end{aligned} \tag{26.22}$$

The nonpaged portion of the executive image, SVAS(nonpaged_exec), is a subset of SVAS(sptreq) when computing the size of the system page table. Its size is variable, depending on the size of the paged portion of the executive.

$$SVAS(nonpaged\_exec) = MMG\$GL\_PGDCOD - MMG\$A\_ENDVEC \qquad (26.23)$$

Notice that the PFN database depends on its own size explicitly (through the NO_PFN_DATA term) and also implicitly through the size of the system page table (Equation 26.24).

In a similar fashion, the size of the system page table depends on its own size explicitly and implicitly through the size of the PFN database.

$$SAVS(spt) = \frac{THE\_REST + SVAS(spt) + SVAS(pfn) + 127}{128} \qquad (26.24)$$

THE_REST represents all contributions to system address space except for the system page table and the PFN database.

$$\begin{aligned}
THE\_REST = \ &SVAS(sptskel) \\
&+SVAS(sptreq) + SVAS(rpb) \\
&+ SVAS(paged\_pool) \\
&+ SVAS(nonpaged\_pool) \\
&+ SVAS(int\_stack) \\
&+ SVAS(scb) \\
&+ SVAS(balance\_slots) \\
&+ SVAS(sysphd) \\
&+ SVAS(gpt)
\end{aligned}$$

26.2.3 Approximation Used by SYSBOOT

For some large values of either VIRTUALPAGECNT or physical memory size, an iterative calculation for the sizes of these two quantities does not converge but rather oscillates about a stable solution.

To avoid this problem, a simplification in the calculation is made. The number of system page table entries set aside for the PFN database does not take into account the fact that the pages occupied by the nonpaged executive are not accounted for in the PFN database.

$$SVAS(pfn) = \frac{18 \times PHYSICAL + 511}{512} \qquad (26.25)$$

This relation replaces Equation 26.20 in the calculation of the size of the system page table. It also greatly simplifies Equation 26.24 because the SVAS(pfn) term no longer depends on SVAS(spt). Instead, SVAS(pfn) is a constant.

586

Because Equation 26.25 errs on the high side in allocating SPTEs for the PFN database, the number of SPTEs set aside for the system page table does not use Equation 26.24 iteratively. Instead, there is a single pass on calculating the size of the system page table.

$$SVAS(spt,0) = \frac{THE\_REST + SVAS(pfn)}{128} \tag{26.26}$$

$$SVAS(spt) = \frac{THE\_REST + SVAS(pfn) + SVAS(spt,0) + 127}{128} \tag{26.27}$$

Because physical pages are not allocated for the PFN database until the system page table size has been calculated, there is no large waste of physical memory. The only effect of these two approximations might be one more physical page allocated for the system page table than is absolutely necessary. The allocation of an extra page would only occur on systems with very large amounts of memory in the first place, so the loss is practically unnoticed.

26.2.4   Renormalization of SPTREQ

The rounding of the size of the system page table to the next highest page boundary can add extra system page table entries to those required to map the entire system. After SYSBOOT has calculated the result of Equation 26.27, it maps the linked executive beginning at the low address end of system address space (80000000) and maps the dynamic portion of system space beginning at the high address end.

Any pages left over after this mapping are put into the pool of system page table entries located by BOO$GL_SPTFREL and BOO$GL_SPTFREH. As SPTEs are needed for further mapping (for example by SYSINIT to map RMS and the system message file or by SYSGEN when loading drivers that require a system virtual page number), these pages are taken from the pool. Once the entire system is mapped, any extra pages (due to rounding as well as an overestimate of the SPTREQ parameter) remain in the pool of system page table entries.

26.3   PHYSICAL MEMORY REQUIREMENTS OF THE EXECUTIVE

Once the sizes of the various pieces of system address space have been calculated, it is possible to list the total physical memory requirements of the executive, the number of pages that are not available for user processes.

26.3.1   Physical Memory Used by the Executive

Table 26-3 lists each piece of the nonpaged executive and either its size in pages or an equation number in Section 26.2 that describes how its size is computed.

Table 26-3: Division of System Virtual Address Space into Nonpaged and Paged Pieces

The following portions of system address space are permanently mapped by SYS-BOOT. The physical pages that they occupy are not accounted for in the PFN database.

Item	Size
Nonpaged Portion of Executive Image	MMG$GL_PGDCOD through MMG$A_ENDVEC
PFN Database	Equation 26.25
Nonpaged Dynamic Memory	Equation 26.14
Interrupt Stack	Equation 26.15
System Control Block	Equation 26.16
System Header	Equation 26.18
System Page Table	Equation 26.27

The following are the pageable portions of the executive. Their total memory cost can never exceed SYSMWCNT.

Item	Size
Paged Executive Routines	MMG$AL_PGDCODEN through MMG$GL_PGDCOD
RMS Image	Size of RMS Image (168 Pages)
System Message File	Size of System Message File (257 Pages)
Paged Dynamic Memory	Equation 26.13
Global Page Table Pages	Equation 26.19

The following portions of system address do not require physical memory accounted for in Equation 26.27.

Item	Reason
XDELTA, INIT, and BUGCHECK	Usually Not Mapped
I/O Space Mapping	I/O Addresses
SVPNs for Disk Drivers	I/O Addresses or Double Mapping
Balance Slot Area	Process Header Pages and Page Table Pages are Charged to Process Working Sets

$$\begin{aligned}
\text{NONPAGED} = \ & \text{SVAS(nonpaged\_exec)} \\
& + \text{SVAS(rpb)} \\
& + \text{SVAS(pfn)} \\
& + \text{SVAS(nonpaged\_pool)} \\
& + \text{SVAS(int\_stack)} \\
& + \text{SVAS(scb)} \\
& + \text{SVAS(sysphd)} \\
& + \text{SVAS(spt)}
\end{aligned} \tag{26.28}$$

This initial sum is the total memory requirement of the nonpaged executive code and data tables. The paged executive (see Table 26-3) also requires physical memory. However, it is reasonable to assume that the system working set is full at all times so that the physical memory requirements of the paged executive are simply SYSMWCNT pages.

Two final items must be taken into account when calculating the number of physical pages used by the executive. The SYSBOOT parameters FREELIM and MPW_LOLIM set low-limit thresholds on the number of pages on the free and modified page lists. These parameters should be included when calculating the number of available physical pages.

$$
\begin{aligned}
\text{MEMORY} = \ &\text{NONPAGED} \\
&+ \text{SYSMWCNT} \\
&+ \text{FREELIM} \\
&+ \text{MPW\_LOLIM}
\end{aligned}
\tag{26.29}
$$

$$
\text{AVAILABLE} = \text{PHYSICAL} - \text{MEMORY}
\tag{26.30}
$$

By working back from Equation 26.30, it is possible to obtain the number of available physical pages in terms of the contents of a SYSGEN parameter file and one more input parameter, the size of physical memory.

26.3.2 System Processes

When attempting to assess the total memory required by the system, one more factor must be taken into account. All memory-resident system processes require a number of pages equal to their respective working set sizes. The following processes are considered to be system processes:

- Job Controller
- Print Symbiont(s) (if any)
- Error Logger Format Process (ERRFMT)
- Operator Communication Process (OPCOM)
- Disk ACP(s) (at least one)
- Magtape ACP(s) (if any)
- Network ACP (NETACP) (if any)
- Remote Terminal ACP (REMACP) (if any)

The amount of memory required by these processes cannot be calculated in closed form as the executive's memory requirements are calculated, for several reasons:

- The memory consumed by a process is its working set size. Automatic working set size adjustment causes this process attribute to vary over time (assuming, of course, that the process in question reaches its working set limit, a reasonable assumption for system processes). The working set of any process in the system is readily available from the Monitor Utility (MONITOR).

- Sharing confuses the issue. However, the DCL command SHOW SYSTEM lists the physical memory used by each process in the system.
- System processes can be outswapped, temporarily reducing the physical memory requirements of those processes to zero.

Because physical memory requirements of system processes vary over time and can be easily obtained from a utility such as MONITOR or with the SHOW SYSTEM command, they are not included in any equations in this chapter. However, their requirements should be taken into account when any type of configuration calculation is made. This chapter has provided a tool for calculating the memory requirements of the executive, a number that is not so readily available.

26.4   SIZES OF PIECES OF P1 SPACE

Most of the pieces of P1 space have predetermined sizes, based on the contents of module SHELL in the executive. This module includes a skeleton P1 page table that is used, to set up an initial P1 page table when a process is created.

Some pieces of P1 space are dynamically configured, with sizes that are determined by a variety of techniques. Table 26-4 lists the pieces of P1 space and how the size of each is determined. The following list includes details about each dynamic portion of P1 space. Like P1 space itself, the list moves toward lower virtual addresses.

1. All of the pieces of P1 space from the debugger symbol table to the process I/O segment have their sizes determined by assembly-time parameters in module SHELL.
2. The P1 window to the process header includes all of the process header except for page table pages (see Table 26-1). The empty pages are included in the P1 window. Section 26.1 relates the size of the process header to the relevant SYSBOOT parameters.
3. The LOGINOUT image maps the selected command language interpreter into P1 space for interactive and batch jobs. (A merged image activation accomplishes this mapping.) The size of the CLI image determines how much space is taken up by the CLI.
4. The SYSBOOT parameter CLISYMTBL determines the number of demand zero pages that are created by LOGINOUT for the CLI symbol table.
5. The special SYSBOOT parameter IMGIOCNT determines the default number of pages that are created by the image activator for the image I/O segment, the RMS impure area for files opened during the execution of a specific image.

The default number of image I/O segment pages can be overridden for a specific image by including the following line as a part of the link time option file:

$$IOSEGMENT = n,[[NO]P0BUFS] \hspace{4em} (26.31)$$

6. The special SYSBOOT parameter EXUSRSTK determines the number of extra pages that are allocated for the user stack by the image activator. These pages are not used for the user stack. Instead, they are at a higher virtual address than the initial value of the user stack pointer.

    These pages allow the operating system to recover if the user stack is corrupted.

7. The size of the user stack is determined by the following option in an options file at link time.

$$STACK = n \hspace{6em} (26.32)$$

The default user stack size is 20 pages.

Because the stack is automatically expanded by the system's access violation handler when the user stack overflows, there is little need for using this option. One possible use might be for an image that requires a large amount of stack space but cannot afford the overhead required for automatic stack expansion at run time.

Table 26-4a: Detailed Layout of P1 Space (Variable Size Portion)

The size of the first portion of P1 space, from the user stack to the P1 window to the process header, is mainly dependent on SYSBOOT parameters. The sizes of each of these pieces may vary for different systems, different processes in the same system, or even different images in the same process.

Item	Global Address of Pointer	Factors That Affect Size	Protection	Owner	Pageable	Mapped by
Low Address End of P1 Space	@PHD$L_FREP1VA (Offset into the Process Header)					
User Stack		STACK = (Link Time Option)	UW	U	Yes	Image Activator
Extra User Stack Pages		EXUSRSTK	UW	U	Yes	Image Activator
Image I/O Segment	@PIO$GW_IIOIMPA + 4 @CTL$AL_STACK + (3*4) (S)	IOSEGMENTS = (Link Time Option)	UREW	E	Yes	Image Activator
Boundary between Process-Permanent and Image-Specific Pieces of P1 Space	@CTL$GL_CTLBASVA (1)					
Per-Process Message Section	@CTL$GL_PPMSG	Size of Message Section	UR	E	Yes	SET MESSAGE Command
CLI Symbol Table		CLISYMTBL	SW	S	Yes	LOGINOUT
CLI Image	@CTL$AG_CLIMAGE	CLI Image Size	UR	S	Yes	LOGINOUT

Table 26-4a: Detailed Layout of P1 Space (Variable Size Portion) *(continued)*

Item	Global Address of Pointer	Factors That Affect Size	Protection	Owner	Pageable	Mapped by
Initial End of P1 Space for Every Process in This System	@MMG$GL_CTLBASVA (2)					
P1 Window to Process Header	@CTL$GL_PHD	Size of the Process Header	SRKW	K	No	Code in SHELL
Channel Control Block Table	@CTL$GL_CCBASE	CHANNELCNT	UREW	K	Yes	Code in EXE$PROCSTRT

@ In the global address column, symbol names preceded by the symbol @ are the addresses of pointers to the specific portions of P1 space. Symbol names with no preceding @ sign are the actual addresses of the areas in question.

(S) Stacks grow toward smaller virtual addresses. This is the reason for the seeming anomaly in the addresses and pointers that delimit the four per-process stacks. The channel control block table also grows toward smaller virtual addresses.

a. Global location CTL$AL_STACK is the address of a four longword array whose elements contain the initial values of the four per-process stack pointers. An array element can be indexed with the access mode as an argument. A fifth longword, preceding the array and accessed with an index of −1, locates the low address end of the kernel stack.

In the table, the explicit multiplications reflect the multiplication by four that is implied by indexed addressing in longword context. That is, CTL$AL_STACK + 3*4 locates the beginning of the user stack. CTL$AL_STACK + 2*4 locates the beginning of the supervisor stack. CTL$AL_STACK + 1*4 locates the beginning of the executive stack. CTL$AL_STACK + 0*4 locates the beginning of the kernel stack. CTL$AL_STACK + (−1*4) locates the end of the kernel stack.

b. The channel number returned to the caller of the Assign Channel system service (or some other system service or RMS call) is a negative byte index from the contents of CTL$GL_CCBBASE to the beginning of the channel control block for the selected channel.

(1) The contents of location CTL$GL_CTLBASVA locate the boundary between the image-specific portion of P1 space (deleted at image exit by routine MMG$IMGRESET) and the process-permanent portion of P1 space.

(2) The contents of global location MMG$GL_CTLBASVA locate the initial size of P1 space, including the linked executive and the P1 window to the process header. All processes have this as their initial size of P1 space. As command language interpreters and other dynamic portions of P1 space such as process-permanent message sections are added, location CTL$GL_CTLBASVA is updated to reflect the change.

Table 26-4b: Detailed Layout of P1 Space (Fixed Size Portion)

The rest of P1 space is fixed in size and locations for all possible systems. The sizes of each of these pieces are determined by assembly time parameters in module SHELL. These pieces are implicitly mapped by the Swapper when the skeleton P1 page tables are swapped in from the shell process at the time that the process is created.

Item	Global Address = Address or Global Address of Pointer	Size in Pages	Protection	Owner	Pageable
Process I/O Segment	PIO$GL_FMLH = 7FFD8E00 @CTL$GL_RMSPP	60 pages	UREW	E	Yes
Per-Process Common for Users	7FFE0600	4 pages	UW	K	Yes
Per-Process Common for DIGITAL	CTL$A_COMMON = 7FFE0E00	4 pages	UW	K	Yes
Compatibility Mode Data Page	CTL$AG_CMEDATA = 7FFE1600 CTL$AL_CMCNTX = 7FFE1600	1 page	UW	K	Yes
VMS User-Mode Data Page	UWVECPAG = 7FFE1800	1 page	UW	K	Yes
Not Currently Used	7FFE1A00	2 pages	NA	K	Yes
Image Activator Context Page	IMGACTCTX = 7FFE1E00	1 page	UREW	E	Yes
Process Allocation Region	CTL$A_PRCALLREG = 7FFE2000	46 pages	UREW	K	Yes
Generic CLI Data Pages	CTL$AL_CLICALBK = 7FFE7C00	6 pages	URSW	S	Yes
Image Activator Scratch Pages	MMG$IMGACTBUF = 7FFE8800 CLIDATAEND	8 pages	UREW	U	Yes
Debugger Context Pages	7FFE9800	4 pages	UW	U	Yes
Vectors for User-Written System Services and Per-Image or Per-Process Messages	CTL$A_DISPVEC = 7FFEA000	2 pages	UREW	K	Yes
Image Header Buffer	MMG$IMGHDRBUF = 7FFEA400 @CTL$GL_IMGHDRBF	1 page	UW	E	Yes
No Access Guard Page	7FFEA600	1 page	NA	K	

Table 26-4b: Detailed Layout of P1 Space (Fixed Size Portion) (continued)

Item	Global Address = Address or Global Address of Pointer	Size in Pages	Protection	Owner	Pageable
Kernel Stack	CTL$GL_KSTKBAS = 7FFEA800 (S) / @CTL$AL_STACK + (−1*4) (S)	3 pages	SRKW	K	No
Executive Stack	CTL$GL_KSPINI = 7FFEAE00 (S) / @CTL$AL_STACK + (0*4) (S)	8 pages	SREW	E	Yes
Supervisor Stack	7FFEBE00 / @CTL$AL_STACK + (1*4) (S)	16 pages	URSW	S	Yes
System Service Vectors	P1SYSVECTORS = 7FFEDE00 / SYS$QIO	16 pages	URKW	K	Yes
P1 Pointer Page	CTL$GL_VECTORS = 7FFEFE00 / @CTL$AL_STACK + (2*4) (S)	1 page	URKW	K	No
Debugger Symbol Table		128 pages			

@ In the global address column, symbol names preceded by the symbol @ are the addresses of pointers to the specific portions of P1 space. Symbol names with no preceding @ sign are the actual addresses of the areas in question.

(S) Stacks grow toward smaller virtual addresses. This is the reason for the seeming anomaly in the addresses and pointers that delimit the four per-process stacks. The channel control block table also grows toward smaller virtual addresses.

a. Global location CTL$AL_STACK is the address of a four longword array whose elements contain the initial values of the four per-process stack pointers. An array element can be indexed with the access mode as an argument. A fifth longword, preceding the array and accessed with an index of −1, locates the low address end of the kernel stack.

In the table, the explicit multiplications reflect the multiplication by four that is implied by indexed addressing in longword context. That is, CTL$AL_STACK + 3*4 locates the beginning of the user stack. CTL$AL_STACK + 2*4 locates the beginning of the supervisor stack. CTL$AL_STACK + 1*4 locates the beginning of the executive stack. CTL$AL_STACK + 0*4 locates the beginning of the kernel stack. CTL$AL_STACK + (−1*4) locates the end of the kernel stack.

b. The channel number returned to the caller of the Assign Channel system service (or some other system service or RMS call) is a negative byte index from the contents of CTL$GL_CCBBASE to the beginning of the channel control block for the selected channel.

27 Powerfail Recovery

For there are moments when one can
neither think nor feel. And if one can
neither think nor feel, she thought,
where is one?

—Virginia Woolf, *To the Lighthouse*

Powerfail recovery support allows suitably equipped VAX/VMS systems to survive power fluctuations and power outages of short duration with no loss of operation. The support is provided by hardware features (battery backup) and VMS software routines.

VMS software support includes a power failure service routine that saves the volatile state of the machine before the power fails, a power recovery routine that restores that state, and device-specific code within many VAX/VMS device drivers. Some drivers are able to resume I/O operations that were in progress when the power failed. Others simply abort the request that was in progress. The VMS operating system also provides process notification by means of power recovery ASTs. The powerfail routine starts at EXE$POWER-FAIL in module POWERFAIL.

27.1 POWERFAIL SEQUENCE

When a fluctuation or drop in operating voltage occurs, the CPU generates a powerfail interrupt. This interrupt causes control to be passed to the routine whose address is stored in offset 12 in the system control block, at the same time raising IPL to 30. The fact that powerfail is an interrupt with a finite IPL associated with it allows powerfail interrupts to be blocked for a short sequence of instructions, avoiding many potential synchronization problems.

The VMS powerfail interrupt service routine saves the volatile machine state (those registers whose contents are not preserved by some sort of battery backup) in main memory (which is preserved by battery backup), either on the interrupt stack or in the restart parameter block. The interrupt stack pointer (ISP) is the last value saved. By checking the value of the saved ISP, the powerfail recovery routine can insure that the interrupt service routine preserved all the required registers. Lists of the registers preserved by the powerfail service routine and restored by the restart routine are found in Tables 27-1 and 27-2. Once the registers have been saved, the powerfail service routine waits in the following tight loop until the hardware generates a HALT operation:

Table 27-1: Data Saved by Powerfail Routine and Restored During Power Recovery

The elements in Group A are restored before memory management is reenabled. The restart parameter block is accessed through its physical address.

Group A

Element	Where Stored
System Base Register	Restart Parameter Block
System Length Register	Restart Parameter Block
Software Interrupt Summary Register	Restart Parameter Block
System Control Block Base Register	Restart Parameter Block
Process Control Block Base Register	Restart Parameter Block
Interrupt Stack Pointer	Restart Parameter Block

The elements in Group B are all restored after memory management has been reenabled, which allows the interrupt stack to be accessed through its normal system virtual address.

Group B

Element	Where Stored
CPU-Specific Processor Registers (See Table 27-2)	Interrupt Stack
Process-Specific Processor Registers P1 Length Register P1 Base Register P0 Length Register P0 Base Register Performance Monitor Enable AST Level Register	Interrupt Stack
Four Per-Process Stack Pointers	Interrupt Stack

The elements in Group C are not restored until the other power recovery steps described in the text are performed and the powerfail interrupt dismissed. The PC/PSL pair are restored by the REI instruction that dismisses the interrupt.

Group C

Element	Where Stored
General Registers (R0 through FP)	Interrupt Stack
Interrupt PC and PSL	Interrupt Stack

```
10$:    BRB 10$
```

The BRB instruction was chosen over an explicit HALT in the software service routine to avoid confusing the restart logic by triggering a restart too soon.

27.2 POWER RECOVERY

The power recovery sequence performs various validity checks in a CPU-dependent fashion and then passes control to the VMS restart routine. This

Table 27-2: CPU-Specific Registers Saved by Powerfail Routine

The following CPU-specific processor registers are saved on and restored from the interrupt stack. Note that there are no CPU-specific processor registers for the VAX-11/730.

Element	CPU
Translation Buffer Disable Register	VAX-11/750
Memory Cache Disable Register	VAX-11/750
SBI Maintenance Register	VAX-11/780

routine restores the saved state of the machine and then notifies each device driver in the system that power has failed so that the drivers can take device-specific action to restore interrupted I/O requests.

27.2.1 Initial Step in Power Recovery

The initial step in recovery from a power failure is performed by either hardware or microcode and is CPU-dependent. The general purpose of any of these routines is to perform the following:

- Verify that the contents of memory survived the power outage
- Locate the power recovery routine through the restart parameter block (RPB)
- Pass control to that routine

A restart parameter block (RPB) is a page-aligned block of physical memory whose first four longwords contain the following:

1. The physical address of the RPB (contents of location equals address of location)
2. The physical address of the restart routine, EXE$RESTART in module POWERFAIL.
3. A checksum of the first 31 longwords in the restart routine
4. A warm restart flag

The restart parameter block is usually stored starting at address 0 (provided that the memory at that location is good). The RPB in the VAX-11/782 must be stored at address 0.

When searching for a restart parameter block, the console subsystem searches for a longword that contains its own address. The contents of the second longword (the restart routine address, EXE$RESTART) are examined to determine that they hold a valid physical address (and not zero, in case a page of zeros passes the first test). If the address is acceptable, the checksum of the first 31 words of the restart routine is calculated. The checksum is then compared to the checksum in the RPB. If the two checksums are equal, the page contains an RPB and the restart routine is intact.

27.2.1.1   **Power Recovery on the VAX-11/730.** When power is restored on a VAX-11/ 730, the console subsystem gains control and proceeds with its normal power on actions. If the AUTO RESTART/BOOT switch on the front of the processor cabinet is in the OFF position, the console program simply prints its prompt on the console terminal and waits for input. (Note that the AUTO RESTART/BOOT switch on the front panel should be switched off when first turning on a VAX-11/730 system to avoid an unnecessary restart attempt.)

If the AUTO RESTART/BOOT switch is in the ON position the console subsystem searches through physical memory for a valid restart parameter block. In searching for the restart parameter block, the contents of memory are tested to determine whether memory successfully survived the power outage.

If an RPB is not located, the restart fails and the console subsystem attempts to bootstrap the system. If the RPB is located, the warm restart inhibit flag (bit<1> in the fourth longword of the RPB) is checked. A bit set indicates that a warm restart has already been attempted and failed. DEFBOO.CMD is then executed in order to bootstrap the system.

If the warm restart inhibit flag is clear, the console subsystem performs the following steps:

- The warm restart inhibit flag is set, to prevent a second restart attempt.
- The address of the RPB + 200 (hex) is loaded into SP.
- A value indicating the cause of the restart is loaded into AP.
- Control is transferred to the restart routine. The address of the restart routine is located in the second longword of the RPB.

27.2.1.2   **Power Recovery on the VAX-11/750.** The console program (see Chapter 24) is the first program that executes in response to a power recovery on the VAX-11/750. This program first checks the setting of the power-on action switch. If the switch is in either the HALT or BOOT position, the console program performs the designated action. If the switch is in either the RESTART/ BOOT or RESTART/HALT position, the console program attempts a restart. Only if the restart fails is the second option (BOOT or HALT) used.

The console program then attempts to locate the restart parameter block. In searching for the restart parameter block, the contents of memory are tested to determine whether memory successfully survived the power outage. This test can identify two different conditions, either of which prevents successful recovery:

- A system that does not have battery backup, in which case, the contents of memory were lost when the power failed.
- A situation where the power was off for longer than ten minutes, the amount of time that battery backup is capable of preserving the contents of memory. (This time depends on the amount of memory present but is not shorter than ten minutes.)

If a valid RPB cannot be located, or if the restart flag is set, the restart attempt has failed and the console program takes its alternative option. If a valid RPB is located, the console program transfers control to the restart routine whose address was stored in the restart parameter block.

27.2.1.3 **Power Recovery on the VAX-11/780.** When power is restored on the VAX-11/780, the console subsystem (LSI-11) goes through the same sequence that it does when a system is being initialized (see Chapter 24). If power is also being restored on the LSI-11, CONSOL.SYS is loaded from the console floppy. No state for the LSI-11 is preserved across a power failure.

The console program then proceeds with its normal power-on actions. If the autorestart switch on the front of the processor cabinet is in the OFF position, or if the warm start inhibit flag maintained by the console program is set, the console program simply prints its prompt on the console terminal and waits for input. (Note that the autorestart switch on the front panel should be switched off when first turning on a VAX-11/780 system to avoid an unnecessary restart attempt.)

If the autorestart switch is in the ON position and the warm start inhibit flag is clear, the console program uses the contents of the command file RESTAR.CMD to direct further action. Before RESTAR.CMD executes, the writeable control store contents are reloaded from the console floppy (from file WCSxxx.PAT). The contents of WCS were not preserved by the battery backup that preserved the contents of main memory. Note that reloading WCS makes power recovery on the VAX-11/780 somewhat slower than in the VAX-11/750, where I/O is not an integral part of power recovery.

The file RESTAR.CMD can contain any valid console commands. The RESTAR.CMD that is distributed with the VMS operating system contains commands designed to restart a running VMS system. (On systems with more than two memory controllers, the UNIBUS adapter is not located at TR 3. On such systems, RESTAR.CMD must be altered so that R1 is loaded with the TR number of the UNIBUS adapter. This step is necessary because the UNIBUS mapping registers are used by ROM restart code as temporary storage.) RESTAR.CMD contains the following lines:

```
HALT                        ! Halt processor
INIT                        ! Initialize processor
DEPOSIT/I 11 20003800       ! Set address of SCB base
DEPOSIT R0 0                ! Clear unused register
DEPOSIT R1 n                ! TR number for UNIBUS adapter
DEPOSIT R2 0                ! Clear unused register
DEPOSIT R3 0                ! Clear unused register
DEPOSIT R4 0                ! Clear unused register
DEPOSIT R5 0                ! Clear unused register
DEPOSIT FP 0                ! No machine check expected
START 20003004              ! Start restart referee
```

Note that RESTAR.CMD is different on the VAX-11/782 multiprocessing system; RESTAR.CMD for the VAX-11/782 is described in Chapter 28.

The START command passes control to the same ROM program that is used during system initialization, except that the program is entered at its restart entry point.

The memory ROM program determines if the contents of main memory are valid. If they are, the ROM program attempts to locate the restart parameter block.

If a valid RPB cannot be found, or if the warm restart flag in the RPB is clear, the ROM program returns control to the console program, which attempts a cold start (bootstrap). This indication is actually made by the memory ROM program writing a "reboot" signal into one of the console registers with the following instruction:

```
MTPR    #^XF02,#PR$_TXDB
```

Otherwise, the memory ROM program passes control to the restart routine (whose address is stored in the RPB). The special uses of the PR$_TXDB register for communication from the VAX-11 CPU to the console program are described in Chapter 19.

27.2.2   Operation of the Restart Routine

The VMS restart routine, EXE$RESTART, receives control with the following conditions:

- In kernel mode
- On the interrupt stack (SP = RPB base + 200 hex)
- With memory management disabled
- At IPL 31

These initial conditions are similar to the entry to VMB, except that the RPB has already been loaded. One more similarity between the entry to the restart routine and VMB is that SP points 200 (hex) bytes past the RPB. This pointer serves two purposes. The contents of SP are used to locate the RPB. The last several longwords in the page that contains the RPB will be used as stack space by the restart routine until the saved interrupt stack pointer is restored.

The restart routine first clears two warm start inhibit flags. One of these flags is CPU-dependent and is cleared by writing a special code into the console transmit data buffer register.

```
MTPR    #^XF03,#PR$_TXDB
```

The other flag is located in the restart parameter block and is cleared with a BICL instruction. The use of these so-called loopbreaker flags is discussed further in Section 27.3.2.

All information stored in the RPB by the powerfail service routine is restored next (see Table 27-1). Most of this information is necessary to turn memory management back on. A dummy P0 page table is set up (just like the one set up by SYSBOOT) so that the page containing the restart routine is mapped as a P0 virtual address that, when translated, yields the identical physical address. Chapter 25 shows how the contents of P0BR are determined to produce this identity mapping.

After the P0 page table is set up, memory management is enabled using the same two instructions used by INIT:

```
        MTPR    #1,#PR$_MAPEN
        JMP     @#10$
10$:
```

(Details of this technique can be found in the beginning of Chapter 25.)

Once memory management has been enabled, the restart routine is able to restore the data that was saved on the interrupt stack. Before the data can be restored, a check is made to determine whether the restart was initiated as a part of powerfail recovery or in response to some other restart condition detected by the console logic. All other reasons for restart are errors. The VMS restart routine simply issues a reason-specific bugcheck (which will result in a cold start, a bootstrap, if the SYSBOOT flag BUGREBOOT is set). By causing a bugcheck, the VMS operating system makes information available about the error condition through a crash dump.

Before moving the saved value of the interrupt stack pointer to the SP, the saved value is checked. If the value is 0, the ISP was not saved in the powerfail interrupt service routine. If this is the case, the bugcheck message, STATENTSVD, software state not saved during powerfail, is issued and a cold restart is attempted.

Table 27-1 indicates the information that is restored from the interrupt stack. The restart routine does not use SP to restore this data. Rather, it uses a scratch register (R6) to traverse the stack to prevent the data on the stack from being overwritten in case another power failure occurs while the data is being restored. This use of a scratch register allows the restart routine to be repeated as many times as necessary without taking any special action.

After everything except the general registers has been restored, the restart routine takes the following steps:

1. A new system time is calculated. (The time-of-year clock kept running while the power was off. Its contents are used to recalibrate EXE$GQ_SYSTIME.)

2. The restart time plus three minutes is computed and stored at the global location EXE$GL_PWRDONE. This value represents the time it may take all hardware components to become fully operational again. Device drivers can use the routine EXE$PWRTIMCHK to make sure that these three minutes have passed before executing restarted $QIOs. The reason the

time is as long as three minutes is that it takes that long for mechanical devices (such as disks) to become operational.

3. The timer queue is scanned. All timer queue elements that have expired have the recalibrated time substituted for their absolute due time. This substitution is done to allow periodic timer requests to reestablish internal synchronization.

   To illustrate the purpose of this step, suppose that a periodic timer request was declared with a period of one minute and the power was off for three minutes. With no adjustment of the absolute due time, three requests would expire immediately following power recovery. The readjustment causes one request to come due immediately, with the next request not occurring until one minute later.

   Note that relative synchronization between several requests may be lost as a result of a power failure. For example, if one request is due to expire in two minutes, a second is due to expire in five minutes (or three minutes after the first), and the power is off for more than five minutes, then both requests will be delivered at the same time. A power recovery AST might be used to allow multiple requests to reestablish their relative synchronization.

4. A power recovery entry is made in the error log.

5. External adapters are initialized.

6. All external devices are notified that a power failure and recovery sequence have occurred. This step is detailed in Section 27.2.3.

7. In the final step the following operations are performed:

   - The SP is set up to point to the saved general registers on the interrupt stack.
   - The general registers are restored.
   - The last sanity check flag, EXE$GL_PFAILTIM, is cleared (see Section 27.3.1).
   - RPB$L_ISP is cleared (so that the powerfail recovery routine will find a 0 if the state is incompletely saved in the next power failure).
   - The powerfail interrupt is dismissed with an REI instruction.

27.2.3 Device Notification

External devices are notified that a power failure has occurred in two stages.

While the power recovery routine is executing (at IPL 31 so that another powerfail interrupt cannot occur), each driver is called at its controller initialization routine for each controller and at its unit initialization routine for each unit. The powerfail bit UCB$V_POWER in the UCB status word UCB$W_STS is set to allow each driver routine to differentiate between power recovery and ordinary initialization.

In addition, the entire I/O database is scanned, looking for units that are expecting interrupts or have timed I/O outstanding. The power recovery routine clears their interrupt-expected bits, sets their timeout-expected bits, and sets their due times to zero. These actions cause each device to appear to have timed out. The check for device timeout occurs as a result of the system subroutine that executes once a second. That routine will not execute until both of the following occur:

1. The hardware clock interrupts (IPL has dropped below 24).
2. The software timer executes as part of the system subroutine that has probably expired while the power was down. (This will not happen until the IPL is lowered below 7.)

Thus, each device that was expecting an interrupt will appear to have timed out. A driver's timeout routine can differentiate between genuine timeout and power failure by checking the UCB$V_POWER bit.

In a VMS system, most of the work done to recover from a power failure occurs in drivers. VMS disk drivers and magnetic tape drivers are capable of restarting whatever request they were processing when the power failed in such a way that the power failure is totally transparent to them. (If a magnetic tape unit lost vacuum, operator intervention is required to reestablish the vacuum and rewind the tape. Once that is done, the driver automatically restarts the I/O request that was in progress when the power failed.)

27.2.4 Process Notification

The VMS operating system also allows processes to be notified, by receiving an AST, that a power failure and subsequent recovery happened. A process requests this notification by using the Set Power Recovery AST system service.

27.2.4.1 $SETPRA System Service. The Set Power Recovery AST system service is an extremely simple service that performs two steps:

- The address of the AST is stored in global location CTL$GL_POWERAST in the P1 pointer page. The access mode in which the AST will be delivered is stored in location CTL$GB_PWRMODE.
- The power AST flag (PCB$V_PWRAST) in the status longword in the PCB is set. This flag will be used by the swapper in scanning the PCB vector following power recovery.

The effect of this system service is disabled as a result of image rundown (see Chapter 21).

27.2.4.2 Delivery of Power Recovery ASTs. The delivery of these ASTs occurs in several distinct steps.

1. The power recovery routine stores the duration of the power failure in location EXE$GL_PFATIM. (This value is simply the current contents of PR$_TODR minus EXE$GL_PFAILTIM, the time at which the power failed.) Nonzero contents in this location act as a trigger to the swapper the next time that it runs.

   Note that no special action is taken at this point to wake up the swapper. In fact, because this routine is running at IPL 31, the swapper could not have its scheduling state changed without potential synchronization problems.

2. A part of the swapper's main loop of execution (see Chapter 17) calls routine EXE$POWERAST if location EXE$GL_PFATIM contains a nonzero value. This subroutine scans the PCB vector and delivers a special kernel mode AST to each process that has the PCB$V_PWRAST flag set. That flag is cleared to prevent multiple ASTs if multiple power failures occur before the process executes.

3. The special kernel mode AST is required because the address (and access mode) of the recovery AST are stored in the P1 space of the requesting process. The special kernel mode AST simply loads the address and access mode from their P1 space locations into the AST control block and queues the recovery AST to the requesting process.

4. Finally, the recovery AST itself is delivered to the requesting process. The AST parameter is the duration of the power failure, in 10 millisecond units.

27.3 MULTIPLE POWER FAILURES

Hardware and software flags exist in combination to prevent infinite looping or related problems in response to a power failure that occurs while either the powerfail service routine is executing or while the restart routine is executing.

27.3.1 Nested Powerfail Interrupts

One of the first steps taken by the powerfail service routine saves the contents of the PR$_TODR register in location EXE$GL_PFAILTIM. This location retains nonzero contents until just before the restart routine issues its REI instruction, dismissing the powerfail interrupt.

If a powerfail interrupt occurs while this location contains a nonzero value (indicating that another failure/recovery is already in progress), this later interrupt is ignored. Some machine state was saved as a result of the first powerfail interrupt. That state will be the one restored eventually by the restart routine.

The previous step is an example of extreme caution that is necessary where power failure is concerned. A naive understanding of the way interrupts are

605

defined in the VAX architecture would expect that a second powerfail interrupt cannot occur while IPL is at or above 30. Because IPL is not lowered until the powerfail interrupt is dismissed, IPL seems to cover this situation. However, if IPL is used to block the powerfail interrupt for a long time, there will be insufficient time to save the volatile machine state when the interrupt is finally granted. The EXE$GL_PFAILTIM check, an extra sanity check that is totally under the control of the software, prevents nested powerfail interrupts on a system that is experiencing some obscure behavior that would otherwise be extremely difficult to diagnose.

27.3.2 Prevention of Nested Restarts

The previous check takes a long time to execute and is designed to prevent a second powerfail interrupt while a first is being serviced. A flag exists to prevent nested restart attempts.

This flag, located in the restart parameter block, is cleared by INIT and by the restart routine, and set by the CPU-specific ROM routine that looks for a valid RPB. If the RPB search routine locates an otherwise valid RPB with the RPB$L_RSTRTFLG set, it assumes that the restart parameter block is in error and aborts the restart attempt. On the VAX-11/750, further action is controlled by the setting of the power on action switch on the front panel. On the VAX-11/780, the console program aborts the restart attempt and prints its prompt on the console terminal.

A second flag, located within the console logic on the VAX-11/780, functions in a similar manner. It is set by hardware at the beginning of the restart and cleared by the restart routine by executing the following instruction:

```
MTPR    #^XF03,#PR$_TXDB
```

If the restart routine detects that this flag is set while attempting a restart, it aborts the restart and takes the same processor-specific action as it would if the restart parameter block flag were set. (There is no analog to this flag on the VAX-11/750. The CPU microcode turns this particular MTPR instruction into a null operation.)

One more bit of caution is evident in the manner in which the recovery routine restores data from the interrupt stack. A scratch register (R6) is used to traverse the stack. If another powerfail interrupt were to occur while data was being restored, no data would be lost due to the push of the PC and PSL onto the interrupt stack because the SP points to the end of the page containing the RPB and not into the middle of the data being restored.

27.3.3 Device Driver Action

Drivers do not have to concern themselves directly with the multiple restart problem. Even though the bulk of driver recovery is done in response to an

IPL 7 software interrupt when a second power failure is possible, drivers are protected by one of the following situations:

- The driver controller and unit initialization routines are called at IPL 31 before EXE$GL_PFAILTIM is cleared. Drivers are protected here by the same sanity checks that VMS uses for itself.
- If the driver does not get called at its timeout entry point before the power fails again, the preserved driver state indicates a unit that has already timed out. When power is finally restored permanently, the driver will be called at its timeout entry point.
- If the driver is in the middle of its timeout routine, it still appears to the system as a unit that has timed out. It will be called at its timeout entry point again when the machine finally stabilizes.
- The driver may succeed in returning control to the operating system with, for example, one of the following calls:

  ```
  WFIxxCH
  IOFORK
  REQCOM
  ```

If the operating system has received control, the request has either been completed or the driver is back into a state (such as expecting an interrupt) where the power recovery logic will cause the driver to be called at its timeout entry point when the power is finally restored.

27.4   POWER FAILURE ON THE UNIBUS

UNIBUS power failure is handled differently on the VAX-11/780 and on the other VAX processors. The UNIBUS is an integral part of the VAX-11/730 and VAX-11/750 processors, whereas the UNIBUS on a VAX-11/780 is connected to the SBI through a UNIBUS adapter (DW780).

27.4.1   UNIBUS Power Failure on the VAX-11/730 and VAX-11/750

The UNIBUS on the VAX-11/730 and the VAX-11/750 cannot experience independent power failure. If power fails on the UNIBUS, it has also failed on the processor. As a result, a powerfail interrupt is generated.

27.4.2   UNIBUS Power Failure on the VAX-11/780

Because a UNIBUS failure on the VAX-11/780 does not necessarily indicate that the entire system is in error, VMS allows UNIBUS errors, including UNIBUS power failure caused by turning off the power to the UBA or the BA-11K, to occur without crashing the entire system.

When such an error occurs, the UBA interrupts on behalf of itself (bit<31>

of the appropriate BRRVR is set). The interrupt service routine for the affected UBA detects that a UBA interrupt (as opposed to a UNIBUS device interrupt) has occurred and transfers control to an error routine that does the following:

- Checks that the interrupt is due to the power failure of the UBA or UNIBUS.
- Writes an error log entry.
- Remaps the system virtual addresses that previously mapped the UBA itself and the UNIBUS I/O page (24 pages in all) so that these pages now point to the so-called black hole page reserved at initialization time.

    This mapping technique prevents subsequent machine checks or related errors from device drivers that reference the UBA or device registers while the UBA or UNIBUS power is off.

If the UNIBUS has gone away either because the power was turned off or for some other reason, devices that were waiting for I/O completion will time out. The program that issued the initial I/O request will receive an appropriate error notification, assuming that no driver is sitting in a tight loop at device IPL waiting for a status bit to change state.

When the power is restored, the system virtual pages are remapped to point to the UBA registers and the UNIBUS I/O page. If any devices were removed while the power was turned off, they will be marked offline as part of the power recovery operation.

This feature has implications for people attempting to debug device drivers. In VAX/VMS Version 1.0, a reference to a nonexistent CSR or other such error caused the system to bugcheck, a drastic but immediate notification that an error had occurred.

The recommended method for debugging UNIBUS device drivers on VAX/VMS Version 2.0 or more recent VMS system is to place an XDELTA breakpoint at global location EXE$DW780_INT (at location 80002EEE in Version 3.0). This technique also allows immediate error notification without taking the system down and without the wait for the system to reboot itself. Of course, the error log can also be examined to obtain information about the error.

28 The VAX-11/782 Multiprocessing System

The one is independent, and its essential nature is to be for itself;
the other is dependent, and its essence is life or existence for
another. The former is the Master, or Lord, the latter the
Bondsman.

—Hegel, *Phenomenology of Mind*

When VAX/VMS Version 3.0 was in the design stages, a large demand was
seen for a more powerful VAX processor. In order to satisfy that demand, a
plan was developed to join two VAX-11/780 processors as a tightly coupled,
asymmetric multiprocessing system. Loosely coupled multiprocessing was
already available through the MA780 shared memory; however, being loosely
coupled, such systems lacked any dynamic load leveling capability. Because
the multiprocessing system was targeted for users with multistreamed, compute-intensive jobs, dynamic load leveling was a necessity.

There were several requirements for the multiprocessing system:

- It must use existing DIGITAL hardware.
- The same version of the VAX/VMS operating system must be able to run
  on the new processor and on any other VAX processor. In addition, applications must be able to run on all processors.
- There were to be no complex changes to existing kernel mode routines.
- Users that did not have the new processor were not to be penalized by the
  increased size of the VAX/VMS operating system.

The VAX-11/782 multiprocessing system consists of two VAX-11/780 processors that use from two to four MA780 shared memory units as common
memory. Both processors are capable of executing instruction streams independently of each other. Both processors address a common pool of memory
in the MA780 shared memory; the local memory on either processor is not
used.

Figure 28-1 depicts the hardware configuration of a VAX-11/782 multiprocessing system (from now on called simply the VAX-11/782). The configuration shown in the figure uses two MA780 shared memory units; note that the
UNIBUS and MASSBUS adapters are attached only to the SBI of the primary
processor. Although I/O devices can be connected to the attached processor,
they will not be recognized by the system.

The primary processor in the VAX-11/782 does computational work, per-

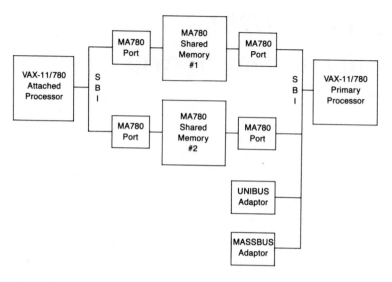

Figure 28-1
Hardware Layout in the VAX-11/782

forms memory management and I/O for the system, and schedules work for itself and the attached processor. The attached processor does computational work but cannot execute kernel mode code on behalf of user processes (system services and exception service routines). An exception or interrupt that causes a change to kernel mode on the attached processor results in an interrupt to the primary processor. The primary processor schedules another job to execute on the attached processor and schedules the kernel mode code to execute on itself.

This chapter describes the internals of multiprocessing on the VAX-11/782. It is assumed that readers are familiar with the concepts of multiprocessing and multiprocessing configurations described in the *VAX-11/782 User's Guide*. Readers interested in hardware-related topics should see the *VAX Hardware Handbook*.

28.1 HOW THE VMS SYSTEM SUPPORTS MULTIPROCESSING

As originally conceived, the copy of the VMS operating system that was run on the VAX-11/782 had to run equally well on the other three VAX processors. The additional software required for the VAX-11/782 could not affect the amount of physical memory required by the VMS operating system running on other VAX processors. To meet this goal, the pieces of multiprocessing code used by the VAX-11/782 are maintained in a separate module and are loaded into nonpaged pool only when multiprocessing is turned on.

In order for these pieces to be included as part of the VMS executive, a number of symbols were added to the executive to indicate the location of branches to the new multiprocessing code. These symbols are termed multiprocessing "hooks." The system control block of the primary processor also contains multiprocessing hooks so that multiprocessing interrupts are routed to the new multiprocessing interrupt service routines. The symbols used as multiprocessing hooks are contained in every copy of the VAX/VMS operating system; however, they are used only by the VAX-11/782 code.

28.1.1 Hooks in the Executive

When multiprocessing is turned on by the DCL command START/CPU, the multiprocessing code is loaded into the system. The instructions at the locations indicated by the hooks are changed to jumps to the multiprocessing code. Three types of hooks are used to link the multiprocessing code into the VMS executive. The hooks and the changes they perform are these:

Symbol Format	Change to Code
MPH$name	The instruction indicated by the hook will be replaced by a jump to multiprocessing code. This hook is used when the multiprocessing routine MPS$name will perform the entire set of actions normally performed by the routine xxx$name.
MPH$nameHK	The instruction indicated by the hook will be replaced by a jump to multiprocessing code. This hook is used when only a few lines need to be changed by multiprocessing, or when supplemental action is necessary.
MPH$nameCONT	Multiprocessing code will return to the normal flow of code at this point. No change is made to the instruction indicated by this hook.

All entry points in the loaded multiprocessing code have the form MPS$name.

When multiprocessing is turned on, the contents of location MPH$nameHK or MPH$name are saved in a storage area in nonpaged pool and the following instruction is inserted in its place:

```
JMP @#MPS$name
```

(Note that the macros used to insert hooks can also create a JSB @#MPS$name instruction; for simplicity, the JMP form is shown in this and the following examples.)

The multiprocessing routines will exit either by returning control to the modified routine's caller (with an RSB or RET instruction, or with an REI instruction, if the routine is an entire new interrupt routine) or by jumping to the MPH$nameCONT location as illustrated by the following code fragment:

```
JMP @#MPH$ASTDELCONT
```

The following code fragment illustrates the use of the MPH$name hook in the queue AST routine in module ASTDEL. Because queuing ASTs is significantly different on the VAX-11/782, the entire routine is replaced.

```
                BRB QEXIT
MPH$QAST::
SCH$QAST::
                MOVZWL ACB$L_PID(R5),R0
```

The following code fragment illustrates the use of the MPH$nameHK and MPH$nameCONT in the routine SCH$ASTDEL:

```
                SETIPL   #IPL$_SYNCH
MPH$ASTDELHK::
                REMQUE   @PCB$L_ASTQFL(R4),R5
                BVS      QEMPTY
MPH$ASTDELCONT::
```

This hook is used to insert multiprocessing code into the routine, rather than to replace code.

Another form of hook is used to modify the SCB. In this case, specific vectors in the SCB are replaced by vectors to multiprocessing interrupt service routines. These routines are invoked by interrupts, and return via the normal REI mechanism.

28.1.2 Hardware Support for Multiprocessing

In terms of hardware, the MA780 shared memory was designed with the idea of multiprocessing in mind. It provides interprocessor interrupts and a multiprocessor selective cache invalidate option.

The MA780 selective cache invalidate option is required in MA780s used in a VAX-11/782 system. This option associates longwords in shared memory with the processor (or processors) using those locations. When one processor performs a write to a longword of shared memory, the MA780 sends a message to the second processor to invalidate the contents of its local cache (but only if the second processor is using the same location). Without this option, every write to shared memory would send cache invalidation messages to both processors, thus increasing overall traffic on both SBIs.

When multiprocessing code is loaded, the software interrupt vectors in the SCB must be modified. The software interrupt level 5 vector is used for the multiprocessing rescheduling routine on the primary processor. (Because this vector is used by XDELTA on single processor systems, XDELTA was moved to the software level 15 interrupt on the VAX-11/782.)

When multiprocessing is turned on, the first MA780's interprocessor interrupt vectors for both processors are modified to point to multiprocessing routines; the MA780 error interrupt vectors remain unchanged. The interprocessor interrupt vectors for any additional MA780s point to unexpected interrupt error handlers. The vectors at IPLs 20 and 21, and IPLs 22 and 23 are loaded redundantly, because the IPL levels interrupted by the MA780 are jumper-selectable. The even-numbered IPLs are the interprocessor interrupts and the odd-numbered IPLs are the error interrupts.

The interrupt service routine MPS$PINTSR is the primary processor's interrupt handler; MPS$SINTSR is the attached processor's interrupt handler. EXE$INT58 handles MA780 error interrupts.

28.2   SYSTEM INITIALIZATION ON THE VAX-11/782

As part of the installation procedures used to install the VAX/VMS operating system on the VAX-11/782, two special console floppy diskettes are created: one for the primary processor, and one for the attached processor. These floppy diskettes contain special command files used to bootstrap the processors of the multiprocessing system.

The primary processor does most of the work of system initialization. It loads the executive into MA780 shared memory and performs all the tasks that are involved in bootstrapping a single processor VAX-11/780 system.

28.2.1   System Initialization on the Primary Processor

The command files on the console floppy for the primary processor set the flag RPB$V_MPM in R5, indicating that VMB is to ignore local memory and to use only the shared memory as main memory. Because there is no bootstrap ROM in the MA780, it is assumed that the first 64K bytes in the MA780 are good. The command file clears error bits in the MA780 registers and defines the starting address for each MA780 memory.

The primary bootstrap routine, VMB, is loaded into the first 64K bytes of memory, starting at physical address 200 (hex) and builds the restart parameter block (RPB) at physical address 0. From this point on, initialization continues as it would on a single processor VAX-11/780 system (see Chapter 24). When the initialization is complete on the primary processor, the VMS operating system will run normally on the primary processor without multiprocessing (using MA780 memory rather than local memory).

28.2.2   System Initialization on the Attached Processor

The attached processor's bootstrap command file clears error bits in the MA780 registers and defines the starting address for each MA780 memory.

These addresses must be identical to those established by the primary processor; hence the need for the new VAX-11/782-specific console floppies. Both processors share the same restart parameter block (RPB). When multiprocessing is turned off, the location RPB$B_WAIT is loaded with a jump-to-self instruction, similar to the following example:

```
DESTINATION:
          .ADDRESS -
                  10$
10$:      JMP      @DESTINATION
```

If the attached processor is rebooted before multiprocessing is turned on again, the attached processor will simply wait in this loop until the DCL command START/CPU is reissued.

Note that it is possible to bootstrap the secondary processor before multiprocessing is turned on only after multiprocessing has been turned on and turned off again. If the VAX-11/782 is being cold started and the attached processor is bootstrapped before multiprocessing is turned on, the bootstrap operation on the attached processor will fail (due to the lack of appropriate data in the RPB$B_WAIT cells in the RPB).

28.2.3 Turning Multiprocessing On

Multiprocessing is turned on by the DCL command START/CPU, which executes the image MP.EXE. MP.EXE performs the following actions:

1. It loads a portion of itself into 8K bytes of nonpaged pool. These 8K bytes contain the following:

   - Data areas used for communication between the two processors
   - Replacement code for several VMS kernel mode routines
   - All special code executed by the attached processor
   - Space for the interrupt stack, system control block, and error log buffers for the attached processor

   The loaded code is a dynamic nonpaged pool data structure that has a standard header. The first two longwords, which usually contain the FLINK and BLINK fields, contain information necessary for deallocating the loadable code from pool. The third longword contains the size and type fields. The symbolic offsets within the multiprocessing code are defined in SYS$SYSTEM:MP.STB.

2. The communication data areas are initialized, and the attached processor's execution state is set to INIT.

3. IPL is raised to 31, to block any system events, and the pages containing the VMS executive are made writeable.

4. Locations within the executive that are identified by multiprocessing

hooks are modified so that control will be transferred to multiprocessing code.

5. The primary processor's SCB is modified to handle multiprocessor scheduling and MA780 interprocessor interrupts.
6. The secondary processor's SCB is initialized.
7. The RPB is modified so that location RPB$B_WAIT contains a jump to the attached processor's initialization and restart routine (which was just loaded as part of the multiprocessing code).
8. The pages containing the VMS executive are marked read only and IPL is lowered to 0.

Once RPB$B_WAIT has been modified, the attached processor can be bootstrapped (if it has not been bootstrapped already). The last console command in the bootstrap command file for the attached processor causes the instruction stored at RPB$B_WAIT to be executed. Before the DCL command START/CPU is issued, this location contains a jump to self; after START/CPU has been issued, this instruction contains the attached processor's initialization routine.

The attached processor's initialization routine then performs the following actions:

• Memory management is turned on, using information in the RPB.
• The interval timer is turned on. The attached processor uses its own interval timer to do CPU-time accounting and quantum-end detection for its processes.
• Any errors are cleared and interrupts are enabled on the MA780 port adapter(s).
• The attached processor's execution state is set to IDLE.
• Finally, the primary processor is interrupted with a rescheduling request.

28.2.4 Turning Multiprocessing Off

The DCL command STOP/CPU is used to turn off multiprocessing on the VAX-11/782. This command invokes the routine MPS$UNLOAD in module MPLOAD. MPS$UNLOAD performs the following functions:

• The primary processor interrupts the attached processor with a stop request. If the attached processor is running a process, it saves the context of the current process and the primary processor adds the process to its scheduling queues.
• The processor state of the attached processor is set to STOP and a jump to self instruction is loaded into the RPB.
• A HALT instruction is issued on the attached processor.
• The pages that contain the VMS executive are made writeable and IPL is raised to 31 to inhibit all system events.

- Each location identified by multiprocessing hooks is replaced with its original contents.
- The primary processor's SCB is restored to its original condition (a single processor SCB).
- IPL is lowered to 7 and the pages containing the multiprocessing code are returned to nonpaged pool.
- The executive is made read only and IPL is restored to 0.

When MPS$UNLOAD completes, the primary processor runs as a single CPU VAX-11/780 and the attached processor either halts or executes the console command file RESTAR.CMD, depending on the position of the RESTART switch on the front panel of the processor cabinet. If the attached processor is bootstrapped by hand, the processor will execute the console command file DEFBOO.CMD and jump to the location RPB$B_WAIT in the restart parameter block. The attached processor will execute the jump to self instruction at RPB$B_WAIT until the DCL command START/CPU is issued.

If, for some reason, the attached processor does not respond to an interrupt after a reasonable amount of time, the primary will assume that the attached processor has failed. In this case, all the steps in turning multiprocessing off are executed, with the exception of deallocating the pages in nonpaged pool. The multiprocessing data is not deleted because it is assumed that an attempt will be made to restart the attached processor. (Note that this action was added in VAX/VMS Version 3.2.)

28.3   SCHEDULING AND INTERRUPTS ON THE VAX-11/782

To simplify synchronization of the scheduler database, the primary processor schedules processes for execution on itself and on the attached processor. Either the attached processor will interrupt the primary for a rescheduling event, or the primary, before scheduling itself, will check the state of the attached processor, to see if it is IDLE. Within the loaded multiprocessing code, the location MPS$GL_STATE contains the execution state of the attached processor. There are six possible execution states: INITIALIZE, IDLE, BUSY, EXECUTE, DROP, and STOP.

Figure 28-2 shows the possible execution states for the attached processor and the possible transitions between the states. As is shown in the figure, certain transitions can be caused only by the primary processor, others can be caused only by the attached processor.

When the multiprocessing code is loaded by the DCL command START/CPU, the attached processor is set to the INITIALIZE state. Once the attached processor has executed its initialization code, it changes its execution

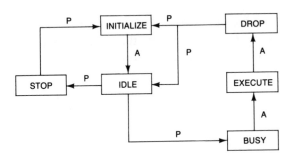

Figure 28-2
Attached Processor Execution States

state to IDLE. The primary processor will schedule work for the attached processor only when the attached processor is in the IDLE state.

28.3.1   Scheduling Processes on the VAX-11/782

When the attached processor needs to be rescheduled, it interrupts the primary processor, using the MA780 interprocessor interrupt capability by issuing the MA780 interprocessor hardware interrupt. The primary processor's interrupt service routine (MPS$PINTSR) requests a rescheduling software level 5 interrupt.

The primary processor's rescheduling routine (MPS$RESCHED) selects a suitable process to run on the attached processor, using the scheduling algorithm that is always used by the VMS operating system (round robin within priority level, highest priority processes scheduled first). If no suitable computable process exists, the execution state of the attached processor is set to IDLE and the processor loops, waiting for the processor execution state to be set to BUSY (by the primary). While waiting, the attached processor also invalidates the contents of the system translation buffer (when indicated by the MA780). To avoid schedule thrashing, the scheduling interrupt routine first insures that the selected process will not be placed back into execution in kernel mode, either directly (by examining the PSL mode bits) or indirectly (by checking for pending AST delivery). When a job is scheduled on the attached processor, the execution state is set to BUSY.

Scheduling for the primary processor is done at IPL 3 (the normal scheduling IPL), with a slightly modified rescheduling interrupt service routine. Because scheduling requests for the attached processor interrupt at IPL 5, scheduling on the attached processor has precedence over scheduling on the primary processor. Before scheduling a process to run on the primary, the slightly modified IPL 3 routine checks the processor state of the attached processor. If the execution state of the attached processor is IDLE, the primary schedules a process to run on the attached processor and sets the execution state to BUSY. A process scheduled to run on the attached processor will run until either it runs out of quantum or it incurs an exception or interrupt. The process will not be taken out of execution if a higher priority process becomes available. However, the process running on the primary processor can be preempted.

28.3.2 Preventing Scheduling on the Attached Processor

Currently the only reason for preventing processes from executing on the attached processor is processes that have created and mapped global sections to specific physical pages (using the PFNMAP option with the $CRMPSC system service). When a process performs an action that disallows it from executing on the attached processor, a location in the process header (PHD$L_MPINHIBIT) is incremented.

A common use of PFN mapping is to access the UNIBUS I/O space. The process's P0 page table is loaded with PFNs that correspond to particular locations in I/O address space. If such a process were to execute on the attached processor, its translated references to the PFN-mapped section would access the attached processor's I/O address space (instead of the primary's I/O address space, where the devices are).

Figure 28-3 shows the relative layout of physical address space in the VAX-11/782. Note that while the processors share common addresses in the MA780 shared memory, each processor has its own I/O address space. Because the I/O address space is different on each processor, processes with PFN-mapped pages are not allowed to run on the attached processor.

28.3.3 Executing Jobs on the Attached Processor

When the attached processor is in the IDLE state, it continuously checks MPS$GL_STATE. When a job is scheduled on the attached processor, the state is set to BUSY. The attached processor detects the change to BUSY, sets the execution state to EXECUTE, and begins to execute the job.

The BUSY and EXECUTE states must be unique so that special conditions, such as powerfail recovery, can be handled correctly. If a powerfail occurs on the attached processor when the execution state is BUSY, the processor simply halts. However, if the execution state is EXECUTE, the attached processor must save the context of its current process and then halt.

A process will be executed on the attached processor until one of the following conditions arises:

- Quantum expiration occurs for the process.
- The process incurs an exception or interrupt that requires a transition to kernel mode.

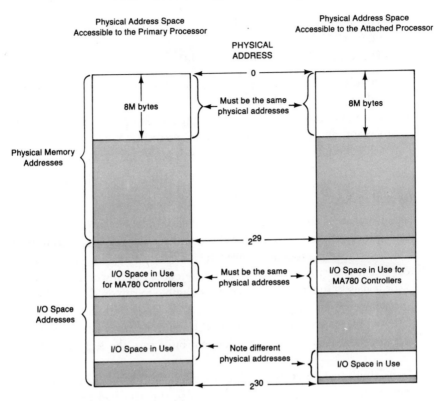

Figure 28-3
Layout of the VAX-11/782 Physical Address Space

If either of these conditions occurs, the attached processor stops executing the process and takes the following actions:

- The attached processor saves the context of the process.
- The execution state is set to DROP.
- The attached processor interrupts the primary processor to request a rescheduling event.

When the primary processor receives the rescheduling interrupt, it performs the following actions:

- It places its current process into the appropriate scheduling queue.
- It locates the process that was executing on the attached processor and places the process into the appropriate scheduling queue.
- It sets the attached processor's state to IDLE.
- It locates a process that is suitable for execution on the attached processor. The following criteria are used for selecting a process:

    —The process must not be executing in kernel mode.

—The current access mode must be less than the value saved in PR$_ASTLVL.

—The value at offset PHD$L_INHIBIT must equal zero.

If no suitable process is available, the attached processor loops until its scheduling state is set to BUSY.

- If a suitable process is found, the process is scheduled on the attached processor, and the execution state is set to BUSY.
- It selects a process to execute on itself.

28.3.4 Detecting Access Mode Transitions

Because process-context kernel mode code can be executed only on the primary processor, it is critical for the attached processor to be able to detect when its current process changes access mode to kernel. For performance reasons, it is desirable to detect when a process running on the primary processor leaves kernel mode and becomes eligible to run on the attached processor (when the attached processor is IDLE). Transitions to kernel mode are detected by exceptions or interrupts; transitions from kernel mode are detected by the AST delivery mechanism built into the REI instruction.

28.3.4.1 Transitions to Kernel Mode.
Almost all exceptions and interrupts cause a transition to kernel mode. The vectors in the attached processor's system control block (SCB) are set up so that only the CHME, CHMS, and CHMU exceptions are vectored to the normal VMS logic. Most other exceptions and interrupts cause an access mode change to kernel and, thus, cause the attached processor to save the current process's context and interrupt the primary processor for a rescheduling event.

28.3.4.2 Transitions from Kernel Mode.
One of the functions of the REI instruction is to request a software level 2 (AST delivery) interrupt whenever an AST is pending for an access mode more privileged than or equal to the access mode to which it is returning. The REI microcode compares the access mode being restored to the access mode in the process register PR$_ASTLVL, the access mode of the AST at the head of the AST queue (see Section 7.1). Because the REI instruction is the only way to return to one of the outer access modes from kernel mode, the AST mechanism can be used as a method of notification that a process is leaving kernel mode.

The IPL 3 scheduling routine will simulate a pending executive mode AST for that process when the following are true:

- There is no process available to execute on the attached processor.
- There are at least two computable processes in the scheduling queues other than the null process.

The process is then scheduled for execution on the primary processor. Eventually, when the process issues the REI instruction to leave kernel mode, an AST delivery interrupt is triggered. The AST delivery interrupt service routine determines that this is a simulated AST and that the attached processor is IDLE. The routine then requests an IPL 3 rescheduling interrupt and dismisses the AST delivery interrupt.

The IPL 3 rescheduling interrupt service routine saves the context of the current process and places it on the appropriate compute queue. Then the interrupt service routine looks for a suitable process to schedule on the attached processor. If the process whose context was just saved is the most suitable process, it is scheduled to run on the attached processor. Note that this simulated AST is scheduled only when the attached processor is IDLE and other computable processes are waiting for execution.

28.3.5   Interrupt Communication

The primary processor will interrupt the attached processor for one of the following reasons:

- When an AST is queued to the process running on the attached processor, the primary processor interrupts the attached processor. Because PR$_ASTLVL is a processor register, it exists on both processors. The value in PR$_ASTLVL on the attached processor can be altered only by code executing on the attached processor.
- When the primary processor detects a fatal bugcheck, it interrupts the attached processor, causes it to save the context of the current process, and sets the execution state to STOP.
- When the DCL command STOP/CPU is issued, the primary processor causes an interprocessor interrupt. The attached processor then saves the context of the current process and sets the execution state to STOP.
- When a system space address becomes invalid, the primary processor causes an interprocessor interrupt to request the attached processor to also make that address invalid. The primary processor waits until it receives an acknowledgment from the attached processor that the address has been made invalid.

The attached processor will interrupt the primary processor for the following reasons:

- When the attached processor signals a rescheduling request. A rescheduling request can occur when the attached processor is first initialized, or when the current process on the attached processor makes a transition to kernel mode. In either case, the attached processor interrupts the primary processor and requests a new process to be scheduled for it.

- When the attached processor has an error log message, it interrupts the primary processor to copy the error log message to the system error log block buffers.
- When a fatal bugcheck occurs on the attached processor, it interrupts the primary processor and requests the primary processor to crash the system.

PART VIII/Miscellaneous Topics

29 Logical Names

Call things by their right names . . . Glass of brandy and water!
That is the current but not the appropriate name: ask for a glass
of fire and distilled damnation.
—Robert Hall, in Olinthus Gregory, *Brief Memoir of the Life of Hall*

Logical names provide a powerful tool for a single process or several processes to use as a communication tool. Logical names also allow the system and application programs to implement a transparent form of device independence and I/O redirection. This chapter describes the internal implementation of logical names.

29.1 LOGICAL NAME TABLES

When a logical name is created, the logical name string and its equivalence name string are put into a data structure called a logical name block. This structure is then inserted into one of three groups of doubly linked lists, depending on whether the logical name is being inserted into the process, group, or system logical name table.

The process logical name table is located in the process allocation region in P1 space. The group and system logical name tables are both allocated from paged dynamic memory.

29.1.1 Logical Name Data Structures

The listheads for the three tables are located through the longword array at global location LOG$AL_LOGTBL. Each of the longwords in this array points to a name table pointer, which, in turn, contains the address of the hash table for the appropriate name table. The name table pointers for the system and group logical name hash tables are stored in longwords at LOG$AL_LOGTBL+8 and LOG$AL_LOGTBL+12 (decimal); the name table pointer for the process logical name hash table is contained in global location CTL$GL_LOGTBL. The hash of the logical name being searched is used as an index into the hash table. Entries in the hash tables point to doubly linked lists of logical name blocks.

The logical name blocks are inserted in the doubly linked lists in increasing lengths of logical name strings. Name blocks with logical name strings of the same length are ordered alphabetically.

The three logical name tables, their hash tables, and their listheads are pictured in Figure 29-1.

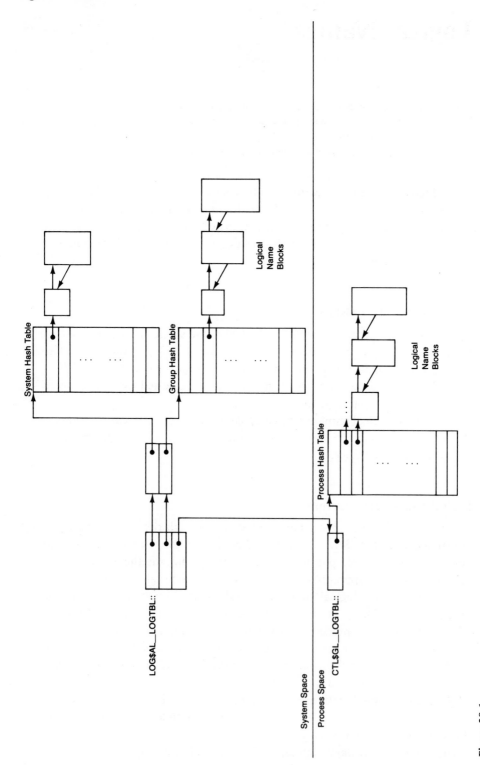

Figure 29-1
Global Listheads for Logical Name Tables

29.1.2   Logical Name Block

The contents of a logical name block are pictured in Figure 29-2. Both the logical name and the equivalence name may be up to 63 characters in length. Before the memory block is allocated, the size required for the sum of the two strings plus the fixed size is rounded up to the next quadword so that, although logical name blocks are of variable length, they are always an integral number of quadwords in length.

The access mode field is only used when a logical name block appears in the process logical name table. When a process logical name is created, its logical name block is inserted into the process logical name table in order of decreasing access mode. In other words, a user mode logical name XYZ appears in the list before a supervisor mode logical name XYZ. When logical name XYZ is translated, the user mode equivalence name rather than the supervisor mode equivalence name is returned.

The group field is only relevant when the logical name block appears in the group logical name table. There is only one group logical name table for the entire system and all group logical name blocks are placed into this list. An operation that searches the group logical name table looks for a match between the group code in the logical name block and the group number of the caller of the system service.

The associated mailbox field is used when the logical name is created as a part of mailbox creation. In addition, the Mount Utility uses this field when it creates a logical name in connection with mounting a volume.

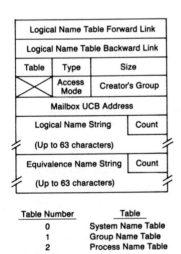

Table Number	Table
0	System Name Table
1	Group Name Table
2	Process Name Table

Figure 29-2
Logical Name Block

627

29.1.3   Searching for a Logical Name

In order to search for a logical name, the logical name services use the routine LOG$SEARCHLOG in module LOGNAMSUB. Figure 29-1 shows the structures used in the search for a logical name.

The search begins by locating the table of logical name pointers at global address LOG$GL_LOGNAM. The logical name table number (indicating system, group, or process logical name table) is used as an index into the table of pointers. When the pointer is located, it is used to point to the name table pointer, which, in turn, points to the appropriate hash table. The logical name is hashed and the resulting value is used as an index into the hash table. The hash table entry located by the index contains the longword listhead for a list of logical name blocks.

As each logical name block is processed, the length of the logical name in the logical name block is compared with the length of the logical name being searched for. If the length of the logical name in the logical name block is less than the length of the logical name being searched for, the block is passed over and the search continues without the costly overhead of a CMPC instruction that is bound to fail.

If the length of the logical name in the logical name block is greater than the length of the logical name being searched for, the search has passed the possible logical name blocks, so the search fails.

If a string is found with the same length, the strings are compared. If the string comparison fails, and the logical name in the logical name block occurs alphabetically before the logical name being searched for, the search has passed the possible logical name blocks, so the search fails.

The failure to locate a logical name indicates the last possible location where the logical name should have been placed. This information is used when inserting a logical name block in the table.

29.1.4   Hashing the Logical Names

The algorithm used to hash the logical names was chosen because it is fast and provides a good distribution within the hash table.

The hashing algorithm is as follows:

1. The size of the logical name string is moved to a longword; this is the base hash value.
2. Four bytes of the string are XORed into the hash longword. The hash is then rotated by nine bits to the left.
3. Step 2 is repeated until there are less than four bytes remaining in the string.
4. The remaining bytes are XORed into the hash longword one byte at a time. After each XOR the hash is rotated by 13 bits.

5. The hash longword is then multiplied by an eight-digit hexadecimal number (71279461 hex).
6. The next longword above the hash longword is cleared, resulting in a quadword whose low-order longword contains the hash and whose high-order longword is zero.
7. The quadword is then rotated by an arithmetic shift to the left. The number of bits to shift is determined by the number of entries in the hash table expressed as a power of two. This value is located through the byte array at global location LOG$AB_HTBLCNT.
8. The value shifted into the high-order longword of the quadword is the index into the hash table.

The process hash table is located in the process allocation region in P1 space when the process is created; the group and system hash tables are both allocated from paged dynamic memory when the system is initialized. The sizes for the system, group, and process hash tables are determined by the SYSBOOT parameters LOGSHASHTBL, LOGGHASHTBL, and LOGPHASHTBL, respectively.

29.1.5 Changes to Speed Logical Name Translation

In VAX/VMS Version 3.0 the logical name translation scheme was modified to reduce the time it took to find (or note the absence of) a logical name. Previous to Version 3.0, the search that took the most time was the search for a nonexistent logical name. Hashing the logical names reduced this time significantly by reducing the average length of the lists of logical name blocks.

In addition, an improvement in efficiency was made by ordering the lists. Previously, the list of logical names was searched until either a match or the end of the list was found. By ordering the lists of logical name blocks, the search does not need to go to the end of a list to determine that a search for a logical name has failed. Failure is indicated as soon as either of the following is true:

- The length of the string in the block is less than the length of the string being searched for.
- The string in the block occurs alphabetically before the string being searched for.

29.2 LOGICAL NAME SYSTEM SERVICES

There are three system services available for logical name manipulation. Logical names can be created, translated, or deleted. Privileges are required to modify the group and system logical name tables. Before discussing the individual services, some checks that are common to more than one of the services are described.

29.2.1   Privilege and Protection Checks

Like any other system services that use access mode as an argument, the logical name system services call the routine EXE$MAXACMODE to maximize the mode passed as an argument with the access mode of the caller (found in the previous mode field of the PSL). A process that wishes to create or delete a group or system logical name must have the appropriate privilege (GRPNAM or SYSNAM respectively).

Several access checks must be made by these services. Because all three services pass at least one string descriptor as an argument (Create Logical Name has two), the read accessibility of both the string descriptor and the string must be checked. Translate Logical Name must check write accessibility of the arguments that are used to pass information back to the caller.

29.2.2   Logical Name Table Mutexes

Both the group and system logical name tables are protected from simultaneous access by mutexes (see Chapter 2). The Translate Logical Name system service locks the table that is currently being searched for read access. This lock does not prevent other processes from reading (translating) logical names in the same logical name table. Logical name creation and deletion both require that the table being modified be locked for write access. This lock prevents other processes from even reading the locked table while the table is being modified.

29.2.3   Logical Name Creation

After the preliminary checks have been made, the Create Logical Name ($CRELOG) system service allocates a block of memory for the logical name block. The block is allocated from the process allocation region for process logical names and from paged dynamic memory for group and system logical names. The size of the block is the sum of the lengths of the logical and equivalence strings plus the size of the constant part of a logical name block. Before the allocation routine is called, the size is rounded to an integral number of quadwords.

After all the parameters have been placed into the allocated block, a search is made for the logical name string in the appropriate logical name table. If the search fails, the logical name block is inserted into the list at the location where the search failed. If an identical logical name already exists, the old name is first deleted and an alternate success status, SS$_SUPERSEDE, is returned to the caller. If the logical name is being put into the process logical name table and an identical name is found with a different access mode, the logical name block is inserted into the table in such a way as to place the highest (least privileged) access mode closest to the beginning of the table.

29.2.4   Logical Name Deletion

After the usual privilege and protection checks are performed, the Delete Logical Name ($DELLOG) system service checks whether this operation is deleting a single logical name or a group of names. If all system names are to be deleted, they are. If all group names are to be deleted, those logical names that have the same group code as the caller are deleted. If all process names are to be deleted, all logical names for the specified access mode and all less privileged access modes are deleted.

The deletion of a single logical name requires that the appropriate table be searched. If the logical name is in the process table, an access mode check is performed. The actual deletion operation first removes the logical name block from the list, clears the UCB$L_LOGADR field in an associated UCB if the LOG$L_MBXUCB in the logical field is nonzero, and finally deallocates the block to the appropriate memory pool.

29.2.5   Logical Name Translation

Logical name translation has several special options that it must check for in addition to the usual privilege and protection checks. If the logical name begins with the underscore character (_), then the equivalence string that is returned is simply the logical name string with the underscore removed. In addition, the caller can specify that the search only occur in some of the tables.

Assuming that none of the tables has been eliminated, the service searches for a match in first the process table, then the group table, and finally the system table. There is no access mode check made for the process table. If a process has the same logical name with more than one access mode, the name associated with the least privileged (largest) access mode is returned. The search of the group table does require that the group numbers match.

30 Miscellaneous System Services

Of shoes—and ships—and sealing wax—
  Of cabbages—and kings—
And why the sea is boiling hot—
  And whether pigs have wings.

—Lewis Carroll, *Through the Looking Glass*

This chapter includes brief discussions of the system services not mentioned in the previous chapters. Although these services do not generally make intensive use of the internal structures and mechanisms of the VMS executive, these descriptions are provided as an informational aid to users of the services and for completeness. Detailed discussions of the arguments, return status codes, required process privileges, and system service options can be found in the *VAX/VMS System Services Reference Manual*.

30.1 COMMUNICATION WITH SYSTEM PROCESSES

Some of the operations often associated with an operating system are performed in the VAX/VMS system by independent normal processes, rather than by code in the linked system image. Examples of this type of system activity include the following:

- Gathering of accounting information about utilization of the system resources
- Managing print and batch jobs and queues
- Communicating with one or more system operators
- Reporting device errors

Four system services are defined in the module SYSSNDMSG to provide communications with the appropriate system processes.

30.1.1 Accounting Manager (Job Controller)

The accounting manager is a part of the job controller (process JOB-_CONTROL running image JOBCTL.EXE). It is responsible for recording the utilization of system resources in the accounting file.

Requests to the accounting manager are sent through the job controller's mailbox by the $SNDACC system service. Explicit $SNDACC requests can

632

be issued by users to request actions normally available through the SET ACCOUNTING command.

The $SNDACC system service routine performs the following operations:

1. The message type is defined as MSG$_SNDACC and the target mailbox is defined as the job controller's mailbox (MBA1:), which is defined in module DEVICEDAT.
2. The request is checked for possible errors such as too large a message, insufficient privilege, or inaccessible data references. (The privilege OPER is required to create a new log file or to enable or disable accounting.)
3. The message buffer is allocated on the current stack (the executive mode stack), and the following information is placed in the buffer:

    *   The message type
    *   The reply mailbox channel (if specified as an optional argument)
    *   The privilege mask, UIC, user name, and account name
    *   The process base priority (see Chapter 10)
    *   The user-defined message text (a required argument)

4. The message is written to the mailbox after changing to kernel mode.

30.1.2   Symbiont Manager (Job Controller)

The symbiont manager is also part of the job controller process. It is responsible for transactions to and from the queue file, including the creation and dispatching of batch and print queues and jobs.

Requests to the symbiont manager are sent to the job controller's mailbox by the $SNDSMB system service. Explicit $SNDSMB requests can be issued by users to request actions normally available through the following DCL commands:

```
ASSIGN/MERGE        SET DEVICE/SPOOLED
ASSIGN/QUEUE        SET QUEUE
DEASSIGN/QUEUE      START/QUEUE
DELETE/ENTRY        STOP/ABORT
DELETE/QUEUE        STOP/QUEUE
INITIALIZE/QUEUE    STOP/REQUEUE
PRINT               SUBMIT
```

The $SNDSMB system service performs exactly the same operations (using common code) as the $SNDACC system service (as described in the previous section), except that the message type is defined to be MSG$_SNDSMB.

The user privilege OPER is required to use any function of $SNDSMB that affects a queue itself (for example, initializing or deleting a queue). $SNDSMB requires GROUP privilege to affect queue entries owned by processes in the caller's group; WORLD privilege is required to affect entries from outside the group.

30.1.3   Operator Communications

Operator communications are handled by a system process (process OPCOM running image OPCOM.EXE). OPCOM has the following responsibilities:

- Defining which terminals are operator terminals and for what class of activity (such as disk or tape operations) these terminals will receive messages
- Replying to or canceling a user request to an operator
- Managing the operator log file

Requests to OPCOM are sent through OPCOM's mailbox by the $SNDOPR system service. Explicit $SNDOPR requests can be issued by users to request actions normally available through the DCL user command REQUEST and the operator command REPLY.

The user privilege OPER is required to call $SNDOPR to enable a terminal as an operator's terminal, to reply to or cancel a user's request, or to initialize the operator communication log file.

With exceptions of a different mailbox (MBA2:), and a different message type (MSG$_OPRQST), $SNDOPR shares common code with $SNDACC and $SNDSMB (described in Section 30.1.1).

30.1.4   Error Logger

As described in Chapter 8, the error logging subsystem consists of three pieces.

- The subsystem itself contains routines that maintain a set of error message buffers. These routines are called by the error logger and device drivers in order that error messages can be written to some available space in one of these buffers.
- The error formatting process (process ERRFMT running image ERRFMT.EXE) is awakened when it is necessary to copy the formatted contents of these error message buffers to the error log file for subsequent analysis.
- The SYE Utility reads the error messages in the error log file and produces an error log report, based on the contents of the error log file and the options selected when SYE was run.

Normal interactions with the error logging routines in the kernel occur in device drivers by issuing device error or device timeout requests. Users can also send messages to the error logger (put messages into one of the error message buffers for later transmission to the error log file) by issuing the $SNDERR system service (this requires the BUGCHK privilege). Unlike the $SNDACC, $SNDSMB, and $SNDOPR system services, the $SNDERR system service has the following characteristics:

- It executes in kernel mode (rather than executive mode).
- It allocates an error message buffer (rather than sending a mailbox message).

The $SNDERR system service routine performs the following actions:

1. The request is checked for access and privilege violations.
2. A buffer is allocated from the error logger's message pool.
3. The message buffer is filled with the message type (EMB$C_SS), the message size, and the message text. An error log sequence number and the current time are also a part of every error message.
4. The buffer is released to the error logging routines for subsequent output to the error log file.

Chapter 8 contains a discussion of the error log routines and a brief description of the ERRFMT process.

30.2   SYSTEM MESSAGE FILE SERVICES

VAX/VMS Version 3.0 provides three levels of message file capability. The creation and declaration of image-specific and process-permanent message files are discussed in the description of the Message Utility in the *VAX-11 Utilities Reference Manual* and the *VAX/VMS Command Language User's Guide*. The system message file (SYSMSG.EXE) is mapped into system address space as a pageable section. This initialization is performed by SYSINIT during system initialization (see Chapter 25).

Two system services provide the capablility for a user to do the following:

- Search for a message text corresponding to a given status code ($GETMSG)
- Write one or more message texts to SYS$OUTPUT ($PUTMSG)

A third procedure (EXE$EXCMSG) does not use the various message files but is also one of the message output procedures that can be invoked as part of condition handling. EXE$EXCMSG is called by EXCEPTION to write the contents of the general registers to SYS$OUTPUT if a condition is not handled in any other way.

30.2.1   Get Message System Service

The Get Message system service ($GETMSG) executes in the mode of the caller. It searches each of the three levels of message files for a match to the status code provided as an argument.

30.2.1.1   Finding the Message Files. The first step of the retrieval of a message involves determining which types of message files have been defined.

1. If an image message section has been defined, then it has been incorporated as a program region image section. The control region location CTL$GL_GETMSG points to the per-image message section vector in the control region (see Chapter 26). The vector is initialized with a value corresponding to an RSB instruction. If an image has defined any message sections, then this vector is changed by the image activator to the following code sequence:

```
JSB    @#<P0-location_1>
JSB    @#<P0-location_2>
  .
  .
  .
JSB    @#<P0-location_n>
RSB
```

These instructions are not executed; rather, the address serves as a pointer to the message sections. Each P0 location is in a different message section (up to a maximum of 41 distinct message sections in a given image). The message section search routine searches one message section at a time.

2. If no match is found in the current section, the message dispatcher searches the next message section given in the P1 space vector, and so on.

3. If no image message section has been defined or the input status value could not be found in any image message section, then a test is made for a process-permanent message section (established by the SET MESSAGE command). The absence of a process-permanent message section is indicated by a zero in the control region location, CTL$GL_PPMSG. If a process-permanent message section has been defined, CTL$GL_PPMSG points to a control region address in a process-permanent section vector (see Chapter 26). The process-permanent message section is searched in a fashion similar to that used for the image section case above.

4. If a process-permanent message section has not been defined or the input status value could not be found in the process-permanent message section, then the system message file is searched. The location EXE$GL_SYSMSG points to a system location in a system section vector. The message section search routine is called to search for the system message file.

If no message file is found or none of the defined message files contains the specified status code, then the status code is inserted into a message indicating that the message is not in the message file, and the service returns with the status code SS$_MSGNOTFND.

30.2.1.2 **Searching a Located Message Section.** When a message section is located, the starting address and length of the message section index are calculated. A binary search of the message section index is then performed to determine if the specified status code is included.

If no message is defined within the section for the specified status code, a check is made in other message sections of the same type. If no further message sections of the same type exist, the search routine returns to the $GETMSG main search procedure. $GETMSG then checks the next type of message section until the system message file has been searched.

If a message corresponding to the specified status code is located within a message section, then the information selected by the $GETMSG FLAGS argument is copied into the user-defined buffer. The search routine returns control to the caller of the $GETMSG system service.

30.2.1.3 **Indirect Message Sections.** Indirect message sections allow users to create more than one message file associated with an executable image. Message files can then be changed without recompiling and relinking the image. Briefly, the executable image contains pointers to a message file, rather than the messages themselves. The DCL commands used to create indirect message sections are described in the *VAX-11 Utilities Reference Manual*.

As a result of creating an indirect message section, two image files are created: one is an executable image, in which the actual message text areas contain the file specification of the second image, a nonexecutable image, which contains the message data.

When the $GETMSG system service searches for a message code and finds a file specification (rather than message text) related to the code, it maps the nonexecutable image specified by the file specification to the end of the current message section (if it has not been mapped already). The newly mapped section contains the actual message text. The search for the message code continues. When the message is found, the information specified by the $GETMSG FLAGS argument is copied into the user-defined buffer.

If the nonexecutable image has already been mapped, the text for the code is in the newly mapped section. $GETMSG then searches for the second occurrence of the message code and processes the code as usual.

30.2.2 **Put Message System Service**

The $PUTMSG system service provides the ability to write one or more error messages to SYS$ERROR (and SYS$OUTPUT if it is different from SYS$ERROR). It executes in the access mode of its caller, and uses $GETMSG to retrieve the associated text for a particular status code.

The following four arguments are passed to $PUTMSG:

1. A message argument vector describing the messages in terms of status codes, message field selection flag bits, and $FAO arguments (see Section 30.5.2).

2. An optional action routine to be called before writing the message texts.
3. An optional facility name to be associated with the first message written. If not specified, the default facility name associated with the message is used.
4. An optional parameter to be passed to the caller's action routine. If not specified, it defaults to zero.

The construction of the message argument vector is discussed in the *VAX/ VMS System Services Reference Manual*. Other uses of the $PUTMSG system service are described in the *VAX-11 Run-Time Library Reference Manual*.

Each argument of the message argument vector is processed as follows:

1. The facility code of the request is determined to be a system, RMS, or standard facility code. Standard facility codes can require $FAO arguments. System messages (facility code 0) and RMS messages (facility code 1) do not use associated $FAO arguments in the message argument vector. System exception messages require $FAO arguments to follow immediately after the message identification in the message vector.
2. $GETMSG is called with the status code and field selections (based upon the selection bits and $FAO arguments).
3. If there are $FAO arguments present and the message is flagged as having at least one $FAO argument, $FAOL is called to assemble all the portions of the message to be written (supplied facility code, optionally specified delimiters, output from $GETMSG).
4. The user's action routine is called, if one was specified.
5. If the action routine returns an error status, the message is not written. Otherwise, the formatted message is written to SYS$ERROR by an RMS $PUT request. If SYS$OUTPUT is different from SYS$ERROR, then the formatted message is also written to SYS$OUTPUT.

When all of the arguments in the message argument vector have been processed, the $PUTMSG system service returns to its caller.

30.2.3 Procedure EXE$EXCMSG

This procedure is used internally by the catch-all condition handler (see Chapter 4) to report a condition that has not been properly handled by any condition handlers further up the call stack. The two input arguments to this procedure are the address of an ASCIZ string and the address of the argument list passed to the condition handlers (see Chapter 4).

The procedure writes a formatted dump of the general registers, the signal array, and the stack, as well as the caller's message text to SYS$OUTPUT (and to SYS$ERROR if different from SYS$OUTPUT). This message appears for all fatal errors that occur in images that were linked without the traceback handler. (Note that most images shipped with the VAX/VMS operating system are linked without the traceback handler.)

Although this procedure has an associated entry point in the system service vector area, it cannot be conveniently called from any languages except VAX-11 MACRO and VAX-11 BLISS-32. This restriction is imposed by the specification of the second argument, which requires access to the general register AP, a capability denied to most high-level languages.

30.3 GET JOB/PROCESS INFORMATION ($GETJPI)

The $GETJPI system service provides selected information about a specified process (which may not necessarily be the process requesting the $GETJPI service). The arguments to $GETJPI include the following:

- The event flag number to set when the service has completed
- The process ID of the process from which information is to be collected
- The process name of the target process
- The address of an item list that includes (for each requested item) which item of information is to be returned, the size and address of the buffer to hold the information, and a location to insert the size of the returned information
- An I/O status block (IOSB) to receive final status information
- The entry point and parameter for an AST routine to be invoked when the system service has completed

A detailed discussion of the format and specification of the item list is described in the *VAX/VMS System Services Reference Manual*.

30.3.1 Operation of the $GETJPI System Service

The $GETJPI system service, executing in kernel mode, performs as follows:

1. The privileges of the current process are checked with regard to the UIC of the target process.
2. The IOSB, if specified, and the event flag are cleared.
3. Each item in the list is checked for the following conditions:

   - The buffer descriptor must be readable and the buffer writable.
   - The requested item must be a recognized one.

4. If these conditions are met, then the requested item can be retrieved. All data about the current process and PCB and JIB data about another process can be obtained without entering the context of the target process. All such information is moved to the user-defined buffers for each corresponding item.

5. If no information remains to be gathered, then the system service returns to the caller after the following action is performed:

   - The specified event flag is set.
   - If an AST was requested, it is queued.
   - If an IOSB was supplied, its values are written.

6. If there is remaining information that could not be retrieved by step 3 above, the information concerns a process other than the caller and is stored either in the target process's control region or process header.

   This information must be retrieved by executing in the context of the target process. In order to execute in the context of the target process, a special kernel mode AST (see Chapter 7) is queued to the target process. Nonpaged dynamic memory is allocated to contain an extended AST control block and an information buffer. (The pool is charged to the JIB$L_BYTCNT quota.) Before the special kernel mode AST is queued, the extended AST control block must be built to contain the normal fields plus descriptors of all of the unsatisfied requests that must be retrieved by executing in the context of the other process. Also, the buffer must be created to receive the retrieved information for transmission to the requesting process.

   The ACB is then queued to the target process with a priority boost of PRI$_TICOM (6); however, if the target process is computable (COM) or computable outswapped (COMO), the target process's priority is boosted only enough to make it equal to the priority of the current process (unless the current process is a real-time process, or the priority is lower than that of the target process).

   If the target process no longer exists, if it is in the suspended (SUSP), suspended outswapped (SUSPO), or the miscellaneous wait (MWAIT) state (see Chapter 10), the block of nonpaged pool is deallocated and an error return is passed back to the caller. The status of SS$_SUSPENDED is returned for the three long wait states of SUSP, SUSPO, and MWAIT. If the process has been deleted or is in the process of being deleted (has the delete pending bit set in the PCB status longword), a status of SS$_NONEXPR is passed back to the caller. Note that the completion mechanisms are all triggered if one of these errors occurs. That is, the event flag is set, a user-requested AST is queued, and an IOSB is written with the failure status.

   The process header contains an image counter at offset PHD$L_IMGCNT. The counter is incremented each time that an image is run down (see Chapter 21). This counter is stored in the extended AST control block in order to prevent the image from requesting information about another process and then exiting, only to have an AST delivered or an IOSB written later on to the requested P0 addresses in another image.

7. Finally, the system service returns to the caller. The caller can either wait for the information to be returned or continue processing.

30.3.2 $GETJPI Special Kernel Mode ASTs

When the target process is not the caller and the information needed resides in the process header or P1 space of the target process, the special kernel mode AST code must execute in the context of the target process (in order to access the information). Once the AST has obtained the information, it must be passed back to the caller's context, in order that it can be written to the caller's address space. The VMS system uses special kernel mode ASTs for both pieces of this operation.

A summary of the operations performed by these special kernel mode ASTs is as follows:

1. When the target process is made executable to execute the special kernel mode AST, the requested information is determined from the extended ACB and stored in the associated system buffer. The completion of the special kernel mode AST routine occurs after the extended ACB is reformatted to deliver a second special kernel mode AST, this time to the requesting process.

2. The second kernel mode AST routine executes in the context of the requesting process. If the image counters do not agree, then the requesting image has gone away. In this case, the block of nonpaged pool is deallocated, the process BYTCNT quota is restored, and the special kernel mode AST simply returns.

   If the image counter in the process header agrees with the image counter in the extended AST control block, the retrieved data is moved from the system buffer into the user-defined buffers. Note that the asynchronous nature of this aspect of the system service requires that the IOSB be probed again for write accessibility. This check insures that the original caller of $GETJPI has not altered the protection of the IOSB in the interval between the call to $GETJPI and the delivery of the return special kernel AST.

3. The event flag is set and the IOSB is written if it was specified (after checking that the buffers are still accessible).

4. If an AST was requested, the AST control block is used for the third time to queue an AST to the requesting process in the access mode of the caller. Otherwise, the ACB is deallocated to nonpaged memory.

30.3.3 Wildcard Support in $GETJPI

The $GETJPI system service also provides the ability to obtain information about all processes in the system (in other words, a wildcard search). A wildcard request is indicated by passing a negative process ID to the $GETJPI system service. The internal routine in $GETJPI that determines the identity of the target process recognizes a wildcard request and passes information back to the caller about the first process in the PCB vector after the swapper and the null process (see Chapter 20).

In addition, the process index field of the caller's PID argument is altered to contain the process index of the target process. When the caller of $GETJPI issues a second call, the negative sequence number (in the high-order word of the process ID) indicates that a wildcard operation is in progress but a positive process index indicates where in the PCB vector the search should continue. Note that the user program will not work correctly if the caller alters the value of the process ID argument between calls to $GETJPI.

The user continues to issue calls to $GETJPI until a status code of SS$_NOMOREPROC is returned, indicating that the PCB vector search routine has reached the end of the PCB vector. An example of the wildcard use of the $GETJPI system service is contained in the *VAX/VMS System Services Reference Manual*.

30.4 GET SYSTEM INFORMATION ($GETSYI)

The Get System Information ($GETSYI) system service provides status and identification information about the system. In VAX/VMS Version 3.0, three pieces of information can be obtained by $GETSYI: the contents of the system ID register, the system version, or the processor type.

To obtain the string containing the system version, $GETSYI (in module SYSGETSYI) performs the following operations:

- $GETSYI copies the quadword value found at global location SYS$GQ_VERSION into the user's buffer.
- The contents of the system ID register are obtained by executing a MFPR (move from processor register) instruction, specifying the system ID register by the symbol PR$_SID.
- The processor type is simply extracted from the contents of the system ID register.

Note that because the information located by $GETSYI is static and immediately obtainable, the $GETSYI system service does not require the AST synchronization mechanisms required by other informational services (for example, $GETJPI and $GETDVI).

30.5 FORMATTING SUPPORT

The final group of system services provides conversion support for time-related requests and for formatted I/O of ASCII character strings.

30.5.1   Time Conversion Services

The time conversion system services are defined in the module SYSCVRTIM. The $NUMTIM system service executes in executive mode and converts a binary quadword time value in system time format (described in Chapter 11) into the following seven numerical word length fields:

- Year (AD)
- Month of year
- Day of month
- Hour of day
- Minute of hour
- Second of minute
- Hundredths of second

A positive time argument is converted into the corresponding absolute system time. A zero-valued time argument requests the conversion of the current system time. A negative time argument is interpreted as a time interval from the current system time.

The $ASCTIM system service executes in the access mode of the caller and converts a system time format quadword into an ASCII character string. The input binary time argument is passed to $NUMTIM. The seven fields returned from $NUMTIM are then converted into ASCII character fields with the selection determined by whether the input time was an absolute or delta time and whether the conversion flag was set, indicating conversion of day and time or only the time portion. The $FAO system service (described in Section 30.5.2) is used to concatenate and format the string components before returning the string to the caller.

The $BINTIM system service executes in the access mode of the caller and converts an ASCII time string into a quadword absolute or delta time. If the input string expresses an absolute time, then the current system time is converted by $NUMTIM to supply any fields omitted in the ASCII string. Each ASCII field is then converted to numerical values and stored in the seven word fields used by $NUMTIM. The seven word fields are then combined into a binary quadword value. The resulting value is negated if a delta time was specified in the ASCII string.

30.5.2   Formatted ASCII Output

The $FAO and $FAOL system services provide formatting and conversion facilities from binary and ASCII input parameters to a single ASCII output string. The two system services execute in the access mode of the caller and use common code. The only difference between them is whether the parameters are passed as a list of arguments ($FAO) or as the address of the first parameter ($FAOL). The control string is parsed character by character. Information that is not preceded by the control character (!) is copied into the output string without further action. When a control character and operation code are encountered in the control string, the appropriate conversion routine is executed to process zero, one, or two of the input parameters to the system service. When the control string has been completely parsed, the service returns to the caller with a normal status code. If the output string length is exceeded, a buffer overflow error status is returned. The description of the $FAO system service in the *VAX/FMS System Services Reference Manual* contains details about how to specify $FAO requests.

31 Use of Listing and Map Files

On the table in the light of a big lamp with a red shade he spread
a piece of parchment rather like a map. . . ."There is one point
that you haven't noticed," said the wizard, "and that is the secret
entrance. You see that rune on the West side, and the hand
pointing to it from the other runes?"

—Tolkien, *The Hobbit*

This book has presented a detailed overview of the VAX/VMS executive. However, the ultimate authority on how the executive or any other component of the system works is the source code for that component. This chapter shows how the listing and map files produced by the language processors and the VAX-11 Linker can be used with other tools to understand how a given component works, or why the system is malfunctioning.

31.1 HINTS IN READING THE EXECUTIVE LISTINGS

The sources for the VAX/VMS operating system are available in two forms. The source listing kit includes microfiche listings for all bundled components except certain compatibility mode utilities. This kit is included with each VAX/VMS system. Source files and command procedures are also distributed on magnetic tape for customers who purchase a source license.

The suggestions made in this chapter emphasize reading the modules that make up the executive and the initialization routines, all of which are written in VAX-11 MACRO.

31.1.1 Structure of a MACRO Listing File

The modules that make up the executive are all written from a common template that includes a module header describing each routine in the module. The general format of a VAX-11 MACRO listing file is described in the *VAX-11 MACRO Language Reference Manual*. Features that are peculiar to listings included in the source listing kit are described here.

31.1.1.1 $xyzDEF MACROs.
One of the first parts of each module that requires explanation is the invocation of a series of macros that define symbolic offsets into data structures referenced in the module. The general form of these macros is shown in the following example, where xyz represents the data structure whose offsets are required:

```
$xyzDEF
```

For example, a module that deals with the I/O subsystem will probably invoke the $IRPDEF and $UCBDEF macros to define offsets into I/O request packets and unit control blocks. Some of the $xyzDEF macros such as $SSDEF, $IODEF, and $PRDEF define constants (system service status returns, I/O function codes and modifiers, and processor register definitions) rather than offsets into data structures.

Structures and constants that are used in system services have their $xyzDEF macros defined in STARLET.MLB, the default macro library that is automatically searched by the assembler. Most of the data structures used by the executive have their macro definitions contained in a special macro library called LIB.MLB. The distinction between these two macro libraries is discussed in Appendix B, where many of the data structures described in this manual are listed.

One way to obtain the symbol definitions resulting from these macros is to look at the symbol table that appears at the end of the assembly listing. However, the information presented there is often incomplete or not in a suitable form. An alternate representation of the data can be obtained from the following sequence of DCL commands:

```
$ CREATE  xyzDEF.MAR
          .TITLE xyzDEF
          $xyzDEF GLOBAL
          .END
          ^Z
$ MACRO xyzDEF+SYS$LIBRARY:LIB.MLBLIBRARY
$ LINK/NOEXE/MAP/FULL xyzDEF
$ PRINT xyzDEF.MAP
```

This command sequence produces a single object module that contains all the symbols produced by the $xyzDEF macro. The argument GLOBAL makes all the symbols produced by the macro global. (This argument must appear in upper case to be properly interpreted by the assembler's macro processor.) That is, the symbol names and values are passed from the assembler to the linker so that they appear on whatever map the linker produces. The full map contains two lists of symbol definitions, one in alphabetical order and one in numeric order.

31.1.1.2   **The Routine Body.** In general, the routines that make up the executive were coded according to strict standards that result in code that is easily maintained. One side effect of these standards is that the code is easy to read for someone attempting to learn how the VMS operating system works.

Several items about the instructions that appear in the module body are worth describing.

- Data structure references are usually made using displacement mode addressing. For example, the following instruction loads the contents of R3 (presumably the address of an I/O request packet) into the IRP pointer field (a longword) in a unit control block pointed to by R5:

```
MOVL      R3,UCB$L_IRP(R5)
```

Such instructions are practically self-documenting. The overall arrangement of data in a particular structure does not need to be known in order to understand such instruction references.

- Whenever a sequence of instructions makes an assumption about the relative locations of fields within a data structure, there is a possibility of failure if the structure should change. In the following two instances such assumptions might be used:

—Two adjacent longword fields could be loaded with a single MOVQ instruction.

—A structure could be traversed using autoincrement or autodecrement addressing.

The ASSUME macro (defined in SYS$LIBRARY:STARLET.MLB) is often used to immediately detect these failures by issuing an assembly-time error. For example, if a device driver wanted to clear adjacent fields in a unit control block, the following instruction and macro sequence sequence would prevent future subtle errors if the layout of the unit control block changed:

```
CLRQ      UCB$L_SVAPTE(R5)
ASSUME    UCB$L_BOFF EQ<UCB$L_SVAPTE + 4>
ASSUME    UCB$L_BCNT EQ<UCB$L_SVAPTE + 6>
```

The options available with this macro can be determined by examining its definition in the microfiche listing in the SYS component.

- There are some commonly used instruction sequences that occur so frequently that the author of a module used an assembly-time macro to represent the instruction sequence. Other instruction sequences, particularly those that read or write the internal processor registers, are more readable if hidden in a macro definition. However, because macros are rarely expanded as a part of the assembler listing, the reader of listing files must be able to locate the macro definitions.

There are three levels at which macros are defined in the VAX/VMS operating system:

—A macro may be local to a module. In this case, the macro definition appears as part of the module header. Such macros are often used to generate data tables used by a single module.

—A macro may be a part of a specific facility, such as DCL or the RSX-11M AME. The macros that are a part of a specific facility are included as part of the microfiche listing for that facility. For example, the DCL microfiche includes not only all modules that make up the DCL images but also the macros that are used to assemble those modules.

—A macro may be used by many components of the operating system. In this case, the macro definition is found on either the SYS microfiche (for example, in SYSDEFxx.MDL or SYSMAR.MAR) or the VMSLIB microfiche (for example, in STARDEFxx.MDL or SSMSG.MDL). Most of the macro definitions in this category are data structure definitions, but there are many common instruction sequences appearing in several components that are defined in the file called SYSMAR.MAR. Note that SYSDEF and STARDEF were divided into four submodules each. The strings AE, FL, MP, or QZ are used to identify the first letters of the structures defined in each module. These strings should be substituted for the string xx.

The definitions of all system macros that are used in building the operating system are included in the macro library SYS$LIBRARY:LIB.MLB that is supplied as a part of the VAX/VMS binary distribution kit. Applications such as user-written device drivers or user-written system services can also use this macro library. Such applications must be reassembled or recompiled with each new release of LIB.MLB, which usually occurs with each major release of the VAX/VMS operating system.

The definitions of all macros that are intended for use in nonprivileged applications such as system service calls can be found in the macro library SYS$LIBRARY:STARLET.MLB that is also supplied as a part of the VAX/VMS binary distribution kit. This macro library is automatically searched by the assembler to resolve undefined macros. Appendix B contains a description of the data structures defined in STARDEF.MDL and SYSDEF.MDL.

- Another search that the reader of listings has to embark on involves looking for destinations of instructions that transfer control or reference static data locations. If the destination or data label is outside the module currently being looked at, the symbol appears in the symbol table at the end of the assembler listing as an undefined global. The module that defines that symbol can be determined with the map file for that component (see Section 31.2).

Symbols that are local to a module are usually easy to find because most of the modules that make up the executive or any other component are not very large. However, the listing files for some modules are longer than 50 pages. There are a couple of steps that can be taken before the reader scans every page of the listing, looking for the place where the symbol is defined.

—The symbol in question or some textual reference to it may appear in the table of contents for this module.

—The value of the symbol appears in the symbol table. Because the assembler includes the value of the current location counter in every line of the listing, the reader can determine approximately where in the listing the symbol is defined.

(This technique is not foolproof. The value of the symbol that appears in the symbol table is relative to the beginning of the PSECT in which the symbol is defined. Modules with more than one relocatable PSECT may have to be searched more carefully.)

31.1.2   The VAX-11 Instruction Set and Addressing Modes

One of the design goals of the VAX-11 instruction set was that it contain useful instructions with a natural number of operands. Thus, there are two- and three-operand forms of the arithmetic instructions ADD, SUB, MUL, and DIV. There are also bit manipulation instructions, a calling standard, character string instructions, and so on. All of these allow the assembly language programmer to produce code that is both efficient and highly readable.

However, there are certain places in the executive where the most obvious choice of instruction or addressing mode was not used, because a shorter or faster alternative was available. Interrupt service routines, routines that execute at elevated IPL, and commonly executed code paths such as the system service dispatcher and the main paths in the pager are all examples where clarity of the source code was sacrificed for execution speed.

One question that must be answered at this point is why there is a concern over instruction length on a machine with practically unlimited virtual address space. There are at least two answers to that question.

Most of the areas where instruction size is an issue are within the permanently resident executive. This portion of the system consumes a fixed percentage of the physical memory that is present in the configuration. Keeping instruction size small is one good way to keep this real memory cost to a minimum.

A second answer is that all three VAX-11 processors make use of an instruction lookahead buffer that contains the next eight bytes in the instruction stream. If the buffer empties, the next instruction or operand cannot be evaluated until the buffer is replenished. By keeping instructions small in key areas, this wait can be avoided and the instruction buffer can be filled in parallel with other CPU operations.

31.1.2.1   Techniques for Increasing Instruction Speed.
This section lists some of the techniques employed to reduce instruction size or increase execution speed. The list is hardly exhaustive but a pattern emerges here that can be applied to other modules in the executive that are not explicitly mentioned here. Each list element consists of a general technique and may also contain a specific example, including the name of the module where this technique is employed.

- The MOVAx and PUSHAx instructions combined with displacement mode addressing are equivalent to an ADDLx instruction with the addition being performed in order to calculate the effective address of the operand. For example, the following two instructions are equivalent:

```
PUSHAB      12(R3)
;
ADDL3       #12,R3,-(SP)
```

However, the PUSHAB instruction is one byte shorter than the ADDL3 instruction and also faster.

- The use of MOVAx and PUSHAx described in the previous item can be combined with indexed mode addressing to accomplish a multiply by 2, 4, or 8. For example, the following instruction multiplies the contents of R1 by 4, adds 4 to the product, and places the result back into R1:

```
MOVAL       @#4R1,R1
```

This instruction is used by the change mode dispatchers (in module CMODSSDSP) to calculate the length of an argument list from the number of arguments.

- The following instruction, found in routine EXE$ALLOCATE in module MEMORYALC, performs two steps at once:

```
MOVAB       (R0)+,R2
```

Its ostensible purpose is to place the address of the allocated block of memory into R2 where it will be picked up by the caller. However, because the allocated block is always at least quadword aligned, the byte context of the instruction forces an increment of R0 by one, setting the low bit of R0. This set bit will be interpreted as a success indicator by the caller.

- When two successive writes to memory occur, the second write must wait for the first to complete. If successive write operations can be overlapped with register-to-register operations, instruction stream references, or other operations that do not generate writes to memory, then some other instruction can begin execution while the memory write is completing.

There are three places in the executive where this technique is used. They are among the most commonly executed code paths in the entire system.

- —The page fault handler saves registers R0 through R5 with three separate MOVQ instructions interspersed among instructions that do not write to memory.
- —The interrupt service routine for the VAX-11/780 UNIBUS adapter also saves R0 through R5 with three MOVQ instructions. Here, the writes to memory are overlapped with references to I/O space addresses, specifically UBA internal registers, as well as register manipulations.
- —The change mode dispatchers for executive and kernel modes build customized call frames on their stacks. As the code examples in Section 9.3.1 illustrate, the writes to memory (the stack operations) are overlapped with register and instruction stream references.

- There are three ways to push registers onto the stack: with a PUSHR mask instruction, with a series of MOVQ instructions to −(SP), or with a series of MOVL instructions to −(SP). Tests on instruction speed show that in general two MOVL instructions are faster than one MOVQ. Thus, in some places in the executive, values are pushed onto the stack with a series of MOVL instructions (for example, EXE$FORKDSPTH in module FORKCNTRL). In other places, values are moved onto the stack in couples, with a series of MOVQ instructions (for example, IOC$IOPOST in module IOCIOPOST). Many MOVQ instructions have not been changed to MOVL instructions simply because no optimizing pass was made on the code.

    The PUSHR instruction is seldom used because it is much slower than either MOVQ or MOVL. PUSHR must interpret its bit mask operand, and then push the registers accordingly.

- When it is necessary to include a test and branch operation, a decision as to which sense of the test to branch on and which sense to allow to continue in line is required. One basis for this decision is to allow the common (usually error-free) case to continue in line, only requiring the (slower) branch operation in unusual cases.

31.1.2.2   Unusual Instruction and Addressing Mode Usage. There are several instances in the executive where the purpose of an instruction is not at all obvious. This list includes the most common occurrences of unusual use of the instruction set and addressing modes.

- There are many instances of the following instruction sequence where the initial setting of the bit has no effect on the flow of control:

```
            BBSS        bit arguments , 10$
    10$:
```

    This sequence is used whenever the bit to be set (or cleared with an equivalent sequence using BBCC) is identified by bit number or bit position.

    In order to set (or clear) the bit with a BISx (or BICx) instruction, a mask must first be created with a 1 in the designated position, requiring either two instructions or an immediate mask that might occupy a longword. (The only exception to this involves a bit in the first six positions, where the mask can be contained in a short literal constant.)

    Note that a BBCS instruction is equivalent to a BBSS instruction when the branch destination is the next instruction. There are some occurrences of BBCS where a BBSS seems to accomplish the same purpose. Probably the choice was made by looking at the usual sense of the bit in question before the instruction and choosing the instruction to avoid the branch in the usual case.

- There are several instances of autoincrement deferred addressing where the need for the increment of the register is not apparent. For example,

both of the following instructions occur in the rescheduling interrupt service routine in module SCHED:

```
INSQUE        (R1),@(R3)+
;
REMQUE        @(R3)+,R4
```

In both cases, R3 contains the address of the listhead of some doubly
linked list before instruction execution. Its contents after the instruction
is executed are irrelevant.

In fact, the increment is totally unnecessary. All that is needed is double
deferral from a register. In other words, the addressing mode @0(R3) would
be equally appropriate if the contents of R3 are not important. However,
deferred byte displacement addressing costs an extra byte to hold the displacement. In this commonly executed code path, the savings of a byte
was extremely important.

It is worth noting that there is no similar problem when a single level of
deferral from a register is required. The assembler is smart enough to generate simple register deferred mode (code 6) when it encounters byte displacement mode with a displacement of zero (0[reg]) in the source code.

- The permanent symbol table of the VAX-11 MACRO assembler recognizes
the mnemonic POPL even though there is no POPL instruction in the
VAX-11 instruction set. The generated code for the following instructions
are identical:

```
POPL        dst
;
MOVL        (SP)+,dst
```

That is, the mnemonic generates two bytes (for instruction opcode and
source operand specifier) plus whatever is required to specify the destination operand.

For example, the following pseudo instruction (the first instruction in
the change-mode-to-kernel dispatcher in module CMODSSDSP) removes
the change mode code from the stack (so that REI will work correctly) and
loads it into R0.

```
POPL        R0
```

A combination of the POPL instruction with an unusual addressing mode
occurs in the exception dispatcher for change-mode-to-supervisor and
change-mode-to-user exceptions where it is necessary to remove the second longword from the stack. The following instruction has the effect of
removing the next-to-last item from the stack and discarding it, leaving
the stack in the state pictured in Figure 31-1:

```
POPL        (SP)
```

- The following instruction, followed by some conditional branch instruc-

POPL dest ≡ MOVL(SP)+, dest

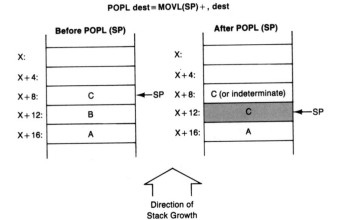

Figure 31-1
Stack Modification Due to POPL (SP) Pseudo Instruction

tion, performs exactly the same function as a TSTQ instruction, which does not exist:

```
MOVQ      R0,R0
```

This curious instruction is found in module SYSSCHEVT, where the Set Timer Request and Schedule Wakeup system services are implemented.

31.1.3   Use of the REI Instruction

The only permissible means of reaching a less privileged access mode from a more privileged mode is through the REI instruction. There are two slightly different techniques that accomplish this mode change.

The most general technique of elevating access mode allows the flow of execution to be altered at the same time. This same technique is also used by the RSX-11M AME to get into compatibility mode. The following instruction sequence accomplishes the desired result:

```
PUSHL     new-PSL
PUSHL     new-PC
REI
```

Note that the many protection checks built into the REI instruction prevent this technique from being used by a nonprivileged user to get into a more privileged access mode or to elevate IPL, two operations that would allow such a user to damage the system. A second technique can be used when it is only necessary to change access mode. No accompanying change in control flow is required. The instruction sequence listed here (patterned after code contained in module PROCSTRT) shows this second technique.

653

```
                    PUSHL           executive-mode-PSL
                    BSBB            DOREI
                      .
                      .                     ;Do processing in
                      .                     ; executive access mode
                      .
                    PUSHL           user-mode-PSL
                    BSBB            DOREI
                      .
                      .
                      .                     ;Do processing in
                      .                     ; user access mode
          DOREI:    REI                     ;REI uses pushed PSL and PC
                                            ; that BSBB put on stack
                      .
                      .
                      .
```

31.1.4   Register Conventions

Each of the major subsystems of the executive uses a set of register conventions in its main routines. That is, the same registers are used to hold the same contents from routine to routine. Some of the more common conventions are listed here.

- R4 usually contains the address of the PCB of the current process. Nearly all system services and the scheduler use this convention. In fact, as illustrated in the code examples in Section 9.3.1, the change-mode-to-kernel system service dispatcher loads the PCB of the caller into R4 before passing control to the service-specific procedure. When it is necessary to store a PHD address, R5 is usually chosen. (Except for the swapper and certain memory management code that executes at IPL 7, R5 contains the address of the P1 window to the process header.)
- The memory management subsystem uses R2 to contain an invalid address and R3 to contain the system virtual address of the page table entry that maps the page. When a physical page is eventually associated with the page, the PFN is stored in R0.
- The I/O subsystem uses two nearly identical conventions, depending on whether it is executing in process context (in the $QIO system service or in device driver FDT routines) or in response to an interrupt. The most common register contents are the current IRP address stored in R3 and the UCB address in R5. In process context, R4 contains the address of the PCB of the requesting process. Within interrupt service routines, R4 contains the virtual address that maps one of the CSRs of the interrupting device. A more complete list of register usage by device drivers and the I/O subsystem can be found in the *VAX/VMS Guide to Writing a Device Driver*.

31.1.5   Elimination of Seldom-Used Code

There are several different techniques that are used to eliminate code and data that are not used very often. For example, none of the programs used during the initialization of a VMS system remains after its work is accomplished. Process creation is an example of a complex system service that does not execute often during the lifetime of a typical system. The VMS executive uses several techniques that allow these routines to do their work as efficiently as possible and yet eliminate them after they have done their work.

31.1.5.1   Eliminating the Bootstrap Programs. The following list illustrates some of the techniques used to remove the bootstrap programs from the system after they have done their work:

1. Both VMB and SYSBOOT execute in physical pages that are not recorded anywhere. When module INIT places all physical pages except those occupied by the permanently resident executive on the free page list, the pages used by VMB and SYSBOOT are included. Their contents are overwritten the first time that each physical page is used.

2. The module INIT is a part of the linked executive and cannot be eliminated quite so easily. Chapter 24 describes how INIT puts the physical pages that it occupied on the free page list after its work was done.

   The routine that puts the physical pages on the free page list performs a straightforward function. However, the unusual part of this step is that this routine was first copied to an unused portion of nonpaged pool, but the pool space was not formally allocated. When the routine has accomplished its work and returned, the code remains until the portion of pool that it occupied is used later on, when the last traces of INIT are eliminated from the system. Note that this technique assumes that no pool allocation takes place until it is done. The fact that IPL remains at 31 while INIT executes insures that no such allocation occurs.

3. The system initialization that takes place in process context can be thought of as a part of the swapper process because the swapper creates SYSINIT, which in turn creates the STARTUP process. Because both SYSINIT and STARTUP are separate processes, however, they disappear after they are deleted (when they have completed their work).

31.1.5.2   Seldom-Used System Routines. The simplest technique used by the system to prevent seldom-used code from permanently occupying memory is to put it into the paged executive. The normal operation of system working set replacement will eventually force those pages that are referenced once and never again out of the system working set.

This technique is used by several system services that are not called very often, such as the Set Time system service, which changes the system time. Process creation and deletion are also events that do not occur very often. Because process creation is spread throughout the system, the following techniques are employed to eliminate the code from the system after the process is created:

1. The routines in the Create Process system service (and also the Delete Process system service and its associated special kernel mode AST) are located in the paged executive.
2. The swapper has a special subroutine that it calls when it inswaps a newly created process from SHELL. This subroutine is located in two of the pages that the swapper just read into memory. Because of the way that the swapper does its I/O, these pages are mapped as P0 pages in the swapper's address space. These pages become the kernel stack of the new process (which cannot execute until the swapper marks the process as COM, after it is finished with the special subroutine). The swapper has succeeded in executing two pages worth of code (that are only used the first time that a process is inswapped) without requiring any physical memory.
3. The final steps of process creation take place in the context of the new process in routine EXE$PROCSTRT, located in the paged executive.

31.1.6 Dynamically Locking Code or Data into Memory

The frequency of use is not the only criterion that is used to decide whether to put a routine into the paged or nonpaged executive. The page fault handler assumes that it will never incur a page fault above IPL 2. (This assumption is enforced by issuing a fatal bugcheck if it is violated.)

Several system services that are not used very often (including Create Process and Delete Process) must elevate IPL to 7 to synchronize access to the scheduler's database. There are several different techniques used to minimize the contribution that these routines make to the nonpaged executive.

31.1.6.1 Locking Pages in External Images.
The simplest technique for locking down pages while executing at IPL 7 is used by privileged utilities that use the $CMKRNL system service. These programs can use the $LKWSET system service to lock down the code and data pages that are referenced while IPL is elevated above 2. This technique is not available to executive routines or user-written system services.

31.1.6.2 Placing Code in the Nonpaged Executive.
This technique puts the smallest possible block of code into the nonpaged executive and places the rest of the routine into the paged executive. A control transfer allows the nonpaged code to execute. The following variation on a routine within the $GETJPI system

service illustrates the technique. The reason that the entire routine cannot exist in pageable pages is because routine EXE$NAMPID returns at IPL 7.

```
        .PSECT YEXEPAGED
        .ENABLE LOCAL_BLOCK
                .
                .                      ;Processing begins in paged
                .                      ; code
        JSB   25$

        .SAVE_PSECT
        .PSECT AEXENONPAGED
25$:    JSB   EXE$NAMPID               ;This is only nonpaged piece
        SETIPL #0
        RSB

        .RESTORE_PSECT
                .
                .                      ;Processing continues in paged
                .                      ; code
```

31.1.6.3   **Dynamic Locking of Pages.** The preceding piece of code only contributes ten bytes to the nonpaged executive. The Create Process and Delete Process system services must execute many more instructions at IPL 7. They employ a technique that dynamically locks one or two pages into memory. (The system cannot use the $LKWSET system service to lock pages into the system working set.) This technique is also necessary for user-written system services that must execute above IPL 2 because they must also lock pages into memory and, in general, cannot use the $LKWSET system service.

   This technique relies on the assumption that once IPL is elevated to IPL$_SYNCH, no events related to page faulting occur, particularly removing a page from the process or system working set.

```
                .
                .                      ;Processing begins in paged
                .                      ; code
BEGIN_LOCK:
            DSBINT   LOCK_IPL
                .
                .                      ;No page faults will occur
                .                      ; here
            ENBINT
                .
                .                      ;Page faults can occur
                .                      ; again
LOCK_IPL:
            .LONG   IPL$_SYNCH
END_LOCK:
            ASSUME <END_LOCK-BEGIN_LOCK> LE 512
```

The key to this technique is that the DSBINT macro cannot successfully complete until both the page containing the instruction and the page containing the source operand are valid. Once the instruction completes (implying that both pages are valid), IPL is set at 7, preventing further paging activity until the IPL is lowered (with the ENBINT macro). The DSBINT macro expands to the following instruction:

```
MTPR    src, #PR$_IPL
```

The ASSUME macro is necessary to make sure that the DSBINT macro and source operand are not more than one page apart, preventing the possibility of an invalid page between the two valid pages, an occurrence that would subvert this technique. Any example of this technique also has some instruction that transfers control so that the longword containing IPL$_SYNCH is not interpreted as an instruction.

A natural question at this point is why the first technique, the one used by $GETJPI, is necessary at all. It seems that the call site to EXE$NAMPID could be locked down using this technique. The answer is that EXE$NAMPID cannot be called above IPL 2. It accesses the caller's argument list, a data reference that could potentially cause a page fault, and page faults are not allowed above IPL 2.

31.2   USE OF MAP FILES

One indispensable tool for reading the executive listings is the map file SYS-.MAP found in directory SYS$SYSTEM. This file was produced when the executive image was linked and contains the system virtual addresses of all global symbols in the executive. More important from the point of view of reading the listings, it contains a cross reference listing of modules that define and reference each global symbol.

The techniques that are described for using this file are also applicable to other map files. Map files for device drivers are necessary when debugging a new device driver. The map files for RMS and DCL are also described because these images do not execute in the usual sense but rather are mapped into system or process virtual address space.

31.2.1   The Executive Map SYS.MAP

There are two main uses for the system map file. One of these occurs when the system crashes. The addresses that are reported either on the console terminal or in the system dump file must be related to actual routines in system address space. The portion of the map that lists in ascending order all program sections that contribute to the executive is useful here. The address in question is compared with each PSECT contribution until the module that defines the symbol is found. The base address of this module is subtracted from the address that is being examined to produce an offset into the correct module. This offset can be used with the assembler listing to locate the instruction or data reference that caused the error.

Such an error situation could arise as a result of a bug in the operating system but more likely is due to some user-written modification to the executive such as a device driver, a customized system service, or simply a procedure that is called through the Change Mode to Kernel or Change Mode to Executive system service. The only limitation to the use of the map in this way occurs when a system virtual address is larger than the highest address in the executive image. This situation probably indicates that the address is found in a routine that is dynamically loaded, such as RMS, a device driver, or CPU-dependent routines. Table 26-2 lists the global pointers that locate each dynamically mapped portion of system address space. By examining the contents of these locations, the component that contains the offending address can be determined.

The second use of SYS.MAP occurs when reading practically any routine in the executive. Due to the modular construction of the VMS system, many routines that are referenced by the routine that is currently being looked at are found in some other module. The simplest way to locate these external symbols is to look in the alphabetical cross-reference map for the external symbol name. The first item of information is the name of the module that defines this symbol. All modules that reference this symbol are listed in succeeding columns.

31.2.2   RMS.MAP, DCL.MAP, and MP.MAP

The same cross-reference capability mentioned for SYS.MAP obviously applies to any component of the operating system that contains many modules. While reading a module in DCL for example, there may be a reference to an external subroutine. The module containing that subroutine can be determined with the cross reference listing in the map file DCL.MAP.

RMS, the loadable multiprocessing code, and the command language interpreters present a second problem to anyone attempting to relate code or data in virtual memory to references in an assembler listing or in a map file. Both images are mapped into a virtual address range that is not known until the mapping occurs. The maps meanwhile contain addresses beginning at 0.

The technique to relate map addresses to virtual memory locations for either of these images is as follows. Despite the fact that RMS and the loadable multiprocessing code are mapped into system virtual address space and DCL is mapped into P1 space, the technique employed in each case is the same.

When RMS is mapped by SYSINIT, the base address of the RMS image is stored in global location MMG$GL_RMSBASE. (The contents of this location are copied to location CTL$GL_RMSBASE in the P1 pointer page by

PROCSTRT when a process is created.) The base address of any command language interpreter is stored in the first longword at global location CTL$AG_CLIMAGE. Because both RMS and DCL are linked as system images with a base address of zero, the contents of these two locations can be used as simple offsets to relate an address extracted from the map to a virtual address in a running system.

For example, if an error occurred at location X in system space, and X was larger than the contents of MMG$GL_RMSBASE, denoted by Y, then the relative offset into the RMS image is simply Y − X. (Obviously, if this difference is larger than the size of the RMS image, then address Y is not in RMS.)

To give an example that goes in the other direction (from a relative address on an assembler listing to a virtual memory location), suppose that we wish to locate a specific instruction in module DCLabcxyz, part of the DCL image. The relative offset in the assembly listing is added to the base address of module DCLabcxyz (taken from DCL.MAP) to form the offset into the DCL image. This sum is added to the contents of global location CTL$AG_CLIMAGE to form the P1 virtual address of the instruction.

The multiprocessing code is described by the map file MP.MAP. When multiprocessing on a VAX-11/782 is turned on, the multiprocessing code is loaded into locations starting at the address specified in global location EXE$GL_MP. Thus, this address can be used as the base address for the multiprocessing image. Note that part of the multiprocessing code is loadable (up to the PSECT named _END, defined in module MPLOAD); the remainder of the multiprocessing code is used to interpret the DCL commands START/CPU, STOP/CPU, and SHOW/CPU, and to load the multiprocessing code into nonpaged pool.

31.2.3   Device Driver Map Files

Device drivers are loaded into nonpaged pool by SYSGEN. The SHOW /DEVICE command to this utility displays among other pieces of information the address range into which the driver image is loaded. The address of the DDT from the driver map (program section $$$115_DRIVER) gives the base address that is used to move between addresses on the assembly listing and system virtual addresses. Debugging device drivers is discussed in more detail in the *VAX/VMS Guide to Writing a Device Driver*.

31.2.4   CPU-Dependent Routines

The base address of the CPU-dependent code (see Chapter 25) can be found in the following way. Location EXE$AL_LOAVEC is the address of the first vector that is loaded by INIT, the machine check handler. That vector contains a JMP instruction to the CPU-dependent machine check handler in nonpaged pool. Because absolute addressing is used with the JMP instruction, the contents of EXE$AL_LOAVEC + 2 are the system virtual address of EXE$MCHK. By subtracting the address of EXE$MCHK obtained from the map file (SYSLOA730.MAP, SYSLOA750.MAP, or SYSLOA780.MAP), the base address of the CPU-dependent image is determined. Note that when reading system dumps with SDA, SDA defines the symbol MCHK to be the contents at EXE$AL_LOAVEC + 2.

31.2.5 Other Map Files

All other map files can also be used for the cross-reference capabilities already mentioned. In addition, most other components of the operating system execute as regular images, and so no base addresses have to be used to locate addresses in virtual address space. The addresses on the map correspond to the virtual addresses that are used when the image executes. The only exceptions to this are shareable images. However, the map file from an executable image that includes a given shareable image can be used to determine the base address of a shareable image in a some instances. The map file cannot be used to determine the base address of nonbased, PIC shareable images; their base addresses are determined at image activation time.

31.3 THE SYSTEM DUMP ANALYZER (SDA)

Because some of the routines and most of the data structures used by the VAX/VMS operating system are loaded or constructed dynamically, the map file is limited in its ability to relate addresses to data structures or routines. In addition, the map file can only supply addresses of static data storage areas in the system, and not their contents. The system dump analyzer is a tool that overcomes these limitations of the map files. The use of the system dump analyzer is described in the *VAX/VMS System Dump Analyzer Reference Manual*. This section mentions several of the many SDA commands that are especially useful when studying how the operating system works.

31.3.1 Global Locations

Many of the dynamic data structures, located in parts of system address space that are beyond the last address in the executive image, are located through global pointers in the static part of the executive (the part found in the image SYS.EXE). These static locations are loaded when the structures in question are created or modified, as a part of either system initialization or some other loading mechanism. By using the SDA command SHOW SYMBOLS /ALL not only the addresses but also the contents of all global locations in the executive are put into SDA's output file. This list, together with the map file

SYS.MAP, enables any data structure to be located in system address space if the global name of the listhead that locates the structure is known. Appendix A contains a complete list of the static data locations used by the system.

31.3.2 Layout of System Virtual Address Space

A second useful application of SDA involves creating a picture of system address space. As Figure 26-2 shows, many of the pieces of system address space are constructed at initialization time. The sizes of the various pieces are determined by SYSBOOT parameters (see Chapter 26). By issuing the SDA command SHOW PAGE_TABLE /SYSTEM, the contents of the entire system page table are listed. This listing, the symbol table described in the previous section, and the executive map file SYS$SYSTEM:SYS.MAP allow an accurate picture of system virtual address space to be drawn. In fact, this technique was used to generate Figures 1-6, 26-1, and 26-2.

31.3.3 Layout of P1 Space

SDA can also be used to obtain the layout of P1 space. Most of the pieces of P1 space (see Figure 1-7 and Table 26-4) are fixed in size. The P1 page tables defined in module SHELL determine the sizes of these pieces of P1 space. Other pieces may not even exist for some processes. In any case, the SDA command SHOW PROCESS/PAGE_TABLES produces a complete layout of P1 space. This technique was used to generate Figure 1-7 and Table 26-4.

31.4 INTERPRETING MDL FILES

There are very many data structures and other system-wide constants used by the executive and other system components. These structures are defined with a special structure definition language called MDL (or Maynard Definition Language). This language allows data structures to be defined from a single source but used in either VAX-11 MACRO or BLISS-32.

When a VMS system is built from source, a preprocessing program called MDL reads all system data structure definitions and produces an output file for each input file. One of these output files contains macro definitions for use by VAX-11 MACRO. The other output file is used by the BLISS compiler to produce BLISS macro definitions. This section is not an exhaustive discussion of every MDL directive. Rather, it attempts to show how the MDL description of a data structure can be related to either a picture of the structure or the resulting VAX-11 MACRO or BLISS-32 definitions.

31.4.1 Sample Structure Definitions

The simplest way to illustrate how a structure is defined is to look at the resultant symbol definitions. One way to accomplish this is to compare the

MDL definition of a given structure with the resultant VAX-11 MACRO or BLISS-32 symbols. These symbols can be found in any listing that uses the structure in question. Alternatively, the command procedure listed in Section 31.1.1.1 can be used.

There are three tables listed here to show the results of simple MDL directives. Individual MDL commands are briefly described in the following sections. Table 31-1 shows the result of the complete MDL definition of the logical name block (pictured in Figure 29-2). Notice that the structure has a variable length. The symbol LOG$K_LENGTH only represents the length of the fixed size portion of the structure, excluding the storage areas for the logical name and equivalence name counted strings.

Table 31-2 illustrates the several uses of the S directive, using excerpts from the definitions for the PCB, the process header, and the timer queue element. Table 31-3 illustrates the eventual results of using MDL to define variable length bit fields. The AST control block is pictured in Figure 7-1. The specific fields within a virtual address are pictured in Figure 15-1.

31.4.2 Commonly Used MDL Commands

This section describes the MDL directives commonly used in defining structures used by the operating system. Emphasis is on reading the MDL files used by the system. A complete syntax of each command is not given. Rather, the features of each directive that are used by the system are emphasized.

31.4.2.1 $STRUCT Directive.
Each structure definition begins with a $STRUCT statement. This statement defines the prefix characters in each symbol definition. For example the following statement defines the PCB structure, where each symbol definition begins with the characters PCB:

```
$STRUCT PCB
```

In the default case (used by the operating system), the next character in each resultant symbol name is the dollar sign ($). Constant definitions can have an underscore (_), a C_, or a K_ as the next character(s). Field definitions have a character (B, W, L, or Q) that represents the size of the field. The naming conventions that MDL symbols adhere to are listed in Chapter 32.

31.4.2.2 F Directive.
Fields in a data structure are defined with the F directive. The name of each field is the first argument of the field definition and forms the balance of a symbol name. The value of the symbol name is set equal to an internal counter. As each field definition is processed, the internal counter value is increased by the size of the field (1, 2, 4, or 8). The default size of a field is four, representing a longword. This default can be overridden by including a second parameter to the F directive. Legal characters are B, W, L, Q,

Table 31-1: MDL Description and Resultant Symbol Definitions for Logical Name Block

MDL Directive	Meaning of Directive	Resultant Symbol Name	Symbol Value (decimal)	Effect on Internal Counter Value
$STRUCT LOG	Begin LOG Structure Definition			
F LTFL,L	Longword Field	LOG$L_LTFL	0	Increase by 4
F LTBL,L	Longword Field	LOG$L_LTBL	4	Increase by 4
F SIZE,W	Word Field	LOG$W_SIZE	8	Increase by 2
F TYPE,B	Byte Field	LOG$B_TYPE	10	Increase by 1
F TABLE,B	Byte Field	LOG$B_TABLE	11	Increase by 1
F GROUP,W	Word Field	LOG$W_GROUP	12	Increase by 2
F AMOD,B	Byte Field	LOG$B_AMOD	14	Increase by 1
F ,B	Skip One Spare Byte	None		Increase by 1 (Even Though No Symbol Defined)
F MBXUCB,L	Longword Field	LOG$L_MBXUCB	16	Increase by 4
L LENGTH	Define Structure Length to This Point	LOGC_LENGTH / LOGK_LENGTH	20 / 20	None / None
F NAME,T,0	A Text String Begins Here	LOG$T_NAME	20	None (Because Size Is Zero)
C SYSTEM,0	Define a Constant	LOG$C_SYSTEM	0	None
C GROUP,1	Define a Constant	LOG$C_GROUP	1	None
C PROCESS,2	Define a Constant	LOG$C_PROCESS	2	None
C NAMLENGTH,64	Define a Constant	LOG$C_NAMLENGTH	64	None
E	Terminate Structure Definition			

and T. The first four possibilities correspond to the logical or integer VAX-11 data types. The T argument indicates a text string, whose size appears as the third argument. (A count [third] argument for any field type increases the internal pointer value by the size of the field multiplied by the count.)

31.4.2.3   **L Directive.** The L directive is used to create a label at a specified point in a data structure. The VMS operating system uses the L directive to define the length of a structure by giving the resultant name the suffix LENGTH.

31.4.2.4   **E Directive.** The structure definition is terminated with an E directive.

31.4.2.5   **S Directive.** It is often desirable to give a field two names. In addition, sub-fields within a field often exist. The S directive defines a symbol with the indicated name and a value derived from the internal pointer when the current F directive was issued. The second argument indicates how far into the current field the subfield exists. The third argument indicates the size of the subfield. For example, the following lines from the PCB structure definition result in a symbol PCB$W_MEM that has the same value as PCB$L_UIC and a second symbol PCB$W_GRP that is two larger than the other two symbols.

```
F    UIC,L
S    MEM,0,W
S    GRP,0,W
```

Table 31-2 shows several examples of the S directive.

31.4.2.6   **C Directive.** The C directive allows a constant or a series of constants to be defined. Depending on what other parameters are supplied, the C directive produces symbols of the form xyzC_name, xyzK_name, or xyz$_name. The example in Table 31-1 illustrates one use of the C directive. There are several other examples of constant definitions in either SYSDEF.MDL or STARDEF.MDL, such as the definitions of the DYN$ symbols that describe dynamically allocated structures or the JPI$ symbols, the codes that describe an information list to the $GETJPI system service.

31.4.2.7   **M and P Directives.** The M and P directives are used together to allow the same fields in a data structure to have different definitions depending on the context in which they are used. For example, the UCB definition contains field definitions at the end of the structure that depend on the device that is described by a given UCB. The M directive (followed by a numeric argument) marks a specific position (internal byte counter value) in the structure. The P directive (followed by a numeric argument) restores the value of the internal counter to the value associated with that numbered mark position.

Table 31-2: Examples of the S Directive Definitions

MDL Directive	Meaning of Directive	Resultant Symbol Name	Symbol Value (decimal)	Effect on Internal Counter Value
$STRUCT PCB	Begin Definition of PCB Structure			
.				
F ARB,L	Longword Field	PCB$L_ARB	132	Increase by 4
F UIC,L	Longword Field	PCB$L_UIC	136	Increase by 4
S MEM,0,W	Word Subfield with Origin of 0	PCB$W_MEM	136	None (Set Subfield Counter to 2)
S GRP,2,W	Word Subfield with Origin of 2	PCB$W_GRP	138	None (Set Subfield Counter to 4)
F LOCKQFL,L	Longword Field	PCB$L_LOCKQFL	140	Increase by 4
.				
L LENGTH	Define Length of PCB	PCB$C_LENGTH PCB$K_LENGTH	156 156	None
E	Terminate PCB Definition			
$STRUCT PHD	Begin Definition of PHD Structure			
.				
F PAGFIL,L	Longword Field	PHD$L_PAGFIL	28	Increase by 4
S PAGFIL,3,B	Byte Subfield with Origin of 3	PHD$B_PAGFIL	31	None

Table 31-2: Examples of the S Directive Definitions (continued)

MDL Directive	Meaning of Directive	Resultant Symbol Name	Symbol Value (decimal)	Effect on Internal Counter Value
F PSTBASOFF,L	Longword Field	PHD$L_PSTBASOFF	32	Increase by 4
.				
F POLRASTL	Longword Field	PHD$L_POLRASTL	200	Increase by 4
S ASTLVL,3,B	Byte Subfield with Origin of 3	PHD$B_ASTLVL	203	None
.				
F P1BR,L	Longword Field	PHD$L_P1BR	204	Increase by 4
.				
E	Terminate PHD Definition			
$STRUCT TQE	Begin Definition of TQE Structure			
.				
F PID,L	Longword Field	TQE$L_PID	12	Increase by 4
S FPC,,L	Subfield with Same Value	TQE$L_FPC	12	None
F AST,L	Longword Field	TQE$L_AST	16	Increase by 4
S FR3,L	Subfield with Same Value	TQE$L_FR3	16	None
F ASTPRM,L	Longword Field	TQE$L_ASTPRM	20	Increase by 4
S FR4,L	Subfield with Same Value	TQE$L_FR4	20	None
F TIME,Q	Quadword Field	TQE$Q_TIME	24	Increase by 8
.				
E	Terminate TQE Definition			

Table 31-3: Sample Variable Length Bit Field Definitions

MDL Directive	Meaning of Directive	Resultant Symbol Names	Symbol Value (decimal)	Internal Bit Counter (before)	Internal Bit Counter (after)
$STRUCT ACB	Begin Definition of ACB Structure				
F RMOD,B	Byte Field	ACB$B_RMOD	11		
V<	Begin Bit Field Definitions				
MODE,2	Bit Field of Size 2 and Origin 0	ACB$V_MODE ACB$S_MODE	0 2	0	2
,2	Skip 4 Spare Bits			2	
PKAST,,,M	Single Bit Field with Mask Definition	ACB$V_PKAST ACB$M_PKAST	4 00000010 (hex)	4	5
NODELETE,,,M	Single Bit Field with Mask Definition	ACB$V_NODELETE ACB$M_NODELETE	5 00000020 (hex)	5	6
QUOTA,,,M	Single Bit Field with Mask Definition	ACB$V_QUOTA ACB$M_QUOTA	6 00000040 (hex)	6	7
KAST	Single Bit Field	ACB$V_KAST	7	7	Beyond Limit
>	End Bit Field Definitions				
F PID,L	Longword Field	ACB$L_PID	12		
E	Terminate ACB Definition				

Table 31-3: Sample Variable Length Bit Field Definitions (continued)

MDL Directive	Meaning of Directive	Resultant Symbol Names	Symbol Value (decimal)	Internal Bit Counter (before)	(after)
$STRUCT VA	Begin VA Bit Field Definitions				
V<	Begin Bit Field Definitions				
BYTE,9,,M	Bit Field of Size 9 and Origin 0	VA$V_BYTE	0	0	9
		VA$S_BYTE	9		
		VA$M_BYTE	000001FF (hex)		
VPN,21,,M	Bit Field of Size 21 and Origin 9	VA$V_VPN	9	9	30
		VA$S_VPN	21		
		VA$M_PFN	3FFFFE00 (hex)		
P1,,,M	Single Bit Field at Bit 30	VA$V_P1	30	30	31
		VA$M_P1	40000000 (hex)		
SYSTEM,,,M	Single Bit Field at Bit 31	VA$V_SYSTEM	31	31	32
		VA$M_SYSTEM	80000000 (hex)		
>	End Bit Field Definitions				
V<	Begin New Set of Bit Field Definitions				
,9	Skip over the First Nine Bits				
VPG,23,,M	Bit Field of Size 23 and Origin 9	VA$V_VPG	9	9	32
		VA$S_VPG	23		
		VA$M_VPG	FFFFFE00 (hex)		
>	End Second Set of Bit Definitions				
E	Terminate VA Definition				

31.4.3   **Bit Field Definitions—the V Directive**

Bit fields require two numbers to completely describe them, a bit position and a size. MDL always defines a bit position (indicated by a V_ in the symbol name). The size of a field (indicated by S_ in the symbol name) is always defined when the field size is different from one. It is often convenient to define a mask symbol (indicated by M_ in the symbol name) that has ones in each bit position defined by the bit field and zeros elsewhere. MDL defines such symbols if so requested.

Because this section is not trying to explain the entire MDL syntax but rather shows what symbols result from a given MDL definition, the simplest way to describe the bit field syntax is with some examples. Table 31-3 includes MDL directives extracted from the definition of the AST Control Block (ACB) that is pictured in Figure 7-1. Note that only the quota field has a mask symbol defined. Table 31-3 also contains the MDL description of the bit fields within a virtual address (see Figure 15-1). The definitions of the PSL bit fields and the STS bit fields (both located in STARDEF.MDL) are more complicated illustrations of the syntax that these examples describe.

32 Naming Conventions

What's in a name? That which we call a rose
By any other name would smell as sweet.
—*Romeo and Juliet* 2, 11

The conventions described in this chapter were adopted to aid implementors in producing meaningful public names. Public names are all names that are global (known to the linker) or that appear in parameter or macro definition files.

Public names follow these conventions for the following reasons:

- Using reserved names insures that customer-written software will not be invalidated by subsequent releases of DIGITAL products that add new symbols.
- Using definite patterns for different uses tells someone reading the source code what type of object is being referenced. For example, the form of a macro name is different from that of an offset, which is different from that of a status code.
- Using length codes within a pattern associates the size of an object with its name, increasing the likelihood that reference to this object will use the correct instructions.
- Using a facility code in symbol definitions gives the reader an indication of where the symbol is defined. Separate groups of implementors choose facility code names that will not conflict with one another.

To fully conform with these standards, local synonyms should never be defined for public symbols. The full public symbol should be used in every reference to give maximum clarity to the reader.

32.1 PUBLIC SYMBOL PATTERNS

All DIGITAL symbols contain a dollar sign. Thus, customers and applications developers are strongly advised to use underscores instead of dollar signs to avoid future conflicts.

Public symbols should be constructed to convey as much information as possible about the entities they name. Frequently, private names follow a similar convention. The private name convention is then the same as the public one with the underscore replacing the dollar sign in symbol names. Private names are used both within a module, and globally between modules of a facility that is never in a library. All names that might ever be bound into a user's program must follow the rules for public names. In the case of internal names, a double dollar sign convention can be used as shown in item 5 in the following list of formats:

1. System service macro names are of the form:

   ```
   $service-name
   ```

   A trailing _S or _G distinguishes the stack form from the separate argument list form. Details about the names of system service macros can be found in the *VAX/VMS System Services Reference Manual.*

   These names appear in the system macro library SYS$LIBRARY:STARLET.MLB and represent a call to one of the VAX/VMS system services or RMS services.

   The following examples show this form of symbol name.

   ```
   $ASCEFC_S   Associate Common Event Flag Cluster
   $CLOSE      Close a File
   $TRNLOG_G   Translate Logical Name
   ```

2. Facility-specific public macro names are of the form:

   ```
   $facility_macroname
   ```

   The executive does not use any symbol names of this form.

3. System macros using local symbols or macros always use names of the form:

   ```
   $facility$macro-name
   ```

   This is the form to be used both for symbols generated by a macro and included in calls to it, and for internal macros that are not documented.

   The executive does not use any symbol names of this form.

4. Status codes and condition values are of the form:

   ```
   facility$_status
   ```

   The following examples show this form of symbol name:

   ```
   RMS$_FNF     File Not Found
   SS$_ILLEFC   Illegal Event Flag Cluster
   SS$_WASCLR   Flag Was Previously Clear
   ```

5. Global entry point names are of the form:

   ```
   facility$entry-name
   ```

   The following examples show this form of symbol name:

   ```
   EXE$ALOPAGED   Allocate Paged Dynamic Memory
   IOC$WFIKPCH    Wait for Interrupt and Keep
                  Channel
   MMG$PAGEFAULT  Page Fault Exception Handler
   ```

   Global entry point names that are intended for use only within a set of related procedures but not by any calling programs outside the set are of the form:

```
facility$$entry-name
```

The executive does not use symbol names of this form. However, the Run-Time Library contains several examples of symbol names that follow this convention, for example:

```
BAS$$NUM_INIT       Initialize the BASIC NUM Function
FOR$$SIGNAL_STO     Signal a FORTRAN Error and Call
                    LIB$STOP
OTS$$GET_LUN        Get Logical Unit Number
```

6. Global entry point names that have nonstandard calls (JSB entry point names) are of the following form, where _Rn indicates that R0 through Rn are not preserved by the routine.

```
facility$entry-name_Rn
```

Note that the caller of such an entry point must include at least registers R2 through Rn in its own entry mask so that a stack unwind will restore all registers properly.

The executive does not use this convention for its JSB entry points. However, the Run-Time Library does contain several examples of its use, for example:

```
COB$CVTFP_R9        Convert Floating to Packed
MTH$SIN_R4          Single Precision Sine Function
STR$COPY_DX_R8      JSB entry to general string
                    copying routine
```

7. Global variable names are of the form:

```
facility$Gt_variable-name
```

The letter G indicates a global variable. The letter t represents the type of variable as defined in Section 32.2.

The following examples show this form of symbol name:

```
CTL$GQ_PROCPRIV     Process Privilege Mask
EXE$GL_NONPAGED     First Free Block in Nonpaged Pool
SCH$GL_CURPCB       Address of PCB of Current Process
```

8. Addressable global arrays use the letter A (instead of the letter G) and are of the form:

```
facility$At_array-name
```

The letter A indicates a global array. The letter t indicates the type of array element as defined in Section 32.2.

The following examples show this form of symbol name:

```
CTL$AQ_EXCVEC       Array of Primary and Secondary
                    Exception Vectors
LOG$AL_LOGTBL       Array of Logical Name Table
                    Listheads
PFN$AW_FLINK        Array of Forward Links for PFN
                    Lists
```

9. In the assembler, public structure offset names are of the form:

```
structure$t_field-name
```

The letter t indicates the data type of the field as defined in Section 32.2. The value of the public symbol is the byte offset to the start of the data element in the structure.

The following examples show this form of symbol name:

```
CEB$L_EFC      Event Flag Cluster (in Common
               Event Block)
GSD$W_GSTX     Global Section Table Index (in
               Global Section Descriptor)
PCB$B_PRI      Current Process Priority (in
               Software PCB)
```

10. In the assembler, public structure bit field offsets and single bit names are of the form:

```
structure$V_field-name
```

The value of the public symbol is the bit offset from the start of the field that contains the datum (and not from the start of the control block).

The following examples show this form of symbol name:

```
ACB$V_QUOTA    Charge AST to Process AST Quota
PSL$V_CURMOD   Current Access Mode
UCB$V_CANCEL   Cancel I/O on this unit
```

11. In the assembler, public structure bit field size names are of the form:

```
structure$S_field-name
```

The value of the public symbol is the number of bits in the field.

The following examples show this form of symbol name:

```
ACB$S_MODE     Access Mode of Requestor (2 bits)
PSL$S_CURMOD   Current Access Mode (2 bits)
PTE$S_PROT     Memory Protection on Page (4 bits)
```

12. For BLISS, the functions of the symbols in the previous three items are combined into a single name used to reference an arbitrary datum. Names are of the following form, where x is the same as t for standard sized data (B, W, L, and Q) and x stands for V for arbitrary and bit fields:

```
structure$x_field-name
```

The macro includes the offset, position, size, and sign extension suitable for use in a BLISS field selector. Most typically, this name is defined by the following BLISS statement:

```
MACRO
       structure$V_field-name =
           structure$t_field-name,
           structure$V_field-name,  ! VAX-11 MACRO V meaning
           structure$S_field-name,
           <sign extension> %;
```

13. Public structure mask names are of the form:

    ```
    structure$M_field-name
    ```

    The value of the public symbol is a mask with bits set for each bit in the field. This mask is not right justified. Rather, it has structure$V_field-name zero bits on the right.

    The following examples show this form of symbol name:

    ```
    CEB$M_VALID    Shared Memory Master CEB is Valid
    PSL$M_CURMOD   Current Access Mode
    PTE$M_PROT     Memory Protection on Page
    ```

14. Public structure constant names are of the form:

    ```
    structure$K_constant-name
    ```

    The following examples show this form of symbol name:

    ```
    PCB$K_LENGTH     Length (in bytes) of Software PCB
    SRM$K_FLT_OVF_F  Code for Floating Overflow Fault
    STS$K_SEVERE     Fatal Error Code
    ```

    For historical reasons, many of the constants used by the executive have the letter C instead of a K to indicate that the object data type is a constant.

    Examples of this form of symbol name are:

    ```
    DYN$C_PCB      Structure Type is Software PCB
    EXE$C_CMSTKSZ  Size of Stack Space Added by
                   Change Mode Handler
    PTE$C_URKW     Protection Code of User Read,
                   Kernel Write
    ```

15. .PSECT names are of the form:

    ```
    facility$mnemonic
    ```

    When these names are put into a library, they have the form:

    ```
    _facility$mnemonic
    ```

    The following examples show symbols of the form facility$mnemonic:

    ```
    COPY$COPY_FILE  File Copying Main Routine Program
                    Section
    DCL$ZCODE       Program Section Section That
                    Contains Most Code for the
                    DCL Command Interpreter
    JBC$MSGOUT      Program Section Containing the Job
                    Controller's Message Output
                    Routine
    ```

    This convention is not adhered to as strictly as the other naming conventions because .PSECT names control the way that the linker allocates virtual address space. Names will often be chosen to affect the relative locations of routines and the data that they reference.

    Some sample .PSECT names from the Run-Time Library show examples of the form _facility$mnemonic:

```
_LIB$CODE     General Library (Read-Only) Code
              Section
_MTH$DATA     Data Section in Mathematics
              Library
_OTS$CODE     Code Portion of Language-
              Independent Support Library
```

The executive does not use this convention when forming its .PSECT names. Rather, it uses names that cause the desired sections to be placed in the correct parts of system space. For example, .PSECT names control those pieces of the executive that are pageable. In addition, .PSECT names allow data areas and code that references that data to be placed within 64K bytes so that word displacement addressing (rather than longword displacement) can be used to reference the data.

The following examples show .PSECT names that are used in the executive:

```
$$$220          One of the First Data Program
                Sections in the Executive
$AEXENONPAGED   Nonpaged Executive Code
YEXEPAGED       Pageable Executive Routines
```

16. Public structure definition macro names are of the form:

```
$facility_structureDEF
```

Invoking this macro defines all symbols of the form structure$xxxxxx.

Most of the public structure definitions used by the VMS operating system do not include the string "facility_" in the macros that define structure offsets. Rather, macros of the following form are used to define structure$xxxxxx symbols:

```
$structureDEF
```

The following examples show these macros:

```
$LOGDEF   Offsets into Logical Name Block
$PCBDEF   Offsets into Software Process
          Control Block
$SSDEF    System Service Status Codes
```

32.2   OBJECT DATA TYPES

Table 32-1 shows the letters that are used for the various data types or are reserved for various purposes.

N, P, and T strings are typically variable length. In structures or I/O records, they frequently contain a byte-sized digit or character count preceding the string. If so, the location or offset is to the count. Counted strings cannot be passed in procedure calls. Instead, a string descriptor must be generated.

Table 32-1: Letters and the Data Types They Indicate

Letter	Data Type or Usage
A	Address
B	Byte Integer
C	Single Character (1)
D	Double Precision Floating
E	Reserved to DIGITAL
F	Single Precision Floating
G	G_floating-point Values
H	H_floating-point Values
I	Reserved for Integer Extensions
J	Reserved to Customers for Escape to Other Codes
K	Constant
L	Longword Integer
M	Field Mask
N	Numeric String (All Byte Forms)
O	Reserved to DIGITAL as an Escape to Other Codes
P	Packed String
Q	Quadword Integer
R	Reserved for Records (Structure)
S	Field Size
T	Text (Character) String
U	Smallest Unit of Addressable Storage
V	Field Position (VAX-11 MACRO); Field Reference (BLISS)
W	Word Integer
X	Context Dependent (Generic)
Y	Context Dependent (Generic)
Z	Unspecified or Nonstandard

(1) In many of the symbols used by VAX/VMS, C is used as a synonym for K. Although K is the preferred indicator for constants, most constants used in VMS are indicated by a C in their name. Some constants, such as lengths of data structures, have both a C form and a K form.

32.3   **FACILITY PREFIX TABLE**

Table 32-2 lists the facility prefixes used by DIGITAL-supplied software. This list will grow over time as new facility prefixes are chosen. No one within DIGITAL is permitted to use a new code without registering it in a common place, thereby insuring that each facility name will be unique.

Note that bit<27>, the customer facility bit, is clear in all of the facility codes listed here. Customers are free to use any of the facility codes listed here, provided that they set bit<27>. The default action of the message compiler is to set this bit.

The location of the facility code within a status code and the meaning of the other fields in the status code are described in Chapter 10 of the *VAX-11 Utilities Reference Manual.*

Table 32-2: Facility Names and Their Prefixes

Prefix	Facility Description	Condition <27:16>
	Nucleus and System Processes	
SYSTEM	System Service Status Codes	0
RMS	RMS Internals and Status Codes	1
DEBUG	Symbolic Debugger	2
CLI	Command Language Interpreters	3
JBC	Job Controller	4
OPCOM	Operator Communication	5
RSX	RSX-11M Application Migration Executive	6
ERF	Error Logger Format Process	8
TRACE	Traceback Facility	9
	Run-Time Library Components	
BLI	BLISS Transportable Run-Time Library	20
LIB	General Purpose Library; Global Sections	21
MTH	Mathematics Library	22
OTS	Language Independent Object Time System	23
FOR	VAX-11 FORTRAN Run-Time Library	24
COB	VAX-11 COBOL Run-Time Library	25
BAS	VAX-11 BASIC Run-Time Library	26
B32	BLISS-32 Specific Run-Time Library	27
SORT	VAX-11 SORT	28
C74	COBOL-74 Specific Run-Time Library	29
PLI	PL/I Run-Time Library	30
XPO	Transportability Support Library	32
PAS	VAX-11 PASCAL Run-Time Library	33
COR	CORAL-66 Run-Time Library	34
APL	VAX-11 APL Run-Time Library	35
STR	String Manipulation Procedures	36
LBR	Librarian Subroutine Package	38
FDV	FMS-32 Forms Driver Library	41
SCR	Screen Formatting Package	44
C	VAX-11 C Run-Time Libary	53
LINK	VAX-11 Linker	100
CREF	Cross-Reference Facility	101
DSUP	Diagnostic Supervisor	102
COPY	COPY	103
BTRAN	AME Back Translator	104
SYSMSG	System Message Maker	105
FORT	VAX-11 FORTRAN Compiler	106
COB74	VAX-11 COBOL-74 Compiler	107
DIFF	File Differences Utility	108
PATCH	VAX-11 Image File Patch Utility	109
PAX	VAX-11 Object Module Patch Utility	110
BLS32	VAX-11 BLISS-32 Compiler	111
APPEND	APPEND	113
MOUNT	Volume Mount	114
DISM	Volume Dismount	115

Table 32-2: Facility Names and Their Prefixes *(continued)*

Prefix	Facility Description	Condition <27:16>
	Utilities and Compilers	
UETP	User Environment Test Package	116
INIT	Volume Initialization	117
HELP	Help Facility	118
SET	SET	119
SHOW	SHOW	120
DIRECT	DIRECTORY	121
AUTHOR	User Authorization Manager	122
INS	INSTALL Utility	123
SYSGEN	System Generation and Driver Loader Utility	124
MACRO	VAX-11 MACRO Assembler	125
MAIL	VAX/VMS MAIL Utility	126
DSM	DIGITAL Standard MUMPS	127
PASCAL	VAX-11 PASCAL Compiler	128
CORAL	CORAL-66 Compiler	129
COBOL	COBOL-79 Compiler	130
SUM	Source Update Merge Utility	132
EDT	DEC Standard Editor	133
LIBRAR	VAX-11 Librarian	134
PLIG	VAX-11 PL/I Level-G Compiler	135
BASIC	VAX-11 BASIC Compiler	137
FUT	Forms Utility	140
COB74T	COBOL-74 to VAX COBOL Translator	143
RENAME	RENAME	144
CREATE	CREATE	145
UNLOCK	UNLOCK	146
DELETE	DELETE	147
PURGE	PURGE	148
TYPE	TYPE	149
RUNOFF	DEC Standard RUNOFF	150
MESSAGE	System Message Compiler	151
CLEDIT	CLI Data Base Editor	155
ACC	Accounting Utility	159
BACKUP	Backup Utility	163
VERIFY	File Structure Verification Utility	165
PHONE	Phone Utility	166
ANALYZE	Analyze Utility	177
CONVERT	Convert Utility	178
EDF	FDL Editor	179
FDL	FDL Utility	180
CC	VAX-11 C Compiler	185
MONTITOR	Monitor Utility	206
SEARCH	Search	215
MP	VAX-11/782 Multiprocessing	239
SDA	System Dump Analyzer	244

Table 32-2: Facility Names and Their Prefixes *(continued)*

Prefix	Facility Description	Condition <27:16>
	Network Support Utilities	
NET	DECnet ACP and NSP Protocol; DTS/DTR	501
DAP	DECnet DAP Procedures and Protocol	502
FAL	DECnet File Access Listener and Protocol	503
NCP	DECnet Network Control Program and Protocol	504
NIC	DECnet NICE Program and Protocol	505
DLE	DECnet Direct Line Executive	506
BSCPTP	2780/3780 BISYNC Point to Point Emulator	507
HLD	DECnet Host Load Protocol	508
REM	DECnet Remote Terminal ACP and Protocol	510
INS3271	3271 Protocol Emulator	511
EVL	DECnet Event Logger	512
XK	3271 Bisynch Protocol Emulator	513
LES	DECnet PSI Layered Environment Services	514
SNA	SNA Application Interface	515
SNADEBUG	SNA Debugging Facility	516
SNARJE	SNA Remote Job Entry	517
SNATERM	SNA 3270 Terminal Facility	518
MOM	DECnet Maintenance Operations Module	519

Individual products such as compilers also get unique facility codes formed from the product name. They must be signed out in the above list. Facility prefixes should be chosen to avoid conflict with file types.

Structure name prefixes are typically local to a facility. Refer to the individual facility documentation for its structure name prefixes. Individual facility structure names do not cause problems because these names are not global, and are therefore not known to the linker. They become known at assembly or compile time only by explicitly invoking the macro defining the facility structure.

For example, the macro $FORDEF defines all of the status codes that can be returned from the VAX-11 FORTRAN support library. The facility code of 24 is included in the upper 16 bits of each of the status codes defined with this macro.

Please note that DIGITAL does not provide a registration service for the customer facility codes.

Appendixes

Appendix A
Executive Data Areas

The writeable executive consists of several dynamically allocated tables as well as statically allocated data structures that are a part of the executive image SYS.EXE. This appendix summarizes all of these data areas, with an emphasis on the static executive database that is related to other material in this book.

The information presented in this appendix was accumulated by incorporating data from the system map (SYS.MAP) with the contents of specific source modules. Information outside the scope of this book is simply summarized. There is no attempt to include every global symbol in SYS.EXE in this appendix. Data blocks (such as unit control blocks or timer queue elements) are referenced as single entities. Global labels within such structures are ignored. Global labels associated with backward link pointers of doubly linked lists are also omitted. Names that appear in the "Global Symbol" column in lower case represent local symbols, names that are only used within the module in which they are defined.

A.1 STATICALLY ALLOCATED EXECUTIVE DATA

The cells that contain the data described in this section can be identified with specific source modules in the executive. Those cells that can be addressed directly with a global name are so indicated. Program section names (.PSECT names) are included in each section title to allow easy location of a given data area. Program sections of zero length declared in module MDAT for the purpose of defining global labels that separate major sections of SYS.EXE are not included here. They are listed in Table 26-2 and can also be found by examining SYS.MAP.

A.1.1 System Service Vector Area ($$$000)

The first four pages of system virtual address space contain the system service vectors. These pages are read only. The global label MMG$A_ENDVEC, defined in module MDAT, represents the high-address end of the system service vector pages.

A.1.2 File System Performance Monitor Data ($$$000PMS)

This area consists of two blocks, both 70 longwords long, used to describe the cumulative behavior of the file ACPs servicing both Structure Level 1 and Structure Level 2. An additional 13 longwords are used to contain information on general file operations.

Global Symbol	Module	Size	Description of Data
PMS$GL_FCP	PMSDAT	70 Longwords	File system statistics for Level 1 ACP
PMS$GL_FCP2	PMSDAT	70 Longwords	File system statistics for Level 2 ACP
PMS$GL_TURN	PMSDAT	Longword	Number of window turns
PMS$GL_SPLIT	PMSDAT	Longword	Number of split I/O transfers
PMS$GL_HIT	PMSDAT	Longword	Number of transfers not requiring window turns
PMS$GL_DIRHIT	PMSDAT	Longword	Number of directory LRU hits
PMS$GL_DIRMISS	PMSDAT	Longword	Number of director LRU misses
PMS$GL_QUOHIT	PMSDAT	Longword	Number of quota cache hits
PMS$GL_QUOMISS	PMSDAT	Longword	Number of quota cache misses
PMS$GL_FIDHIT	PMSDAT	Longword	Number of file ID cache hits
PMS$GL_FIDMISS	PMSDAT	Longword	Number of file ID cache misses
PMS$GL_EXTHIT	PMSDAT	Longword	Number of extent cache hits
PMS$GL_EXTMISS	PMSDAT	Longword	Number of extent cache misses
PMS$GL_OPEN	PMSDAT	Longword	Number of currently opened files
PMS$GL_OPENS	PMSDAT	Longword	Total number of file opens

A.1.3 Process Database ($$$000_STACKS)

Module PDAT defines kernel mode stacks for two system processes: the null process and the swapper process. Note that the global symbols for the swapper's kernel stack points to the base (high address) of the stack.

Global Symbol	Module	Size	Description of Data
	PDAT	32 Longwords	Short stack for the null process
SWP$A_KSTK	PDAT	160 Longwords	Kernel mode stack for swapper

A.1.4   **Miscellaneous Bugcheck Information ($$$025)**

Module BUGCHECK maintains two longwords about a fatal bugcheck in progress.

Global Symbol	Module	Size	Description of Data
fatal_spsav	BUGCHECK	Longword	Fatal bugcheck in progress stack pointer
EXE$GL_BUGCHECK	BUGCHECK	Longword	Saved fatal bugcheck code

A.1.5   **Data Structures for Drivers Linked with the Operating System ($$$100)**

Module DEVICEDAT contains data structures for the devices that are linked as a part of the executive image SYS.EXE. These devices are the null device (NL:), mailboxes, and the console terminal. The data structures for device OPA0 (the console port driver) are assembled into the VAX/VMS operating system. The terminal class driver is loaded and linked to the console port driver by INIT; the other terminal port drivers are loaded by the SYSGEN command AUTOCONFIGURE.

There are unit control blocks for three mailboxes set aside in DEVICEDAT. Unit control block zero is a skeleton UCB that is copied into any other UCB when a mailbox is created. The job controller's mailbox and OPCOM's mailbox also use preallocated UCBs.

Global Symbol	Module	Size	Description of Data
IOC$GL_DEVLIST	DEVICEDAT	Longword	Listhead of DDBs of all devices in the system
IOC$GL_ADPLIST	DEVICEDAT	Longword	Listhead of all adapter control blocks
IOC$GL_DPTLIST	DEVICEDAT	Quadword	Listhead of driver prolog tables
TTY$GL_DPT	DEVICEDAT	Longword	Terminal class driver DPT pointer
SYS$GL_BOOTDDB	DEVICEDAT	52 Bytes	Device data block for system disk
SYS$GL_BOOTUCB	DEVICEDAT	252 Bytes	Unit control block for system disk (22 extra longwords)
OPA$GL_DDB	DEVICEDAT	52 Bytes	Device data block for console terminal

Global Symbol	Module	Size	Description of Data
OPA$UCB0	DEVICEDAT	320 Bytes	Unit control block for console terminal (24 extra longwords)
OPA$CRB	DEVICEDAT	84 Bytes	Channel request block for console device
opa$idb	DEVICEDAT	32 Bytes	Interrupt dispatch block for console device
MB$GL_DDB	DEVICEDAT	52 Bytes	Device data block for mailbox
MB$UCB0	DEVICEDAT	132 Bytes	Unit control block template used in mailbox creation (not linked into mailbox DDB's UCB list)
SYS$GL_JOBCTLMB	DEVICEDAT	116 Bytes	Unit control block for job controller's mailbox (Unit 1)
SYS$GL_OPRMBX	DEVICEDAT	132 Bytes	Unit control block for operator's Mailbox (Unit 2)
NL$GL_DDB	DEVICEDAT	52 Bytes	Device data block for null device
NL$GL_UCB0	DEVICEDAT	132 Bytes	Unit control block for null device
NET$WCB	DEVICEDAT	48 Bytes	Window control block for network pseudo device
sys_crb	DEVICEDAT	72 Bytes	Channel request block for mailbox devices

A.1.6   Driver Prolog Tables ($$$105_PROLOGUE)

The driver prolog tables for these drivers are also assembled and linked into the executive image. The contributions to this part of the writable executive come from the three driver modules (MBDRIVER, NLDRIVER, and CONINTDSP) that are linked with SYS.EXE.

Global Symbol	Module	Size	Description of Data
MB$DPT	MBDRIVER	57 Bytes	Driver prolog table for mailbox driver
NL$DPT	NLDRIVER	57 Bytes	Driver prolog table for null device driver
OP$DPT	CONINTDSP	57 Bytes	Driver prolog table for console terminal device driver

A.1.7 Linked Driver Code ($$$115_DRIVER)

There is a read only section (six pages long) that contains the driver code for these drivers as well as code for the MA780 shared memory, the DR780 interface, and interrupt dispatch code for the MASSBUS adapter. This section is bounded by the two global labels MMG$AL_BEGDRIVE and MMG$AL_ENDDRIVE, defined in module MDAT.

A.1.8 Memory Management Data ($$$210)

The memory management data consists mainly of listheads for dynamically allocated structures.

Global Symbol	Module	Size	Description of Data
PFN$AL_HEAD	ALLOCPFN	3 Longwords	Pointers to the heads of the free, modified, and bad page lists
PFN$AL_TAIL	ALLOCPFN	3 Longwords	Pointers to the tails of the free, modified, and bad page lists
SCH$GL_FREECNT	ALLOCPFN	Longword	Free page count
SCH$GL_MFYCNT	ALLOCPFN	Longword	Modified page count
pfn$al_count	ALLOCPFN	Longword	Bad page count
PFN$GL_PHYPGCNT	ALLOCPFN	Longword	Count of available physical pages
SCH$GL_FREEREQ	ALLOCPFN	Longword	Free pages required by the swapper
SCH$GL_MFYLIM	ALLOCPFN	Longword	Modified page list high limit
PFN$AL_HILIMIT+8	ALLOCPFN	Longword	Bad page list high limit
SCH$GL_FREELIM	ALLOCPFN	Longword	Free page list low limit
SCH$GL_MYFLOLIM	ALLOCPFN	Longword	Modified page list low limit
PFN$AL_LOLIMIT+8	ALLOCPFN	Longword	Bad page list low limit
SCH$GL_MFYLIMSV	ALLOCPFN	Longword	Saved high limit threshold of modified page list
SCH$GL_MFYLOSV	ALLOCPFN	Longword	Saved low limit threshold of modified page list
	PAGEFAULT	16 Longwords	Page fault statistics for Monitor Utility

Global Symbol	Module	Size	Description of Data
MPW$AL_PTE	WRTMFYPAG	Longword	Pointer to modified page writer PTE array
MPW$AW_PHVINDEX	WRTMFYPAG	Longword	Pointer to process header vector index array used by the modified page writer
MPW$GL_BADPAGTOTAL	WRTMFYPAG	Longword	Total number if pages placed on the bad page list
MMG$GL_IACLOCK	SYSIMGACT	Longword	Image activator interlock
MMG$GL_PFNLOCK	SYSLKWSET	Longword	Countdown counter of pages remaining that may be locked in memory

A.1.9 Page Fault Monitor Data ($$$215)

The page fault monitor subsystem maintains three longwords of impure data.

Global Symbol	Module	Size	Description of Data
PFM$GL_SIZE	SYSSETPFM	Longword	Size of allocated block
PFM$GL_PMBLST	SYSSETPFM	Longword	Pointer to PMB list block
	SYSSETPFM	Longword	Count of processes using monitor

A.1.10 Scheduler Data ($$$220)

The scheduler's database is defined primarily in module SDAT. This module contains the queue headers for each of the scheduling states and related counters. Several other modules (particularly SWAPPER) also contribute to this program section.

Global Symbol	Module	Size	Description of Data
	SDAT	Quadword	Spare quadword to terminate outswap scheduling scan
SCH$AQ_COMH	SDAT	32 Quadwords	Listheads for computable states for all 32 software priority levels

A.1 Statically Allocated Executive Data

Global Symbol	Module	Size	Description of Data
SCH$AQ_COMOH	SDAT	32 Quadwords	Listheads for computable out-swapped states for all 32 software priority levels
SCH$AQ_WQHDR	SDAT	132 Bytes (132 = 11*12)	Wait queue headers for 11 wait states (wait queue header for CEF state not used)
SCH$GL_CURPCB	SDAT	Longword	Address of PCB of current process
SCH$GL_COMQS	SDAT	Longword	Queue summary longword for COM state
SCH$GL_COMOQS	SDAT	Longword	Queue summary longword for COMO state
SCH$GB_SIP	SDAT	Byte	Swap in progress flags
SCH$V_SIP		Bit	Swap in progress
SCH$V_MPW		Bit	Activity of modified page writer
SCH$GB_RESCAN	SDAT	Byte	Queue reordering notification flags
SCH$V_REORD		Bit	Indicates RELPFN has reordered the queue
MMG$GB_FREWFLGS	SDAT	Byte	SWAPPER/FREWSLE communication flags
MMG$V_NOWAIT		Bit	Do not allow FREWSLE to enter a resource wait state for pages from the modified list
MMB$V_NOLASTUPD		Bit	Do not allow FREWSLE to update WSLAST
SCH$GW_PROCCNT	SDAT	Word	Current number of processes which require swap file (does not count NULL or SWAPPER)
SCH$GW_PROCLIM	SDAT	Word	Maximum number of processes that this system allows
		Word	Spare for alignment
SWP$GL_SLOTCNT	SDAT	Longword	Count of available swap slots
SCH$GQ_CEBHD	SDAT	Quadword	Listhead for common event blocks
SCH$GW_CEBCNT	SDAT	Word	Number of common event blocks

Executive Data Areas

Global Symbol	Module	Size	Description of Data
SCH$GW_DELPHDCT	SDAT	Word	Number of process headers of already deleted processes
SWP$GL_SHELL	SDAT	Longword	Shell process swap address
SWP$GL_INPCB	SDAT	Longword	PCB address of process being swapped into memory
SWP$GL_ISPAGCNT	SDAT	Longword	Inswap page count
SWP$GW_IBALSETX	SDAT	Word	Balance slot index for inswap process
SWP$GB_ISWPRI	SDAT	Byte	Priority of inswap process
		Byte	Spare for alignment
SWP$GL_ISWPPAGES	SDAT	Longword	Count of inswapped pages
SWP$GL_ISWPCNT	SDAT	Longword	Count of inswaps performed
SWP$GL_OSWPCNT	SDAT	Longword	Count of outswaps performed
SWP$GL_HOSWPCNT	SDAT	Longword	Count of header outswaps
SWP$GL_HISWPCNT	SDAT	Longword	Count of header inswaps
SCH$GL_RESMASK	SDAT	Longword	Resource wait mask vector
SCH$GB_PRI	SDAT	Byte	Priority of current process
		3 Bytes	Spare for alignment
SWP$GL_SWTIME	OSWPSCHED	Longword	Earliest time for next exchange swap
EXE$GL_PWRDONE	POWERFAIL	Longword	End time for power recovery interval
EXE$GL_PWRINTVL	POWERFAIL	Longword	Allowable recovery interval in 10 millisecond units
ioroutine	SWAPPER	Longword	Address of proper (read or write) build packet routine
ioea	SWAPPER	Longword	I/O end action routine
rwsswp	SWAPPER	Longword	Remaining working set swap address
rsvapte	SWAPPER	Longword	Remaining system virtual address of page table entries

Global Symbol	Module	Size	Description of Data
rpgcnt	SWAPPER	Word	Remaining page count
oswppgs	SWAPPER	Word	Outswap page count
oswppcb	SWAPPER	Longword	Address of PCB of outswap process
SWP$GW_BALCNT	SWAPPER	Word	Count of processes in balance set (swapper and null processes not counted)
SCH$GW_SWPFCNT	SWAPPER	Word	Count of successive outswap schedule failures

A.1.11   Memory Management Data ($$$222)

This program section contains the data cell contribution of module MDAT to the executive. MDAT also defines global labels that separate data areas from read-only sections and that separate pageable code from nonpaged routines. In addition, MDAT allocates patch areas for the executive.

Global Symbol	Module	Size	Description of Data
PHV$GL_PIXBAS	MDAT	Longword	Address of process index array
PHV$GL_REFCBAS	MDAT	Longword	Address of process header reference count array
EXE$GL_CONFREG	MDAT	Longword	Address of nexus device type byte array
MMG$GL_SBICONF	MDAT	Longword	Address of a long-word array containing the nexus slot virtual addresses
EXE$GL_NUMNEXUS	MDAT	Longword	Maximum nexus number possible on the system
MMG$GL_RMSBASE	MDAT	Longword	Pointer to base address of RMS image
MMG$GL_GBLSECFND	MDAT	Longword	Last global section table entry found when deleting page file backing store addresses
MMG$GL_GBLPAGFIL	MDAT	Longword	Remaining page file available for global sections

A.1.12 Process Data for System Processes ($$$230)

Two processes exist as a part of the system image. They are the swapper and the null process. In addition, there exists a system header containing the system page table (see Chapters 14 and 26) and a system PCB to support system paging.

Global Symbol	Module	Size	Description of Data
nulphd	PDAT	376 Bytes	Minimal process header (fixed portion only) for null process
SCH$GL_NULLPCB	PDAT	156 Bytes	PCB for null process
swpphd	PDAT	376 Bytes	Minimal process header (fixed portion only) for swapper process
SCH$GL_SWPPCB	PDAT	156 Bytes	PCB for swapper process
MMG$AL_SYSPCB	PDAT	156 Bytes	System PCB
SCH$GL_PCBVEC	PDAT	Longword	Address of PCB vector of longwords
SCH$GL_MAXPIX	PDAT	Longword	Maximum process index for this system
SCH$GL_SEQVEC	PDAT	Longword	Address of sequence vector of words

A.1.13 Console Interrupt Dispatch Data ($$$250)

The console device driver maintains a small amount of impure storage.

Global Symbol	Module	Size	Description of Data
op_vector	CONINTDSP	14 Longwords	Vectors for console terminal driver prolog tables
curr	CONINTDSP	Byte	Current unit expecting output completion
next	CONINTDSP	Byte	Next unit awaiting output
data	CONINTDSP	Word	Next data for output

A.1.14 SYSCOMMON—Miscellaneous Executive Data ($$$260)

Module SYSCOMMON contains most of the miscellaneous listheads, counters, semaphores, and other data that is not directly tied to one of the major subsystems. Module ERRORLOG also makes a significant contribution to this program section.

Global Symbol	Module	Size	Description of Data
EXE$GL_FLAGS	SYSCOMMON	Longword	System flags longword (see Section A.1.17)
EXE$GQ_ERLMBX	SYSCOMMON	Quadword	Descriptor of error log mailbox
		Word	Unit number (0 => none)
		Word	Spare for alignment
		Longword	Process ID of assigner
EXE$GL_USRCHMK	SYSCOMMON	Longword	Address of system-wide user-written change mode to dispatcher
EXE$GL_USRCHME	SYSCOMMON	Longword	Address of system-wide user-written change mode to executive dispatcher
SWI$GL_FQFL	SYSCOMMON	6 Quadwords	Fork queue listheads for IPL levels 6 to 11 (IPL 7 used only as a place holder)
LOG$AL_LOGTBL	SYSCOMMON	3 Longwords	Addresses of pointers to hash tables for system, group, and process logical name tables
	SYSCOMMON	2 Longwords	Pointers to hash tables for system and group logical name tables
LOG$AB_HTBLCNT	SYSCOMMON	3 Bytes	Number of entries in system, group, and process logical name hash tables (expressed as a power of two)
		Byte	Spare for alignment
LOG$AL_MUTEX	SYSCOMMON	4 Words	Mutexes for system and group logical name tables
EXE$GL_SYSUCB	SYSCOMMON	Longword	Address of system disk UCB
FIL$GT_DDDEV	SYSCOMMON	14 Bytes	Counted ASCII string for default device (SYS$SYSDEVICE)
FIL$GT_TOPSYS	SYSCOMMON	10 Bytes	Counted ASCII string for top-level directory in use on default device
		2 Bytes	Spare for alignment

Global Symbol	Module	Size	Description of Data
FIL$GQ_CACHE	SYSCOMMON	Quadword	File read cache descriptor
EXE$GQ_BOOTCB_D	SYSCOMMON	Quadword	Descriptor for boot control block
EXE$GL_SAVEDUMP	SYSCOMMON	Longword	Number of blocks to release to the page file when a dump in the page file is copied
IOC$GL_PSFL	SYSCOMMON	Quadword	Listhead for I/O postprocessing queue
IOC$GL_IRPFL	SYSCOMMON	Quadword	Listhead for IRP lookaside list
IOC$GL_IRPREM	SYSCOMMON	Longword	Address of partial packet
IOC$GL_IRPCNT	SYSCOMMON	Longword	Current count of allocated IRPs
IOC$GL_IRPMIN	SYSCOMMON	Longword	Minimum size of request that can be allocated an IRP
IOC$GL_SRPFL	SYSCOMMON	Quadword	Listhead for SRP lookaside list
IOC$GL_SRPSIZE	SYSCOMMON	Longword	Size of an SRP
IOC$GL_SRPMIN	SYSCOMMON	Longword	Minimum size of request that can be allocated an SRP (not used)
IOC$GL_SRPSPLIT	SYSCOMMON	Longword	Boundary between SRP and IRP lookaside lists
IOC$GL_SRPREM	SYSCOMMON	Longword	Address of remaining packets
IOC$GL_SRPCNT	SYSCOMMON	Longword	Current count of allocated SRPs
IOC$GL_LRPFL	SYSCOMMON	Quadword	Listhead for LRP lookaside list
IOC$GL_LRPSIZE	SYSCOMMON	Longword	Size of an LRP
IOC$GL_LRPMIN	SYSCOMMON	Longword	Minimum size of request that can be allocated an LRP
IOC$GL_LRPSPLIT	SYSCOMMON	Longword	Boundary between LRP lookaside list and the main portion of nonpaged pool

Global Symbol	Module	Size	Description of Data
IOC$GL_LRPREM	SYSCOMMON	Longword	Address of remaining packets
IOC$GL_LRPCNT	SYSCOMMON	Longword	Current count of allocated LRPs
IOC$GL_POOLFKB	SYSCOMMON	6 Longwords	Fork block for pool expansion
IOC$GL_PFKBINT	SYSCOMMON	Longword	Fork block interlock (0=free)
IOC$GL_AQBLIST	SYSCOMMON	Longword	ACP queue block listhead
IOC$GQ_MOUNTLST	SYSCOMMON	Quadword	System-wide mounted volume list
IOC$GQ_BRDCST	SYSCOMMON	Quadword	Terminal broadcast message listhead
IOC$GL_CRBTMOUT	SYSCOMMON	Longword	List of CRBs to scan for timeouts
EXE$GL_GSDGRPFL	SYSCOMMON	Quadword	Listhead for group global section descriptor list
EXE$GL_GSDSYSFL	SYSCOMMON	Quadword	Listhead for system global section descriptor list
EXE$GL_GSDFREFL	SYSCOMMON	Quadword	Listhead for global section descriptor block lookaside list
EXE$GL_GSDDELFL	SYSCOMMON	Quadword	Listhead for global section descriptor block delete pending list
EXE$GL_WCBDELFL	SYSCOMMON	Quadword	Listhead for window control block delete queue for GSD windows
EXE$GL_SYSWCBFL	SYSCOMMON	Quadword	Listhead for system window control block list
EXE$GL_SYSWCB	SYSCOMMON	42 Bytes	Window control block (with one retrieval pointer) for system image SYS.EXE
PMS$GL_KERNEL	SYSCOMMON	6 Longwords	Timer statistics for time spent in each access mode, on the interrupt stack, and in compatibility mode
EXE$GL_ABSTIM	SYSCOMMON	Longword	Absolute time in seconds (for device driver timeout)
		Longword	Spare for alignment

Global Symbol	Module	Size	Description of Data
EXE$GQ_SYSTIME	SYSCOMMON	Quadword	System time in units of 100 nanoseconds
EXE$GL_PFAILTIM	SYSCOMMON	Longword	Contents of PR$_TODR at last power failure
EXE$GL_PFATIM	SYSCOMMON	Longword	Duration of most recent power failure (in units of 10 milliseconds)
EXE$GL_TQFL	SYSCOMMON	Quadword	Timer queue listhead
devicetim	SYSCOMMON	32 Bytes	Timer queue element for system subroutine
EXE$AL_TQENOREPT	SYSCOMMON	32 Bytes	Permanant last entry in timer queue
IOC$GL_MUTEX	SYSCOMMON	2 Words	I/O database mutex
EXE$GL_CEBMTX	SYSCOMMON	2 Words	Common event block list mutex
EXE$GL_PGDYNMTX	SYSCOMMON	2 Words	Paged dynamic memory mutex
EXE$GL_GSDMTX	SYSCOMMON	2 Words	Global section description list mutex
EXE$GL_SHMGSMTX	SYSCOMMON	2 Words	Shared memory global section descriptor list mutex
EXE$GL_SHMMBMTX	SYSCOMMON	2 Words	Shared memory mailbox list mutex
EXE$GL_ENQMTX	SYSCOMMON	2 Words	Enqueue/dequeue tables mutex (not used)
EXE$GL_KFIMTX	SYSCOMMON	2 Words	Known file table mutex
EXE$GL_KNOWNFIL	SYSCOMMON	Longword	Address of known file list vector
KFI$GL_F11AACP	SYSCOMMON	Longword	Address of KFI for system disk ACP
EXE$GL_GPT	SYSCOMMON	Longword	Address of first free global page table entry
	SYSCOMMON	Longword	Dummy count of number of GPTEs in listhead
SYS$GQ_VERSION	SYSCOMMON	Quadword	ASCII string that contains system version number
SYS$GW_IJOBCNT	SYSCOMMON	3 Words	Current counts of interactive, network, and batch logins

A.1 Statically Allocated Executive Data

Global Symbol	Module	Size	Description of Data
EXE$GW_SCANPIX	SYSCOMMON	Word	Process index of next process to check for priority boost
EXE$GL_SYSMSG	SYSCOMMON	Longword	Address of system-wide message section
EXE$GL_USERUNDWN	SYSCOMMON	Longword	Address of system-wide user rundown service vector
EXE$GL_NONPAGED	SYSCOMMON	Longword	IPL at which nonpaged pool allocation will occur
	SYSCOMMON	Longword	Address of first free block of nonpaged pool
	SYSCOMMON	Longword	Dummy size of zero for listhead
EXE$GL_SPLITADR	SYSCOMMON	Longword	Address of boundary between LRP and IRP lookaside lists
EXE$GL_PAGED	SYSCOMMON	Longword	Address of first free block of paged pool
	SYSCOMMON	Longword	Dummy size of zero for listhead
RMS$GL_SFDBASE	SYSCOMMON	Longword	Address of shared file database
EXE$GL_SHBLIST	SYSCOMMON	Longword	Address of shared memory control block list
EXE$GL_RTBITMAP	SYSCOMMON	Longword	Address of real-time SPTE bitmap
MCHK$GL_MASK	SYSCOMMON	Longword	Function mask for current machine check recovery block
MCHK$GL_SP	SYSCOMMON	Longword	Saved stack pointer for return at end of recovery
EXE$GL_MCHKERRS	SYSCOMMON	Longword	Count of machine checks since bootstrap
EXE$GL_MEMERRS	SYSCOMMON	Longword	Count of memory errors since bootstrap
IO$GL_UBA_INT0	SYSCOMMON	Longword	Count of UBA interrupts through vector 0
EXE$GL_BLAKHOLE	SYSCOMMON	Longword	Physical page used to remap addresses of adapters that have experienced power failure

Global Symbol	Module	Size	Description of Data
IO$GL_SCB_INT0	SYSCOMMON	Longword	Count of unexpected SCB interrupts
EXE$GL_TENUSEC	SYSCOMMON	Longword	Number of time loops executed in 10 microseconds
EXE$GL_MP	SYSCOMMON	Longword	Pointer to multiprocessor code (when loaded into pool)
EXE$GL_SITESPEC	SYSCOMMON	Longword	Longword that is available to privileged users
EXE$GL_INTSTKLM	SYSCOMMON	Longword	Top of interrupt stack
LCK$GL_IDTBL	SYSCOMMON	Longword	Address of lock ID table
LCK$GL_NXTID	SYSCOMMON	Longword	Pointer to next lock ID to use
LCK$GL_MAXID	SYSCOMMON	Longword	Maximum lock ID
LCK$GL_HASHTBL	SYSCOMMON	Longword	Address of resource hash table
LCK$GL_HTBLCNT	SYSCOMMON	Longword	Number of entries in resource hash table (expressed as a power of two)
LCK$GL_TIMOUTQ	SYSCOMMON	Quadword	Listhead for lock timeout queue (for deadlock detection)
LCK$GL_PRCMAP	SYSCOMMON	Longword	Address of process bitmap
LCK$GB_MAXDEPTH	SYSCOMMON	Byte	Maximum number of sublocks allowed
		3 Bytes	Spare for alignment
EXE$GL_SYSFLAGS	SYSCOMMON	Longword	System-wide status flags
EXE$V_BLKHOLBSY	SYSCOMMON	Bit	Blackhole page busy
EXE$GL_ACMFLAGS	SYSCOMMON	Longword	Accounting manager control flags
EXE$GL_SVAPTE	SYSCOMMON	Longword	SVAPTE for PTE that maps the blackhole page
EXE$GQ_BLKHOLWQ	SYSCOMMON	Quadword	Listhead for blackhole page wait queue

Module ERRORLOG makes a significant contribution to program section $$$260. Most of the space is occupied by two 512-byte error message buffers.

Global Symbol	Module	Size	Description of Data
buf1	ERRORLOG	512 Bytes	First error log buffer
buf2	ERRORLOG	512 Bytes	Second error log buffer
ERL$AL_BUFADR	ERRORLOG	2 Longwords	Addresses of two error log buffers
ERL$GB_BUFIND	ERRORLOG	Byte	Current buffer allocation indicator
ERL$GB_BUFFLAG	ERRORLOG	Byte	Buffer status flags
ERL$GB_BUFPTR	ERRORLOG	Byte	Format process (ERRFMT) buffer indicator
ERL$GB_BUFTIM	ERRORLOG	Byte	Format process wake up timer
ERL$GL_ERLPID	ERRORLOG	Longword	Process ID of error format processs
ERL$GL_SEQUENCE	ERRORLOG	Longword	Universal error sequence number

A.1.15   Statistics Used by the Monitor Utility ($$$270NP)

Module PMSDAT contains most of the data that is presented by the Monitor Utility.

Global Symbol	Module	Size	Description of Data
PMS$GL_DIRIO	PMSDAT	Longword	Number of direct I/O operations
PMS$GL_BUFIO	PMSDAT	Longword	Number of buffered I/O operations
PMS$GL_LOGNAM	PMSDAT	Longword	Number of logical name translations
PMS$GL_MBREADS	PMSDAT	Longword	Number of mailbox read operations
PMS$GL_MBWRITES	PMSDAT	Longword	Number of mailbox write operations
PMS$GL_TREADS	PMSDAT	Longword	Number of terminal read operations
PMS$GL_TWRITES	PMSDAT	Longword	Number of terminal write operations
PMS$GL_IOPFMPDB	PMSDAT	Longword	Address of performance data block
PMS$GL_IOPFMSEQ	PMSDAT	Longword	Master I/O packet sequence number
PMS$GL_ARRLOCPK	PMSDAT	Longword	Number of local packets arriving (DECNET class)

Executive Data Areas

Global Symbol	Module	Size	Description of Data
PMS$GL_DEPLOCPK	PMSDAT	Longword	Number of local packets departing (DECNET class)
PMS$GL_TRCNGLOS	PMSDAT	Longword	Cumulative transit congestion loss (DECNET class)
PMS$GL_RCVBUFFL	PMSDAT	Longword	Number of receiver buffer failures (DECNET class)
PMS$GL_ENQNEW	PMSDAT	Longword	Number of lock requests (LOCK class)
PMS$GL_ENQCVT	PMSDAT	Longword	Number of conversion requests (LOCK class)
PMS$GL_DEQ	PMSDAT	Longword	Number of locks dequeued (LOCK class
PMS$GL_ENQWAIT	PMSDAT	Longword	Number of waiting locks (LOCK class)
PMS$GL_ENQNOTQD	PMSDAT	Longword	Number of requests not queued (LOCK class)
PMS$GL_DLCKSRCH	PMSDAT	Longword	Number of deadlock searches performed (LOCK class)
PMS$GL_DLCKFND	PMSDAT	Longword	Number of deadlocks found (LOCK class)
PMS$GL_CHMK	PMSDAT	Longword	Number of CHMK exceptions
PMS$GL_CHME	PMSDAT	Longword	Number of CHME exceptions
PMS$GL_PAGES	PMSDAT	Longword	Number of physical pages of memory configuration
PMS$GW_BATCH	PMSDAT	Word	Number of current batch jobs
PMS$GW_INTJOBS	PMSDAT	Word	Number of interactive users
PMS$AL_READTBL	PMSDAT	10 Longwords	Histogram to count number of characters per terminal read operation
PMS$AL_WRITETBL	PMSDAT	10 Longwords	Histogram to count number of characters per terminal write operation
PMS$GL_READCNT	PMSDAT	Longword	Total number of terminal characters read since bootstrap

Global Symbol	Module	Size	Description of Data
PMS$GL_WRTCNT	PMSDAT	Longword	Total number of terminal characters written since bootstrap
PMS$GL_PASSALL	PMSDAT	Longword	Number of reads in PASSALL mode
PMS$GL_RWP	PMSDAT	Longword	Number of read-with-prompt reads
PMS$GL_LRGRWP	PMSDAT	Longword	Number of read-with-prompt reads of more than 12 characters
PMS$GL_RWPSUM	PMSDAT	Longword	Total number of characters read in prompt mode
PMS$GL_NOSTDTRM	PMSDAT	Longword	Number of reads not using standard terminals
PMS$GL_RWPNOSTD	PMSDAT	Longword	Number of read-with-prompt reads not using standard terminals
PMS$GL_LDPCTX	PMSDAT	Longword	Number of LDPCTX instructions
PMS$GL_SWITCH	PMSDAT	Longword	Number of switches from the current process
PMS$GB_PROMPT	PMSDAT	4 Bytes	RTE input prompt
PMS$GL_DOSTATS	PMSDAT	Byte	Flag to turn statistics code on and off
		3 Bytes	Spare for alignment

A.1.16   **Entry Points for CPU-Dependent Routines ($$$500)**

Module SYSLOAVEC contains entry points for each CPU-dependent routine; module SCSVEC contains entry points for the loadable SCS code (SCS is described in Chapter 19). Each entry point contains a JMP instruction (with absolute addressing). The destination of each JMP is altered by INIT to point to the appropriate routine in the CPU-dependent image SYSLOAxxx.EXE (SYSLOA730.EXE, SYSLOA750.EXE, or SYSLOA780.EXE) that is loaded into nonpaged pool by INIT.

There are two types of routines here. Those routines that are entered through the system control block must have their entry points longword aligned. Each of these routines has two spare bytes to preserve longword alignment. Other routines can have the six-byte JMP instructions packed together.

Global Symbol	*Module*	*Size*	*Description of Data*
EXE$AL_LOAVEC	SYSLOAVEC		Address of start of vectors
EXE$MCHK	SYSLOAVEC	8 Bytes	Machine check exception service routine
EXE$INT54	SYSLOAVEC	8 Bytes	Interrupt service routine for SCB vector 54
EXE$INT58	SYSLOAVEC	8 Bytes	Interrupt service routine for SCB vector 58
EXE$INT5C	SYSLOAVEC	8 Bytes	Interrupt service routine for SCB vector 5C
EXE$INT60	SYSLOAVEC	8 Bytes	Interrupt service routine for SCB vector 60
UBA$INT0	SYSLOAVEC	8 Bytes	Interrupt service routine for UNIBUS vector 0
UBA$UNEXINT	SYSLOAVEC	6 Bytes	Interrupt service routine for unexpected UNIBUS interrupts
ECC$REENABLE	SYSLOAVEC	6 Bytes	Reenable memory error timers
EXE$INIBOOTADP	SYSLOAVEC	6 Bytes	Initialize device adapter
EXE$DUMPCPUREG	SYSLOAVEC	6 Bytes	Dump CPU-specific registers to error log buffer
EXE$REGRESTOR	SYSLOAVEC	6 Bytes	Restore CPU-specific registers on power recovery
EXE$REGSAVE	SYSLOAVEC	6 Bytes	Save CPU-specific register at power failure
EXE$INIPROCREG	SYSLOAVEC	6 Bytes	Initialize processor registers
EXE$TEST_CSR	SYSLOAVEC	6 Bytes	Test UNIBUS CSR for existence
IOC$PURGDATAP	SYSLOAVEC	6 Bytes	Purge UNIBUS buffered datapath
EXE$DW780_INT	SYSLOAVEC	6 Bytes	DW780 UBA adapter error interrupt routine
EXE$RH780_INT	SYSLOAVEC	6 Bytes	RH780 MBA adapter error interrupt routine
CI$INITIAL	SYSLOAVEC	6 Bytes	Initialize CI adapter

Global Symbol	Module	Size	Description of Data
CI$INT	SYSLOAVEC	6 Bytes	Interrupt service routine for CI adapter
UBA$INITIAL	SYSLOAVEC	6 Bytes	Initialize UNIBUS adapter
INI$MPMADP	SYSLOAVEC	6 Bytes	Initialize multiport memory
EXE$SHUTDWNADP	SYSLOAVEC	6 Bytes	Shut down any (all) adapters
EXE$MCHK_ERRCNT	SYSLOAVEC	Longword	Pointer to error counters in machine check routine
EXE$LOAD_ERROR	SYSLOAVEC	Byte	HALT instruction (initial destination of JMP instructions in vectors)
SCS$GQ_CONFIG	SCSVEC	Quadword	Listhead for system descriptor blocks
SCS$GQ_DIRECT	SCSVEC	Quadword	Listhead for directory of processes in cluster
SCS$GL_BDT	SCSVEC	Longword	Buffer descriptor table for SCS block transmissions
SCS$GL_CDL	SCSVEC	Longword	Connection descriptor table pointing to list of SCS connections
SCS$GL_RDT	SCSVEC	Longword	Response descriptor table
SCS$GL_MCLEN	SCSVEC	Longword	Not used
SCS$GL_MCADR	SCSVEC	Longword	Pointer to CI port microcode paged pool
SCS$AL_LOAVEC	SCSVEC		Address of start of vectors
SCS$ACCEPT	SCSVEC	6 Bytes	Perform SCS accept
SCS$ALLOC_CDT	SCSVEC	6 Bytes	Allocate connection descriptor table
SCS$ALLOC_RSPID	SCSVEC	6 Bytes	Allocate Response ID
SCS$CONFIG_PTH	SCSVEC	6 Bytes	Configure with path to remote system
SCS$CONFIG_SYS	SCSVEC	6 Bytes	Configure with System ID
SCS$CONNECT	SCSVEC	6 Bytes	Perform SCS connect
SCS$DEALL_CDT	SCSVEC	6 Bytes	Deallocate connection descriptor table
SCS$DEALL_RSPID	SCSVEC	6 Bytes	Deallocate response ID
SCS$DISCONNECT	SCSVEC	6 Bytes	Perform SCS disconnect
SCS$ENTER	SCSVEC	6 Bytes	Insert an entry in SCS directory

Global Symbol	Module	Size	Description of Data
SCS$LISTEN	SCSVEC	6 Bytes	Perform an SCS listen operation
SCS$LOCLOOKUP	SCSVEC	6 Bytes	Look up a path block
SCS$REMOVE	SCSVEC	6 Bytes	Remove an entry in SCS directory
IOC$THREADCRB	SCSVEC	6 Bytes	Place CRB in SCS timer queue
SCS$RESUMEWAITR	SCSVEC	6 Bytes	Resume when CRB is dequeued
SCS$UNSTALLUCB	SCSVEC	6 Bytes	Resume when UCB is dequeued
SCS$LKP_RDTCDRP	SCSVEC	6 Bytes	Search a response descriptor table for a CDRP
SCS$LKP_RDTWAIT	SCSVEC	6 Bytes	Search a response ID wait queue for a CDRP

A.1.17 Table of Adjustable SYSBOOT Parameters ($$$917)

As described in Chapter 25, the executive image contains a copy of the working value of each SYSBOOT parameter. This table of values is written into the memory image of the executive by SYSBOOT and copied back to the executive disk image by SYSINIT. Global label MMG$A_SYSPARAM, defined in module MDAT, locates the beginning of the parameter area. Global label EXE$A_SYSPARAM, defined in module SYSPARAM, has the same value.

In the following list, the name of each parameter is included as a part of its description. Table A-1 lists the SYSGEN parameters alphabetically and indicates the names of the cells where each parameter is stored.

Global Symbol	Module	Size	Description of Data
EXE$GQ_TODCBASE	SYSPARAM	Quadword	Base value of time-of-day clock in system time format (not a parameter)
EXE$GL_TODR	SYSPARAM	Longword	Base value in time-of-year clock (not a parameter)
SGN$GW_DFPFC	SYSPARAM	Word	Default page fault cluster size (PFCDEFAULT)
SGN$GB_PGTBPFC	SYSPARAM	Byte	Default page table page fault cluster size (PAGTBLPFC)

Global Symbol	Module	Size	Description of Data
SGN$GB_SYSPFC	SYSPARAM	Byte	Page fault cluster factor for system paging (SYSPFC)
SGB$GB_KFILSTCT	SYSPARAM	Byte	Number of known file lists (KFILSTCNT)
		Byte	Spare for alignment
SGN$GW_GBLSECNT	SYSPARAM	Word	Global section count (GBLSECTIONS)
SGN$GL_MAXGPGCT	SYSPARAM	Longword	Global page count (GBLPAGES)
SGN$GL_GBLPAGFIL	SYSPARAM	Longword	Global page file page limit (GBLPAGFIL)
SGN$GW_MAXPRCCT	SYSPARAM	Word	Maximum process count (MAXPROCESSCNT)
SGN$GW_PIXSCAN	SYSPARAM	Word	Maximum number of processes to scan for priority boosting (PIXSCAN)
SGN$GW_MAXPSTCT	SYSPARAM	Word	Process section count (PROCSECTCNT)
SGN$GW_MINWSCNT	SYSPARAM	Word	Minimum working set size (MINWSCNT)
SGN$GW_PAGFILCT	SYSPARAM	Word	Number of page files (PAGFILCNT)
SGN$GW_SWPFILES	SYSPARAM	Word	Number of swap files (SWPFILCNT)
SGN$GW_SYSDWSCT	SYSPARAM	Word	Size of system working set count (SYSMWCNT)
SGN$GW_ISPPGCT	SYSPARAM	Word	Size in pages of interrupt stack (INTSTKPAGES)
SGN$GL_EKTRASTK	SYSPARAM	Longword	Amount of interrupt stack that must remain free when performing deadlock searches (DLCKEXTRASTK)
SGN$GL_BALSETCT	SYSPARAM	Longword	Balance set count (BALSETCNT)
SGN$GL_IRPCNT	SYSPARAM	Longword	Count of preallocated I/O request packets (IRPCOUNT)

Global Symbol	Module	Size	Description of Data
SGN$GL_IRPCNTV	SYSPARAM	Longword	Maximum number of IRPS allowed on the IRP lookaside list (IRPCOUNTV)
SGN$GL_MAXWSCNT	SYSPARAM	Longword	Maximum size of process working set (WSMAX)
SGN$GL_NPAGEDYN	SYSPARAM	Longword	Number of bytes of nonpaged pool (NPAGEDYN) (Truncated to page boundary by SYSBOOT)
SGN$GL_NPAGEVIR	SYSPARAM	Longword	Maximum size of nonpaged pool (NPAGEVIR)
SGN$GL_PAGEDYN	SYSPARAM	Longword	Number of bytes of paged pool (PAGEDYN) (Truncated to page boundary by SYSBOOT)
SGN$GL_MAXVPGCT	SYSPARAM	Longword	Maximum virtual page count (VIRTUALPAGECNT)
SGN$GL_SPTREQ	SYSPARAM	Longword	Number of additional SPTEs to allocate (SPTREQ)
SGN$GL_EXUSRSTK	SYSPARAM	Longword	Extra user stack space (in bytes) allocated by image activator (EXUSRSTK)
SGN$GL_LRPCNT	SYSPARAM	Longword	Initial number of packets in the LRP lookaside list (LRPCOUNT)
SGN$GL_LRPCNTV	SYSPARAM	Longword	Maximum number of LRPs allows on the LRP lookaside list (LRPCOUNTV)
SGN$GL_LRPSIZE	SYSPARAM	Longword	Size of an LRP (LRPSIZE)
SGN$GL_LRPMIN	SYSPARAM	Longword	Smallest allocation request that can be allocated an LRP (LRPMIN)

706

A.1 Statically Allocated Executive Data

Global Symbol	Module	Size	Description of Data
SGN$GL_SRPCNT	SYSPARAM	Longword	Initial number of packets in SRP lookaside list (SRPCOUNT)
SGN$GL_SRPCNTV	SYSPARAM	Longword	Maximum number of SRPs allows on the SRP lookaside list (SRPCOUNTV)
SGN$GL_SRPSIZE	SYSPARAM	Longword	Size of an SRP (SRPSIZE)
SGN$GL_SRPMIN	SYSPARAM	Longword	Smallest allocation request that can be allocated an SRP (SRPMIN)
SGN$GW_PCHANCNT	SYSPARAM	Word	Permanent I/O channel count (CHANNELCNT)
SGN$GW_IMGIOCNT	SYSPARAM	Word	Default number of pages mapped for image I/O segment (IMGIOCNT)
SCH$GW_QUAN	SYSPARAM	Word	Length (in 10 milliseconds units) of quantum (QUANTUM)
MPW$GW_MPWPFC	SYSPARAM	Word	Modified page writer cluster factor (MPW_WRTCLUSTER)
MPW$GW_HILIM	SYSPARAM	Word	High limit threshold of modified page list (MPW_HILIM)
MPW$GW_LOLIM	SYSPARAM	Word	Low limit threshold of modified page list (MPW_LOLIM)
MPW$GB_PRIO	SYSPARAM	Byte	Priority at which modified page writes will be queued (MPW_PRIO)
SWP$GB_PRIO	SYSPARAM	Byte	Priority at which swapper I/O requests will be queued (SWP_PRIO)

Executive Data Areas

Global Symbol	Module	Size	Description of Data
MPW$GL_THRESH	SYSPARAM	Longword	Limit below which modified page writer will not reclaim pages (MPW_THRESH)
SGN$GL_WAITLIM	SYSPARAM	Longword	Limit above which processes creating modified pages must wait until pages have been released from modified page list (MPW_WAITLIMIT)
SGN$GW_WSLMXSKP	SYSPARAM	Word	Number of working set list entries to skip in modified scan of WSL (SKIPWSL)
MMG$GL_PHYPGCNT	SYSPARAM	Longword	Maximum number of physical pages to use (PHYSICALPAGES)
SCH$GL_PFRATL	SYSPARAM	Longword	Low limit page fault rate threshold (PFRAIL)
SCH$GL_PFRATH	SYSPARAM	Longword	High limit page fault rate threshold (PFRATH)
SCH$GL_PFRATS	SYSPARAM	Longword	Page fault rate threshold for system paging (PFRATS)
SCH$GL_WSINC	SYSPARAM	Longword	Working set increment (WSINC)
SCH$GL_WSDEC	SYSPARAM	Longword	Working set decrement (WSDEC)
SCH$GW_AWSMIN	SYSPARAM	Word	Minimum value of automatic working set adjustment (AWSMN)
SCH$GL_AWSTIME	SYSPARAM	Longword	Working set measurement interval (in 10 msec units) (AWSTIME)

Global Symbol	Module	Size	Description of Data
SCH$GL_SWPRATE	SYSPARAM	Longword	Swap rate for compute-bound jobs (SWPRATE)
SGN$GL_SWPPGCNT	SYSPARAM	Longword	Number of pages to attempt to shrink a working set before attempting outswap (SWPOUTPGCNT)
SGN$GL_SWPINC	SYSPARAM	Longword	Swap file allocation increment value (SWPALLOCINC)
SCH$GW_IOTA	SYSPARAM	Word	Amount of time (in 10-msec units) to charge against quantum when process goes into wait state (IOTA)
SGN$GW_LONGWAIT	SYSPARAM	Word	Amount of time elapsed for a LEF or HIB process to be scheduled as a longwait process (LONGWAIT)
SCH$GW_SWPFAIL	SYSPARAM	Word	Number of outswap failures to happen before modifying selection algorithm (SWPFAIL)
SGN$GL_VMSD1	SYSPARAM	Longword	DIGITAL-reserved parameter (VMSD1)
SGN$GL_VMSD2	SYSPARAM	Longword	DIGITAL-reserved parameter (VMSD2)
SGN$GL_VMSD3	SYSPARAM	Longword	DIGITAL-reserved parameter (VMSD3)
SGN$GL_VMSD4	SYSPARAM	Longword	DIGITAL-reserved parameter (VMSD4)
SGN$GL_VMS5	SYSPARAM	Longword	DIGITAL-reserved parameter (VMS5)
SGN$GL_VMS6	SYSPARAM	Longword	DIGITAL-reserved parameter (VMS6)
SGN$GL_VMS7	SYSPARAM	Longword	DIGITAL-reserved parameter (VMS7)

Executive Data Areas

Global Symbol	Module	Size	Description of Data
SGN$GL_VMS8	SYSPARAM	Longword	DIGITAL-reserved parameter (VMS8)
SGN$GL_USERD1	SYSPARAM	Longword	Parameter reserved for users (USERD1)
SGN$GL_USERD2	SYSPARAM	Longword	Parameter reserved for users (USERD2)
SGN$GL_USER3	SYSPARAM	Longword	Parameter reserved for users (USER3)
SGN$GL_USER4	SYSPARAM	Longword	Parameter reserved for users (USER4)
SGN$GL_EXTRACPU	SYSPARAM	Longword	Extra CPU time after CPU time expiration (EXTRACPU)
EXE$GL_SYSUIC	SYSPARAM	Longword	Maximum group code for system UIC (SYSUIC)
IOC$GW_MVTIMEOUT	SYSPARAM	Word	Time before abandoning mount verification attempt (MVTIMEOUT)
IOC$GW_MAXBUF	SYSPARAM	Word	Maximum buffered I/O request size (MAXBUF)
IOC$GW_MBXBFQUO	SYSPARAM	Word	Default buffer quota for mailbox creation (DEFMBXBUFQUO)
IOC$GW_MBXMXMSG	SYSPARAM	Word	Default maximum message size for mailbox creation (DEFMBXMXMSG)
IOC$GW_MBXNMMSG	SYSPARAM	Word	Default number of messages for mailbox creation (DEFMBXNUMMSG))
SGN$GL_FREELIM	SYSPARAM	Longword	Low limit threshold of free page list (FREELIM)
SGN$GL_FREEGOAL	SYSPARAM	Longword	Number of pages to attempt to free when the size of the free list is less than FREELIM (FREEGOAL)

Global Symbol	Module	Size	Description of Data
SGN$GL_GROWLIM	SYSPARAM	Longword	Number of pages that must exist on the free list for processes to add pages to their working sets above WSQUOTA (BORROWLIM)
SGN$GL_BORROWLIM	SYSPARAM	Longword	Number of pages that must exist on the free list for processes to extend their working set lists above WSQUOTA (GROWLIM)
EXE$GL_LOCKRTRY	SYSPARAM	Longword	Number of retries when attempting to lock a multiprocessor data structure (LOCKRETRY)
IOC$GW_XFMXRATE	SYSPARAM	Word	Maximum data rate
IOC$GW_LAMAPREG	SYSPARAM	Word	Number of UNIBUS map registers to preallocate for LPA11 (LAMAPREGS)
EXE$GL_RTIMESPT	SYSPARAM	Longword	Number of preallocated SPTEs for connect to interrupt (REALTIME_SPTS)
EXE$GL_CLITABL	SYSPARAM	Longword	Number of pages for CLI symbol table (CLISYMTBL)
LCK$GL_IDTBLSIZ	SYSPARAM	Longword	Size of the lock ID table (LOCKIDTBL)
LCK$GL_HTBLSIZ	SYSPARAM	Longword	Size of the resource hash table (RESHASHTBL)
LCK$GL_WAITTIME	SYSPARAM	Longword	Deadlock detection timeout period (DEADLOCK_WAIT)
SCS$GW_BDTCNT	SYSPARAM	Word	Number of buffer descriptor table entries allocated for SCS (SCSBUFFCNT)

Global Symbol	Module	Size	Description of Data
SCS$GW_CDTCNT	SYSPARAM	Word	Number of connect descriptor table entries allocated for SCS (SCSCONNCCNT)
SCS$GW_RDTCNT	SYSPARAM	Word	Number of response descriptor table entries allocated for SCS (SCSRESPCNT)
SCS$GW_SCSMAXDG	SYSPARAM	Word	Maximum SCS datagram size (SCSMAXDG)
SCS$GW_MAXMSG	SYSPARAM	Word	Maximum SCS sequenced message size (SCSMAXMSG)
SCS$GW_FLOWCUSH	SYSPARAM	Word	SCS flow control cushion (SCSFLOWCUSH)
SCS$GB_SYSTEMID	SYSPARAM	Byte	SCS system ID (SCSSYSTEMID)
		7 Bytes	Spare for alignment
SCS$GW_PASTRTRY	SYSPARAM	Word	Number of CI will attempt to START (PASTRTRY)
SCS$GW_PASTMOUT	SYSPARAM	Word	Wakeup interval for CI port driver (PASTIMOUT)
SCS$GW_PAPPDDG	SYSPARAM	Word	Number of datagram buffers to queue for START (PASTDGBUF)
SCS$GW_PAPOLINT	SYSPARAM	Word	Time between polls (PANUMPOLL)
SCS$GW_PAPOOLIN	SYSPARAM	Word	Time between checks for SCS applications waiting for pool (PAPOOLINTERVAL)
SGN$GW_TPWAIT	SYSPARAM	Word	Amount of time to wait for the time of day to be entered when booting (TIMEPROMPTWAIT)
SCS$GB_UDABURST	SYSPARAM	Byte	Maximum number of longwords that the host is willing to accept per transfer (UDABURSTRATE)

Global Symbol	Module	Size	Description of Data
LOG$GL_HTBLSIZ	SYSPARAM	Longword	Size of system logical name hash table (LOGSHASHTBL)
LOG$GL_HTBLSIZG	SYSPARAM	Longword	Size of group logical name hash table (LOGGHASHTBL)
LOG$GL_HTBLSIZP	SYSPARAM	Longword	Size of process logical name hash table (LOGPHASHTBL)
EXE$GL_DEFFLAGS	SYSPARAM	Longword	System flags longword (not a parameter itself)
EXE$V_BUGREBOOT		Bit	Automatic reboot on bugcheck (BUGREBOOT)
EXE$V_CONCEALED		Bit	Enable use of concealed devices (CONCEAL_DEVICES)
EXE$V_CRDENABLE		Bit	CRD error enable (CRDENABLE)
EXE$V_BUGDUMP		Bit	Write system dump on bugcheck (DUMPBUG)
EXE$V_FATAL_BUG		Bit	Make all bugchecks fatal (BUGCHECKFATAL)
EXE$V_JOBQUEUES		Bit	Enable job controller queues (JOBQUEUES)
EXE$V_MULTACP		Bit	Create separate ACP for each volume (ACP_MULTIPLE)
EXE$V_NOAUTOCNF		Bit	Inhibit autoconfiguration of I/O devices (NOAUTOCONFIG)
EXE$V_NOCLOCK		Bit	Do not start interval timer (NOCLOCK)
EXE$V_NOCLUSTER		Bit	Inhibit page read clustering (NOCLUSTER)
EXE$V_POOLPGING		Bit	Enable paging of paged pool (POOLPAGING)
EXE$V_REINITQUE		Bit	Create a new JBCSYSQUEUE.EXE (REINITQUE)
EXE$V_SBIERR		Bit	Enable detection of SBI errors (SBIERRENABLE)

Executive Data Areas

Global Symbol	Module	Size	Description of Data
EXE$V_SETTIME		Bit	Prompt for system time in SYSBOOT (SETTIME)
EXE$V_SHRF11ACP		Bit	Enable sharing of file ACP (ACP_SHARE)
EXE$V_SAVEDUMP		Bit	Save dump from page file (SAVEDUMP)
EXE$V_SSINHIBIT		Bit	Inhibit system services on a per-process basis (SSINHIBIT)
EXE$V_SYSPAGING		Bit	Enable paging of pageable system code (SYSPAGING)
EXE$V_SYSUAFALT		Bit	Select alternate authorization file (UAFALTERNATE)
EXE$V_SYSWRTABL		Bit	Leave entire executive writeable (WRITABLESYS)
EXE$V_RESALLOC		Bit	Enable resource allocation checking (RESALLOC)
EXE$GL_MSGFLAGS	SYSPARAM	Longword	Mount message flags
EXE$V_DISMOUMSG		Bit	Inform operator console of dismounts (DISMOUMSG)
EXE$V_MOUNTMSG		Bit	Inform operator console of mounts (MOUNTMSG)
TTY$GL_DELTA	SYSPARAM	Longword	Delta time for dialup timer scan (TTYSCANDELTA)
TTY$GB_DIALTYP	SYSPARAM	Byte	Dialup flags (DIALTYPE) (1 => United Kingdom 0 => elsewhere)
TTY$GB_DEFSPEED	SYSPARAM	Byte	Default speed for terminals (TTY_SPEED)
TTY$GB_RSPEED	SYSPARAM	Byte	Default receive speed (TTY_RSPEED)
TTY$GB_PARITY	SYSPARAM	Byte	Default parity (TTY_PARITY)
TTY$GW_DEFBUF	SYSPARAM	Word	Default terminal line width (TTY_BUF)

A.1 Statically Allocated Executive Data

Global Symbol	Module	Size	Description of Data
TTY$GL_DEFCHAR	SYSPARAM	Longword	Default terminal characteristics (TTY_DEFCHAR)
TTY$GL_DEFCHAR2	SYSPARAM	Longword	Default terminal characteristics (second longword) (DEFCHAR2)
TTY$GW_TYPAHDSZ	SYSPARAM	Word	Size type-ahead buffer (TTY_TYPAHDSZ)
TTY$GW_ALTYPAHD	SYSPARAM	Word	Alternative type-ahead buffer size (TTY_ALTYPAHD)
TTY$GW_ALTALARM	SYSPARAM	Word	Alternative type-ahead buffer alarm size (TTY_ALTALARM)
TTY$GW_DMASIZE	SYSPARAM	Word	DMA size
TTY$GW_PROT	SYSPARAM	Word	Default terminal allocation protection (TTY_PROT)
TTY$GL_OWNUIC	SYSPARAM	Longword	Default terminal owner UIC (TTY_OWNER)
TTY$GW_CLASSNAM	SYSPARAM	Word	Default terminal class name prefix (TTY_CLASSNAME)
TTY$GB_SILOTIME	SYSPARAM	Byte	Default silo timeout value for DMF-32 (SILOTIME)
SYS$GB_DFMBC	SYSPARAM	Byte	Default multiblock count (RMS_DFMBC)
SYS$GB_DFMBFSDK	SYSPARAM	Byte	Default multibuffer count for sequential disk I/O (RMS_DFMBFSDK)
SYS$GB_DFMBFSMT	SYSPARAM	Byte	Default multibuffer count for magtape I/O (RMS_DFMBFSMT)
SYS$GB_DFMBFSUR	SYSPARAM	Byte	Default multibuffer count for unit record devices (RMS_DFMBFSUR)
SYS$GB_DFMBFREL	SYSPARAM	Byte	Default multibuffer count for relative files RMS_DFMBFREL)

Executive Data Areas

Global Symbol	Module	Size	Description of Data
SYS$GB_DFMBFIDX	SYSPARAM	Byte	Default multibuffer count for indexed files DFMBFIDX)
SYS$GB_DFMBFHSH	SYSPARAM	Byte	Default multibuffer count hashed (RMS_DFMBFHSH)
SYS$GB_RMSPROLOG	SYSPARAM	Byte	Default Default RMS prolog value (RMS_PROLOGUE)
SYS$GW_RMSEXTEND	SYSPARAM	Word	Default file extend quantity (RMS_EXTEND_SIZE)
SYS$GW_FILEPROT	SYSPARAM	Word	Default file protection (RMS_FILEPROT)
PQL$AL_DEFAULT+4	SYSPARAM	12 Longwords	Table of process quota list default values (see Table 20-3)
PQL$AL_MIN+4	SYSPARAM	Longwords	Table of process quota list minimum values (see Table 20-3)
PQL$AB_FLAG+1	SYSPARAM	12 Bytes	Table of process quota list flags
ACP$GW_MAPCACHE	SYSPARAM	Word	Number of blocks in bitmap cache (ACP_MAPCACHE)
ACP$GW_HDRCACHE	SYSPARAM	Word	Number of blocks in file header cache (ACP_HDRCACHE)
ACP$GW_DIRCACHE	SYSPARAM	Word	Number of blocks in file directory cache (ACP_DIRCACHE)
ACP$GW_WORKSET	SYSPARAM	Word	ACP working set size (ACP_WORKSET)
ACP$GW_FIDCACHE	SYSPARAM	Word	Number of cached index file slots (ACP_FIDCACHE)
ACP$GW_EXTCACHE	SYSPARAM	Word	Number of cached disk extents (ACP_EXTCACHE)
ACP$GW_EXTLIMIT	SYSPARAM	Word	Fraction of disk to cache (ACP_EXTLIMIT)
ACP$GW_QUOCACHE	SYSPARAM	Word	Number of quota file entries to cache (ACP_QUOCACHE)

Global Symbol	Module	Size	Description of Data
ACP$GW_SYSACC	SYSPARAM	Word	Default access for system volumes (ACP_SYSACC)
ACP$GB_MAXREAD	SYSPARAM	Byte	Maximum number of blocks to read at once for directories (ACP_MAXREAD)
ACP$GB_WINDOW	SYSPARAM	Byte	Default window size for system volumes (ACP_WINDOW)
ACP$GB_WRITBACK	SYSPARAM	Byte	Enable deferred cache write back (ACP_WRITEBACK)
ACP$GB_DATACHK	SYSPARAM	Byte	ACP datacheck enable flags (ACP_DATACHECK)
ACP$V_READCHK		Bit	Do datacheck on reads
ACP$V_WRITECHK		Bit	Do datacheck on writes
ACP$GB_BASEPRIO	SYSPARAM	Byte	ACP base software priority (ACP_BASEPRIO)
ACP$GB_SWAPFLGS	SYSPARAM	Byte	ACP swap flags (ACP_SWAPFLGS)
ACP$V_SWAPSYS		Bit	Swap ACPs for /SYSTEM volumes
ACP$V_SWAPGRP		Bit	Swap ACPs for /GROUP volumes
ACP$V_SWAPPRV		Bit	Swap ACPs for private volumes
ACP$V_SWAPMAG		Bit	Swap magtape ACPs
SYS$GB_MXPRTSYM	SYSPARAM	Byte	Maximum number of print symbionts AXPRINTSYMB)
SYS$GB_DEFPRI	SYSPARAM	Byte	Default priority for job initiations (DEFPRI) (also upper limit on "cruncher" process priority)
SYS$GW_IJOBLIM	SYSPARAM	Word	Limit for interactive jobs (IJOBLIM)
SYS$GW_BJOBLIM	SYSPARAM	Word	Limit for batch jobs (BJOBLIM)
SYS$GW_NJOBLIM	SYSPARAM	Word	Limit for network jobs (NJOBLIM)
SYS$GW_RJOBLIM	SYSPARAM	Word	Limit for remote terminal jobs (RJOBLIM)

Table A-1

SYSBOOT Parameter	Cell Name
ACP_BASEPRIO	ACP$GB_BASEPRIO
ACP_DATACHECK	ACP$GB_DATACHK
ACP_DIRCACHE	ACP$GW_DIRCACHE
ACP_EXTCACHE	ACP$GW_EXTCACHE
ACP_EXTLIMIT	ACP$GW_EXTLIMIT
ACP_FIDCACHE	ACP$GW_FIDCACHE
ACP_HDRCACHE	ACP$GW_HDRCACHE
ACP_MAPCACHE	ACP$GW_MAPCACHE
ACP_MAXREAD	ACP$GB_MAXREAD
ACP_MULTIPLE	EXE$V_MULTACP (EXE$GL_DEFFLAGS)
ACP_QUOCACHE	ACP$GW_QUOCACHE
ACP_SHARE	EXE$V_SHRF11ACP (EXE$GL_DEFFLAGS)
ACP_SWAPFLGS	ACP$GB_SWAPFLGS
ACP_SYSACC	ACP$GW_SYSACC
ACP_WINDOW	ACP$GB_WINDOW
ACP_WORKSET	ACP$GW_WORKSET
ACP_WRITEBACK	ACP$GB_WRITBACK
AWSMIN	SCH$GW_AWSMIN
AWSTIME	SCH$GL_AWSTIME
BALSETCNT	SGN$GL_BALSETCT
BJOBLIM	SYS$GW_BJOBLIM
BLPAGFIL	SGN$GL_GBLPAGFIL
BUGCHECKFATAL	EXE$V_FATAL_BUG (EXE$GL_DEFFLAGS)
BUGREBOOT	EXE$V_BUGREBOOT (EXE$GL_DEFFLAGS)
CHANNELCNT	SGN$GW_PCHANCNT
CLISYMTBL	EXE$GL_CLITABL
CONCEAL_DEVICES	EXE$V_CONCEALED (EXE$GL_DEFFLAGS)
CRDENABLE	EXE$V_CRDENABL (EXE$GL_DEFFLAGS)
DEADLOCK_WAIT	LCK$GL_WAITTIME
DEFMBXBUFQUO	IOC$GW_MBXBFQUO
DEFMBXMXMSG	IOC$GW_MBXMXMSG
DEFMBXNUMMSG	IOC$GW_MBXNMMSG
DISMOUMSG	EXE$V_DISMOUMSG (EXE$GL_MSGFLAGS)
DLCKEXTRASTK	LCK$GL_EXTRASTK
DUMPBUG	EXE$V_BUGDUMP (EXE$GL_DEFFLAGS)
EXTRACPU	SGN$GL_EXTRACPU
EXUSRSTK	SGN$GL_EXUSRSTK
FREEGOAL	SGN$GL_FREEGOAL
FREELIM	SGN$GL_FREELIM
GBLPAGES	SGN$GL_MAXGPGCT
GBLSECTIONS	SGN$GW_GBLSECNT
GROWLIM	SCH$GL_GROWLIM
IJOBLIM	SYS$GW_IJOBLIM
IMGIOCNT	SGN$GW_IMGIOCNT
INTSTKPAGES	SGN$GW_ISPPGCT
IOTA	SCH$GW_IOTA
IRPCOUNT	SGN$GL_IRPCNT

Table A-1 *(continued)*

SYSBOOT Parameter	Cell Name
IRPCOUNTV	SGN$GL_IRPCNTV
JOBQUEUES	EXE$V_JOBQUEUES (EXE$GL_DEFFLAGS)
KFILSTCNT	SGN$GB_KFILSTCT
LAMAPREGS	IOC$GW_LAMAPREG
LOCKIDTBL	LCK$GL_IDTBLSIZ
LOCKRETRY	EXE$GL_LOCKRTRY
LOGGHASHTBL	LOG$GL_HTBLSIZG
LOGPHASHTBL	LOG$GL_HTBLSIZP
LOGSHASHTBL	LOG$GL_HTBLSIZ
LONGWAIT	SCH$GW_LONGWAIT
LRPCOUNT	SGN$GL_LRPCNT
LRPCOUNTV	SGN$GL_LRPCNTV
LRPMIN	SGN$GL_LRPMIN
LRPSIZE	SGN$GL_LRPSIZE
MAXBUF	IOC$GW_MAXBUF
MAXPRINTSYMB	SYS$GB_MXPRTSYM
MAXPROCESSCNT	SGN$GW_MAXPRCCT
MAXSYSGROUP	EXE$GL_SYSUIC
MINWSCNT	SGN$GW_MINWSCNT
MOUNTMSG	EXE$V_MOUNTMSG (EXE$GL_MSGFLAGS)
MPW_HILIMIT	MPW$GW_HILIM
MPW_LOLIMIT	MPW$GW_LOLIM
MPW_PRIO	MPW$GB_PRIO
MPW_THRESH	MPW$GL_THRESH
MPW_WAITLIMIT	MPW$GL_WAITLIM
MPW_WRTCLUSTER	MPW$GW_MPWPFC
NJOBLIM	SYS$GW_NJOBLIM
NOAUTOCONFIG	EXE$V_NOAUTOCNF (EXE$GL_DEFFLAGS)
NOCLOCK	EXE$V_NOCLOCK (EXE$GL_DEFFLAGS)
NOCLUSTER	EXE$V_NOCLUSTER (EXE$GL_DEFFLAGS)
NPAGEDYN	SGN$GL_NPAGEDYN
NPAGEVIR	SGN$GL_NPAGEVIR
ORROWLIM	SCH$GL_BORROWLIM
PAGEDYN	SGN$GL_PAGEDYN
PAGFILCNT	SGN$GW_PAGFILCT
PAGTBLPFC	SGN$GB_PGTBPFC
PANUMPOLL	SCS$GB_PANPOLL
PAPOLLINTERVAL	SCS$GW_PAPOLINT
PAPOOLINTERVAL	SCS$GW_PAPOOLIN
PASTDGBUF	SCS$GW_PAPPDDG
PASTIMOUT	SCS$GW_PASTMOUT
PASTRETRY	SCS$GW_PASTRTRY
PFCDEFAULT	SGN$GW_DFPFC
PFRATH	SCH$GL_PFRATH
PFRATL	SCH$GL_PFRATL
PFRATS	SCH$GL_PFRATS
PHYSICALPAGES	MMG$GL_PHYPGCNT

Table A-1 *(continued)*

SYSBOOT Parameter	*Cell Name*
PIXSCAN	SGN$GW_PIXSCAN
POOLPAGING	EXE$V_POOLPGING (EXE$GL_DEFFLAGS)
PROCSECTCNT	SGN$GW_MAXPSTCT
QUANTUM	SCH$GW_QUAN
REALTIME_SPTS	EXE$GL_RTIMESPT
REINITQUE	EXE$V_REINITQUE (EXE$GL_DEFFLAGS)
RESALLOC	EXE$V_RESALLOC (EXE$GL_DEFFLAGS)
RESHASHTBL	LCK$GL_HTBLSIZ
RJOBLIM	SYS$GW_RJOBLIM
RMS_DFMBC	SYS$GB_DFMBC
RMS_DFMBFHSH	SYS$GB_DFMBFHSH
RMS_DFMBFIDX	SYS$GB_DFMBFIDX
RMS_DFMBFREL	SYS$GB_DFMBFREL
RMS_DFMBFSDK	SYS$GB_DFMBFSDK
RMS_DFMBFSMT	SYS$GB_DFMBFSMT
RMS_DFMBFSUR	SYS$GB_DFMBFSUR
SAVEDUMP	EXE$V_SAVEDUMP (EXE$GL_DEFFLAGS)
SBIERRENABLE	EXE$V_SBIERR (EXE$GL_DEFFLAGS)
SCSBUFFCNT	SCS$GW_BDTCNT
SCSCONNCNT	SCS$GW_CDTCNT
SCSFLOWCUSH	SCS$GW_FLOWCUSH
SCSMAXDG	SCS$GW_MAXDG
SCSMAXMSG	SCS$GW_MAXMSG
SCSRESPCNT	SCS$GW_RDTCNT
SCSSYSTEMID	SCS$GB_SYSTEMID
SETTIME	EXE$V_SETTIME (EXE$GL_DEFFLAGS)
SPTREQ	SGN$GL_SPTREQ
SRPCOUNT	SGN$GL_SRPCNT
SRPCOUNTV	SGN$GL_SRPCNTV
SRPMIN	SGN$GL_SRPMIN
SRPSIZE	SGN$GL_SRPSIZE
SSINHIBIT	EXE$V_SSINHIBIT (EXE$GL_DEFFLAGS)
SWPALLOCINC	SWP$GW_SWPINC
SWPFAIL	SCH$GW_SWPFAIL
SWPFILCNT	SGN$GW_SWPFILES
SWPOUTPGCNT	SWP$GL_SWPPGCNT
SWPRATE	SCH$GL_SWPRATE
SWP_PRIO	SWP$GB_PRIO
SYSMWCNT	SGN$GW_SYSDWSCT
SYSPAGING	EXE$V_SYSPAGING (EXE$GL_DEFFLAGS)
SYSPFC	SGN$GB_SYSPFC
TBSKIPWSL	SGN$GW_WSLMXSKP
TIMEPROMPTWAIT	SGN$GW_TPWAIT
TTY_ALTALARM	TTY$GW_ALTALARM
TTY_ALTYPAHD	TTY$GW_ALTYPAHD
TTY_BUF	TTY$GW_DEFBUF
TTY_CLASSNAME	TTY$GW_CLASSNAM

Table A-1 *(continued)*

SYSBOOT Parameter	Cell Name
TTY_DEFCHAR	TTY$GL_DEFCHAR
TTY_DEFCHAR2	TTY$GL_DEFCHAR2
TTY_DIALTYPE	TTY$GB_DIALTYP
TTY_DMASIZE	TTY$GW_DMASIZE
TTY_OWNER	TTY$GL_OWNUIC
TTY_PARITY	TTY$GB_PARITY
TTY_PROT	TTY$GW_PROT
TTY_RSPEED	TTY$GB_RSPEED
TTY_SCANDELTA	TTY$GL_DELTA
TTY_SILOTIME	TTY$GB_SILOTIME
TTY_SPEED	TTY$GB_DEFSPEED
TTY_TYPAHDSZ	TTY$GE_TYPAHDSZ
UAFALTERNATE	EXE$V_SYSUAFALT(EXE$GL_DEFFLAGS)
UDABURSTRATE	SCS$GB_UDABURST
USER3	SGN$GL_USER3
USER4	SGN$GL_USER4
USERD1	SGN$GL_USERD1
USERD2	SGN$GL_USERD2
VIRTUALPAGECNT	SGN$GL_MAXVPGCT
VMS5	SGN$GL_VMS5
VMS6	SGN$GL_VMS6
VMS7	SGN$GL_VMS7
VMS8	SGN$GL_VMS8
VMSD1	SGN$GL_VMSD1
VMSD2	SGN$GL_VMSD2
VMSD3	SGN$GL_VMSD3
VMSD4	SGN$GL_VMSD4
VTIMEOUT	IOC$GW_MVTIMEOUT
WRITABLESYS	EXE$V_SYSWRTABL (EXE$GL_DEFFLAGS)
WSDEC	SCH$GL_WSDEC
WSINC	SCH$GL_WSINC
WSMAX	SGN$GL_MAXWSCNT
XFMAXRATE	IOC$GW_XFMXRATE

The rest of module SYSPARAM consists of other system-wide parameters the values of which are not directly adjustable with SYSBOOT or SYSGEN; rather their values depend directly on the values of one or more adjustable parameters.

Executive Data Areas

Global Symbol	Module	Size	Description of Data
SWP$GL_SHELLSIZ	SYSPARAM	Longword	Pages required for shell process
SWP$GW_BAKPTE	SYSPARAM	Word	Number of process header pages for process header page arrays
SWP$GW_EMPTPTE	SYSPARAM	Word	Number of empty process header pages for working set list expansion
SWP$GW_WSLPTE	SYSPARAM	Word	Number of process header pages for fixed area, working set list, and process section table
SWP$GB_SHLP1PT	SYSPARAM	Byte	Number of P1 page table pages required for SHELL
		Byte	Spare for alignment
SWP$GL_BSLOTSZ	SYSPARAM	Longword	Size (in pages) of balance slot
SWP$GL_MAP	SYSPARAM	Longword	Address of swapper's I/O page table
SWP$GL_PHDBASVA	SYSPARAM	Longword	Base address of process header window
SGN$GL_PHDAPCNT	SYSPARAM	Longword	Count of SHELL header pages
SGN$GL_PHDLWCNT	SYSPARAM	Longword	Count of longwords in process header
SGN$GL_P1LWCNT	SYSPARAM	Longword	Count of longwords to end of P1 page table
SGN$GL_PHDPAGCT	SYSPARAM	Longword	Count of all process header pages excluding page table pages
SGN$GL_PTPAGCNT	SYSPARAM	Longword	Count of page table pages
MMG$GL_CTLBASVA	SYSPARAM	Longword	Initial low address end of P1 space
EXE$AL_STACKS	SYSPARAM	2 Longwords	Array of kernel mode system space stacks
		Longword	Address of swapper's kernel stack
EXE$GL_INTSTK		Longword	Address of interrupt stack

Global Symbol	Module	Size	Description of Data
MMG$GL_GPTBASE	SYSPARAM	Longword	Base address of global page table
MMG$GL_GPTE	SYSPARAM	Longword	Address of first GPTE (pseudo SPTE) at end of system page table
MMG$GL_MAXGPTE	SYSPARAM	Longword	Highest GPTE Address
MMG$GL_MAXSYSVA	SYSPARAM	Longword	Highest system virtual address (plus one)
MMG$GL_SPTBASE	SYSPARAM	Longword	Base virtual address of system page table
MMG$GL_SPTLEN	SYSPARAM	Longword	Length of system page table
MMG$GL_SYSPHD	SYSPARAM	Longword	Virtual address of system header
MMG$GL_SYSPHDLN	SYSPARAM	Longword	Size (in bytes) of system header
SWP$GL_BALBASE	SYSPARAM	Longword	Base virtual address of balance slot area
SWP$GL_BALSPT	SYSPARAM	Longword	Base virtual address in system page table for mapping balance slots
MMG$GL_SBR	SYSPARAM	Longword	Physical address of system page table (Duplicates contents of PR$_SBR)
MMG$GL_NPAGEDYN	SYSPARAM	Longword	Virtual address of beginning of nonpaged pool
MMG$GL_NPAGNEXT	SYSPARAM	Longword	Next virtual address for nonpaged pool extension
MMG$GL_IRPNEXT	SYSPARAM	Longword	Next virtual address for IRP list extension
MMG$GL_LRPNEXT	SYSPARAM	Longword	Next virtual address for LRP list extension
MMG$GL_SRPNEXT	SYSPARAM	Longword	Next virtual address for SRP list extension
MMG$GL_PAGEDYN	SYSPARAM	Longword	Virtual address of beginning of paged pool
MMG$GL_MAXPFN	SYSPARAM	Longword	Maximum PFN accounted for in PFN database
MMG$GL_MINPFN	SYSPARAM	Longword	Minimum PFN in PFN database
EXE$GL_RPB	SYSPARAM	Longword	Virtual address of restart parameter block

Global Symbol	Module	Size	Description of Data
BOO$GL_SPTFREL	SYSPARAM	Longword	Virtual page number of lower end of pool of unused SPTEs
BOO$GL_SPTFREH	SYSPARAM	Longword	Virtual page number of upper end of pool of unused SPTEs
EXE$GL_SCB	SYSPARAM	Longword	Virtual address of system control block
EXE$GB_CPUDATA	SYSPARAM	16 Bytes	System-specific information
EXE$GB_CPUTYPE	SYSPARAM	Byte	CPU type read from PR$_SID
		3 Bytes	Spare for alignment
PFN$A_BASE	SYSPARAM	8 Longwords	Addresses of eight PFN database arrays
PFN$AL_PTE		Longword	Address of PTE array
PFN$AL_BAK		Longword	Address of backing store address array
PFN$AW_REFCNT		Longword	Address of reference count array of words
PFN$AW_FLINK		Longword	Address of combined forward link/global share count of words
PFN$AW_SHRCNT		Longword	
PFN$AW_BLINK		Longword	Address of combined backward link/working set list index array of words
PFN$AW_WSLX		Longword	
PFN$AW_SWPVBN		Longword	Address of swap image virtual block number array of words
PFN$AB_STATE		Longword	Address of STATE array of bytes
PFN$AB_TYPE		Longword	Address of TYPE array of bytes
EXE$GT_STARTUP	SYSPARAM	33 Bytes	Counted ASCII string of name of startup command file

A.1.18   Remainder of Executive Image

The rest of the executive image consists of read-only code areas, read-only tables, and patch space. All other data areas are dynamically created as a part of system initialization.

Global label MMG$FRSTRONLY, defined in module MDAT, locates the beginning of the nonpaged executive routines. The paged executive is delimited by the labels MMG$AL_PGDCODEN, also defined in MDAT.

A.2   DYNAMICALLY ALLOCATED EXECUTIVE DATA

Many of the data structures and areas of system address space are not a part of the executive image but instead are constructed when the system is initialized. The sizes of some of these areas depend on the values of SYSBOOT parameters. Other areas depend on the particular physical configuration.

A.2.1   Restart Parameter Block

The restart parameter block (RPB) is filled in at initialization time with bootstrap parameters. The power failure interrupt service routine loads the volatile machine state into the RPB before the system halts. During power recovery, the restart parameter block allows the console logic to determine whether memory contents survived the power outage. The use of the restart parameter block is discussed in Chapters 24 and 27.

A.2.2   PFN Database

The PFN database consists of several arrays, contents of which describe the state of each page in physical memory. (To save memory, pages that contain the permanently resident executive are not accounted for in the PFN data base.) The PFN arrays are described in Chapter 14. Their use during page fault resolution is discussed in Chapter 15. PFN array manipulation during swapper operations is discussed in Chapter 17.

A.2.3   Paged Dynamic Memory

Paged dynamic memory contains all system-wide dynamically allocated structures that do not have to be permanently resident. Typical structures allocated from paged dynamic memory are listed in Chapter 3.

A.2.4   Nonpaged Dynamic Memory

Nonpaged pool contains all dynamically allocated structures that must be resident at all times. These structures may contain either code or data. There are actually two pool areas here. The normal nonpaged pool uses the same allocation routine as is used for paged pool. This pool area can have blocks of any size allocated from it. A second pool area of nonpaged pool contains three lists of fixed-size blocks (the lookaside lists), linked together so that a block may be inserted or removed with the INSQUE and REMQUE instructions. The contents of this second area are often called the lookaside lists. The use of nonpaged pool is described in Chapter 3.

A.2.5 Interrupt Stack

The interrupt stack is used to service all hardware interrupts and all software interrupts except AST delivery.

A.2.6 System Control Block

The system control block is strictly speaking not a writeable data structure, although entries are sometimes modified by the executive debugger XDELTA, by the DCL commands START/CPU and STOP/CPU, and by SYSGEN code used to connect MA780 shared memory.

A.2.7 Balance Slot Area

The balance slot area is devoted exclusively to process headers. Any resident process has its process header in one of the balance slots. Balance slots are described in Chapter 14. Their use by the swapper is discussed in Chapter 17.

A.2.8 System Header

The system header is a system analogue to process headers. It allows system code to be pageable. The structures within the system header that are often altered are the system working set list and the system section table that contains global section table entries.

A.2.9 System Page Table

The portion of the system page table that undergoes the most change is that part that maps the balance slot area. Other operations can cause other areas of the system page table to change.

A.2.10 Global Page Table

The global page table is a pseudo extension of the system page table that allows GPTEs to be accessed with SVPNs. The global page table is altered when global sections are created and deleted. In addition, GPTEs can change as a result of page faults.

A.3   PROCESS-SPECIFIC EXECUTIVE DATA

Some process-specific data is stored in the process header. That data is accessible (subject to synchronization considerations) whenever the process is resident. Most of the process-specific data is found in P1 space. P1 space is only addressable when the process is the current process. The executive uses ASTs that execute in process context when it is necessary to acquire or modify such data from some other process.

A.3.1   P1 Pointer Page

The P1 pointer page is a permanent member of the process working set. The entire pointer page is defined in executive module SHELL.

Global Symbol	Data Area	Size	Description of Data
CTL$GW_NMIOCH	P1 Pointer Page	Word	Number of I/O channels
CTL$GW_CHINDX	P1 Pointer Page	Word	Maximum channel index
CTL$GL_RMSPP	P1 Pointer Page	Longword	Pointer to RMS process I/O segment
CTL$GL_RMSIP	P1 Pointer Page	Longword	Pointer to RMS image I/O segment
	P1 Pointer Page	Longword	Maximum extent (low address limit) of kernel stack
CTL$AL_STACK	P1 Pointer Page	Longword	Initial value of kernel stack pointer
	P1 Pointer Page	Longword	Initial value of executive stack pointer
	P1 Pointer Page	Longword	Initial value of supervisor stack pointer
	P1 Pointer Page	Longword	Initial value of user stack pointer
CTL$GL_LOGTBL	P1 Pointer Page	Longword	Pointer to process logical name table
		Longword	Spare
CTL$GL_CMSUPR	P1 Pointer Page	Longword	Address of change mode to supervisor handler
CTL$GL_CMUSER	P1 Pointer Page	Longword	Address of change mode to user handler
CTL$GL_CMHANDLR	P1 Pointer Page	Longword	Address of compatibility mode handler
CTL$AQ_EXCVEC	P1 Pointer Page	8 Longwords	Addresses of primary and secondary exception handlers for each of the four access modes

Executive Data Areas

Global Symbol	Data Area	Size	Description of Data
CTL$GL_THEXEC	P1 Pointer Page	3 Longwords	Termination handler listheads for executive, supervisor, and user access modes
CTL$GQ_COMMON	P1 Pointer Page	Quadword	Descriptor (size and address) of per-process common area
CTL$GL_GETMSG	P1 Pointer Page	Longword	Address of per-process page dispatcher
CTL$AL_STACKLIM	P1 Pointer Page	4 Longwords	Limit on stack size for each access mode
CTL$GL_CTLBASVA	P1 Pointer Page	Longword	Low address end of permanent part of P1 space
CTL$GL_IMGHDRBF	P1 Pointer Page	Longword	Address of image activator's image header buffer
CTL$GL_RUNDNFLG	P1 Pointer Page	Longword	Image rundown control flag
RND$V_IACLOCK		Bit	Image activator lock must be reset
CTL$GL_PHD	P1 Pointer Page	Longword	Address of P1 window that doubles maps the process header pages that are not page table pages
CTL$GQ_ALLOCREG	P1 Pointer Page	Quadword	Listhead for the process allocation region
CTL$GQ_MOUNTLST	P1 Pointer Page	Quadword	Listhead for the process private mounted volume list
CTL$T_USERNAME	P1 Pointer Page	12 Bytes	User name for process (blank-filled ASCII string)
CTL$T_ACCOUNT	P1 Pointer Page	8 Bytes	Account name for process (blank-filled ASCII string)
CTL$GQ_LOGIN	P1 Pointer Page	Quadword	System time at process creation
CTL$GL_FINALSTS	P1 Pointer Page	Longword	Exit status of latest image to execute
CTL$GL_WSPEAK	P1 Pointer Page	Longword	Peak working set size for process
CTL$GL_VIRTPEAK	P1 Pointer Page	Longword	Peak virtual size for process
CTL$GL_VOLUMES	P1 Pointer Page	Longword	Count of mounted volumes
CTL$GQ_ISTART	P1 Pointer Page	Quadword	Image activation time

Global Symbol	Data Area	Size	Description of Data
CTL$GL_ICPUTIM	P1 Pointer Page	Longword	Initial image CPU time
CTL$GL_IFAULTS	P1 Pointer Page	Longword	Initial image fault count
CTL$GL_IFAULTIO	P1 Pointer Page	Longword	Initial image fault I/O count
CTL$GL_IWSPEAK	P1 Pointer Page	Longword	Image working set peak
CTL$GL_IPAGEFL	P1 Pointer Page	Longword	Image page file peak usage
CTL$GL_IDIOCNT	P1 Pointer Page	Longword	Initial image direct I/O count
CTL$GL_IBIOCNT	P1 Pointer Page	Longword	Initial image buffered I/O count
CTL$GL_IVOLUMES	P1 Pointer Page	Longword	Initial image volume mount count
CTL$T_NODEADDR	P1 Pointer Page	7 Bytes	Remote node address
CTL$T_NODENAME	P1 Pointer Page	7 Bytes	Remote node name (counted ASCII)
CTL$T_REMOTEID	P1 Pointer Page	17 Bytes	Remote node ID
		Byte	Spare for alignment
CTL$GQ_PROCPRIV	P1 Pointer Page	Quadword	Permanent process privilege mask
CTL$GL_USRCHMK	P1 Pointer Page	Longword	Address of per-process change mode to kernel dispatcher
CTL$GL_USRCHME	P1 Pointer Page	Longword	Address of per-process change mode to executive dispatcher
CTL$GL_POWERAST	P1 Pointer Page	Longword	Address of power recovery AST for process
CTL$GB_PWRMODE	P1 Pointer Page	Byte	Access mode for power recovery AST AST
CTL$GB_SSFILTER	P1 Pointer Page	Byte	System services inhibit filter mask
		2 Bytes	Spare for alignment
CTL$AL_FINALEXC	P1 Pointer Page	4 Longwords	Address of last chance exception handlers for each of the four access modes
CTL$G_CCBBASE	P1 Pointer Page	Longword	Address of base of I/O channel area
CTL$GQ_DBGAREA	P1 Pointer Page	Quadword	Descriptor (size and address) for debug symbol table
CTL$GL_RMSBASE	P1 Pointer Page	Longword	Pointer to base of RMS image

Global Symbol	Data Area	Size	Description of Data
CTL$GL_PPMSG	P1 Pointer Page	2 Longwords	Address of process-permanent message section
CTL$GB_MSGMASK	P1 Pointer Page	Byte	Default message display flags
CTL$GB_DEFLANG	P1 Pointer Page	Byte	Default message language
CTL$GW_PPMSGCHN	P1 Pointer Page	Word	Channel to process-permanent message section
CTL$GL_USERUNDWN	P1 Pointer Page	Longword	Per-process vector to user rundown service
CTL$GL_PCB	P1 Pointer Page	Longword	Address of process control block
CTL$GL_RUF	P1 Pointer Page	Longword	Pointer to recovery unit blocks (unused)
CTL$GL_SITESPEC	P1 Pointer Page	Longword	Site-specific per-process cell
CTL$GL_KNOWNFIL	P1 Pointer Page	Longword	Process known file list pointer
CTL$AL_IPASTVEC	P1 Pointer Page	8 Longwords	Vector for IPAST addresses
CTL$GL_CMCNTX	P1 Pointer Page	Longword	Address of the AME context page
CTL$GL_IAFLNKPTR	P1 Pointer Page	Longword	Address of IAF list (used by the debugger)

A.3.2 Other P1 Space Data Areas

The layout of P1 space is pictured in Chapter 1 and detailed in Chapter 26. Table 26-4 lists the global labels that delimit each area in P1 space. The remainder of this appendix summarizes data locations in specific P1 areas that are defined in module SHELL. The areas are presented in order of decreasing P1 virtual addresses. That is, the CLI data pages are presented first and occupy the highest P1 address range. The process I/O segment occupies the lowest P1 address range of the areas presented here and is listed last.

A.3.2.1 Data Pages for Command Language Interpreter. Module SHELL sets aside an area for the generic CLI data pages.

Global Symbol	Size	Description of Data
CTL$AL_CLICALBK	2 Longwords	Call back vector for CLI
CTL$AG_CLIMAGE	2 Longwords	Virtual address range into which CLI is mapped
CTL$AG_CLIDATA		Rest of CLI data area

A.3.2.2   **Process Allocation Region.** The process allocation area is a per-process pool area constructed exactly like paged and nonpaged dynamic memory. It initially requires two longwords. One longword describes the initial size of the block. The other contains a zero, indicating that there are no other unused blocks in the pool.

Size	Description of Data
Longword	Initial forward link (contains zero)
Longword	Initial size of region

A.3.2.3   **Compatibility Mode Context Page.** Another P1 data area that module SHELL defines symbols for is the page used by the compatibility mode exception service routine.

Global Symbol	Size	Description of Data
CTL$AL_CMCNTX	10 Longwords	General register contents stored by exception service routine
	7 Longwords	Saved R0 through R6
	1 Longword	Saved compatibility mode exception code
	2 Longwords	Saved exception PC and PSL rest of page Used by compatibility mode emulator

A.3.2.4   **Process I/O Segment.** The process I/O segment is used to hold all of the RMS context that exists for the life of the process. This includes all information about process permanent files, as well as pointers into the image I/O segment, the RMS context area that only exists while an image is active. There is a second area in SHELL called the process I/O segment. This portion of P1 space is no longer used.

Global Symbol	Size	Description of Data
PIO$GL_FMLH	2 Longwords	Free memory listhead for process I/O segment
PIO$GL_IIOFSPLH	2 Longwords	Free memory listhead for image I/O segment
PIO$GW_STATUS	Word	RMS overall status
PIO$GT_ENDSTR	16 Bytes	End of data string
PIO$GW_DFPROT	Word	Default file protection
PIO$GB_DFMBC	Byte	Default multiblock count (RMS_DFMBC)

731

Executive Data Areas

Global Symbol	Size	Description of Data
PIO$GB_DFMBFSDK	Byte	Default multibuffer count for sequential disk I/O (RMS_DFMBFSDK)
PIO$GB_DFMBFSMT	Byte	Default multibuffer count for magtape I/O (RMS_DFMBFSMT)
PIO$GB_DFMBFSUR	Byte	Default multibuffer count for unit record devices (RMS_DFMBFSUR)
PIO$GB_DFMBFREL	Byte	Default multibuffer count for relative files (RMS_DFMBFREL)
PIO$GB_DFMBFIDX	Byte	Default multibuffer count for indexed files (RMS_DFMBFIDX)
PIO$GB_DFMBFHSH	Byte	Default multibuffer count hashed (RMS_DFMBFHSH)
PIO$GB_RMSCOMPAT	Byte	Contains values representing current versions of RMS images
PIO$GB_RMSPROLOG	Byte	Structure level for RMS files
PIO$GW_RMSEXTEND	Word	Extend quantity for RMS files
	Byte	Spare for alignment
PIO$GT_DDSTRING	84 Bytes	Default directory string
PIO$GL_DIRCACHE	2 Longwords	Directory cache listhead
PIO$GL_DIRCFRLH	Longword	Free list for directory cache nodes (singly linked)
PIO$GW_PIOIMPA	35 Longwords	Process I/O segment context area
PIO$GW_IIOIMPA	41 Longwords	Image I/O segment context area
PIO$AL_RMSEXH	4 Longwords	RMS termination handler control block
	13 Longwords	Free area that fills rest of page

Appendix B
Data Structure Definitions

This book has described the VMS operating system primarily in terms of the data structures that are used by the various components of the executive. The data structures used by the VMS operating system are defined in a language called MDL (Chapter 31) in one of two groups of files. These files also define most of the symbolic constants mentioned throughout this book.

- Four files contain all structure and constant definitions used internally by the VMS operating system. The location of a particular facility's definitions is determined by the initial letter of the facility name. The file names have the form [SYS.SRC]SYSDEFxx.MDL, where "xx" represent the letters AE, FL, MP, or QZ. The two letters indicate the initial letters of the facilities contained in that file. The resultant macro definitions are stored in the special macro library SYS$LIBRARY:LIB.MLB used to assemble all components of the VMS operating system and are available to users for special applications such as user-written device drivers and system services.
- Four files named [VMSLIB.SRC]STARDEFxx.MDL contain all structure and constant definitions that are available for general applications (such as system service calls). Again, "xx" represents the letters AE, FL, MP, or QZ. The resultant macro definitions are stored in the default macro library SYS$LIBRARY:STARLET.MLB (as well as LIB.MLB).
- Miscellaneous definitions mentioned in this book are defined in other files. In particular, the file [VMSLIB.SRC]SSMSG.MDL defines all symbols of the form SS$_name.

The distinction between the files in SYSDEFxx.MDL and STARDEFxx.MDL is that structures and constants defined in STARDEF, because they are stored in the library STARLET.MLB and are used in conjunction with system services, will probably not change from release to release. Structures and constants defined in SYSDEF (and stored in LIB.MLB) carry no such guarantee, requiring that programs that use such structure definitions must be reassembled and relinked with each major release of the VAX/VMS operating system. The use of LIB.MLB in assembly language source programs (or LIB.L32 in BLISS-32 programs) is in this way analogous to programs linked with SYS$SYSTEM:SYS.STB that must be relinked with each major release of the VAX/VMS operating system.

This appendix summarizes the primary data structures used by the components described in this book. A somewhat arbitrary division of data structures is made in order to keep the size of this appendix manageable. Table B-1 lists all the data structures and constants defined in SYSDEF and STARDEF, showing how this arbitrary division is made. Only the first two classes are described in any detail in this appendix or elsewhere in this book.

Table B-1: Summary of Arbitrary Division of Data Structures in This Appendix

Structures defined by STARDEFxx.MDL				Structures defined by SYSDEFxx.MDL			
System-Wide Data Structures							
ACC	CHF	DMP	PLV	ACB	ARB	BRD	CEB
PSL	SEC	STS		EMB,CRDEF		EMB,HDDEF	
				FKB	GSD	IAF	IFD
				IHA	IHD	IHI	IHP
				IHS	ISD	JIB	KFH
				KFI	KFP	LKB	LOG
				MBX	MCHK	MPM	MTX
				PCB	PFL	PFN	PHD
				PQB	PRM	PTE	PTR
				RBM	RPB	RSB	SHB
				SHD	SHL	TQE	VA
				WQH	WSL		
Symbolic Constants							
IAC	JPI	MSG	PQL	BTD	CA	DYN	IO730
PR	PRT	PRV	SYI	IO750	IO780	IPL	NDT
				PRI	RSN	SGN	STATE
Structures Used by the I/O Subsystem							
CR	DC	DEV	DIB	ADP	AQB	CCB	CDRP
IO	LA	LP	MT	CDDB	CDL	CDT	CIBDT
PCC	TT	TT2	XA	CIBD	CIBHAN	CIFQDT	CRB
XF	XM	XW		DDB	DDT	DPT	IDB
				IRP	IRPE	MBA	MSCP
				PB	PDT	RCT	RDT
				RD	SCS	SCSMSG	SDIR
				TAST	TTY	UBA	UBI
				UCB	VEC		

Table B-1: Summary of Arbitrary Division of Data Structures in This Appendix *(Continued)*

Structures defined by STARDEFxx.MDL			Structures Used by the File System		Structure defined by SYSDEFxx.MDL		
ATR	FIB	FID	MNT	AIB	BBS	CXB	EO1
				EO2	EO3	FCB	HD1
				HD2	HD3	MTL	MVL
				NMB	RVT	RVX	VCA
				VCB	VL1	WCB	

Miscellaneous Data Structures							
ACR	CLI	CLISERV	OPR	ACM	ABD	ACF	CIN
CLIVERB	SMQ	DJI	SQH		EMB,BCDEF	EMB,DVDEF	
SJH	SYM	SMR	USG		EMB,ETDEF	EMB,MCDEF	
SQR		TPA			EMB,SBDEF	EMB,SEDEF	
					EMB,SSDEF	EMB,SUDEF	
					EMB,TSDEF	EMB,UEDEF	
					EMB,UIDEF	EMB,VMDEF	
				ERL	ICP	IHX	IMP
				PBH	PDB	PIB	PMB
				PRQ	RDP	UAF	

The five classes of structures that are listed here are:

- Data structures used by memory management, the scheduler, and miscellaneous components. There is at least one figure or table in this book that describes each of these structures.
- Constants such as condition codes, scheduling state codes, data structure types, and so on.
- Data structures and device-specific constants used by the I/O subsystem, including device drivers.
- Data structures used by the file control processes and related utilities such as MOUNT and INIT.
- Miscellaneous data structures and constants. Some of these are defined in the manuals of the VMS documentation set.

B.1 EXECUTIVE DATA STRUCTURES

This first section mentions each data structure that is described in this book, including a brief summary of the structure and references to a more complete description elsewhere in the book. Three data structures, the software PCB, the process header, and the job information block, are partially described in several places throughout the text. They are described here in their entirety, with references to other partial descriptions.

B.1.1 ACB—AST Control Block

Purpose:	Describes pending AST for a process.
Usual Location:	AST queue with listhead in software PCB.
Allocated from:	Nonpaged pool.
Special Notes:	ACBs are usually a part of a larger structure, an I/O request packet (IRP) or a timer queue element (TQE).

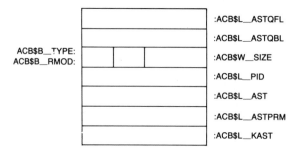

Figure B-1
Layout of an ACB

B.1.2   ACC—Accounting and Termination Message Block

Purpose:	Used to send a termination message to the job controller when a process is deleted. The same message is also sent to the termination mailbox of the creator of the process. The structure is also used in the Send Message to the Accounting Manager system service.
Usual Location:	The termination message resides on the kernel stack.
References:	Table 22-1.

B.1.3   ARB—Access Rights Block

The access rights block currently consists of the privilege mask and UIC located at the end of the software PCB. That is, the ARB is currently a part of the software PCB. The ARP pointer (PCB$L_ARB) currently points to this overlaid data structure. Figure B-24 shows an ARB within a software PCB. Figure B-15 shows that the first four longwords in a JIB can also be considered an ARB. Program references that use the ARB pointer in the software PCB to locate the ARB or any fields within the ARB (such as a privilege mask) will continue to work without modification should the ARB become an independent data structure in a future release of the VAX/VMS operating system.

Purpose:	Defines process access rights and privileges.
Location:	Currently a part of the software PCB.
References:	Table 21-1, Figures B-15 and B-24.

B.1.4   BRD—Broadcast Message Descriptor Block

Purpose:	Contains broadcast message.
Usual Location:	In terminal broadcast list (listhead IOC$GL_BRDCST).
Allocated from:	Nonpaged pool.

B.1.5   CEB—Common Event Block

Purpose:	Contains description and wait queue for common event flag cluster.
Location:	In common event block list (listhead SCH$GQ_CEBHD). (Master CEBs are located in shared memory and pointed to by a field in the slave CEB located in the common event block list on each processor.)
Allocated from:	Nonpaged pool. (Master CEBs are allocated from a CEB table located in shared memory.)

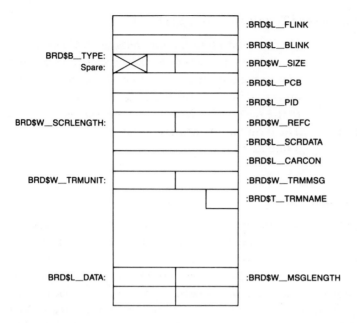

Figure B-2
Layout of a Broadcast Descriptor Block

B.1.6   CHF—Condition Handler Argument List Arrays

Purpose:	Describes condition or exception to condition handler.
Usual Location:	On stack of access mode in which exception or condition occurred.
Special Notes:	The $CHFDEF macro defines offsets into not only the primary argument list but also the signal and mechanism arrays.

B.1.7   DMP—Header Block of System Dump File

Purpose:	Describes contents of dump file.
Location:	First virtual block of SYS$SYSTEM:SYSDUMP.DMP or any other dump file.

B.1.8   EMB—Error Log Message Block

Purpose:	Describes a particular error log entry in one of the error log buffers. There are several different forms of error message. They are all invoked with the $EMBDEF macro with one of several second parameters. For example, invoking the follow-

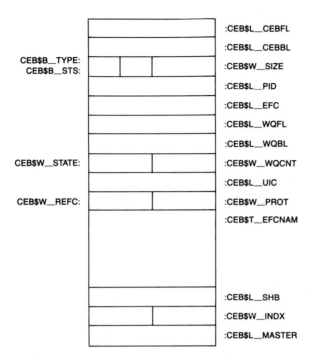

Figure B-3
Layout of a Common Event Block

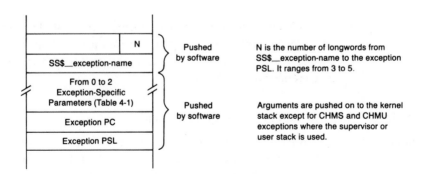

Figure B-4
Layout of a Condition Handler Argument List Array

Data Structure Definitions

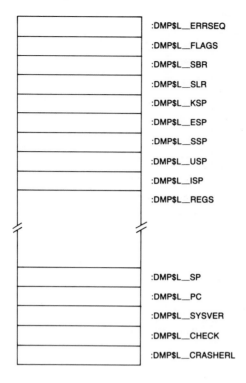

:DMP$L__ERRSEQ

:DMP$L__FLAGS

:DMP$L__SBR

:DMP$L__SLR

:DMP$L__KSP

:DMP$L__ESP

:DMP$L__SSP

:DMP$L__USP

:DMP$L__ISP

:DMP$L__REGS

:DMP$L__SP

:DMP$L__PC

:DMP$L__SYSVER

:DMP$L__CHECK

:DMP$L__CRASHERL

Figure B-5
Layout of a System Dump File Header Block

ing macro (from module ERRORLOG) defines symbols of the form shown following the macro instruction:

```
$EMBDEF<DV,SU,TS,UI>
EMB$x_DV_abc
EMB$x_SU_abc
EMB$x_TS_abc
EMB$x_UI_abc
```

Almost all of the error message formats are related to a specific type of error. Only one type of error message buffer, the crash/restart error message (associated with a fatal bugcheck), is referenced in this book.

B.1.8.1   EMB,CR—Crash/Restart Error Log Entry Format

Purpose: Defines offsets for error log entries associated with fatal bugchecks. (Nonfatal bugchecks result in a slightly different form of entry, designated by BC instead of CR.)

References: Table 8-1.

B.1.8.2   EMB,HD—Longword Header for All Entries

The first longword in all error log entries is a header that defines the rest of the record.

Purpose: Describes the rest of the error log entry.
References: Table 8-1.

B.1.9   FKB—Fork Block

Purpose: Stores minimum context for driver process or system timer subroutine.

Usual Location: First six longwords of device unit control block or timer queue element of system subroutine.

Allocated from: Nonpaged pool (except for statically allocated TQE or UCB).

Special Notes: The one use of a system timer subroutine in VMS is a statically allocated timer queue element.

B.1.10   GSD—Global Section Descriptor

Purpose: Contains identifying information about a global section.

Usual Location: Group or system GSD list. (Shared memory GSDs are located in shared memory.)

Allocated from: Paged pool. (Shared memory GSDs are allocated from pages in shared memory set aside for shared memory GSDs.)

Special Notes: There are three different forms of GSD:

- Normal global section descriptor
- Descriptor for PFN-mapped section
- Descriptor for section that resides in shared memory

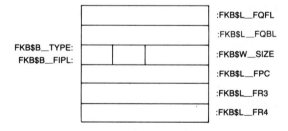

Figure B-6
Layout of a Fork Block

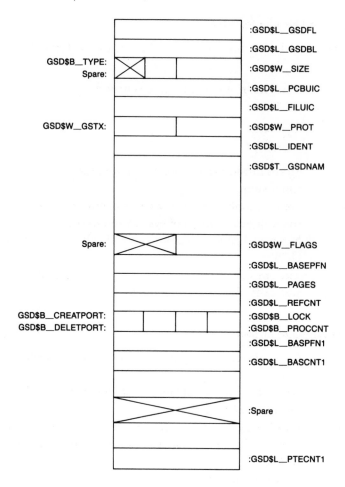

Figure B-7
Layout of a Global Section Descriptor

B.1.11 IAC—Image Activation Control Flags

Purpose: Describes activation options to the Image Activation system service.

Usual Location: Fourth argument in argument list to system service.

References: Section 21.1.1.

B.1.12 IFD—Image File Descriptor Block

Purpose: Returns information about image from image activator to its caller.

Usual Location: In address space of caller of image activator.

References: Section 21.1.1.

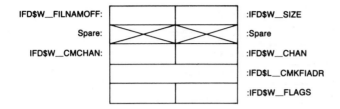

Figure B-8
Layout of an Image File Descriptor

B.1.13   IHx—Image Header Fields

The image header contains several records that fully describe the image. The IHx structures define the fields within each record.

B.1.13.1   IHA—Image Header Transfer Address Array

Purpose: Defines transfer address(es) for image.
References: Figure 21-9.

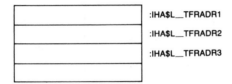

Figure B-9
Layout of an Image Header Transfer Address Array

B.1.13.2   IHD—Image Header Record Definitions. This is the first record in the image header. Among other things, this portion of the image header contains offsets to the other records. The layout of an image header descriptor is shown in Figure B-10.

Purpose: Describes the rest of the image header.

B.1.13.3   IHI—Image Header Identification Section. This section contains such information as the image name and the date and time that the link was performed. The layout of an image header identification section is shown in Figure B-11.

B.1.13.4   IHP—Image Header Patch Section. This section describes the patch level of the image. The layout of an image header patch section is shown in Figure B-12.

B.1.13.5   IHS—Image Header Symbol Table and Debug Section. For executable images that have included DEBUG support, this section locates the debug

Data Structure Definitions

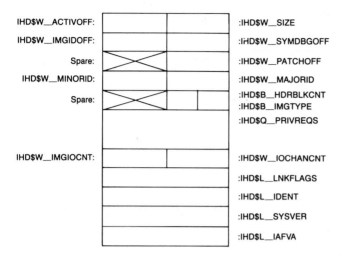

Figure B-10
Layout of an Image Header Descriptor

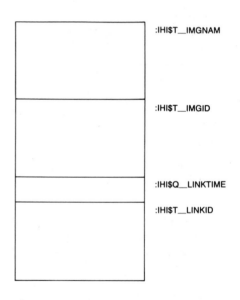

Figure B-11
Layout of an Image Header Identification Section

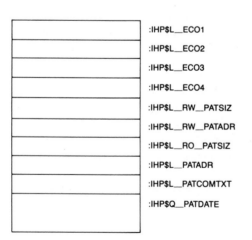

Figure B-12
Layout of an Image Header Patch Section

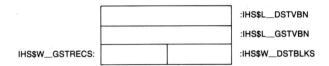

Figure B-13
Layout of an Image Header Symbol Table

symbol table within the image file. For shareable images, this section locates the universal symbol table at the end of the image file.

B.1.14   ISD—Image Section Descriptor

Purpose: Describes virtual address range and corresponding informa-
            tion (virtual block range, global section name) to the image
            activator.

Location: Image header.

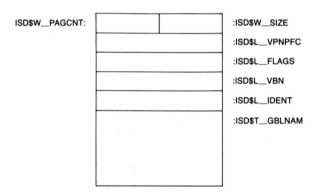

Figure B-14
Layout of an Image Section Descriptor

B.1.15   JIB—Job Information Block

The job information block appears in several figures in this book. Figure B-15 shows all of the fields currently defined in this structure. Some of these fields are not currently used.

Purpose: Contains quotas pooled by all processes in the same
                 job.

Location: Pointed to by PCB$L_JIB field of all PCBs in the same
                 job.

Allocated from: Nonpaged pool.

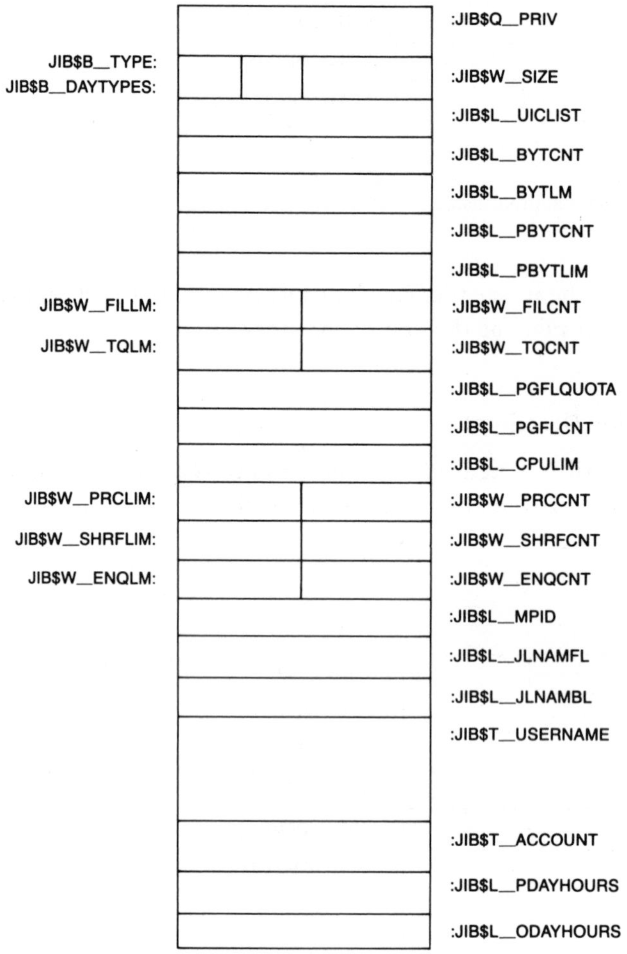

Figure B-15
Detailed Layout of Job Information Block (JIB)

B.1.16 KFH—Known File Header

Purpose: Contains image header for any known image that is installed /HEADER_RESIDENT.

Usual Location: Located through KFI$L_IMGHDR pointer in KFI for that known image.

Allocated from: Paged pool.

B.1.17 KFI—Known File Entry

Purpose: Describes an image that has been made known to the system with the Install Utility.

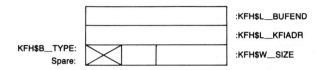

Figure B-16
Layout of a Known File Header

Usual Location:	In one of the known file lists. There is one list for each directory that has images installed from it.
Allocated from:	Paged pool.

B.1.18   KFP—Known File Pointer Block

Purpose:	**Acts as listhead for all KFIs in a given directory.**
Usual Location:	**In known file list (listhead EXE$GL_KNOWNFIL).**
Allocated from:	**Paged pool.**

B.1.19   LKB—Lock Block

Purpose:	Contains information about a lock request to the lock manager.
Allocated from:	Nonpaged pool.

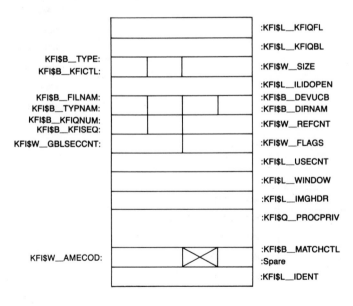

Figure B-17
Layout of a Known File Entry

Data Structure Definitions

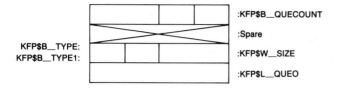

Figure B-18
Layout of a Known File Pointer Block

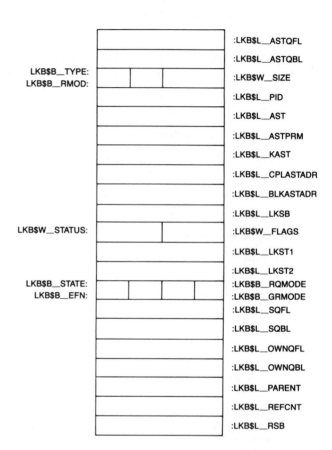

Figure B-19
Layout of a Lock Block

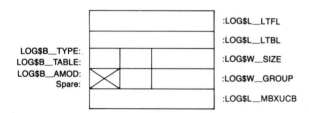

Figure B-20
Layout of a Logical Name Block

748

B.1.20 LOG—Logical Name Block

Purpose: Contains logical and equivalence name strings for a given logical name.

Usual Location: In one of three logical name tables: process, group, or system.

Allocated from: Paged pool for group and system logical names, process allocation region for process logical names.

B.1.21 MBX—Shared Memory Mailbox Control Block

Purpose: Describes each mailbox that exists in shared memory.

Usual Location: Pages in shared memory dedicated to mailbox control blocks.

B.1.22 MCHK—Machine Check Error Mask Bit Definition

Purpose: Describes particular set of machine check errors that a block of kernel mode code wishes to protect itself against.

References: Section 8.3.

B.1.23 MPM—Multiport Memory Adapter Registers

Purpose: Symbolic names for registers that control operation of MA780 multiport memory.

Location: I/O pages set aside for this adapter.

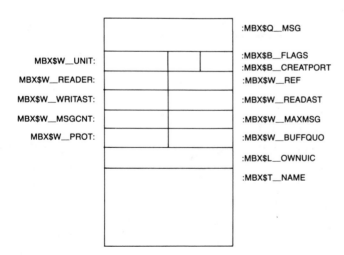

Figure B-21
Layout of a Shared Memory Mailbox Control Block

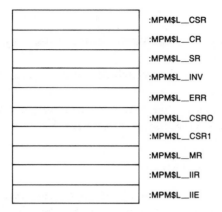

:MPM$L_CSR
:MPM$L_CR
:MPM$L_SR
:MPM$L_INV
:MPM$L_ERR
:MPM$L_CSRO
:MPM$L_CSR1
:MPM$L_MR
:MPM$L_IIR
:MPM$L_IIE

Figure B-22
Layout of Multiport Memory Adapter Registers

B.1.24 MTX—Mutex (Mutual Exclusion Semaphore)

Purpose:	Mutexes control process access to protected data structures.
Usual Location:	Statically allocated longwords in module SYSCOMMON.

31
17 16 15
0
Status
Ownership Count
Write-in-Progress or
Write Pending Flag

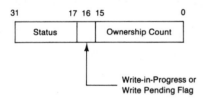

Figure B-23
Layout of a Mutual Exclusion Semaphore

B.1.25 PCB—Process Control Block

The term process control block can refer to two different structures in the VAX literature. All software documentation including this book refers to the software process control block as simply PCB and always prefixes the hardware process control block with the word "hardware."

B.1.25.1 Software Process Control Block. The software PCB appears in several figures in this book. However, each of these figures shows only those fields related to the purpose of the particular figure. The software PCB is illustrated in Figure B-24.

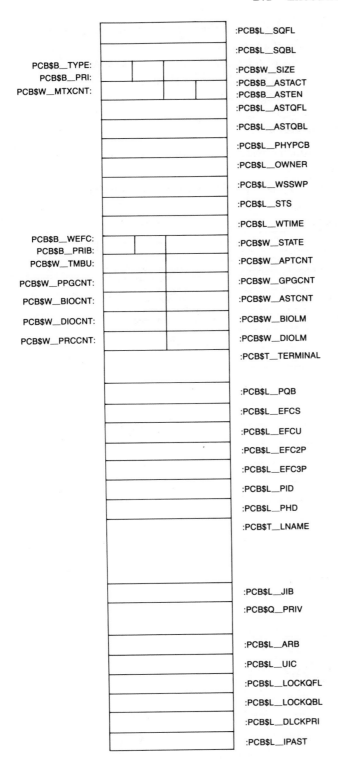

Figure B-24
Detailed Layout of Software Process Control Block

Purpose:	Contains all the permanently resident information about a process.
Location:	One of the scheduling state queues. Also pointed to by one of the PCB vector elements.
Allocated from:	Nonpaged pool.

B.1.25.2 Hardware Process Control Block

Purpose:	Contains hardware context of a process while it is not executing.
Location:	Part of the fixed portion of the process header.

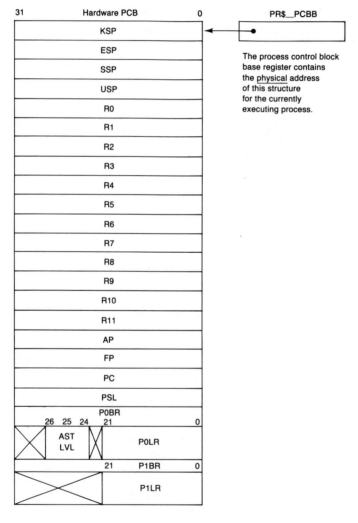

Figure B-25
Layout of the Hardware Process Control Block

752

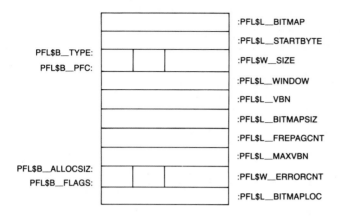

Figure B-26
Layout of the Page File Control Block

B.1.26   PFL—Page File Control Block

Purpose: Contains data needed by pager to read from page file
                      and by modified page to write to page file.

Allocated from: Statically allocated in module SWAPFILE.

B.1.27   PFN—PFN Database Definitions

The $PFNDEF macro defines fields in the STATE, TYPE and BAK array elements.

Purpose: PFN data base describes dynamic physical pages.

Usual Location: Separate area in system address space.

References: Figures 14-9 through 14-13.

B.1.28   PHD—Process Header

The process header contains process-specific memory management data and other process context that can be swapped. Offsets into the fixed portion of the process header are defined with the $PHDDEF macro.

Purpose: The process header contains all process context that
                      must reside in system space but can be outswapped.

Usual Location: Process headers always reside in the balance slot area
                      in system space. Process header pages that are not page
                      table pages are double mapped by a range of P1 space
                      addresses.

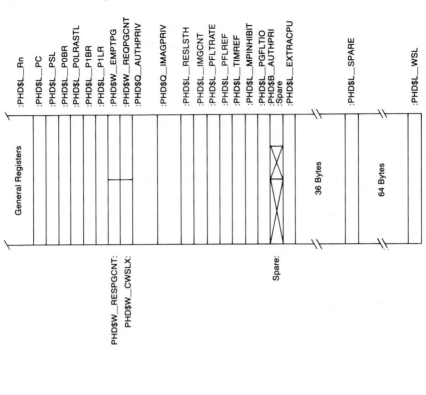

Figure B-27
Layout of the Process Header

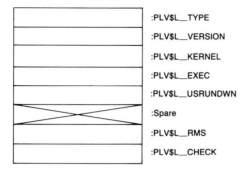

Figure B-28
Layout of a Privileged Library Vector

B.1.29   PLV—Privileged Library Vector

Purpose: Describes privileged shareable image (containing user
                    written system services) to the image activator.
Usual Location: Part of privileged shareable image, usually residing in
                    P0 space.

B.1.30   PQB—Process Quota Block

Purpose: Used during process creation to store new process pa-
                    rameters that belong in the process header and in P1
                    space until those areas are accessible.
Usual Location: Pointed to by longword (PCB$L_EFWM field) in the
                    PCB.
Allocated from: Nonpaged pool.

B.1.31   PRM—Parameter Descriptor Block

Purpose: Used by SYSBOOT and SYSGEN to fully describe each
                    adjustable parameter.
Usual Location: Address space of SYSBOOT or SYSGEN program.

B.1.32   PSL—Processor Status Longword

Purpose: Describes state of processor.
Location: Processor internal register.

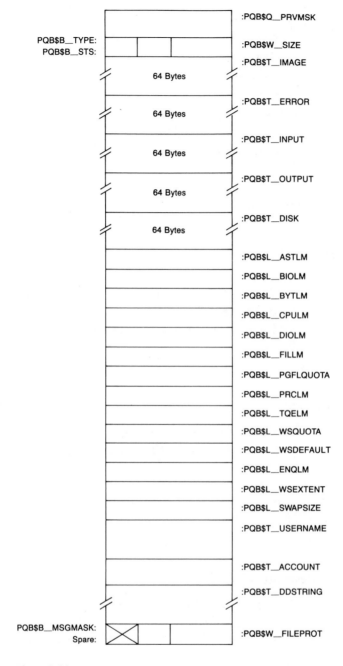

Figure B-29
Layout of a Process Quota Block

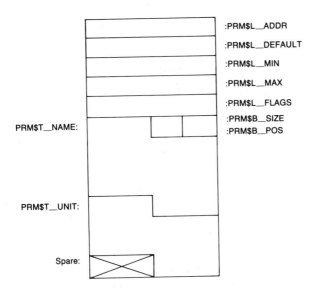

PRM$T__NAME:

:PRM$L__ADDR
:PRM$L__DEFAULT
:PRM$L__MIN
:PRM$L__MAX
:PRM$L__FLAGS
:PRM$B__SIZE
:PRM$B__POS

PRM$T__UNIT:

Spare:

Figure B-30
Layout of a Parameter Descriptor Block

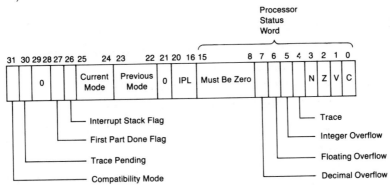

Figure B-31
Layout of the Processor Status Longword

B.1.33 PTE—Page Table Entry Formats

Purpose: Describes state and location of each. virtual page

Usual Location: Process header contains P0 and P1 page tables that describe process address space. The system page table in the system header contains the system page table.

References: The various forms of a PTE are shown in Figure 14-3.

B.1.34 PTR—Pointer Control Block

Purpose: Acts as block header for arbitrary data structure. The VMS operating system uses one to contain the array of

757

Data Structure Definitions

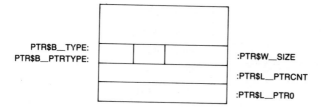

Figure B-32
Layout of a Pointer Control Block

pointers to swap file table entries and page file control blocks. A second is used to contain the array of pointers to each known file list.

Usual Location: At the head of most data structures.

Allocated from: The page file and swap file vector is statically allocated in module SWAPFILE. The known file listhead is allocated from nonpaged pool by SYSINIT.

B.1.35   **RBM—Real-Time Bitmap**

Purpose: Describes available SPTEs for connect-to-interrupt driver.

Usual Location: Pointed to by EXE$GL_RTBITMAP.

Allocated from: Nonpaged pool.

B.1.36   **RPB—Restart Parameter Block**

Purpose: Used by powerfail and recovery routines to save volatile processor state. Used by the bugcheck routines to locate the bootstrap I/O driver and associated subroutines.

Usual Location: Physical page zero on system with no bad memory in the first 64K bytes.

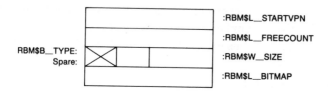

Figure B-33
Layout of a Real-Time Bitmap

758

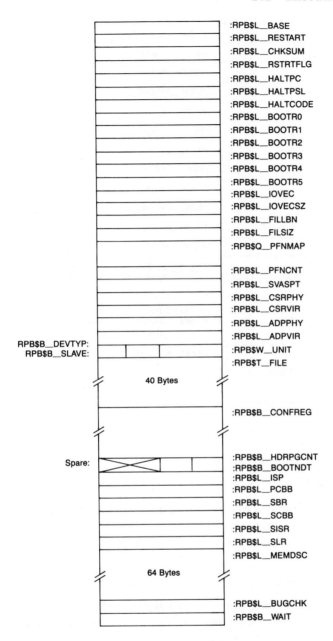

Figure B-34
Layout of the Restart Parameter Block

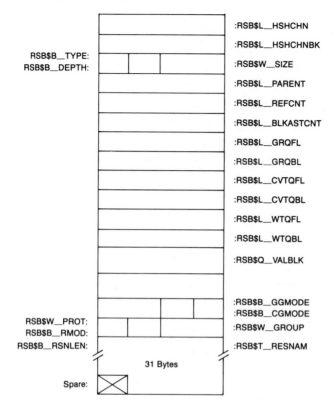

Figure B-35
Layout of a Resource Block

B.1.37 RSB—Resource Block

Purpose: Contains information about a resource locked by the lock manager.

Allocated from: Nonpaged pool.

B.1.38 SEC—Section Table Entry

Purpose: Describes a process, global, or system section.

Usual Location: In process or system header in area allocated for section table entries.

B.1.39 SHB—Shared Memory Control Block

Purpose: Describes shared memory connected to specific processor.

Usual Location: In list of shared memory control blocks (listhead EXE$GL_SHBLIST) in processor local memory.

Allocated from: Nonpaged pool.

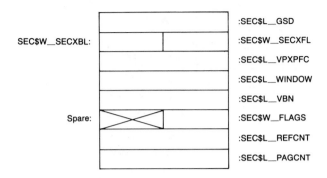

Figure B-36
Layout of a Section Table Entry

B.1.40 SHD—Shared Memory Data Page

Purpose: Initial description of a specific shared memory controller.

Usual Location: Last physical page of shared memory. (Its processor-specific virtual address is stored in the shared memory control block on each port connected to the shared memory.)

B.1.41 STS—Return Status Field Definitions

Purpose: Describes return status from procedure (including system service). Describes condition name to condition handler.

References: The field definitions are found in the *VAX-11 Run-Time Library Reference Manual*.

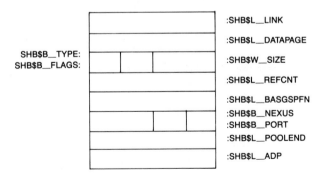

Figure B-37
Layout of a Shared Memory Control Block

Data Structure Definitions

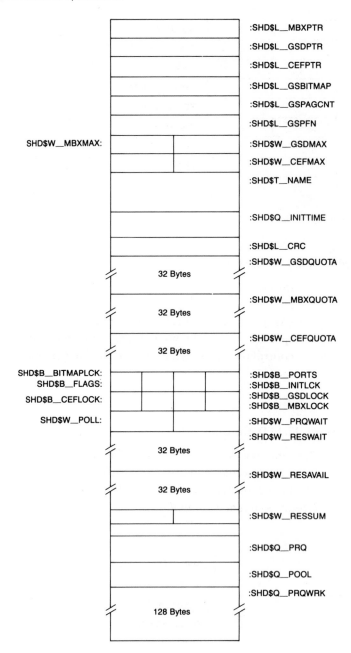

Figure B-38
Layout of a Shared Memory Data Page

762

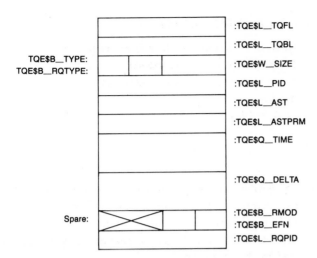

Figure B-39
Layout of a Timer Queue Element

B.1.42   TQE—Timer Queue Element

Purpose: Describes pending timer or scheduled wakeup request.
Location: In timer queue (listhead EXE$GL_TQFL).
Allocated from: Nonpaged pool.

B.1.43   VA—Virtual Address Field Definitions

Purpose: Selects a page table and virtual page number for the address
                      translation mechanism and page fault handler.
References: Figure 15-1.

B.1.44   WQH—Scheduler Wait Queue Header

Purpose: Listhead for all PCBs of processes in given scheduling
                      state.
Usual Location: Statically allocated in module SDAT.

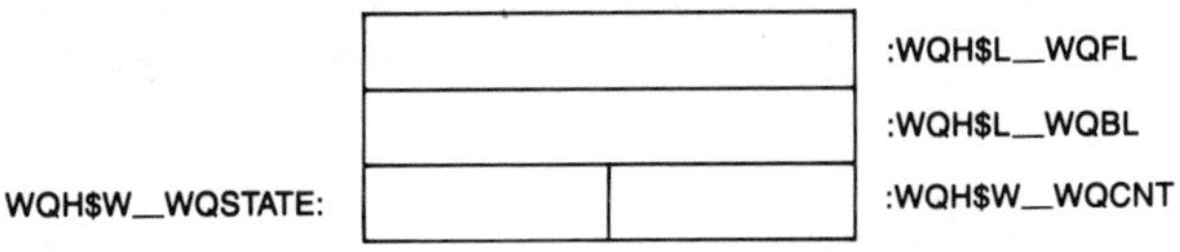

```
                  ┌──────────────────────┐ :WQH$L__WQFL
                  ├──────────────────────┤ :WQH$L__WQBL
WQH$W__WQSTATE:   ├───────────┬──────────┤ :WQH$W__WQCNT
                  └───────────┴──────────┘
```

Figure B-40
Layout of the Scheduler Wait Queue Header

B.1.45   **WSL—Working Set List Entry Field Definitions**

Purpose:	Describes virtual page that is a member of process or system working set.
Usual Location:	In working set list in process or system header.
References:	Figures 14-4 and 14-5.

B.2   **CONSTANTS**

The files SYSDEF and STARDEF define many system-wide symbolic codes that identify structures, resources, quotas, priorities, and so on. Many of these constants are listed in either the *VAX/VMS System Services Reference Manual* or the *VAX/VMS I/O User's Guide*. Those that are most closely tied to the material presented in this book are listed here.

B.2.1   **BTD—Bootstrap Device Codes**

The bootstrap device codes are used to interpret the contents of R0 to VMB, the primary bootstrap program.

```
BTD$K_MB         0    MASSBUS Device
BTD$K_DM         1    RK06RK07
BTD$K_DL         2    RL02
BTD$K_DQ         3    RB02RB80
BTD$K_UDA        17   UDA
BTD$K_HSCCI      32   HSC on CI
BTD$K_CONSOLE    64   Console Block Storage Device
```

The bootstrap device type codes are listed in Table 24-6.

B.2.2   **CA—Conditional Assembly Parameters**

The conditional assembly parameters control whether certain code is included when components of the VMS operating system are assembled. These parameters were important during the initial development of the VMS operating system but are no longer used. All simulator code has been removed. All measurement code (used by the Monitor Utility) is always included.

```
CA$_SIMULATOR      1    VMS System Running on Simulator
CA$_MEASURE        2    Accumulate Statistics for MONITOR
CA$_MEASURE_IOT    4    Count IO Transactions for MONITOR
```

B.2.3   **DYN—Data Structure Type Definitions**

All structures allocated from nonpaged and paged dynamic memory have a unique code in a type field (at offset xyz$B_TYPE = 10). SDA uses the contents of this field when formatting dumps of pool and in automatic formatting of a data structure with the FORMAT command. The results of invoking the $DYNDEF macro are summarized in Table B-2.

Table B-2: Dynamic Data Structure Type Codes

Symbolic Name	Code	Structure Type
DYN$C_ADP	1	Adapter Control Block
DYN$C_ACB	2	AST Control Block
DYN$C_AQB	3	ACP Queue Block
DYN$C_CEB	4	Common Event Block
DYN$C_CRB	5	Channel Request Block
DYN$C_DDB	6	Device Data Block
DYN$C_FCB	7	File Control Block
DYN$C_FRK	8	Fork Block
DYN$C_IDB	9	Interrupt Dispatch Block
DYN$C_IRP	10	I/O Request Packet
DYN$C_LOG	11	Logical Name Block
DYN$C_PCB	12	Software Process Control Block
DYN$C_PQB	13	Process Quota Block
DYN$C_RVT	14	Relative Volume Table
DYN$C_TQE	15	Timer Queue Element
DYN$C_UCB	16	Unit Control Block
DYN$C_VCB	17	Volume Control Block
DYN$C_WCB	18	Window Control Block
DYN$C_BUFIO	19	Buffered I/O Buffer
DYN$C_TYPAHD	20	Terminal Type-Ahead Buffer
DYN$C_GSD	21	Global Section Descriptor
DYN$C_MVL	22	Magnetic Tape Volume List
DYN$C_NET	23	Network Message Block
DYN$C_KFI	24	Known File Entry
DYN$C_MTL	25	Mounted Volume List Entry
DYN$C_BRDCST	26	Broadcast Message Block
DYN$C_CXB	27	Complex Chained Buffer
DYN$C_NDB	28	Network Node Descriptor Block
DYN$C_SSB	29	Logical Link Subchannel Status Block
DYN$C_DPT	30	Driver Prologue Table
DYN$C_JPB	31	Job Parameter Block
DYN$C_PBH	32	Performance Buffer Header
DYN$C_PDB	33	Performance Data Block
DYN$C_PIB	34	Performance Information Block
DYN$C_PFL	35	Page File Control Block
DYN$C_SFT	36	Swap File Table Entry
DYN$C_PTR	37	Pointer Control Block
DYN$C_KFH	38	Known File Image Header
DYN$C_RVX	39	Relative Volume Table Extension
DYN$C_EXTGSD	40	Extended Global Section Descriptor
DYN$C_SHMGSD	41	Shared Memory Global Section Descriptor

Table B-2: Dynamic Data Structure Type Codes *(Continued)*

Symbolic Name	Code	Structure Type
DYN$C_SHB	42	Shared Memory Control Block
DYN$C_MBX	43	Mailbox Control Block
DYN$C_IRPE	44	Extended I/O Request Packet
DYN$C_SLAVCEB	45	Slave Common Event Block
DYN$C_SHMCEB	46	Shared Memory Master Common Event Block
DYN$C_JIB	47	Job Information Block
DYN$C_TWP	48	Terminal Driver Write Packet ($TTYDEF)
DYN$C_RBM	49	Real Time SPT Bitmap
DYN$C_VCA	50	Disk Volume Cache Block
DYN$C_SPECIAL	128	Code That Defines Beginning of Special Codes
DYN$C_SHRBUFIO	128	Shared Memory Buffered I/O Buffer

B.2.4 **IO7xx—I/O Space Address Specifications**

The division of physical address between main memory addresses and I/O space addresses is CPU dependent.

B.2.4.1 **IO730—VAX-11/730 Physical Address Space Definitions.** Physical address space on the VAX-11/730 is defined by a 24-bit address and is partitioned into physical memory addresses (15M bytes, 000000 through EFFFFF) and I/O space addresses (1M Byte, F00000 through FFFFFF).

```
IO730$AL_IOBASE   F20000 (hex)   Start of IO Space
IO730$AL_PERNEX   2000 (hex)     Size of Register Space for
                                 Each Nexus
IO730$AL_NNEX     16 (dec)       Maximum Nexus Number
O$AL_UBOSP        FC000 (hex)    Address of UNIBUS 0
                                 Address Space
```

B.2.4.2 **IO750—VAX-11/750 Physical Address Space Definitions.** Physical address space on the VAX-11/750 is defined by a 24-bit address and is evenly divided between main memory (Phys.Addr.<23> = 0) and I/O space addresses (Phys.Addr.<23> = 1). Ten of the sixteen slot positions are fixed. Thus it is possible to identify the address space for UBI0 registers and MASSBUS 0 registers.

```
IO750$AL_IOBASE   F20000 (hex)   Base Address of Register
                                 Space for Slot 16
O$AL_MBBASE       F28000 (hex)   Base Address of Register
                                 Space for MASSBUS 0
IO750$AL_UBBASE   F30000 (hex)   Base Address of Register
                                 Space for UNIBUS 0
IO750$AL_NNEX     16 (dec)       Number of Adapters (Nexus)
IO750$AL_PERNEX   2000 (hex)     Size of Register Space for
                                 Each Nexus
IO750$AL_UBOSP    FC0000 (hex)   Base Address of UNIBUS 0
                                 Address Space
```

Adapter assignments for the first ten slots are fixed. The following constants describe these assignments:

```
IO750$C_SL_MEM0    0    Memory Controller
IO750$C_SL_MPM0    1    Multiport Memory 0
IO750$C_SL_MPM1    2    Multiport Memory 1
IO750$C_SL_MPM2    3    Multiport Memory 2
IO750$C_SL_MB0     4    MASSBUS 0
IO750$C_SL_MB1     5    MASSBUS 1
IO750$C_SL_MB2     6    MASSBUS 2
IO750$C_SL_MB3     7    MASSBUS 3
IO750$C_SL_UB0     8    UNIBUS 0
IO750$C_SL_UB1     9    UNIBUS 1
```

B.2.4.3 **IO780—VAX-11/780 Physical Address Space Definitions.** Physical address space on the VAX-11/780 is defined by a 30-bit address and is evenly divided between main memory (Phys.Addr.$<29>$ = 0) and I/O space addresses (Phys.Addr.$<29>$ = 1).

```
IO780$AL_IOBASE    20000000 (hex)    Base Address of Register
                                     Space for TR 0
IO780$AL_NNEX            16 (dec)    Number of Adapters (Nexus)
IO780$AL_PERNEX       2000 (hex)    Size of Register Space for
                                     Each Nexus
IO780$AL_UB0SP     20100000 (hex)    Base Address of UNIBUS 0
                                     Address Space
```

B.2.5 **IPL—Processor Priority Level Definitions**

IPL levels that are used for synchronization and other purposes by the VMS operating system are given symbolic names.

```
IPL$_ASTDEL     2    AST Delivery Interrupt
IPL$_SCHED      3    Rescheduling Interrupt
IPL$_IOPOST     4    IO Postprocessing Interrupt
IPL$_QUEUEAST   6    Fork Level Used for AST Queuing
IPL$_SYNCH      7    System-Wide Synchronization Level
IPL$_TIMER      7    Software Timer Interrupt
IPL$_SCS        8    SCS Synchronization Level
IPL$_MAILBOX   11    Fork IPL for Mailbox Driver
IPL$_HWCLK     24    Hardware Clock Interrupt
IPL$_POWER     31    Block Powerfail Interrupt
```

A powerfail interrupt causes IPL to be raised to 30, not 31. Raising IPL to 31 blocks all interrupts and serious conditions until IPL is lowered.

The IPL values used for synchronization are listed in Table 2-1. Those values that correspond to software interrupt IPL values are also listed in Table 6-1.

B.2.6 **JPI—$GETJPI Data Identifier Definitions**

The $JPIDEF macro is used in argument lists to the $GETJPI system service to identify those data elements that are being requested. The symbolic names defined by this macro are listed in Part II of the *VAX/VMS System Services Reference Manual.*

B.2.7 MSG—System-Wide Mailbox Message Types

The $MSGDEF macro defines codes to identify mailbox messages. The symbolic names defined by this macro are listed in the *VAX/VMS System Services Reference Manual.*

B.2.8 NDT—Nexus (Adapter) Device Type

Each external adapter has an associated code that is used by VMB, INIT, and the power recovery routine to determine which adapter-specific action should be taken to (re)initialize each adapter.

```
NDT$_MEM4NI        8    4K Memory - Not Interleaved
NDT$_MEM4I         9    4K Memory - Interleaved
NDT$_MEM16NI      16    16K Memory - Not Interleaved
NDT$_MEM16I       17    16K Memory - Interleaved
NDT$_MB           32    MASSBUS
NDT$_UB0          40    UNIBUS 0
NDT$_UB1          41    UNIBUS 1
NDT$_UB2          42    UNIBUS 2
NDT$_UB3          43    UNIBUS 3
NDT$_DR32         48    DR32
NDT$_CI           56    CI
NDT$_MPM0         64    Multiport Memory 0
NDT$_MPM1         65    Multiport Memory 1
NDT$_MPM2         66    Multiport Memory 2
NDT$_MPM3         67    Multiport Memory 3
NDT$_MEM64NIL    104    64K Memory, Not Interleaved,
                        Lower Controller
NDT$_MEM64EIL    105    64K Memory, Externally Interleaved,
                        Lower Controller
NDT$_MEM64NIU    106    64K Memory, Not Interleaved,
                        Upper Controller
NDT$_MEM64EIU    107    64K Memory, Externally Interleaved,
                        Upper Controller
NDT$_MEM64I      108    64K Memory, Internally Interleaved
```

B.2.9 PQL—Process Quota List Codes

The $PQLDEF macro defines symbolic codes that are passed to the Create Process system service. These symbols are listed in Part II of the *VAX/VMS System Services Reference Manual.*

B.2.10 PR—Processor Register Definitions

The $PRDEF macro defines symbolic names for the processor internal registers. Some of these registers are defined as part of the VAX architecture and are found in all processors. Others are specific to a single CPU. The internal processor registers are listed the *VAX/VMS System Services Reference Manual*. Processor registers are described in the *VAX Hardware Handbook*.

B.2.11   PRI—Priority Increment Class Definitions

The $PRIDEF macro defines the priority increment classes. These constants are typically loaded into R2 before SCH$CHSE or SCH$CHSEP is called to make a process computable.

```
PRI$_NULL      0    No Priority Boost
PRI$_IOCOM     1    IO Completion
PRI$_RESAVL    2    Resource Available
PRI$_TIMER     2    Timer Request Complete
PRI$_TOCOM     3    Terminal Output Completion
PRI$_TICOM     4    Terminal Output Completion
```

Table 10-3 shows the correspondence between increment classes and the actual boosts.

B.2.12   PRT—Protection Field Definitions

The $PRTDEF macro defines the different contents of the protection field in a page table entry. (The $PTEDEF macro defines similar constants, except that the PRT$C_xxx symbols are values in the range from 0 to 15 while the PTE$C_xxx symbols have shifted these values into bit positions<30:27>.)

```
PRT$C_NA          0    No Access
PRT$C_RESERVED    1    Reserved
PRT$C_KW          2    Kernel Write
PRT$C_KR          3    Kernel Read
PRT$C_UW          4    User Write
PRT$C_EW          5    Executive Write
PRT$C_ERKW        6    Executive Read, Kernel Write
PRT$C_ER          7    Executive Read
PRT$C_SW          8    Supervisor Write
PRT$C_SREW        9    Supervisor Read, Executive Write
PRT$C_SRKW        10   Supervisor Read, Kernel Write
PRT$C_SR          11   Supervisor Read
PRT$C_URSW        12   User Read, Supervisor Write
PRT$C_UREW        13   User Read, Executive Write
PRT$C_URKW        14   User Read, Kernel Write
PRT$C_UR          15   User Read
```

B.2.13   PRV—Privilege Bit Definitions

The $PRVDEF macro defines symbolic names for all recognized VMS privileges. The symbolic names produced by this macro are described in Part II of the *VAX/VMS System Services Reference Manual*.

B.2.14   RSN—Resource Name Definitions

The $RSNDEF macro defines constants that indicate the particular resource a process is waiting for when it is in the MWAIT state. The resource number is stored in the PCB$L_EFWM field in the PCB.

```
RSN$_ASTWAIT     1    Wait for Delivery of an AST
RSN$_MAILBOX     2    Wait for Mailbox Space
RSN$_NPDYNMEM    3    Wait for Nonpaged Pool Space
RSN$_PGFILE      4    Wait for Space in the Page File
RSN$_PGDYNMEM    5    Wait for Paged Pool Space
RSN$_BRKTHRU     6    Terminal Broadcast
RSN$_IACLOCK     7    Image Activation Interlock
RSN$_JQUOTA      8    Job Pooled Quota
RSN$_LOCKID      9    Lock IDs
RSN$_SWPFILE     10   Swapping File Space
RSN$_MPLEMPTY    11   Modified Page List Empty
RSN$_MPWBUSY     12   Modified Page Writer Busy
RSN$_MAX         13   Maximum Resource Number
```

B.2.15   SGN—SYSGEN Parameter Constant Definitions

The $SGNDEF macro is used to define defaults values for SYSGEN.

```
SGN$C_BALSETCNT    24      Number of Processes in Balance Set
SGN$C_DFWSCNT      100     Default Working Set Count
SGN$C_DFWSQUOTA    120     Default Working Set Quota
SGN$C_GBLSECCNT    40      Global Section Count
SGN$C_MAXGPGCNT    2048    Global Page Count
SGN$C_MAXPAGCNT    16384   Physical Memory Size in Pages
SGN$C_MAXPGFL      4096    Default Maximum Paging File
SGN$C_MAXPSTCNT    5       Maximum Number of PST Entries
SGN$C_MAXVPGCNT    8192    Maximum Process Virtual Size (Pages)
SGN$C_MAXWSCNT     1024    Maximum Working Set Size (Pages)
SGN$C_MINWSCNT     10      Minimum Working Set Size (Pages)
SGN$C_NPAGEDYN     26624   Nonpaged Dynamic Pool Size
SGN$C_NPROCS       64      Maximum Number of Processes
SGN$C_PAGEDYN      16384   Paged Dynamic Pool Size (Bytes)
SGN$C_PHYPAGCNT    4096    Actual Physical Page Count
SGN$C_SYSDWSCNT    40      Default System Working Set Count
SGN$C_SYSVECPGS    4       Number of Pages of System
                           Service Vectors
SGN$C_SYSWSCNT     96      System Working Set Count
```

B.2.16   SS—System Service Completion Codes

The $SSDEF macro defines all system wide status codes. The *VAX/VMS System Services Reference Manual* lists the symbolic names of all SS$_name symbols. (These symbols are defined in a separate file called [VMSLIB.SRC]SSMSG.MDL.)

B.2.17   STATE—Scheduling States

The $STATEDEF macro defines symbolic names for all scheduling states. Note that the prefix for each of the symbols is SCH$C_ and not STATE$C_.

```
SCH$C_COLPG    1    Collided Page Wait
SCH$C_MWAIT    2    Miscellaneous Wait
                    (Resource Wait)
                    (Mutex Wait)
SCH$C_CEF      3    Common Event Flag Wait
SCH$C_PFW      4    Page Fault Wait
SCH$C_LEF      5    Local Event Flag Wait (Resident)
SCH$C_LEFO     6    Local Event Flag Wait (Outswapped)
SCH$C_HIB      7    Hibernating (Resident)
SCH$C_HIBO     8    Hibernating (Outswapped)
SCH$C_SUSP     9    Suspended (Resident)
SCH$C_SUSPO   10    Suspended (Outswapped)
SCH$C_FPG     11    Free Page Wait
SCH$C_COM     12    Computable (and Resident)
SCH$C_COMO    13    Computable (Outswapped)
SCH$C_CUR     14    Current Process
```

B.3   DATA STRUCTURES USED BY THE I/O SUBSYSTEM

There are two classes of symbolic definitions used by the I/O subsystem. Data structures used by device drivers are pictured the *VAX/VMS Guide to Writing a Device Driver* ("Device Drivers" in the tables following). Symbolic definitions specific to each device class are listed in the appropriate chapters of the *VAX/VMS I/O User's Guide* ("I/O User's Guide" in the tables following). The I/O function codes and device information block are also described in the *VAX/VMS System Services Reference Manual* ("System Services" in the tables following). The SCS and CI related data structures can be obtained by looking at the microfiche listings.

B.3.1   I/O Data Structures Defined in SYSDEF

The following data structures are defined in SYSDEF and stored in LIB.MLB.

Structure Name	Acronym	Described in
Adapter Control Block	ADP	Device Drivers
ACP Queue Block	AQB	
Channel Control Block	CCB	Device Drivers
Class Driver Request Packet	CDRP	Table 19-2
Class Driver Data Block	CDDB	
SCS Connection Descriptor List	CDL	
SCS Connection Descriptor Table	CDT	
CI Buffer Descriptor Table	CIBDT	
CI Buffer Descriptor Format	CIBD	
CI Buffer Handle Format	CIBHAN	

Data Structure Definitions

Structure Name	Acronym	Described in
CI Free Message/Datagram Queue Descriptor Table	CIFQDT	
Channel (Controller) Request Block	CRB	Device Drivers
Device Data Block	DDB	Device Drivers
Driver Dispatch Table	DDT	Device Drivers
Driver Prolog Table	DPT	Device Drivers
Interrupt Dispatch Block	IDB	Device Drivers
I/O Request Packet	IRP	Device Drivers
I/O Request Packet Extension	IRPE	Device Drivers
MASSBUS Adapter Register Offsets	MBA	Device Drivers
Mass Storage Control Protocols	MSCP	
SCS Path Block	PB	
Port Descriptor Table	PDT	
MSCP Replacement and Caching Table	RCT	
SCS Response Descriptor Table	RDT	
SCS Response Descriptor Format	RD	
SCS Message Definitions	SCS	
SCS Connection Management Message Format	SCSCMG	
SCS Directory Entry	SDIR	
Terminal AST Packet	TAST	
Terminal Driver Write Request Block	TTY	
UNIBUS Adapter Register Offsets	UBA	Device Drivers
UNIBUS Interconnect Register Offsets	UBI	Device Drivers
Unit Control Block	UCB	Device Drivers
CRB Interrupt Transfer Vector Structure	VEC	Device Drivers

B.3.2   I/O Data Structures Defined in STARDEF

The following data structures are defined in STARDEF and stored in both STARLET.MLB and LIB.MLB:

Structure Name	Acronym	Described in
Card Reader Status Bits	CR	I/O User's Guide
Device Adapter, Type, and Class Definitions	DC	I/O User's Guide
Device Characteristics	DEV	I/O User's Guide
Device Information Block	DIB	I/O User's Guide System Services
I/O Function Code Definitions	IO	I/O User's Guide, System Services
LPA-11 Characteristics	LA	I/O User's Guide
Line Printer Characteristics	LP	I/O User's Guide
Magtape Status Bits	MT	I/O User's Guide
Printer/Terminal Carriage Control Specifiers	PCC	
Special Symbols for Terminal Driver	TT	I/O User's Guide
Additional Terminal Driver Symbols	TT2	I/O User's Guide

Structure Name	Acronym	Described in
DR11-W Device Characteristics	XA	I/O User's Guide
DR32 Command Table and Packet Definitions	XF	I/O User's Guide
DMC-11 Status and Characteristics	XM	I/O User's Guide
Software DDCMP Definitions	XW	

B.4   DATA STRUCTURES USED BY FILES-11

The data structures used by the file ACPs and associated utilities such as INIT and MOUNT are outside the scope of this book and are listed here for completeness. Any incidental references are indicated. The ANSI magnetic tape labels are pictured in the *VAX-11 Record Management Services Reference Manual* ("RMS Reference"). The attribute list descriptor (ATR) and file identification block (FIB) are described in the *VAX/VMS I/O User's Guide*.

B.4.1   File System Data Structures Defined in SYSDEF

The following data structures are defined in SYSDEF and stored in LIB.MLB.

Structure Name	Acronym	Described in
ACP I/O Buffer Packet	AIB	
ACP Message to Bad Block Scan	BBS	
Complex Chained Buffer	CXB	
EOF1 ANSI Magnetic Tape Label	EO1	RMS Reference
EOF2 ANSI Magnetic Tape Label	EO2	RMS Reference
EOF3 ANSI Magnetic Tape Label	EO3	RMS Reference
File Control Block	FCB	
HDR1 ANSI Magnetic Tape Label	HD1	RMS Reference
HDR2 ANSI Magnetic Tape Label	HD2	RMS Reference
HDR3 ANSI Magnetic Tape Label	HD3	RMS Reference
Mounted Volume List Entry	MTL	
Magnetic Tape Volume List	MVL	
File Name Block	NMB	
Relative Volume Table	RVT	
Relative Volume Table Extension	RVX	
Volume Cache Block	VCA	
Volume Control Block	VCB	
VOL1 ANSI Magnetic Tape Label	VL1	RMS Reference
Window Control Block	WCB	

B.4.2   File System Data Structures Defined in STARDEF

The following data structures are defined in STARDEF and stored in both STARLET.MLB and LIB.MLB:

Structure Name	Acronym	Described in
Attribute List Description	ATR	I/O User's Guide
File Identification Block	FIB	I/O User's Guide
File Identification	FID	
Flag Bits for the $MOUNT System Service		System Services

B.5   MISCELLANEOUS DATA STRUCTURES AND CONSTANTS

This section lists the data structures and constants that are defined in SYSDEF.MDL or STARDEF.MDL but are not mentioned in this book. A description of any of these structures can be obtained by looking at the microfiche listing of the file in which the structure is defined. Very few of these structures are described elsewhere in the documentation set. The connect-to-interrupt facility is described in the *VAX/VMS Real-Time User's Guide* ("Real-Time" in the table following). Some of the symbiont manager request codes are listed in the *VAX/VMS System Services Reference Manual*. The TPARSE control block is pictured in the *VAX-11 Run-Time Library Reference Manual* ("RTL Reference" in the table following). The accounting record structure is shown in the *VAX-11 Utilities Reference Manual* ("Utilities" in the table following).

B.5.1   Miscellaneous Data Structures Defined in SYSDEF

The following data structures are defined in SYSDEF and stored in LIB.MLB:

Structure Name	Acronym	Described in
Generalized Name String Descriptor	ABD	
Configuration Control Block	ACF	
Accounting Manager Definitions	ACM	Utilities
Connect-to-Interrupt Definitions	CIN	Real-Time
Error Log Allocation Buffer Header	ERL	
Change Image Section Protection	ICP	
Cross Linker Image Header Format	IHX	
RMS Impure Area Offset Definitions	IMP	
Performance Buffer Header	PBH	
Device Performance Data Block	PDB	
Performance I/O Information Block	PIB	
Interprocessor Request Block Definitions	PRQ	
Remote Device Protocol Definitions	RDP	
User Authorization File Record Format	UAF	

B.5.2   Miscellaneous Data Structures Defined in STARDEF

The following data structures are defined in STARDEF and stored in both STARLET.MLB and LIB.MLB:

Structure Name	Acronym	Described in
Command Language Interface Definition	CLI	
CLI Service Request Codes	CLISERV	
Generic Codes for Command Verbs	CLIVERB	
Detached Job Initiate Message	DJI	
Operator Communication Message Types	OPR	
Symbiont Manager Job Record Header	SJH	
Symbiont Manager Queue Header	SMQ	
Symbiont Manager Request Codes	SMR	System Services
Symbiont Queue Header Record	SQH	
Symbiont Manager Queue Record	SQR	
Symbiont Queue Record Envelope Structure	SYM	
TPARSE Control Block	TPA	RTL Reference
Disk Usage Accounting File	USG	

B.5.3 Error Log Message Buffers Defined in SYSDEF

The error log message buffers are defined in SYSDEF and are stored in LIB.MLB. The $EMBDEF macro, with one of fourteen different parameters, defines the various error message buffers used by the error logger. The buffer header and the error log entry for system crashes are described in Table 8-1. They are included in this list for completeness.

Structure Name	Acronym
Buffer Header	EMB,HDDEF
Entry Type Definitions	EMB,ETDEF
Nonfatal Bugcheck Error	EMB,BCDEF
Crash/Restart Error (Fatal Bugcheck)	EMB,CRDEF
Device Error	EMB,DVDEF
Machine Check Log	EMB,MCDEF
SBI Faults and Asynchronous Write Errors	EMB,SBDEF
Soft ECC Errors and SBI Alert	EMB,SEDEF
System Service Messages	EMB,SSDEF
System Startup Message	EMB,SUDEF
Time Stamp Message	EMB,TSDEF
UNIBUS Error Summary	EMB,UEDEF
UNIBUS Adapter Undefined Interrupt	EMB,UIDEF
Volume Mount/Dismount Message	EMB,VMDEF

Index

$ADJSTK system service, 344
$ALLOC system service, 396
$ASCTIM system service, 643
$ASSIGN system service, 393, 394
$BINTIM system service, 643
$BRDCST system service, 408
$CANCEL system service, 402
$CANTIM system service, 222
$CANWAK system service, 222
$CMEXEC system service, 179
$CMKRNL system service, 179
$CNTREG system service, 345
$CRELOG system service, 630
$CREMBX system service, 402
$CREPRC system service, 443
$CRMPSC system service 346
    in shared memory, 304
$DALLOC system service, 396
$DASSGN system service, 393
$DCLCMH system service, 165
$DELLOG system service, 631
$DELMBX system service, 407
$DELPRC system service 492
    operation, 492
$DELTVA system service, 345
$DEQ system service
    operations, 254, 255
$DERLMB system service, 150
$ENQ system service
    operations, 250
$EXIT system service 234, 482
    operation of, 482, 483
$EXPREG system service, 342
$FAO system service, 643
$GETDVI system service, 411
$GETJPI system service 639
    operation of, 639
    special kernel mode ASTs, 139
    wildcard support, 641
$GETMSG system service, 635
$GETSYI system service, 642
$IMGSTA system service 481
    operations of, 481
$LCKPAG system service, 358
$LKWSET system service, 357
$NUMTIM system service, 642, 643
$PURGWS system service, 357
$PUTMSG system service 637
    operation of, 637
$QIO system service
    description of, 397, 398
$SCHDWK system service 222
    operation, 220
$SETIME system service, 215
$SETIMR system service
    operation of, 222
$SETPRA system service, 604

$SETPRT system service, 359
$SETPRV system service, 490
$SETRWM system service, 195
$SETSFM system service, 178, 179
$SETSSF system service, 179
$SETSWM system service, 359
$SNDACC system service, 632
$SNDERR system service, 634
$SNDOPR system service 634
    operation of, 634
$SNDSMB system service, 633
$STRUCT (MDL directive), 663
$TRNLOG system service, 631
$ULKPAG system service, 358, 359
$ULWSET system service, 358, 359
$UPDSEC system service, 338
$WAITFR system service, 228
$WFLAND system service, 228
$WFLOR system service, 228

Abnormal image termination, 514
Abort
    type of exception, 68
ACB (AST control block)
    contents of, 127
    creation of, 129
    in image rundown, 487
    layout of, 736
ACC (Accounting message block)
    layout of, 737
Access mode
    and ASTs, 130
    transitions on VAX-11/782, 620
    used with ASTs, 127
Access rights block, 446, 737
Accounting
    of process deletion, 495
Accounting manager
    communication with, 632
Accounting message block, 737
ACP (Ancillary control process)
    intervention, 419
    introduction to, 8
    necessary functions in bootstrap, 542
    system disk initialization, 564
Adapter
    device types, 768
Adapter configuration, 104
Addressing mode
    unusual usage, 651
.ADDRESS (Macro directive)
    address relocation fixups, 477, 478
Address space
    control region, 26
    creation of, 342
    deletion of, 344

Address space *(continued)*
   introduction to, 24
   program region, 26
   virtual, 5
Adjust Stack system service, 344
Algorithms
   for logical name hashing, 628
Allocate Device system service, 396
Allocation
   device, 396
   of lookaside lists, 50
   of virtual memory, 346
ALLOCPFN (PFN list manipulation routines)
   data areas described by, 687
Altering page protection, 359
Alternate page and swap files, 295, 299
AME (Applications migration executive)
   activation of, 476
Applications migration executive, 476
ARB (Access rights block)
   description of, 446
   layout of, 737
Architecture
   of the VAX family, 13
Arithmetic exceptions, 72
ASCII time strings, 643
Assigning channels, 393
Assign I/O Channel system service, 393, 394
Assignment
   of local device, 394
ASSUME (macro), 647
AST level processor register, 127
ASTs (Asynchronous system traps)
   access mode and queuing, 130
   accounting, 223
   attention, 140, 143
   delivering, 126
   delivery interrupts, 125, 133
   delivery mechanism, 133
   exit path, 136
   interrupts, 117
   lock manager, 253
   out-of-band, 143, 146
   piggyback, 130
   power recovery, 604
   process deletion, 492, 493
   queuing, 127
   special kernel mode, 130, 136, 137
   spurious, 133
   unwinding, 92
   and wait states, 198
ATTACH (DCL command)
   operation of, 507
Attached processor (VAX-11/782)
   description of, 609
   executing jobs, 618
   initialization of, 613
   preventing scheduling on, 618
Attention ASTs 140
   delivery of, 141
   examples of, 142
   flushing list, 142
   terminal driver, 142, 143
AUTOCONFIGURE (SYSGEN command)
   in STARTUP, 565
Automatic working set adjustment 354
   at quantum end, 190

Backing store address 280
   modified pages, 334
Bad blocks
   in disks, 416
Bad page list
   links in, 283, 284
BAK array
   in PFN database, 280
Balance slots 292
   arrays, 293
   size of, 294, 584
Base time values, 215
Batch jobs, 499
Battery backup, 214
BBSS instruction, 651
Bit fields
   in MDL, 665, 666, 670
Black hole page
   allocation of, 557
BLINK array
   in PFN database, 283, 284
Blocking AST
   lock manager, 253
BOOT58
   VAX-11/750 bootstrap, 527, 528
Bootblock program
   VAX-11/750, 527
Bootstrap 521, 99
   conversational, 546
   device codes, 764
   device driver, 542
   file operations, 542
   I/O, 542
   processor-specific, 521
   of VAX-11/782, 614
Bootstrap programs
   primary, 530
   secondary, 542
BORROWLIM (SYSBOOT parameter) 275
   in automatic working set size adjustment,
      356
BRD (Broadcast descriptor block)
   description of, 408
   layout of, 737
Broadcast descriptor block, 408
Broadcast system service, 408
Buffered I/O, 401
Buffer pages
   double mapping, 439
BUG_CHECK (macro), 150
Bugchecks 150
   information data areas, 684, 685, 99
   mechanism for, 150
   operation of, 151
BUGCHECK (Software bugcheck routines)
   data areas described by, 685

Call frame
   change mode services, 166
   condition handlers, 79
Call stack
   unwinding, 84
Cancel I/O on Channel system service, 402
Cancel Timer system service, 222
Cancel Wakeup system service, 222

Card reader
  unsolicited input to start batch job, 502
Catch-all condition handler 79, 95
  operations of, 462
  in process creation, 461
Cathedral windows
  definition of, 417
  description of, 297
CCB (Channel control block)
  in device assignment, 393, 394
CEB (Common event block)
  description of, 197
  layout of, 737
  master and slave, 240, 307
CEF wait state, 197
Change mode
  condition handling, 65
  dispatching, 165, 166
  to executive dispatcher, 168
  to executive vectors, 163
  handlers, 165
  instructions, 164, 165
  to kernel dispatcher, 168
  to kernel vectors, 163
Channel control block, 393, 394
Channel deassignment
  in image rundown, 487
Channels
  assigning and deassigning, 393
  to terminals, 428
CHME instruction, 165
CHMK instruction, 165
CI (Computer interconnect)
  DECnet communications, 420
  port driver (PADRIVER), 421
Class drivers 420
  I/O processing, 422
  terminal, 422
CLIs (Command language interpreters)
  condition handlers, 97
  data pages, 730
  and image execution, 508
  initialization of, 509
  mapping at process creation, 504
  user-written, 179
Clocks
  hardware, 212
  interval, 212
  powerfail, 215
  software, 214, 215
Clustered reads, 329
Cluster size
  page read maximum, 332
C (MDL directive), 665
CMI (Computer to memory interconnect),
  102
CMODSSDSP (Change mode dispatcher), 168
CNDRIVER (DECnet class driver), 420
Coding techniques
  instruction speed, 649
  register conventions, 654
COLPG wait state 193
  and pager, 340
Command file
  site-specific startup, 565
Common event flags 197, 225, 226
  affecting computability, 231

clusters, 240
clusters in shared memory, 307
permanent, 227
Common event flag wait state, 197
Communication
  interprocess, 225, 235
  using global sections, 239
  using MA780, 239
COMO scheduling state, 191
Compatibility mode
  context page, 730, 731
  exceptions, 74
  image activation, 476
Computable states, 191
COM scheduling state, 191, 206
Conditional assembly parameters, 764
Condition handlers
  action of, 83
  argument list arrays, 738
  call frame for, 79
  catch-all, 79, 95, 461, 462
  default, 95
  establishing, 77
  last chance, 79
  LIB$SIGNAL, 75
  removing, 78
  search for, 78
  search termination, 79
  used by CLI, 97
Condition handling, 61
Configuration-dependent routines
  initialization of, 555
CONINTDSP (Console terminal class driver)
  data areas described by, 692
CONINTERR (Connect-to-interrupt driver),
  115
Connect-to-interrupt mechanism, 115
Console block storage device
  I/O, 438
Console floppy, 438
Console interface 435
  in VAX-11/730, 435
  in VAX-11/750, 436
  in VAX-11/780, 436
Console subsystems
  VAX-11/730, 521
  VAX-11/750, 524
  VAX-11/780, 528
Console terminal 435
  data areas, 685
  data transfers, 437
  DPT initialization, 556
  driver prolog tables, 686
  interrupt dispatch data, 692
  interrupt dispatching, 437
  port driver, 424
Console TU58, 438
Context
  hardware, 3
  software, 3, 4, 5
Context switching
  hardware assistance, 207
CONTINUE (DCL command), 515
Contract Region system service, 345
Control
  of processes, 225
Control C processing, 514

Control region
  introduction to, 26
Control Y processing, 514
Conventions
  naming, 671
  register, 654
  for sharing event flags, 229
Conversational bootstrap, 546
Conversion deadlocks, 256
Convert ASCII String to Binary Time system
  service, 643
Convert Binary Time to ASCII String system
  service, 643
Convert Binary Time to Numeric Time
  system service, 642, 643
Copy-on-reference pages
  page faults, 315
Crash/restart
  error log entry formats, 740
Create and Map Section system service, 346
Create Logical Name system service, 630
Create Mailbox system service, 402
Create Process system service, 443
Creation
  of address space, 342
  of mailboxes, 402, 403
  of processes, 443
  of virtual addresses, 342
CUR scheduling state, 198

Data areas
  executive, 681, 682, 683
Database
  PFN, 279
Data management
  concepts of, 8
Data structures
  description of, 733
  global pages, 286
  lock manager, 244
  logical name, 625
  miscellaneous, 774
  page and swap files, 295
  shared memory, 302
  for swapping, 292
  type definitions, 764
DCL (DIGITAL command language)
  activation of, 508
  command processing loop, 509
  initialization of, 509, 510, 511
  termination of, 513
Deadlocks
  conversion of, 256
  detection of, 256
  lock manager, 255
  multiple resource, 257
  search, 256
  search example, 261
  unsuspected, 259
  victim selection, 262
DEADLOCK_WAIT (SYSBOOT parameter),
  256
Deallocate Device system service, 396
Deallocation
  device, 396, 397

  of pool, 51
Deassign I/O Channel system service, 393
DEBUG (DCL command) 515
  exceptions, 72
Debugger
  in image activation, 481
  watchpoint implementation, 359
Declare Error Log Mailbox system service,
  150
DECnet
  class driver (CNDRIVER), 420
  device driver, 429
Default
  condition handlers, 95
  depth in SYS$UNWIND, 89
DEFPRI (SYSBOOT parameter), 366
Delete Logical Name system service, 631
Delete Mailbox system service, 407
Delete Process system service, 492
Delete Virtual Address system service, 345
Deletion
  of address space, 344
  of mailboxes, 402, 407
  of pages and scheduling, 345
  of processes, 492
  of subprocesses, 496
  of virtual addresses, 342
Delivery
  of ASTs, 133
  of attention ASTs, 141
  of out-of-band ASTs, 144
Delta time
  modified by $SETIME, 216
Demand zero pages 273
  page faults for, 317
Dequeue Lock Request system service, 254,
  255
Dequeuing locks (lock manager), 250
DEVICEDAT (Executive device data)
  data areas described by, 685
Device drivers 414
  bootstrap, 542
  class and port drivers, 420
  data areas, 685
  errors in, 147
  magnetic tape, 419
  mailbox driver, 430
  map files, 660
  multiple restarts, 606
  network, 429
  pseudo, 428
  terminal driver, 422
Device information
  device dependent, 412
  device independent, 411
Devices
  allocation and deallocation of, 396
  informational services for, 411
  IPL, 33
  notification of powerfail, 603
Direct I/O
  completion, 400
  in memory management, 299
  and swapper, 374, 375, 376
Disk drivers 414
  ACP intervention, 419

bad block handling, 416
no ACP intervention, 418
offset recovery, 416
Dispatchers
change mode, 165, 166
system services, 162, 178
user-written, 174
user-written system-wide, 178
DR32
interrupts on, 112
DSBINT (macro), 30
DUDRIVER (MSCP class driver), 421
Dynamic address space
size of, 576
Dynamic bad block handling
disk drivers, 416
Dynamic memory
allocation example, 43, 44
allocation of, 42, 43
deallocation of, 45
size of, 578
use of, 53

ECC error recovery
disk drivers, 414
Elapsed time cell, 215
EMB (Error log message block)
layout of, 738
E (MDL directive), 665
ENBINT (macro), 31
Enqueue Lock Request system service, 250
Entry points
naming conventions, 672
Equivalence name string, 625
ERRFMT process 147
overview, 149
waking, 149
Error detection
VAX-11 RMS, 174
Error handling, 147
Error log
buffers in SYSINIT, 563
crash/restart entries, 740
header entries, 741
message buffers definitions, 775
ERRORLOG (Error logger)
data areas described by, 698
Error logger 147, 634
allocation of message buffer, 148
mailbox, 149, 150
operation of, 148
Error log message block, 738
Errors
device driver, 147
logging, 147
Event flags 225
in communication, 235, 236, 237, 238
ownership conventions, 229
posting, 230
setting and clearing, 229
shared, 229
in shared memory, 240
system services, 228
Event reporting, 199, 200

Exceptions
description of, 63
handlers for traceback, 482
hardware, 63
in kernel or executive mode, 96
primary and secondary vectors, 78
service routines, 68
software, 74
vector handlers, 78
EXE$EXTENDPOOL (Extend nonpaged pool), 56
EXE$FORK, 121
EXE$GL_ABSTIM, 215
EXE$GQ_SYSTIME 214
calculated, 216
EXE$GQ_TODCBASE, 215
EXE$IMGFIX (Address Relocation Fixup system service) 476
operation of, 479
EXE$NAMPID (Check name or PID), 231, 232
Execution
scheduling, 183
selection of processes, 205
states of (VAX-11/782), 616
Executive
dynamic locking of pages, 657
initialization of, 550
locating modules, 659
map file for, 658
memory requirements of, 587
multiprocessing hooks in, 611
reading listings of, 645
size of image, 585
Executive data
dynamically allocated, 725
read-only areas, 724
statically allocated, 683
Executive data structures, 736
Executive mode
AST, 174
exceptions, 96
EXIT (DCL command), 516
Expand Region system service, 342
Expansion
of nonpaged pool, 56
External adapters
VAX-11/730, 102
VAX-11/750, 102
VAX-11/780, 103
External symbols
locating, 659

Facilities
prefixes for, 676, 677
FDT routines, 399
File operations
bootstrap, 542
FILES-11 Data structures, 773
File system
data area, 683
Filtering
system services, 179
Fixups
address relocation, 476

FLINK array
  in PFN database, 283, 284
Floating slots
  VAX-11/750, 102
Flushing
  attention AST list, 142
  modified page list, 370, 380
  out-of-band AST list, 145
F (MDL directive), 663
Forced exit, 234
Fork
  dispatcher, 122
  IPL, 33
  layout of block, 741
  processing, 35, 121
Formatted ASCII Output system service, 643
Formatting support system services, 642
FPG wait state
  and pager, 339
  in scheduling, 193
FREEGOAL (SYSBOOT parameter), 360
FREELIM (SYSBOOT parameter), 360
Free page list
  identification of pages, 282
  links in, 283, 284
  scan by swapper, 380
  swapper actions, 360
Function decision table, 399

G^ (Addressing mode)
  address relocation fixups, 477, 478
Get Device/Volume Information system
    service, 411
Get Job/Process Information system service,
    139, 639
Get Message system service, 635
Get System Information system service, 642
Global locations
  examining with SDA, 661
  naming conventions, 672
  symbols, 659
Global pages
  data structures, 286
  page faults for, 319
  page faults for copy-on-reference, 317, 322
  page faults for page-file backing-store
      pages, 323
  page faults for page file pages, 317
  page faults for read-only, 319
  page faults for read/write, 322
  page table, 273, 289
  process PTEs, 291, 292
  and swapper, 376
  swapper resolution for read-only, 384
Global page table
  size of, 585
Global page table entry, 288
Global page table index, 273
Global sections
  in communication, 239
  creation of, 346, 347
  shared memory, 304
Global section table entry, 287
GPTE (Global page table entry), 288
GPTX (Global page table index), 273

Granularity
  of pool allocation, 49
GROWLIM (SYSBOOT parameter), 275
GSD (Global section descriptor)
  description of, 286
  layout of, 741
GSTE (Global section table entry), 287

Hardware
  context (in rescheduling), 203
  exceptions caused by, 63
  interrupts 98, 100
  process control block layout, 752
  VAX-11/782, 612
Hardware clock
  interrupt service routine, 123, 217
Hardware context
  definition of, 3
Hash chains
  lock manager, 249
Hashing
  logical name algorithm, 628
Hash tables
  lock manager, 248
  for logical names, 625
Hibernation, 232
HIBO wait state, 192
HIB wait state, 192
Hooks
  VAX-11/782, 610, 611

IDC (Integrated disk controller), 102
IFD (Image file descriptor block)
  layout of, 742
Image activation 463, 464
  compatibility mode images, 476
  control flags described, 742
  from DCL, 509, 510, 511
  debugger, 481
  image startup, 480
  image with no global sections, 467
  implementation, 465
  known images, 474, 476
  overview, 467
  shareable images, 472
  system service, 465
  traceback handler, 481
Image activator
  SYSIMGACT, 464
  user-written system services, 176
Image file
  location using PSTE, 277
Image file descriptor block, 742
Image header
  fields, 743
  identification section, 743
  patch section, 743
  record definitions, 743
  symbol table, 743
  transfer address array, 743
Image initialization
  from DCL, 509, 510, 511
Images
  definition of, 5, 6
  exit, 482

initialization, 463
interrupted states, 515
privileged, 9
privileged shareable, 175
run down of, 485
termination from DCL, 513
Image section descriptor, 745
Image startup 480
traceback handler, 95
transfer vector array, 480
Image termination (abnormal), 514
Indirect message sections, 637
Infinite loop
in unwind, 88
INIADP (Adapter initialization routine), 557
INILOA (Loadable initialization code)
in INIT, 555
Initial bootstrap
VAX-11/730, 521
VAX-11/750, 524
VAX-11/780, 528
Initialization
of executive, 550
of images, 463
of I/O adapters, 557
of operating system, 548
in process context, 559
of shared memory, 302
swap file, 372
system bootstrap, 521
of VAX-11/782, 613
Initial quantum
and outswap selection, 366
INIT (Processor initialization)
control from SYSBOOT, 547
described, 548
executive initialization, 550
Install Utility
in image activation, 474
Instructions
CHMx, 164, 165
increasing speed, 649
interlocked, 302
size, 649
unusual usage, 651
Instruction set
introduction to, 14
VAX-11, 649
Inswap
candidate selection, 362, 382
example, 386
final processing, 389
operation, 381, 389
pages with I/O in progress, 384
process header, 382
Interactive jobs 499
and LOGINOUT, 503
Interlocked instructions, 302
Internal errors
machine check, 156
Interprocess communication, 235
Interprocessor communication
interlocked instructions, 302
Interrupt dispatching
hardware, 98, 100, 99
MA780, 112

Interrupted images
state of, 515
Interrupt priority level
See IPL
Interrupts
AST delivery, 125, 133
communication (VAX-11/782), 621
connection to, 115
console terminal, 437
DR32, 112
hardware, 98
MA780, 112
MASSBUS, 109
reschedule process, 124
rescheduling, 202
software, 117
UNIBUS, 105
on VAX-11/782, 616, 621
Interrupt service routines 104
buffered I/O completion, 401
DR32 (DR750 and DR780), 112
hardware, 98
hardware clock, 217
I/O completion, 400
MASSBUS, 109
powerfail, 596
restrictions, 104
software, 119
software timer, 123, 218
UNIBUS, 105
Interrupt stack
initialization, 546
size of, 578
Interval
clock, 212
count register, 214
quantum expiration, 218
Invalid page
handler, 269
Invalid PTE
forms, 270
Invalid virtual address
pager action, 310
I/O
adapter initialization, 557
address space specifications, 765, 766
address space (VAX-11/782), 618
bootstrap, 542
buffered, 401
cancellation, 402
class driver, 422
device dependence, 399
device independence, 398
direct, 400
pager, 328
postprocessing, 399, 400
process context data areas, 730, 731
queuing requests for, 397, 398
subsystem concepts, 6
swapper, 300
system services, 393
I/O completion
buffered, 401
direct, 400
I/O data structures
defined in STARDEF, 772

I/O data structures *(continued)*
  defined in SYSDEF, 771
  swapper, 372
I/O in progress
  inswap of pages, 384
  swap during, 286
I/O postprocessing 123
  special kernel mode AST, 137
  synchronization, 35, 36
IOTA (SYSBOOT parameter), 188
IPL 3 32, 99, 33, 34
  interrupt, 121
  interrupt service routine, 202
  and pager, 309, 310
  symbolic definitions, 767
IPL$_QUEUEAST (IPL 6), 33
IPL$_SYNCH (IPL 7)
  use of, 31
IPL$_TIMER (IPL 7), 123
IPL (Interrupt priority level)
  in allocation of nonpaged pool, 47
  device, 33
  for hardware, 98
  software interrupt levels, 117
  used in synchronization, 30
IRPs (I/O request packets)
  allocation of, 50
  description of, 50
  use in memory management, 299
ISD (Image section descriptor)
  layout of, 745

JIB (Job information block)
  layout of, 745
  in process creation, 443
Job controller 633
  process creation, 499
  use by $SNDACC, 632
Job information block, 443, 745

Kernel
  hardware implementation of, 13
  of operating system, 6
Kernel mode
  ASTs, 130
  exceptions, 96
  and VAX-11/782, 620
Kernel stack not valid
  condition handling, 65
Kernel subsystems
  interface, 9
KFH (Known file header)
  layout of, 746
KFI (Known file entry)
  layout of, 746
KFP (Known file pointer block)
  layout of, 747
Known file entry, 746
Known file header, 746
Known file pointer block, 747
Known images
  image activation of, 476
  initial activation of, 474

Large request packets, 50
Last chance condition handler, 79
LDPCTX instruction 210
  use in executive, 211
LEFO wait state, 191
LEF wait state, 191
LIB$ESTABLISH (Establish condition
    handler), 78
LIB$FREE_VM (Free virtual memory from
    program region), 346
LIB$GET_VM (Get virtual memory in
    program region), 346
LIB$REVERT (Remove condition handler),
    78
LIB$SIGNAL (Signal condition) 75
  operation of, 75
Listing files
  reading, 645
  routine body, 646
  symbol table, 648
  table of contents, 648
LKB (Lock block)
  description of, 245
  layout of, 747
L (MDL directive), 665
Local device
  assignment of, 394
Local event flags, 225
Lock conversions, 254
Lock database
  accessing, 249, 250
Lock ID table, 247
Lock manager 244
  ASTs, 253
  in communication, 238
  data structure initialization, 555
  data structures, 244
  deadlocks, 255
  granting locks, 252
  lock conversions, 254
  lock ID table, 247
  parent locks, 250
  queuing and dequeuing locks, 250
  resource hash table, 248
  sublocks, 250
  timeout queue, 256
  waiting locks, 253
Lock Page in Memory system service,
    358
Lock Pages into Working Set system
    service, 357
Locks
  granting, 252
  queuing and dequeuing, 250
Logging errors, 147
Logical name blocks 627
  layout of, 749
Logical names 625
  in communication, 239
  data structures, 625
  logical name blocks, 625
  searching, 627, 628
  system services, 629
  tables, 625
LOGINOUT 503
  image, 503

operations in batch jobs, 505
operations in logout, 516
Logout
description of, 516
LONGWAIT (Process swapping flag), 367, 368
Lookahead buffer
optimizing instructions for, 649
Lookaside lists
allocation from, 50
description of, 50
initialization of, 56
size of, 578
LRPs (Large request packets)
allocation of, 50
description of, 50

MA780
adapter registers, 749
interprocessor communcation, 239
interrupts, 112
interrupts (VAX-11/782), 114
interrupt vectors (VAX-11/782), 612, 613
used in VAX-11/782, 609
Machine check 156
condition handling, 65
error mask bit definitions, 749
recovery blocks, 160
recovery from, 161
Macros
BUG_CHECK, 150
DSBINT, 30
ENBINT, 31
naming conventions, 645, 672
RPTEVT, 200
SAVIPL, 31
SETIPL, 30
SOFTINT, 118
Magnetic tape
drivers, 419
Mailbox driver
attention ASTs, 143
data areas, 685
DPT initialization, 556
driver prolog tables, 686
MBDRIVER, 430
Mailboxes
in communication, 238
creation in shared memory, 405
creation of, 402, 403
deletion of, 407
error log, 149, 150
read request, 432
in shared memory, 240, 307
write request, 434
Map files
nonbased images, 659
reading, 645
using, 658
Mapping information
for disk drivers, 417, 418
Masks
naming conventions, 674, 675

MASSBUS
adapters on VAX-11/750, 102
interrupt service routines, 109
Master CEB 307
in communication, 240
MBDRIVER (Mailbox device driver), 430
MBX (Shared memory mailbox control block)
layout of, 749
MCR (Monitor console routine)
activation of, 508
MDAT (Memory management data)
data areas described by, 691
MDL (Maynard definition language)
commands, 663
files, 662
MEMORYALC (Memory allocation)
routines described, 42
Memory allocation
dynamic, 42
Memory management
avoiding window turns, 417
concepts of, 6, 7, 8
data areas, 687, 691
I/O, 299
swapper, 370
system services, 341
turning on, 548
wait states, 193, 199
Message buffer
error logger, 148
Message files
finding, 635
open by SYSINIT, 564
Message sections 636
indirect, 637
searching, 636
Miscellaneous wait state, 195
M (MDL directive), 665
Modem polling
repeat request, 222
Modified page list
flush by swapper, 380
flushing, 370
identification of pages, 282
links in, 283, 284
swapper actions, 360
Modified pages
backing store address, 334
writing, 370
Modified page writer
completion, 337, 338
nonreentrancy, 301
operation of, 333
page table arrays, 299
PTE array, 300
write clustering, 334
Modified page writes
clustering, 300
completion, 337, 338
example, 337
pager, 333
Monitor console routine, 508
Monitor Utility
data areas, 699
Mount verification
cancellation of, 120

Index

MPW_WRTCLUSTER (SYSBOOT
  parameter), 335, 373
MSCP (Mass storage control protocol)
  class driver (DUDRIVER), 421
  description of, 420
Multiply active signals 79, 80, 81
  unwinding, 88
Multiprocessing
  hooks, 610, 611
  loading code, 612
  reading map files, 660
  turning off, 615
  turning on, 612, 613, 614
Mutexes
  description of, 36
  layout of, 750
  locking for read access, 37
  locking for write access, 38
  logical name table, 630
  unlocking, 39
  wait states, 196
MWAIT state 195
  resource name definitions, 769, 770

Naming conventions 671
  object data types, 676
Nested restarts
  prevention of, 606
NETACP (Network ancillary control process)
  operations of, 429
NETDRIVER (Network device driver), 429
Network ACP, 429
Network device
  assign channel, 395
  driver, 429
  NETDRIVER, 429
Next interval count register, 214
Nexus
  device types, 768
NLDRIVER (Null device driver), 428, 429
Nonbased images
  reading maps, 659
Noncontiguous virtual I/O
  disk drivers, 417
Nonpaged dynamic memory
  use of, 55
Nonpaged executive
  adding code, 656
  size of, 587
Nonpaged pool
  allocation example, 43, 44
  allocation of, 42, 43
  deallocation of, 45
  dynamic expansion of, 56
  expansion of, 56
  initialization by INIT, 554
  initialization of, 56
  size of, 55, 578
  synchronization of, 47
  use by SYSINIT, 561
  use of, 55
Nonreentrancy
  swapper and modified page writer, 301
Null device
  data areas, 685

DPT initialization, 556
driver prolog tables, 686
NLDRIVER, 428, 429
Null process
  kernel mode stack, 684

Object data types
  naming conventions, 676
Offset recovery, 416
OPCOM (Operator communications process)
  description of, 633, 634
Operating system
  initialization of, 548
Operator communications, 633, 634
OSWPSCHED (Swap scheduler)
  data areas described by, 691
Out-of-band ASTs 143
  delivery of, 144
  flushing list, 145
Outswap
  candidate selection, 366, 373, 374
  example, 376
  operation, 373
  partial, 379, 380
  process body, 374
  process header, 379, 381
Outswap process listheads, 362
Ownership
  of event flags, 229

PADRIVER (CI port driver), 421
Pageable executive
  load by SYSBOOT, 546
Paged dynamic memory
  use of, 53
Page deletion
  and scheduling, 345
Paged pool
  mutex protection of, 47
  use of, 53
Page fault monitor
  data areas, 688
Page faults 308
  for copy-on-reference pages, 315
  for demand zero pages, 317
  description of, 269
  for global copy-on-reference pages, 317, 322
  for global page-file backing-store pages, 323
  for global page file pages, 317
  for global pages, 319
  for global read-only pages, 319
  for global read/write pages, 322
  handler, 269
  for pages in image file, 310, 311
  for pages in page file, 317, 318, 319
  for process private pages, 310
  for transition states, 314
PAGEFILE.SYS (System page file)
  open by SYSBOOT, 545
Page files
  alternate, 299
  backing store address, 280
  control blocks, 295
  control blocks used by swapper, 372

control block vector initialization, 556
data structures, 295
initialization of, 562
open by SYSBOOT, 545
open by SYSINIT, 562
page location in, 271
space allocation, 335
structure, 295
virtual block number, 271
Page protection
  altering, 359
Pager
  compared with swapper, 361, 362
  hardware action, 308
  initial action, 309
  IPL requirements, 309, 310
  modified page writing, 333
  operation, 308
  page read clustering, 329
  skipping WLSEs, 328
  working set list replacement, 326
  working set list scan, 326
Page reads
  completion, 332
  pager, 329
Pages
  demand zero, 273
  locking and unlocking, 357
  locking into memory, 358
  page faults for image file, 310, 311
  page faults for page file, 317, 318, 319
  reference count, 284
  in transition, 273
  unlocking, 358, 359
Page selection
  $UPDSEC system service, 338
Page share count, 285
Page table
  matching conditions in scan, 329
Page tables
  global, 289
  P0 and P1, 268
  process, 269
  system, 289
Page writes
  swapper, 300
Page zero
  use, 284
Paging
  compared with swapping, 361, 362
  dynamics of, 308
  I/O, 328
  and scheduling, 339
Parameter block
  system, 566
Parameter descriptor block, 755
Parameter files
  used by SYSBOOT, 566
  used by SYSGEN, 570
Parent locks, 250
Pause capability
  COBOL or FORTRAN, 514
PAUSE (VAX-11 FORTRAN command), 515
PCB (Process control block)
  layout of, 750
  in process creation, 443

system, 287
used in scheduling, 183
vector in process creation, 452
PDAT(System process data)
  data areas described by, 684, 692
Permanent event flags, 227
Per-process system service dispatcher, 174
PFN database 279
  BAK array, 280
  BLINK array, 283, 284
  definitions, 753
  FLINK array, 283, 284
  PTE array, 279
  REFCNT array, 284
  SHRCNT array, 285
  size of, 585
  STATE array, 280, 281, 282
  SWPVBN array, 286
  TYPE array, 283
  WSLX array, 286
PFN-mapped sections
  on VAX-11/782, 618
PFW state 193
  and pager, 339
Physical address space definitions
  VAX-11/730, 766
  VAX-11/750, 766
  VAX-11/780, 767
Piggyback ASTs, 130
P (MDL directive), 665
PMSDAT (File system performance monitor)
  data areas described by, 683, 684, 99, 699
Pointer control block, 757
Polling
  by modem, 222
Pool
  dynamic, 42, 43
  granularity of allocation, 49
  nonpaged, 43, 44
  paged, 43, 44
  use by SYSINIT, 561
Pooled quotas 450
  return on subprocess deletion, 497
Port drivers 420
  terminal, 422
Post event flag, 230
Postprocessing
  I/O, 399, 400
Powerfail
  condition handling, 65
  detection by clock, 215
  detection by swapper, 370
  device notification, 603
  interrupt, 596
  interrupt service routine, 596
  IPL, 32
  multiple, 605
  nested, 605
  operation, 596
  process notification, 604
  recovery, 596, 597
  restart routine, 601
  on UNIBUS, 607
POWERFAIL (Powerfail interrupt service
    routine)
  data areas described by, 691

Power recovery
  delivering ASTs, 604
  initial steps, 598
  special kernel ASTs, 140
  VAX-11/730, 598, 599
  VAX-11/750, 599
  VAX-11/780, 600
P0 page tables, 268, 269, 99
P1 pointer page
  contents, 727
PQB (Process quota block)
  description of, 450
  layout of, 755
PR$_ASTLVL (Mode of current deliverable
    AST)
  computing new value, 132
  and software interrupts, 125
  use of, 127
PR$_ICCS (Interval clock), 212
PR$_ICR (Interval count register), 214
PR$_NICR (Next interval count register),
    214
PR$_SIRR (Software interrupt request
    register), 118
PR$_SISR (Software interrupt summary
    register), 118
PR$_TODR (Time-of-day clock), 214
Preallocated request packets, 49, 50
Primary exception vectors, 78
Primary processor (VAX-11/782)
  description of, 609
  initialization of, 613
  rescheduling routine, 617
Priority
  adjustments of, 187
  boosts by system events, 201
  changing, 234
  quantum end adjustments of, 188
  software, 184
  software real-time, 185
Priority increment classes
  definitions of, 769
Private sections
  creation of, 346, 347
Privileged images
  introduction to, 9
Privileged library vector
  layout of, 755
Privileged shareable images, 175
PRM (Parameter descriptor block)
  layout of, 755
Process
  allocation region, 730, 731
  initialization of data structures, 559
  I/O segment, 730, 731
  notification of powerfail, 604
Process allocation region
  description of, 53
  granularity of, 49
Process body
  outswap, 374
  outswap example, 376
  rebuilding by swapper, 383
Process context
  initialization in, 559

Process creation 443
  context of new process, 458
  control flow, 444
  detached quotas, 450
  establishing quotas, 450
  and job controller, 499
  operations of, 448
  operations off, 444
  process ID fabrication, 452
  shell process, 454
Process deletion 492
  in context of deleting process, 493
  example, 497
  special kernel mode AST, 138, 492, 493
  with subprocesses, 496
  termination mailbox, 494
Processes
  AST accounting, 223
  changing name, 235
  communication, 235
  concepts of, 3, 21
  control and communication, 225
  control by system services, 231
  controlling computability, 231
  creation of, 443
  data structures, 267
  establishing quotas, 450
  exit, 234
  forced exit, 234
  priority (normal range), 186
  removal from execution, 204
  rescheduling, 204
  run down of, 485
  scheduling on VAX-11/782, 617
  scheduling state, 183
  selection for execution, 205
  state change, 197, 198
  suspend and resume, 233
  swap mode, 359
  time accounting, 217
Process header
  configuration, 454, 455
  inswap, 382
  layout of, 753
  memory management pieces, 267
  outswap, 379, 381
  page arrays, 279, 371, 574, 575
  pages, 381
  partial outswap, 379, 380
  P1 window to, 383
  rebuild by swapper, 382
  size of, 572
  storage, 292
  use by swapper, 370
  vector initialization, 555
Process ID
  creation of, 452
  negative, 452
Processor
  register definitions, 768
Processor-dependent routines
  entry points, 701
  in INIT, 555
  initialization of, 558
  map files, 660

Processor-specific code, 545
Processor status longword, 755
Processor status word, 755
Processor time limit, 190
Process page tables 269
  rebuild by swapper, 383, 384
  size of, 572, 573
  use by swapper, 371
Process priority
  initialization of, 447
Process private pages
  page faults for, 310
Process privileges
  checks by system services, 231
  in image activation, 488
  masks, 488
Process PTEs
  for global pages, 291, 292
Process section table 270, 271, 276
  size of, 573
Process suspension
  special kernel mode AST, 138
PROCSTRT (Process startup)
  operation of, 458
Program region
  introduction to, 26
Protection field
  definitions of, 769
PSECTS
  naming conventions, 675
Pseudo device drivers, 428
PSL (Processor status longword)
  layout of, 755
P1 space
  examining with SDA, 662
  in process deletion, 495
  size of pieces, 590
PSTE (Process section table entry)
  description of, 276
  lists, 276
PSTX (Process section table index)
  description of, 270, 271
PSW (Processor status word)
  layout of, 755
PTE array
  modified page writer, 300
  in PFN database, 279
  swapper, 373
PTE (Page table entry)
  description of, 269
  formats, 757
  forms, 270
  pager use, 310
PTR (Pointer control block)
  layout of, 757
PUDRIVER (UDA50 port driver), 421
Purge Working Set system service, 357
Put Message system service, 637
P1 window to process header, 383

Quantum
  IOTA adjustment, 188
  and outswap selection, 366

Quantum end
  detection, 218
  operations, 189
  priority adjustment, 188
  on VAX-11/782, 618
QUANTUM (SYSBOOT parameter), 188
Queue I/O system service, 397, 398
Queues
  process scheduling states, 191
Queuing
  ASTs, 127
  ASTs by access mode, 130
  locks, 250
Quotas
  pooled, 450
  process, 450
  return on subprocess deletion, 497

Rabbit hole page
  allocation of, 557
RBM (Real-time bitmap)
  layout of, 758
Read completion
  pager, 332
Reading listings, 645
Read-only executive data areas, 724
Reads
  clustered in pager, 329
Real-time bitmap, 758
Recalibration
  with $SETIME, 216
  clocks, 214
REFCNT array
  in PFN database, 284
Reference count
  for pages, 284
Registers
  conventions, 654
  interval clock, 212
REI instruction
  in AST delivery, 126
  introduction to, 21
  in return from system services, 172
  use of, 653
REMACP (Remote ancillary control process)
  operations of, 430
Remote terminals 430
  RTTDRIVER, 429, 430
Reporting system events, 199, 200
Request packets
  initialization of, 56
  preallocated, 49, 50
Requests
  timer, 218
Rescheduling interrupt, 124, 202
Reserved instruction fault, 74
Resignaling
  in condition handler, 62
  after exception, 84
Resources
  control of, 22
  hash table (lock manager), 248
  name definitions, 769, 770

Resource wait
  introduction to, 40
  miscellaneous, 195
Restarts
  powerfail, 601
  prevention of nested, 606
Resume process 233
  operation, 233
Return
  status field definitions, 761
Return path for system services, 172
RPB (Restart parameter block)
  in bootstrap, 535
  layout of, 758
  locating after powerfail, 598
  location, 284
RPTEVT (macro), 200
RSB (Resource block)
  description of, 246
  layout of, 760
RTPAD
  operations of, 430
RTTDRIVER (remote terminal driver), 429,
    430

SAVIPL (macro), 31
SBI (Sychronous backplane interconnect)
  VAX-11/780, 103
SCA (Systems communication architecture)
  implementation on VAX/VMS, 420
  I/O processing, 422
Scatter/Gather
  in memory management, 299
SCB (System control block)
  in bootstrap, 535
  hardware interrupts, 100
  interrupt dispatching, 100
  loaded by SYSBOOT, 546
  size of, 578
SCH$ASTDEL (AST interrupt service
    routine), 133
SCH$LOCKR (Lock mutex for read access),
    37
SCH$LOCKW (Lock mutex for write access),
    38
SCH$POSTEF (Post event flag)
  operation of, 230
SCH$QEND (Quantum end routine), 188
SCH$RESCHED (Rescheduling routine), 204
SCH$RSE (Report system event), 200
SCH$RWAIT (Wait for resource), 40
SCH$SWPWAKE (Wake swapper process),
    361
SCH$UNLOCK (Unlock a mutex), 39
Scheduled wakeup
  operations, 223
Scheduled Wakeup system service, 220
Scheduler
  data areas, 688
  start new process, 449
  wait queue header layout, 763
Schedule Wakeup system service, 222
Scheduling 183
  computable states, 191

  concepts of, 8
  interrupt at quantum end, 190
  and page deletion, 345
  and paging, 339
  prevention on VAX-11/782, 618
  process states, 183
  of a swap, 362
  on VAX-11/782, 616, 617
  wait states, 191
Scheduling states
  symbolic names, 770, 771
SCSLOA (Load SCS code)
  in INIT, 555
SCS (Systems communication services)
  definition of, 420
  loadable image, 555
SCSVEC (Loadable SCS code)
  data areas described by, 704
SDA (System dump analyzer)
  description of, 154, 661
SDAT (Scheduler data)
  data areas described by, 688
SEARCH_RESDLCK (Deadlock search
    routine), 258
Secondary exception vectors, 78
Section table
  in system PCB, 287, 288
Section table entry
  layout of, 760
Selection
  of inswap candidates, 362
  of process for execution, 205
Selective cache invalidation
  in VAX-11/782, 612
Semaphores
  lock manager, 244
Send Message to Accounting Manager system
    service, 632
Send Message to Error Logger system service,
    634
Send Message to Operator system service,
    634
Send Message to Symbiont Manager system
    service, 633
Serialized access, 35
SETIPL (macro), 30
Set mode requests
  processing, 432
Set Power Recovery AST system service, 604
Set Privilege system service, 490
Set Process Swap Mode system service, 359
Set Protection on Pages system service, 359
Set Resource Wait Mode system service, 195
Set System Service Failure Exceptions system
    service, 178, 179
Set System Service Filtering system service,
    179
Set System Time system service, 215
SETTIME (SYSBOOT flag), 562
SET WORKING_SET (DCL command), 354
Shareable image list
  in image activation, 477, 478
Shareable images
  activation of, 472
  privileged, 175

Share count
  for pages, 285
Shared event flags
  ownership conventions, 229
Shared memory
  in bootstrap, 302
  common event flag clusters, 307
  communication, 239
  control block layout, 760
  control structures, 302
  create and map sections, 304
  data page layout, 761
  data structures, 302
  global sections, 304
  interlocked instructions, 302
  mailbox creation, 405
  mailboxes, 307
  virtual mapping, 302
Shared memory mailbox control block, 749
Shell process, 297, 454
SHRCNT array
  in PFN database, 285
Shrinking
  of working set, 366
Signaling software status, 75
Site-specific STARTUP command file, 565
Slave CEB 307
  in communication, 240
Slots
  balance, 292
  in CMI, 102
Small request packets, 50
S (MDL directive), 665
Smithsonian base date, 214, 215
SOFTINT (macro), 118
Software
  exceptions, 72, 74
  signaling status, 75
Software clocks, 214, 215
Software interrupts 117
  AST delivery, 125, 133
  request register, 118
  service routines, 119
  summary register, 118
Software priority 184
  adjustment of, 187
  real-time, 185
Software timer
  interrupt service routine, 123, 218
Space allocation
  page file, 335
SPAWN (DCL command)
  operation of, 506
Special kernel mode ASTs 130
  $GETJPI, 640
  lock manager, 253
  piggyback, 130
  uses, 136, 137
Spooled device
  assignment of, 394, 395
SPTEs (System page table entries)
  free, 587
SPTREQ (SYSBOOT parameter)
  renormalization, 587
Spurious ASTs, 133

SRPs (Small request packets)
  allocation of, 50
  description of, 50
Stack
  expansion of user, 343
  use in exceptions, 63
STARLET.MLB
  description of, 648
START/CPU (DCL command), 611
STARTUP (System startup process) 561, 564
  described, 564
  initialization of, 561
  operations, 564
State
  changes in, 197, 198
  process scheduling, 183
  queues, 191
  transitions, 200
  transitions on VAX-11/782, 616
STATE array
  in PFN database, 280, 281, 282
STOP/CPU (DCL command), 615
STOP (DCL command), 516
STOP (VAX-11 COBOL command), 515
Sublocks, 250
SUBMIT (DCL command), 500, 501, 502
Subprocesses
  creation of, 445
  process deletion, 496
Subsystems
  error logging, 147
  I/O, 393
Summary longword, 206
Supervisor mode
  bugchecks, 151
  termination handler, 508, 509
Suspend process 233
  operation, 233
SVPCTX instruction 207
  use in executive, 210
SWAPASAP (Process swapping flag), 368
Swap files
  alternate, 299
  data structures, 295
  initialization of, 372, 563
  open by SYSINIT, 562
  structure, 295, 297
Swap mode
  process, 359
SWAPOGOAL (Process swapping flag), 368
Swapper
  activity, 368, 369
  data areas described by, 691
  flush modified page list, 380
  global pages, 376
  inswap example, 386
  inswap final processing, 389
  inswap of process header, 382
  I/O, 300, 372
  I/O map, 374
  kernel modestack, 684
  main loop, 369
  memory management, 370
  and modified page writer, 299
  nonreentrancy, 301

Swapper *(continued)*
    outswap candidates, 366
    outswap operation, 373
    page file control blocks, 372
    pages with direct I/O in progress, 374, 375, 376
    process, 361
    PTE array, 373
    rebuild process body, 383
    rebuild process header, 382
    rebuild process page tables, 383, 384
    rebuild working set list, 383, 384
    resolution of global read-only pages, 384
    responsibilities, 360
    scan of free page list, 380
    scan of working set list, 374
    selection of inswap candidate, 382
    selection table, 366
    shrink candidates, 366
    triggering events, 368, 369
    trimming, 357
    wake, 361
Swapper map
    allocation by INIT, 556
Swapping 360
    compared with paging, 361, 362
    data structures, 292
    overview, 360
Swap scheduling, 362
Swap space 297
    allocation of, 372
    expansion of, 297
SWP$SHELINIT (Shell initialization)
    operations of, 455, 456, 458
SWPFAIL (SYSBOOT parameter), 367
SWPRATE (SYSBOOT parameter), 362, 363, 364, 365, 366
SWPVBN array
    in PFN database, 286
SYE Utility, 634
Symbiont manager, 633
Symbols
    naming conventions, 671
Symbol tables
    in listing files, 648
Synchronization 30
    by IPL, 31, 32
    IPL example, 33
    in pool allocation, 47
SYS.STB (System symbol table) 658
    concepts of, 9
SYS$INPUT (Process permanent file)
    creation of, 447, 448
SYS$OUTPUT (Process permanent file)
    creation of, 447, 448
SYS$RUNDOWN internal system service, 485
SYSBOOT (Secondary bootstrap program)
    approximations, 586
    data areas, 704
    description of, 542
    operations of, 543
    parameters and system virtual address space, 576
    use of parameter files, 566
SYSCOMMON (Miscellaneous system data)

    data areas described by, 692, 693, 698, 99
SYSDUMP.DMP (System dump file) 154
    header block layout, 738
    open by SYSBOOT, 545
SYSGEN (System Generation Utility) 565
    parameter constant definitions, 770
    use of parameter files, 570
SYSIMGACT (Image activator), 464
SYSINIT (System initialization process) 560, 561
    description of, 561
    operation, 561
    pool usage, 561
SYSLOAVEC (System loadable routines)
    data areas described by, 701, 702, 704
SYSLOAxxx (CPU-dependent loadable image)
    in INIT, 555
SYSPARAM (SYSBOOT parameters)
    data areas described by, 704, 717, 99, 718, 99, 719, 99, 720, 99, 721, 99, 99, 722
SYSSETPFM (Page fault monitor)
    data areas described by, 688
SYSTARTUP.COM (Site-specific startup command file), 565
System control block
    See SCB
System data structures, 733
System events 197
    priority boosts, 201
    reporting, 199, 200
System executive
    miscellaneous data, 692
System header 287
    configured by SYSBOOT, 546
    size of, 584
System initialization
    bootstrap, 521
    loading terminal driver, 424
    on VAX-11/782, 613
System map files
    using, 658
System message files
    finding, 635
    open by SYSINIT, 564
    system services, 635
System page table 289
    size of, 576, 577, 585
System parameter block, 566
System PCB, 287
System procedures
    periodic, 221
System processes
    ERRFMT, 147
    memory requirements for, 589
    process data areas, 691, 692
    SYSINIT, 560, 561
Systems communication architecture, 420
Systems communication services, 420
System section table 287, 288
    size of, 584
System services
    device information, 411
    dispatching, 162, 178
    filtering, 179
    formatting support, 642
    I/O, 393

logical names, 629
macro naming conventions, 672
memory management, 341
miscellaneous, 632
privilege checks, 231
process control, 231
return path, 171, 172
system message file, 635
timer, 222
timer conversion, 642, 643
user-written, 174
vector area, 683
vectors, 162
wait states, 198
System time 212
    setting, 562
    updating, 217
System virtual address space
    examining with SDA, 662
    introduction to, 24
    size approximations, 586
    size of, 572, 576
    and SYSBOOT parameters, 576

Table of contents
    in listing files, 648
Tape, 419
TBSKIPWSL (SYSBOOT parameter), 328
Terminal driver 422
    assembling, 422, 423
    attention ASTs, 142, 143
    full duplex operation, 425, 426
    initialization of, 556
    linking, 424
    out-of-band ASTs, 143
    type-ahead buffer, 428
Terminals
    class driver, 425
    controllers, 428
    port drivers, 422
    remote, 430
    TTDRIVER, 422
    unsolicited input to start process, 499
Termination handlers
    in image exit, 482
    list processing, 484
    supervisor mode, 508, 509
Termination mailbox
    in process deletion, 494
Time
    base values, 215
    recalibration, 214
    updating, 217
Timekeeping, 212
Time-of-day clock, 212, 214
Timeout queue
    lock manager, 256
TIMEPROMPTWAIT (SYSBOOT parameter),
    214, 562
Timer 212
    requests, 218
Timer queues 217
    description of, 218
    element in, 218
    lock manager, 256

Timer requests
    repeating, 221
    servicing, 220
Timer system services, 222
TQE (Timer queue element)
    layout of, 218, 763
Traceback handler 95, 482
    in image activation, 481
Transfer address array
    layout of, 743
Transfer vector array
    image startup, 480
Transition
    page in, 273
Transition states
    page faults for, 314
Translate Logical Name system service, 631
Translation not valid
    condition handling, 65
Traps
    exceptions caused by, 68
TR numbers
    VAX-11/780, 103
TTDRIVER
    terminal class driver, 422
Type-ahead buffer
    terminal driver, 428
TYPE array
    in PFN database, 283

UCB (Unit control block)
    in device assignment, 393, 394
UDA50 port driver (PUDRIVER), 421
UNIBUS
    interrupt service routines, 105
    power failure, 607
UNIBUS adapters
    VAX-11/750, 102
UNIBUS interrupts
    servicing, 105
    VAX-11/780, 106
Unit control block, 393, 394
Unlocking pages
    from memory, 358, 359
    from working set, 358, 359
Unlock Page from Memory system service,
    358, 359
Unlock Page from Working Set system
    service, 358, 359
Unsuspected deadlocks, 259
Unwind
    in condition handler, 62
    example, 85
    after exception, 84
Update Section File on Disk system service,
    338
User interface
    concepts of, 9
User mode
    bugchecks, 151
User stack
    automatic expansion of, 343
    overflow exception, 72
User-written code
    CLIs, 179

User-written code *(continued)*
  dispatcher, 174
  dispatcher (system-wide), 178
  system services, 174

VAX-11
  addressing modes, 649
  instruction set, 14, 649
VAX-11/730
  console interface, 435
  console subsystem, 521
  external adapters, 102
  initial bootstrap, 521
  machine check, 157
  physical address space definitions, 766
  power recovery, 598, 599
  UNIBUS power failure, 607
VAX-11/750
  console interface, 436
  console subsystem, 524
  external adapters, 102
  initial bootstrap, 524
  machine check, 157
  physical address space definitions, 766
  power recovery, 599
  UNIBUS power failure, 607
VAX-11/780
  console interface, 436
  description of, 609
  detecting access mode transitions, 620
  external adapters, 103
  hardware configuration, 609
  hardware support, 612
  initial bootstrap, 528
  interrupts, 616
  I/O address space, 618
  machine check, 159
  MA780 interrupts, 114
  physical address space definitions, 767
  power recovery, 600
  scheduling, 616
  scheduling prevention, 618
  UNIBUS interrupts, 106
  UNIBUS power failure, 607
VAX architecture, 13
VAX-11 MACRO
  listing file structure, 645
VAX-11 RMS
  dispatching, 171
  error detection, 174
  initialization of, 563
  return path for services, 173
Vectors
  change mode to executive, 163
  change mode to kernel, 163
  system service, 162
Victim selection
  lock manager, 262
Virtual address
  creation and deletion of, 342
  deletion of, 345
  field definitions, 763
Virtual address space
  definition of, 5
  limits on creation of, 342, 343

Virtual block number
  page file, 271
Virtual I/O
  disk drivers, 417
Virtual mapping
  shared memory, 302
Virtual memory
  controlled allocation, 346
VMB (Primary bootstrap program) 530
  operation of, 535
V (MDL directive), 665, 666, 670
Voluntary wait states, 191

Wait for Logical AND of Event Flags system
    service, 228
Wait for Logical OR of Event Flags system
    service, 228
Wait for Single Event Flag system service, 228
Waiting locks 253
  granting, 255
Wait states 191
  and AST delivery, 198
  event flag, 227, 228
  memory management, 193, 199
  mutex, 39
  system service, 198
  VAX-11 RMS, 173
  voluntary, 191
Wake from hibernation, 232
Wakeup
  scheduled, 220
Waking
  ERRFMT process, 149
Warning messages
  page file full, 335
Watchpoints
  debugger implementation of, 359
WCB (Window control block)
  definition of, 417
  description of, 297
  mapping information, 417, 418
Window control block, 417
Windows, cathedral, 417
Window turns
  definition of, 417
Working set
  automatic adjustment, 354
  lock pages into, 357
  reduction, 357
  replacement (pager), 326
  unlock pages from, 357
Working set list 269, 273
  dynamic portion, 275
  expansion of, 277
  expansion (quantum end routine), 190
  rebuild by swapper, 383, 384
  scan by pager, 326
  scan during outswap, 374
  size of, 275, 573
  swapper scan, 300
  use by swapper, 371
Working set shrinking
  candidate selection, 366
Write clustering
  modified page write, 300

modified page writer, 334
Write completion
  $UPDSEC system service, 339
WRTMFYPAG (Modified page writer)
  data areas described by, 688
WSLE (Working set list entry)
  description of, 275
  empty, 326
  field definitions, 764
  reuse by pager, 326
  skipping (by pager), 328
  use by pager, 327
WSLX array
  in PFN database, 286

XDELTA
  in VAX-11/782, 612
XFDRIVER (DR32 driver), 112